CRITICAL SURVEY OF GRAPHIC NOVELS

HISTORY, THEME, AND TECHNIQUE

CRITICAL SURVEY OF GRAPHIC NOVELS

HISTORY, THEME, AND TECHNIQUE

Editors

Bart H. Beaty

University of Calgary

Stephen Weiner

Maynard Public Library

SALEM PRESS

A Division of EBSCO Publishing

Ipswich, Massachusetts

Library of Congress Cataloging-in-Publication Data

Critical survey of graphic novels : history, theme, and technique / editors, Bart H. Beaty, Stephen Weiner.
      p. cm. -- (Critical survey of graphic novels)
Includes bibliographical references and indexes.
ISBN 978-1-58765-957-7 (hardcover) -- ISBN 978-1-58765-958-4 (ebook) 1. Graphic novels. 2. Comic books, strips, etc. I. Beaty, Bart. II. Weiner, Stephen, 1955- III. Title: History, theme, and technique.
 PN6725.C7536 2012
 741.5'0973--dc23
                        2012019474

First Printing

Printed in the United States of America

CONTENTS

PUBLISHER'S NOTE

Graphic novels have spawned a body of literary criticism since their emergence as a specific category in the publishing field, attaining a level of respect and permanence in academia previously held by their counterparts in prose. Salem Press's *Critical Survey of Graphic Novels* series aims to collect the preeminent graphic novels and core comics series that form today's canon for academic coursework and library collection development, offering clear, concise, and accessible analysis of not only the historic and current landscape of the interdisciplinary medium and its consumption, but the wide range of genres, themes, devices, and techniques that the graphic novel medium encompasses.

The combination of visual images and text, the emphasis of art over written description, the coupling of mature themes with the comic form—these elements appeal to the graphic novel enthusiast but remain a source of reluctance to other readers. Designed for both popular and scholarly arenas and collections, the series provides unique insight and analysis into the most influential and widely-read graphic novels with an emphasis on establishing the medium as an important academic discipline. We hope researchers and the common reader alike will gain a deeper understanding of these works, as the literary nature is presented in critical format by leading writers in the field of study.

History, Theme, and Technique is the fourth title of the *Critical Survey of Graphic Novels* series, in conjunction with *Heroes and Superheroes*; *Independents and Underground Classics*; and *Manga*. This title collects more than seventy essays on the evolution of the graphic novel, from its conceptual beginnings to widespread acceptance. This volume covers the unique process of creating a product both in art and in word: historical overviews track the complex development of this important art form, while the survey of key themes, genres, and events, albeit far from exhaustive, will help define the major milestones and provide an important foundation for future research.

SCOPE AND COVERAGE
This single-volume set includes over seventy essays covering themes and concepts of graphic novels, including genres, time periods, foreign-language tradi-

tions, social relevance, and craftsmanship. A wide spectrum of other genres is also presented in critical format, ranging from the nationalistic, such as Japanese manga and African graphic novels, to the traditional, such as Westerns, science fiction, and the archetypal superhero genre and mythos. This set also provides insight into various aspects of the industry, from techniques such as lettering, inking, and illustration, to the production and distribution of graphic novels and the significance of comic book conventions. Issues of readership and literacy, library collection development, and censorship are also covered.

ORGANIZATION AND FORMAT
The essays in *History, Theme, and Technique* appear in three topical sections: History, which traces the evolution of the medium before exploring a wealth of cultural and historical topics; Theme, arranged in alphabetical order and covering a wide range of storytelling across genres from the funny animal genre to action and adventure; and Technique, which examines the operations involved in creating and publishing graphic novels. Each essay is three to four pages in length and is divided into the following sections:

- **Definition–**describes the time period, genre, or step in the creation process in two or three sentences for the reader.
- **Introduction–**provides a brief overview of the topic for the reader before delving into more concentrated topics within the essay.
- **Impact–**covers the theme, genre, or time period and its influence on the medium of graphic novels itself, and literature in general.
- **Bibliography–**lists secondary print sources for further study and examination, annotated to assist readers in evaluating focus and usefulness.

APPENDIXES AND OTHER SPECIAL FEATURES
Special features provide tools for further research and points of access to the wealth of information and content contained in *Critical Survey of Graphic Novels*. This includes a listing of major graphic novel awards, a guide to online resources, and a general bibliography. In

addition, the glossary includes terms and techniques pertinent to the study and understanding of graphic novels. A cumulative timeline discusses significant events and influential graphic novel predecessors and spans the ancient world through the Middle Ages and the Renaissance to the present.

Finally, our comprehensive recommended reading list of over 1,100 titles reflects the complexity and diversity of the graphic novel medium, extending far beyond the preeminent and core series of today's canon. Titles are sorted by three distinct genres—heroes and superheroes; independents and underground classics; and manga—and include author, artist, publisher, and publication date.

The single-volume set also features over 100 pictures, including cover images and panels from influential and referenced works. A subject and name index is also included.

ACKNOWLEDGMENTS
Many hands went into the creation of this work, and Salem Press is grateful for the effort of all involved. This includes the original contributors of these essays, whose names can be found at the end of each essay and also found in the "Contributors List" that follows the Introduction. Special mention must be paid to Lisa Schimmer, who played an invaluable role in shaping some of the reference content. Finally, we are indebted to our editors, Bart Beaty, Professor of English at the University of Calgary, and Stephen Weiner, Director of Maynard Public Library in Maynard, Massachusetts, for their advice in selecting works and their writing contributions. Both are published in the field of comics and graphic novels studies. Beaty is the author of *Fredric Wertham and the Critique of Mass Culture*, *Unpopular Culture: Transforming the European Comic Book in the 1990s*, and *David Cronenberg's "A History of Violence."* Weiner is the author or co-author of *The 101 Best Graphic Novels*, *Faster than a Speeding Bullet: The Rise of the Graphic Novel*, *The Hellboy Companion*, *The Will Eisner Companion*, and *Using Graphic Novels in the Classroom*. Their efforts in making this resource a comprehensive and indispensible tool for students, researches, and general readers alike is gratefully acknowledged.

INTRODUCTION

In his 2005 book, *Alternative Comics: An Emerging Literature*, comics scholar Charles Hatfield termed the graphic novel an "art of tensions." In his keen analysis of comic storytelling, he identified the push and pull of formal considerations as one of the central formal features of comics reading. One might take his observation further and note that the very form of the graphic novel is one that stems from a series of related contradictions.

Perhaps the most striking contradiction about the graphic novel is that it is both so new and so very old. The practice of crafting narratives from images dates back to antiquity, and the mass production and circulation of storytelling images arose with the birth of the printing press in the fifteenth century. Comics, as a distinct cultural form, most frequently traces its roots back to the publications of Swiss artist Rodolphe Töpffer in the 1830's, while the comic book, as an industry, is a product of the printing houses that dotted midtown Manhattan in the 1930's. The graphic novel, essentially a long-form comic book, entered into the mainstream in the 1970's, the product of cartoonists who were strikingly cognizant of the immense debt that they owed to the practitioners who had shaped the cartoon, the comic strip, and the comic book before them. And while in many ways the very idea of a novel-length graphic work is still a work in progress, a genre undergoing definition, the history of the comics form—upon which it is so dependent—is long and varied. This volume takes as one of its key themes the task of establishing these chronologies.

For readers approaching the graphic novel from related fields such as literature and art history, the most striking contradiction is surely the tension that exists between word and image. The very term "graphic novel," which appends the first term to the second as an adjectival modifier, cuts to the heart of the contradiction. What is the dominant element? Is it the text that makes the work akin to traditional literary novels, or the images that supply the graphics? This is a contradiction that need not be resolved. In the best works found in the graphic novel tradition, these elements are brought together so seamlessly that Matt Madden and Jessica Abel titled their how-to guide for producing graphic novels *Drawing Words and Writing Pictures*. As this volume shows, the most skilled graphic novelists have such a facility with the elements of the graphic novel that the contradiction is made to disappear entirely.

The success of comic books around the globe has been primarily driven by the popularity of certain key characters: superheroes like Batman and Spider-Man in the United States, adventurers like Tintin and Lucky Luke in Europe, and fantastical creatures like the Pokémon in Japan. These character-driven comics routinely mine the past as a source of stories; many of the works that we now consider graphic novels found their origins in ongoing monthly or weekly serializations. To this end, the graphic novels are collections of works that were previously conceptualized as discrete, but related units. In contrast, many contemporary graphic novels have eschewed these connections to ongoing characters. One of the fundamental shifts in the way graphic novels have distinguished themselves from the larger field of comics has been the focus on works that are complete in themselves and which are not tied to larger publishing continuities. The industrial practices that have facilitated this contradictory transformation are explored in depth in this volume.

Unlike the literary novels from which they take part of their name, graphic novels are not always—perhaps not even predominantly—produced by a single creator. In the history of comics, creative teams, which can include writers, pencillers, inkers, letterers, colorists, and other technical specialists, have been the norm, and continue to be. Well-integrated teams of equals such as René Goscinny and Albert Uderzo (the writer and illustrator of *Astérix*) are like Rodgers and Hammerstein—better together than apart. Yet recent decades have placed a disproportionate emphasis on the single-minded graphic novel auteur, the creator who both writes and draws, overseeing the entire aesthetic package. Inherently, there is no single best practice when it comes to the production of great work in the graphic novel format, though many critics and artists might pass the time arguing otherwise. This volume takes no sides in this debate, and opts instead to feature analyses and biographical information on many of the key figures to have worked in the form, no matter what roles they may have played.

Unlike older and better-established fields such as literature, painting, music, and drama, in which many of the greatest works remain in the now distant past, the graphic novel is a young form. A relative infant, the graphic novel is being transformed on a nearly daily basis as new works are added to the quickly growing canon and new storytelling innovations are discovered. Though it owes debts to its cognate forms, the graphic novel is still in its period of experimentation and growth, and it seems inevitable that the advances of today will soon be transformed by the artists of tomorrow. Though its roots are in the past, the graphic novel is remarkably forward-looking; it is an art form whose time has arrived, and this volume is a testament to its increasing centrality in our culture.

Bart Beaty

CONTRIBUTOR LIST

Karley Adney
ITT Technical Institute

Maaheen Ahmed
Jacobs University

Kane Anderson
*University of California, Santa
Barbara*

Ted Anderson
Golden Valley, MN

Bart Beaty
University of Calgary

Richard A. Becker
Pasadena, CA

Adam Bessie
Diablo Valley College

Beth Blakesley
*Washington State University
Libraries*

Arnold T. Blumberg
University of Baltimore

Mark Brokenshire
Hove, South Australia, Australia

Rachel Cantrell
Texas A&M University, Commerce

Terry Joseph Cole
*LaGuardia Community College-
CUNY*

Anthony Coman
University of Florida

Michel De Dobbeleer
Ghent University, Belgium

Gail A. de Vos
University of Alberta

Thomas Donaldson
University at Albany (SUNY)

Lance V. Eaton
Emerson College

Jack Ewing
Boise, ID

Camila Figueiredo
*Universidade Federal de Minas
Gerais*

Sergio C. Figueiredo
Clemson University

Theresa Fine-Pawsey
*Durham Technical Community
College*

Jean-Paul Gabilliet
University of Bordeaux, France

Jessica Gamache
Western Connecticut State University

Diana Green
*Minneapolis College of Art and
Design*

Robert Greenberger
Fairfield, CT

Jim Haendiges
Dixie State College of Utah

Kaitlan Huckabone
University of Waterloo

Sam Julian
Mountain View, California

Emily Laycock
Lancaster University

Pascal Lefèvre
University of Leuven

Celeste Lempke
University of Nebraska, Kearney

Héctor Fernández L'Hoeste
Georgia State University

Laurie Lykken
Century College

June M. Madeley
*University of New Brunswick, Saint
John*

Melissa Mallon
Wichita State University Libraries

Stephen Marchand
University of Rhode Island

Michelle Martinez
Sam Houston State University

Jessica McCall
Las Vegas, NV

Ora C. McWilliams
University of Kansas

B. Keith Murphy
Fort Valley State University

Robert J. Paradowski
Rochester Institute of Technology

Marco Pellitteri
London Metropolitan University

Mark C. Rogers
Walsh University

Gabriel Romaguera
University of Rhode Island

Joseph Sanders
Western Michigan University

Elizabeth D. Schafer
Loachapoka, AL

Cord Scott
Loyola University, Chicago

Amanda Sheppard
Eastern Kentucky University

Matthew J. Smith
Wittenberg University

Fredrik Strömberg
University of Malmö

Susan Sylvia
Acushnet, MA

P. L. Thomas
Furman University

Robert G. Weiner
Texas Tech University

Stephen Weiner
Maynard Public Library

Nathan Wilson
Tulsa, OK

Daniel Yezbick
Forest Park College

Shan Mu Zhao
Surrey, British Columbia

CRITICAL SURVEY OF GRAPHIC NOVELS

HISTORY, THEME, AND TECHNIQUE

HISTORY

ANCIENT TIMES TO 1920: THE EVOLUTION OF SEQUENTIALLY IMAGED NARRATIVES

Definition

Those who see the graphic novel as the culmination of a long history broadly define the term as a collection of sequential pictorial, symbolic, or other images intended to tell a story, communicate information, or elicit an aesthetic response. Sequentially imaged narratives from a wide range of cultures have been identified as precursors to the graphic novel.

Introduction

Some aficionados of graphic novels point to Will Eisner's *A Contract with God* (1978) as the first such work; in 2003, *Time* magazine published an article entitled "The Graphic Novel Silver Anniversary" that, despite caveats, reinforced this date. Others have pointed out that Richard Kyle used the term in a 1964 newsletter, and as scholars explored the history of comic books, they began to find extended-form precursors published earlier in the century. Cognizant of the wide variety of themes treated by creators under the umbrella term of "graphic novel," some analysts discovered less obvious forerunners created in earlier centuries, and, after in-depth analyses of the intentions and accomplishments of many graphic novelists, some historians have even traced the graphic novel's roots to Paleolithic times.

Prehistoric and Ancient Precursors

Archaeologists and other explorers have discovered examples of the earliest art created by *Homo sapiens* in caves and other locations throughout the world. Using a variety of techniques, scientists have determined that these works, largely depicting animals, date to the Upper Paleolithic period (40,000-10,000 B.C.E.). Two of the most famous of these sites are the caves of Lascaux in southwestern France and Altamira in northern Spain.

Altamira, with its multicolored images of bison, horses, and other animals, has come to be known as the "Sistine Chapel of Paleolithic Art." The images influenced later artists such as Pablo Picasso, who deeply admired them, and comic book artist Bernet Toledano, who created the *Altamiro de la cueva* series in the 1960's. The nearly two thousand images in the Lascaux caves include animals as well as various abstract symbols. Spiritual, magical, and even astronomical interpretations have been proffered to explain some of the groupings, such as the famous Great Hall of the Bulls. Others theorize that certain collocations or overlapping of images might represent a hunting narrative.

Works of art from ancient Egypt, Greece, and Rome have also been cited as precursors to the

The caves of Altamira, with its multicolored images of bison and other animals, influenced generations of artists. The caves were first discovered in 1869; a proper archaeological exploration in 1875 revealed the paintings. (Robert Frerck)

graphic novel. At first glance, Egyptian hiero-glyphs—sequences of images representing animals, humans, jars, water, and so on—would seem to imply some kind of narrative, but these glyphs actually stand for sounds in an ancient Egyptian language. On the other hand, the sequences of paintings found on papyri and tomb walls do tell stories, including how crops were harvested and boats were built. Similarly, the friezes and other decorated parts of Greek build-ings sometimes include sculptural or carved depic-tions of stories from Greek mythology. In the Roman Empire, artists continued this tradition not only in public buildings but also in private homes and busi-nesses. Early Christians adapted some of these methods in re-creating stories from the Old and New Testaments, for example, in panels on the sarcophagi of their dead.

The Middle Ages Through the Early Modern Period

Two new methods sometimes used to tell stories through sequential images came to prominence during the Euro-pean Middle Ages: tapestries and stained glass. A tap-estry is a cloth interwoven with varicolored, symbolic designs for decorative purposes or with biblical or historical scenes to tell a story. The Bayeux Tapestry tells the story of the Norman conquest of Eng-land in 1066, communicating through several hundred images and many words such important historical events as the Battle of Hastings.

Stained glass, used in medieval ca-thedrals, served both decorative and narrative purposes. Because many me-dieval worshipers were illiterate, the panels of stained-glass windows were often used to tell stories from the life of Christ or from the Old Testament. For example, the stained-glass windows of Canterbury Cathedral in England are often called the "poor man's Bible," since the artists used sequential sections to recount Old Testament stories as well

as the birth, public life, passion, and resurrection of Christ as depicted in the Gospels.

The use of stained glass for narrative purposes con-tinued through the Renaissance and into the modern eras. However, new narrative techniques came into prominence during the Renaissance. Several Renais-sance artists notably engaged in a competition to depict the biblical story of the sacrifice of Isaac through se-quential panels on the bronze doors of the baptistery of San Giovanni in Florence, Italy. Other artists used fresco techniques to tell sequential stories from the Bible. During the High Renaissance, Michelangelo brought the narrative fresco technique to its peak in his Sistine Chapel depiction of the Christian story of salva-tion, from the creation of the universe to the Last Judgment.

During the Reformation, Protestant artists used the woodcut technique to make multiple prints of sequen-tial stories depicting the corruption of the Roman Catholic Church and the Pope as the Antichrist. Lu-theran artists such as Lucas Cranach told the story of Christ from a Protestant perspective. In the seven-teenth century, Roman Catholic artists such as Peter Paul Rubens responded with narrative history pictures

Job's Complaint by William Blake; the English poet and artist reinvigorated the medieval illuminated book by creating a revolutionary blend of visual imagery and literary text. (Corbis)

in a variety of media and formats, including large frame paintings, ceiling paintings, panels, and even textiles.

In the late eighteenth and early nineteenth centuries the English poet and artist William Blake reinvigorated the medieval illuminated book by creating a revolutionary blend of visual imagery and literary text that he hoped would purify human imaginations and rescue viewers and readers from the corruptions engendered by a soulless industrialized society. In Blake's illuminated books, from *Songs of Innocence* (1789) to *Jerusalem: The Emanation of the Giant Albion* (1804-1820), images are often dialectically interrelated to the text and serve as a conduit for the poet's highly personal mythology, reminiscent to modern readers of certain contemporary graphic novelists.

From Short- to Long-Form Comic Books
Although the terms "comics," "comic strips," and "comic books" have been traced to the early twentieth century in the United States, historians have seen these forms as derivative of caricatures and cartoons of earlier centuries. According to several historians of comic books, Rodolphe Töpffer, a Swiss schoolmaster and the creator of *Histoire de M. Vieux Bois* (c. 1839), is the father of this genre. Published in English under the title *The Adventures of Mr. Obadiah Oldbuck* in 1842, Töpffer's work is considered by some to be the United States' first comic book. In forty pages of pictures and captions, the work tells of the amorous adventures of Mr. Oldbuck.

At the end of the nineteenth century, the first widely popular American comic books owed their origins to comic strips that were first published in the Sunday supplements of newspapers. Richard Felton Outcault's *The Yellow Kid*, an exploration of an Irish immigrant youngster and the ethnic tensions he encounters in an urban setting, became a great success for the *New York Journal*. The strips were collected in book form as *The Yellow Kid in McFadden's Flats* (1896).

In the early twentieth century, hundreds of newspapers printed syndicated comic strips such as Winsor McCay's *Little Nemo in Slumberland* (1907), which centers on the dreams of a child from a middle-class

family. The styles of the comic-strip artists were sometimes influenced by such movements as Art Nouveau and cubism. Less sophisticated but more popular were the strips focused on family life from a broadly comedic perspective. Rudolph Dirks's *Katzenjammer Kids*, recounting the escapades of mischievous German immigrant children Hans and Fritz, went on to become the longest-running comic in the United States. George McManus's *Bringing Up Father*, which ran from 1913 to 2000, deals with the comedic conflicts between nouveau riche Irish immigrant Jiggs and his shrewish wife, Maggie. The strips were collected into books and also inspired a Broadway play.

Flemish artist Frans Masereel is often cited by graphic novelists as an influence on their work. He began to publish "image novels," composed of expressionistic woodcuts, in Europe in the 1910's. In such works as *Mon livre d'heures* (1919; *Passionate Journey*, 1922), Masereel dissects urban life and the state of the world in the post-World War I period. The German writer Thomas Mann compared the wordless *Passionate Journey* to a black-and-white film and praised the spiritual insights occasioned by the young protagonist's journeys.

Distinctive for having a female protagonist, Russ Westover's *Tillie the Toiler* comic strips began to appear in 1921. The stories concern the trials and tribulations of a young working girl and manifest an early feminist outlook. Tillie is often more clever, more insightful, and wittier than the male characters, though she exhibits the typical penchant of the flapper for fancy dresses and fascinating men. The strips were so popular that they were collected into several books and inspired two films. The comic strip continued to be published through the 1950's.

Impact
The many styles, stories, and viewpoints found in the forerunners of graphic novels have explicit analogues and counterparts in contemporary examples of the form. Many modern graphic novelists have acknowledged their debt to such early works, and they have drawn on several of the works' techniques and themes. Thus, creators have helped to unify the long history of developments that led from cave paintings with

collocated images to the complex, often long, and creatively artistic form of the modern graphic novel.

Robert J. Paradowski

Bibliography

Gabilliet, Jean-Paul. *Of Comics and Men: A Cultural History of American Comic Books*. Translated by Bart Beaty and Nick Nguyen. Jackson: University Press of Mississippi, 2010. Chronicles the development of the American comic book industry, beginning with the comics of the 1930's and continuing into the Modern Age.

McCloud, Scott. *Understanding Comics: The Invisible Art*. New York: HarperPerennial, 1994. Uses the comic book format to explore the definition, language, and historical development of the comic book and the graphic novel.

Sabin, Roger. *Comics, Comix, and Graphic Novels*. London: Phaidon Press, 1996. Provides a history of the development of both mainstream and underground comics and graphic novels from the seventeenth century to the Modern Age.

1920's-1950's: EARLY STORYTELLING ATTEMPTS A FORMAT SIMILAR TO THE MODERN GRAPHIC NOVEL

Definition

Although the graphic novel as a form became popular in the 1970's and 1980's, many books published in earlier decades could be considered graphic novels. The history of fictional graphic narratives published in the United States between 1920 and 1950 demonstrates the genre's reliance on European influences.

Introduction

When Richard Felton Outcault created *The Yellow Kid* in 1895, he did not realize that he was starting a cultural revolution. Newspaper comics became enormously popular, but these comics were generally not collected until 1933, when Max Gaines published *Famous Funnies* to repackage and preserve newspaper comics. The comic book industry g r e w out of Gaines's vision, and it could be argued that the comics magazine (then sixty-four pages long) was the progenitor of the graphic novel. However, publishers had been experimenting with graphic narratives prior to the publication of *Famous Funnies*.

European artists, influenced by Renaissance art, had tried telling stories using only illustrations. Shortly after Europeans experimented with the form, American artists and publishers began to produce works primarily relying on silent visual narratives as well as books that used words and pictures. Many of these books were collections of previously published cartoons, but unlike *Famous Funnies* and its imitators, these collections were hardbound and contained the work of a single cartoonist or single cartoon. Paralleling the humorous comic strips were attempts to tell longer, more complete stories using pictures only or pictures accompanied by words.

The early American graphic novelists relied heavily on two European storytellers who used woodcut narratives,

Frans Masereel and Otto Nückel. Masereel produced a successful string of wordless woodcut novels beginning with *Debout les morts* (arise ye dead) in 1917. Probably his most famous works were *Mon livre d'heures* (1919; *Passionate Journey*, 1922) and *Die Stadt* (1925; *The City*, 1972). Masereel's books deal with mature themes with a sense of humor and also have political components.

Nückel's contribution to the development of narrative storytelling was one book, *Schicksal: Eine Geschichte in Bildern* (1930; *Destiny: A Novel in Pictures*, 1930), containing more than two hundred lead-cut prints and telling the story of an impoverished woman in the nineteenth century. Books such

He Done Her Wrong. (Courtesy of Fantagraphics Books)

as these inspired some Americans to create their own graphic narratives.

Early Wordless Graphic Novels

The chief American creator of graphic narratives in the 1920's and 1930's was Lynd Ward. Like Masereel's, Ward's stories were broad. Unlike Masereel's, his pieces did not include humor. Another difference between the two was that Masereel worked in woodcuts (with the grain of the wood), while Ward worked in wood engravings (against the grain of the wood). Ward's output was impressive. Between 1929 and 1937, he produced six wordless graphic narratives: *Gods' Man* (1929), *Madman's Drum* (1930), *Wild Pilgrimage* (1932), *Prelude to a Million Years* (1933), *Song Without Words* (1936), and *Vertigo* (1937).

It is unclear why Ward moved on to other forms after *Vertigo*, but it is clear that he provided a framework for what would later become the graphic novel form as well as inspiration for cartoonists of the 1930's, many of whom cite his influence. Ward eventually went on to commercial and critical success as a children's writer and illustrator, winning the Caldecott Medal in 1953 for *The Biggest Bear* (1952).

Another experiment in the graphic narrative form was cartoonist Milt Gross's *He Done Her Wrong: The Great American Novel and Not a Word in It—No Music Too* (1930), a semivaudevillian tale of westward expansion that countered the seriousness of Ward's earlier work. The pages consist of one or two black-and-white illustrations surrounded by a generous white border that highlights the comic effect.

Early Graphic Novels with Words

As publishers continued to experiment with formats, several early graphic novels appeared in print. One such book was James Thurber's "parable in pictures" *The Last Flower* (1939). Thurber's earlier graphic collections, *The Seal in the Bedroom and Other Predicaments* (1932) and *Men, Women, and Dogs: A Book of Drawings* (1943), were both bound cartoon collections with no consistent narrative. *The Last Flower* differed, telling one long story about a war and its aftermath. The story is presented in "picture book" style, with the simple images and text appearing on facing pages.

Another early graphic novelist was Don Freeman, who became a commercial success as a children's writer and illustrator with the Corduroy books. In his satire *It Shouldn't Happen* (1945), Freeman tells the story of Private Bedlington, who is transformed into a dog by trauma. The dialogue appears on the same pages as the ink and watercolor illustrations. Another pre-graphic novel was Crockett Johnson's *Barnaby* series, a family oriented strip collected in a book series and published in the 1940's. The drawings are simple, with two cartoon panels per page, and include dialogue.

A final early graphic novel was Virginia Lee Burton's *Calico the Wonder Horse, or the Saga of Stewy Stinker* (1950), a children's story in which a special horse saves the day. The story is told in a series of scratchboard illustrations, and the narrative writing

Author and cartoonist James Thurber; his graphic parable *The Last Flower* (1939) is often considered an early graphic novel. (Raimondo Borea)

appears on the same pages as the illustrations. Due in part to the success of such children's stories, many publishing houses came to believe that the comic book format appealed to children only.

Impact

It is difficult to gauge the impact of such precursors on the development of the graphic novel format because these publications, with the exception of Ward's work, were sporadic and did not capture the popular imagination. In addition, no reliable sales statistics exist for these books. It is fair to assume that sales were not extraordinary; if they had been, the graphic novel would have become a steady arm of the publishing field by 1950. One theory as to why the serious graphic narrative did not take during this time is that, with the explosion of comic book magazines, the idea that stories told in cartoon format were for children only became a notion deeply embedded in the public consciousness.

However, it is not difficult to gauge the effect these early graphic novels had on their creators, who used the works to fuel their careers. Many creators had successful careers as writers and artists for children. Burton created *Mike Mulligan and His Steam Shovel* (1939) and *Katy and the Big Snow* (1943). Thurber created *Many Moons* (1943). Johnson produced *Harold and the Purple Crayon* (1955) and many other books for children. Ward is best known for his picture book *The Biggest Bear*, although he was a prolific writer and illustrator of children's books, and the wordless book *Silver Pony* (1973). Freeman created the Corduroy series, beginning with *Corduroy* (1968), and, like the other early proponents of the graphic novel form, wrote and illustrated numerous children's books.

The contribution of these early writers and artists is best understood in retrospect. Their books provide a historical basis for cartoon storytelling and graphic novels as the form continues to reach out beyond the traditional comic book readership.

Stephen Weiner

Bibliography

Avermaete, Roger. *Frans Masereel*. New York: Rizzoli, 1976. Discusses Masereel's life and career and contains illustrations, color plates, and samples of his many wordless novels.

Beronä, David A. *Wordless Books: The Original Graphic Novels*. New York: Abrams, 2008. Studies early wordless graphic novels and includes lengthy discussions of Ward and Gross as well as Europeans such as Masereel.

Thurber, James. *Writings and Drawings*. New York: Literary Classics of the United States, 1996. Collects all of Thurber's work, from his early cartoons for *The New Yorker* to his attempts at creating a narrative form.

Ward, Lynd. *Six Novels in Woodcuts*. New York: Library of America, 2010. Includes all six of Ward's woodcut novels as well as his writings and a lengthy introduction by graphic novelist Art Spiegelman.

1960's: THE FOUNDATIONS OF TODAY'S GRAPHIC NOVELS

Definition

During the 1960's, a period typically considered to fall within the Silver Age of comics, publishers adjusted to cultural changes and introduced a number of major characters and concepts that would greatly shape the industry. Long-form comics continued to develop, becoming more similar to the graphic novels of later decades.

Introduction

The Silver Age of comics usually evokes images of brightly colored costumes, wisecracking adolescent sidekicks, heavy-handed morality, and a monochromatic divide between good and evil. Some remember these comics with nostalgic fondness for their innocence and optimism. Others are critical of their naïveté, limited character development, and juvenile nature.

Love them or hate them, these early stories have an important place in the history of the medium as precursors of graphic novels. Many of the conventions of the modern comics medium were established and built upon during the 1960's, and many writers and artists who were raised on these stories went on to steer the comics medium toward the legitimacy enjoyed by the graphic novel form.

Comics as a medium cannot be condensed into a singular form for the 1960's. While the decade certainly opened with simplistic story lines and two-dimensional characters, a number of developments within the comic book industry had a lasting effect, updating the comics for an ever-maturing readership and cultivating a loyal fan base that would ensure the survival of the medium.

The Comics Code and Its Aftermath

The comic book medium began the 1960's in the wake of a moral backlash that had left the industry with little choice but to regulate itself in accordance with mainstream conservative values. While this self-regulation stifled creativity, it also was the catalyst for a number of innovations that would have a lasting effect on the industry, paving the way for experimentation during

The Fantastic Four #1 debuted in November, 1961, and was an immediate success. (Courtesy of Marvel Comics)

the late 1960's and 1970's and allowing for newfound acceptance of the graphic novel as a literary form during the 1980's.

As the comic book industry entered the 1960's, it was still recovering from the devastating effects of the publication of psychiatrist Fredric Wertham's anti-comics book *Seduction of the Innocent* (1954) and the subsequent Senate subcommittee hearings on connections between comics and juvenile delinquency. The Comics Code Authority, which had been voluntarily established by publishing companies in order to avoid government regulation, placed considerable restrictions on the content of comic books. The establishment of the Comics Code had effectively obliterated horror and violent crime comics, leaving superhero comics with relatively little competition.

With the Comics Code forbidding depictions of the supernatural, violent crime, and corrupt or inept authority figures and demanding that good triumph over evil without exception, realism had essentially been eliminated from the superhero subgenre. These restrictions left writers with limited avenues of storytelling and led to a series of story lines about romantic mishaps, sidekicks and superpets, grandiose supervillains with giant novelty traps, and fantastic excursions into outer space.

The characters (as well as the creative teams behind them) were trapped in a perpetual loop of simplistic storytelling in which heroes always prevailed, all loose ends were resolved at the end of each adventure, and the status quo was preserved at all costs. Story arcs rarely extended beyond a monthly issue, and characters remained relatively unchanged over time. This left comic books in a somewhat static form, allowing casual readers to come and go as they pleased but effectively limiting the readership to the preteen and young-adult market.

Heroes for a New Age
With the advent of television, coupled with a loss of interest in the new style of comics among older readers, sales steadily declined as the 1960's approached. DC Comics set about revamping some of its original Golden Age characters in the hope of capturing a new generation of readers. The company had already enjoyed some success in 1956 with a new incarnation of the Flash. Now the secret identity of Barry Allen, this new version of the hero was given a sleek red costume and a scientific edge. As the 1950's drew to a close, Golden Age favorites such as Green Lantern and Hawkman were also reinvented, redrawn to be more modern and scientific and less supernatural in origin.

While these new characters enjoyed varied levels of success, it was not until 1960, when DC combined its superhero lineup under the banner of the Justice League of America, that the characters became more widely known. Drawing on the original concept of the Justice Society of America as well as on the military and science team stories of the 1950's, the superhero team was

extremely popular. The team had a lasting impact on the comics world, necessitating the creation of the DC Multiverse and prompting struggling rival Marvel Comics to launch its own superpowered team in 1961.

Birth of the Multiverse
While the Justice League of America was a commercial success, it also generated continuity issues for DC Comics. The new Flash, Barry Allen, had already been established in 1956 as an avid comic book reader who had based his superhero identity on his favorite comic book character, Jay Garrick, the Flash of the Golden Age. While characters such as the Flash and Green Lantern had been reinvented for the new scientific age, more popular characters such as Superman, Batman, and Wonder Woman had remained relatively unchanged. In previous adventures these characters had interacted with the Golden Age version of the Flash, Jay Garrick, who was now being portrayed as a fictional character.

This and a number of other continuity issues were addressed in "Flash of Two Worlds," in *The Flash*, issue 123 (1961), a story in which Barry Allen punctures an interdimensional barrier and finds himself on Earth 2, the parallel-universe home of the Golden Age incarnations of the DC superheroes, including the original Flash. Jay Garrick's comic book appearance in Barry Allen's universe is explained as the product of subconscious extrasensory perception on the part of writer Gardner Fox, a real-life writer for DC Comics. The Multiverse yielded an abundance of Silver Age story lines in the DC Comics Universe and was used as the proving ground for experimental characters and alternate time line tales known as "Imaginary Stories."

Rise of Marvel Comics
In 1961, a struggling company that had been known as Timely Comics during the 1930's and Atlas Comics during the 1950's rebranded itself as Marvel Comics. Tasked with creating a superhero team to compete with DC's Justice League, writer Stan Lee and artist Jack Kirby devised a new take on the superhero that secured Marvel Comics' place as a serious contender in the industry. *The Fantastic Four* debuted in November,

American marines patrolling through the streets of Hue during the Vietnam War. In the late 1960's, comics began to explore taboo themes, including the divisive war in Vietnam. (Getty Images)

1961, and was an immediate success. Modeled after the nuclear family, the team was composed of four heroes who fought and bickered with one another and displayed human character flaws such as ego, jealousy, and impatience. This injection of realism resonated with comics readers, who could easily identify with the characters.

With the success of *The Fantastic Four*, Lee and Kirby went on to create a multitude of new Marvel Comics superheroes and stories that were based on societal interest and anxiety about atomic power, scientists and the military, male identity, and the growing civil rights and counterculture movements. The creative team at Marvel Comics soon realized that their core readers were college students who were inspired by the realism of the characters and the social relevance of the stories. Lee and artist Steve Ditko further challenged the conventions of the superhero subgenre by reinventing the adolescent sidekick as the teen protagonist. Spider-Man debuted in 1962 in *Amazing Fantasy*, issue 15, and was an instant success, with the character going on to become the "mascot" character for Marvel Comics.

Comics Go Underground

In the late 1960's, a number of artists who were disillusioned with the restrictions of working in the mainstream arena began to write, draw, and independently publish their own comic books. Sold in record stores and head shops, these publications did not need to abide by the Comics Code and gained the moniker "comix" because of the "X-rated" nature of their content. The comix firmly placed the comic book medium within the realm of mature-adult entertainment, exploring sex, drugs, and political taboos such as opposition to the Vietnam War. With less emphasis on artistic finishing and more on substance and satire, the comix have been likened to a return to the newspaper cartoon origins of mainstream comics. Many underground comics were based on autobiographical accounts of the artists' childhoods, the drudgeries and difficulties of daily life, and experimentation with hallucinogenic drugs such as LSD.

The importance of the underground comics movement to the development of the graphic novel cannot be overlooked. The movement was led by artists such as Robert Crumb, Kim Deitch, Spain Rodriguez, S. Clay Wilson, and, later, Harvey Pekar and Art Spiegelman. These artists challenged the perception of comics as a child's medium and sought to explore and experiment with the comic book form well into the 1970's. Pekar and Spiegelman in particular became major forces in the legitimization of the graphic novel medium and the introduction of comics into mainstream literature.

Impact

The progression of the comic book medium during the 1960's can be held as a cultural mirror to the tumultuous nature of the decade. While it may be tempting to dismiss the comic books of the early 1960's as childish and formulaic, they were the springboard for a series of creative leaps that led to the modern graphic novel. The subgenre of superhero fiction is often decried as being less legitimate than its more "literary" peers, but it was the adaptability of the subgenre, and the creativity of its writers and artists, that helped the comic book medium survive the stagnation of the early 1960's.

Inventions of necessity such as character reboots and the parallel universes of the DC Multiverse have become staples of the medium, and they eventually provided a platform for two of the most famous graphic novels in publishing history: Frank Miller's *Batman: The Dark Knight Returns* (1986) and Alan Moore's *Watchmen* (1986-1987), reinterpretations of the "imaginary tales" of the 1960's and reinventions of existing characters in alternative realities. The popularity of the Justice League of America can be linked to the rise of Marvel Comics and with it a greater emphasis on character realism and social commentary. By creating characters and story lines that tapped into the interests and anxieties of a maturing readership, Marvel Comics was instrumental in the creation of a loyal fan base that helped the medium survive the introduction of television and reach a wider, more mature audience.

As the counterculture movement gained strength in colleges around the United States and the rest of the Western world, the phenomenon of underground comics provided an avenue for experimentation with the form and inspired a new generation of mainstream writers and artists in the early 1970's to see the value of the medium as a tool for social commentary. Ironically, one of the more prominent artists of the underground movement, Spiegelman, brought mainstream legitimacy to the graphic novel with the publication of *Maus* in 1986.

Accordingly it can be said that the 1960's represent the formative years of the graphic novel.

Although the graphic novel form did not officially appear until the following decade, many of the developments that led to its creation, such as experimentation with the comic book form, social realism, and autobiographical narrative, can be traced to the innovations of the 1960's.

Mark Brokenshire

Bibliography

Genter, Robert. "With Great Power Comes Great Responsibility: Cold War Culture and the Birth of Marvel Comics." *The Journal of Popular Culture* 40, no. 6 (2007): 957-978. Provides an outline of the rise of Marvel Comics, with a particular focus on the transition from conservatism to counterculture and the development of Marvel's adult fan base.

Jenkins, Henry. "Just Men in Tights: Rewriting Silver Age Comics in an Era of Multiplicity." In *The Contemporary Comic Book Superhero*, edited by Angela Ndalianis. New York: Routledge, 2009. Examines the comics ages in the context of wider genre theory and explores the enduring popularity of the Silver Age incarnations of superheroes and their adaptation to modern publications.

Lopes, Paul Douglas. *Demanding Respect: The Evolution of the American Comic Book*. Philadelphia: Temple University Press, 2009. Discusses the moral panic over comics during the 1950's as well as the aftermath during the 1960's and the subsequent evolution of fan culture.

1970's: Social Justice, Self-Discovery, and the Birth of the Graphic Novel

Definition

The comics industry evolved significantly throughout the 1970's, responding to the amendment of the Comics Code, the rise of cultural relevance in superhero comics, and the contributions of the underground comics movement. The decade also marked the first official appearance of the graphic novel.

Introduction

For comic books, the 1970's could be seen as a period of both consolidation and refinement of the advances to the medium that were made in the 1960's. Growing public acceptance of comic books, along with an increasing drive for realism, relevance, and social commentary among the new generation of writers and artists, led to an amendment of the Comics Code and opened up new avenues for mainstream comics stories. In keeping with the desire for relevance, characters such as Superman, Wonder Woman, and Batman, who had remained relatively untouched for decades, were finally updated. New characters from diverse ethnic, social, and religious backgrounds were introduced into mainstream superhero comics, and previously submissive female characters finally found their voices and asserted their independence.

The underground comics movement was fertile soil for the advancement of the comic book form, with notable figures such as Harvey Pekar, Art Spiegelman, and Will Eisner working to explore the form's potential beyond escapist fantasy, guiding it in the direction of more literary storytelling and urban realism. Although the movement declined in the 1970's, its focus on experimentation and challenging boundaries provided the basis for the first official appearance of a graphic novel in 1978.

The Social Justice League

At the beginning of the 1970's, the mainstream comic book industry was becoming stagnant. While DC Comics and Marvel Comics had made some headway in building a mature readership during the 1960's, they were still hampered by the restrictions of the Comics

African American characters such as Luke Cage debuted in the 1970's. (Courtesy of Marvel Comics)

Code. With many of the original comics creators beginning to retire, a new generation of left-leaning writers and artists began to push for more realism and social commentary in the superhero subgenre.

These writers and artists, along with educators and public officials who were beginning to see the potential of comic books as tools for reaching young adults, successfully lobbied for amendments to the Comics Code. In 1971, for the first time in seventeen years, the Comics Code was revised to allow for more graphic depictions of drug abuse, organizational corruption, and the supernatural, provided these depictions were for the purpose of social commentary or, in the case of supernatural creatures, were in the context of a literary tradition.

Titles such as *Green Lantern-Green Arrow* (1970-1971) by Dennis J. O'Neil and Neal Adams and *The Amazing Spider-Man* (1963-1998) by Stan Lee tackled racism, misogyny, state corruption, drug abuse, and other serious issues. Green Arrow's former sidekick, Speedy, was revealed to be a heroin addict, while Spider-Man's best friend, Harry Osborne, overdosed on narcotics. These stories brought new credibility to the superhero subgenre as it entered a decade of reinvention and self-examination.

Diverse Heroes

Characters such as Superman, Batman, Wonder Woman, and the X-Men were updated during the 1970's. The X-Men, who had started as a small band of American teenagers, were reinvented as an international team of mutants of varying age and background. Some of the more popular characters introduced during this time include the Canadian Wolverine and the African American Storm. Both of these characters have remained staples of the X-Men series.

For the first time, African American, Native American, Asian, and Jewish characters were introduced into superhero comics as leading characters rather than as sidekicks or members of supporting casts. African American characters such as Blade, Luke Cage, and Green Lantern John Stewart debuted during the 1970's, although many of these characters were subsequently criticized as overtly stereotypical and akin to characters from the blaxploitation films of the same era.

Seeking to capitalize on the women's liberation movement, creators attempted to depict female characters as more assertive and independent, to mixed success. Some characters were positive role models, career women and respected leaders, but others tended to veer toward clichéd stereotypes of volatile feminists who erupted into scathing outbursts at the slightest provocation. Wonder Woman was stripped of her powers and transformed into a boutique owner and martial artist for a time before being restored to her former self following a campaign by *Ms.* editor Gloria Steinem.

The exploration of realistic social issues was introduced through more diverse characters and topical story lines. Many of these updates gave characters much-needed depth and laid the foundations for longer story arcs that were later compiled into graphic novel releases. Characters such as Superman and Wonder Woman eventually became diluted because of their popularity in other media such as film (Christopher Reeve starred as Superman in a string of films beginning in 1978, and Lynda Carter played Wonder Women in a television series that ran from 1975 to 1979). However, O'Neil's work on *Batman* during the 1970's would continue to inform the character in later decades, forming the basis of Frank Miller's gritty characterization of Batman in his 1986 graphic novel *Batman: The Dark Knight Returns*.

Ascension from the Underground

The underground comics movement that began during the 1960's and continued into the 1970's was an area of avant-garde experimentation and self-exploration. Although the movement eventually waned as a result of distribution problems and antiobscenity laws, it formed the basis of an ongoing alternative comics scene, inspired a new generation of writers and artists, and was the birthplace of two landmark titles in the history of comics and graphic novels: *American Splendor* (1976-1991; 1993-2008) and *Maus* (serialized 1980-1991).

American Splendor began as a collaborative project between Pekar and underground comics pioneer Robert Crumb but eventually involved a host of other artists. First appearing in *The People's Comics* in 1972 and then as its own title in 1976, *American Splendor* was an autobiographical series that drew upon the daily drudgeries of Pekar's life and his experiences as a file clerk at the Cleveland Veterans Administration hospital. *American Splendor*'s realistic portrayal of a mundane working-class lifestyle won Pekar an American Book Award (1987) and earned a fan following that would last for decades. *American Splendor* is considered one of the first exemplars of the "literary" potential of the comic book. Pekar's contribution to the comic book and graphic novel medium was that of stark realism, without the support of satire or fantasy.

Spiegelman tested the boundaries of the medium's potential throughout the 1970's, and he also showcased the "comix" of other artists as the coeditor of the

Feminist Gloria Steinem led a campaign to restore Wonder Woman's powers and traditional costume in the 1970's. The editor of *Ms. magazine*, Steinem placed the character on the cover of the magazine's first stand-alone issue in 1972. (Bettmann/Corbis)

anthology *Arcade* (1975-1976). In 1972, an early incarnation of Spiegelman's critically acclaimed *Maus* appeared in the pages of *Funny Aminals*, as did "Prisoner on the Hell Planet," a short piece about the impact of his mother's suicide, a topic later covered in *Maus*. As the creator of the first graphic novel to win a Pulitzer Prize (1992), Spiegelman is a pivotal figure in the history of graphic novels. His work during the 1970's as both a writer and an editor laid much of the groundwork for the medium's success in the following decades.

Introducing the "Graphic Novel"

The introduction of the graphic novel is commonly credited to Eisner, who published *A Contract with God, and Other Tenement Stories* in 1978. Eisner was said to have coined the term while pitching the project to publishers who were anxious about printing a "comic book." These are both somewhat contentious issues among comics historians; the term "graphic novel" is commonly accepted to have been coined as early as 1964 by Richard Kyle in an Amateur Press Association newsletter, and many historians consider *A Contract with God* to be not a

graphic novel but an anthology of comics stories.

What cannot be debated is that Eisner successfully used the term graphic novel to alter perceptions of the comic book medium and guide it toward the legitimacy that it would enjoy in later decades. Best known in the mainstream comics industry for having created *The Spirit* in 1940, Eisner nevertheless drew a great deal of inspiration from the more avant-garde world of underground comics. After meeting Spiegelman and several other comix artists at conventions in the early 1970's, Eisner is said to have been inspired by their dedication to advancing the comics medium and set out on his own mission to showcase the literary possibilities of comic book storytelling.

In *A Contract with God*, Eisner taps into the autobiographical style made famous by the underground comics movement to write about the hardships of life as a Jewish immigrant in the United States during the Great Depression of the 1930's. The graphic novel is divided into four vignettes about different residents of the Bronx tenement in which Eisner grew up, and it would later form part of a trilogy about Jewish life in the United States. *A Contract with God* is considered to be one of the first comics to combine the techniques of mainstream comics with the stark realism and social commentary of the underground to create a new direction for the medium.

Impact

The years 1970 through 1979 form the core of what is referred to as the Bronze Age of comics, an era of self-examination, experimentation, and reinvention of the characters, the creative teams, and the medium itself. As the Golden Age writers and artists began to retire, a new generation sought to assert its own influence on the medium and continue the work its mentors had pioneered. Many notable graphic novel writers and artists began their careers during the 1970's, including Alan Moore and Frank Miller, who both went on to write landmark superhero graphic novels during the 1980's.

Underground comics, which began as protests against the restrictions of the Comics Code, became a source of inspiration to writers and artists who saw that the potential of the comics medium surpassed the escapist fantasy of superhero stories. Writers and artists such as Pekar, Eisner, and Spiegelman injected the realism of urban life and recaptured the interest of a generation of former comic book readers. Experimentation with the form, which had been in progress since the 1960's, culminated in the creation of the first official graphic novels. By the 1970's, the comics medium had finally progressed to the point that it could produce meaningful, relevant stories that showcased the potential of the comic book form. Readers who had been raised on increasingly sophisticated comics were ready to embrace the next step in the evolution of comic books, in the form of graphic novels.

Mark Brokenshire

Bibliography

Gardner, Jared. "Autobiography's Biography, 1972-2007." *Biography* 31, no. 1 (2008): 1-26. Provides an overview of some of the autobiographical comics artists of the 1970's, including Justin Green, Pekar, and Spiegelman, along with visual examples of their work.

Madrid, Mike. *The Supergirls: Fashion, Feminism, and the History of Comic Book Heroines*. Ashland, Oreg.: Exterminating Angel Press, 2009. Devotes an entire chapter to female superheroes during the 1970's, examining the shortcomings and successes of the character changes made during the decade.

Weiner, Stephen. *Faster than a Speeding Bullet: The Rise of the Graphic Novel*. New York: NBM, 2003. Follows the development of the graphic novel and devotes a chapter to Eisner's *A Contract with God and Other Tenement Stories*.

1980's: The Graphic Novel Grows Up

Definition

In the 1980's, graphic novels gradually arrived in bookstores, specialty shops, and some libraries. As popular auteurs developed ambitious stories, their burgeoning readership welcomed a new format that could better accommodate demanding works from mainstream and alternative publishers.

Introduction

By the beginning of the 1980's, the term "graphic novel" had become a convenient euphemism that helped creators and publishers legitimize the unique aesthetics of comics art and facilitated the merchandising of relatively long and expensive texts. The 1980's became a watershed decade, with many publishers realizing that the new format could generate both substantive sales and positive press. It is telling that Frank Miller's *Batman: The Dark Knight Returns* and the first volume of Art Spiegelman's *Maus* both appeared in 1986 to enormous critical acclaim and financial success. The public's appreciation of comics, from superhero comic books to avant-garde works, was changing by mid-decade as readers, creators, and publishers paid more attention to long-term continuity and intricate storytelling. Old forms and genres were enthusiastically deconstructed, while bold new systems of comics syntax that could sustain more elaboration and complexity than before arose. The graphic novel market provided such texts with convenient, respectable frameworks through which the public could appreciate them.

Alternative Comics at the Forefront of the Industry

As publishers such as RAW Books, Fantagraphics Books, Aardvark-Vanaheim, Eclipse Comics, First Comics, and Comico Comics turned toward edgier subject matter than had been published previously, the nascent graphic novel market instigated a vehement campaign for cultural legitimization. The most important text to benefit from this trend is undoubtedly Spiegelman's *Maus*. As an avant-garde homage to Spiegelman's family, underground comics, and the "funny animal" milieu, the story fuses fiction, history, and design in graphic novel form, consolidating and amplifying its impact beyond the original miniature pull-out pamphlets from *RAW* magazine.

Throughout the 1980's, *RAW*'s graphic novels increased the medium's immediate impact as well as its legacy. *RAW*'s series of one-shots showcased innovative works such as Gary Panter's *Jimbo* (1982), Ben Katchor's *Cheap Novelties: The Pleasures of Urban Decay* (collected in 1991), Charles Burns's *Big Baby* (1989-1991), and Sue Coe and Holly Metz's *How to Commit Suicide in South Africa* (1983). Coe and Metz's novel remains one of the most affecting and nightmarish sequential exercises of any period. More frenetic and ruthlessly uncompromising in its imagery than Coe's biography of Malcolm X or her later work focusing on animal rights (*Dead Meat*, 1995; *Sheep of Fools*, 2005), *How to Commit Suicide in South Africa*, a composite of radical political awareness, experimental art publishing, and comic book mediation, stands as an extreme example of how completely graphic novels changed the perception of comics as "funny books."

Fantagraphics Books pioneered multicultural comics with its collections of *Love and Rockets* (first published 1982-1996), created by Gilbert, Jaime, and Mario Hernandez. The original magazine borrowed extensively from experiments in the 1960's underground, the 1980's punk and new wave movements, and even Magical Realism. As fairly expensive and obscure black-and-white comics, *Love and Rockets* could not gain serious attention beyond local, limited fan bases. Collected as graphic novels, however, the series was able to reach a wider audience.

Similar compilation strategies informed the first collections of Dave Sim's unique *Cerebus* (1977-2004) project from Aardvark-Vanaheim. The graphic novel also served as a useful form for collecting Dave Stevens's on-again, off-again *The Rocketeer* back-up stories and one-shots, which were published as a collected volume in 1991. Matt Wagner's *Grendel* (1983-   ) and

Mage: The Hero Discovered (1982-1984) received similar treatment by Comico, as did Howard Chaykin's sexy science-fiction farce *American Flagg!* (1983-1988), published by First Comics.

A longtime comics iconoclast, Chaykin also embraced the new format with his *Time2* graphic novels (1986, 1987), which stand among his most revealing projects. Wagner's *Mage* was compiled in a number of editions, but his lesser-known work *Grendel: Devil by the Deed* (1986) stands as an especially elegant treatment of his signature antihero. Ironically, Wagner and Chaykin also discovered the first limitations of the graphic novel format. When smaller companies such as Eclipse Comics, Comico, and First Comics eventually

failed, many of the original processing materials for *American Flagg!*, *Time2*, *Grendel*, and *Mage* were lost or put at risk. The early graphic novels that first collected these independent works had limited printings and eventually drifted into obscurity.

Years later, Chaykin's *American Flagg!* and Wagner's original *Grendel* stories did receive scrupulous graphic novel treatments, but neither artist enjoyed the sustained attention lavished on more mainstream practitioners such as Miller and John Byrne. Similarly, Coe's books, like many of the *RAW* one-shots, remain scarce and difficult to appreciate as virtuoso relics of their times. Equally compelling is the problem of Richard and Wendy Pini's self-published *ElfQuest* (1978-1985), a rollicking fantasy that garnered a cultish fan base almost from its first publication. By the early 1990's, the series had been so overcollected and recompiled that it experienced something of a repackaging burnout.

Graphic Novels Go Mainstream

Before the 1980's, annuals, treasuries, digests, and trade collections of superhero comics, funny animals material, and comic-strip reprints were quite familiar. Though such collections were hardly graphic novels by modern definitions, their booklike design, high page count, and generally reverential attitude toward the reprisal of previously ephemeral material lent credence to the concept of more comprehensive products.

Before the publication of Miller's and Alan Moore's deconstructions of the Cold War superhero in the mid-1980's, both Marvel and DC had already initiated graphic novel imprints to test the capacities of the direct-market system. In fact, the Marvel Graphic Novel line of high-priced, slickly bound books began in 1982 with Jim Starlin's popular *Death of Captain Marvel*. Soon after, Chris Claremont and Brent Anderson produced *X-Men: God Loves, Man Kills* (1982), a story that would influence X-Men media for decades. Marvel Comics also released graphic novels through its Epic Comics imprint.

A visual history of apartheid is depicted in *How to Commit Suicide in South Africa*, published by Knockabout Comics in 1983.(Courtesy of Knockabout Comics)

DC Comics, on the other hand, avoided the use of high-profile characters in graphic novels until mid-decade. In 1983, it initiated a line of fantasy and science-fiction graphic novels that featured lavish stand-alone tales and avant-garde story forms. Notable installments included Pat Mills and Kevin O'Neill's *Metalzoic* (1986) and Jack Kirby's long-delayed Fourth World reprisal, *The Hunger Dogs* (1985). The seven-volume DC Science Fiction Graphic Novel series followed, running from 1985 to 1987, with adaptations of works by Ray Bradbury, Harlan Ellison, and Frederik Pohl.

DC Comics also experimented with a compromise between traditional pamphlet comics and full-blown graphic novels: a square-bound prestige format that was longer, higher quality, and, at almost three dollars, more expensive than the average seventy-five-cent comic book. The results proved fruitful for several miniseries, especially for Miller's four-part *Batman: The Dark Knight Returns*, Marv Wolfman and George Pérez's two-part *History of the DC Universe* (1986), and Moore and Brian Bolland's *Batman: The Killing Joke* (1988). However, it was the compilation of Miller's complete *Batman: The Dark Knight Returns* and Moore and Dave Gibbons's *Watchmen* (1987) that cemented graphic novels as a legitimate medium. DC continued its experiments with Batman books such as Mike W. Barr and Jerry Bingham's *Batman: Son of the Demon* (1987) and Grant Morrison and Dave McKean's *Batman: Arkham Asylum* (1989) as well as extensions of the prestige square-bound formats in series such as Chaykin's *Blackhawk* (1987) and Mike Grell's *Green Arrow: The Longbow Hunters* (1989).

Both major publishers developed four- and six-issue miniseries and twelve-issue maxiseries throughout the 1980's, planning to repurpose them as graphic novels eventually. Works that were reformatted from limited series include Moore and David Lloyd's *V for Vendetta* (1982-1985; 1988-1989), Wolfman and Pérez's *Crisis on Infinite Earths* (1985-1986), and Jim Shooter and Mike Zeck's *Marvel Super Heroes Secret Wars* (1984-1985).

Impact

The 1980's was a decade of immense variety and experimentation with comic book forms. At the same time, the long-term castration of the traditional superhero was underway as part of a much larger expression of popular resentment about the declining state of inner cities and American industry during the period. Even Spider-Man's switch to a macabre and parasitic black costume in *Marvel Superheroes Secret Wars* suggests a darkening of the generally idealistic ethics of superhero conflict. Add to this the ascendance of morally ambiguous vigilantes such as the Punisher and Grendel and skeptical everyday heroes such as *Locas*'s Maggie and Hopey, *Mage*'s Kevin Matchstick, *American Splendor*'s Harvey Pekar, and the protagonist from *Reid Fleming, the World's Toughest Milkman*, and the comics landscape of the 1980's seems to search resiliently for strength, heroism, and understanding. In many ways, the decade became the quintessential era of furious

The Marvel graphic novel line of high-priced, slickly bound books began in 1982 with Jim Starlin's popula*r Death of Captain Marvel.*. (Courtesy of Marvel Comics)

exploration across the comics medium. Much of this discovery and diversity helped to foster stronger industry commitment to the developing graphic novel.

Daniel Yezbick

Bibliography

Gabilliet, Jean-Paul. *Of Comics and Men: A Cultural History of American Comic Books*. Translated by Bart Beaty and Nick Nguyen. Jackson: University Press of Mississippi, 2005. Provides a history of comic books as cultural phenomena and aesthetic signifiers and a survey of the medium conversant with French theories of comic book semiotics.

Weiner, Stephen. *Faster than a Speeding Bullet: The Rise of the Graphic Novel*. New York: NBM, 2003. Includes a concise history of the medium as well as a guide to the most influential graphic novels of the 1980's and 1990's.

Wright, Bradford. *Comic Book Nation: The Transformation of Youth Culture in America*. Baltimore: Johns Hopkins University Press, 2001. Studies comic books and superheroes as American cultural icons and includes a chapter on the evolution of comic books and graphic novels in the 1980's and 1990's.

1990'S: COMICS AS LITERATURE

Definition

During the 1990's, the graphic novel medium was on the road to legitimization. Over the course of the decade, great writers and artists rose to the forefront, some comics came to be regarded as works of literature, and graphic novels handled themes not seen previously in the medium.

Introduction

Graphic novels came to be regarded as legitimately literary in the 1990's, in large part because of mainstream media attention, inclusion in bookstores, and increasing recognition of the superhero genre. Prior to the 1990's, large publishers such as Marvel Comics and DC Comics were slow to adapt to the graphic novel format. Rarely would either company release a graphic novel of original content. There was some dabbling in original stories in book-bound form during the 1970's and 1980's, but mostly, publishers reprinted collected runs of superhero comics.

The mass-merchandizing phenomenon that had taken off with the *Star Wars* films in the late 1970's and early 1980's continued into the 1990's. This proved to be beneficial to the comics industry, as the 1989 film

After the success of Tim Buton's *Batman* (1989), bookstores increasingly began to carry comic books and graphic novels. (Courtesy of Sunset Boulevard/Corbis)

Batman, directed by Tim Burton, had a wide range of licensing contracts across different media. The film's popularity led to an increase in interest in the superhero. Because of the success of the film, bookstores began to carry more comic books and graphic novels. Frank Miller's 1986 graphic novel *Batman: The Dark Knight Returns* particularly resonated with readers, demonstrating the ability of graphic novels to tell complex, mature stories to a wide audience.

Throughout much of the 1990's, comic book publishers sought to increase revenues by marketing comics to collectors and encouraging them to buy multiple copies. To that end, publishers released comics with variant covers, foil, embossing, and other gimmicks. The marketing technique for graphic novels was the opposite, as publishers wanted wide distribution to make comics more inclusive.

Writers and Artists

During the 1990's, many artists imitated other artists, creating house styles for publishers. Image Comics, one of the largest comics companies at the time, was founded in the wake of a dispute between Marvel and a group of its creators, including Jim Lee and Todd McFarlane, who were upset about the lack of negotiation in their contracts and the lack of creator ownership opportunities. Although Image Comics first published works set in a superhero universe like those of Marvel and DC, by the late 1990's, the company began to experiment with stories in other genres and with original graphic novels.

While many comics of the day were visually striking, they lacked substance. However, the nonsuperhero realm of 1990's comics was dominated by a stable of rising writers. Many of the industry's most popular creators, such as Alan Moore, Grant Morrison, Neil Gaiman, and Warren Ellis, were British writers who were rising in prominence in the United States during the 1990's.

Moore was the first writer of the group to become widely known in the United States. He was primarily known for *Watchmen* (1987), but throughout the 1990's, he worked on the superhero book *Supreme*, which played with the Superman archetype. Moore revived some of the larger-than-life ideas of the Golden Age and Silver Age that other creators had eliminated in favor of more realistic superheroes, proving that some of the less realistic ideas of those ages could still resonate with contemporary audiences. Moore also worked on nonsuperhero works such as *From Hell* (1989-1996), about Jack the Ripper. In 1999, Moore founded America's Best Comics, a publishing imprint that allowed Moore and other creators to experiment with form and genre.

Comics as Literature

The defining moment of legitimization for the comics medium occurred when Art Spiegelman won the Pulitzer Prize Special Citation in 1992 for *Maus*, which chronicles Spiegelman's father's experience as a Holocaust survivor. The first volume was published in 1986; a second volume was published in 1992, and both volumes were collected into a complete novel in 1993. Widely recognized by the mainstream literary establishment as a work of legitimate literature, *Maus* encouraged readers to consider the literary nature of the graphic novel medium as a whole.

Vertigo, an imprint of DC Comics, was a driving force for comics as literature during the 1990's, and it co-opted the term "graphic novel" to describe collected editions of its nonsuperhero work. Throughout much of the 1990's, Vertigo republished Gaiman's *The Sandman* (1989-1996) in hardcover volumes and trade paperbacks. The series received much critical acclaim and went through several printings. Likewise, Morrison's series *The Invisibles* (1994-2000) was published as individual issues and republished in collected volumes throughout the 1990's, as was Ellis's series *Transmetropolitan* (1997-2002).

As graphic novels began to be accepted as literature, works such as Scott McCloud's critically acclaimed *Understanding Comics* (1993) helped readers better

Ghost World. (Courtesy of Fantagraphics Books)

understand the form. McCloud's book, presented in the form of a comic narrated by the author's avatar, explains how the reader interprets the comics form and describes the techniques used to convey the story.

New Themes and Plots

Increasingly, DC Comics began to trust the original graphic novel format, releasing many of its titles under the Paradox Press banner. Paradox's publications included *The Big Book Of* series (1994-2000), which explored a different theme in each volume. Paradox also released English editions of the manga series *Gon* (1992-2002) by Masashi Tanaka. The wordless story tells the adventures of a hungry dinosaur who often gets in tangles with other animals. The publication of *Gon* and similar books illustrates the increasing influence of manga during the 1990's. Another important graphic novel published by Paradox during the 1990's was *Road to Perdition* (1998), written by Max Allen Collins and illustrated by Richard Piers Rayner, which would inspire a 2002 film adaptation.

A number of other companies successfully published graphic novels during the 1990's. Oni Press was founded in 1997 by Joe Nozemack and Bob Schreck and went on to publish many original graphic novels. Dark Horse Comics, founded during the previous decade, republished limited series such as Frank Miller's *300* (1998) in graphic novel format. Some of Dark Horse's graphic novels won Eisner Awards, including Moore's *A Small Killing* (1991), Joe Kubert's *Fax from Sarajevo* (1996), and Mike Mignola and John Byrne's *Hellboy: Seed of Destruction* (1994). Dark Horse also gained mainstream attention for its licensed products, publishing comic books based on preexisting properties such as *Star Wars* and *Alien vs. Predator* (both beginning in 1992).

The diversity of themes and plots and the talent of the writers working in the field allowed comics to become a more respected genre during the 1990's than it ever had been before. Though slice-of-life tales, gangster stories, and tales of wayward dinosaurs did not always fit into the mainstream comic book form, the graphic novel proved to be the ideal form through which to tell such stories. Through the publishing and marketing efforts of independent publishers and specialized imprints and the groundbreaking work of writers such as Moore, Gaiman, Morrison, Ellis, and Miller, graphic novels became both critically and commercially successful.

Impact

The first graphic novel to earn mainstream acclaim, *Batman: The Dark Knight Returns* called attention to the literary potential of graphic novels. Comics creators such as Spiegelman and Will Eisner saw the graphic novel as the final legitimization of the medium and a further extension of the art. The publication of a number of high-profile graphic novels throughout the 1990's confirmed the medium's status as a legitimate form of literature, with novels such as Spiegelman's *Maus* garnering recognition from the mainstream literary establishment.

During the 1990's, the definition of the graphic novel expanded to include trade paperback collections of ongoing series. Many of the early serialized works of small presses found new life as graphic novels. For example, Daniel Clowes's *Ghost World* (1997) was originally published in his Fantagraphics series *Eightball*.

Collections of the Vertigo series *The Sandman* sold well throughout the 1990's. Publishers adapted a model in which they released comic books in both hardcover and paperback format. *The Sandman* series drew mainstream attention to the existence of comic books for adult readers, and this series and others were soon shelved in bookstores. Graphic novels became a staple product line of chain bookstores such as Borders and Barnes & Noble.

In another major development, small presses put their trust in writers, publishing many original graphic novels and marketing them based on the writers' reputations and existing fan bases. Marvel, DC, and, to a lesser extent, Dark Horse raced to find the next breakout writers and artists, at times signing them to relatively generous exclusive contracts. This focus on writers would greatly shape the comic book industry over the course of the following decades.

Ora C. McWilliams

Bibliography

Lopes, Paul Douglas. *Demanding Respect: The Evolution of the American Comic Book*. Philadelphia: Temple University Press, 2009. Provides a short history of the evolution of the comic book in the United States with an eye toward comics' legitimization.

Wolk, Douglas. *Reading Comics: How Graphic Novels Work and What They Mean*. Cambridge, Mass.: Da Capo Press, 2007. Examines the comics form, looking at how several creators in the industry have applied their art, including Eisner, Miller, Morrison, and Moore.

Wright, Bradford W. *Comic Book Nation: The Transformation of Youth Culture in America*. Baltimore: Johns Hopkins University Press, 2003. Links events in the history of the United States, such as U.S. involvement in World War II, to events in the comic book industry.

2000'S: FROM NOVELTY TO CANON

Definition

Since 2000, the acceptance of graphic novels as a valid form of literature has gained momentum, undeniably shaping both the medium and its contributors and influencing its future. As graphic novels are increasingly found in libraries and academic arenas, the popularity of serious graphic texts and the expansion of the medium to include historical texts and graphic adaptations raise concerns about the already complicated classification and definition of the term "graphic novel."

One! Hundred! Demons! (Courtesy of Sasquatch Books)

Introduction

While anthologies have broadened their contents to reflect the interests and experiences of a more diverse faculty and student population, the inclusion of comics in textbooks still surprises readers, for despite the diversity promoted by publishers, comics are one of the last media still struggling to earn respect in academia. However, academic publishers have recognized the validity of the medium and have included "graphic essays" (usually excerpts from graphic novels) in readers, anthologies, and other textbooks. From chapters of Art Spiegelman's *Maus* (1986, 1991) in American literature anthologies to excerpts from Lynda Barry's *One! Hundred! Demons!* (2000-2001) in college readers, graphic texts are working their way into the American literary consciousness.

During the 2000's, many serious graphic novels—including Marjane Satrapi's *Persepolis* (2000-2003) and Gene Luen Yang's *American Born Chinese* (2006), countless manga titles, and graphic histories of such events as the signing of the U.S. Constitution and Hurricane Katrina—were published. The medium asserted itself as one that accommodates many genres, including graphic histories, graphic biographies, and graphic mythology, and as the genres have multiplied, so has readership. While declining sales might contradict the popularity or cultural reach of graphic novels, libraries play a key role in recognizing the validity of

the medium by meeting readers' demand for graphic texts, building and expanding graphic novel collections in both young-adult and adult reader sections.

Significant Publications

A number of notable graphic novels chronicling significant historical events or serving as graphic memoirs or graphic biographies were published during the 2000's. Of these, several have garnered critical attention and awards, such as Joe Sacco's *Safe Area Goražde* (2000) and Satrapi's *Persepolis*, both winners of Eisner Awards (Satrapi won the award for *Persepolis 2*, published in 2004). Though *Maus* earned a Pulitzer Prize Special Citation in 1992, it was not until the 2000's that graphic novels began to be more frequently noticed by both critics writing for publications that do not focus exclusively on comics art and juries for awards that are not limited to graphic or comics work. For example, Alison Bechdel's *Fun Home* (2006) was a finalist for the 2006 National Book Critics Circle Award.

As the pervasion of graphic novels into areas dominated by written texts continued throughout the 2000's, the publication of graphic novels tackling such significant subjects as war, politics, gender and sexuality, and racism increased. Other novels published during the period borrow from the more traditional superhero and horror comics to comment on the state of the modern world; these include Mark Millar's *Kick-Ass* (2008-2010), which questions the morality and necessity of vigilante justice, and Robert Kirkman's *The Walking Dead* (2003-   ), which takes the zombie genre in a direction more akin to Cormac McCarthy's *The Road* (2006) than George A. Romero's *Night of the Living Dead* (1968).

That graphic novelists tackle such significant subjects is not a new development. However, the frequency with which authors have used the medium and the positive critical and public receptions of such works suggest that those working in the medium, from publishers to writers and artists, are heeding a call to validate it by demonstrating the depth and breadth of its potential.

Graphic Novels in Libraries

The role of public and academic libraries in the readership and reception of graphic novels has shifted the focus of the medium from long-form texts based on popular serial comics characters (Batman, the X-Men, Spider-Man) to texts that could be more accurately described as graphic nonfiction, graphic memoirs, and graphic historical fiction. The inconsistent application of such descriptions and the general lack of agreement on those labels or on appropriate categorization by readership seem to be particularly problematic for libraries, in which the location and classification of graphic novels vary dramatically.

Periodicals such as *Library Journal* have made efforts to provide guidance to librarians, particularly by publishing reviews to help them select texts appropriate for their collections. However, the industry struggles to reach those who have yet to accept the graphic novel as a valid medium, or at least as a medium appropriate for and targeted at adult readers. For example, articles written to help librarians build graphic novel and comic collections frequently assume that such collections are for young adults. As a result, many graphic novel collections in

public libraries appear in young-adult collections, and graphic novels that are not appropriate for young-adult readers are omitted from collections. The omission of notable texts, or of collections altogether, is still the subject of much campaigning in library journals and other relevant publications.

The Academic Study of Graphic Novels

Like libraries, academic programs also struggle to classify the study of graphic novels and comic texts. The University of Florida became the first university to establish a graduate program in comics studies in the United States; it is part of the graduate English program. Courses in graphic novels and comics are found in visual media studies, English and literature, and graphic design programs, and professors and lecturers across disciplines have introduced graphic texts into their courses.

While such a lack of centralized study of graphic texts seems promising in that it suggests that the medium is versatile and valuable, decentralization poses a problem in the development of theory and praxis.

From Alison Bechdel's *Fun Home,* a finalist for the 2006 National Book Critics Circle Award. (Courtesy of Mariner Books)

Many who primarily or exclusively study graphic novels are based in English or literature departments; such placement is logical if one considers the graphic novel purely a literary text. However, the visual element of graphic novels is as significant as the written content, as is the relationship between the word and the image. Any academic studying the medium must be knowledgeable in not only literary theory but also visual theory. No doubt those studying comics and graphic novels find themselves proficient in both concentrations, a trend that coincides with movements in K-12 education toward multiple types of literacy, addressing students' ability to engage with written, visual, and audio media.

In fact, the decentralization of the study of graphic novels and comics speaks not to the failure of libraries or institutions of higher education to "find a home" for these texts but to the innate complexity of the texts. To those inclined to order and to organization, the ad hoc nature of the study of graphic novels is uncomfortable; to readers of graphic novels, issues of classification are no surprise, for such a limitless medium will naturally present limitless options for study.

Impact

As suggested by the direction that both creators and students of graphic novels have taken since 2000, one might expect the medium of comics and graphic novels to continue to flourish in areas deemed more credible by academics and libraries: for example, history, biography, and literary fiction. Whether creators are responding to criticism or whether the graphic novel has, at last, found its niche has yet to be seen. However, as in any medium, from poetry to painting, one can certainly expect a range of work, from simplistic texts with commercial appeal to mature texts with complex themes. The lasting power not only of individual texts and authors but also of specific subgenres of the medium is not yet known.

Spiegelman's *Maus*, a work frequently anthologized and widely studied by academics, has found its place in the literary canon, and it is clear that the reading public continues to embrace graphic novels as legitimate texts. However, which texts join *Maus* and which are relegated to trend is less certain. As is true with most any medium, those texts possessing social or cultural significance and those demonstrating original or "mature" use of the medium will continue to be held in high esteem.

Theresa Fine-Pawsey

Bibliography

Gordon, Ian. "Let Us Not Call Them Graphic Novels: Comic Books as Biography and History." *Radical History Review*, no. 106 (Winter, 2010): 185-192. Uses three graphic novels about politics to determine the appropriate classification of the texts and argues that the term graphic novel is a "marketing tool" for publishers.

Gravett, Paul. *Graphic Novels: Everything You Need to Know*. London: Aurum, 2005. Covers everything from the definition of the term graphic novel to readers' questions about graphic novels, also providing a list of thirty essential works.

Griffith, Paula A. "Graphic Novels in the Secondary Classroom and School Libraries." *Journal of Adolescent and Adult Literacy* 54, no. 3 (November, 2010): 181-189. Addresses the concerns of educators and librarians and provides concrete guidelines and suggestions for using graphic novels in the classroom and building school library collections.

Weiner, Steven. *The 101 Best Graphic Novels*. New York: NBM, 2005. Provides an introduction and a history of the medium for unfamiliar readers and lists significant graphic novels for young-adult or adult readers.

African American Portrayal: The Depiction of Black History, Culture, and Experience Through Sequential Art and Text

Definition

African American graphic novels collect previously published black-oriented comic books or present original material from an African American perspective through a series of words and images. African Americans as featured characters were rarities in comic books before the 1960's and in graphic novels before the 1990's. In the twenty-first century, however, African American graphic novels have flourished, offering a variety of subjects appropriate for all audiences.

Introduction

Born in the 1970's, graphic novels are offspring of comic books, which debuted in the 1930's. Likewise, comic books are descendants of early twentieth century pulp fiction and late nineteenth century major metropolitan newspaper comic strips.

Like all minorities in the United States, African Americans were considered fair game for cartoonists. Comics were originally aimed at lower-class citizens and new immigrants. Funny papers satirized perceived national or racial characteristics even as they provided cheap visual entertainment for illiterate minorities that were the subjects of humor.

In a time when they were politely called "colored" or "Negroes," African Americans, because of skin tone, were distinctive wherever they showed up in comics. In domestic settings, African Americans (typically shown as menial laborers or unemployed) were invariably depicted as balloon-lipped, kinky-haired, lazy simpletons in tattered clothing, who walked barefoot, ate watermelon, and spoke in dialect.

One reason for ethnic stereotyping was the nature of the early medium. Newspaper comic strips did not allow space for development of secondary characters, so artists resorted to visual shorthand. A figure with side curls and a hooked nose was instantly recognizable as Jewish. A hulking blond was a Swede. A dark-skinned character was an African American.

Black Panther. (Courtesy of Marvel Comics)

Early comics stereotypes also perpetuated prevailing attitudes of the dominant force in American society toward ethnic groups. The Caucasian majority saw those who were somehow different—in physical attributes, languages or accents, clothing, religion, or customs—as outside the mainstream.

African Americans Fade into the Background

By the advent of comic books, most other ethnic groups had been assimilated into American society. At a glance, they were physically indistinguishable from other citizens and their stereotypes became increasingly anachronistic, thus, less interesting fodder for visually weighted comic strips.

Because of their distinctive appearance, African Americans were an exception. The Civil War had abolished slavery in the United States, and African Americans were afterward supposedly free and equal. The reality, however, was quite different. This difference was reflected in comics, which maintained racial stereotypes of the previous century with little public objection. Popular comic strips or books such as *Moon Mullins* (with a black servant called Mushmouth), which began in 1923, perpetuated the derogatory image of African Americans.

In the Deep South especially, Jim Crow laws had been imposed both as revenge for Civil War defeat and as reinforcement for the concept of white supremacy. Laws promulgated segregation and added literacy requirements or poll taxes to vote, disenfranchising millions of African Americans and poor whites from participating in the process of democracy and thereby robbing them of political power.

Those who spoke out against the system's unfairness faced elimination: Between the 1880's and the 1960's, some thirty-five hundred African American men, women, and children were lynched at the hands of the Ku Klux Klan or other vigilante groups. Those who bore injustice without protest continued to live on the fringes of society as second-class citizens and, in essence, became invisible.

In Search of a Positive African American Identity

The advent of comic books did little to improve the image of black people. One of the first admirable dark-skinned characters to appear was Lothar, the muscular sidekick in Lee Falk's crime-fighting *Mandrake the Magician* comic strip and books (first appearing in 1934). African royalty, Lothar's "otherness" was emphasized by his fez, leopard-skin clothing, and broken English. In later incarnations, Lothar dressed and spoke better, but he remained subordinate to Mandrake.

In the early 1940's, influential cartoonist Will Eisner helped institute a comic book version of the film convention of black sidekicks, such as Stepin Fetchit and Willie Best, as comic relief. Eisner introduced a detective called the Spirit and gave him the dark-skinned assistant Ebony White, who exhibited all the worst stereotypical characteristics and traits.

African Americans began to make positive inroads in comics representation following World War II, in which many African Americans had served with distinction. In 1947, the year Jackie Robinson became a true-life hero by breaking major-league baseball's color barrier, the short-lived independent publisher All-Negro Comics introduced realistically drawn black heroes Ace Harlem, a private detective, and Lion Man, a tribal African. At the beginning of the Civil Rights movement in the mid-1950's, Atlas Comics (later Marvel Comics) produced *Jungle Tales* (1954-1955), starring nonstereotypical African hero Waku, prince of the Bantu.

In 1959, DC Comics released *Our Army at War*, featuring Sgt. Rock of Easy Company. Among the unit's soldiers (in contrast to the U.S. military's actual wartime policy of segregation) was a black man named Jackie Johnson. Four years later, Marvel also rewrote history, inducting African American Gabe Jones into the Stan Lee-Jack Kirby series *Sgt. Fury and His Howling Commandos* (1963-1981).

Not until 1965 did the first featured black hero debut. He was Lobo, a former slave turned gunfighter and righter of wrongs in the Wild West after the Civil War. He appeared in a two-issue series from Dell Comics.

Stepping into the Comic Book Limelight

Passage of the Civil Rights Act of 1964 helped inspire positive black comic book characters. In 1966, Marvel introduced a mainstream superhero named T'Challa, an African prince known as Black Panther, in the supporting cast of the Lee-Kirby creation *Fantastic Four*, which debuted in 1961. He later starred in an eighteen-issue story arc in *Jungle Action* (1972-1976), considered an early graphic novel, and continued to fight crime in his own series.

In 1969, Marvel introduced the first African American superhero, the Falcon, in *Captain America* (1968-1996), and he has continued to appear sporadically ever since. Three years later, Marvel premiered another featured black hero, the invulnerable, eponymous detective from *Luke Cage, Hero for Hire*, who continues

Captain America and The Falcon. (Courtesy of Marvel Comics)

informally investigating cases in the twenty-first century as Cage.

Thanks to blaxploitation movies of the 1960's and 1970's, black characters burgeoned in comic books and graphic novels. Some were ordinary, decent citizens, such as newspaperman Robbie Robertson in *Amazing Spider-Man.* Some were superheroes or superheroines (such as Storm of the X-Men, who later married Black Panther, or Dark Horse Comics' character Martha Washington, a 1990 creation from Frank Miller). Some were even supervillains, including female genius and Captain America opponent Nightshade. It took many decades, but by the 1990's, African American characters had finally become regular and significant members in the world of sequential art.

Impact

With the institution of Black History Month, the inauguration of the first black U.S. president, the establishment of independent publishers, and the development of talented black writers and artists, African American comic book and graphic novel characters have proliferated as never before in the early twenty-first century. Stereotypes of earlier comics have vanished, replaced in public consciousness by troubling new stereotypes to overcome. These include the uniform depiction of black men as angry and violent, the portrayal of black women as purely sexual creatures, and the characterization of the hip-hop culture as solely antiauthority and misogynistic.

Because of their power to appeal through evocative words and pictures, graphic novels play an increasingly important role in diluting the overt and covert racism that still permeates American life. Graphic novels offer wide diversity in style and subject matter. Works such as *The Prison-Ship Adventure of James Forten, Revolutionary War Captive* (2011) and *Best Shot in the West: The Adventures of Nat Love* (2012) highlight the deeds of forgotten or neglected historical black figures. Others such as *Black Jack: The Ballad of Jack Johnson* (2010) and *I See the Promised Land: A Life of Martin Luther King, Jr.* (2004) present heroes to admire. Still others—such as *Sentences: The Life of M.F. Grimm* (2007), the cautionary tale of a real-life hip-hop artist; *Stuck Rubber Baby* (1995), an autobiographical story of black and white gay lovers; and *Incognegro* (2008), a mystery centered on a black man passing as white—entertain even as they illuminate. Like no other medium, graphic novels have the ability to reach reluctant readers, to show the way conditions were in the past and how they could be in the future.

Jack Ewing

Bibliography

Chaney, Michael A. *Fugitive Vision: Slave Image and Black Identity in Antebellum Narrative*. Bloomington: Indiana University Press, 2008. An illustrated work dealing with the post-Civil War writings of former slaves, which have influenced the way African Americans see themselves in the modern world.

Duffy, Damian, and John Jennings. *Black Comix: African American Independent Comics, Arts, and Culture*. Brooklyn: Mark Batty, 2010. An illustrated discussion of the twenty-first century proliferation of independent black comics and graphic novels, featuring interviews with many of the major artists and writers in the genre.

Strömberg, Fredrik. *Black Images in the Comics: A Visual History*. Seattle: Fantagraphics, 2003. A profusely illustrated history showing the changing depiction of African Americans in newspaper comic strips, comic books, and graphic novels from the early twentieth century.

AFRICAN GRAPHIC NOVELS: AFFIRMATIONS OF NATIONAL IDENTITY

Definition

This essay explores graphic novels written and illustrated by writers and artists who identify themselves as African and create for a predominantly African audience. Tracing the historical development of such works from colonial to contemporary African nations, the essay takes into consideration issues of colonialism and postcolonialism, varying cultures and traditions, concerns with literacy, and how graphic literature is distributed throughout the continent and the world.

Introduction

Poor distribution, a reliance on English and French, widespread illiteracy, and prices considered expensive

for "disposable material" are issues that have affected graphic novels in Africa. Still, writers and artists have adjusted to their audiences, argued with governments to improve distribution, relied on various organizations to distribute under the guise of "educational comics," and challenged African, French, and Belgian publishers to produce their works. African creators make more use of pictures than words, keeping the dialogue simple, and encourage readers to share the books rather than throw them out. At least in part, all of this is to counter the Eurocentric ideas of the comics that appeared in Africa until the 1970's and to provide either a more Afrocentric perspective or, at least, a national one, since a number of writers and artists are Africans

Marguerite Abouet's hugely popular series of books centered on the life of a young woman in a cheerful Ivory Coast suburb show an Africa far away from stereotypes of war and disease. (AFP/Getty Images)

of European descent who identify themselves as African rather than European. Gone are the days when British writers and artists such as Dave Gibbons and Brian Bolland were hired to produce comic books such as *Powerman* (collected into an English graphic novel entitled *Powerbolt*, featuring an African version of Superman) for a readership more used to imports of Marvel Comics, DC Comics, or Disney characters.

There is a wide variety of African comics, and many of these are either published as graphic novels or collected, because of story-line continuity, into graphic novels. Some of the comics rely on European authors; others are cultural hybrids, coproduced by African artists and European writers. Still others are African (not necessarily black African, but produced by artists and writers who identify themselves as Africans by nationality). The latter deal in particular with politics, sports, societal events, and traditions. There are still a number of comics and graphic novels that are published anonymously, either because of political and religious concerns or because they are published through organizations such as the Red Cross and other nongovernmental organizations (NGOs).

The audience for African graphic novels has also changed and grown. Originally, comics were generally thought of as being for children, but with the rise of satire magazines such as *Bitterkomix* in South Africa and the more expensive graphic novels such as *Aya* (2005-2010; a kind of soap-opera series featuring the Ivory Coast), they are increasingly being consumed by adults and by the newly affluent in some African nations. Though most often written in French or English, African comics and graphic novels are easily read because of simple word use and a reliance on pictures. In fact, some artists and writers, such as Kenyan Anthony Mwangi and Congolese Fifi Makuna with Christophe N'Galle Edimo, produce work without any words whatsoever. In the latter's graphic novel *Les Enfants*, Makuna and Edimo create a variation of Victor Hugo's *Les Misérables* (1862) in which a starving child gets stuffed in a tire and set on fire for stealing purses. Some artists and writers choose to use *fumetti* or *fotoromanzi*, Italian-originated forms of photographs with dialogue. There are an increasing number of comics also written in Arabic. These, like Japanese manga, must be reproduced

backward, read from what westerners would consider the last page to the first page, and be read, in their original language, from right to left.

Comic strips, books, and graphic novels fall into two types. The first is educational, which are biographical (several in South Africa on Nelson Mandela) or deal with social problems, notably AIDS (*I Need to Know* from Botswana), hygiene (UNICEF's seventy-four-page "novel" *Facts of Life*), abuse of women, illegal migration, agriculture (*Eating with Hope* from South Africa), and concerns about illiteracy and the benefits of education.

The second type of graphic novel is pure entertainment. These stories usually begin as magazines and, depending on popular response, are collected. One of the most notable is a magazine entitled *Serial Killer* published in Nigeria, which features murder mysteries. The most popular of these serialized stories are frequently collected and released as graphic novels. South Africa's *Supa Strikas*, based on a popular English strip, *Roy of the Rovers* (1954-1993), features a popular soccer team and its star player. Rwanda's *De wraak van Bakamé* (2010; the revenge of Bakamé) features an anthropomorphic trickster rabbit who reinforces folktales and tradition. The *Goorgoolu* series from Senegal has been turned into a play and a live television series and has been collected in a series of graphic novels.

Creators

The artists and writers labeled European are usually from Western Europe or the United States. They create works that are distributed exclusively in Africa to an African audience. An example would be Serge Saint-Michel and Bernard Dufossé, French artists who published the magazines *Calao* and *Kouakou* from Paris, which feature new African artists and writers. These creators are sometimes hampered by not knowing local customs or traditions.

During the 1970's, there was an increasing number of graphic works being produced by a combination of European, American, and African writers and artists. Critics of African graphic literature label these works as a combination of "northern thought" and "southern artwork," which suggests that the writer is "guiding" the artist, who is African. There is an assumption that colonizers and postcolonizers know more about the culture than those within the culture. While some of this production is collaborative, some of it is not. Stereotypes of African culture still infiltrate the work. Nonetheless, many African artists like this form of production because it gives them exposure, helps them financially, and usually guarantees the reprinting of the comics as a graphic novel in Europe.

African creators are those artists and writers who consider themselves African by nationality, whether white or black. They constitute the largest number of comics creators and graphic novelists on the African continent. Their work is usually nationalistic, acknowledging history, culture, and tradition. It is often produced first in Africa, encouraging their respective nation's economies, and is produced with an African audience in mind.

Reversal of Eurocentric Stereotypes
Hergé (Georges Prosper Remi), a Belgian artist-writer, created *Les Aventures de Tintin* (1929-1976; *The Adventures of Tintin*, 1930-1976), twenty-three completed graphic novels that frequently made use of African stereotypes, depicting all Africans without nationality and with one look and human qualities that rendered them as humorous, rather than as three-dimensional personalities. Hergé's influences were other works of popular culture, particularly Edgar Rice Burroughs's Tarzan series, showing Africans to be passive, unintelligent, and ineffectual and, thus, worthy to be controlled by Europeans; these novels were popular throughout Africa. Still, a number of contemporary African artists and writers such as T. T. Fons (Alphonse Mendy, of *Goorgoolou*) and Joe Dog (Anton Kannemeyer, a founder of *Bitterkomix*) credit Hergé as their inspiration to produce radically new graphic works that reverse prior stereotypes.

Other writers and artists reverse the stereotype perpetuated in the United States of connecting African and African American characters with animals or nature (e.g., Marvel Comics' Black Panther and Storm and DC Comics' Vixen and Black Lightning) by dealing with daily African life rather than with superheroics. An example of this reversal of stereotypes might be the Albert Cossery and Golo (Guy Nadeau) graphic novel

Mendiants et orgueilleux (2009) from Cairo. The graphic novel is based on Cossery's novel of the same name, published in 1955 and translated into English as *Proud Beggars* (1981). The work focuses on Cairo's slums and their various inhabitants trying to succeed in life: notably, Gohar, a former university professor who works as a bookkeeper in a brothel; Yeghen, a drug dealer; El Kordi, a revolutionary; Naila, a prostitute who Gohar would like to marry; Set Amina, the madam of the bordello; and Nour El Din, a corrupt politician. These characters encompass a variety of lifestyles and hopes in Egypt, and their comedic interaction allows for satiric commentary on Egypt's people and government.

Postcolonialism and African Graphic Novels
During the 1960's, with many African nations becoming independent after European colonization, there was a rise in African comic books, many self-published and tribal. These books are called *kinoseires*, and few are available. They were written in native languages, such as Lingala, Tshiluba, and Kikongo, and featured local news events and gossip. As nations became independent, there was a rise in the publication of newspapers and magazines and a wider introduction to television. New publications encouraged new artists and writers, while television encouraged certain formats that these artists and writers would follow, such as the soap opera or detective drama.

The soap opera set the format for graphic novels such as the Aya series, written by Marguerite Abouet and drawn by Clément Oubrerie. The series features a teenage girl, Aya, on the Ivory Coast (Côte d'Ivoire) during the 1970's. The novels contain discussions and depictions of history and culture but focus primarily on female-male relationships. An interesting aspect of the series is that it highlights a period during the 1970's when the Ivory Coast was benefiting from its former colonial status with France. Agriculturally rich, the Ivory Coast has been a major producer of coffee, timber, cocoa, and bananas. Referred to at the time as the Paris of West Africa, Aya's city, Abidjan, is transnational, featuring people, fashion, and music from all over the world, but especially from France and the United States. The series was first published in 2007, by which time the Ivory Coast had become impoverished, Francophobic, and embroiled in civil war. One of the criticisms of the text, therefore, is that it harks back to an era when Eurocentric empowerment made the country better rather than identifying positively with its Africanness, separate from European influences.

Issues in Modern African Graphic Novels

Most popular contemporary African graphic novels for an older audience are either satirical or naturalistic, dealing with current issues, communal values, government insensitivity and corruption, racial strife, and redemption. The latter is particularly common of white writers and publishers, as in Conrad Botes and Anton Kannemeyer's *Bitterkomix* in postapartheid South Africa, and frequently represents guilt or sympathy for black South African violence. In white writer Andy Mason's *Vusi Goes Back* (1982), South African history is revealed from the point of view of a black grandfather to his grandson. Kannemeyer's *Bloedrivier* (1995) argues that the black Africans should have "killed the colonialist pigs" upon first contact. He revisits this issue in his other graphic novels *Heaven Help Us* (1998) and *Fear of a Black Planet* (2008). Another frequent contributor to *Bitterkomix*, Paddy Bouma serialized and then published a graphic novel entitled *The Guilty Bystander*, in which a white South African reevaluates the way he and his family participated in apartheid.

Black African artists and writers have different concerns, though many of these concerns involve revising history and telling myth from a black African perspective. In a series of graphic novels entitled *Mandrill* (1998-   ), Congolese artist-writer Barly Baruti focuses on French colonization of Africa. Eric Salla, another Congolese creator, uses photos from newspapers to recreate life in the country beginning in the 1930's. *Africavi* (2008), by the Togolese brothers Anani and Mensah Accoh, takes place starting in the seventeenth century, when Africato, king of a small African village, enlists his men to search for European ice, which becomes a symbol of Eurocentric values. In his journey, he has to agree with many of his people that African values are as important as European.

Feminism and African Graphic Novels

African ideals of women's rights have radically changed in the graphic novels world. Most of the artists and writers support the idea of women in nontraditional roles and, either gently or overtly, make those around them aware of this shift.

Samba Ndar Cisse's graphic novel *Oulaï: Pour que cesse l'excision* (2005; Oulaï: To end infibulation) argues against female circumcision. The novel shows a blood-soaked girl who runs toward the reader. In the novel, after the event, a woman says she will never allow this to happen to her daughter. Cisse does not make her African nation known, preferring to be known as an expatriate who resides in France.

La Vie de Pahé (2006; the life of Pahé), an autobiographical graphic novel by Gabonese writer-artist Patrick Essono, begins by describing his father's life as village chieftain with ten wives. The wives yell at the father, "a real polygamist," to which Pahe's father responds, "Zip it, chickies." Though gentle in nature, the novel suggests the changes occurring in Africa; the son is not as successful as the father is in getting women to "zip it."

A number of series are focused on the health of the country's peoples, though most of these are published in the United States. One such series is *Emma Says* (1994), published by the AIDS Technical Assistance Project, created by Lahoma Smith Romocki, and written and drawn by unnamed writers and artists. Emma is a middle-aged African woman who goes about sharing wisdom about women's health care, particularly in regards to AIDS.

Censorship and African Graphic Novels

In 2007, Egyptian writer-artist Magdy El Shafee created the first graphic novel published for adults in his country, entitled *Metro* (English translation, 2012). The novels were confiscated by the police, and El Shafee and his publisher were put in jail, charged with creating and disseminating work that was "offensive to public morals." While the work contains depictions of sexuality, it may have been banned for it revelations about governmental corruption.

Many African artists and writers have found themselves unable to work in their native lands and have become expatriates, shipping their work back to Africa for consumption. Along with Belgian Carl Norac, Simon Mbumbo, a Cameroonian, writes and draws a comic strip collected into a graphic novel entitled *Hisham et Yseult* (2005; Hisham and Isolde), inspired by the European medieval tale *Tristan und Isolde* (1210; *Tristan and Isolde*, 1899). Hisham is an African refugee, while Isolde is biracial from a family that defines itself as French. The cultural clash, particularly the introduction of a biracial love affair, displayed in the novel forced Mbumbo from Cameroon.

Patrice "Pat" Masioni was born in the Democratic Republic of Congo. He has created graphic novels on Rwandan genocide, but his most popular work is *L'Appello* (2005), in which a series of dreams by discontented Africans become acknowledged and, in some cases, realized. Nigerian cartoonist Tayo Fatunla lives and works in London. Salla saw his drawings destroyed by the police and was granted political asylum in the Netherlands.

In some African nations, African artists and writers are continually challenged because of concerns over antinationalism or historical revision. They are also jeopardized by challenging culture and tradition. Some who remain on the continent choose to censor themselves, preferring not to release works until a time when their work will seem more acceptable.

Impact

Popular in many African nations, African graphic novels have also earned fan bases in France, Belgium, the Netherlands, England, and the United States. African artists and writers have started to work outside Africa, writing and illustrating a variety of projects. The Tanzanian artist Godfrey Mwampembwa has done animated cartoons for MTV. Masioni has published a series of graphic novels in the Netherlands about the Plains Indians of the United States. Mauritania's Man Keong Leval created a medieval saga published in England. A show of African graphic artists was displayed at the prestigious Studio Museum in Harlem in New York City. Similar shows have also taken place in France and throughout Africa, allowing nations to cross borders by identifying common concerns.

Within Africa, there has been a rise in the number of artists and writers associations. These have encouraged fan clubs and better publication quality and distribution for graphic novels. Abetted by increased popularity, artists and writers are able to request and receive more money for their creations.

The major impact of these graphic novels lies in their ability to reshape the African landscape. Whether by increasing literacy, aiding in health concerns, dealing with communal or national news, reinforcing or reinterpreting folk culture, or reshaping stereotypical portrayals of African peoples, these novels aid and serve the continent's emergence as a literary and artistic force in the twenty-first century.

Terry Joseph Cole

Bibliography

Barnard, Rita. "Bitterkomix: Notes from the Post-Apartheid Underground." *South Atlantic Quarterly* 103, no. 4 (Fall, 2004): 719-754. Distinguishes between the interests of black and white African artists and writers, focusing on South Africa's *Bitterkomix* and the graphic novels that have come out of that magazine. Attempts slight comparisons between this "adult" satire magazine and other forms of African comics.

"An Inventory of the Comic Strip in Africa." *Africultures*, January, 2011. http://www.africultures.com/php/index.php?nav=article&no=5470. A history of the publication of various forms of comics in Africa, giving useful references for artist/writer associations as well as publishers of African comics.

Repetti, Massimo. "African Wave: Specificity and Cosmopolitanism in African Comics." *African Arts* 40, no. 2 (Summer, 2007): 16-35. An incisive historical essay by a curator of international events of African comics and graphic novels. Leans toward a Eurocentric view regarding how Europeans have helped to develop the African market for graphic novels and comics in general.

AWARDS FOR GRAPHIC NOVELS: RECOGNIZING EXCELLENCE

Definition

This essay will describe and discuss the major awards given to graphic novels, including the Eagle, Kirby, Eisner, Harvey, Ignatz, and Hugo awards, as well as various awards given to manga.

Introduction

For most media, various awards are created to recognize excellence. Comic arts are no exception, and graphic novels have typically been included to some extent from the beginning of most comics awards. In several cases, graphic novels and anthologies were initially combined into a single prize. As they become more prominent, graphic novels have been awarded their own prizes; in fact, for some awards, there is more than one category for graphic novels.

Eagle and National Comic Awards

The Eagle Awards were first given in 1977, created and funded by a group of comic book dealers and fanzine editors in the United Kingdom. Beginning with the 1979 awards, separate awards have been given in some categories for works from the United Kingdom and from the United States. The awards were on hiatus from 1981 to 1983. In 1986, the first Eagle Award for Favorite Graphic Novel was given to Howard Chaykin's *American Flagg!: Hard Times* (1985). During another hiatus, the National Comics Award took the place of the Eagle Awards in the United Kingdom but had a graphic novel-related category only once, in 1999. That award was for Best Collected Series or Graphic Novel and was given to *Superman: For All Seasons* (1988), a series of comic books. The Eagle Awards returned in 2000 and have since been a component of England's annual comics convention. Volumes from Alan Moore's *The League of Extraordinary Gentlemen* (1999-) won the Favorite Original Graphic Novel award in the 2008 and 2009. Moore also won with Gene Ha for *Top 10: The Forty-Niners* (2005), and other winners include Brian K. Vaughn's *Pride of Baghdad* (2006) and Brian Azzarello and Joe

Kubert's *Sgt. Rock: Between Hell and a Hard Place* (2003).

Kirby, Eisner, and Harvey Awards

The first major award for graphic novels in the United States was named for Jack Kirby and was initially awarded in 1985. The Kirby Award existed for only a brief time, though. The award was created by *Amazing Heroes* magazine, which was published by Fantagraphics Books, and the program was run by Dave Olbrich, who was a Fantagraphics employee when the award began. Because of a dispute between Olbrich and Fantagraphics over the ownership of the award, the Kirby was discontinued after 1987, and two new awards emerged. Fantagraphics created and administers the Harvey Award, named for Harvey Kurtzman, and Olbrich began the Eisner Award, named for Will Eisner.

The Kirby Award was given for a number of specific genres or publications, including Best Single Issue, Best Continuing Series, Best Black and White Series, Best Finite Series, Best New Series, Best Graphic Album, Best Artist, Best Writer, Best Writer/Artist, Best Art Team, Best Cover, and Best Comics Publication. Moore dominated the awards for the three years of their existence. He, Stephen R. Bissette, and John Totleben won Best Continuing Series for all three years of the Kirby Awards for their work with *Swamp Thing* (1984-1987), and Moore won Best Writer all three years, twice for *Swamp Thing* and once for *Watchmen* (1986-1987). Moore's work was also recognized in other categories, including a Best Single Issue for *Swamp Thing* in 1985, and Best New Series in both 1986 and 1987, for *Miracleman* (1985-1989) and *Watchmen*, respectively. Moore and Dave Gibbons won the 1987 award for Best Writer/Artist Team for *Watchmen*.

The Will Eisner Comic Industry Award was established in 1987 and began conferring its awards at the 1988 Comic-Con International: San Diego. Olbrich continued to manage the award until 1990, when Jackie Estrada took over. Until his death in 2005,

Eisner participated in the awards ceremonies each year. The Eisners, often called the Oscars of comics, are awarded for a wide range of categories, including graphic novels. An open call for nominations is sent to publishers each year, and nominating and judging panels are named to work at Comic-Con. The award for Best Graphic Album was given to Moore and Gibbons for *Watchmen* in 1988 and to Moore and Brian Bolland for *Batman: The Killing Joke* (1988) in 1989. Since 1991, there have been two awards for graphic novels, one for new material and a second for reprinted items. Award winners include *Stuck Rubber Baby* (1995), *Blankets* (2003), *Fax from Sarajevo* (1996), *One Hundred Demons* (2000-2001), *Safe Area Goražde* (2000), and *American Born Chinese* (2006).

The Harvey Award is coordinated by Fantagraphics. They began in 1987 after the demise of the Kirby Award. Professionals in the field of comics have an open vote to determine the nominees for each category. The top five in each category are listed on a final ballot. The award has been presented at major fan conventions including WonderCon, the Dallas Fantasy Fair, and comics conventions in Pittsburgh, Chicago, and Baltimore, as well as at events hosted by the Museum of Comic and Cartoon Art. There are numerous categories of Harvey Awards, with two awards given for graphic novels. From 1988 to 1990, there was one award for Best Graphic Album, and since 1991, there have been two awards offered, one for original work and one for previously published material.

The 1988 Harvey Award was bestowed on Moore and Gibbons for *Watchmen*, and Moore also won in 1989 for *Batman: The Killing Joke* and again in 2000 for *From Hell* (1989-1996). Moore has also been awarded the Best Writer prize seven times. Over the years, the winners of the Harvey Award for Best Graphic Album of Original Work have included *Our Cancer Year* (1994), *Stuck Rubber Baby*, *Blankets*, *Fax from Sarajevo*, *The Golem's Mighty Swing* (2001), *Last Day in Vietnam* (2000), *Scott Pilgrim Gets It Together* (2007), and Scott McCloud's *Understanding Comics* (1993).

Maus is the only graphic novel or comic book that has been recognized by the Pulitzer Prize. (Courtesy of Pantheon Books)

Ignatz Awards

The Ignatz Awards began in 1997 and are awarded at the Small Press Expo, which is held annually in Bethesda, Maryland (except in 2001, when the awards were canceled because of the terrorist attacks of September 11). The prize is named for a character in George Herriman's "Krazy Kat" comic strip. A five-member panel selects the nominees, and those attending the expo vote for the winners, who are then announced during the event. Initially, the awards included a single category for graphic novel or collection, but these were split into two distinct awards in 2005.

The Ignatz Award distinguishes graphic novels from comics by page count and type of binding. Other categories for the awards include Outstanding Artist, Outstanding Story, Promising New Talent, Outstanding

Series, Outstanding Comic, Outstanding Minicomic, and Outstanding Online Comic. An award for Outstanding Debut was given from 2000 to 2008. Since 2005, the winners of the graphic novel award have included Marjane Satrapi's *Persepolis 2* (2004), Anders Nilsen's *Don't Go Where I Can't Follow* (2006), Mariko Tamaki and Jillian Tamaki's *Skim* (2008), Alex Robinson's *Tricked* (2005), Chris Ware's *Acme Novelty Library #19* (2008), and James Sturm's *Market Day* (2010).

Hugo Awards and Others

The Hugo Awards had recognized graphic novels just once before 2009, when the award for Best Graphic Story was introduced. Moore and Gibbons won a Hugo for *Watchmen* in 1988, in the Other Forms category. This has caused confusion over the years, because the award was created under the "special category" rule. Each WorldCon is able to create a special award to be given at its event. In 1988, the WorldCon committee decided to have a category for "anything that doesn't qualify for one of the other categories," and *Watchmen* was the winner. This type of award has not been repeated. Kaja and Phil Foglio won the Best Graphic Story in the first three years of the award, for volumes from their series about Agatha Heterodyne, *Girl Genius*.

Mainstream awards have begun to recognize graphic novels in recent years. In the United States, the National Book Award had its first graphic novel finalist in 2007, Gene Luen Yang's *American Born Chinese*. In the United Kingdom in 2001, Chris Ware's *Jimmy Corrigan: The Smartest Kid on Earth* (1993-2000) was the first graphic novel to win a major award, when it won the Guardian First Book Award. In 2010, Matt Phelan's *The Storm in the Barn* (2009) was the first graphic novel to win the Scott O'Dell Award for Historical Fiction, given for excellence in children's and young-adult literature; Phelan's award caused some controversy among educators.

One major exception to the relatively recent attention from mainstream awards is the Pulitzer Prize Special Citation, which was given to Art Spiegelman for *Maus: A Survivor's Tale* (1986, 1991) in 1992. The Pulitzer Prize Special Citation has been given since 1917 and has often honored musicians and composers. A pictorial history of the Civil War won this prize in 1961, but *Maus* is the only graphic novel or comic book to have been awarded a Pulitzer Prize.

Manga Awards

The Shogakukan Manga Award has been given to manga since 1955. Until 1976, there was a single award given. After creating a general category, other categories have emerged. There are awards given for a children's work, a work specifically for boys (*shōnen*), a work specifically for girls (*shōjo*), and the general award, also referred to as a young-adult award. Occasionally awarded is a special prize for lifetime achievement or other particular honors. Shogakukan is a major publisher of manga, and its works have often been awarded the prizes.

The Kodansha Manga Award began in 1977 and is given annually for manga published serially during the previous year. Sponsored by Kodansha, a major publisher of manga, they initially were given in two categories, *shōnen* and *shōjo*. In 1982, a general award was added, and in 2003, Kodansha began giving an award for children's manga.

The Tezuka Osamu Cultural Prize was founded in 1997. It is named in honor of Osamu Tezuka, often heralded as the father of manga and anime. This prize recognizes artists that follow in his style, which introduced the prominent eyes considered typical in manga and anime. Awards are given in four categories, including a Grand Prize, a Creative Award for a particularly innovative work, a Short Story Award, and a Special Award, given to someone who worked to promote the culture of manga.

The Manga Taishō is an award that began in 2008. The nominating committee is composed mostly of people who work in bookstores. The Manga Taishō is given to works with eight or fewer volumes and intends to reward relatively new contributors to the genre; awards are not given to those who have become popular over long careers.

Impact

The range of awards given to graphic novels attests to the power and impact that graphic novels have had in both classrooms and popular culture. Also, the fact that graphic novels are being considered for major publishing awards from established institutions signals the genre's shift from the fringe to mainstream legitimacy.

Beth Blakesley

Bibliography

Estrada, Jackie. "The Eisner Awards: A Brief History." *Comic-Con International*, n.d. http://www.comic-con.org/cci/cci_eisners_faq.shtml. Written by the second Eisner Awards administrator. Discusses the emergence and evolution of the awards.

Gravett, Paul. *Graphic Novels: Stories to Change Your Life*. London: Aurum, 2005. Accessible guide to graphic novels that provides information about a number of important contributions to the genre.

Hahn, Joel. "Comic Book Awards Almanac." *Hahn Library*, 2006. http://www.hahnlibrary.net/comics/awards. Provides an overview of numerous awards, including the Kirby, Eisner, Harvey, Ignatz, Eagle, and Kodansha awards, along with other awards for comics given in Sweden, Germany, Spain, and Italy.

Kannenberg, Gene. *Five Hundred Essential Graphic Novels: The Ultimate Guide*. New York: Collins Design, 2008. Provides overviews of key graphic novels, including many award winners.

CENSORSHIP AND THE GRAPHIC NOVEL

Definition

Censorship is defined as the exertion of control over creative works. This article details historical and contemporary issues surrounding censorship and the graphic novel format and examines in detail the effect on the content and nature of graphic novels, the relationship between comic book censorship and the Comics Code Authority (CCA), and the censorship of graphic novels in libraries.

Introduction

The censorship of graphic novels has been closely tied to the problems experienced by their comic book antecedents. The most obvious reason for censorship is the often adult nature of graphic novels. Frequently, as a result of misconception or misclassification, the books are targeted to youth when the subject matter is in fact aimed at adults. Even though graphic novels stand alone as a medium, the common perception of comics as children's literature has given graphic novels a stigma that is hard to erase. Consequently, many challenges result from the fact that graphic novels have been mistaken for reading material that is appropriate for children.

A discussion of the history of censorship in graphic novels could not take place without mention of the CCA, an independent and self-regulating body established during the 1950's. The group was unique because of its membership: comic book publishers that set out to censor any material that might cause offense. Although never officially applied to graphic novels, the Comics Code inadvertently helped shape the nature of early graphic novel content. During the 1960's, specialty retailers who were not subject to the code began to disregard the intentions of the CCA and produce "underground comics," self-published and small-press comic books. These comics dealt with subject matter long repressed, including sex, drugs, race, and war—material that eventually led to the emergence of the format known as the graphic novel.

As graphic novels have gained ground and begun to appear more prominently on shelves in libraries and bookstores, their visibility has also risen. As a result, concerned parents, librarians, and community leaders occasionally challenge the content and educational level of the graphic novel format. Challengers vary in the resolutions they seek; some may demand removal of graphic novels from collections, while others may simply request the materials be shelved in a restricted area. Some libraries even encounter mutilation of graphic novels as a more direct form of censorship.

Adult Nature of Graphic Novels

Historically, comics and graphic novels have often been viewed as material for children. Many graphic novels, however, contain complex characters and adult subject matter. This distinction is one that, when overlooked, can lead to censorship or challenges.

By definition, graphic novels are heavily dependent on visual images. Challengers of graphic novel collections in libraries and schools may feel that images are more powerful or persuasive than written words, especially where young children are concerned. Additionally, when paging through a graphic novel, the graphical images or depictions of certain circumstances may appear more obvious to would-be censors than textual descriptions. This applies to images of drug use, violence, and gore, but most often to images of nude figures or sexual situations.

Censorship of comic books and graphic novels based on adult content was largely influenced by the CCA. The Comics Code was embraced by comics publishers of wholesome content, such as the *Archie* series, published by John L. Goldwater. These publishers attempted to stifle other, more daring works in order to highlight their own age-appropriate comics. Other publishers, including Irving Klaw, required artists such as John Scott Coutts to alter his artwork to cover exposed breasts or undesirable images. Many artists resisted and went underground with their work. Coutts made the required alterations but continued to offer the unaltered issue by mail order.

The content of some graphic novels has also led to charges of obscenity in some communities. In January,

1995, a British customs official filed charges against British publishing company Knockabout Comics when he found objectionable the sexual content in Robert Crumb's *My Troubles with Women* (1992). Knockabout Comics was charged with importing obscene materials but was cleared in court after lawyers proved the satirical nature of the work.

Comics Code Authority

Despite generally being considered a children's genre, comic books nonetheless failed to escape the scrutiny of Joseph McCarthy-era critics. One critic in particular, psychiatrist Fredric Wertham, published a book called *Seduction of the Innocent* (1954), in which he suggested a link between comic books, teen suicide, aggression, and communism. The hysteria brought about by Wertham's charges ultimately led to Senate hearings on comic books and juvenile delinquency.

In response to the hearings and general anticomics sentiment of the period, comics publishers created a group called the Comic Magazine Association of America (CMAA) in order to regulate the content of new comics. Their regulations came in the form of the CCA, which banned any text or images that could be considered to include so-called offensive content: excessive violence, adultery, death, gore, or sexual situations. Other taboo topics included the portrayal of vampires, werewolves, or zombies. The CCA mandated both that good must triumph over evil and authority figures always be presented respectfully. Any comic book that complied with the code received a stamp of approval on its cover; any comic book that did not was banned.

Despite the publishers' regulations, some comics creators and authors fought the code. The Comic Book Legal Defense Fund (CBLDF) was created in 1986 by creators and sellers of comics to fight censorship. During the 1980's, since specialty re-

tailers were free from the regulations of the CCA, many comic books and graphic novels began appearing without the CCA seal of approval. Many of these titles dealt with sex and drugs, such as Howard Chaykin's *American Flagg!* (1983-1989) series, published by First Comics.

Modern comics publishers have ignored the code because of the ability to distribute comics through specialty comics stores and direct mail. Also, because the CCA does not apply to graphic novels, many publishers reprint comics as graphic novels. The exempt status of graphic novels has allowed genres such as horror and crime, which were once censored under the CCA, to flourish.

Censorship in Libraries

Contemporary censorship of graphic novels often occurs in school- or public-library settings, where it can take one of several forms: challenges to graphic novel collections, theft or mutilation of materials, or even

Alison Bechdel's graphic novel *Fun Home: A Family Tragicomic* faced censorship for its adult themes.(Coutesy of Mariner Books)

self-censorship by librarians or library staff that make purchasing and shelving decisions. Self-censorship can include neglecting to purchase a graphic novel title because of its content or deciding to restrict access to graphic novel materials by shelving them behind a public service desk.

Challenges can arise from many different sources both inside and outside the library. In many cases, challenges center on obscene content, which can include sex, nudity, and offensive language. In the case of school libraries, challengers are often parents or members of the community who debate the educational value of graphic novels in the library's collection and wish to have the materials removed from the shelves. Librarians can prepare for challenges by ensuring that all staff understand collection policies and are made aware of the procedures set in place for complaints. Likewise, library employees should provide their patrons with facts about the policies as well as background material related to graphic novels and the library's collection.

A subtler, arguably more destructive, type of censorship is caused by theft or mutilation of graphic novels in a library's collection. Damage to a collection may be at the hands of library patrons or staff members who object to a title but, for whatever reason, refrain from voicing their opinion. Theft or mutilation can be related to a specific title or even the concept of the graphic novels format.

Many experts encourage librarians to create guidelines for purchasing, displaying, and shelving graphic novels in order to minimize this type of censorship. In a joint effort, the CBLDF, the National Coalition Against Censorship, and the American Library Association published a document with suggested guidelines.

Impact

Graphic novels have been afflicted by the same prejudices that plagued comic books during the 1940's and 1950's. The content of the majority of graphic novels puts them at risk for challenges and censorship. Additionally, the perception that graphic novels and comic books are the same has meant that graphic novels are often incorrectly labeled as children's literature.

Would-be censors, including parents and religious groups, use this mislabeling to support the claim that graphic novels are inappropriate for public and school libraries.

Despite these issues, graphic novels have enjoyed a somewhat more contextual freedom than their comic book siblings. Since graphic novels have not been subjected to the CCA's seal of approval, their authors have license to push the envelope on a number of themes, including sex, war, and the occult—all topics that have been considered taboo at some point in comic books. Likewise, the book-length format has allowed for more in-depth and substantive intellectual content than is typically found in comic books. However, as long as graphic novels are labeled as children's literature because of their visual nature, they will continue to be in danger of being censored.

Melissa Mallon

Bibliography

Cornog, Martha, and Erin Byrne. "Censorship of Graphic Novels in Libraries." In *Graphic Novels Beyond the Basics: Insights and Issues for Libraries*, edited by Martha Cornog and Timothy Perper. Santa Barbara, Calif.: Libraries Unlimited/ABC-CLIO, 2009. Contains statistical data garnered from surveys administered to libraries regarding challenges to graphic novel collections. Also discusses why materials are challenged and how to handle these challenges.

Gravett, Paul. *Graphic Novels: Everything You Need to Know*. London: Aurum, 2005. Colorful book covering many aspects and genres of graphic novels. Each chapter contains sample pages from relevant graphic novels. Also includes a list of print and online resources. Especially useful for the study of adult subjects in graphic novels.

National Coalition Against Censorship, American Library Association, and Comic Book Legal Defense Fund. "Graphic Novels: Suggestions for Librarians." *National Coalition Against Censorship*, December 10, 2006. http://www.ncac.org/graphic novels.cfm. Provides a brief history of graphic novels and offers concrete suggestions for librarians, including where to shelve materials, talking points for media relations, and sample "challenging" questions and answers.

Nyberg, Amy Kiste. *Seal of Approval: The History of the Comics Code*. Jackson: University Press of Mississippi, 1998. An in-depth look at the history and consequences of the CCA. Discusses the modern significance of the code and its relationship to graphic novels.

Versaci, Rocco. *This Book Contains Graphic Language: Comics as Literature*. New York: Continuum, 2007. Discusses graphic novel censorship, political imagery, and other adult topics in comics and graphic novels. Includes sample illustrations from graphic novels to support the text.

Wright, Bradford. *Comic Book Nation: The Transformation of Youth Culture in America*. Rev. ed. Baltimore: Johns Hopkins University, 2003. Considered by many to be a seminal work on comics. Does not specifically discuss graphic novels but has several chapters on the controversies surrounding comics during the 1940's and 1950's. Contains specific details on the Senate Subcommittee to Investigate Juvenile Delinquency.

CLASSICAL COMICS: GRAPHIC NOVEL ADAPTATIONS OF CLASSICAL LITERATURE

Definition

The terms "graphic story" and "graphic novel" were first used by American comics critic and magazine publisher Richard Kyle to describe the growing number of stories that included narrative artwork. Such publications were meant to offer an alternative to comic books that were printed on poor-quality paper and had limited story lines. The Gilberton Company published the *Classic Comics* series, later known as *Classics Illustrated*, in graphic novel format to introduce school-age children to classic literature.

Introduction

Between 1941 and 1971, the Gilberton Company coupled narrative artwork with classic literature in the series *Classic Comics*, later renamed *Classics Illustrated*. The founder of the company, Albert Lewis Kanter, designed the series to expose school-age children to literary classics such as Alexandre Dumas's *Les Trois Mousquetaires* (1844; *The Three Musketeers*, 1846) and Herman Melville's *Moby-Dick* (1851). In an effort to provide faithful adaptations of the original works, each issue averaged sixty pages, which was a substantial increase over the average comic book size. Many of the classics that were selected for publication were action-oriented in order to appeal to the series' young audience. The publications were purchased primarily by parents hoping to provide a literary base for their children.

Because of the nature of the series' content, *Classics Illustrated* issues were exempt from the regulations of the Comics Code Authority (CCA), a regulatory commission that oversaw the appropriateness of content in comic books. This was in part because Kanter refused to declare that the series needed monitoring. In addition to this uncommon exemption, Gilberton was ahead of its time in the publishing field in that its staff included an African American scriptwriter and artist as well as female artists and scriptwriters.

One criticism of the series was that students were using the abbreviated scripts as substitutes for reading

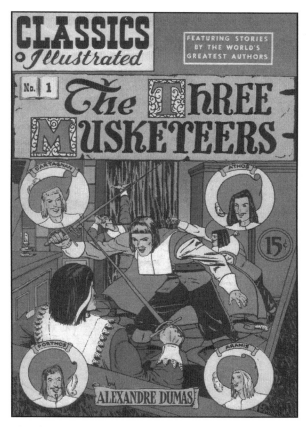

The Three Musketeers (Courtesy of First Classics Inc.)

the actual literary works. Additionally, the series received criticism for subpar artwork, particularly in the earliest issues. In the late 1940's, Gilberton hired artist Jerry Iger and his comics studio, which employed well-known artists such as Robert Webb and Matt Baker, to provide the drawings. The affiliation with these artists ended in the mid-1950's, at which time Kanter sought freelance workers.

In 1962, Kanter's son, William, supervised the publication of thirteen new issues of *Classics Illustrated* in England, but none of these titles was issued in the United States. Ultimately, the series was overtaken by technological advancements and the rise of juvenile paperback classics. By the release of the final issue, however, the titles were published in twenty-six languages and in thirty-six countries. The series also inspired many spin-off publications, including *Classics Illustrated Junior*, *Picture Progress*, *Classics Illustrated Special Issues*, and *The World Around Us— Classics Illustrated*.

In 1989, First Comics, Berkley Books, and Classics Media Group published a new *Classics Illustrated* series in trade paperback. These publications included adaptations of Charles Dickens's *Great Expectations* (1860-1861), Nathaniel Hawthorne's *The Scarlet Letter* (1850), and Robert Louis Stevenson's *Treasure Island* (1883). Contributors to the artwork in this series included Bill Sienkiewicz, Kyle Baker, Dan Spiegle, Rick Geary, and Gahan Wilson. The series ended in 1991.

Albert Kanter: Creator of *Classic Comics/ Classics Illustrated*

Kanter was the eldest son of a family that fled from Russia to Nashua, New Hampshire, in 1904. When his father became ill in 1913, Kanter quit high school to help support his family by working as a door-to-door salesman. Kanter moved around frequently in an effort to improve his life. While in Savannah, Georgia, he married Rose Ehrenrich, with whom he had three children, Henry, William, and Saralea.

Because of the Great Depression, Kanter and his family moved to New York, where he worked as a publisher's representative for Colonial Press and, subsequently, Elliott Publishing Company. While there, he worked selling remaindered comic books in bulk lots. Combining his growing admiration for comics with his ever-present love of literature, Kanter formulated the idea of introducing classic literary works to young audiences through comic books.

Meyer Levy, an acquaintance of Kanter's friend Raymond Haas, partnered with Kanter on the *Classic Comics/Classics Illustrated* endeavor. They contracted the Jacquet Shop to illustrate the first issues of the series, published between 1941 and 1944. The first issue, which was published in October of 1941, was an adaptation of *The Three Musketeers*. The 250,000-copy print run cost $8,000 to produce.

The Jacquet Shop

The Jacquet Shop, led by Lloyd Jacquet of Funnies, Inc., was the team of artists that illustrated the earliest issues of *Classic Comics*. These initial issues are generally considered to have the most inferior artwork in the series, in part because Gilberton was unable to pay the premium fees needed to contract first-rate illustrators.

Malcolm Kildale, a member of the Jacquet Shop, adapted and illustrated the first issue of the series. Although he was considered competent in his field, his illustrations lacked the sophistication and polish needed for critics to look favorably on his work. Kildale's general technique was criticized, but he was credited with energetic character drawings, each of which contributed to a successful narration. The villains were appropriately portrayed, and the comic as a whole held true to the spirit of the original work. This was a significant accomplishment, as many of the subsequent comics did not accurately reflect the original works.

Kildale was also the art director and editor of the second comic, the adaptation of Sir Walter Scott's *Ivanhoe* (1819), which was published in December, 1941. Although Kildale was credited with the cover artwork, Edd Ashe and Ray Ramsey drew the panels. This comic was criticized for its lack of detail in the panel backgrounds as well as for its lack of strong character personalities. The original plotline, however, was generally adhered to, and the battle scenes were a strong point.

The third comic, Dumas's *The Count of Monte Cristo* (*Le Comte de Monte-Cristo*, 1844-1846; English translation, 1846), was published in March, 1942, and is generally considered to be the worst of the first three titles. In particular, the adapted script was a mass of scattered subplots that did not adhere to the story line of the original text. The illustrations were considered weak, though the cover art created by Ramsey was deemed enthralling.

Ramsey went on to contribute to the fourth comic, an adaptation of James Fennimore Cooper's *The Last of the Mohicans* (1826), which was published in August, 1942. The character depictions and cover art in this comic were considered better than those of the previous books. This adaptation was the last in the series with artwork created by the Jacquet Shop.

Other Artists

Twenty-two issues of the *Classic Comics/Classics Illustrated* series were produced in the first three years of the series' run. Critics view these issues as subpar in comparison to both comic book industry standards and the subsequent issues in the series. In the late 1950's and early 1960's, artists such as Jack Kirby, Reed Crandall, George Evans, Joe Orlando, and Al Williamson provided higher-quality artwork that improved the reputation of the series.

Louis Zansky, whose use of fluid lines and expansiveness greatly improved the series' art, began to contribute to the series with the fifth issue, the adaptation of *Moby-Dick* (1851); he also adapted the novel for this comic. Zansky's use of heavy brush strokes in his artwork for some of the Sherlock Holmes comics lends the issues a more whimsical style, and his contribution to the adaptation of Miguel de Cervantes's *Don Quixote* (*Don Quixote de la Mancha*, 1605, 1615; English translation, 1612-1620) displays an impressionistic flare that confirms his ability to portray different artistic styles. Zansky worked for Gilberton Company until 1944 but continued to contribute to comics later in the series.

Another notable artistic contributor was Stanley Maxwell Zuckerberg, who used heavily accented foregrounds and characters in his panels. Zuckerberg's wife, Lillian Chestney, was also an artist for Gilberton. Her artwork displayed an ornate style that included twinkling stars and bejeweled clothing. This style offered a childlike quality to the comics. Many other notable artists contributed to the *Classic Comics/Classics Illustrated* series, including Jack Hearne, Rudy Palais, and Norman Nodel.

Impact

For decades comics were widely known for their violence and sexual content. In 1948, *Time* magazine re-

ported that juvenile comic book readers were copying the crimes that they were reading about in print. In a series of hearings, the U.S. government attempted to determine if comic books contributed to the delinquency of minors. Although there was no action taken as a result of the case, the CCA was created to monitor the appropriateness of comics.

Kanter did not want to work under CCA scrutiny and maintained that his company's literary comics were not in need of such inspection. *Classics Illustrated* was criticized for its violent cover art for the adaptations of Stevenson's *Strange Case of Dr. Jekyll and Mr. Hyde* (1886) and Victor Hugo's *Hunchback of Notre Dame* (*Notre-Dame de Paris*, 1831; English translation, 1833); however, Kanter's series demonstrated comic books could have educational value. By providing children with the basic story lines of classics, the comics encouraged their appreciation for the stories to grow, allowing them to foster a love of literature.

Susan Sylvia

Bibliography

Gravett, Paul. *Graphic Novels: Everything You Need to Know*. New York: HarperCollins, 2005. Offers an overview of some of the best-known artists to work in the comic book industry and examines common comic book themes and famous works, including adaptations of literary classics.

Jones, William B. *Classics Illustrated: A Cultural History, with Illustrations*. Jefferson, N.C.: McFarland, 2002. Traces the evolution of the publishing company that founded the *Classics Illustrated* series and provides an in-depth examination of the artists who contributed to the artwork in the series.

Sabin, Roger. *Comics, Comix, and Graphic Novels: A History of Comic Art*. New York: Phaidon, 1996. Covers the rise of comics, including literary adaptations, and reviews thematic comics topics. Also highlights some of the various artistic styles and artists who have contributed to the industry.

COLD WAR AND GRAPHIC NOVELS, THE

Definition

Comic books reflected shifts in American culture during the prolonged Cold War period, providing commentary and catharsis while suffering from censorship that forever altered the comic book industry and the medium's methods of telling stories.

Introduction

In the years following World War II, the United States was a study in contradictions. Americans were victors in war but faced a new conflict with former ally the Soviet Union, entered the age of atomic power and wielded responsibility for employing this energy of the future but feared its use against the United States, and built a prosperous, family-oriented country but stifled increased female independence. Those in power were indebted to the nation's young people for their role in fighting the war but feared the emerging youth culture and its independent ways of thinking. Americans were desperate for entertainment that reflected their fears and would provide catharsis but were scared of their desires and willing to crusade against the very media for which they yearned. In the midst of all this turmoil, the still-young comic book industry walked a fine line, capturing this era of rapid, painful transition in American culture but also becoming one of the nation's chosen targets for vilification.

The superhero genre, so successful during the 1930's and 1940's, suffered in the 1950's with a rapid decline in sales, perhaps because the United States' enemy was no longer an easily portrayed Axis stereotype but the more amorphous threat of communist infiltration. Some heroes still tried to maintain their past relevance. One was Captain America, who briefly tussled with communists in the 1950's and whose former Nazi nemesis, the Red Skull, had a convenient appellation that could be exploited.

Ironically, costumed crime fighters often depended on maintaining secret identities and now had to fight enemies whose principal advantage was their use of subterfuge. Thus, the superhero genre gave way to other genres in comics: romance, Westerns, humor,

Set in the Cold War-era of the of the Czech Republic, *A Jew in Communist Prague* depicts the adolescence of a young Jewish boy. (Courtesy of Nantier Beall Minoustchine Publishing)

and, perhaps most important, horror. The growing popularity of shocking, gory horror comics was an obvious cry for catharsis from a nation gripped by fear.

Crypt of Censorship

In the 1940's and 1950's, a movement led by psychologists, newspaper pundits, and government officials blamed comics for the corruption of the nation's youth, even suggesting they were part of a deliberate campaign to weaken American culture for an impending communist invasion. EC Comics and its over-the-top brand of horror storytelling and subversive military comics, in which the true terrors of the Korean War were portrayed, became the centerpiece of a highly publicized crusade that resulted in a Senate subcommittee investigation. Aided by psychiatrist Fredric Wertham and his anticomics book, *Seduction of the Innocent* (1954), the hearings led directly to the collapse of the popular EC Comics horror line and the formation of the comics industry's self-regulatory censor, the Comics Code Authority.

Fearing further government interference, surviving publishers offered propaganda that exposed the evils of those invisible invaders from overseas. One of the most famous is *Blood Is the Harvest* (1950), published by the Catechetical Guild. The Catholic Guild's *Treasure Chest*, issue 2 (1961), features the first chapter of a ten-

One of the most influential graphic novels ever conceived, *Watchmen* (1986-1987) serves as a commentary on the dangerous game of mutually assured destruction played by the world's superpowers. (AP Photo)

part story titled "This Godless Communism," with an introductory letter from Federal Bureau of Investigation director J. Edgar Hoover proclaiming communism as "the most serious threat facing our way of life." The story features biographies of communist leaders and claims that their cause is the product of the devil himself. Such comics told American children that the Cold War was not only a political and ideological conflict but also a holy war.

Birth of Atomic Age Heroes

Just before the Cold War reached a dramatic peak during the Cuban Missile Crisis, the superhero genre surged back into popularity. Arguably the most profound effect of the Cold War on comics was the introduction of the atom-charged Marvel Comics pantheon of superheroes. Editor and writer Stan Lee crafted virtually every one of them as a response to the United States' roiling culture of contradictions. The dysfunctional family unit of the Fantastic Four, transformed by strange cosmic rays, reflected the desire for Americans to rely on traditional domestic roles but also illustrated the tensions that underlay the pretense. The Incredible Hulk, a creature born of a device not unlike an atomic bomb, was the raging, übermasculine alter ego of Dr. Robert Bruce Banner, a sensitive man struggling with the responsibility of wielding destructive forces from within and without while symbolizing the shift in gender roles facing American men.

Marvel's flagship hero, Spider-Man, was an intellectual, socially isolated teenager, the embodiment of many of his comics' readers and part of the new youth culture that both amazed and disturbed the nation's adults just as Spider-Man's bizarre antics thrilled and terrified the people he defended. In one of Marvel's most subversive commentaries on the era, Iron Man is a life-preserving, armored heroic guise built by former arms manufacturer Tony Stark, a millionaire playboy who pays a terrible price for his role in the military-industrial complex when he falls into communist hands and suffers a near-fatal wound. In that blend of guilt and responsibility, conscience and complicity, Marvel defined the Cold War United States.

If This Be Détente

Throughout the early history of Marvel Comics, its heroes frequently battled Russian or Far Eastern archenemies, international spy organizations such as HYDRA and A.I.M., and other representatives of the so-called worldwide communist conspiracy. The 1960's and 1970's, however, were marked by increasing social and political unrest during and after the Vietnam War, and American entertainment began to offer a more nuanced, ambivalent look at the Cold War, the country's position in the world, and the decisions its leaders were making. Even staunch symbols of American ideals such as Captain America began to question their place in society, and for a time, this patriotic hero left his star-spangled uniform behind and assumed the more ambiguous identity of Nomad.

Following a period of détente, the Cold War surged one more time in the late 1970's and early 1980's after the Russian invasion of Afghanistan in 1979. Sometimes dubbed the "Second Cold War," this period of conflict sparked a renewed media focus on the threat of communism and the potential for global thermonuclear war. One of the most significant examples of the late-era Cold War in graphic novels is British comics creators Alan Moore and Dave Gibbons's *Watchmen* (1986-1987). One of the most influential graphic novels ever conceived, it serves as a commentary on the dangerous game of mutually assured destruction played by the world's superpowers. *Watchmen* is not only a deconstruction of the superhero genre and a metacommentary on the comics medium but also a satire of the tensions between the United States and the Soviet Union in which the nuclear-powered Dr. Manhattan serves as the literal embodiment of brinksmanship. The story concludes with the suggestion that perhaps society's most feared outcome of the Cold War, total annihilation, was inevitable.

Impact

The end of the Cold War did come, but not in the way so many feared. In 1989, the Berlin Wall, which served as one of the most potent symbols of the divide between the Western and communist cultures, came down. In 1991, the Soviet Union was officially dissolved. For all intents and purposes, the United States had won the Cold War, if for no other reason than that it outlasted its opponent. As the world shifted to other battles no less profound, the comics medium also moved on to reflect the world outside its pages. Communism and the Cold War became parts of comics history but are themes that continue to resonate through the medium.

Marvel Comics characters still carry the era within their radiation-mutated DNA, and the fear of industry-wide censorship that led to the creation of the Comics Code is still felt by creators and fans, although the code is defunct. In the twenty-first century superhero genre, a number of comics offer intriguing takes on the evocative historical period of the Cold War. The three-issue miniseries *Superman: Red Son* (2003), for example, dares to take the quintessential American icon and transplant him into an alternate reality in which his rocket ship landed in the Soviet Union and Superman became a dedicated crusader for communism. In the comic book pages, history and its myriad possibilities, as well as all the fear and tension that fueled the decades-long Cold War, are only a few panels away.

Arnold T. Blumberg

Bibliography

Genter, Robert. "With Great Power Comes Great Responsibility: Cold War Culture and the Birth of Marvel Comics." *Journal of Popular Culture* 40, no. 6 (December, 2007): 953-978. Analyzes Marvel's superheroes, from the Fantastic Four to the Hulk, and Stan Lee's use of them to reflect aspects of Cold War culture.

Hajdu, David. *The Ten-Cent Plague: The Great Comic-Book Scare and How It Changed America*. New York: Farrar, Straus and Giroux, 2008. Provides a detailed account of the comic book censorship movement, controversial comics stories published at the time, and the Cold War-era politics that motivated the individuals involved.

Jones, Gerard. *Men of Tomorrow: Geeks, Gangsters, and the Birth of the Comic Book*. New York: Basic Books, 2004. Discusses the formation of the comics industry in the United States and includes anecdotal portraits of many of the prominent players and their sociopolitical leanings.

COMIC BOOK AGES: A HISTORY AS ORGANIZED BY READERS

Definition

In discussing the history of comic books and graphic novels, fans have created rough chronological categories to segregate periods of output and development characterized by shifting trends and critical reception.

Introduction

As comic books evolved into their modern format, collectors and fans of the medium began to organize the sum total output from the different publishers into eras. The beginnings and endings of eras remain points of debate among historians of the field. Nevertheless, the creation of such categories has allowed fans to discuss, analyze, and debate the relative merits of material published during specific time periods.

Graphic storytelling has existed since the first cave paintings. Since then, images have been used to tell stories in one way or another; examples of early graphic storytelling include the Codex Zouche-Nuttall, a 36-foot-long pre-Columbian folded manuscript telling of the Mixtec leader Eight Deer Tiger Claw, and the Bayeux Tapestry, a 230-foot-long embroidered cloth that tells of the Norman conquest of England in 1066. In the eighteenth century, poet William Blake carefully integrated words with pictures in books such as *The Marriage of Heaven and Hell*, a forerunner of the graphic novel.

Collection of old comic books. (Ted Streshinsky/Corbis)

Generally accepted as the oldest American comic is *The Adventures of Mr. Obadiah Oldbuck* (1841), an English translation of Rodolphe Töpffer's *Histoire de M. Vieux Bois* (c. 1839) serialized in the popular *Brother Jonathan* magazine. As printing technology continued to improve, others experimented with graphic storytelling in newspapers, magazines, and books, including American artist Lynd Ward, who began producing wordless woodcut graphic novels with *Gods' Man* (1929).

Victorian Age and Platinum Age

The *Overstreet Comic Book Price Guide* uses the term Victorian Age to describe the first age of comics, a period in which comic strips such as *The Adventures of Mr. Obadiah Oldbuck,* took shape in newspapers and magazines. The Yellow Kid became the first significant recurring comic strip character; his 1895 debut led to an explosion of merchandising and the publication of a collection of *Yellow Kid* strips in 1897. The book measured 5 inches by 7 inches, sold for fifty cents, and was described as a comic book on the back cover—the first such use of the term.

Overstreet terms the period from 1883 to 1938 the Platinum Age. During this era, comic strips gained popularity and began to be collected in magazines or comic books, often used as promotional giveaways. In 1928, George T. Delacorte, Jr., and Eastern Color teamed up to produce such compilations, beginning with *The Funnies*, which established the sixty-four-page format. In 1933, *New Funnies* became the first recognizable comic book, reprinting a variety of comic strips. Publishers unwilling to pay the newspaper syndicates for the rights to reprint strips soon began to pay cheaply for original content. Malcolm Wheeler-Nicholson founded National Allied Publications with the idea of producing a comic with all new material that he could own and exploit. *New Comics* (1935) is recognized as the first comic book to contain all original material, and National Allied Publications later evolved into DC Comics.

Golden Age

Superman's debut in issue 1 of *Action Comics* in June, 1938, is universally recognized as the beginning of the Golden Age, during which superheroic figures rapidly took over the comics. DC Comics' success inspired countless imitators and flooded the market with dozens of titles. During this period, *Classics Illustrated* flirted with the graphic novel format by producing lengthy comic book adaptations of classic novels. From 1941 to 1971, these publications helped children comprehend great works from around the world. They were published periodically and released on newsstands like standard comic books.

Comic book writer Arnold Drake and illustrator Matt Baker experimented with the graphic novel form with *It Rhymes with Lust*, published by St. John Publications in 1950. At 128 pages, it was the longest graphic story to be published in the United States. The work's success led St. John to publish *The Case of the Winking Buddha* (1950) by pulp novelist Manning Lee Stokes and illustrator Charles Raab; the latter title did not sell well, and the concept was abandoned.

Many argue that the Golden Age ended as superheroes faded from popularity in the years following World War II, but few agree on the era's final year. The most commonly accepted year is 1951, the year in which DC Comics reduced its heroes to Superman, Batman, and Wonder Woman and Fawcett Comics stopped publishing comics about Captain Marvel. Three years later, the Comics Code Authority (CCA) formed to enforce the newly created Comics Code, which would restrict the content of mainstream comics for the next several decades.

Silver Age

DC Comics revived the Flash in 1956 with issue 4 of *Showcase*, ushering in the Silver Age of comics. Readers were treated to new superheroes and revived heroes, and many companies followed the superhero trend. DC's success prompted Atlas Comics publisher Martin Goodman to charge editor Stan Lee with creating a new heroic team. Lee's creation of the Fantastic Four in 1961 and the subsequent success of the company, which became known as Marvel Comics, have caused some to refer to the era as the Marvel Age.

The term "graphic novel" was coined in November, 1964, by writer Richard Kyle in a newsletter circulated to all members of the Amateur Press Association

(APA). The term was slow to catch on, although fellow APA member Bill Spicer adapted it for the title of his fanzine *Graphic Story Magazine*. Artist Gil Kane and writer Archie Goodwin collaborated on *His Name Is . . . Savage!*, which Kane self-published in 1968. At the same time, Marvel published the black-and-white magazine *Spectacular Spider-Man*. Neither gained a following, but both were significant steps toward longer graphic narratives. Undaunted, Kane published his next project, *Blackmark*, in paperback form in 1971. *Blackmark* is arguably the first true graphic novel, as it was an original story in book form.

By 1970, the content of comics indicated a shift in direction. In *The Comic Book Heroes* (1997), Will Jacobs and Gerard Jones argue that the Silver Age ended in 1970, at which time Denny O'Neil and Neal Adams took over *Green Lantern* and produced stories taken from news topics of the day. Others argue that the age ended in 1973 with the death of Spider-Man's girlfriend, Gwen Stacy, in *Amazing Spider-Man*, issue 122.

Bronze Age and Modern Age

By the early 1970's, the CCA had rewritten its standards, which led to an increase in horror, occult, and sword-and-sorcery titles. Many small companies vanished during this period, including Gold Key Comics, Harvey Comics, and Charlton Comics, while DC Comics and Marvel Comics struggled with rising production costs. The direct-sales channel, in which retailers could purchase comics directly from the publishers or dedicated distributors, was created and led to the establishment of independent comic book shops. Such shops provided small, independent publishers such as Eclipse Comics with the opportunity to reach a wider readership. Several self-published comics, including Wendy and Richard Pini's *ElfQuest* (1978-1985), helped pioneer the format of collected editions.

The term graphic novel began to gain traction during these years. It was used to describe *Bloodstar* (1976), based on a story from Conan creator Robert E. Howard and adapted by Richard Corben, and George Metzger used it in his *Beyond Time and Again* (1976). Jim Steranko's digest-sized *Chandler: Red Tide* (1976) was called both a graphic novel and a visual novel, though

The Spectacular Spider-Man magazine #1 (July 1968). (Courtesy of Marvel Comics)

the work is more commonly considered an illustrated novel than a work of graphic narrative. In 1978, Eclipse published writer Don McGregor and artist Paul Gulacy's *Sabre: Slow Fade of an Endangered Species*, the first graphic novel sold in the direct market. That same year, Lee and Jack Kirby produced *The Silver Surfer* (1978), a graphic novel with an original story featuring a character first introduced in *Fantastic Four* more than a decade earlier.

What many cite as the first graphic novel, Will Eisner's *A Contract with God, and Other Tenement Stories* (1978), was actually published after *Sabre* and *The Silver Surfer*. Exploring serious themes about religion and life, the work was in many ways more a novel than the publications that preceded it. Eisner used the term graphic novel to describe the work, as many companies refused to consider publishing a comic book. In the wake of Eisner's critical success, the term graphic novel became more accepted than graphic album, a term coined by Terry Nantier when he began publishing European works in the United States.

The Bronze Age is often described as ending in 1985. At that time, DC Comics celebrated its fiftieth anniversary by rewriting its continuity and setting the stage for new ways of telling stories.

The Modern Age is often described as beginning in 1986. In this watershed year, a number of notable long-form works, including Frank Miller's *Batman: The Dark Knight Returns*, were published. These works found their way into bookstores, introducing graphic storytelling to new readers. Other terms used to describe the Modern Age include Copper Age, Iron Age, and Dark Age, reflecting the tone of stories published during this period. More publishers entered the field, producing creator-owned or company-owned works, and this increase in publications, along with marketing tactics such as the release of special editions and variant covers, created a speculator market that allowed creators and retailers to reap massive profits. When the bubble burst during the 1990's, it drove many publishers from the field and caused many retailers to fold.

Impact

Graphic storytelling has been a part of human creative expression since the earliest cave paintings. As printing technology improved, so too did the ability to communicate through both words and pictures. Comic book fandom was a natural spin-off from science-fiction fandom, which coalesced in the mid-twentieth century; these fans began writing about characters and publishers and in so doing created the chronological divisions that have become key to discussions of comic book history. Because of the established community of fans, publishers were able to tailor works to core readers, allowing for experimentation in content and format and giving rise to traditional comic books and collected editions, both of which have come to be called graphic novels. The changes in comics formats allowed comics to be sold in bookstores, attracting new readers and introducing foreign works, notably manga, to US audiences.

Robert Greenberger

Bibliography

Benton, Mike. *The Comic Book in America*. Dallas, Tex.: Taylor, 1989. Provides a generalized overview of the comic book field from the Golden Age forward, touching on ages, genres, and significant events, with heavy emphasis on illustrations.

Jones, Gerard, and Will Jacobs. *The Comic Book Heroes*. Rocklin, Calif.: Prima Books, 1997. Examines the comic book field from the Silver Age to the Modern Age and looks at the forces that shape the comics industry.

Schumer, Arlen. *The Silver Age of Comic Book Art*. Portland, Oreg.: Collectors Press, 2003. Surveys the Silver Age of comic books and discusses the maturing illustrators who ushered in a new brand of storytelling.

COMIC BOOK CONVENTIONS AND CULTURAL PRACTICE

Definition

A comic book convention is an organized and publicized gathering that attracts people with a desire to interact with others who share an interest in comic books and associated popular culture.

Introduction

Comic book conventions may occupy a single hotel meeting room or fill an entire convention center. They may attract a few dozen people for a single afternoon or hundreds of thousands for a week. They may be called "comic con," "comicon," or some variation thereof and can be referenced colloquially as "con" and, sometimes, "show." There are, in essence, a whole host of events that have been labeled as comic book conventions by those who create them, and a whole host of activities may be associated with each.

Nonetheless, there are some features that cons seem to hold in common. They are typically open to the public and actively solicit attendance, for which there is most often an admission fee. Most established cons are held on an annual basis. Though many cons have comic books as the central focus, there has always been overlap with other forms of popular culture, especially science fiction. The overlap with other forms of media has become increasingly visible, in no small part the result of the crossover appeal that has come with increased licensing of comic book properties into other media. Most readers of comic books are also consumers of other forms of entertainment, such as television and video games, and cons have expanded to incorporate features addressing these interests.

While regard for the medium and its talented contributors remains a key motivator behind support of comic book conventions, cons are also sites of commerce. Like comics specialty shops, they not only provide social support for those attracted to the medium but also serve as sites for sales and the promotion of the industry.

While most conventions continue to be grassroots initiatives, the efforts of franchisers such as Wizard World to acquire, rename, and market conventions strategically reminds observers that these events are potentially lucrative attractions.

A Brief History of Comic Book Conventions

In the early 1960's, comic book fans became increasingly successful in networking with one another thanks in part to editors such as Julie Schwartz at DC Comics and Stan Lee at Marvel Comics, who published the addresses of fans who wrote to their letters pages. Initially, these fans circulated self-published magazines, or fanzines, among their virtual community, but many of them longed for face-to-face interaction with their fellow comics fans. Science fiction enthusiasts had been holding conventions of their own since 1939. However, not until March, 1964, did a group of comics fans get together for a coordinated event: Jerry Bails, a college professor in Michigan often credited as the "father of comics fandom," organized and hosted a score of his fellow comics fans for a weekend. In May, another event was held in Chicago, and later that month, teenagers Dave Szurke and Bob Brosch successfully organized what is considered to be the first formal

2011 Comic-Con in San Diego. (Sandy Huffaker/Corbis)

comic book convention at the Hotel Tuller in Detroit. Later that summer, the inaugural New York Comic Con hosted the first professional guests at a convention.

In the next year, conventions began to pop up in cities across the country. While these events proliferated, few continued for many consecutive years, as they were largely dependent on the organizers' interest, energy, and financial stability. These were almost all grassroots rather than corporate initiatives. Marvel Comics did try its hand at hosting conventions in the mid-1970's but desisted after only a couple of years. Conventions would have to grow significantly before corporations would take an interest in managing them.

The longest continually running, and best attended, comic book convention in the United States is Comic-Con International: San Diego (CCI). Founded in 1970 as the Golden State Comic-Con, CCI has grown to become a popular culture phenomenon, drawing more than 125,000 attendees and overflowing the spacious San Diego Convention Center each summer. Part of CCI's rapid expansion in the early twenty-first century has been its proximity to and favor with Hollywood, which has taken to CCI as a means to test market and promote many of its forthcoming blockbuster projects.

Participants

A number of different kinds of people are involved in a comic book convention. The most essential to the process of holding a convention are organizers, the people who help coordinate and promote the event. Organizers are often enthusiasts themselves, but they stage conventions for an even wider audience. That audience is composed of fellow fans, those who want to be involved in a dialogue about comics and associated cultures. Some fans express their status in visually distinct ways such as dressing in costume for the convention, an activity known in some circles as "cosplay."

In order to entice fans to attend, organizers will recruit several other groups to participate in the convention. Vendors are comics and specialty shop owners, publishers, art dealers, and others who have items for sale or trade. Over the years, some events have seen an increasing number of promoters become a part of the convention scene. These are people (for example "booth babes") who work for publishers, television and

film production companies, and other mass media producers who are present to promote current and upcoming media products.

Perhaps the single most enticing draw for fans is the presence of comic book professionals, typically referred to as "pros," and other celebrities who are guests of the convention. The guest list (and the implied opportunity to meet these famous figures) is highly touted in convention promotions. The pros may agree to sign autographs, give presentations, or appear in other venues throughout the convention. Their ranks include comic book professionals such as *Batman* writer Grant Morrison and Hollywood actors such as *Iron Man* star Robert Downey, Jr. A notable number of celebrities from older television shows and films are often found signing autographs at conventions. For example, Lou Ferrigno, a star of the 1970's *Incredible Hulk* television series, is a familiar fixture on the convention circuit.

Programming

Typically, most of the activity at comic book conventions takes place in the exhibit hall (also known as the dealer's room), where fans and vendors gather to buy and sell comic books (new and old), graphic novels, trade paperbacks, art, action figures, T-shirts, and every conceivable product associated with the industry. Vendors are assigned to "tables" or "booths," which are designated areas in which they display their merchandise and conduct business with potential buyers. Many comics vendors are proprietors of their own comic book specialty stores, and most of their marketing efforts are unsophisticated. Many erect backdrops with their most valuable items (back issues, for example) and display additional items on a table in front of them (long boxes of comics, for example).

Comic book conventions also typically provide some forum for interaction between fans and pros, such as autographing sessions. Sometimes multiple guests will be arranged in a row, or "artists' alley," in a distinct section or room of the convention space apart from the vendors. The degree and amount of formality associated with this interaction seems inversely related to both the size of the convention and the star power of the pro; that is, obtaining an autograph from Marvel Comics creator Stan Lee, for example, at CCI is more difficult to accomplish than having a conversation with a writer of independent comics at a regional convention.

Formal presentations are also frequent convention activities; they usually take place in a space other than the exhibit hall, and they can feature any combination of pros and fans speaking on a number of industry-related topics. Such presentations include, but are not limited to, new project announcements, interviews, and fan-led discussions of the content of comics. These presentations are scheduled in advance and are typically promoted in some public manner, such as being previewed in a convention program or announced over a public address system.

Other activities that might take place at a convention include social gatherings such as after-hours parties, costume contests, charity auctions, and awards ceremo-

nies recognizing those in the industry. At some conventions, there are even conference-style research presentations made by academics (for example, the Comics Arts Conference). The variety of activities made available to attendees results from some combination of the convention's size, longevity, and fiscal strength and the imagination and initiative of its organizers.

Impact

Although quantifying the impact of conventions on the production of graphic novels is difficult, numerous creator-told anecdotes indicate that the gatherings have influenced the creative directions of many careers and played a role in shaping some of the art form's most memorable works. Pros have recounted how successful collaborations have emerged after meeting a colleague at a convention. Indeed, because so much of the work of comics creation is done in geographic isolation, conventions provide some of the rare opportunities for pros to meet in person.

The conventions have also contributed to the growing sense of awareness about graphic novels in the wider culture. With mainstream media increasingly providing coverage that goes beyond treating conventions as havens for social misfits, the events help raise the profile of comics as a legitimate medium for the expression of ideas.

The most enduring impact of conventions, however, is likely the sense of community that they have fostered among fans and between fans and professionals. Because of the open and often cordial interactions between fans and pros, the comics industry demonstrates a level of interactivity that is atypical in other mass media, where fans rarely gain audiences with their favorite creative personalities, much less influence the direction of their work, as comics fans have done.

Matthew J. Smith

Actor Robert Downey, Jr., who portrays the Marvel Comics' superhero Iron Man, speaks to fans during a panel discussion at the 2009 Comic-Con. (Sandy Huffaker/Corbis)

Bibliography

Comic-Con: Forty Years of Artists, Writers, Fans, and Friends. San Francisco: Chronicle Books, 2009. A detailed and highly illustrated history of Comic-Con International: San Diego from its origins to its fortieth anniversary.

Pustz, Matthew J. *Comic Book Culture: Fanboys and True Believers*. Jackson: University Press of Mississippi, 1999. An extensive ethnography of comic book culture largely focusing on the comic book store as a locus of activity but also addressing the role of conventions.

Schelly, Bill. *The Golden Age of Comic Fandom*. Seattle: Hamster Press, 1999. A history recounting in detail the early years of comics fandom, from its initial publications to its first meetings, based on personal experience and interviews.

THE COMICS CODE: ITS ORIGIN AND EFFECTS ON THE COMICS INDUSTRY

Definition

The Comics Code was a self-imposed censorship system on comics in the United States created in 1954 and revised in 1971 and 1989. The code prevented the depiction of sexuality, brutal crimes, and drug use and generally ensured that comics would be suitable for young readers. The code is frequently blamed for reinforcing the notion that comics are strictly for children.

Introduction

The Comics Code was created in response to criticism that comics were harmful to young readers. As comics emerged as a mass medium during the 1940's, cultural critics, religious and civic authorities, and intellectuals began condemning them in editorials reprinted in newspapers across the United States. In 1948, a number of publishers formed the Association of Comics Magazine Publishers (ACMP) in order to regulate the content of their publications, but this organization rapidly imploded.

Criticism of comics did not receive major public attention until after World War II, when the superhero genre began to wane in popularity, to be replaced by crime and horror comics, and comics were linked with the rising problem of juvenile delinquency. The most vocal opponent of comics, Fredric Wertham, accused them of inspiring or even teaching children to commit crimes. The attacks on the industry culminated in a 1954 Senate subcommittee hearing on comics.

In response to the mounting public criticism of comics, publishers created the Comics Magazine Association of America (CMAA) in September of 1954. The enforcement arm of the CMAA, the Comics Code Authority (CCA), modeled its Comics Code on the ACMP code of 1948, the codes of individual publishers, and the Motion Picture Production Code (also known as the Hays Code) that regulated the film industry. The Comics Code forbade depicting "indecent . . . exposure"; presenting crime "in such a way as to create sympathy for the criminal"; using "profanity, obscenity, smut, [or] vulgarity"; treating divorce "hu-

morously"; or ridiculing any religious or racial group. Subsections of the code detailed exactly what could and could not be shown, particularly with regard to depictions of crime and horror. Those comics that passed were given the CCA stamp on the cover; those that did not could still be printed, but many distributors would refuse to carry unapproved comics. Thus, although the CCA could not legally compel publishers to change their comics, those that did not would not have their comics distributed to retailers.

The code's effect on comics was immediate. Several publishers went out of business between 1954 and 1956, including EC Comics, which was known for its high-quality horror comics. Comics sales in general fell, and horror and crime comics virtually disappeared from the stands as superheroes made a resurgence. As the direct market system, in which publishers sold comics directly to independent comic book shops, took over during the 1980's, the importance of the code waned. The rise of independent publishers and comics lines aimed specifically at adults during the 1990's further hastened the demise of the code. By the twentieth-first century, the CMAA and the CCA had lost virtually all of their power, and the code ceased to have any real effect on the industry.

Senate Hearings on Comics

The most immediate cause of the creation of the Comics Code was the series of public hearings of the Senate Subcommittee on Juvenile Delinquency in 1954. During the hearings, the committee, a unit of the Senate Judiciary Committee, was led by Senator Estes Kefauver, a Democrat from Tennessee. The subcommittee met April 21-22 and June 4 in New York, where it heard twenty-two witnesses. The list included psychiatrists, publishers, retailers, and strip cartoonists (including Walt Kelly and Milton Caniff), but the two most important witnesses by far were Wertham and William Gaines, publisher of EC Comics.

Wertham essentially rephrased the arguments he had made in his articles and book, linking depictions of crime and horror in comics to juvenile delinquency. The committee was receptive to Wertham, giving him time to make a statement before questioning him, and members clearly agreed with the broad strokes of his argument. Gaines, on the other hand, was essentially forced to defend the content of the comics he published to the committee members. Famously, he was shown the cover of one of his comics, which featured a man with a bloody ax holding up a woman's severed head, and asked whether he felt it was in good taste. He replied, "Yes, sir, I do, for the cover of a horror comic." Gaines's testimony was widely reported by the media.

The committee's investigation and findings made clear the extent of the criticism facing the comics industry. It led almost directly to the founding of the CMAA later in 1954.

Fredric Wertham

Wertham played a major role in the creation of the code. While Wertham was not the first person to attack comics as potentially harmful to young readers, he was the most vocal and well-known critic of comics. Born in 1895 in Munich, Germany (he became an American citizen in 1927), Wertham was a practicing psychiatrist who primarily treated poor or disadvantaged patients. Through his work with criminals and juvenile delinquents, Wertham became certain that comic books presented a great danger to children. Beginning in the late 1940's, Wertham wrote a number of articles for popular magazines on the dangers of comics, and in 1954, he published his most famous book, *Seduction of the Innocent*. Wertham accused comics of not only encouraging criminal behavior in children but also containing sexual subtexts—for example, Wertham perceived the relationship between Batman and Robin as a homoerotic one. Wertham became a recognized expert on the comics industry and was a major witness in the Senate hearings of 1954.

Wertham's arguments about comics had their flaws. Given the popularity of the medium, it is no surprise that many criminals read comics; many law-abiding, psychologically healthy people did also. However, Wertham was looking at violence on a social, not individual, level. He was concerned about media depictions of violence as symptomatic of larger problems in society, and he was not trying to censor comics because of prurience. Though his attacks on comics may have led to the oppressive restrictions of the Comics Code, Wertham was not quite the villain many comics fans have painted him to be.

Impact

The code's effect on comics was immediate and severe, forcing several publishers out of business and contributing to a significant decrease in sales. Superhero comics returned to the forefront, and comics with supposedly questionable subject matter were essentially blacklisted. However, the direct market system of the 1980's circumvented the code, and in the 1990's, independent comics aimed at adults ignored the code altogether. Marvel Comics stopped using the code's seal of approval in 2001, and other publishers followed its lead. As of 2012, the code was no longer in use by any major comics publisher.

Ted Anderson

Bibliography

Beaty, Bart. *Fredric Wertham and the Critique of Mass Culture*. Jackson: University Press of Mississippi, 2005. An in-depth examination of the life and works of Wertham, discussing his impact not only on comics but also on psychoanalysis.

Hajdu, David. *The Ten-Cent Plague: The Great Comic-Book Scare and How It Changed America*. New York: Farrar, Straus and Giroux, 2008. An examination of the anticomics hysteria that led to the Comics Code and the latter's immediate impact.

Jones, Gerard. *Men of Tomorrow: Geeks, Gangsters, and the Birth of the Comic Book*. New York: Basic Books, 2004. A history of the comic book industry that focuses on the larger-than-life personalities of those involved.

Wright, Bradford W. *Comic Book Nation: The Transformation of Youth Culture in America*. Baltimore: Johns Hopkins University Press, 2001. A history of the mainstream American comics industry from its birth to the end of the twentieth century.

"COMICS" VS. "GRAPHIC NOVELS": IS IT ALL IN THE BINDING?

Definition

The terms "comics" and "graphic novels" both describe works that use sequential images to tell stories. However, they also refer to different formats in which comics are published; the former implies monthly magazines, the latter a book. Calling comics graphic novels lends the medium literary worth; however, equating the two terms has been controversial because some feel the latter term suggests that comics should aspire to be like novels.

Introduction

Comics have been increasingly recognized as a major form of literature, and related terminology is fluid and frequently debated. The terms comics and graphic novels are interchangeable when they refer to the medium of using pictures to tell stories. However, they can also refer to different ways in which the medium is presented. Comics brings to mind amusing newspaper comic strips or thin monthly magazines, whereas graphic novels refers to thicker books that have a kind of literary gravitas.

The link between comics and humor comes from the first newspaper comics published in the late 1800's, which were called "comic weeklies" and later simply "comics." Later illustrated stories have been called comics even though they may be neither humorous nor published weekly. In discussions of motion pictures, "films" refers to films in the plural and "film" can refer to one film or the entire medium; "comic" in the singular, however, is not used to designate the comics medium. The term can only refer to one work or volume or serve as an adjective.

The "comic book," also called a "monthly," or "floppy," refers to a monthly issue of typically around thirty-two pages, a format that has been used the most in the comics industry by American publishers such as Marvel and DC. (Getty Images)

As comics scholarship has spread and deepened, academics and industry insiders, recognizing the confusion surrounding the term comics and its inability to describe all of the titles in circulation adequately, have proposed a range of different naming conventions. One of the most popular terms in circulation is graphic novels, which was invented to disassociate works from the "childishness" of comics. The term was first used by Richard Kyle in 1964 in a Comics Amateur Press Alliance newsletter and was later popularized by Will Eisner, who marketed his 1978 comic *A Contract with God* as a graphic novel. Before the 2000's, the term was sometimes understood to mean violent or pornographic novels, but wide usage has made the compound noun accurately understood.

Compared to the term comics, which technically only communicates that the stories are funny, graphic novels more accurately describes the medium's use of pictures to tell stories, and the term is also a better description for comics in book form. However, use of the term has generated new questions. If *Ultimate Spider-Man*, for example, is a comic in monthly issues, does it become a graphic novel after it is bound? If so, does a different binding automatically put it in the same category as a work such as Art Spiegelman's *Maus* (1986, 1991), or do other descriptors need to be applied to differentiate between bound comics and stand-alone graphic novels? Also, even although "graphic novel" does sound more literary than "comic," there have been debates over whether it should be used as a substitute, as some have found the term too contrived. Others have pointed to its inaccuracy; the word "graphic" may highlight the medium's use of images, but "novel" suggests a long fictional story. Exploring the naming conventions for different formats of comics has helped the medium diversify and open artistic possibilities.

Further Distinctions

Comics can be used as an umbrella term to mean all types of graphic publications, regardless of format. Under this definition, a "comic strip" refers to a comic of two or more panels and up to a page in length, often featuring recurring characters if it is serialized. A "cartoon" is a single-image comic. The "comic book," which also can be called a "monthly," a "pamphlet," or a "floppy," is a monthly issue that is approximately thirty-two pages in length; this is the most common format used by American publishers such as Marvel Comics and DC Comics.

Comic strips have been published in North America since the late 1800's; however, during the 1930's, the comic book format was initiated by Max Gaines, a salesman for Eastern Color Printing, as a way to collect previously published newspaper comic strips and boost their sales. A subcategory under comics, graphic novels refers specifically to book-length, completed stories published in one or more bound volumes; however, the term is also applied to volumes of collected comic book series. Sometimes, to differentiate between graphic novels featuring previously unpublished content and those reprinted from serialized comic books, the former are referred to as "original graphic novels" ("OGNs"), while the latter are referred to as "trade paperbacks" ("trades" or "TPBs"). Most comic book series are collected into paperbacks, so the few hardcover collections can still be generally referred to as trade paperbacks.

Some original graphic novels may be serialized in independent magazines before being issued in a bound volume, and comic books may be collected into volumes; however, for most of comics publishing history, comic book series were issued only in the monthly format, sold at newsstands with other newspapers and magazines, and disposed of after reading. As readers began to collect comics in the 1970's, publishers responded by printing collections. Because original graphic novels and graphic novel collections have become extremely popular, some have predicted that comics as a whole may transition into being published only as graphic novels. However, comic book publishers have established a pattern for working with the monthly comic book through many decades, and comic book creators and readers maintain that comic books have a unique storytelling structure and will continue to draw audiences.

Differences in Publication Format

In terms of publication, there have been a few major differences between serialized comic books and original graphic novels: production process, publication format, and content. First, as a result of the structure of major comic book publishers in the United States, publishers often own the rights to characters and divide writing, penciling, inking, lettering, and coloring duties among their employees. A series or character can outlive its initial individual creators; for example, Superman was created by Jerry Siegel and Joe Shuster in 1932 but is owned by DC Comics and remains an active character in the DC Universe. Original graphic novels grew out of underground comics, which developed outside the mainstream comic book production structure. They are often produced by an individual or a self-selected team who retains the rights to the characters and the work as a whole.

Second, comics and graphic novels differ in terms of publication format, which leads to differences in story structure. Because the earliest comic books reprinted short comic strips, the first superhero comic books also featured short, completed stories centered on a stable cast rather than stories developed over several issues. In modern publishing, stories tend to be framed in one issue to create a satisfying monthly reading experience. Although many modern serialized comic books are written with a completed story as a target, early series may continue to tell short stories indefinitely, based on publisher discretion. In contrast, the plot in original graphic novels may build and resolve itself through the entire story and does not necessarily require a specific story structure within a set number of pages.

Third, stories published in the serialized comic book format have overwhelmingly been superhero and crime-fighting stories. Original graphic novels, on the other hand, are particularly noted for covering more personal stories or nonfiction narratives.

Naming Strategies

Before the wide production of graphic novels, comics referred to comic strips and serialized comic books, which are fast reads compared to prose novels and are associated with humor and entertainment. Thus, comics have largely been regarded as a disreputable and juvenile element of popular culture. Fredric Wertham's 1954 criticism of comics, *Seduction of the Innocent*, further confirmed this perspective in the minds

of many educators by arguing that comics teach children violent behavior and lax social values. In addition, the production of comic book series, divided among many individuals with apparently limited roles, has been seen as a form of industrial mass production and not necessarily art or literature. One approach to changing the public perception of comics is to rename all comics "graphic novels" to distance them from such associations. Because the term graphic novels has literary connotations, another approach is to affix nonfiction or literary comics with a more realistic or serious label to distinguish them from comic book series meant primarily to entertain.

The increase in the number of comics published in the graphic novel format has helped comics become more mainstream. Comics published in the graphic novel format can be more welcoming to new comics readers than those in serial format. They are distributed through the more familiar environment of the bookstore, look like other books, and are more likely to contain complete stories or story arcs; therefore, they do not necessarily ask readers to wait as the series progresses monthly. In addition, original graphic novels have drawn more attention than comics from educators, who have seen in them more literary value, and this has helped readers understand that comics are not all about superheroes.

Others believe, however, that avoiding the term comics panders to a vague idea of literary worth and that there is no need for comics to be similar to prose literature. Scholarship has revealed that comic strips that were previously considered junk reading have relevance in their ability to chart changing social anxieties in North America. Labeling certain titles as graphic novels to set them apart from other comics is particularly contentious. First, a difference in naming creates a hierarchy within comics. Comic books would still be considered childish and remain obscure, when, in reality, they can be mined as rich cultural texts. Second, while there is no inherent link between publication format and content, because series published in the monthly comic book format have been predominantly superhero stories and original graphic novels have been personal or nonfiction stories, format and content have often been conflated. Labeling personal and nonfiction stories as graphic novels risks entrenching the belief that monthly comic books are not a suitable format for personal stories and nonfiction and that original graphic novels should not tell superhero or action stories. This would limit experimentation with different formats of comics.

Impact

As industry professionals, librarians, and academics have grappled with the terms comics and graphic novels and tried to pin down their attributes, they have also come to understand the publication possibilities for comics as a medium and how different forms of publication can affect the reading experience. Despite both differences between the uses of comics and graphic novels and the debates around their similarities, the two terms have remained flexible. Comics writer Neil Gaiman has noted that while his *Sandman* series (1989-1996) was published serially as a comic book, many people have subsequently referred to it as a graphic novel. The differences between the two terms are also lessening as more and more serialized comic books are being collected into trade paperbacks. Readers, librarians, and academic scholars have begun to distinguish between comic books and graphic novels based on publication format rather than content.

Realizing that monthly comic books do not necessarily have to contain superhero stories can help readers read more widely. Many libraries and bookstores have a graphic novels section; while this takes marketing concerns into consideration, as many readers are drawn to comics as a format regardless of genre, one space for all comics encourages readers to consider formats to be similar rather than different.

Original graphic novels are still more likely than serialized comics to be used as teaching materials in schools and universities. However, as more comics are published in the graphic novel format, comics in general have become more socially accepted. On the other hand, maintaining the term comics to denote all forms of graphic storytelling is a part of a larger push in the arts and humanities to close the perceived gap between high and low culture, and it emphasizes that comics need not be elevated to literary status to be an important aspect of culture. Superhero comics, comic strips, and Web comics are regularly discussed at academic conferences and in scholarly journals, and the older term comics is increasingly looked upon favorably.

The debate regarding terminology has also generated suggestions for more precise terms. Many acclaimed graphic novels, such as *Maus* and Marjane Satrapi's *Persepolis* (2000-2003), are not fiction, and calling them novels would be as misleading as calling a serious story a comic. "Graphic narrative" has been proposed to cover all comics, and sometimes more precise terms such as "graphic nonfiction" and "graphic memoir" are also used.

Shan Mu Zhao

Bibliography

Chute, Hillary. "Comics as Literature? Reading Graphic Narrative." *PMLA* 123, no. 2 (2008): 452-465. Focuses on nonfiction graphic novels and their representation of history and critically reassesses the term graphic novel, suggesting the use of "graphic narrative" to describe nonfiction.

Couch, Chris. "The Publication and Formats of Comics, Graphic Novels, and Tankobon." *Image [&] Narrative* 1, no. 1 (December, 2000). http://www.image andnarrative.be/inarchive/narratology/chriscouch. htm. Traces the development of the monthly comic book and the graphic novel forms as well as their influences, such as pulp-fiction magazines.

Weiner, Robert G., ed. *Graphic Novels and Comics in Libraries and Archives: Essays on Readers, Research, History, and Cataloguing.* Jefferson, N.C.: McFarland, 2010. Deals directly with how naming has affected the delivery and reception of comics in libraries and examines how grouping comics together or throughout the library according to subject matter affects reader access.

DISTRIBUTION OF GRAPHIC NOVELS: HISTORY AND PRACTICE

Definition

Distribution refers to the method by which goods are moved from the producer to the consumer, in this case the different channels in the comic book and graphic novel industry by which comics are moved from publishers to retailers and readers. Two important categories of distribution in the comics industry are independent distribution and direct distribution.

Introduction

The method by which a product reaches consumers is generally not considered to have much influence on the consumers or the product itself. However, the various distribution systems used in the comics industry have had a powerful and lasting effect on comic books and graphic novels. How comics are distributed has been

an integral part of the medium's history, and a thorough understanding of the distribution systems used helps to reveal the causes of various changes in the industry, such as the increasing isolation of comics from the mass market that began during the 1970's. Each distribution system has created changes at several levels, producing dramatic effects on the overall health of the industry and even altering the content that is produced to suit particular distribution systems.

The main distribution channels employed in North America beginning in the twentieth century include independent distribution, direct distribution to comic book stores, bookstore distribution, and digital distribution. None of these has ever completely replaced the others, but some have come close, much to the detriment of the entire industry. The influences of various

Customers wait in line at the Forbidden Planet comic book store in Manhattan in 1992; by 1993, there were about 9,400-10,000 comic book shops in the United States. (AP Photo)

distribution channels, and more specifically, what occurs when one of those channels comes to dominate the others, present an interesting demonstration of the problems of monopoly and of the importance of diversity. No single distribution system can "save" comics, as has been shown repeatedly by previous rescue attempts such as direct distribution. Instead, the interaction of various distribution channels tends to provide the best opportunities for growth.

Independent Distribution

In their original transition from strip to book, comics were treated as part of the magazine industry and sold alongside magazines in pharmacies, newsstands, and grocery stores. While this system, known as independent distribution, helped comics reach a wide audience and still exists in a much-reduced form, several problems eventually arose.

For readers, one of the main problems was the system's unreliability; customers could not be sure when a comic they wished to buy would be available at a store, if it became available at all. Another difficulty was that these stores tended to sell random assortments of comics and had little interest in tailoring their selections to an audience. For the retailers, comics were a nuisance that produced only a small profit margin while taking shelf space from more valuable products.

For the publishers, the costliest problem was that retailers were reimbursed for unsold comics, sometimes without even having to prove that they had received them, a system that at best removed incentive to sell the comics and at worst encouraged fraud. During the 1970's, Marvel Comics reported that as few as three of every ten comics sold to retailers actually went on to be sold to readers. With the comics market much smaller than in the Golden Age, this costly practice became impossible to maintain, leading to a financial crisis for the industry in the late 1960's and early 1970's.

Direct Distribution

Comics fan and distributor Phil Seuling is generally credited with introducing the idea of direct distribution in 1973. He approached several major publishers to purchase comic books directly for retail without having to rely on the preexisting distributors. As part of the deal between the retailers and the publishers, direct-market distribution allows retailers to purchase comics at a larger discount than the independent distributors receive, with the stipulation that the retailers cannot return unsold copies of the comics they order.

In 1979 and 1980, there was a brief explosion in the number of distributors when Marvel Comics began selling to any direct distributor that could meet its minimum sales requirement of three thousand dollars. However, while the number of comic book stores continued to grow over the course of the 1980's, competition greatly reduced the number of distributors to only a remaining few by the early 1990's, the top three being Diamond Comic Distributors, Capital City Distribution, and Heroes World Distribution.

By 1993, there were about ten thousand comic book shops in the United States. By 1995, the number had dropped to between six and seven thousand. Comics collecting, encouraged by the establishment of comic book stores, created a speculator-driven bubble; when the bubble burst in 1994, many customers were driven away. In 1996, further problems arose when Marvel Comics signed a deal with Heroes World in an attempt to control the distribution of its product. This deal led to a "distributor war" that further decreased the number of retailers to approximately forty-five hundred. The "war" ended with one company, Diamond Comic Distributors, possessing a monopoly of the direct-distribution system.

The distribution system that saved the mainstream North American comics industry during the 1970's contributed to its near collapse during the 1990's and its subsequent stagnation. Direct distribution had become a victim of its own success. The system was incredibly effective at serving its already established audience, having virtually ended the independent distribution system that provided mainstream visibility; however, with comics locked away in specialty comic book stores out of sight of most audiences, comics stopped attracting new readers and have struggled to reestablish an audience.

Comic Book Stores

Direct distribution led to the proliferation of the comic book specialty store for the first time during the 1970's.

Over the course of the decade, the number of stores increased from approximately thirty to several thousand across the United States. These stores became the first venues dedicated to selling comics instead of treating them as an afterthought.

For comic book stores, direct distribution offers several advantages over independent distribution. Because the low cost of comics made them a low priority to the independent distributors, publishers would often delay delivering the comics by at least a week. Meanwhile, direct distributors competed to provide comics to retailers as quickly as possible, giving comic book stores the clear advantage of being able to sell their products sooner. In addition, since most retailers entered the business because of their preexisting interest in comics, the inability to return unsold comics was

American Splendor was first published and distributed independently by the author, Harvey Pekar. (Mark Duncan/AP/Corbis)

mitigated for the retailers; they already knew what readers were interested in, so they could order exactly as many comics as they thought would sell. Also, retailers found it desirable to maintain a small stock of unsold issues. Rather than being a financial liability, comics that remained unsold could be stored as back issues and sold for higher prices than they would have commanded when they were first published. These back issues also turned into collector's items, which helped draw a new audience for comic books.

Bookstore Distribution

As part of the independent-distribution system, bookstores predated direct distribution but had been largely eclipsed by it by the 1990's. However, in the first decade of the twenty-first century, bookstores became increasingly popular retailers of graphic novels. Bookstore distribution increased the availability and popularity of graphic novels, since bookstores prefer to stock reading material that resembles what they have already sold, instead of the serialized single issues popular in comic book stores. The availability of graphic novels in bookstores also increased mainstream media and academic interest in graphic novels, introducing the medium to a wider audience.

By providing graphic novels with the opportunity to appeal to a new audience outside the comic book store, bookstores have changed the medium in several significant ways. The success in bookstores of manga publishers VIZ Media and TOKYOPOP and independent publishers such as Top Shelf Comics, Fantagraphics Books, and Drawn and Quarterly has encouraged the comics industry to experiment with a more diverse range of works and genres. The growing market for graphic novels also led to changes in serialized comics; more stories are being written with the forethought of collecting them as hardcover or paperback books to be sold in bookstores and consequently feature plot arcs that last for the length of an average trade paperback.

Digital Distribution

The Internet has led to a new form of distribution, typically referred to as digital distribution, which relies on the sale of comics from publisher to reader as pure, digitized information. Previously, the distribution of comics using the Internet took several forms, ranging from the creation of Web comics that are produced explicitly and entirely for reading on the Internet to the ability to order comics online from brick-and-mortar stores. However, few comics were produced as print comics and simultaneously delivered digitally. The proliferation of tablets and e-book readers, however, has led most mainstream publishers to make comics available for purchase via online applications such as comiXology, with major publishers opening their own application stores in 2010.

Digital distribution is expected to help comics reach mainstream audiences in the same way that book stores helped graphic novels. Readers using digital distribution tend to buy a wide range of comics rather than restrict themselves to the superhero genre. At the same time, the instantaneous nature of the Internet experience encourages a greater interest in periodical pamphlets as opposed to graphic novels. Digital distribution has its own set of challenges, including digital piracy and problems of ownership; however, with the Internet's ability to reach a mass, international audience, digital distribution may revitalize the comics industry.

Impact

The role that different distribution channels have played in shaping comics as a medium is difficult to overestimate; direct distribution alone has been credited with both saving and destroying the comics industry in North America. Direct distribution made it possible for customers to find all the comics they wanted in one place on a reliable basis. Comic book stores have provided a place for the development of a "comics culture," one that particularly orients itself around the superhero genre. However, that culture can seem intimidating, to the point of keeping new readers out of comic book stores. Similarly, story lines that require multiple issues to resolve increased in popularity with direct distribution, since readers could ensure that they acquired every issue. However, the increasingly complex story lines, combined with a focus on superhero comics at the expense of diversity in other genres, has also prevented new readers from finding an entry point into comics.

Distribution systems have also affected the comics' producers. For a period during the 1980's, direct distri-

bution increased competition among comic book publishers when distributors such as Pacific Comics and Eclipse Comics began publishing their own comic books in order to have more products to distribute. This increased competition led publishers to compete for talented writers and artists, which led large publishers such as Marvel Comics and DC Comics to offer better deals to comic book creators and allow some creators to retain ownership of their characters and works.

How comics are perceived has also changed with distribution systems. When comics were sold exclusively through newsstands, they reached a wide audience but were generally treated as ephemeral products because of their association with magazines. The establishment of specialty stores serving a narrow audience of preestablished fans helped segregate comics from mainstream interests but also led to expectations of a more "mature" product to suit its aging readers. The transition to the bookstore led to an increased interest in graphic novels with more diverse genres and a sense of increased literary legitimacy, and digital distribution seems to be changing who reads comics and why they read them.

Kaitlan Huckabone

Bibliography

Dean, Michael. "A Comics Journal History of the Direct Market." *The Comics Journal*, February 15, 2010. http://www.tcj.com/history/a-comics-journal-history-of-the-direct-market-part-one. Provides a history and evaluation of the direct market's effect on both mainstream and independent comics from the 1970's to the 1990's.

Eisner, Will. "Teaching and Learning Sequential Art for Comics in the Print and Digital Age." In *Comics and Sequential Art: Principles and Practices from the Legendary Cartoonist*. Rev. ed. New York: W. W. Norton, 2008. Explores some of the differences between traditional print distribution and online distribution in terms of artistic challenges, technology, process, delivery, and reading experience.

McCloud, Scott. *Reinventing Comics*. New York: HarperCollins, 2000. Reviews the history, process, and consequences of different distribution methods, particularly direct distribution, and includes early speculation on the effects of digital distribution.

EDUCATIONAL COMICS

Definition

Comics and graphic novels have been used for several decades for the purpose of teaching people to understand and operate machinery or learn educational concepts. The educational comic as a teaching tool, in both professional and educational formats, has been part of the comic book field for years. Educators continue to find new ways to teach readers through comic book illustrations.

Introduction

From their inception, comic books and their long-form cousins, graphic novels, have served to entertain the masses. As the medium expanded in the late 1930's, comic books were derided by many as a poor form of entertainment. However, with the entry of the United States into World War II, the need to train military personnel quickly and effectively led to unorthodox methods. Any means of reaching the serviceman was explored. A 1942 study commissioned by the University of Chicago concluded that soldiers who read manuals that used visual explanations were seven times more likely to retain the material presented. If a soldier could remember basic principles taught in visual form, he could very well save his life on the battlefield.

After World War II, comics illustrations continued to be used in the military and civilian fields. Comic books were used to teach subjects ranging from literature to history and scientific principles. In the 1950's, *Classics Illustrated* was the leader in the market to reach readers in an educational context, and titles from that line often ranged across the social and hard sciences.

In the Modern Age, graphic novels have been produced by more companies in an attempt to capture the academic market. With more students being visually motivated than before, the graphic novel fits an expanding niche. As publishing companies try to grow markets, new forms of education have evolved to the point that graphic novels are no longer merely fodder for poor readers but are actual learning tools for students of all ages and abilities.

Early Forms of Instruction

One of the first people to experiment with comic illustrations as a teaching tool was the comic book creator Will Eisner. While at the Aberdeen Proving Grounds in Maryland in the early days of U.S. involvement in World War II, he used the series *Joe Dope* to teach soldiers about maintenance. These single-panel illustrations were not sequential in format. Self-contained stories for civilians included titles such as *USA is Ready* and *Our Army and Our Navy*. They told readers how to identify Allied and enemy aircraft, hold scrap-metal drives, or administer first aid.

Military books that used comics to tell stories or morals included the Coast Guard book *Adventure Is My*

Two boys look at educational comic books with the theme of atomic energy. (Corbis)

Career, written by *Captain America* creator Joe Simon, and the U.S. Marine Corps' *Tokyo Straight Ahead*. The former told of the history and purpose of the Coast Guard and, most important, how the Coast Guard was a proper branch of the armed forces. *Tokyo Straight Ahead* was written to teach soldiers how to adapt to the reality of combat. One story depicted Marines shooting surrendering Japanese soldiers only to see that the surrender was a ruse; the Japanese soldiers were hiding weapons on them. This seeming cruelty was born out of battles, and the stories taught lessons that would keep an American soldier alive in battle. The military stories often used humor to teach a deadly subject. These titles were a substantial contribution to the field of educational comics at the time.

Education After the Comics Code
The postwar accusations that comics corrupt American youth also affected the way that comics were written. By the 1950's, the industry adopted the Comics Code, which noted that comics should be used for moral purposes. At the same time, many comic book publishers realized that comics could educate readers in a positive manner.

The use of comics to teach soldiers proved worthwhile to the extent that the U.S. Army published a booklet entitled *PS Preventative Maintenance Monthly*. While not a graphic novel in the full extent, it relied heavily on specific characters and copious illustrations to demonstrate maintenance on vehicles and weapons. It was meant as a supplementary text to the standard military maintenance manuals. Eisner continued to illustrate and edit this book, and in 1971, he was replaced by another comic book legend, Joe Kubert.

The troops particularly benefited from these illustrations because parts and procedures could be drawn in ways that photographs could not effectively or accurately demonstrate. The pinnacle of Eisner's work was the 1969 manual on the maintenance of the M16A1 battle rifle. The booklet was small but effective in terms of conveying what needed to be done to maintain a weapon in combat.

Like propaganda comic books, educational comics and graphic novels were used to indoctrinate children and readers about concepts such as communism. *Is*

This Tomorrow? is but one example. Graphic novels were also used to refute the argument prevalent in the 1950's that comics were the first step toward degeneracy. *Classics Illustrated* published many famous literary works in a simple, visually assisted form. While some critics charged that this detracted from the actual book, the publishers responded by saying that reading *Classics Illustrated* novels was the first step, and readers would then want to read the actual books.

Embracing the New Medium
The most prolific American writer of educational comics is Larry Gonick. He first utilized comics in an educational format in 1977, with the book *Blood from a Stone: A Cartoon Guide to Tax Reform*. Soon after, he started producing graphic novels that dealt with various topics, including a *Cartoon History of the Universe* (1977-1992), as well as books that covered topics ranging from statistics to physics to sex. His work is still reproduced through various publishers and serves as a model for other companies. Most of Gonick's work was published in the 1990's, when other companies were expanding their production into the graphic novels field.

The DC Comics imprint Paradox Press has told history through illustration. While its most successful comics focus on crime (*Road to Perdition*, 1998) or are manga reprints (*Gon*, 1992-2002), the series *The Big Book of . . .* (1994-2000) centers on lesser-known historical aspects of real life and events. The series utilized little-known history or myth as a way to inform readers of a general subject. These comics were popular enough that the series totaled seventeen books. While the books did spark an interest in the odd aspects of history, their true legacy extended well past the series. Many of the artists in the *Big Book of . . .* series also worked on their own historical graphic novels. Rick Geary contributed to the Paradox publications and produced several of his own graphic novels of various figures from the Victorian era of crime, from Jack the Ripper to the first documented serial killer in American history, Herman Mudgett.

Teaching People to Interpret Comics
Educators have increasingly sought to reach students through a variety of media. Graphic novels have be-

come one way of expanding discussions and reading in the classroom. However, many people either had the misconceived notion of comics as having poor stories and character development or thought that the graphic novel was not appropriate.

Two writers published books to explain the medium and its impact. Eisner's *Graphic Storytelling and Visual Narrative* (1996) broke down the basic components of the comics story, as well as the symbolism of weaponry or shading. His book has been used by those teaching basic comic book appreciation. A more substantial book that discusses the use of comics in a wider academic role is Scott McCloud's *Understanding Comics: The Invisible Art* (1993). His book details why the medium is not merely pictures and how it uses imagination to accurately tell stories in a wider concept. The success of this book allowed McCloud to write a follow-up, *Reinventing Comics*, in 1999.

Graphic novels have also become a way to teach modern aspects of literature and history. Joe Sacco infused the comics medium with aspects of classic journalism. His works center on areas of conflict and include *Palestine* (1993-1995), *Safe Area Goražde* (2000), *The Fixer* (2003, 2005), and *Footnotes in Gaza* (2009).

Political comics include *Silk Road to Ruin* (2006) and *To Afghanistan and Back* (2002) by Ted Rall. *Macedonia* (2007), by Harvey Pekar, Heather Roberson, and Ed Piskor, recounts how the United Nations looked at eliminating the violence in the Balkans through peaceful means. A graphic novel that tells of political malfeasance is *Brought to Light* (1989), which was published by the Christic Institute. The writers described how U.S. intervention in Central America under the Ronald Reagan administration (1981-1989) led to several acts of terrorism.

Education in the Schools

Many companies that specialize in textbooks for children have expanded into graphic novels as a way to teach young readers the stories of the United States. Some companies have turned to specific aspects to find their niche. For example, Puffin Graphics, a Penguin imprint, specializes in retelling the classics of literature, from graphic novels of Bram Stoker's *Dracula*

(1897) and Mary Shelley's *Frankenstein* (1818) to a manga version of William Shakespeare's *Macbeth* (1623). Osprey Graphic Novels specializes in battles of American history from the Civil War and World War II. Its twelve-title series was written by several famous comic book writers, including Larry Hama of *GI Joe: A Real American Hero* (1982-1994) fame. Rosen has published biographies of famous historical figures, from Abraham Lincoln and George Washington to Harriet Tubman, Sitting Bull, and Spartacus. It also published a series that dealt with the unexplained (creatures like aliens and places like the Bermuda Triangle) and world mythology.

Other books have tried to teach or, at least, distill the basic aspects of American history or science into simple forms. Graphic novels in this area include the *Stuff of Life* (2008) on genetics, Gonick's works on science and history, and Jim Ottaviani's biographies of scientists (*Sus-*

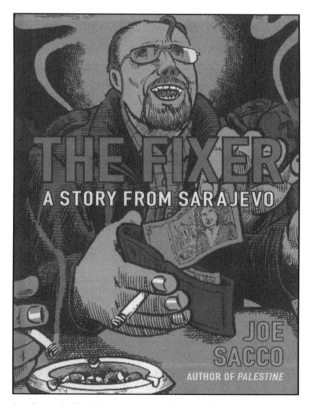

Joe Sacco infused the comics medium with aspects of classic journalism in works such as *The Fixer*. (Courtesy of Drawn & Quarterly)

pended in Language, 2004, on physicist Niels Bohr, and *Dignifying Science*, 2003, on famous female scientists).

Robert Crumb reentered the graphic novels field with a version of the Old Testament. One history-based graphic novel, *A People's History of American Empire* (2008; based on historian Howard Zinn's *A People's History of America*, 1980) sought to tell of the abuses of American society in an illustrated format. Paul Buhle and a group of collaborators used their talents to tell of the history of the Industrial Workers of the World in *Wobblies!* (2005). Finally, Hill and Wang took the bold step of using the graphic novel format to tell the facts of September 11, 2001 (9/11) with its book the *9/11 Report: A Graphic Adaptation* (2006), which was followed by *After 9/11: America's War on Terror (2001-   )* (2008). Some companies have tried to reintroduce historical figures through comics, be they Martin Luther King, Jr., Che Guevara, J. Edgar Hoover, or Reagan.

Impact

While the comics medium has been derided by some as weakening the field of literature, others have seen comics as a way to communicate basic concepts and as springboards to reading literary masterpieces. The educational potential of comics is vast, as demonstrated by the number of companies that have expanded to publish some form of educational comics. Whether this trend can be sustained is debatable. Nonetheless, the graphic novel has already shown its educational worth.

Cord Scott

Bibliography

Carter, James Bucky, ed. *Building Literary Connections with Graphic Novels: Page by Page, Panel by Panel*. Urbana, Ill.: National Council of Teachers of English, 2007. A compilation of essays that discuss the issues surrounding the use of comics in the classroom.

Eisner, Will. *Graphic Storytelling and Visual Narrative*. New York: W. W. Norton, 2008. An excellent overview of how comics can be used to tell stories and how elements of literature are critical to graphic novels.

McCloud, Scott. *Understanding Comics: The Invisible Art*. New York: HarperPerennial, 1994. Summarizes how to effectively read and interpret comic books from panel art to spaces between panels and interpretations of images.

Sabin, Roger. *Comics, Comix, and Graphic Novels*. London: Phaidon, 2001. A concise history of the comic book industry. Includes the origins of and major movements in the industry as well as contributions from comics creators from around the world.

Wolk, Douglas. *Reading Comics: How Graphic Novels Work and What They Mean*. Cambridge, Mass.: Da Capo Press, 2007. Discusses the academic approaches to reading comics and graphic novels. Highlights notable comics from the Modern Age.

Wright, Nicky. *The Classic Era of American Comics*. London: Prion Books, 2009. A history of the comic book medium, focusing on its early years.

EUROPEAN GRAPHIC NOVELS: THE RICH DIVERSITY OF THE EUROPEAN CONTINENT SINCE 1960

Definition

Even before the widespread use of the English term "graphic novel," works were published in Europe that, in retrospect, can be considered belonging to this category, because the themes and visual narration of these works had artistic ambitions and they aimed at an adult readership.

Introduction

Though the one-shot is the prototypical form of the graphic novel, in practice, most graphic novels are published in limited series of albums. For comics publishers worldwide, it is more lucrative to split a graphic

novel into various volumes than to compile the work in one expensive volume. For example, the 361 pages of *L'Ascension du Haut Mal* (1996-2003; *Epileptic*, 2005) were originally published in six albums, and it took the author, David B., about seven years to finish the work. Only in exceptional cases (such as the French or Dutch translations of *Jimmy Corrigan*, 1993-2000, or *Blankets*, 2003) have companies risked publishing a work in one volume.

Just as the material presented in a graphic novel may be varied, the themes, narratives, and graphics can be extremely diverse. Furthermore, it is important to stress that graphic novels, or comics in general, do not

Blueberry comics, set in the American Old West, began publication in Europe in 1963. (Courtesy of Dargaud)

have the same impact in every European state. In Greece or the Baltic states, for example, comics remain a marginal cultural form, while in France or Belgium, for example, comics seem almost constitutional to their respective cultures. This explains why critically acclaimed graphic novels of non-French authors (such as the Italian Lorenzo Mattotti, the Argentinean José Muñoz, or the Spanish Miguelanxo Prado) were first published in French—and often in better quality—before they were published in the native language of the authors.

Historically speaking, some European graphic narratives published before 1960 can be considered forerunners of the adult graphic novel; examples include Gustave Doré's *Histoire dramatique, pittoresque et caricaturale de la Sainte Russie* (1854) or Frans Masereel's *Histoires sans paroles* (1920). However, from the early twentieth century until the mid-1960's, most comics produced in Europe were primarily targeted to children and were considered low cultural phenomena without any artistic value.

One can see various stages in the evolution of graphic novels in Europe beginning in the 1950's, and the genre evolved somewhat differently in each country. One could argue that, in general, the first period of the graphic novel in Europe ran from the early 1960's to the late 1980's, followed by a second period of further growth and development beginning in the 1990's.

Major Shifts from 1960 to 2010

There are remarkable differences between the European comics culture of 1960 and that of 2010, in terms of both production and public reception. In 1960, almost all European comics were meant for children and were published in serial form. By 2010, however, a considerable number of one-shots were targeted specifically to adults. In 1960, the title of the series was the most important selling point; however, in the contemporary marketplace, who wrote and illustrated the book has become more important than the title.

Though Europe is not a homogenous cultural market, the media industries (helped by European Union legislation) are paving the way for a more integrated approach to dissemination. Since the 1980's,

publishing houses that started small as family enterprises have merged into international conglomerates. For example, three important francophone publishers (Dargaud, Lombard, and Dupuis) became part of Média-Participations, and they occupy more than one-third of the French comics market.

Though the number of comics publishers has increased enormously since 1960, the comics market is dominated by a limited number of conglomerates. On the whole, the number of book editions has increased; from 1960 to 1980, the number of graphic albums increased in France tenfold. Since 2000, the industry has exploded, with a record number of more than five thousand titles in 2010. In 1960, comics production was still strongly rooted in the press, be it in the general press or in specialized comics magazines; book editions (called "albums" in French and Dutch) existed, but in limited number. Since 1960, the perception of comics has shifted drastically from a cultural form perceived as entertainment for children to an medium with a rich and varied culture, capable of producing high quality works for adults. Admittedly, not all has changed; some of most popular series of the past, such as *Astérix* (1961-1979), *Lucky Luke* (1949-1967), and *Blake et Mortimer* (1946-   ) remain best sellers in many European countries.

Emergence of Graphic Novels

Cultural recognition of the comics medium began in the 1960's, when comics specialists and fans began forming associations, such as *Club des bandes dessinées* and *Het Stripschap*. These associations organized festivals (Lucca Comics and Games in Italy, Angoulême International Comics Festival in France), gave exhibitions (for example, *Bande dessinée et figuration narrative* in 1967 in the Louvre Museum*)*, and published fanzines (such as *Stripschrift*, *Linus*, and *Phénix*) and books on comics. The first generation of comics scholars came soon after.

Furthermore, in the 1960's, the comics market was evolving. The baby boomers became young adults in the 1960's and 1970's; consequently, some publishers tried to deliver products adapted to their age and taste. The new protagonists, seen in *Blueberry* (1963-   ) and *Corto Maltese* (first published in 1967), for example, looked and acted quite differently from the classic heroes. Before, women characters were rather scarce, but an increasing number of young attractive women became protagonists, including the eponymous characters of *Barbarella* (1964) and *Valentina* (first published in 1967).

The constraints on children comics—the result of self-imposed industry rules of conduct—could no longer be justified in relation to publications for adults. Everything that was forbidden in comics for children, from explicit violence to explicit sex and radical political ideas, became possible in comics for adults.

As more adult comics were published, the themes and styles evolved and broadened. Many existing children's genres, such as science fiction, history, and humor, were reconceptualized for an adult readership. Moebius changed the approach to science fiction in *Le garage hérmetique de Jerry Cornelius* (1976-1980;

Streak of Chalk is an example of the variety among European graphic novels since 1990. (Courtesy of Nantier Beall Minoustchine Publishing)

The Airtight Garage, 1993), and Jacques Tardi took a realistic approach to World War I in *C'était la guerre des tranchées: 1914-1918* (1993; *It Was the War of the Trenches*, 2010).

The evolution of the industry was not only significant on the thematic level; it was also important on the graphic level. Various artists explored more artistic techniques than ever before. Some artists such as Alex Barbier, Enki Bilal, Mattotti, and Jacques de Loustal tried new color possibilities in graphic novels, while draftsmen such as Hugo Pratt, Dino Battaglia, Muñoz, and Edmond Baudoin explored the expressiveness of black and white. The possibilities of the medium were tried out by authors such as Régis Franc and Renato Calligaro.

Instrumental in the first decades for the development of adult comics were the various new magazines for teens and adults. These included *Linus* and *Frigidaire* in Italy, the revamped *Pilote*, *Charlie*, *L'Écho des Savanes*, *Métal Hurlant*, *Fluide glacial*, and *(A SUIVRE)* in France, *Strapazin* and *Boxer* for the German language, *El Víbora* and *Madriz* in Spain, *De Vrije Balloen* in the Netherlands, and *Relax* in Poland.

Widespread Breakthrough and Diversification

Though interesting graphic novels were produced throughout the 1980's, the enthusiasm of the publishers was curbed at the beginning of the decade because consumers lost interest in the comics magazines and did not buy enough albums. However, thanks to the worldwide popularity and critical success of the American graphic novel *Maus* (1986, 1991), both the media and comics readers recognized that the medium was growing up. At that moment, a new generation of authors who grew up reading comics wanted to push the frontiers even further. However, because the European comics industry was in a rather conservative mode, the new generation had no other outlet than self-publishing, often doing so in groups such as L'Association in Paris or Frigo in Brussels. Also, comics enthusiasts started magazines for alternative work; these include the Polish *Produkt* (1999-2004) and the Slovenian *Stripburger* (1992-   ).

The scholarly legitimacy of comics was raised. Scores of dissertations were written on comics; comics museums opened their doors in Brussels, Angoulême, Groningen, and Lucca; various training facilities for comics artists were organized; and some governments developed subsidy systems for stimulating local and original creations. It is reasonable to state that without this support the second revival of graphic novels would probably not have had the same magnitude.

The French-language terrain remained a shining example of the medium, with artists such as Blutch, Nicolas de Crécy, David B., Dominique Goblet, Emmanuel Guibert, Pascal Rabaté, and Bastien Vivès. New voices were raised in other European countries as well: German artists Martin tom Dieck, Jochen Gerner, and Jens Harder; Swiss artist Thomas Ott; Dutch artists Olivier Schrauwen and Brecht Evens; Spanish artists Raúl (Fernández Calleja), Federico del Barrio, Prado, Felipe H. Cava, Ricardo Castells, and Max (Francesc Capdevila Gisbert); Italian artists Gipi (Gianni Pacinotti), Igort, and Stefano Ricci; Swedish artists Gunnar Lundkvist and Max Andersson; and Eastern European artists Danijel Zezelj, TBC (Tomaz Lavric), Jaroslav Rudiš, and Jaromír 99.

From the limited number of graphic albums that have been translated in English, the following titles give an idea of the variety among European graphic novels since 1990: Marjane Satrapi's subjective documentary *Persepolis* (2000-2003), Schrauwen's humorous and parodic *Mon fiston* (2006; my boy), Moebius's New Age science-fiction cycle *Eadena* (first published in 1983), Prado's magical realistic *Trazo de tiza* (1992-1993; *Streak of Chalk*, 1994), Guibert's biographical *La Guerre d'Alan* (2000; *Alan's War*, 2008), Mattotti and Jerry Kramsky's graphic adaptation of the classic horror novel *Dr. Jekyll and Mr. Hyde* (2002), and Harder's wordless *Leviathan* (2003).

Impact

The impact of European graphic novels on the history of comics is difficult to evaluate because, though European artists are often held in high esteem among "enlightened" critics, fans, and colleagues from other continents, only a small portion of European comics are available in English or Japanese. At the academic level,

there are two associations for the study of European comics, the International Bande Dessinée Society and the American Bande Dessinée Society, which edits the peer-reviewed journal *European Comic Art*.

Despite the various efforts that have been made to introduce European comics in other countries, most translation projects have not found commercial success. However, the interactions between various comics-producing countries are growing—Moebius, for example, collaborated with both American and Japanese authors.

Unlike other sectors of popular culture, most European comics markets are not dominated by anglophone cultural industries. Never before has there been so much interest in the general media for graphic novels—though this interest in terms of European contributions is generally limited to a few superstars, such as Bilal, Moebius, or Satrapi. Even the biggest European comics festivals, such as Angoulême, do not have the same impact as the film festivals of Cannes, Venice, or Berlin. Comics are still progressing toward becoming an accepted form of culture.

Pascal Lefèvre

Bibliography

Beaty, Bart. *Unpopular Culture: Transforming the European Comic Book in the 1990's*. Toronto: University of Toronto Press, 2007. An introduction to the scene of "alternative" European comics beginning in the 1990's.

Gravett, Paul. *Graphic Novels: Stories to Change Your Life*. London: Aurum, 2005. An introduction to masterpieces of the medium from all around the world, including various European graphic novels by artists such as Bilal, David B., Mattotti, Moebius, Pratt, and Tardi.

Grove, Laurence. *Comics in French: The Bande Dessinée in Context*. New York: Berghahn Books, 2010. A comprehensive introduction to francophone comics and their sociological implication.

Sabin, Roger. "Worldcomics." In *Adult Comics: An Introduction*. London: Routledge, 1993. A brief historical look at adult comics in Europe, focusing mostly on the evolution in the francophone region.

Feminism in Graphic Novels

Definition

The relationship between feminist ideologies and graphic novels has been problematic throughout the history of the medium. Long seen as a medium that primarily engaged male interests and thus promoted antifeminism, graphic novels have been a site of contention, both promoting and opposing feminist issues.

Introduction

Throughout its history, graphic literature has had a problematic relationship with feminism, the gender ideology that holds that women should be accorded the full political, economic, and social rights of citizenship that men have been granted. From its beginning, the comic book industry can be seen as antifeminist in its orientation, a notion established by imitation, particularly in adventure-oriented genres. In past adventure stories, creators constructed tales of heroism that projected an image of inferior femininity that could not be perceived by the audience as threatening to male power. Creators tended to cast female characters as literary foils against which heroes' masculinity was contrasted, often showing women as less decisive and less able than their male counterparts. According to these comics, women's limited role in the public sphere was for the best; it was better for men to do the lion's share of the hard work, mental or physical, because men were better suited to these tasks than women, whose femininity rendered them inferior.

However, the graphic novel industry's tendency to resist feminism or to promote antifeminism has not been static. Rather, it has waxed and waned, with some creators favoring more progressive notions of gender and others favoring the status quo. Additionally, creators have changed their approach to the portrayal of women in response to external social pressures, at different times reacting to advocacy groups that were opposed to and in favor of feminism. Antifeminism continues to be a characteristic present in much modern graphic literature, yet the industry remains a site of contention with regard to the issue of feminism.

Ms. Marvel became the foremost incarnation of the industry's portrayal of feminism, going as far as modeling the heroine's alter ego after Gloria Steinem, in both profession and appearance. (Courtesy of Marvel Comics)

The Golden Age

In its early days, the industry generally reproduced existing popular forms, such as Westerns, jungle adventures, and hard-boiled detective or funny-animal stories. As such, the industry replicated the gender ideology embedded in the subtext of these preexisting forms, which held that, on one hand, white heterosexual men rightly held dominant social power in American society and, on the other, women should play a subordinate and subservient role, largely limited to that of lover, wife, and mother. Creators communicated female subservience by typically "casting" male characters in leading, heroic roles and portraying women as passive and timid, constantly under threat and in need of male support and rescue. When comics did feature female characters who were not reliant on masculine protection, they tended to be villains, conniving femmes fatales, as typified by the Dragon Lady in Milton Caniff's comic strip *Terry and the Pirates*, and, therefore, symbolically opposing the proper social order.

Creators were willing to experiment with the medium's gender values, even in this early phase of development. The most significant example of creator experimentation with pro-feminist values came in 1940 with DC Comics development of the character Wonder Woman. William Moulton Marston consciously developed Wonder Woman to redress the "bloodcurdling masculinity" that he saw within the superhero genre and comics as a whole. Marston made Wonder Woman into an icon of feminism not only by imbuing her with power and independence and casting her as a leading character but also by having the her confront villainous males seeking to subjugate women and expand masculine power through force.

During the Golden Age, DC Comics and other companies created several other female superheroes and occasionally cast female characters as leads in other genres, most commonly jungle adventures. Creators did not imbue these characters with the explicit sense of feminism that defined Wonder Woman. However, as creators cast these characters in lead roles, these stories can be considered nominally feminist, in that they portrayed women as able to do the same work (confronting villains, saving the day) as a man.

The Silver Age Retreat from Feminism

The 1950's saw a development that would reinforce, and in fact, codify, the industry's antifeminist orientation: The comics industry's adoption of the 1954 Comics Code, a set of industry-wide rules governing acceptable graphic literature content, cemented the antifeminist orientation of mainstream producers. Companies within the industry banded together to create the code in response to the growing influence of the anticomics movement, which caught the attention of American lawmakers in the early years of the decade,

in large measure because of the work of psychiatrist Fredric Wertham. Wertham argued that reading comics did not simply prevent readers from consuming better cultural products but could (and did, in his estimation) do readers psychological harm by encouraging criminal and sexually deviant behaviors. Wertham specifically criticized Wonder Woman as a character that encouraged sexual deviance (lesbianism) in readers because the character did not seek to marry or raise children. When creating the Comics Code, industry leaders responded directly to Wertham's criticisms by establishing rules both mandating that creators portray marriage and family life as the ideal outcomes of romantic plots and forbidding portrayal of any sexual perversion.

With these rules and the popularization of romance stories, the comics industry reinforced the contemporary movement within American society, which sought to limit women's roles in public life and codify the idealization of homemaking that scholars referred to as domestic containment. The rules encouraged creators to imbue female characters with a narrowly defined vision of femininity that could not be seen as threatening to male power, not only in romance comics but also within adventure-oriented features, such as the superhero genre.

By demonizing Wonder Woman, Wertham, in essence, created an alternative and antithetical archetype for future female superheroes. As Wonder Woman was strong and stoic, aloof from "normal" male-female relations, and a leading character, future heroines (such as Marvel Comics' Invisible Girl) would be weak, emotional, devoted to the heterosexual and patriarchal order, marginal, and limited to appearing almost exclusively in team books, where they were outnumbered by male characters by a wide margin.

Second-Wave Feminism, 1970-1972

The comics industry confronted second-wave feminism throughout the 1970's, and early in the decade, creators portrayed women's liberation as a spurious, perhaps dangerous movement. In Marvel's *Avengers*, volume 1, issue 83 (December, 1970), the male leads confront a team of female superheroes duped into fighting against male chauvinism by a female villain in disguise. The creators metaphorically suggested that feminism is a hollow ideology because the villain is not truly trying to advance the cause of women but using feminism as a ploy to destroy the Avengers so that she might rule the Earth.

Neither "The Fury of the Femizons" (Marvel's *Savage Tales*, issue 1, May, 1971) nor "All Men Are but Slaves" (DC's *Adventure Comics*, issue 417, March, 1972) explicitly refer to feminism or women's liberation directly. Nonetheless, in each, an alien society is created as a result of women's rejections of hegemonic male rule and the narrative details the society's abuses, clearly making second-wave feminism the subtext. While creators of both stories make clear that there are problems with patriarchal society, they communicate just as clearly that a matriarchal society, a possible consequence of second-wave feminism if taken to a logical extreme, is as problematic, if not more so. They implied that feminists would take revenge on men for the years of female oppression, reducing men to slaves, and that feminism was not a form of progressive thought but, rather, a regressive gender ideology.

In a third example from Marvel, *Our Love Story*, issue 18 (August, 1972), creators produced an issue "Dedicated to the fearless, fabulous females of Women's Lib!" in which the female lead, Brandy, feels torn between her feminist principles and her search for love. Ultimately, love triumphs but only because the male romantic interest stops worrying about offending Brandy's "women's lib attitude," takes charge of the relationship, and moves it forward toward marriage, suggesting domesticity is more important than women's equality.

Second-Wave Feminism, 1973-1980

The industry seemed to change its portrayal of feminism in response to feminist criticism. The editors of *Ms.* magazine (including iconic feminist leader Gloria Steinem) published a series of editorials celebrating the original feminist virtues of the industry's most prominent female character, Wonder Woman, and criticizing DC's more recent antifeminist treatment of the character. In response to this criticism, and taking account of the television industry's creation of several pro-

grams featuring heroines as the central characters (most notably Wonder Woman), creators began developing female superheroes who presented a more powerful vision of femininity. This was accomplished by either amplifying the superhuman powers of existing characters, such as Wonder Woman or Marvel Girl (renamed the Phoenix), or creating new features with leading female characters, such as DC's Black Orchid, Rima the Jungle Girl, and Isis; Marvel's the Cat, Red Sonja, and Ms. Marvel; and Charlton's the Bionic Woman.

These female characters can be read as feminist because they were empowered in several ways. First, creators made many of these heroines the leading characters in the features and comics in which they appeared, a reversal of the previous trend. These characters were professional career women in addition to being superheroes (creators never depicted their domesticated predecessors as having jobs). Also, the feminist heroines were able to stand toe-to-toe with most any male character. Lastly, antagonists became embodiments of the patriarchal oppression against which the feminists struggled, making each victory a victory for women's rights. Ms. Marvel became the foremost incarnation of the industry's portrayal of feminism, going as far as modeling the heroine's alter ego after Gloria Steinem, in both profession and appearance.

However, in grafting this ideology to the superhero convention, creators subtly negated feminism as well. As creators always return the world to "normal" when a villain is defeated, the patriarchal order is protected; thus, these heroines preserve the very system that they ostensibly seek to reform as feminists. Further, creators made these heroines behave in a manner similar to their male counterparts; by using violence, the medium's primary mode of conflict resolution, female heroes, in essence, conformed to male standards. The underlying message creators projected with these "feminist" characters was that women could be equal to men, so long as they acted like men.

After 1980: The Backlash Against Feminism and Beyond

In 1980's, the comics industry quickly backed away from its tentative embrace of feminism in a move that

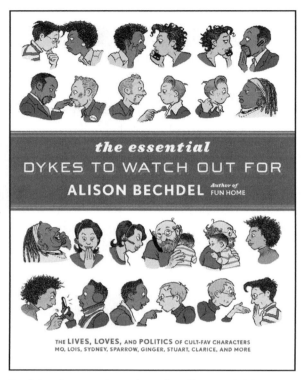

Feminism is a prominent theme in Allison Bechdel's *Dykes to Watch Out For.* (Courtesy of Houghton Mifflin Harcourt)

paralleled the "backlash" against second-wave feminism in popular culture and politics. Companies canceled most of the series featuring female leading characters within the first few years of the decade, returning female characters to secondary roles. While this was a symbolic humiliation in itself for the feminist heroines, mainstream creators initiated a pattern of destructive victimization and/or humiliation of female characters, a misogynistic current that prevailed through the 1980's: Some suffered physical abuse (for example, the Wasp, Black Canary, and Batgirl); a few were deprived of their power (Ms. Marvel and Storm); some lost their identities (the Cat, Ms. Marvel, and the Phoenix); some were raped (Ms. Marvel); and several were killed outright (the Phoenix, Spider-Woman, Supergirl, and Wonder Woman). Creators did not simply discard feminism as a character trait, they thoroughly destroyed it in a grand gesture of symbolic annihilation that restored white heterosexual men to the posi-

tion of exclusive privilege enjoyed before the popularization of second-wave feminism.

The comics industry shifted from general distribution outlets to direct retail sales during the 1980's. The industry's move to direct sales has brought mixed results with regard to the portrayal of feminism. Companies became free of the restrictions on content created by the Comics Code. One result has been that creators increasingly portray female characters as little more than sex objects. An obvious indicator of this trend has been the expansion of explicitly pornographic comics in the decades since the move to direct sales.

Small publishers, however, have benefited from direct sales. Some of these companies have produced powerful alternative images of femininity, more congruent with feminism than those of mainstream producers bound by established genres (and established gender ideologies). One example is Frank Miller and Dave Gibbon's series *The Life and Times of Martha Washington in the Twenty-first Century* (1990-2007). Mainstream producers have also rehabilitated many of the female characters (such as Ms. Marvel and Red Sonja) that served as signifiers of feminism, suggesting a softening in the industry's antifeminist attitude.

Impact

The comics industry's long history of antifeminism has left a lasting impression on graphic literature, suggesting that the medium is a preserve of males. The industry's most enduring contribution to American culture, the superhero genre, seems particularly defined by this tradition of antifeminism. However, while they have most often favored an antifeminist orientation, creators have been open enough to feminism that there is a level of ambivalence regarding the issue of gender equity in the comics world.

Some of the enduring icons of feminism within graphic literature have transcended the medium, such as Wonder Woman and Red Sonja. The industry may have retreated from explicit endorsement of feminism during the 1980's, but creators never fully returned to the passive, domesticated, limited vision of femininity that prevailed through the 1960's. Lastly, female creators are becoming more of a presence within the industry, with figures such as Gail Simone advocating, with their work and public statements, for a more sophisticated portrayal of womanhood, which suggests that the graphic literature industry may yet become reconciled to the principles of feminism.

Thomas Donaldson

Bibliography

Beaty, Bart. *Fredric Wertham and the Critique of Mass Culture*. Jackson: University Press of Mississippi, 2005. Presents the anticomics movement that helped codify antifeminism in the industry. Stands as the most thorough and objective work on Wertham published to date and successfully elevates the discourse about Wertham by examining the entire body of his work regarding the effects of popular culture on its consumers.

Faludi, Susan. *Backlash: The Undeclared War Against American Women*. New York: Crown, 1991. Definitive work to date on the growth of antifeminism in American political and popular culture that accompanied the rise of the New Right of the 1980's. Gives perspective on how antifeminism became a major theme of popular discourse at the close of the twentieth century.

Inness, Sherrie A. *Tough Girls: Women Warriors and Wonder Women in Popular Culture*. Philadelphia: University of Pennsylvania Press, 1999. Examines how the entertainment industry capitalized on and co-opted second-wave feminism. Contains a small section devoted to graphic literature, focusing on characters such as Elektra and Martha Washington. Discusses the rise of adventure-heroine programming in the mid-1970's, which helped impel the comics industry to embrace feminism more positively.

Nyberg, Amy Kiste. *Seal of Approval: The History of the Comics Code*. Jackson: University Press of Mississippi, 1998. Looks at the larger history of the anticomics movement beyond the work of Wertham, who is often erroneously portrayed as the sole force behind the campaign to regulate comic book content. Includes the text of various editions of the Comics Code in the appendix.

Robinson, Lillian S. *Wonder Women: Feminisms and Superheroes*. New York: Routledge, 2004. Examines the manner in which feminist principles have been communicated within the superhero genre since the 1940's. Focuses mostly on developments during the 1940's and early 1990's; briefly touches on the antifeminism of the 1960's. Provides insight into the impact the editors of *Ms.* magazine had on the comics industry in the early 1970's.

Strömberg, Fredrik. "Sexual Slander." In *Comic Art Propaganda: A Graphic History*. New York: St. Martin's Griffin, 2010. Demonstrates that creators expressed feminism and antifeminism through comic book imagery in a variety of ways across time, companies, and genres.

FILM ADAPTATIONS: FROM PRINTED PAGE TO SILVER SCREEN

Definition

Since its inception, cinema has sought material from other media, such as literature, plays, video games, and comics. Although adapting film from comics and graphic novels is not a new phenomenon, there has been a boom in this kind of adaptation in the twenty-first century. The upsurge has two explanations: First, comics and graphic novels have gained more critical respectability; second, advances in digital technology have allowed for more sophisticated production of unrealistic images in film.

Introduction

The most popular inspiration for film adaptation comes from novels. However, other media has also been combed for stories. Film adaptations of comics date from as early as 1900, with a series produced by the Edison Film Company inspired by Frederick Burr Opper's *Happy Hooligan* cartoon strip.

This relationship between comics and film is natural because both arts are essentially narrative, telling stories through sequences of images. Comics and films share both aesthetic qualities and formats. If there are evident resemblances, there are also important differences, which influence the way these media are produced and received by audiences.

Since 2000, nearly fifty film adaptations of comics have been released, and the trend does not show signs of slowing. There is also a good prospect for sequels, prequels, and remakes of previous works.

There are two reasons for the rediscovery of comics as source texts for profitable films. Beginning with the release of *Maus* in 1986, comics have gained increasing critical respectability. *Maus* proved that comics can deal with mature themes and can be addressed to an adult audience, revelations that have helped expand the popularity of the comics medium. The second reason for the increase in adaptations is the development of digital technology in cinema. Adaptations are not limited to plot, characters, and dialogue of comics; technology allows filmmakers to re-create the appearances of comics on screen.

From Comics to Graphic Novels

The narrative structure of graphic novels—with a beginning, middle, and end—is closer to that of films than the never-ending narrative structure of superhero comic books. The approximation between the narrative structure of films and graphic novels perhaps makes the job of the screenwriter easier because there are fewer choices for dialogue and narrative events.

Comics-to-film adaptations also differ from film adaptations of graphic novels because graphic novels are, for the most part, written and drawn by a single artist. Because superhero comic book series have been drawn by several artists in many different styles, there is no single, stable iconic meaning to characters, and the

Actor Christopher Reeve plays the comic-book hero in the 1978 film *Superman*. The success of Richard Donner's film marked the inauguration of the blockbuster era for comics cinema and the beginning of a period of several motion picture adaptations of comic books. (Getty Images)

comics do not always have unique defining styles. Unlike comics superheroes such as Batman or Superman, which have already become mythical figures with multiple incarnations, graphic novels have only one version, to which comics readers refer when watching film adaptations. The drawn image of the graphic novel bears the "signature" of its artist, which should somehow transfer to the screen. Because of the similar narrative structure of graphic novels and films and the unique visual style of graphic novels, when the latter are adapted, audiences tend to compare films to the graphic novels in a more rigid manner than they do in the case of film adaptations of comic books.

Historical Overview to 2001

Before the 1970's, films based on comics were mainly intended for children, and the special effects were drearily primitive. The success of Richard Donner's 1978 *Superman* marked the inauguration of the blockbuster era for comics cinema and the beginning of a period of adaptations of comic books. However, for a long time, the works that followed were not as successful as Clark Kent's story.

At about the same time, during the 1970's but especially since the second half of the 1980's, graphic novels started attracting academic and critical attention. However, film adaptations of graphic novels in the United States did not become popular until the 2000's. With the exception of *Swamp Thing* (1982) and *The Crow* (1994) (and their respective sequels), no other remarkable films based on graphic novels were produced.

In 2001, three films marked the beginning of a new period for film adaptations of graphic novels: Henry Selick's *Monkeybone*, Terry Zwigoff's *Ghost World*, and Albert and Allen Hughes's *From Hell*. Selick's *Monkeybone* was based on a graphic novel called *Dark Town* (1995), by Kaja Blackley. *Ghost World* adapted Daniel Clowes's graphic novel of the same name, which first appeared in his *Eightball* series from 1993 to 1997. Lastly, *From Hell* adapted Alan Moore's eponymous graphic novel about the legendary murderer Jack the Ripper, which had been published in several volumes from 1989 to 1996 and later compiled in a single-volume work in 1999. Despite their different

genres and styles, together, these three works represented a new niche in the film industry.

Historical Overview, 2001-2010

With the relative success of these three film adaptations in 2001, several other films were released in the following years. Sam Mendes's *Road to Perdition* (2002), based on a graphic novel by Max Allan Collins, was a major hit, especially because of its five-star cast that included Tom Hanks, Paul Newman, Jude Law, and Daniel Craig.

Stephen Norrington's *The League of Extraordinary Gentlemen* (2003) was an adaptation of the eponymous work by Moore and Kevin O'Neill, which depicts a league of heroes formed by popular characters in literature of the Victorian era, such as Allan Quatermain, Captain Nemo, and Dorian Gray. *American Splendor* (2003), directed by Shari Springer Berman and Robert Pulcini, is a realistic depiction of the life of Harvey Pekar, the author of the comics series *American Splendor* (1976-1991; 1993-2008) and the graphic novel *Our Cancer Year* (1994). The film, with Paul Giamatti playing Pekar (who also appears in some scenes as himself), acquired cult status and received several positive critical reviews.

David Cronenberg's *A History of Violence* (2005), adapted from the 1997 work by John Wagner and Vince Locke, captures the source text's noirish atmosphere and received positive critical appraisal. In *Sin City* (2005), director Robert Rodriguez worked with comics artist Frank Miller to adapt the latter's series; the result is the most aesthetically faithful adaptation ever produced in comics cinema. In 2006, another graphic novel was adapted to film: *V for Vendetta*, directed by James McTeigue and starring Natalie Portman and Hugo Weaving, reenacts Moore and David Lloyd's dystopian fiction.

Two other films adaptations also did well at the box office: David Slade's *30 Days of Night* (2007), an adaptation of a three-issue horror comic series by Steve Niles and Ben Templesmith, and Zack Snyder's *300* (2006), from Frank Miller's fictional retelling of the Battle of Thermopylae. In 2009, Moore and Dave Gibbons's dystopian masterpiece *Watchmen* was brought to the screen by Snyder. The science-fiction graphic novel *The Surrogates* (2005-5006), by Robert Venditti and Brett Weldele, became a 2009 film directed by Jonathan Mostow.

In 2010, three works reaffirmed the successful formula of film adaptations of graphic novels: Matthew Vaughn's *Kick-Ass*, inspired by a graphic novel by Mark Millar and John Romita, Jr.; Edgar Wright's *Scott Pilgrim vs. the World*, based on Bryan Lee O'Malley's graphic novel; and Robert Schwentke's *Red*, based on a three-issue comic series by Warren Ellis and Cully Hamner.

Digital Technology in Cinema

Digital technology has had a strong influence on adaptations of comic books and graphic novels. In fact, it can be said that recent advances in digital technology have had a decisive role in the boom of this kind of film. Digital technology allows for the re-creation of fantastic worlds and characters and can make action scenes look more sophisticated. Special effects also have been used to reproduce the comics look on screen.

One of the most striking characteristics in *Sin City* is the directors' attempt to closely match the noirish look of the source text. In the film, actors do not perform before real-life landscapes but in front of a green screen, which is later filled by digitally created images in a process called computer-generated imagery (CGI). CGI is also used for certain characters' features to call attention to specific elements, such as glasses, lips, and eyes.

Another film in which the resemblance to the source text has attracted audiences' attention is Snyder's *300*. The film manages to digitally reconstruct the look of the graphic novel—with Lynn Varley's beautiful aquarelle colors—in a totally artificial manner but nevertheless extremely close to the original work.

Impact

With some positive critical reviews and, in many cases, successful box-office returns, film adaptations of comics and graphic novels will likely continue. The growth in this kind of adaptation has affected the film industry, emphasizing digital special effects and making these adaptations more likely to be visual spectacles than other types of films.

The rediscovery of comics by the film industry may also help popularize graphic novels because film audiences will probably look for source texts after viewing the films. This may reaffirm the position of graphic novels as a nonjuvenile subcategory within the comics medium and, as a consequence, also contribute to the academic recognition of this kind of adaptation. Thus, even though theoretical works that approximate both arts remain scarce, it is expected that film adaptations of comics and graphic novels will become a fruitful area for future academic research.

Also, while graphic novels may inspire other successful films to come, the converse may also be true. Readers may expect an increase in the number of graphic novels with a cinematographic quality and structure, written and illustrated with the intention of being adapted to screen or perhaps even as marketing tools to be sold across different media.

Camila Figueiredo

Bibliography

Booker, Keith M. *May Contain Graphic Material*: *Comic Books, Novels, and Films*. Westport, Conn.: Praeger, 2007. Examines some of the most successful film adaptations of comic books and graphic novels since 1978, focusing on aspects of production and reception.

Christiansen, Hans-Christian. "Comics and Films: A Narrative Perspective." In *Comics and Culture: Analytical and Theoretical Approaches to Comics*, edited by Anne Magnussen and Hans-Christian Christiansen. Copenhagen: Museum Tusculanum Press, 2000. Analyzes how cinematic devices are used differently in comics and in films, constructing different notions of time, space, and identification.

Gordon, Ian, Mark Jancovich, and Matthew P. McAllister, eds. *Film and Comic Books*. Jackson: University Press of Mississippi, 2007. Analyzes the problems of adapting one medium to another, audience expectations, recurrent themes, and aspects of reception and reaction, discussing different genres of comics and of films.

Groensteen, Thierry. "Du 7e au 9e Art: L'Inventaire des singularités." *CinémAction* (Summer 1990):16-28. Analyzes the differences between comics and films in terms of the field of expression, process of creation, and mode of articulation. Considered a reference work in the field for its thorough examination of the steps of production of each medium.

Lacassin, Francis. "The Comic Strip and Film Language." *Film Quarterly* 26, no. 1 (1972): 11-23. Translated by David Kunzle. Draws a parallel between the properties of comic strip and film language, proving that comic strips developed their "basic expressive resources" before the influence of cinema.

Folklore, Mythology, and the Comic Book Format: A Contemporary Tradition

Definition

Comic book creators borrow themes, archetypes, and ideas from traditional and contemporary folklore to build their own narratives, histories, heroes, villains, and origin stories, creating a strong connection and sense of community with their audience. Folklore, which includes myths, legends, and folk and fairy tales, is in the public domain and thus freely available for anyone to adapt, adopt, retell, or rework in any medium.

Introduction

Folklore—consisting of traditional customs, superstitions, myths, legends, folktales, riddles, proverbs, motifs, and songs—has infused the world of Western comic books from its beginnings. While the majority of comic book creators construct their own histories, heroes, villains, and legends for their stories, they consciously and subconsciously borrow themes and ideas from traditional and contemporary folklore and depend upon folklore and folklore theory for the development

Author and artist Eric Shanower used the comics medium to retell the Trojan War in *Age of Bronze*. (Courtesy of Image Comics)

of their narratives. Like any written version of folklore, these too are necessarily interpretation because the thought world of a literate culture is so different from that of the oral cultures from which the stories came.

Traditional prose narratives, along with those of poetic folklore such as ballads, epics, and sagas, are, by their very nature, concise and spare in details, focusing primarily on plot. The folkloric style leaves gaps in the story line and in the concrete visualization of characters and settings, which can be filled by illustrations, narration, and dialogue in comic book panels. The ages, physical appearances, and personalities of characters, as well as their relationships, as shown through facial expressions and posture, become visible. Buildings, furniture, and clothing in the illustrations suggest a time and place in which the story is set, while the colors, shading, style, panel shape, and font used by the illustrator set the overall tone of the graphic story.

There are four basic ways that folklore has been employed in the comic book format. First, and most evident throughout comic book publishing, there are straightforward comic book adaptations of folklore, which by virtue of the graphic format, involve an element of interpretation in the rendering of the story. Second, a large body of work reworks folklore, extending the tales or altering them to renew the stories and adapt them from their traditional structure and cultures. A third method of employing folklore is the use of stock motifs, themes, and characters in the telling of original stories, frequently reconstructing the characters, their origin stories, and their relationships with other folklore characters in entirely new settings. Inserting partial or entire tales into ongoing story lines, rather than constituting the main action, is the fourth way that folklore is commonly used in comic books.

The most evident change in the use of folklore by contemporary comic book creators is that folklore is most often reworked rather than retold; the intersection between the world of folklore and the world of comic books has become stronger than ever before. There is concern, however, that people in modern society are no longer as conversant with traditional folklore and may not recognize the allusions, reworkings, and adaptations being employed.

Straightforward Adaptations of Traditional Folklore

Straightforward adaptations have been adapted only to fit the comic book mode of storytelling, retaining the basic story line, main characters, and original setting, both time and place, of the tale being modified. In successful adaptations, dialogue and the pacing of the traditional oral stories are well served with thoughtful panel arrangements, evocative illustrations, and adept speech balloons. The timeless relevance and archetypal characters and themes of myths and legends are treated to great effect in Eric Shanower's *Age of Bronze* (1998-   ) series about the Trojan War, Erik Evensen's *Gods of Asgard* (2007), and both Gareth Hinds's *Beowulf* (2007) and Chris Ryall and Gabriel Rodriguez's *Beowulf* (2007), the latter based on the eponymous film by Neil Gaiman. Two other highly recommended titles are mpMann and A. David Lewis's *Some New Kind of Slaughter, or, Lost in the Flood (and How We Found Home Again): Diluvian Myths from Around the World* (2007) and P. Craig Russell's *The Ring of the Nibelung* (2002), retelling Richard Wagner's Ring cycle opera based on Germanic folklore. Traditional English and Scottish ballads are superbly illustrated in Charles Vess's *Book of Ballads* (2004), and Derek McCulloch and Shepherd Hendrix explore a traditional American ballad in their *Stagger Lee* (2006).

Since the beginning of North American comic book production, a multitude of sequential reproductions of folk and fairy tales have been published for audiences of all ages. Modern titles include compilations of tales such as *Little Lit: Folklore and Fairy Tale Funnies* (2000), edited by Art Spiegelman and Françoise Mouly; Jonathan Vankin's *The Big Book of Grimm* (1999); and *Trickster: Native American Tales* (2010), edited by Matt Dembicki with key participation from Native American storytellers and artists. Equally successful are single-edition comic book variants of traditional tales, such as Will Eisner's *The Princess and the Frog* (1999) and *Sundiata: A Legend of Africa* (2003) for younger readers and Hinds's *Bearskin* (1998) for older audiences.

Reworkings of Traditional Folklore

A renaissance has been underway in the creative re-working of traditional folklore in popular culture, including the world of comics. The new narratives extend stories established in the traditional tales by placing the newly crafted story lines in a different setting or playing with genre. Reworking the folklore may include a major transformation of setting in tales from diverse cultures. Both *Rapunzel's Revenge* (2008), by Shannon and Dale Hale and illustrated by Nathan Hale, and *Seven Sons* (2006), by Alexander Grecian and Riley Rossmo, are single tales newly realized in the American Wild West. A series of Jewish folktales in Steve Sheinkin's *Rabbi Harvey* series (2006-   ) also take place in the legendary Wild West.

Other reworkings may result from the illustrative style employed to tell the tale, as in Michael Nicoll Yahgulanaas's *Red: A Haida Manga* (2009). Still others arise from the incorporation of recognizable superheroes in the story line, as in Terry LeBan and Rebecca Guay's *Green Lantern: 1001 Emerald Nights* (2001), in which the comic book character Green Lantern meets the mesmerizing Scheherazade from the *Alf layla wa-layla* (fifteenth century; *Arabian Nights' Entertainments*, 1706-1708).

In another successful example, the nursery tale of the Three Little Pigs is reworked in J. D. Arnold and Richard Koslowski's *BB Wolf and the Three LPs* (2010) to tell a dark tale of murder, the blues, and retribution in the Mississippi Delta in the early part of the twentieth century. A horror series aimed at older readers, *Grimm Fairy Tales* (2005-   ), incorporates the retelling of folklore tales as a teaching tool into a larger frame story that, while clever, eclipses the story line with pinup artwork.

Among the first titles that come to mind when discussing reworkings of mythology is that of Thor, who first appeared in comics in 1962. However, this character has little in common with his traditional Norse mythological counterpart other than the ability to control thunder and lightning, the magic hammer, and his homeland of Asgard. *Thor: Son of Asgard* (2007), by Akira Yoshida and Greg Tocchini, does attempt to connect the character more directly to his mythological pedigree.

Mike Mignola's *Hellboy* incorporates elements from world myth and folklore, and regularly features characters from African and European folk traditions, among others. (Courtesy of Dark Horse Comics)

Folklore Characters Reconstructed

Along with the reworking of entire tales, there is a wide variety of narratives incorporating folklore motifs, themes, and both well-known and lesser-known characters in comic book series. This is particularly effective in Gaiman's *The Sandman* series (1989-1996), in which characters from classical mythology, such as Hecate, Morpheus, and Orpheus, interact with characters from the fairy realm and elsewhere. *The Sandman* paved the way for other series in which characters from nursery rhymes, folk and fairy tales, myths, and legends coexist on the same stage. Japanese folklore motifs and characters are intertwined with characters from Japanese history in Stan Sakai's *Usagi Yojimbo* (1987-   ). Mike Mignola's *Hellboy* (1994-   ) incorporates entire stories from the world of folklore as well as renowned characters from Russian folklore such as Baba Yaga and Koshchei the Deathless. Titles as diverse as Nick Percival's *Legends: The Enchanted* (2010), Bill Willingham's *Fables* (2002-) and *Jack of Fables* (2006-), and Linda Medley's *Castle Waiting* (1996-2010) all epitomize the model of incorporating classic folklore characters and motifs into original and vibrant tales.

Numerous folklore characters are found in multiple comic book universes. In addition to Hellboy, the horrific witch Baba Yaga manifests herself in *Fables* and *The Books of Magic* (1990-1991). The Faerie Queen is found in *The Sandman*, *The Books of Magic*, and Mike Carey and Jon Bolton's *God Save the Queen* (2007), while Bigfoot, Wendigo, and other legendary monsters coexist in the Grecian and Rossmo series *Proof* (2007-), Beau Smith's *Wynonna Earp: The Yeti Wars* (2010), Doug TenNapel's *Flink* (2007), and Marian Churchland's *Beast* (2009). These types of appearances are too numerous to list but provide hours of amusement for readers of comic books and folklore.

Folklore in Ongoing Story Lines

Folklore allusions abound in the comic book format, particularly in the superhero and fantasy genres but often in surprising places. Several examples of this phenomenon stand out. In Mat Johnson and Warren Pleece's *Incognegro* (2008), the main character escapes captivity by emulating the actions of the traditional trickster Brer Rabbit. A concise version of the traditional tale is told within the story line so that audiences unfamiliar with the tale are aware of what has just occurred. Other trickster characters and motifs are also present throughout the comic book world. In the short story "Street Magic" in *Minor Miracles* (2000), Eisner reworks a Jewish trickster tale as part of a lesson in surviving gang warfare in the Bronx in the early twentieth century. David Mack sprinkles Native American tales and folklore motifs in *Daredevil: Echo—Vision Quest* (2004) in his tale of Maya Lopez's search for her identity. *Sloth* (2006), by Gilbert Hernandez, incorporates contemporary urban legends in its story line, while Gene Luen Yang integrates the ancient Chinese myth of the Monkey King in *American Born Chinese* (2006).

Impact

Folktales and fairy tales have often been considered light entertainment for young listeners and readers, and, indeed, many picture-book retellings have been aimed at the juvenile audience. The use of folklore in comic books, however, has moved many of these reworkings away from the expected reading audience. A quick glance through the examples mentioned above shows that many of the comics are published in imprints aimed at mature readers, whether the folklore being used is a classic folktale or a more serious myth. Classical Greek, Roman, and Norse gods and heroes have been the prototypes for many comic book superheroes, and, thus, the idea of borrowing folklore has been part of the comic book culture from its beginnings. Collecting folklore references in the comic book format has become an almost overwhelming task as titles referring to mythology, legends, and folklore continue to be published with varying success; comic book writers such as Gaiman, Mignola, and Willingham have succeeded in creating enduring series imbued with folklore that have increased the popularity of the marriage between folklore and comics. Yet it seems ironic that at a time when most of society is becoming less aware of folklore, comic book creators are drawing on those traditional stories more and more frequently.

Gail A. de Vos

Bibliography

Altmann, Anna E., and Gail A. de Vos. *Tales, Then and Now: More Folktales as Literary Fictions for Young Adults*. Englewood, Colo.: Libraries Unlimited, 2001. A companion volume to *New Tales for Old*. Discusses comic book reworkings of four folktales and five literary fairy tales by Hans Christian Andersen.

De Vos, Gail A. *Stories from Songs: Ballads as Literary Fictions for Young Adults*. Westport, Conn.: Libraries Unlimited, 2009. Explores various renditions of traditional ballads in both North America and Western Europe and their literary reworkings, including graphic novels. Covers tragic love stories, murder ballads, otherworld beings, and tricks and disguises.

De Vos, Gail A., and Anna E. Altmann. *New Tales for Old: Folktales as Literary Fictions for Young Adults*. Englewood, Colo.: Libraries Unlimited, 1999. Gathers a number of popular folktale reworkings in a variety of genres and formats that appeal to young adults. Discusses Cinderella, the Frog King or Iron Henry, Hansel and Gretel, Little Red Riding Hood, Rapunzel, Rumpelstiltskin, Sleeping Beauty, and Snow White.

Lewis, A. David, and Christine Hoff Kraemer, eds. *Graven Images: Religion in Comic Books and Graphic Novels*. New York: Continuum, 2010. Identifies the unique advantages of the comics medium for religious messages; analyzes how often and in what ways comics communicate such messages; contextualizes the religious messages in comic books; and articulates the significance of the innovative theologies being developed in comics.

FROM SAVAGE TALES TO HEAVY METAL: HOW MAGAZINES FOR MATURE AUDIENCES INFLUENCED THE RISE OF THE GRAPHIC NOVEL

Definition

Adult-oriented titles were the forerunners of the graphic novel. Often printed as serialized strips, they became increasingly popular and were sometimes reproduced as collections.

Introduction

When *Evergreen Review*, a counterculture publication, successfully released a serialization of the French comic strip *Barbarella* in 1965, the nature of comic books changed. While anthologizing comics series had been a practice in Europe, the concepts of serialization and creating novel-length comics was new.

Jean-Claude Forest's *Barbarella* was first published in France in 1962. It is frequently referred to as the first comic book for adults because, though it was science fiction, the heroine, Barbarella, made frequent use of her sexuality to escape dangerous situations. The fact that adult-oriented material, featuring graphic sexuality, violence, and language, was marketable was not lost on other publishers.

Early Adult-Oriented Publications in America

During the 1960's, Warren Publishing, a mainstream publisher, released *Creepy* (1964-1983), *Eerie* (1966-1983), and *Vampirella* (1969-1983) after the demise of Entertaining Comics' lines of horror and science fiction. Works from Warren appealed to adult audiences because they highlighted artistic detail by using blacks, whites, and grays, rather than color; were sold on the magazine rack rather than in the comics section; and featured Frank Frazetta's paintings of fantasy and science-fiction nudes on the cover. However, their stories were mostly one-shots, which, save for some of the early *Vampirella* stories, could not be collected into a single novel.

In 1970, Robert Hoffman, Henry Beard, and Douglas Kenney founded a national version of the satirical magazine *National Lampoon*. The magazine heavily relied on comics and, in fact, had two special issues devoted to comics: *National Lampoon Presents the Very Large Book of Comical Funnies* (1975) and *National Lampoon Presents French Comics (the Kind Men Like)* (1977). The comics featured graphic sex and violence, all with satirical intent, and were created by underground and alternative cartoonists, such as Vaughn Bodé, Shary Flenniken, and Tina Robbins, as well as mainstream artists and writers, including Neal Adams, Frazetta, Edward Gorey, and Gahan Wilson.

In 1971, Marvel Comics entered the adult market because of editor Stan Lee's desire to break away from the Comics Code. In 1968, Marvel had released *The Spectacular Spider-Man*, a magazine-format publication. The stories, though they seemed reengineered for mature audiences, were simply variations of stories that had appeared earlier in the comic book magazine. The magazine was not a great success, but Lee tried again, against the advice of his publisher, Martin Goodman. *Savage Tales* was the result, but the magazine, never a favorite of the publisher, limped through only two years of irregular publishing before being canceled.

Sal Quartuccio Publishing (SQP) began in 1973 with the intention of publishing pinup books of fantasy and comics art by predominantly European artists. Slowly, however, it began to release serialized European comics in graphic novel format. It published Enrique Villagrán's classic *Teach Me!* (2002), about a trio of bisexual female teachers. SQP also produced *Hot Stuf'* (1974), a sexually explicit comic book that led to the fantasy-horror graphic novel *Demon Baby: Hell on Heels* (1996).

In 1976, NBM Publishing came into existence, and in 1977, it began repackaging a number of European serials that were heavy on sex and violence, starting with *Racket Rumba*, a detective spoof by French creator Loro. NBM was among the first publishers to perceive the worth of the graphic novel, and it is considered responsible for introducing artist-writers such as Enki Bilal, Hugo Pratt, and Milo Manara to U.S. audiences.

When *Heavy Metal* first appeared in 1977, it surprised readers: It contained color throughout and featured stunning covers. It was based on a French science-fiction and fantasy comics magazine for mature audiences titled *Metal Hurlant*. The American version featured both European and American artists and writers; stories were often serialized and then collected into albums.

Changing Audiences, Changing Creator Benefits

The fledgling success of alternative, or underground, comics during the 1960's and 1970's suggested that there was a mature audience looking for comics. The rise of specialty comic book stores both encouraged and allowed for a variety of magazines and early graphic novels. Writers and artists did not necessarily recognize that they were fostering the birth of the graphic novel, but they did understand and respond to the fact that many of the magazines for mature readers allowed them to explore issues that would not have been publishable by mainstream publishers because of the Comics Code. Issues of sexuality, gender, drugs, popular culture, and politics came to the fore, and writers and artists explored a variety of genres, including autobiography, biography, satire, mystery, fantasy, and science fiction. Another benefit of publishing in magazines such as *Heavy Metal* or *Epic Illustrated* was that publishers gave contractual control of material to the creators, instead of demanding ownership of it, as popular comic book franchises did.

Mainstream Publishers

Marvel Comics tried to make use of its most popular franchises in the magazine format. The company had already been cited in popular magazines and newspapers as appealing to a more mature audience than DC Comics, for example, with emphasis on a known real world where characters seemed to meet daily to deal with personal dilemmas as much as saving the universe. The first issue of *Savage Tales* seemed to hold some promise. A Conan the Bar-

barian story, adapted by Roy Thomas and Barry Windsor-Smith, was more graphically violent and included more nudity than would have been allowed in monthly comic books. The other stories were more mundane, though they dealt with contemporary social issues: Sergius O'Shaughnessy and Gene Colan's "Black Brother," highlighted racial issues, and Lee and John Romita's "Femizons" dealt with feminism. "Man-Thing" and "Ka-Zar," both previously published as comic books, rounded out the first issue. While boasting artwork from such major mainstream artists as John Buscema, Adams, Mike Kaluta, and Boris Vallejo, neither writers nor artists could figure a way to make the new magazine work. Low sales, coupled with Goodman's concern about

Heavy Metal began publishing in 1977 and relied initially on the stories which appeared in *Metal Hurlant*. (Courtesy of Martine Franck/Magnum Photos)

challenging the Comics Code Authority, caused the magazine to be published sporadically.

Marvel enjoyed more success with *Epic Illustrated* (1980-1986), possibly because the magazine made use of writers and artists who were not familiar with a "house style" and had a greater investment in their own work, as Marvel offered creator's rights for the first time. *Epic Illustrated* was influenced by *Heavy Metal* magazine. While some stories made use of popular Marvel characters, most were new fantasy and science fiction, created and illustrated by John Byrne, Jeffrey Jones, Jim Starlin, Stephen R. Bissette, John J Muth, and Rick Veitch, among others. Unlike *Savage Tales*, *Epic Illustrated* was printed in color. It attracted readers with covers by Frazetta, the Brothers Hildebrandt, and Richard Corben.

While DC Comics is not known for any direct forays into magazines for mature readers, magazines such as *Heavy Metal* and *Epic Illustrated* clearly influenced the development of the company. DC's Vertigo imprint features comic books and graphic novels for mature readers interested in nonsuperhero fare. The stories have a variety of themes and make use of explicit art, violence, and language.

Behind the scenes, however, DC is recognized for its business acumen in deciding to align with the French publisher Les Humanoïdes Associés, which originally published *Metal Hurlant*. The two companies partnered to publish much of the original work from *Metal Hurlant* in English in graphic novel format. The relationship was tempestuous, with arguments over format, what to publish, and how many novels to release in any given month. Still, these releases helped to raise the profile of *Metal Hurlant*.

Heavy Metal

Heavy Metal, the American version of *Metal Hurlant*, began publishing in 1977. It relied initially on the stories that appeared in *Metal Hurlant*, though increasingly made use of Spanish, Latin American, British, and American writers and artists. *Heavy Metal*'s early publisher, Leonard Mogel, and editors Sean Kelley and Valarie Marchant brought in writers and artists such as Howard Cruse, Howard Chaykin, Bernie Wrightson, and Arthur Suydam. The magazine was later bought by

Kevin Eastman (of *Teenage Mutant Ninja Turtles* fame), who became the new publisher and editor; many of its graphic novels and art books are published by Metal Mammoth.

While the magazine is known for highlighting the erotic in science fiction and fantasy contexts, editorial censorship has occasionally become an issue, with artists asked to redraw panels or with cover art that was considered sexually overt partially printed on the front of the magazine and in full on the front inside cover.

For each issue, both the front and back covers are used to display awe-inspiring art by artists such as Frazetta, Wrightson, Luis Royo, Olivia De Berardinis, Chris Achilleos, and H. R. Giger. The covers from the first twenty-five years of the magazine have been compiled into a book, and the artwork and stories have also inspired two cartoon movies, *Heavy Metal* (1981) and *Heavy Metal 2000* (2000).

One unusual feature of the magazine is its tactic of changing written literature to visual literature. *Heavy Metal* has re-created stories by Harlan Ellison, Ray Bradbury, William S. Burroughs, Stephen King, Robert Silverberg, and even John Milton as graphic narratives. Many of the stories are fatalistic or nihilistic. Another unusual feature is the inclusion of essays, reviews, and interviews with writers, artists, musicians, and film directors. These two features have given the magazine a sense of seriousness that appeals to a sophisticated mature reader.

Impact

Magazines for mature audiences encouraged the creation of graphic novels. Increasingly, readers wanted to read the complete story as quickly as possible, rather than wait for installments. Publishers were attracted to the idea of the graphic novel because a book-length volume of comics could be placed in both bookstores and comics specialty shops; also, albums have longer shelf lives, possibly attracting more customers over time.

Collections of serialized works from adult-oriented magazines helped launch the graphic novel, which can be either a collection of serialized work or a new work written especially for the format. The use of comic book techniques in works of Maurice Sendak (especially *In the Night Kitchen*,

1970), Jules Feiffer (*Tantrum*, 1979), and Shel Silverstein (*A Light in the Attic*, 1981) also suggested that comics could attract adults in addition to children.

From adult-oriented magazines such as *Epic Illustrated* came Starlin's *Dreadstar* saga (1982-   ); an early version of *Cerebus* (1977-2004), the warrior aardvark created by Dave Sim; and a series of Michael Moorcock's Elric of Melniboné stories, written by Roy Thomas and penciled by P. Craig Russell. *Savage Tales* also introduced stories that would be collected in graphic novels, such as *The 'Nam* (1987-   ), focusing on actual soldiers' accounts from the Vietnam War, written by Doug Murray and illustrated by Michael Golden. *Heavy Metal* begot a series of graphic novels featuring the violent *RanXerox*, which influenced the images of the aliens in George Lucas' *Star Wars* series, and Corben's Den stories, about a man who solves everything through sex and violence in an untold time and space.

During the 1980's, magazines such as *RAW*, edited by Art Spiegelman and Françoise Mouly, were published. These often large, oversized magazines introduced readers to works such as Spiegelman's *Maus* (1986).

Terry Joseph Cole

Bibliography

"Full Cover Gallery." *Heavy Metal Magazine*, 2012. http://www.heavymetal.com. Includes little history on *Heavy Metal* magazine itself, but this information can be gleaned from the front covers, which highlight the authors and artists featured in each issue.

Pilchner, Tim. *Erotic Comics 2: A Graphic History from the Liberated 70's to the Internet*. New York: Abrams ComicArts, 2008. A critical history of erotic content in comics, beginning in the 1970's. Highlights comics magazines for mature audiences. Also includes sections on *Barbarella*, NBM, and *Heavy Metal*.

Workman, John, ed. *Heavy Metal: Twenty-Five Years of Classic Covers*. Rockville Centre, N.Y.: Heavy Metal, 2002. Provides wonderful graphics. Introductions by Workman, the original art editor for *Heavy Metal*, and by artists such as Richard and Wendy Pini, Royo, and Simon Bisley.

Gender Evolution in Graphic Novels

Definition

Gender, a socially constructed demarcator for traits generally associated with one sex, has long been presented in the graphic novels genre of literature. Gender is now thought to be a continuum ranging from feminine to masculine with androgyny in the middle. Graphic novels have portrayed men and women at many points on this continuum, bending traditional conventions since the beginning of the genre.

Introduction

While gender theorists such as Michel Foucault and Judith Butler have evaluated and redefined gender, graphic novels reinvent gender roles in pronounced ways. Graphic novels' predecessors, comic books, often represented gender in binary ways: Women were either superheroines, such as Wonder Woman or Ms. Marvel, or damsels in distress, such as Lois Lane. Similarly, men were either the "alpha" of humanity (examples include Superman, a hero whose name elicits an image of perfect masculinity) or the subordinate, feminized sidekick, such as Batman's Robin, who never seemed to outgrow his "wonder boy" status.

As the genre has grown from the Marvel classics and superheroes, gender distinction has become a muddy area. Writers such as Alison Bechdel and Bryan Lee O'Malley have presented men and women as creatures of duality, embracing the androgyny of their characters. Bechdel's *Fun Home* (2006), a memoir about her closeted homosexual father, their relationship, and her childhood home (a funeral home), presents Bechdel's struggle with gender identity, both hers and her father's. O'Malley's Scott Pilgrim is a timid man who, in order to secure a relationship with the girl of his dreams, must defeat her seven evil exes: six alpha males and a lesbian. Pilgrim is an awkward, nonviolent, and unlikely hero. Conversely, his girlfriend is dark and mysterious, exuding ample masculine energy.

The Japanese graphic novel genre, manga, has also revolutionized the way gender is represented in the graphic novel. Manga often deals with homosexuality and transgender issues, and gender is often questioned.

Scott Pilgrim's Precious Little Life. (Courtesy of Oni Press)

Gay characters are presented without question, and the stories are built around their lives, while androgyny is built into the characters' personas. *Shōjo* mangas, produced specifically for girls, are often written to reveal an ideal feminine character, although this trend is evolving to present more androgynous characters. One need not look far in the genre of graphic novels to find gender definitions and redefinitions along a continuum of masculinity and femininity.

"Super-AlphaMale-Man"

Traditional graphic novels and their comic book predecessors often portray characters that fit the mold of the "alpha male." He is a hero—strong, intelligent, agile, and ready with a solution. A fantastic example of this motif can be found in Jeph Loeb and Tim Sale's revisionist version of the Superman series, *Superman: For All Seasons* (1998). Each of the seasons is narrated by a different member of Superman's cast of characters. "Spring," narrated by Clark Kent's father, reveals Clark's life before becoming Superman. As expected, Clark is the son of a man's man, a farmer who provides for his family with his bare hands. Furthermore, as Clark grows, his powers become stronger at a rapid rate. When he goes to get a haircut, he realizes he can see through walls and his hair breaks the barber's scissors. A tornado strikes Smallville, and Clark saves a man from an explosion at a gas station. This message is clearly one that is applicable to all pubescent males. As male characters' sex drives grow and their shoulders spread, the tradition is to highlight masculine power: strength, good looks, and the ability to woo any woman.

Alpha males need not be quite so obvious in graphic novels. In O'Malley's *Scott Pilgrim* series (2004-2010), each of Ramona's male exes, in his own way, represents pure masculinity. From the first evil ex (Matthew Patel, whose mystical powers enable him to summon women as he may see fit) to the last (Gideon Gordon Graves, a wealthy, self-sufficient entrepreneur who is well-versed in fencing), each of Ramona's lovers has been sure of himself, confident, and incredibly ambitious. Scott, who at the outset does not seem to be more than an awkward, mediocre musician, must overcome these alpha males to achieve the status himself.

Damsel to the Rescue

The traditional view of femininity has been part of graphic novels since the beginning of the genre. *Shōjo* mangas often represent women as passive, willing, and dutiful. These women are seen as the good wife or the wise mother, who speaks traditional passive Japanese. Similar passivity can be seen in American graphic literature. The alpha males of graphic novels cannot be without their girlfriends. However, it would seem that these women are of little value in their world and are desperate to tie down the superheroes through matrimony. As brilliantly as Lois Lane has been portrayed throughout the Superman sequences, even she is not safe from becoming little more than a clingy girl, per-

petually attempting to secure marriage and even willing to marry Satan for a little attention (which happens in *Superman's Girlfriend Lois Lane*, issue 103). Apparition, otherwise known as Phantom Girl, has her soul bound to her boyfriend upon her death. Green Lantern's girlfriend is strangled by a supervillain and stuffed into a refrigerator.

A marked gender difference occurs within the superhero genre. While superheroes have traditionally taken their girlfriends for granted, nearly every popular female in the traditional superhero niche has faced an array of horrible fates. Stephanie Brown became Batman's first female sidekick in 2004. To do so, she needs to create her own Robin costume and demand that Batman train her. While she was physically capable of saving Batman from a serial killer, she was not adept enough to avoid setting off a gang war. Although this sort of chaos is not uncommon in comics, Stephanie is tortured to death with a power drill by a supervillain because she is not skilled enough to avoid causing trouble. Further, some of the most influential superheroines (Ms. Marvel, Power Girl, and Wonder Woman) are at some point depowered, raped, and/or impregnated "magically," providing a clear picture to readers what "a woman's place," traditionally, is supposed to be.

Gender Evolution

Although it is crucial to understand both the highly masculinized prototypes and the often unappreciated, devalued feminine characters in traditional graphic novels, depictions of gender have evolved in the genre. Frequently, androgyny serves as a means for creating depth in characters. Joss Whedon's *Buffy the Vampire Slayer Season 8* (2007-2011), a graphic novel extension of the popular television series, features a main character who is a prime example of the advanced, androgynous female. Buffy is physically strong, strong-willed, and opinionated. She is feared by much of the world and is considered a terrorist.

Although she is not the dainty female portrayed in much of the *shōjo* mangas or the brain-dead girlfriend of a superhero, Buffy is still feminine. Her body is not exaggerated for male fantasy, but it is not hidden to hide her sex, which represents the more fluid, accepting standards of postfeminism. Buffy is involved in a love triangle between two men, both alpha types, but is not swayed by one or the other to deny who she is. This woman can have it all and will not be unfairly punished for having power like her predecessors.

In *V for Vendetta* (1982-1985; 1988-1989), Alan Moore depicts an androgynous lead. V, a masked man bent on destroying a totalitarian regime, wears a mask and a cape. He has a male voice but does not exhibit any secondary sex characteristics. V is often soft with Evey, the female lead character, who eventually falls in love with him. However, he is also vengeful, adept with and knowledgeable about explosives, and strong. On the other hand, Evey exhibits clear female sex characteristics. Because V saves Evey from a man who is about to rape her, she then becomes clingy and overly dependent upon him. As the story line progresses, V stages Evey's imprisonment and torture to make her aware of the sort of circumstances that he faced and that led him to choose a life dedicated to vengeance. Evey survives, as did V, and eventually becomes his successor. This progression of story line suggests that, male or female, anyone is capable of mass terrorism and vengeance.

Impact

In the twentieth century, visual media displayed few variations of gender roles, particularly, the June Cleaver-type domesticated woman and the John Wayne alpha male. Graphic literature has generally followed the same trajectory in terms of its depiction of gender, having grown from ten-cent comic books that parents refused to let their sons read to an expansive collection of literature that depicts a wide array of gender roles and identities.

Graphic literature still includes superhero fiction. However, it also includes fantasy, science fiction, horror, comedy, erotica, and creative nonfiction. In each niche and in every genre, the hypermasculine brute supervillain or damsel in need of rescuing may still exist. Despite the stereotypical presentation of such characters, they have appealed to many.

A growing number of educators are pushing for graphic novels to be appreciated as an art form. The graphic novel has allowed the comics tradition to ex-

pand from a primarily preadolescent male audience to an audience that includes women and men of all ages and education levels. Despite long-held beliefs that people must be either masculine or feminine, the majority of psychological professionals support a push toward androgyny for optimal mental health. As more youth are gaining access to quality graphic literature, children who did not like to read traditional texts not only are learning to enjoy reading but also are expanding their understanding of their own masculinity and femininity. Also, because of the rise in likable characters that are both masculine and feminine, children will gain a wider understanding of humanity.

Amanda Sheppard

Bibliography

Anders, Charlie. "Supergirls Gone Wild: Gender Bias in Comics Shortchanges Superwomen." *Mother Jones* July 30, 2007, 71-73. With a somewhat humorous tone, discusses the history of subjugating women in comic books. Provides a list of popular heroines and the fates that they meet. Examines how women have been viewed in the world of the superhero.

Carinci, Sherrie, and Pia Lindquist Wong. "Does Gender Matter? An Exploratory Study of Perspectives Across Genders, Age, and Education." *International Review of Education* 55, nos. 5-6 (2009): 523-540. Attempts to understand how a variety of factors, including age and education levels, impact perceptions of gender and other arenas of life.

Caselli, Daniela. "*Androgyny in Modern Literature* (review)." Review of *Androgyny in Modern Literature*, by Tracy Hargreaves. *MFS Modern Fiction Studies* 54, no. 4 (Winter, 2008): 926-929. Looks at ways androgyny influences literature, including whether having androgynous characters affects how deeply characters are understood.

Goldstein, Lisa, and Molly Phelan. "Are You There God? It's Me, Manga: Manga as an Extension of Young Adult Literature." *Young Adult Library Services* 7, no. 4 (July, 2009): 32-38. Explores graphic literature as an introduction to reading for children. Notes how manga provides girls with the ability to mentally experiment with different sexual orientations. Suggests that young adults are growing up exposed to more open portrayals of sex and gender than their parents did.

Ho, J. D. "Gender Alchemy: The Transformative Power of Manga." *Horn Book Magazine* 83, no. 5 (September/October 2007): 505-512. Focuses on the "boy-love" genre of manga. Explores how manga may be able to allow youth both to experience life from a variety of different perspectives and to understand different sexual orientations and attitudes.

Krensky, Stephen. *Comic Book Century: The History of American Comic Books*. Minneapolis: Twenty-First Century Books, 2008. Provides a detailed look at how comic books influenced American culture (and vice versa) in the twentieth century. Highlights the changing face of comic books during wartime and the evolution of masculinity.

Lefkowitz, Emily S., and Peter B. Zeldow. "Masculinity and Femininity Predict Optimal Mental Health: A Belated Test of the Androgyny Hypothesis." *Journal of Personality Assessment* 87, no. 1 (August, 2006): 95-101. Examines the belief held by psychologists that embracing the masculinity and femininity inherent in all people is a step toward mental health.

Ueno, Junko. "'Shojo' and Adult Women: A Linguistic Analysis of Gender Identity in *Manga* (Japanese Comics)." *Women and Language* 29, no. 1 (2006): 16-25. Examines graphic novels aimed at young girls and women. Analyzes the speech presented by female characters in these novels.

Wolk, Douglas. *Reading Comics: How Graphic Novels Work and What They Mean*. Cambridge, Mass.: Da Capo Press, 2007. An excellent overview of the graphic novel genre, containing a section on theory and history as well as an extensive list of book reviews and commentary. Provides information about writing, understanding, and enjoying the genre.

THE HISTORICAL IMPACT OF FILM

Definition
From the beginnings of the comic book industry to the Modern Age, films and graphic novels have exerted mutual influence on each other. Silent films of the 1920's have inspired comics such as *Batman*, and later films based on sequential art and comic book characters have been both critically acclaimed and successful at the box office.

Introduction
The relationship between films and comics and graphic novels, collectively understood as "sequential art," has a long and complex history. For example, Batman co-creator Bob Kane credits films such as *The Mark of Zorro* (1920), *The Bat* (1926), and the latter's sound remake, *The Bat Whispers* (1930), as inspiration for Batman. The dark and brooding cityscapes of *The Bat* are recognizable models for Gotham City. The Bat in the eponymous film is a criminal; nonetheless, Kane saw value in using the bat motif as a means to scare criminals. Batman's main nemesis, the Joker, was inspired by Conrad Veidt's performance as Gwynplaine in *The Man Who Laughs* (1928).

Film adaptations of graphic novels have become critical and box-office successes; these include *Superman* (1978), *Spider-Man* (2002), and *The Dark Knight* (2008). By the early twenty-first century, works of sequential art were being adapted into films in record numbers as Hollywood film studios strove to option as many graphic novels as they could, and some of the resulting adaptations have received mainstream critical attention. In 2010, the film version of Warren Ellis and Cully Hamner's graphic novel *Red* (2009) was nominated for a Golden Globe Award in the Best Motion Picture-Comedy or Musical category. Sequential art has become a major influence on the film industry, but the inverse is also true: Films have had an enormous influence on comics and graphic novels.

The Early Influence of Film
Film slightly predates the advent of modern paneled comic strips, and the film medium has had a long, mutu-

Poster for *Superman and the Mole Men* (1951); it is the first theatrical feature film based on the character Superman. (Getty Images)

ally influential relationship with sequential art. The influence of film on comics dates at least to the 1928 publication of the hardback collection *Texas History Movies*. Originally published in the *Dallas Morning News* as a comic strip, *Texas History Movies* was illustrated by Jack Patton and written by John Rosenfield, Jr. The series presents Texas history through a sequence of illustrated panels reminiscent of frames from a film. Comics were sometimes thought of as "printed movies" because a sequence of individual panels resembled strips of individual celluloid frames. During the era of silent film, both films and comics told stories using pictures and text.

Characters and stories from films have influenced comics since the industry's infancy in the mid-1930's. Will Eisner's "Muss 'Em Up Donovan," published late in the decade, features characters directly influenced by filmic portrayals by actors such as James Cagney in the gangster and crime pictures of the era. Pulp heroes of the 1930's such as Tarzan, Flash Gordon, and Buck Rogers appeared in both comics and films, and silver-screen cowboys such as Gene Autry and Roy Rogers also found their adventures being told in four-color print. When crime comics grew in popularity in the late 1940's and early 1950's, the boundaries between films noirs such as *The Maltese Falcon* (1941) and comics such as the Dashiell Hammett-penned *Secret Agent X-9* (1945) became somewhat unclear.

Graphic Adaptations of Television Shows and Films

During the 1950's and 1960's, many television shows spawned their own comic book counterparts, including *Have Gun Will Travel* (1957-1963), *Lassie* (1954-1974), *Car 54, Where Are You?* (1961-1963), *77 Sunset Strip* (1958–1964), *The Lone Ranger* (1949–1957), and *Star Trek* (1966-1969). Perhaps the earliest long-form paperback publications issued concurrently with a television series were the 1959 *Steve Canyon* books by Milton Caniff. The publication of comics and graphic novels based on television shows is a practice that has continued into comics' Modern Age, with graphic novels related to shows such as *Fringe* (2008-   ), *The X-Files* (1993-2002), *Buffy the Vampire Slayer* (1997-2003), and *True Blood* (2008-   ) proving commercially successful.

Feature films began to have a major impact on graphic novels in the 1970's, when the success of Marvel Comics' paperback graphic novel adaptation of *Star Wars* (1977) by Roy Thomas and Howard Chaykin showed there was a market for graphic novel tie-ins to feature films. Other graphic novel adaptations followed, including adaptations of *Star Trek: The Motion Picture* (1979), *Dragonslayer* (1981), and *Dune* (1984). Even the James Bond film *For Your Eyes Only* (1981) was adapted into a graphic novel, published by Marvel. These relatively

early graphic novels highlight the beginning of the market for sequential art adaptations of feature films.

In the late 1980's and early 1990's, many comics publishers produced comics and graphic novels based on films and film series, particular science-fiction and horror franchises. Probably the best-known example is the *Aliens vs. Predator* crossover series (beginning in 1989), which combines elements from the films *Alien* (1979) and *Predator* (1987) and the associated franchises; the series later inspired two film adaptations of its own. Dark Horse Comics also published graphic novels based on such properties as *The Terminator* (1984) and *Planet of the Apes* (2001).

A cottage industry has developed for graphic novels based on popular film franchises that are themselves based on literary properties. For example, Stephenie Meyer's Twilight series (2005-2008) has been adapted into a series of blockbuster films. In turn, the success of the films influenced the creation of a series of graphic novel adaptations.

Directors

The relationship between comics and film has also influenced graphic novel writers and artists to direct films, particularly those based on their own works. Renowned writer and artist Frank Miller codirected *Sin City* (2005), based on his series of graphic novels, with filmmaker Robert Rodriguez. Miller went on to direct the feature film *The Spirit* (2008), based on the influential work of comics artist, early graphic novelist, and sequential-art theorist Eisner. Artist Dave McKean directed *MirrorMask* (2005), a film written by comics writer, novelist, and screenwriter Neil Gaiman, and Gaiman himself directed *A Short Film About John Bolton* (2003), a fictionalized film about the titular comics artist.

Conversely, filmmakers such as J. Michael Straczynski (creator of *Babylon 5*) and Joss Whedon (creator of *Buffy the Vampire Slayer* and *Firefly*) have written comics and graphic novels. Straczynski had a long run on *Amazing Spider-Man*, and Whedon wrote more than twenty issues of *Astonishing X-Men*. A number of individuals have worked in both film and comics and established successful careers in both fields. As Hollywood directors and studios increasingly use graphic novels as source material and film and graphic novels become more entwined, this creative overlap will likely continue to have significant effects on both industries.

Impact

Although the U.S. film industry took to adapting graphic novel properties at a breakneck pace during the late twentieth and early twenty-first centuries, film and sequential art have long had reciprocal influence. Graphic novel adaptations of films and television series have demonstrated how such media have directly influenced graphic novels and comics production. Likewise, graphic novels provide a never-ending source of story material and ideas from which filmmakers can draw. In the mid-1970's, artist Jack Kirby quipped that comic book and graphic novel properties "will be where all of Hollywood will come every year to look for the idea for next year's movies." Kirby may have been off by a few decades, but his statement has certainly proven prophetic.

Robert G. Weiner

Bibliography

Booker, M. Keith. *May Contain Graphic Material: Comic Books, Graphic Novels, and Film*. Westport, Conn.: Praeger, 2007. Discusses the evolution of the comics behind the feature films, focusing on popular superhero comics and films as well as nonsuperhero films based on sequential art.

Gordon, Ian, Mark Jancovich, and Matthew P. McAllister, eds. *Film and Comic Books*. Jackson: University Press of Mississippi, 2007. Collects essays on a wide range of topics, including the challenges faced in adapting comics to the screen and comics-related movies such as *Unbreakable* (2000).

Hughes, David. *Comic Book Movies*. London: Virgin Books, 2003. Provides a history and discussion of comic book-related movies up to 2003, including cast lists, plot synopses, and critical evaluations.

HISTORY AND USES OF THE TERM "GRAPHIC NOVEL"

Definition

The term "graphic novel" came into currency at the end of the 1970's to describe comic-strip narratives published in book form as opposed to the periodical pamphlets called "comic books," circulated since the 1930's. It has come to be used in the book trade to refer to any nonperiodical book featuring comics. In academia it designates auteur comic-strip narratives produced outside mainstream periodical comic books. It is used occasionally in the plural as a synonym for "comics."

Introduction

The history of the designation "graphic novel" should not be mistaken for the elusive, fan-centric, and ultimately sterile debate about the "first" graphic novel. Rather, this history concerns how, in contemporary American usage, the term came to refer to books of comics, regardless of the discrepancy between the commercial meaning of the term in the book trade and its scholarly meaning in academia.

Prior to the 1970's, American comics were either syndicated newspaper comic strips, the most popular of which were collected in cheap paperbacks, or periodical newsstand comic books. The overwhelming majority of comics readers had no familiarity whatsoever with book-form comics such as the so-called albums that had become the high-end segment of comics publishing in francophone Europe with the publication of best-selling series such as *Les Aventures de Tintin* (1929-1976; *The Adventures of Tintin*, 1958-1991) and *Astérix* (1961-1979, *Asterix*, 1969-1975).

Out of several terms coined during the 1970's to encapsulate the concept (graphic album, comic album, and picture novel, among others), "graphic novel" was co-opted by both the book industry and the specialty comic store market to label usually expensive, high-production-value books designed for bookstores instead of newsstands. The general public became gradually aware of the term beginning in 1986, following the increasing media coverage granted to contemporary comics that were breaking out of mainstream formats in both tone and theme.

The term graphic novel was first used by fan-writer Richard Kyle in November, 1964, in issue 2 of *Capa-Alpha*, a newsletter associated with an Amateur Press Association comics gathering with a few dozen subscribers. In his "Wonderworld" column, Kyle stated he would use the terms "graphic story" and "graphic novel" to describe the artistically serious "comic book strip,'" which, in his mind, referred to outstanding comics such as Harvey Kurtzman's and Bernard Krigstein's EC Comics stories. Kyle used the term again in the "Graphic Story Review" column he contributed to Bill Spicer's *Fantasy Illustrated*, issue 5 (1966).

In its early incarnation, the term referred not to long-form comics, complete-in-one-volume stories, or European albums but to an implicit aesthetic agenda summarized by Kyle as "great artistic creativity . . . that no child could have appreciated—but which would have electrified many intelligent adults, if they'd permitted themselves to read 'comic books.'" The initial vagueness of the notion, the slight pompousness of the term, and its risqué overtones explain why it failed to catch on outside the subcultural circles of comics fandom.

Rise of a Trade Term

By the mid-1970's the term gradually rose from obscurity to become a catchword in the book trade. Three books described as graphic novels in their editorial blurbs were published in 1976: Richard Corben's *Bloodstar* and George Metzger's landscape format *Beyond Time and Again* were expensive, low-print-run hardcovers, while Jim Steranko's *Chandler: Red Tide* was a mass-market, digest-sized paperback.

Except for the shared sobriquet, the books were quite different. Nonetheless, the term stuck in the book trade. "Graphic novels" was used once in a paragraph heading in Ray Walters's "Paperback Talk," in the January 22, 1978, issue of *The New York Times* in which he explained that the previous year's unprecedented success of science-fiction and fantasy publications (such as the adaptations of the films *Star Wars*, 1977, and *Close Encounters of the Third Kind*, 1978) had encouraged the book industry to explore these genres. In fact, at this time, two publishers were about to release "large-format paperbacks that depend upon pictures as much as words to tell their stories"; the two titles were Corben's *Neverwhere* (1978), published by Ballantine, and Jack Katz's *The First Kingdom* (1978), published by Pocket/Wallaby.

Katz was an essential, if inconspicuous, participant in the late 1970's popularization of the term. In 1973, he came up with the idea of a mammoth 768-page sustained comic-strip narrative, *The First Kingdom*, which he sold to his publisher Bud Plant as a "graphic novel." He used the same term in an August 7, 1974, letter to Will Eisner: "What I am starting is a graphic novel in which every incident is illustrated." Eisner would have been responsive to the concept. In an interview granted to John Benson in 1968, he had expressed his interest in "the so called 'graphic story,' . . . a whole novel in comic form." It is no wonder that "graphic novel" was the term that occurred to him when he started pitching the project that became *A Contract with God, and Other Tenement Stories* (1978); the softcover edition of the book bore the subtitle "A Graphic Novel by Will Eisner." Still, the term did not appear in the introduction, where he placed his work under the aegis of Lynd Ward's woodcut novels instead. Hence, although Eisner did not coin the term graphic novel, *A Contract with God* popularized the term within the comic book industry.

Breaking into Bookstores and Mainstream Culture

In the 1980's, the emerging direct-distribution market embraced the graphic novel as one of the formats designed for specialty bookstores. The Marvel Graphic Novels, a line launched in 1982, were glorified vehicles for otherwise fairly traditional superhero narratives or new concepts liable to be turned into continuing titles. The format established by Marvel (8.5-inch-by-11-inch softcover one-shots printed on quality paper and written and illustrated by big-name creators) became the template of the graphic novel lines issued by DC Comics and various alternative publishers of the day, including Pacific Comics, Eclipse Comics, and First Comics.

While they thrived in the direct market, graphic novels were a tiny niche market for regular bookstores by the mid-1980's. According to an article in the May, 1987, issue of the trade publication *American Bookseller*, the attention paid to comics by mainstream media had turned graphic novel into "an industry buzz-word" even though most booksellers at first saw it as "a two or three-book field," referencing Art Spiegelman's *Maus* (1986), Harvey Pekar's *American Splendor* (first published in 1976), and Frank Miller's *Batman: The Dark Knight Returns* (1986). Over the following fifteen years, the book

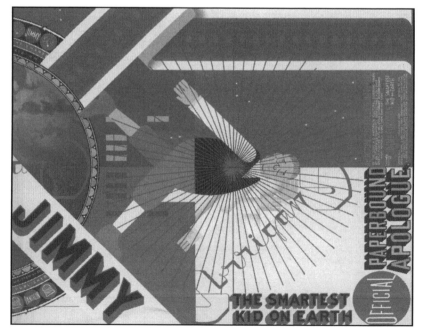

The first graphic novel to win a major award in the UK was Chris Ware's *Jimmy Corrigan: The Smartest Kid on Earth*, which won the Guardian First Book Award for 2001 (Courtesy of Pantheon Books)

trade gave up its decades-long reluctance to carry nonperiodical comics.

By the late 1980's, it seemed that the term was about to go mainstream and become the label that would eventually dissociate comic art from its traditional connotations of juvenile entertainment and lowbrow escapism, as had been happening in western Europe since the 1970's. The term subsequently became a marketing category encompassing trade paperback or hardback reprints of syndicated strips or periodical comic books, original graphic novels, and translations of foreign material, including manga. Throughout the 1990's, general bookstores moved books featuring comics from "humor" sections to newly created "graphic novels" sections.

Many saw the Pulitzer Prize awarded to *Maus* in 1992 as a signal of definitive cultural recognition. The same could be said about the entry of graphic novels into libraries. However, in a 1998 piece for *The New York Times Book Review*, Tom De Haven pointed out a persistent cultural reticence among college students and highbrow types: Visibly, graphic novels had not managed to overcome the stigma of comics. However, the positive reception of several high-profile books in the following decade, such as *Jimmy Corrigan* (2000), *In the Shadow of No Towers* (2004), *Black Hole* (2005), and *Fun Home* (2006), turned the tables and settled the graphic novel in middlebrow-to-highbrow culture.

Impact

Regardless of the public and media interest in the format, various criticisms of the term have risen among creators. Some say graphic novels is a marketing term that lumps together the best and worst of the industry's output. Others have argued it is an unnecessarily pretentious way to designate comic books. Still others have come up with alternate appellations—"picture novella" (Seth), "comic-strip novel" (Dan Clowes)— as tongue-in-cheek responses to what they perceive as the term's increasingly commercial connotations.

It is undeniable that the popularization of the term "graphic novel" has played a major role in the cultural acceptance of comics art. As far as the genre's long-term history is concerned, the simultaneous shift of the industry's dominant economic model from magazine to book publishing has been a fairly unique example of Europeanization (or, arguably, Japanization) of an American popular cultural medium.

Jean-Paul Gabilliet

Bibliography

Couch, Chris. "The Publication and Formats of Comics, Graphic Novels, and Tankobon." *Image [&] Narrative* 1 (December, 2000). http://www.imageand narrative.be/inarchive/narratology/chriscouch.htm. Examines the parallel histories of book-form comics in the United States, Europe, and Japan by comparing such factors as readership demographics, economic models, and cultural specificities.

Gabilliet, Jean-Paul. *Of Comics and Men: A Cultural History of American Comic Books*. Translated by Bart Beaty and Nick Nguyen. Jackson: University Press of Mississippi, 2010. Provides a history of the U.S. comic book industry that charts the evolution of comic books and graphic novels in terms of cultural hierarchy and legitimization.

Hatfield, Charles. *Alternative Comics: An Emerging Literature*. Jackson: University Press of Mississippi, 2005. Discusses long-form comics as a literary form and underscores the impact of production contexts on the critical interpretation of graphic novels.

LATINO IDENTITY: AN ACCOUNT OF OTHERNESS

Definition

Though conventional wisdom traces the first Latino presence in graphic novels to the Hernandez brothers' *Love and Rockets* (1981-1996), substantial evidence points to the appearance of Latino characters in graphic narratives from an earlier date, particularly in superhero comics.

Introduction

In 1981, along with his brothers Jaime and Mario, Gilbert Hernandez self-published the first issue of *Love and Rockets*, a comic book series later released by Fantagraphics Books, virtually redefining the field of graphic novels throughout much of the 1980's and 1990's. In it, the Hernandez brothers explored the world of Southern California from a previously unexplored perspective, that from the Mexican American barrio. The text also repeatedly ventures into many other contexts; in fact, part of this series takes place beyond American national borders, specifically in a small Latin American enclave called Palomar. Central to the whole project was a reassertion and redefinition of Latino identity in the U.S. mainstream.

Since *Love and Rockets* explored many forms of difference—ethnic, racial, social, regional, and gender—its influence on the depiction of Latinos in graphic novels is significant. However, Latinos were present in mainstream graphic narratives from an earlier time. Thus, it is important to consider the chronological evolution of Latino identity in superhero comics. Marvel Comics and DC Comics have both played significant parts in this process. Marvel's catalog of Latino characters is larger and more eclectic than DC's, but both follow the same general patterns in terms of how they engage minority identities.

Initially, most Latino characters emerged from or were situated south of the U.S.-Mexican border and represented malignant interests. In due time, they made the transition to U.S. soil, landing in the urban ghetto of the 1970's. Later, as Latinos ascended socially and joined the mainstream, more generic identities were proposed and celebrated, in some cases revising earlier constructs.

Love and Rockets. (Courtesy of Fantagraphics Books)

With Latinos in the sight of the media industry, comics introduced more elaborate story lines set abroad, depicting Latin American origin with an unusual degree of detail. In this sense, the evolution of Latino identity in graphic novels is, like those of many other minorities, an ongoing process. Along the way, a small assortment of independent creators such as the Hernandez brothers emerged and had tangential influence on the consideration of Latino identity.

Early Latino Presence

It is difficult to suggest a first date for the presence of Latinos in graphic narratives, particularly when many characters appeared in formats that would eventually evolve into the graphic novel. However, within the context of the Cold War (an ideal excuse for inclusion), the first instance of a Latino presence is a rather surprising

　　　　　　　　　　　　　　　　　　Critical Survey of Graphic Novels

one: In 1963, Iron Man (Tony Stark) was created by Stan Lee, Larry Lieber, Don Heck, and Jack Kirby. The case is an indication of the degree of invisibility of Latinos in mainstream U.S. culture. A Long Island whiz kid who attends MIT from the age of fifteen, Tony Stark is the son of Maria Collins Carbonell Stark. The mother's surname, of Catalan origin and fairly common in the Spanish-speaking Caribbean, points to Stark's overlooked descent. Even if considered on a second-generation basis (if Collins Carbonell were the full surname, Stark's grandparents would have been Latino), the family name ratifies his Latin origin.

Tony Stark is an anomaly. Initial Latino presence in comics came in the form of villains, with an eventual transition to "good guys" south of the U.S.-Mexican border. Also in 1963, Esteban Corazón De Ablo, also known as Diablo (devil), appears as the rival of the Fantastic Four. A mix of Dracula and Faust, Diablo evinces the fact that initially Hispanic presence was partial to European extraction, rather than Latin American.

Eventually, more specifically Latin American characters surfaced. For instance, Juan Meroz (El Tigre or Kukulcan), an enemy of the X-Men who is loosely based on the Aztec god Quetzalcoatl, appeared in 1966. A year later, Iron Man killed Crusher, a South American communist agent linked to a Fidel Castro-like dictator. In 1975, Crusher was resurrected under the name Juan Aponte and fought Daredevil.

During the 1970's, a lineage of criminal brothers from Puerto Rico—Ramón, Jaime, and Philip García, playing the roles of Señor Suerte and Señor Muerte—confronted Luke Cage. Another Puerto Rican, Hector Ayala, also known as White Tiger, appeared in 1975. By the time of Ayala, though, using Puerto Rico (and New York) as a beachhead, Latino characters had landed on U.S. soil, evincing traces of benevolence. The luck of immigrants is mixed, though. Ayala attends college, but soon dark circumstances send him to prison; upon fleeing, he is shot and dies, a fate of many early Latino heroes or villains.

Transition to U.S. Context

The transition for Latino characters to an affirmative role on U.S. soil is not straightforward. Along the way,

Marvel employed characters such as Tarantula (1974), El Jaguar (1975), Windeagle (1976), and Cheetah (1977), most of whom die or end in prison, giving Latino identity a rather disposable quality.

In 1979, there was a novelty, perhaps the first confrontation between a Latino superhero, the mutant known as El Águila (real name Alejandro Montoya), and his Spanish nemesis, Conquistador. At this point, representation of things Spanish was still a jumble of medieval clichés and leitmotifs, and Montoya's costume, except for the coloring, is remarkably similar to Zorro's. Even his rivals largely replicate a fairly rudimentary reading of a Spanish context. This aspect is particularly pertinent, since it condones the perception of a culture burdened by history.

By 1981, Mexicans were no longer perceived as foreigners, though they were relegated to the Southwest. Ironically, the pace in the creation of Latino superheroes and villains contrasted markedly with the Hernandezes' struggle for visibility amid the graphic novel scene of the 1980's. While Marvel offered Firebird, a Latina member of the Avengers, DC offered Bushmaster, who assisted Batman and Robin in South America. In this sense, though both of the major publishers were celebrating Latino identity in a positive light, DC still framed its location abroad.

In 1984, DC's approach changed with the appearance of Vibe, a former gang member from Detroit. Marvel, however, continued to produce idiosyncratic Latino characters, such as the mutants Empath (1984) and Rictor (1987), the villains Armadillo (1985) and Riptide (1986), and Poison (1988) and La Bandera (1989). In 1985 and 1987, two new DC characters appeared: Wildcat, who dies when the villain Eclipso kills her, and Gangbuster, who becomes a fugitive after Superman's apparent death.

During the 1980's, Latinos were imagined in graphic narratives in relation to urban demise, as a fractional consequence of the white flight of the 1970's. Thus, while the Hernandezes were transgressing conventions, Latino characters in DC and Marvel publications were still struggling for affirmative representation.

Spider-Man 2099, created in 1992, features the first Latino Spider-Man. (Courtesy of Marvel Comics)

Exploring Difference

By the late 1980's, DC became more adventurous in its efforts, trying to make up for lost time. While the Hernandezes were pushing the envelope with their characters, some of whom were openly gay or bisexual, mainstream publishers were only beginning to explore. Consequently, new Latino characters in mainstream narratives tended to embrace contemporary controversies reluctantly.

In 1988, Gregorio de la Vega (Extraño), a Peruvian from Trujillo and DC's first gay Latino superhero, debuted. A member of the New Guardians, Extraño (Spanish for "strange") is eventually confirmed to be HIV-positive, following a clash with a creature called Hemo-Globin. Though his powers are essentially those of a magician, Extraño's bent for justice and love is what makes him especially popular with colleagues.

Thus, while pretending inclusivity, DC effectively legitimated every conceivable cliché related to gay men, fixating the context of their identity politics. Eventual reframing resulted from gradual, more comprehensive assessment through the 1990's.

In 1989, a second version of Diablo debuted. As a Latino councilman from Dos Rios, Texas, Rafael Sandoval was a superhero dedicated to solving the customary problems of the border: drug trafficking and human smuggling. Hence, the association of Latinos with illegal activities began to cater to a more ideological bent.

In 1991, Pantha debuted as the only living result of genetic alterations started by a criminal organization called the Wildebeest Society. While not DC's forte, animalization is sporadically reserved for Latino representation. At first, Pantha is known only as Subject X-24. Ultimately, in an alternate time line, it is revealed that Pantha's true name is Rosabelle Mendez and that she had been a veterinarian student at New York University. Pantha dies early, at the hands of Superboy.

In 1992, Renée Montoya, a Dominican police officer, appeared. In *Gotham Central* (2003-2006), a series about the city's police department, Two-Face outs her as lesbian, much to the chagrin of her religious parents, who disown her. Disgusted by corruption in the police force, Montoya resigns and gradually becomes an alcoholic. Montoya is befriended by the Question, a Charlton Comics superhero who fights crime with ruthless methods. Montoya joins him, trains with his mentors, and, upon his death from cancer, takes up his mantle as the new Question. Through it all, Montoya even manages to have a romantic dalliance with Batwoman Kate Kane.

Subsequently, Montoya has appeared in comic book series such as *Countdown* (2007-2008) and *Final Crisis* (2008-2009). In short, she became the darling representation of imperfection. She is disgraced in numerous ways: She is gay, disowned, alienated, and alcoholic. Thus, what is unanimously interpreted and celebrated as an exploration of difference, supposedly indicting the conservative sexual mores of the Latino community, for practical purposes, offers little affirmation in exchange.

Better exploration of difference at the superhero level took place at approximately the same time that the Hernandez brothers revolutionized the graphic novel. Their representation of Latino identity, while certainly more idiosyncratic than the one proposed by mainstream comics publishers, appeared in tune with a new, common sensibility, more open than before to the contemplation of Latinos and Hispanics within the larger U.S. mainstream. Some of the Hernandezes' most beloved characters, including Luba, Penny Century, Maggie, and Hopey, signal true novelty in terms of gender, as they are granted centrality within an overall narrative. With their quirky, convoluted sagas featuring an ample assortment of strong female characters, the Hernandezes break down a number of stereotypes sustained by DC and Marvel.

Going Mainstream

During the 1990's, by which time the Hernandez brothers had solidified their reputation, Latinos embodied all sorts of nefarious characters in conventional superhero narratives, with contradictory results. Coming from the fictional Caribbean island of Santa Prisca, the villain Bane breaks Batman's back. Bane's home is an amalgam of Latin clichés: it has both an illegal drug trade and a large black population from the days of the slave trade. Though thuggish, Bane is highly intelligent and occasionally depicted fighting alongside Batman, making the transition from rival to associate.

After dealing with forceful racial (John Stewart) and gender (Jade) difference in the Green Lantern series, DC addressed Latino presence, if only tangentially, when in 1994, Kyle Rayner, the son of Mexican American CIA agent Gabriel Vasquez, became the latest Green Lantern. The year 1996 was a watershed, with new characters such as Aztek, a short-lived member of the Justice League of America. Former New York City police detective Alex Sanchez became the third Firebrand. Hero Cruz, arguably the first gay Latino superhero of African descent in the DC Universe, debuted in 1997. Aside from his surname, there is not much Latino about Cruz, who in many fan circles is considered more African American than Latino.

Coming of Age

The 2000's marked a multiplicity of Latino representation in graphic novels: heightened presence in super-

hero volumes, the maturity of the Hernandezes, the rise of a few independent authors, and even the occasional importation of talent.

Chicanos (2005-2007), the work of Argentineans Carlos Trillo and Eduardo Risso, so popular in Europe and South America, was brought to the United States. Jessica Abel's *La Perdida* (2001-2005), chronicling a young woman's trip to Mexico in search of her origins, made a big splash in the graphic novels field, earning some recognition. Having attained a certain degree of success with his comic strip *La Cucaracha*, Lalo Alcaraz published *Migra Mouse* (2004) and illustrated Ilan Stavans's *Latino U.S.A.: A Cartoon History* (2000).

Héctor Cantú and Carlos Castellanos issued several collected volumes of their work in *Baldo* in the early 2000's. With an ideological bent, 1960's icon Spain Rodriguez published *Che: A Graphic Biography* (2008), eliciting mixed reviews. On a similar topic, but with an alternative perspective, Inverna Lockpez authored *Cuba: My Revolution* (2010), illustrated by Dean Haspiel and colored by José Villarrubia.

Lastly, in an effort to appeal to a growing Latino population, DC and Marvel created teen superheroes of Hispanic descent. DC revived its *Blue Beetle* series in 2006, with a Latino, Jaime Reyes, as the new hero. Marvel introduced Anya Corazon, a Latina with a spiderlike persona named Araña. In addition, characters such as Acrata, Iman, and El Muerto point to the greater specificity of Latino heroes in the general catalog of mainstream publishers.

In a way, the 2000's represented a coming-of-age for Latinos in graphic novels. For the average reader, Latinos have been present since the Hernandezes emerged. In truth, the Latino presence bears a longer record. Nevertheless, the variety of offerings in the 2000's validated the notion that Latinos are visible in a more comprehensive fashion than ever.

Impact

Latino identity has certainly contributed greatly to the acceptance of the graphic novel as a publishing standard. The Hernandez brothers, through *Love and Rockets*, are closely linked to this process. Subsequent volumes such as *Palomar: The Heartbreak Soup Sto-*

ries (2003) or *The Girl from H.O.P.P.E.R.S.* (2007) have been even more influential.

Along the way, the complementary yet steady participation of Latinos in superhero narratives has encouraged the eventual acceptance of the graphic novels format within the field of comics. Thus, Latino identity, by forcing authors to embrace new means of representation, contributes handsomely to the modern age of graphic narratives. Introducing characters that reflect a diverse United States, both ethnically and culturally, authors and illustrators have empowered the medium and legitimated new formats.

Furthermore, the variety of titles available attests to the many ways in which Latinos seek to problematize and redefine their own condition, beyond the stranglehold or privilege of other groups or economic interests. In this sense, the graphic novel has served well as a vehicle for the representations of the many experiences that describe the travails, predicaments, and achievements of Latinos.

Héctor Fernández L'Hoeste

Bibliography

Aldama, Frederick Luis. *Your Brain on Latino Comics: From Gus Arriola to Los Bros Hernandez.* Austin: University of Texas Press, 2009. Reviews a number of Latino comics authors, generally emphasizing alternative, independent efforts. Includes images and lengthy interviews.

McGrath, Karen. "Gender, Race, and Latina Identity: An Examination of Marvel Comics' *Amazing Fantasy* and *Araña*." *Atlantic Journal of Communication* 15, no. 4 (2007): 268-283. Focuses on objectification, misrepresentation, and racial stereotyping of Araña, a teenage Latina character from Marvel Comics. Contains an image of the character.

Saxey, Esther. "Desire Without Closure in Jaime Hernandez' *Love and Rockets*." *ImageText* 3, no. 1 (Summer, 2006). http://www.english.ufl.edu/image text/archives/v3_1/saxey/. A scholarly article focusing on the relationship between Hopey and Maggie, two of the Hernandez brothers' most important characters.

Scott, Darieck. "Love, Rockets, Race, and Sex." *The Americas Review: A Review of Hispanic Literature and Art of the USA* 23, nos. 3-4 (Fall/Winter, 1995): 73-106. Describes how the Hernandez brothers' work compares with mainstream comics in terms of race, sexuality, and even fan mail.

LIBRARY COLLECTION DEVELOPMENT AND GRAPHIC NOVELS

Definition

An estimated ten million people read comic books and graphic novels annually. Therefore, adding graphic novels to public-library collections broadens collections overall, introduces readers of prose to graphic novels, and brings in comics readers who might otherwise not visit public libraries. When assembling a collection, librarians must make a number of important decisions related to selecting, purchasing, cataloguing, circulating, and promoting graphic novels.

Introduction

Public-library administrators have debated how far to delve into popular culture since Andrew Carnegie first endowed public libraries in 1883, and graphic novels have been subject to the same kind of debate librarians once held over romance novels and science-fiction books. In reality, public libraries have collected graphic novels on occasion without labeling them graphic novels. Hergé's *Les Aventures de Tintin* (1929-1976; *The Adventures of Tintin*, 1958-1991), a staple of children's collections, is an early European graphic novel series. The *Peanuts* collections by Charles M. Schulz and Walt Kelly's *Pogo* books fall into a similar category. Other graphic novels from trade publishers, such as Jules Feiffer's *Tantrum* (1979), also found their way into public libraries.

However, beginning in the 1980's, graphic novels originating from comic book publishers became more popular, and librarians were forced to wrestle with this emerging format, which was poorly reviewed in library literature and unavailable from library vendors. Early graphic novels from comics publishers suffered from the same stigma that comic books had following the Senate Subcommittee on Juvenile Delinquency hearings in 1954. At that time, the comic book industry almost closed down because of charges that the material it published contributed to juvenile delinquency. Because most graphic novels were published by independent publishers, librarians had difficulty selecting, purchasing, and cataloging them.

Another challenge for librarians was determining the intended readership of graphic novels. Because of the visual nature of the comics medium, displaying and promoting graphic novels that were not targeted to children was problematic. However, as more and more graphic novels with adult themes and adult images became available, adding these materials to library collections became necessary. Though these challenges may have been a deterrent to stocking graphic novels in libraries, the high circulation of these books and their importance as doorways to other kinds of reading made collecting graphic novels an important task for librarians. Not surprisingly, these books often fell outside of the collection-development policies of many libraries; thus, new policies had to be developed.

Collecting Graphic Novels

As graphic novels became more popular, they began to be reviewed in collection-development journals such as *Voice of Youth Advocates*, *Booklist*, *School Library Journal*, *Library Journal*, and *Publishers Weekly*, guiding librarians in selecting appropriate materials for their collections. Prior to reviews appearing in these journals, keeping up-to-date with graphic novel publishing schedules and content was difficult.

Librarians struggled with where to place graphic novels in the library collections. Some books, such as *Astérix* (1961-1979; *Asterix*, 1969-1975), clearly belonged in the children's section. Others, such as Art Spiegelman's *Maus* (1986, 1991), just as clearly belonged in the adult collection. Other books were more difficult to place, another reason reviews in library literature proved invaluable. The reviews often signified for whom the book was intended.

Graphic novel collections in the juvenile library seemed a natural fit. Comics for children seemed beneficial: The content was appropriate, and reading graphic novels often proved to be a springboard to other reading. Graphic novels also drew teenagers into libraries. However, it is difficult to argue that graphic novels also attracted adult readers. One restriction was budget. Another restriction was the appropriateness of the graphic novels. Although public libraries carry movies and prose books with sexual or abrasive content, purchasing graphic novels, in which these qualities were expressed through artwork, left a library open to complaints or criticism. Reviews from library literature became a necessary component of selecting, explaining, and defending the inclusion of graphic novels in public libraries.

Types of Graphic Novels

Just as there are many kinds of prose novels, there are several different types of graphic novels. Some have specific appeal, while others have a broad appeal. Subgenres include superhero stories, human-interest stories, manga, nonfiction, adaptations and spin-offs, and satirical novels.

Superhero stories generally involve recognizable characters such as Superman and may evoke a more mature aspect of the character than readers might expect. An example of a superhero text with mature content is *Daredevil: Born Again* (1987), by Frank Miller and David Mazzucchelli.

Human-interest stories cover a broad range of subjects and are similar to what one might find in prose fiction. An example might be *Wilson* (2010), by Daniel Clowes.

Manga are Japanese comics that are an outgrowth of anime (Japanese animation). The artwork is often more cartoony than in American graphic novels. Manga is not genre specific and covers a wide range of subjects. Funny animal stories, another category, feature animals such as Donald Duck but endow these characters with human traits and conflicts.

Nonfiction graphic novels are not novels in the traditional sense but are still narrative in nature. These may be instructional or autobiographical, as in the case of Spiegelman's *Maus*. Adaptations and spin-offs contain stories of well-known characters such as Dracula. Satirical novels question political systems or social mores. The work of cartoonists such as Robert Crumb and Harvey Kurtzman exemplify the latter genre.

Shelving, Displaying, Circulating, and Outreach

Because of the strong visual impact of graphic novels, shelving them has proved to be a double-edged sword:

These books naturally draw attention to themselves but not always in a positive fashion. Teenagers who might be attracted to a popular graphic novel such as Alan Moore's *Watchmen* (1987) might find their parents repelled by the book's violent imagery. However, librarians found that displaying graphic novels together, with a face-out display, often increased their circulation because of the strong visual statement and the ease with which readers could access them.

Shelving these books brought another challenge: Many graphic novels are larger than trade books but are paperbound. As a result, standing them vertically often put strain on the paper binding. The paper binding became another reason to display the books face out on a stand, from which the binding can receive proper support.

Circulating graphic novels has also proved challenging. Most graphic novels are paperbacks and wear out with repeated borrowing. For this reason, some libraries reinforce or rebind the books or purchase more expensive hardcover editions. Theft has also been a problem, as graphic novels are costly. To counter theft, many librarians clearly identify these books as library property. Some go as far as to deface the books slightly to minimize their resale value on the collector's market. Graphic novels may also be used effectively in outreach programs such as book talks and classroom visits to spark interest in the library program.

Library Inclusion Challenges and Graphic Novel Placement

Because graphic novels have both visual and prose currency, patrons can find either parts of or a whole graphic novel visually objectionable, depending on community standards. As a result, graphic novels may be challenged. To counter these challenges, librarians may refer to the library's collection-development policy. Graphic novels may be justified as part of a popular-culture collection or as one aspect of youthful doorways to learning. Other libraries refer specifically to collecting graphic novels in their collection-development policies. If a graphic novel is challenged, it is wise to follow the same procedures one implements in any challenge to library materials.

Where graphic novels are placed is an important aspect of warding off challenges. When grouped together,

Library board president Anita Wright, left, and Amy Crump, director of the Marshall Public Library, look at a graphic novel at the library in Marshall, Missouri. (AP Photo)

displayed, and advertised, graphic novels may circulate well, justifying increasing the collection. However, placing graphic novels in age-appropriate sections of the library, rather than together, makes it more difficult to challenge the inclusion of graphic novels in libraries. Spreading graphic novels throughout libraries may positively affect overall circulation as well. Many librarians have never received challenges against graphic novels.

Impact

As public libraries began collecting and circulating graphic novels in the 1980's and 1990's, the impact was wide-ranging. Graphic novels added significantly to the appeal of public libraries and brought in patrons who might otherwise not have used library services. In this way, graphic novel collections have served as advertisements for both the texts themselves and library services in general. Many libraries boast of high circulation of graphic novel collections, and other libraries have noted that total circulation increased after they included graphic novels in their collections.

Placing graphic novels in public libraries has helped legitimize the comics format. Public-library

sponsorship of graphic novels through collection and promotion as well as through a series of professional conferences held from 1998 to 2002 educated library patrons and the general public about how the comics field had evolved. The visibility afforded by these collections and conferences emboldened major publishing houses to develop graphic novels imprints, thus making graphic novels more readily available to libraries and the reading public.

Stephen Weiner

Bibliography

Carter, James Bucky. *Building Literacy Connections with Graphic Novels.* Urbana, Ill.: National Council of Teachers of English, 2007. Presents articles about how to teach specific graphic novels, many of which include classroom exercises and black-and-white illustrations.

Gorman, Michele. *Getting Graphic! Using Graphic Novels to Promote Literacy with Preteens and Teens.* Worthington, Ohio: Linworth, 2003. Focuses on practical issues librarians face when collecting graphic novels and includes a bibliography of graphic novel recommendations.

Gravett, Paul. *Graphic Novels: Everything You Need to Know.* New York: Collins Design, 2005. Provides an overview of the graphic novels field and an illustrated discussion of seminal works and serves as a readers' advisory tool.

Pawuk, Michael. *Graphic Novels: A Genre Guide to Comic Books, Manga, and More.* Westport, Conn.: Libraries Unlimited, 2007. Organizes and describes more than twenty-four graphic novels and includes a cartoon preface touching on collection-development issues and the history of comics and graphic novels.

Weiner, Robert G. *Graphic Novels and Comics in Libraries and Archives: Essays on Readers, Research, History, and Cataloging.* Jefferson, N.C.: McFarland, 2010. Covers a range of topics of interest to public library, school, and academic librarians regarding graphic novels, including a graphic-novels-collection evaluation.

LITERACY AND THE GRAPHIC NOVEL: PREJUDICE, PROMISE, AND PEDAGOGY

Definition

Since comics hit the newsstands at the beginning of the twentieth century, they have been immensely popular, especially with juveniles, preteens, and young adults. This popularity sparked a debate over how reading comics affects literacy in general. Through most of their history, comics have been seen as distractions from "real" reading and learning. In the late twentieth and early twenty-first centuries, however, many teachers and librarians came to see educational promise in comics as a new way to enrich student literacy.

Introduction

The comics medium was immediately popular with children as well as adults. The full-color strips of the early twentieth century, such as Richard F. Outcault's *Yellow Kid* or *Hogan's Alley*, were born of a fierce competition among newspapers seeking to attract wider audiences. The early strips acted as lures for those with limited English literacy, which at the time was a significant population. However, the strips soon found wide appeal across social classes, diverse cultures, and gender lines and became permanent and popular fixtures in newspapers.

Despite the popular success of comics, the new art form's contentious history was vividly illustrated from the start. In a time when one-tenth of the population was totally illiterate, comics could connect and communicate without prejudice. However, by providing accessibility, comics also provoked great dread: People wondered how the art form would affect literacy and how the captivating, full-color stories would affect a person's ability to read pictureless text. For most of their popular history, comics were seen as distractions that dulled the wits of readers, and their popularity pointed toward widespread illiteracy.

With the rise of graphic novels since the 1980's, however, an expanding group of parents, tutors, teachers, professors, and librarians have questioned the widely accepted view of comics and have seen comics as a boon to reading. While graphic novels have re-

ceived literary praise and considerable positive attention from literacy and education experts, they are still plagued by the same doubts and fears that met *The Yellow Kid*. As graphic novels move from the fringe and into libraries and classrooms, the debate about whether comics present peril or promise for reading still rages.

Who Reads Graphic Novels?

In the United States, comic books and graphic novels are still widely perceived as most appropriate for preteen and young-adult boys. This is not because the graphic novel form is inherently more appealing to this gender and age group. Rather, the American public's narrow perception of the intended audience of graphic novels owes itself largely to the work of psychiatrist Fredric Wertham and his 1954 anticomics manifesto, *Seduction of the Innocent*.

In the late 1940's and early 1950's, Wertham led a charge against comics with mature themes and images, a public assault that ended in a hearing before the Senate and, subsequently, the 1954 creation of the Comics Code Authority (CCA), which censored comic books. No mainstream comic books could be published without the approval of the CCA. As a result of the CCA, American comic books became juvenile. For decades, the primary comics readers were juvenile, preteen, and young-adult boys and men, an audience publishers and distributors focused on vigorously.

Since the late 1980's, the graphic novel readership has broadened from an audience of young men to one that is diverse and mainstream. While young men are still the dominant readers of comic books, young women have become an important segment of the readership. Manga, an enormous segment of the American comics market, draws far more female than male readers.

American publishers such as DC Comics have responded to this trend, distributing more content for young women. More broadly, mainstream book publishers such as Random House and Norton are publishing and promoting graphic novels, and bookstores have entire sections devoted to them. Graphic novels can be found and read by anyone.

Can Graphic Novels Cause Illiteracy?

Since their introduction in Sunday newspapers, comics have been accused of making readers (especially children) illiterate. This criticism was especially harsh as comic books became a primary form of entertainment for children in the late 1930's and early 1940's. Beyond causing "juvenile delinquency," Wertham asserted that comic books were a primary cause of the increasing number of children who had reading troubles.

Comic strips and comic books are seen as inferior reading material because of both form and content.

Young man reading a Japanese comic book in a store in Kyoto, Japan. Home to the flourishing manga publishing industry, Japan also has one of the highest literacy rates in the world. (David Clapp)

First, the form allows readers to use visual cues to make sense of the text. Thus, readers can "read" a comic without actually reading or understanding any words. It has been argued that this form, by its nature, diminishes readers' abilities to read print text. Second, the content itself is perceived as juvenile and thus, even when understood, is considered to provide the reading equivalent of junk-food calories.

Like comic strips and comic books, graphic novels are widely seen as inferior reading materials and are believed to contribute to reading disabilities. In 2010, Ben Bova, a prolific science-fiction writer, argued that graphic novels are inherently shallow and by their nature cannot explore the depth of thought that a print novel can. In essence, he argued that the form limits the quality of the content. To Bova, graphic novels represent part of a march toward an increasingly illiterate society—the same claim made by newspaper readers one hundred years before and by Wertham sixty years earlier.

The Gateway Drug (to Reading)

While Wertham claimed comics were a gateway to illiteracy, since the 1990's, an expanding group of librarians, reading scholars, and English instructors have described comics as a gateway that leads students toward reading rather than from it. Many librarians and teachers believe graphic novels are a means of engaging reluctant or resistant readers.

In the early 1990's, graphic novels did not have their own category in libraries or their own collection areas. As graphic novels and manga have gained legitimacy and popularity, librarians have taken notice and have started to make a home for them on the shelves. Librarians have noted that when available, graphic novels circulate in high numbers. Just as publishers used comic strips to attract a wider audience to their newspapers at the beginning of the twentieth century, librarians have used graphic novels to attract juveniles, preteens, and young adults to the library.

Some have argued that graphic novels lure a wider audience to the library, especially those who otherwise would avoid it. Once in the library, these readers become more comfortable there and ultimately come to use the library for noncomics purposes such as research and finding print books to read. In this way, graphic novels act as a gateway to the library, a means to engage the patron, and a way to encourage them to develop further literacy practices.

Educators, especially English teachers, see graphic novels as a means to lure reluctant readers into print books. They argue that young-adult readers can more easily relate to the themes in young-adult graphic novels, and in a visual-oriented culture, the images in graphic novels can act as a bridge to the world of books. They hope that by reaching out to their students' interests and to their visual way of learning as well as by making reading "fun," they can encourage students to connect with books and become more motivated to read in general.

Classrooms Illustrated

In the days of Wertham, comic books were something to be smuggled into classrooms inside "real" books. In later decades, they have increasingly become textbooks themselves; graphic novels, manga, and comics in general have entered classrooms at all levels, from kindergarten through college. Educational publishers have responded to this trend, publishing textbooks in "graphic novel" formats and including excerpts of graphic novels in print literature anthologies.

Beyond motivating students, many educators use graphic novels because they find them especially accessible for students learning to read in English or struggling with learning or reading disabilities. For example, teachers provide graphic novel adaptations of famous texts—such as the *Classics Illustrated* series, which provides illustrated versions of William Shakespeare's plays and Charles Dickens's novels, among other works. The students may read the graphic novel version instead of the print text, or they may read it in accompaniment with the text, as a support. In either case, graphic novels provide

a bridge to more challenging print-based reading, and students will ultimately leave the pictures behind as they advance in skill.

Other educators argue that reading comics is not a bridge to a superior print literacy but an end in itself. The theory of New Literacy claims that in a multimedia world, literacy involves the ability not only to read print but also to read words and images together. Thus, graphic novels provide an ideal media for teaching students to read and think critically in the digital era, in

Maus: A Survivor's Tale. (Courtesy of Pantheon Books)

which most of the texts they encounter on a daily basis will be closer to comics than print text.

The Graphic Novel as Literature

As graphic novels have gained greater literary acclaim, they have increasingly become part of the curriculum in general high school and middle school education. Educators treat graphic texts such as Art Spiegelman's Pulitzer Prize-winning Holocaust narrative *Maus* (1986, 1991) as works of literature to be studied, with literary devices to be explored and significance to be explained in academic essays and similar assignments.

Graphic novels are also finding a place in higher education. Anthologies of literature and first-year composition readers include graphic literature, and professors assign graphic novels such as *Maus* in English and other humanities courses. There is also an increasing number of literature courses at the community-college and university levels focused solely on graphic novels. Further, scholars present and publish articles on graphic novels, and there is a small body of book-length scholarly criticism.

Comics are not part of the mainstream educational experience for most students or a serious part of teacher education. Many educators will not use graphic novels in the classroom on the grounds that they are not "real literature" and, as such, represent a dilution of the curriculum. Further, research into comics and literacy is still in its infancy, with little knowledge to definitively settle the debate and demonstrate conclusively the value that comics have for education.

Impact

The early twenty-first century has been a pivotal moment in the history of comics, which have been a popular, though often maligned, literary form. Graphic novels have increased comics' visibility, bringing stronger sales and a broader, more diverse audience to the art form. Ironically, it the success of graphic novels that has in part undermined its legitimacy: The explosion of big-budget Hollywood films based on comics—such as *Iron Man* (2008) and *Thor* (2011)—appears to reinforce the prejudice that comics are purely popular culture, more entertaining, action-packed distractions than human expressions worth study, analysis, and serious consideration. Thus, public opinion is generally that graphic novels and comics are, as they were considered to be at the beginning of the twentieth century, juvenile entertainment. At the same time, graphic novels have found their way into more and more libraries and classrooms, an idea all but unthinkable in the days of *Yellow Kid*.

As Wertham's long shadow fades, graphic novels may play a significant role in twenty-first century American education and subsequently raise a generation of students who see comics not as a debased form of reading but as a legitimate art form worthy of appreciation. Ultimately, given comics' tumultuous history with literacy and how prone education is to fads, it is unclear what impact schools will have on graphic novels, what impact graphic novels will have on schools, and how both, together, will affect the face of literacy.

Adam Bessie

Bibliography

Cary, Stephen. *Going Graphic: Comics at Work in the Multilingual Classroom*. Portsmouth, N.H.: Heinemann, 2004. Looks at practical ways to integrate comics into a classroom with second-language learners, providing examples of classroom activities and samples of various graphic novels.

Hadju, David. *The Ten Cent Plague: Great Comic Book Scare and How It Changed America*. New York: Farrar, Straus and Giroux, 2008. Chronicles the history of comics, focusing in particular on the controversies of the 1950's, and includes key insights about how comics have come to be viewed as a debased art form.

Wolk, Douglas. *Reading Comics: How Graphic Novels Work and What They Mean*. Cambridge, Mass.: Da Capo Press, 2007. Provides a scholarly critique of acclaimed graphic novels, focusing on works from a range of eras and subgenres.

ONLINE GRAPHIC NOVELS: BOUNDLESS BEGINNINGS

Definition

Online graphic novels, or Web comics, refers to any graphic narrative that is created with computer-based technologies and distributed on the Internet. Web comics may incorporate animation, sound, or other media that are otherwise inaccessible to print comics, as long as the basic design of the online graphic novel still represents that of its print relatives. Print comics that have been copied to CD-ROMs or related devices are not considered online graphic novels.

Introduction

The comics medium has always relied heavily on its capacity for hybridity. Able to blend written text seamlessly with pictures, comics have engraved themselves on the global literary scene in a way that print, film, radio, and countless other media could never accomplish. The innovation of Web comics at the beginning of the twenty-first century has continued comics' tradition of combining forms by taking the familiar graphic novel design seen in print since the 1930's and using modern computer and Internet technologies to reinvent the potential of comics. For the first time, comics artists are able to experiment with animation, music, and interconnectivity in a way that print comics never could.

Print Comics vs. Web Comics

Famous graphic novelist Will Eisner defined comics as "sequential art." Comics scholar Scott McCloud devoted his graphic novel *Understanding Comics* (1993) to the expansion of that definition to "juxtaposed pictorial and other images in deliberate sequence." McCloud proposed that comics are created by physically placing images next to each other to construct a narrative. However, when a graphic novel is created on the Internet, this idea of juxtaposing pictorial images can become easily lost. When Web comics artists tell their graphic narratives one panel at a time, with links moving the reader from panel to panel, the physical juxtaposition of the images no longer applies.

Not all Web comics abandon the familiar print comics design. In fact, most adhere to the conventions of the printed graphic novel genre. However, the idea that Web comics are not bound to this familiar design suggests that while Web comics and print comics are similar art forms with a common history, Web comics have begun to establish themselves as a unique medium. As Web comics continue to separate themselves from the print world and their true potential continues to be explored, a new definition applicable only to Web comics will emerge and help distinguish them from their print ancestors.

Because they are online, Web comics enjoy the benefit of real-time feedback from their audience. Online graphic novelists often use forums, blogs, and social networking sites to connect directly with their audience and obtain feedback instantaneously upon the publication of each Web comic they create. In addition, the Internet has freed online graphic novelists from the restrictions of print. They are no longer bound by page count; their stories can be as long or short as they need to be. Creators are also free to utilize music, sound effects, and "sprites," two-dimensional figures animated against a two-dimensional background, to bring their work to life.

The Internet has broadened the audience for and increased accessibility to print comics as well. However, this increased accessibility to print comics does not fall under the realm of online graphic novels.

History

The idea of using computers as an artistic tool goes back to the computing industry's beginnings, when computers could do little more than calculate mathematical equations and send short textual messages and code between connected terminals. As the computer evolved and developed an ability to see, create, and edit pictures, its artistic potential has risen exponentially.

In the years before the Internet became readily available, comics began to break into the new digital market. Comics publishers used CD-ROMs to make their product available to consumers who were interested in reading comics but swept up in the computer

Web comic artist Michael Terracciano, creator of *Dominic Deegan: Oracle for Hire,* does his illustrations from his apartment and updates the online comic at 3:00 A.M. each day. (*Boston Globe* via Getty Images)

industry. However, the online graphic novel was not born until the dawn of the twenty-first century.

In their early days, Web comics faced several limitations to their production and distribution. Even after artists were given a means of drawing pictures and having them immediately read by a computer, they were still hindered by slow Internet connections, which made downloading Web comics a lengthy and frustrating process for potential readers. Also, early computer monitors had an extremely low resolution, as they were intended to either read text or see pictures but were not ideal for doing both simultaneously. As Internet technologies continue to evolve, with higher resolution monitors, high-speed Internet connections, and new software programs constantly working to revolutionize how users interact online, comics artists are finding a broader audience, who may have previously been unexposed to the comics art form.

Production

Print comics have been the victims of business throughout their entire existence. When comic books were created in the 1930's, the medium was not considered artistic or literary. Artists were paid to create hu-

morous, patriotic, inspirational, or controversial graphic narratives, but they did not necessarily consider their work to be legitimate expressions of their imaginations. In time, they began creating graphic novels of greater thematic and artistic sophistication. However, as the artistic possibilities of the comics form were explored, the business aspect of the industry remained as omnipotent and omnipresent in the process as ever.

In addition to innovative technologies that simplify the act of creating and sharing comics online, e-commerce has enabled comics artists to monetize their own work. Furthermore, they can do so without interference from the publishing companies that had controlled every aspect of the industry. Now, artists can create the content they envision and charge the average consumer what they consider a fair price. By cutting out the expenses of publishing and distributing hard copies of graphic novels, the artists are able not only to maintain artistic integrity in their work but also to receive a much higher percentage of the revenue their comics generate. However, this has not proven to be the most profitable avenue for Web comics artists to follow. Much like the underground comics movement of the 1960's, Web comics are unrestricted in terms of their content. Profanity, sexually explicit images, and gratuitous violence are common in the medium. This tends to limit Web comics' appeal to a more specific audience. Ultimately, the market will decide how successful these independent self-publishing comics artists will be.

Another area in which Web comics have an advantage over print texts is their capacity to teach young students about any of a seemingly infinite spectrum of topics. Increasingly, students are using computers and the Internet as invaluable teaching tools, and Web comics are proving to be an ideal bridge between an entertaining medium with which students are at least somewhat familiar and the educational atmosphere of a school setting. Therefore, reading comics online about a historical narrative, a scientific experiment, or other subjects relevant to their studies is proving to be an effective way to help students understand and retain knowledge in school.

Impact

Print comics have found a variety of different purposes during their relatively short existence. Created exclusively to tell fictional stories to young readers, comics have spread into countless subgenres, including memoir and nonfictional narratives, educational texts, analytical texts, and even airplane safety diagrams demonstrating the proper procedure for putting on an oxygen mask. The new genre of Web comics has begun to follow suit. The breadth of Web comics' content is quickly becoming as vast as that of print comics or any print medium.

Joseph Sanders

Bibliography

Fenty, Sean, Trena Houp, and Laurie Taylor. "Web Comics: The Influence and Continuation of the Comix Revolution." *ImageText* 1, no. 2 (Winter, 2005). http://www.english.ufl.edu/imagetext/archives/v1_2/group/index.shtml. In-depth comparison between the Web comics uprising and the underground comics revolution of the 1960's. Focuses mostly on the content created during both comics movements.

Kratina, Al. "Internet Liberates Comic Book Artists." The (Montreal) Gazette, November 14, 2008, E1. Examines the potential of Web comics to generate revenue outside of the typical publishing environment in which comics have traditionally existed.

Lamb, Annette, and Larry Johnson. "Graphic Novels, Digital Comics, and Technology-Enhanced Learning." *Teacher Librarian* 36, no. 5 (June, 2009): 70-75. Looks at graphic novels and Web comics written for young audiences as a form of both entertainment and education.

McCloud, Scott. *Reinventing Comics*. New York: Perennial, 2000. Provides an in-depth look at various "revolutions" within the comics industry, including the creation and distribution of digital comics. Analyzes Web comics as a continuation of the broader comics genre.

Meskin, Aaron. "Comics as Literature?" *British Journal of Aesthetics* 49, no. 3 (July, 2009): 219-239. Within a broader debate about whether comics are legitimate literary works, Meskin looks briefly at Web comics and their continued reliance on hybridity, which he argues print comics are built on.

Pornography in Graphic Novels: Criticism and Censorship

Definition

This essay considers the uses of sexuality, the erotic, and the pornographic in graphic novels since the 1920's. Under discussion are the shifting definitions of erotica and pornography, readership, and historical and social changes in moral values in the United States. Censorship and responses to it are also covered.

Introduction

Pornography's appearance in comics formats arguably enhanced the potential for the creation of graphic novels. Soldiers returning to the United States at the end of World War I had been introduced to risqué comics and sexually explicit artwork from Europe. In France, a series of men's magazines that frequently contained bawdy cartoons or pinups were available.

Beginning in the 1920's, a new magazine format emerged, often sold illicitly in bars, popularly called Tijuana bibles (though they were neither from Mexico nor religious in nature). These books were crudely drawn and written, only six to eight pages, and small in size (frequently 3 inches by 2 inches), although a number of them ran to sixteen or thirty pages of varying sizes. They sold for between two and five dollars, expensive compared to comic books for children, which sold for five cents.

The Tijuana bibles featured comic-strip characters, movie stars, and other popular celebrities. Readers could be certain that by the end of the strip, the participating characters would be publicly caught in an embarrassing sexual situation. This made the sexual horseplay in the books at once titillating and innocently humorous.

The rise of men's magazines in the 1950's, particularly Hugh Hefner's *Playboy* (first published in 1953), provided a new outlet for erotic comic strips that were frequently reproduced as graphic novels. From *Playboy* came Harvey Kurtzman and Will Elder's *Little Annie Fanny* (1962-1968), an always naïve, voluptuous character placed in unwanted sexual situations. Because of both the humor and the fact that Annie never actually en-

Gemma Bovery (1999) reimagines Gustave Flaubert's *Madame Bovary* (1857; English translation, 1886), a novel often banned or censored because of the main character's willingness to live out her fantasies. (Courtesy of Pantheon Books)

gaged in sex, the strip's creators labeled it as satire. Since the strips were often sequential, they were collected and published in a graphic novel format by *Playboy*.

Other magazines followed suit, notably *Evergreen Review*, a 1960's popular culture and news magazine for young adults that published the English translation of Frenchman Jean-Claude Forest's *Barbarella*, a science-fiction work for adults. The monthly serialization was collected into a graphic novel and published initially by Evergreen Press when it was made into a successful film starring Jane Fonda. Like *Little Annie*

Fanny, the series contained nudity but no explicit sex. Evergreen's production paved the way for adult comics magazines such as *Heavy Metal*.

The Comics Code and Underground Comics

During the 1950's, psychiatrist Fredric Wertham published *Seduction of the Innocent*. In his text, he argued that juvenile delinquency was partially motivated by popular culture, including comic books. His argument was aggressively pursued by the U.S. Senate, and after seeing the possibility of government legislation, comic book publishers established the Comics Magazine Association of America (CMAA). The organization established a suborganization named the Comics Code Authority, which established a list of rules in 1954 that comics had to meet in order to receive a seal of approval. Some rules directly addressed sexuality and what might be deemed pornographic, labeling "nudity" and even "suggestive posture" in illustrations as grounds for nonapproval. Women were also supposed to be drawn "without exaggeration of physical qualities."

The Comics Code effectively made comic books primarily entertainment for children. But during the 1960's, in the midst of challenges to traditional thought, the antiwar, Civil Rights, women's, and gay and lesbian movements encouraged a new group of comics creators, self-named "underground," who avoided major publishers and ignored the Comics Code. Through self-publishing or forming small publishing houses, they produced material for a mature audience, dealing with contemporary issues, including sexuality. Publishing sporadically and frequently using the serial format, a number of their works were collected, published, and sold as graphic novels beginning in the 1970's.

The underground comics were partly salable because of the rise of comic book specialty shops, which encouraged comics fans to leisurely peruse a variety of titles, mainstream, underground, and some clearly for older audiences.

Influenced by both the writers and the artists of the 1960's and the increasing ineffectiveness of the Comics Code, writers, artists, and publishers started publishing some comics for mature readers. Many fans with disposable income began to prefer collected stories to serialized stories, which in turn encouraged some publishers to hire artists and writers to produce new, longer works.

Sexuality in the Graphic Novel

The Sexuality Information and Education Council of the United States comments in its statement of purpose, "One cannot, not be sexual." The double negative emphasizes that all humans are sexual, regardless whether they acknowledge their sexuality. As in other forms of art, graphic novels posit sexuality as simply a life experience. Usually, sexual acts are not depicted in the books and are a logical part of the narrative. Sexuality in mainstream graphic novels has become more commonplace, especially since the early 1990's. Marvel Comics, with its MAX imprint, and DC Comics, with its Vertigo imprint, have both published comics and graphic novels that explore sexual themes.

Charles Burn's *Black Hole* (1995-2004) is a semiautobiographical, science-fiction tale of teenagers in the mid-1970's. The characters are obsessed with sex, and a nameless spreading disease mutates teenagers who have unprotected intercourse, creating a parallel with the early attitude toward the AIDS crisis. Craig Thompson's *Blankets* (2003) focuses on what it feels like to sleep next to someone for the first time when one has been raised in a rigid Christian environment and both girlfriend and boyfriend have taken chastity vows.

Depictions of alternative sexual behavior in graphic novels have led to threats of censorship in some parts of the United States. Fantagraphics Books, which originally relied largely on its erotic imprint, Eros Comix, to finance mainstream works, became successful with titles such as *Love and Rockets* (1981-1996), featuring a love affair between the two major female characters. Despite sex scenes, which are integrated subtly and without sensation, the two characters, Maggie and Hopey, have been adopted as positive images by lesbian rights movements.

Gay writer and artist Howard Cruse began creating comics for gay underground magazines and became an award-winning graphic novelist for his semiautobiographical novel, *Stuck Rubber Baby* (1995). The work focuses on growing up in the American South during the 1960's and coming to grips with racism and homosexuality at the same time.

Alison Bechdel's *Dykes to Watch Out For* (1983-2008) is a serialized strip that has been collected into a variety of graphic novel formats. The strip focuses on the stories of a group of mostly lesbian friends. Bechdel is also known for *Fun Home: A Family Tragicomic* (2006). Autobiographical in nature, it was among the first graphic novels to make *The New York Times*' hardcover nonfiction best-seller list.

Eroticism in the Graphic Novel

Eroticism implies that the narrative does not simply integrate sexuality but, rather, that sexuality is the major theme of the novel. These works tend to be graphic and serve to titillate. Frequently, they depend on humor, particularly satire, to tone down their visual effect, though they can be quite serious in nature.

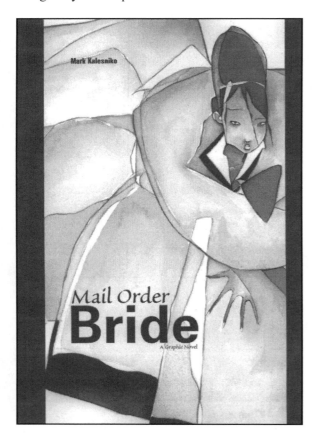

Mail Order Bride. (Courtesy of Fantagraphics Books)

Posy Simmonds's *Gemma Bovery* (1999) reimagines Gustave Flaubert's *Madame Bovary* (1857; English translation, 1886), a novel often banned or censored because of the main character's distaste for her husband and willingness to live out her fantasies. Gemma is a similar character, who is flawed by an inability to distinguish between sex and love. While the novel is funny, it opens in tragedy: The main character has been dead for three weeks, almost as if Simmonds needs to punish Gemma for her willfulness.

In Pat McGreal, Stephen John Phillips, and Jose Villarrubia's *Veils* (1999), a Victorian Englishwoman is transported to an Arabian country by her domineering husband and becomes aware of her sexuality in the company of a sultan's concubines. In *Mail Order Bride* (2001), by Mark Kalesniko, a Canadian husband runs awry of his Korean wife, whom he has "ordered" from a pornography catalog, and is disappointed because she is quite virginal, save when she is alone with another woman.

A graphic novel that is often the subject of legal cases involving pornography in comics is *Omaha the Cat Dancer* (1984-1995, 2006-   ), a soap opera by Kate Worley, Reed Waller, and James Vance. The main character, Omaha, is a stripper. It seems what provokes the most negative criticism is that the protagonist is also a cat. In fact, all of the characters are anthropomorphic but, at the same time, are anatomically human, which has caused critics to label the series pornographic because of perceived bestiality.

Pornography and "Pornographies" in Graphic Novels

Debate over what is considered pornography in graphic novels exists, but artist Robert Crumb, for example, diverts the issue by saying, "It's only lines on paper, folks." This is certainly less elaborate than writer Alan Moore's argument, in response to criticism of his and Melinda Gebbie's novel *Lost Girls* (1991-1992), that "pornographies" are "our secret gardens where seductive paths of words and images lead us to the wide, blinding gateway of our pleasure, beyond which things may only be expressed in a language that is beyond literature, beyond all words." Crumb's and Moore's definitions of pornography suggest that identifying graphic novels as pornographic is a deliberate attempt to tease the imagination to enter these "secret gardens," though to some these "gardens" may appear as dark and deserted alleyways.

Robert Crumb's *My Troubles with Women* (1992) focuses on semiautobiographical episodes as a stereotypically nerdy weakling dealing with the women around him. These women are always perceived as extremely sexual and voluptuous, though usually dominated. They are more than willing to do his sexual bidding, and he is quite varied in his requests. This has caused his work to be labeled as misogynistic, though Crumb seems to be making fun of himself and his fantasies more than of women.

Lost Girls harks back to Sir James Barrie's Victorian play and novel *Peter Pan: Or, The Boy Who Wouldn't Grow Up* (pr. 1904, pb. 1928). Barrie thought of men as boys who fight against growing up and who use women as mother figures. The ultimate mother figure in *Peter Pan* is Wendy, who shows up in *Lost Girls* along with Alice from Lewis Carroll's *Alice's Adventures in Wonderland* (1865) and Dorothy from Frank Baum's *The Wonderful Wizard of Oz* (1900). Meeting in 1913, each character deconstructs the story in which she originally appeared, using her sexual experiences.

Censorship

When the Comics Code was revised in 1971, it focused primarily on curtailing portrayals of rape and "illicit sexual relations," a code term covering premarital, extramarital, and homosexual sex. Despite the loosening and eventually abandonment of the code, pornography and censorship has remained an issue in the comics industry.

In 1986, comics specialty stores came under scrutiny when the manager of a Chicago store was arrested for "possession and sale of obscene materials," mainly a graphic novel from the *Omaha the Cat Dancer* series. The publisher of the series, Denis Kitchen of Kitchen Sink Press, organized a fund-raiser to hire a lawyer for the manager of the store. The manager was acquitted on First Amendment grounds. Kitchen used the remaining money from his fund-raiser to establish the Comic Book Legal Defense Fund (CBLDF), which

has argued in numerous cases for freedom of speech in comic strips, books, and graphic novels. Paralleling the work of the CBLDF, Bechdel works with a number of lesbian and gay writers and artists to secure money for those sued for the creation, publication, and distribution of lesbian, gay, bisexual, and transsexual comics.

Lost Girls came under immediate criticism for displaying "child pornography," since the women featured are all children in their original texts and detail their experiences from the original texts to their present. In England and the United States, some retailers said they would not stock the book for fear of prosecution. In France, where depicting a nude child in a sexual context is outlawed, the publisher suspended production of the French edition.

Manga

Manga has been the subject of controversy because of depictions of child pornography. *Bunkoban* and *tankōbon* collections have become increasingly popular in English translations released in the United States by companies such as VIZ Media, TOKYOPOP, Fantagraphics' Eros Comix imprint, and even DC Comics' CMX imprint. In the case of manga, the differences in culture and perceptions of sexuality between Western and Eastern cultures must be considered. In Japan, the age of sexual consent is thirteen. There are no sodomy laws, so homosexuality was never outlawed. Child pornography was only outlawed in 1999, as the Japanese culture became increasingly acculturated to Western moral philosophy. In 1999, the first ruling affecting graphic depictions of sexuality in comics was put in place: Article 175 of the Japanese penal code prohibits the depiction of explicit sexual intercourse and adult genitalia in comics.

Testing the law, many artists and writers continued to convey such depictions, but upon turning them into their publishers, found their work redrawn, blocked out by pixilation, covered by representational visuals, or simply erased. This led to the creation of *lolicon*, a genre featuring nude children (by drawing younger, cuter-looking characters, Article 175 could be subverted). Graphic novels such as Kaworu Watashiya's *Kodomo no jikan* (2005-   ;

Nymphet, English publication canceled) is representative of this subgenre.

In addition, manga has subgenres known as *shōnen-ai* and *yaoi*, both written by women for predominantly female readers but featuring gay characters. *Shōnen-ai* tends to be more literary, similar to the soft-core sexuality found in a typical Western romance novel, and geared toward an audience of adolescent girls. An example of *shōnen-ai* is Akimi Yoshida's *Banana Fish* (1985-1994).

Yaoi, produced for an audience of women, is more sexually explicit, though historical and social issues are often incorporated. The gay Japanese artist and writer Tagame Gengoroh published *Kimi yo shiru ya minami no goku* (2007; do you remember the south island's POW camp?), a *yaoi* manga focusing on events in a Japanese prisoner-of-war camp run by the United States during World War II. Both *shōnen-ai* and *yaoi* also attract bisexual and homosexual male readers.

Impact

Sexuality, erotica, and pornography have existed in the arts of every culture from primitive times. Readers' interest in erotic comic strips and book formats encouraged the collection of completed series. Though sexuality is more widely depicted than it was in the past, sexual mores still challenge the placement of some graphic novels in bookstores, libraries, and classrooms. As more erotic and pornographic literature is published in graphic novel format, various types of censorship issues, particularly corporate and legal, come to the fore, especially concerning distribution to age-appropriate audiences.

The use of sexuality, erotica, and pornography has made comics more appealing to an adult audience. It has refreshed the field by allowing the coexistence of superheroes and funny animals with story lines based on more realistic human experiences and desires.

Modern adult graphic novels have certainly shown themselves to be literary and artistic, not at all like Tijuana bibles. Attempts at censorship in the United States have caused the demise of the Comics Code Authority and brought about organizations such as the CBLDF, fighting to maintain First Amendment rights.

A growing concern that will create censorship challenges are erotic and pornographic comics that appear online before they are released in graphic novel form. The Internet is a nebulous space and difficult to censor. When these comics begin to appear in print, they are likely to face censorship from a variety of sources.

Terry Joseph Cole

Bibliography

Gravett, Paul. *Graphic Novels: Stories to Change Your Life*. London: Aurum, 2005. Superior introductory survey of graphic novels that opens with a discussion of the differences between graphic novels and comic books and a rationale for why these texts should appeal to readers who do not read comic books. Gives clues for how to read graphic novels. Examines thirty novels in detail.

Pilchner, Tim. *Erotic Comics: A Graphic History from Tijuana Bibles to Underground Comix*. New York: Abrams, 2008. Uses graphics and text to give a history of erotica in comics from the 1920's to the late 1960's. Foreword discusses what makes a work erotic. Surveys a variety of subsections, including women artists, bondage and fetishism in art, and the rise of the Comics Code.

_____. *Erotic Comics 2: A Graphic History from the Liberated '70's to the Internet*. New York: Abrams, 2008. Excellent use of graphics and comics history. Explores censorship issues, the creation of writer and artist organizations to fight censorship, and issues that may create challenges to censorship in future.

A POSTMODERN ART FORM: GRAPHIC NOVELS AS POSTMODERN "TEXTS"

Definition

Postmodernism and postmodern theories of art can shed light on the medium of graphic novels and its importance. In general, the medium relies on two art forms—textual writing and the visual arts—and the combination of these two traditionally separate arts is a performance of postmodern theories that value the deconstruction of their differences.

Introduction

According to literary theorist Jean-François Lyotard, writing in *Condition postmoderne: Rapport sur le savoir* (1979; *The Postmodern Condition: A Report on Knowledge*, 1984), the postmodern act of writing takes place when "the artist and the writer . . . are working without rules in order to formulate the rules of what *will have been done*" according to "the paradox of the future (*post*) anterior (*modo*)." As it relates to the graphic novel, this paradox takes place as the deconstruction of the divisions between the writing and visual arts, as they are used without concern for the rules associated with each in order to formulate a new art form. The graphic novel is best reflected in terms of this postmodern writing since the division between someone who composes texts and someone who composes works of art is eliminated as the two forms are combined—two of the most notable practitioners of this combined art form are Art Spiegelman and Chris Ware.

One of the most misunderstood concepts surrounding postmodernism is that it moves past the modern with the assumption that (theoretical) modernism has nothing left to offer; however, as Lyotard's definition suggests, postmodern writers compose without regard to established theories of textual composition or art criticism. Comics theorist Scott McCloud's exploration of the art form suggests that comics and graphic novels have always been postmodern despite attempts to define each as a fixed medium; he claims that defining comics is an ongoing process. While McCloud has been critiqued for his

Notable works originating in the alternative comics movement include Craig Thompson's *Blankets* (2003). (Courtesy of Top Shelf Productions)

seemingly simplistic understanding of comics, it is precisely this view that not only allows graphic novels to be viewed as postmodern but also opens the medium to new and inventive ways of composing with image and text.

The juxtaposition of McCloud's view of comics as an art form that continues to defy any fixed definition and Lyotard's description of the postmodern writer as someone who works to formulate new rules of composing (in this case, graphic novels) proposes that comics and graphic novels are essentially postmodern texts that can teach the reader ways of reading and writing in a postmodern age. Moreover, these new ways of writing are worked out apart from any distinct field of study, which is seen in Ware's explanation of the general comics artist as someone who is a trained artist but who does feel at home in the prescribed industry. To think of graphic novels in this way would be to think of them in terms of a postmodern art form interested in formulating new methods of thinking and composing without regard for any previously established rules of writing or art.

Alternative Comics

The term "alternative comics" generally refers to comics and graphic novels that diverge from the mainstream superhero comics that have dominated the industry. Often experimental, alternative comics take on a wide range of genres and artistic styles that are uncharacteristic of traditional approaches to and understandings of the genre.

One of most important alternative comics anthologies was *RAW*, a magazine started by Spiegelman and Françoise Mouly. In *Alternative Comics: An Emerging Literature* (2005), critic Charles Hatfield claims that alternative comics were an outgrowth of the underground comics movement of the 1960's. While claiming that there is a direct correlation between the rise of postmodernism and the alternative comics movement would be problematic, the approach to composing comics in this movement parallels many of the same sentiments and methods usually proposed by postmodern theorists (namely, exploration rather than illustration). However, the alternative comics movement has tended to focus on content (genre and aesthetic style) rather than on form. Notable works originating in the alternative comics movement include Dave Sim's *Cerebus* (1977-2004), Jeff Smith's *Bone* (1991-2004), and Craig Thompson's *Blankets* (2003).

One alternative comics artist who has pushed the form of comics further into postmodernism is Ware. His graphic novel *Jimmy Corrigan, The Smartest Kid on Earth* (1993-2000) features a design that parallels the fragmented narrative of the main character. While alternative comics have historically tended to address the traditional content of the medium, the next iteration of alternative comics, as

Ware's work suggests, will experiment with the formal elements of the medium.

Exceeding the System of Comics

When proposing that comics are a postmodern art form, thinking in terms of systems becomes counterproductive. In *The System of Comics* (2007), theorist Thierry Groensteen proposes that for a work to be a comic book or graphic novel, its composition must follow a "spatio-topical" system (broadly defined), but this is precisely what postmodernism seeks to break apart. One reason for exceeding this way of thinking is that systems only allow for a certain number of possibilities. The system that Groensteen looks to affirm is one that "defines an ideal"; a postmodern perspective would be wary of any claims to ideal forms.

To exceed Groensteen's systematic approach and the sequential history of comics that McCloud describes is to think of comics as an art form that has consistently enacted the sort of work that other artists and art movements have been moving toward—particularly, breaking the division between life and art. In finding new ways of composing comics from a postmodern perspective, the systems of comics will give way to innovative forms of composing with images and text. As postmodern "texts," comics present an art form that has little concern for the formal and aesthetic qualities required of other arts. As such, any systematic approach to graphic novels, at least from a postmodern perspective, would contradict the historical importance of the medium.

Impact

The effects of postmodern theories on the graphic novel medium are varied. Since the development of the alternative comics movement during the 1980's, postmodern theories have greatly influenced the significant area of study that deals with the form of comics, asking whether graphic novels must be cohesive narratives or if there are other ways of thinking about their composition.

While contemporary perspectives on the graphic novel continue to adhere to its definition as "sequential art," some of the medium's most popular artists have started to experiment with the form, commenting on the form through the stories they create. For example, in *Promethea: Book 5* (2005), Alan Moore suggests that comics stimulate imagination by combining words

Cerebus, considered part of the alternative comics movement, focuses more on content than form.. (Courtesy of Aardvark-Vanheim)

and images. In part, one of the impacts of postmodernism on the graphic novel is the invention of the medium as an art form interested in exploring new ways of composing the experiences of life rather than commenting on art, which has led artists to begin composing comics as if the previously established rules are only guidelines.

By returning to the basic principles of combining images and words or composing narratives through images alone, comics artists influenced by postmodern theories seem to be attempting to reframe the medium as an art form. The difference between a medium and an art form, in this example, has to do with the ways in which the works are composed: A medium adheres to the systems and rules established through years of practice, whereas an art form continually explores new ways of composing works of art. Overall, postmodernism may be one of the key factors in the resurgence of interest in the graphic novel.

Sergio C. Figueiredo

Bibliography

Ellis, Warren. *Do Anything: Thoughts on Comics and Things*. Rantoul, Ill.: Avatar Press, 2010. Explores an alternative history of comics from a postmodern perspective and discusses the comics medium as one open for experimentation.

Lyotard, Jean-François. *The Postmodern Condition: A Report on Knowledge*. Translated by Geoff Bennington and Brian Massumi. Minneapolis: University of Minnesota Press, 1984. Articulates postmodernism in a way that contributes to the understanding of graphic novels as works of art that adhere to the postmodern theory of working without a set of boundaries.

McCloud, Scott. *Understanding Comics: The Invisible Art*. New York: HarperCollins, 1994. Provides information about historical contributions to contemporary understandings of comics and graphic novels and suggests that comics are open to the creation of new meanings through postmodern approaches to writing and art.

Molotiu, Andrei, ed. *Abstract Comics*. Seattle: Fantagraphics Books, 2009. Offers examples of postmodern comics, including works by Robert Crumb and those influenced by the work of artists such as Marcel Duchamp and Jackson Pollock.

Moore, Alan. *Alan Moore's Writing for Comics*. Rantoul, Ill.: Avatar Press, 2007. Critiques the comparison of comics with cinema and cinematic techniques and proposes some ways of breaking away from this comparison to move comics into new and interesting unexplored domains.

Spiegelman, Art, and R. Sikoryak. *The Narrative Corpse: A Chain-Story by Sixty-Nine Artists!* Richmond, Va.: RAW Books, 1995. Serves as an example of a postmodern work created by sixty-nine comics artists, including influential figures such as Daniel Clowes, Crumb, Will Eisner, McCloud, and Ware.

Ware, Chris. *The ACME Novelty Library*. New York: Pantheon, 2005. Examines and critiques traditional comics from a Marxist perspective and inserts a design structure that breaks the sequentiality that both Eisner and McCloud suggest is at the heart of the medium.

PROPAGANDA IN GRAPHIC NOVELS: SEX, WAR, AND POLITICS!

Definition

Propaganda is a form of communication that aims to influence a specific group to think in a certain way. Through techniques such as omitting certain facts, putting a deliberate spin on a message, and aiming for an emotional rather than a rational response, propaganda is expected either to change an audience's attitudes or to amplify ideas with which it already agrees.

Introduction

Though perhaps unexpected, the combination of propaganda and graphic novels is a rather common amalgam. Propaganda was once a neutral term, until the Nazis and leaders of the Russian Soviet state used propaganda during World War II to "sell" the ideas of fascism and communism, respectively, imbuing the word with a negative connotation.

Comics are naturally fit for propaganda because they catch the eye and keep readers enthralled. Speech balloons, captions, and onomatopoetic words give life and meaning to still images. Also, two or more images form a sequence, leading readers' eyes across the paper. Furthermore, the iconographic way in which many comics display images is inherent in the way one views the world and, thus, speaks directly to the readers.

Propaganda is abundant in graphic novels, especially if the scope is not limited to the negative interpretation of the term. Many graphic novels try to transmit ideas to readers, good or bad, and this includes comics used to promote more "wholesome" ideas and not just easily condemned comics that try to persuade readers to do or think things that most people would deem unacceptable.

Religious Propaganda in Graphic Novels

There are many examples of outright religious propaganda in comics, and throughout the years, a number of comics have been created to spread the "good word." These comics have been made by those intent on convincing people of the "right" way of thinking and who

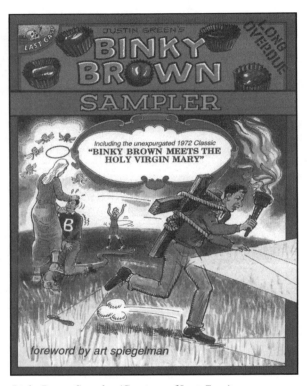

Binky Brown Sampler. (Courtesy of Last Gasp)

are prepared to utilize the accessibility, direct appeal, and impact that comics have.

Most of these comics deem communicating the message more important than how it is communicated. Graphic novels that focus on biblical stories include *Picture Stories from the Bible* (1942-1946), *The Picture Bible* (1979), *The Lion Graphic Bible: The Whole Story from Genesis to Revelation* (2004), and *The Manga Bible: From Genesis to Revelation* (2008). Underground comics legend Robert Crumb produced *The Book of Genesis* (2009), the first in the genre to actually include all the words from the first book of the Bible and not just make an opportunistic selection.

There are also comics that try to communicate negative ideas about religion. One of the earliest was Justin Green's *Binky Brown Meets the Holy Virgin Mary* (1972), later collected in *Binky Brown*

Sampler (1995). In this story, Green experiences neurosis, which he blames on his Catholic upbringing, even though he later finds that his condition is attributable to obsessive-compulsive disorder.

Political Propaganda in Graphic Novels

Comics have been used extensively as a political tool as well. The ways comics have treated the issues varies, though. Some graphic novels deal with political issues but try to give the impression of impartiality. In *The 9/11 Report: A Graphic Adaptation* (2006), Sid Jacobson and Ernie Colón turn the report issued by the 9/11 Committee into an interesting comic. Another example of a political comic book is the European Union's "infotainment" album *Troubled Waters* (2003).

Some graphic novelists are more open about their intentions, as in the case of the collective of Swedish artists who thought that the history books used in school were too biased toward a right-wing interpretation and created a Marxist history book—aptly titled *The History Book* (1974). Other graphic novels that explore political topics include *The Adventures of Tintin: Breaking Free* (1988), an anarchist take on the classic Belgian character; *Brought to Light: A Graphic Docudrama* (1989), in which Alan Moore and others try to make sense of CIA activities in South America; and *In the Shadow of No Towers* (2004), in which Art Spiegelman discusses American politics before and after 9/11.

Some graphic novels intend to entertain but carry political messages just the same. In the French-Belgian tradition, for example, cartoonists have often used parody to discuss politics. *Astérix* (1961-1979; *Asterix*, 1969-1975) is a good example of this technique; the scriptwriter René Goscinny wrote serious contemporary political satire into what was otherwise a humorous adventure comic set in the distant past. In the United States, the superheroes genre is most popular, and it too is rife with political messages. *Civil War* (2006-2007), a major crossover written by Mark Millar, clearly comments on American post-9/11 politics in general and the much-debated Patriot Act in particular.

War Comics

The basic premise of war, with two antagonists who naturally have opposing views, lends itself to stories that are filled with emotions, opinions, and propaganda. Comics dealing with war are often produced by cartoonists who frame stories from their subjective points of view.

There are many ways in which war can be featured in comics: War can be part of another genre (superheroes, fantasy, or historical fiction), used as the setting for dramatic story lines about the fate of people in dreadful times, or used to make a political point. Also, there is the genre of war comics that often depicts the heroism of war, making obvious pro-war statements.

Antiwar graphic novels that make statements against war are not hard to find, however. One of the subtler examples is *When the Wind Blows* (1982), by British creator Raymond Briggs, which depicts an elderly couple experiencing the effects of an atomic war. Another effective antiwar comic book is *Barefoot Gen* (1973–1974, 1975–1987), by Keiji Nakazawa, a ten-volume story about the horrors of the Hiroshima bombing. The most blatantly propagandistic antiwar graphic novel is probably *Addicted to War: Why the U.S. Can't Kick Militarism* (2004), by Joel Andreas.

Racism in Comics

Problematic ideas of race appear in numerous graphic novels and are often used for propagandist purposes. The genre of comics is essentially a narrative art form. To get a readable flow, images are often reduced to iconic simplicity, but in doing so, artists often resort to using stereotypical characteristics of groups of people, many of which are construed as racist.

The most blatant and unsettling racist images can be found in early graphic novels. In early volumes of *Les Aventures de Tintin* (1929-1976; *The Adventures of Tintin*, 1930-1976)—such as *Tintin in the Land of the Soviets* (1930), *Tintin in the Congo* (1931), *Tintin in America* (1932), and *Cigars of the Pharaoh* (1934)—Hergé did scant research about the countries to which he sent his protagonist, and thus, he transmitted many ideas about "the other" from a Belgian perspective to readers all over the world.

Graphic novels have also been used to counter racist images with more positive depictions. One of the best-known examples of this is Spiegelman's *Maus* (1986), in which he tells the story of his father's experience during the Holocaust, transmitting ideas about what actually happened during this time in history as well as of Jews and Jewish culture.

Another important cartoonist who worked to dispel stereotypes was Will Eisner, who made a number of graphic novels showcasing Jewish characters, themes, and culture. Eisner's most propagandist effort, though, was the graphic novel *The Plot: The Secret Story of the Protocols of the Elders of Zion* (2005), in which he set out to disprove a fraudulent anti-Semitic text. Other graphic novels with similar themes or subject matters are *American Born Chinese* (2006) by Gene Luen Yang, *Arab in America* (2008) by Toufic El Rassi, and *Judenhass* (2008) by Dave Sim.

Sex as Propaganda

Examples of how graphic novels are used to reinforce the heterosexual, male-dominated social order abound, existing in almost every graphic novel, at least when read from a gender perspective. However, there are also comics that seek to punctuate the normative model and show alternatives and that often try to convey important messages about sexuality in stories meant to entertain. *The Tale of One Bad Rat* (1995), by British artist Bryan Talbot, tells the story of a young girl's plight in order to convey a message about incest and the need for resilience and self-assertion. *Lost Girls* (2006), by Alan Moore and Melinda Gebbie, uses female characters from classic British and American children's novels to show that human sexuality can be depicted in an explicit but nonpornographic way.

Graphic novels have also been used to convey the experiences of homosexuality. *Stuck Rubber Baby* (1995) by Howard Cruse is set in the American South during the 1960's and tells the story of a man grappling with his homosexuality against a backdrop of the Civil Rights movement. Other examples that include the theme of homosexuality include Alison Bechdel's *The Essential Dykes to Watch Out For* (2008), a soap-opera-like story with almost only homosexual characters, and *Fun Home: A Family Tragicomic* (2006), an

The Tale of One Bad Rat. (Courtesy of Dark Horse)

autobiographical story of reckoning with her own homosexuality and that of her father.

Impact

The urge to convey ideas, thoughts, and opinions to audiences is probably as old as humanity itself and can, in varying degrees, be found in all forms of communication. Finding examples of propaganda in comics is not hard because of the visual nature of the art form. The inherent aestheticism of comics is something that many creators, organizations, and institutions have been aware of and have tried to exploit.

In the modern form of graphic novels, propaganda has been used in numerous ways. The most common is probably a subtle communication of ideas through the way characters are depicted and the stories are told, using both visual and textual elements to convey ideas of how the world is to be interpreted. In many comics, proving a deliberate propagandist intent can be hard, but because of this, their effects can be farther reaching than comics with obvious didactic purposes.

Looking at graphic novels from a historical perspective, stories that have propagandist purposes have become more common as the art form has matured. More artists have embraced the technique, realizing the potential for using it to persuade audiences of their points of view.

Fredrik Strömberg

Bibliography

Conroy, Mike. *War Comics: A Graphic History*. Lewes, England: Ilex Press, 2009. A popular-culture study of American and English comics that contain themes of war. Amplified with a large number of illustrations.

Riches, Adam, Tim Parker, and Robert Frankland. *When the Comics Went to War: Comic Book War Heroes*. Edinburgh, Scotland: Mainstream, 2009. Does not specifically examine war in graphic novels but, rather, in British comics in general. Contains a large number of illustrations.

Strömberg, Fredrik. *Black Images in the Comics: A Visual History*. Seattle: Fantagraphics Books, 2012. An image-heavy history of how black people have been portrayed in comics from all over the world. Introduction by Charles Johnson.

_____. *Comic Art Propaganda: A Graphic History*. New York: St. Martin's Griffin, 2010. A general, popular-culture approach to the subject of propaganda in comics, with a plethora of illustrations.

REVISING SUPERHERO HISTORY: COMICS, CHARACTERS, AND MULTIMEDIA

Definition

Though born in comic books, superheroes have become so ubiquitous in multimedia that encountering superhero imagery seems to be a daily occurrence. The word "superhero" traces back to as early as 1917 as "a public figure of great accomplishments" but gained most prominence when heroes moved from comic books into other popular-culture media.

Introduction

Born from mythology and popular-culture sources such as 1920's pulp fiction, the American superhero carries an extensive lineage. Superhero history falls into the various agreed-upon ages of comics: Stone Age (prior to 1938), Golden Age (1938-1956), Silver Age (1956-1970), Bronze Age (1970-1985), Dark Age (1985-1998), and Modern Age (1998-).

Superhero comics serve as source material for advertisements, films, television, and video games. While comic books remain in publication, mainstream access to superheroes largely comes from multimedia revisions, revamps, and remakes. A notable trend with superheroes is the growing transmedial interconnectedness—that is, the world building that links the printed page with other media. What follows are conflicting narratives of each generation's superheroes and the ability for serious enthusiasts and casual fans to reconcile competing versions of the same characters. For example, Superman of the *Smallville* television series (2001–2011) is not the Superman of the *Young Justice* (2010-) cartoon, the one of *Batman: Brave and the Bold* (2008-) cartoon, or the one seen in many comic books.

Parallel to their growing prominence, superheroes have gone from adult fair to children's medium, from camp plaything to serious film subject, and back again. Thus, the history of superheroes is a shadow history of the United States, providing insight into how cultural points of view shift over time.

The Golden Age

While characters such as Dr. Occult, Lee Falk's the Phantom, the Green Hornet, and the Crimson Avenger all predate Superman's first appearance in 1938, the accepted generic conventions of the superhero first coalesced in Superman, marking the beginning of the Golden Age. Prior to Superman's appearance, prototypical superheroes existed mainly in newspaper strips; Superman was the first to appear in comic books with original material. Following the somewhat surprising success of Superman, the Bat-Man (later simply Batman) debuted in 1939.

The Golden Age included an explosion of superhero characters created to cash in on the success of Superman. These include the first Human Torch, the Sub-Mariner, Captain Marvel, Robin, the Spirit, Plastic Man, Wonder Woman, and Captain America. The rampant production of superhero characters and stories often relied on a formulaic pattern without ongoing story continuity. In essence, the Golden Age was an age of serial contact with largely interchangeable superheroes. Themes guiding superhero stories during this time included dealing with absent, dead, or otherwise lost parents and the need to defend and sustain a sense of positive idealism.

How superheroes maintained positivity changed over time, however. Superheroes battled more gangsters when mobsters headlined the news, and then stories acquired a jingoistic bent with characters battling Nazis during World War II.

Meanwhile, Superman's radio show (1940), cartoon (1941), and live-action serials (1948) plastered the superhero across multimedia formats. The Superman radio show introduced a transmedial aspect by creating Kryptonite as a foil to Superman. The early connection between comics and other media serves as evidence for superheroes carrying cultural appeal behind the page.

The Golden Age ended partly because of changes in distribution methods, the widespread consumption of television, and outcry from psychologist Fredric Wertham. By this point, the comic book industry's self-regulating Comics Code restricted the content in comic books, and all but a few characters (Superman, Batman, and Wonder Woman, most notably) stopped appearing.

The Silver Age

The Silver Age began with the re-conception of the Golden Age character the Flash as a more explicitly science-based hero. The Silver Age responded to the space race and featured many science-fiction-influenced heroes, including the Legion of Super-Heroes, a revised Green Lantern, the Fantastic Four, the Hulk, Spider-Man, Iron Man, and the X-Men.

The age included much of the idealism of the Golden Age but with a growing sense of unease. Significant in this age was the influx of Marvel Comics characters. Unlike DC Comics characters, which generally maintained a lighthearted, almost camp sensibility, Marvel injected psychological realism into its stories, challenging the neat conception of superheroes as superidealized humans. Spider-Man/Peter Parker struggled with everyday problems such as paying rent and dating, just as the Thing of the Fantastic Four wrestled daily with his monstrous appearance. Nonetheless, superheroes remained largely a white male phenomenon.

In a change from the Golden Age, Silver Age stories included situations in which the heroes did not always win or, at the very least, did not escape difficult situations completely unscathed. Late in the Silver Age, continuity took hold in comics and created a rich history of interlocking stories, particularly with the Marvel superheroes. The continuity did not extend to the media representations of superheroes, however; the cartoons and television shows, with their interchangeable episodes, seemed more in line with the Golden Age themes than with those of the Silver Age. Significantly, the highly rated *Batman* live-action television series (1966-1968) debuted in this era and left a lasting impression on American's popular understanding of superheroes. The Silver Age ended in 1970, largely as the result of shifting cultural mores in the United States.

The Bronze Age

The shiny heroes of the Silver Age did not fit with the more pessimistic social climate of the Bronze Age. By this time, the superheroes' luster had faded. Some

The controversial *Batman: A Death in the Family* saw the demise of Jason Todd, the second Robin. (AP Photo)

called this period "the death of comic book innocence," for the Bronze Age included the death of Spider-Man's girlfriend Gwen Stacy and Batman's return to dark avenging detective.

In 1970, DC's space-faring Green Lantern and the left-wing archer Green Arrow teamed up as "Hard-Traveling Heroes" to confront real-world problems such as racism, pollution, and drug abuse. In 1971, the revision of the Comics Code opened the door for the return of horror with new, dark heroes such as Swamp Thing and Ghost Rider.

Major comic book publishers also introduced more minority characters to reflect the diversity of the United States and to capitalize on the blaxploitation and kung fu crazes of the time. Making their debuts were urban-inspired African American characters such as Power

Man/Luke Cage, Black Lighting, and the mutant Storm of the X-Men. The X-Men were revised from white middle-class teenagers to a highly diverse lineup that included the clawed Canadian hero Wolverine. Also, the violent vigilante the Punisher began slaughtering criminals throughout the Marvel Universe in a manner that would prefigure the Dark Age.

Meanwhile, technology advanced, and the potential for special effects grew. Accordingly, superhero projects exploded, including the live-action television series *Shazam!* (1974-1977), *Wonder Woman* (1975-1979), and *The Incredible Hulk* (1978-1982); the cartoons *Spider-Man* (1967-1970) and *Super Friends* (1973-1977); and films such as *Swamp Thing* (1982) and the Superman franchise starring Christopher Reeve, beginning in 1978.

The end of the Bronze Age remains in dispute. While the Golden Age and Silver Age possess more definitive beginnings and endings, the boundaries of the Bronze Age, the Dark Age, and the Modern Age are less firmly established.

The Dark Age

The Dark Age began in the 1980's and was so named for both the shift to "grim and gritty" dark heroes and the rise and fall of comics publishing that occurred in the 1990's. The age is generally characterized by a darkening of heroes and predominance of new antiheroes.

In 1985, DC attempted to reorganize and revise more than forty years of stories with the *Crisis on Infinite Earths* (1985-1986), obliterating its own continuity to various degrees. This event's aftermath included reboots of flagship characters Superman and Wonder Woman.

Another starting point of the age may be Frank Miller's gritty depictions of Batman's future and past in *Batman: The Dark Night* (1986) and *Batman: Year One* (1987). At the same time, independent presses introduced characters such as the Teenage Mutant Ninja Turtles and Miracleman, Alan Moore's critique of superheroes. Moore's further dystopian dismantling of superheroes, *Watchmen* (1986-1987), continued the darkening of superhero comics by deconstructing the social and political utility of character archetypes.

Other aspects of the grim side of superheroes included the crippling and sexual assault of Barbara Gordon/Batgirl in Moore's *Batman: The Killing Joke* (1988) and the controversial *Batman: A Death in the Family* (1988-1989), in which Robin Jason Todd dies, partly because fans voted for his demise. Marvel followed the dark trend with the angst-ridden X-Men, the spin-offs of which became the company's best-selling franchise. Antiheroes, such as the mutant Cable, turn the teenage New Mutants team into a pro-mutant strike force, or X-Force. By 1988, Spider-Man's most significant villain of the age, Venom, brought bitter justice to some and psychopathic serial violence to others.

Following the deconstruction of the genre, superheroes were rebuilt when director Tim Burton revitalized the genre with the 1989 film *Batman*. Drawing popular attention back to comics, the film incited the comic book explosion of the early 1990's. Key to this era were the overspeculation of superhero comic books with stunt story lines like the "Death of Superman" and "Knightfall," with Superman, Batman, and many other highly recognizable DC characters being temporarily replaced by new and often bloodthirsty versions.

At the same time, alternative voices in the superhero genre somewhat destabilized the dominance of the major publishers DC and Marvel. Image Comics, an independent press serving as a confederation of established illustrators, began to publish *Savage Dragon* (1986-), *Spawn* (1992-), and *Witchblade* (1995-). Known for both its style of characters, with bulging muscles and exaggerated breast sizes, and for action-oriented stories, Image wrapped a shiny exterior around its gritty heroes. In reaction to all the brutality in mainstream comics, the tongue-in-cheek *Tick* (1988-1993) appeared as a lighthearted spoof of the superhero genre and comic fans in general.

Milestone Comics began publishing stories with neglected minority characters and story lines with such characters as Static, Hardware, and Xombi. Though their tenure with Milestone was short-lived, the characters, diverse in race and sexual orientation, later entered the mainstream DC Universe.

Perhaps the largest coup in terms of superheroes came from DC's Vertigo imprint. Coinciding with the so-called British invasion of creators, this division moved in a markedly different direction from the big-stunt events of

DC's flagship characters and instead took superheroes in a postmodern direction. Peter Milligan's *Shade the Changing-Man* (1990-1996), Grant Morrison's *Animal Man* (1988-1990) and *Doom Patrol* (1989-1993), and Neil Gaiman's *The Sandman* (1989-1996) transitioned lesser-known Silver Age characters into more mature properties. As these titles moved further away from questions of superheroics, they were collected under the Vertigo Comics umbrella outside of the main DC Universe.

The end of the Dark Age may best be signified by the fall of the Batman film franchise with the Joel Schumacher-directed *Batman and Robin* (1997). Largely lambasted for its camp portrayals and odd, sexualized costumes, the production cast doubt on the success of superhero films until Bryan Singer's *X-Men* (2000).

In the Dark Age, superheroes experienced increased visibility and transformation in other media. The connection between comics and other media continued with the television show *Lois and Clark: The New Adventures of Superman* (1993-1997). Additionally, *Batman: The Animated Series* begat further series within the same animated universe and created a franchise that eventually brought obscure characters mainstream attention.

The Modern/Multimedia Age

Many fans and comics studies scholars offer different opinions in regards to the Modern Age of superheroes, particularly as to whether it exists as its own era or as an extension of the Dark Age or even the Silver Age. The Modern Age may be best understood as the contemporary production in superhero comic books and media.

One point of transition between ages may be September 11, 2001 (9/11), and the comic book industry's response to the terrorist attack. Marvel and DC, as well as numerous independent publishers, produced comics to aid in fund-raising after the terrorist attacks. In the aftermath of 9/11, the superhero has been increasingly questioned and placed in political situations; for example, in *Civil War* (2006-2007), heroes are asked to register with the government in a nod to U.S. Homeland Security initiatives. Superhero narratives have grown increasingly complex, with current story lines making more transparent political statements.

In terms of multimedia, beginning in the 1980's, the video- and computer-game market relied on superheroes as big draws and made superheroes interactive phenomena. Each superhero film or cartoon garnered its own game adaption, thus creating an interactive aspect to superheroes. *Marvel vs. Capcom* and *Mortal Kombat vs. DC Universe* even used existing video-game universes to expand the reach of iconic superheroes. Similarly, multiplayer online role-playing games (MORGs) such as *City of Heroes* (2004) and *DC Universe Online* (2011) create whole worlds and digital social systems for superhero fans. Indeed, the digital realm may be the next big profit center for superheroes and their stories.

Impact

The comic book and graphic novel industry has always been dominated by the superhero genre. Al-

In the aftermath of 9/11, political overtones have become more prominent in superhero comics. In Marvel Comics' *Civil War* event, for example, heroes were asked to register with the government in a nod to Homeland Security initiatives. (Courtesy of Marvel Comics)

though largely still relegated to the puerile morass of popular culture, in reality, superheroes compose a rich tapestry of American history and are big business globally. Superhero history further reveals how the comic books have made use of transmedia, connecting marketing and products long before television and film companies followed suit.

In any medium, the nature of the superhero is one of change, transformation, revision, and redeployment. As American and global cultures change, so do superheroes. Anyone born since the 1930's has been touched by the wide reach of superheroes and their history.

Kane Anderson

Bibliography

Coogan, Peter. *Superhero: The Secret Origin of a Genre*. Austin, Tex.: MonkeyBrain Books, 2006. Seeks to define the superhero as a distinct genre of American entertainment. Addresses how the ages of superhero comic books reflect an introduction, solidification, deconstruction, and reinscription of the genre's components.

Daniels, Les. *Comix: A History of Comic Books in America*. New York: Bonanza Books, 1971. An early contribution to comics studies scholarship. Examines comic books as an artistic medium from a historiographic perspective and considers other roots of modern comics such as horror stories and funny animal books.

Knowles, Christopher. *Our Gods Wear Spandex: The Secret History of Comic Book Heroes*. San Francisco: Weiser Books, 2007. Attempts to establish a link between modern mainstream superhero characters and Western mythologies. While more speculative than scholarly, this text further breaks down superheroes into archetypes such as messiah and wizard.

Levitz, Paul. *Seventy-five Years of DC Comics: The Art of Modern Mythmaking*. Köln: Taschen, 2010. Provides access to decades of history of DC Comics' superhero publications, including rare and full-sized art samples. Breaks down the superhero ages with time lines on foldout pages that highlight the important points in the periods.

Reynolds, Richard. *Super Heroes: A Modern Mythology*. Jackson: University Press of Mississippi, 1994. Examines superheroes as modern myth while paying particular attention to projects such as *Batman: The Dark Knight Returns* and *Watchmen*. Evaluates the artistic value of the graphic novel format versus that of monthly serials.

Wandtke, Terrance R., ed. *The Amazing Transforming Superhero! Essays on the Revision of Characters in Comic Books, Film, and Television*. Jefferson, N.C.: McFarland, 2007. Looks at how superheroes have changed in relation to social mores over decades and across media. Confronts issues of canonicity and continuity. Examines the tensions between audiences celebrating the newest versions of characters while mastering their dense histories.

SUPERHEROES AS TWENTIETH CENTURY AMERICAN MYTHOLOGY: NEW GODS FOR A NEW WORLD

Definition

Myths are stories that explain to members of a culture who they are, from whence they came, their role in the universe, and what the future holds for them. As Americans staggered out of the Great Depression and toward World War II, the mythic tales that had served to convey the society's moral codes no longer seemed to fit the realities of the late 1930's. Superheroes, led by Superman, built new mythologies that became dominant cultural motifs for much of the remainder of the twentieth century.

Introduction

The mythologies, both religious and secular, upon which the United States was built had grown thin and tired by 1938. The country was in the midst of the Great Depression and faced another world war. The tales of the Founding Fathers taught in schools and those of supernatural gods taught on the Sabbath no longer offered young Americans the same balm or hopes for a better future. However, with the launch of *Action Comics* and its dashing protagonist, Superman, both a new type of myth and a new type of god were born.

The new stories and deities that followed created textual tapestries that offered young readers a worldview in which the forces of light always overcame the forces of darkness. The tales spoke of the sweetness of success achieved through individual bravery and hard work. These myths advocated many of the same moral structures as their American predecessors but did so in a way that was more exciting, topical, and timely than the old myths. With its simple plots, complex symbolic language, and exciting and imaginative art, superhero mythology proved to be a powerful means of communicating American societal values. In the twenty-first century, superheroes and the comic book form are still used to instruct, indoctrinate, and proselytize.

In the Beginning Was the Cape

Prior to the dawn of the superhero, the heroes of American popular literature had one troublesome trait: They tended to be human. These human heroes were not overly interesting or much of a match for the colorful and daring villains they faced. In 1938, issue 1 of Detective Comics' *Action Comics* hit the newsstands, and American forms of storytelling, as well as myths and legends, were forever changed. The cover of that breakthrough book features a stunning young godling, dressed in blue tights and sporting a scarlet cape, effortlessly destroying an automobile by holding the vehicle above his head and slamming it into a hillside while the human villains flee in terror.

Superman was created by Jerry Siegel and Joe Shuster and, like so many of the character's ancient forebears, is a sun god, or god of light, in that his powers come directly from the sun. As a god of light, he established a clear moral framework for his followers, and through the stories of his adventures, he showed his followers the righteous path. He was a messianic god, sent from the heavens by his father to use his godlike powers to save mankind. He was also a patriarchal god in that from him, many others were born.

The instant commercial success of Superman turned the comic book business into a major industry. All other comics publishers looked for their own spandex-clad gods, leading to a dramatic surge in the creation of costumed heroes.

Enter the Gods of War

DC Comics and other publishers were quick to fashion other gods and goddesses to capitalize on Superman's commercial success. Among the critical early additions was Fox Publications' Blue Beetle, who first appeared in *Mystery Men Comics* and originally gained his power by wearing a blue chain-mail outfit and eating his potent "vitamin 2-X." Thus, he was a demigod, his powers a gift from the gods of, in this case, nutrition.

In 1940, Fawcett Comics introduced Captain Marvel, a solar deity whose powers came from a magic "occult" word that, when spoken, turned the young Billy Batson into a supremely powerful being. Timely Comics (later Marvel Comics) added gods of fire and water to the mix with the Human Torch, a synthetic

Captain America Bicentennial Battles. (Courtesy of Marvel Comics)

human who caught fire when exposed to oxygen, and Prince Namor the Sub-Mariner, who starred in Timely's *Marvel Comics* beginning in late 1939.

By 1940, most Americans realized that war against the Axis Powers was inevitable, and comic book publishers were quick to send the new gods to the front of the fighting to delineate clearly the proper moral beliefs all good Americans should hold concerning the pending conflict. Martin Goodman, Timely's publisher, announced in 1938 that he would use his publishing line as a propaganda weapon against Adolf Hitler. Perhaps the hardest punch he landed was with the publication of *Captain America Comics*, issue 1.

Created by the team of Joe Simon and Jack Kirby, Captain America was a new breed of American demigod, as his powers came as a gift from the gods of science. Artist Kirby explained that Captain America was created when the United States "needed a super

patriot." The cover of the first issue depicts Captain America punching Hitler, and he kills Nazi sympathizers in his origin story.

World War II bred scores of superpatriots, including the Young Allies, who worked with the British Secret Intelligence Service. In 1941, Quality Comics introduced Uncle Sam, a godly superhero, in *Uncle Sam Quarterly* and Blackhawk, a superaviator who led a band of guerrillas fighting for the Allies, in *Military Comics*.

Superheroes also played godlike roles in the allegories spun about future wars; however, American antipathy toward those conflicts often led the heroes to spout mixed messages. Both Captain America and Nick Fury, agent of S.H.I.E.L.D., were resurrected for the Cold War, but at times, they seemed to be sending a message of wariness of the government rather than the one of all-out patriotism seen during World War II.

Marvel's *Thor* is one of the more notable comic characters borrowed from the realm of mythology. (Courtesy of Marvel Comics)

Multiple Pantheons for Multiple Universes

As comics matured as an art form, two practices increased the role of the divine in graphic novels. The first was borrowing gods, demigods, or heroes from pantheons outside the realm of comics. Among the more notable of these characters was Marvel Comics' Thor, who was cast out of Asgard in the 1962 *Journey into Mystery*, issue 83, to learn humility. DC's best known contribution was the Amazon Wonder Woman, a blend of Aphrodite (goddess of love) and Mars (god of war) concocted by psychologist William Moulton Marston. The character premiered in *All Star*, issue 8, in 1941.

Other creators developed entire pantheons fully peopled with gods and goddesses. Kirby created the Fourth World for DC. This epic saga played out across three titles in 1971: *The New Gods*, *The Forever People*, and *Mister Miracle*, which pitted an evil faction of gods led by Darkseid against the righteous followers of the Highfather. DC's Vertigo line also hosted another of the great comic book pantheons, the Endless, in Neil Gaiman's *The Sandman* (1989-1996). The Endless embody the most powerful forces of nature, such as Death, Dream, Delirium, and Destruction.

Impact

The mythological aspect of superheroes was the main reason for the first explosion in comic book sales and popularity in the late 1930's and early 1940's and was also why so many of the superheroes quickly became cultural icons. The adventures of the godlike superheroes were the twentieth century's version of the myths and religious texts of the preceding epochs of human history. These colorful tales were simple wonder tales through which strict moral codes were passed from one generation of Americans to the next. The serial nature of the stories allowed publishers to create entire universes in which the theogony, or stories of the lives of the gods, could be played out.

The theogony, which kept readers coming back to follow the exploits of their favorite heroes, allowed for the moral codes embedded in the stories to be reinforced. Without their moral teachings, superhero comic books would have had little lasting impact on their young readers and would likely have been quashed because of their violence, as horror comics were in the 1950's. Although the Comics Code Authority toned down violence in superhero tales, it tended to strengthen the moral stances of the books' protagonists. Readers of superhero comics recognized the significance of comics in their moral upbringing.

B. Keith Murphy

Bibliography

Feiffer, Jules. *The Great Comic Book Heroes*. New York: Dial Press, 1965. Provides a firsthand account of coming of age during the initial explosion of comic book heroes and explains the cultural impact of these texts.

Goulart, Ron. *Over Fifty Years of American Comic Books*. Lincolnwood, Ill.: Mallard Press, 1991. Chronicles the publishing history of the first half century of modern comic books, from *Famous Funnies* (1935) through the beginning of the direct market and independent press boom of the late 1980's.

Knowles, Christopher. *Our Gods Wear Spandex: The Secret History of Comic Book Heroes*. San Francisco: Weiser Books, 2007. Traces the history of theocratic symbolism of superheroes and divides the pantheon into such respective types of gods as wizards, golems, and messiahs.

Underground Comix Movement: Words and Pictures out of the Mainstream

Definition

Underground comics offer a decidedly different emphasis in subject matter and presentation than traditional comics. Intended for adults rather than juveniles, underground comics frequently employ profane language and graphically depict violence, sexual situations, drug abuse, or other generally unacceptable behavior. They often satirize or criticize society's institutions and attitudes.

Introduction

Underground comics are legitimate descendants of a bastardized art form. Though linked in public perception to the countercultural movement of the 1960's and 1970's, they were conceived during the 1920's, with the advent of Tijuana bibles. Tijuana bibles were cheap, anonymously created booklets of pornographic cartoons using characters from newspaper comic strips (such as Popeye, Little Orphan Annie, and Mickey Mouse) or public figures (such as Cary Grant, Mae West, or Al Capone) to humorously and explicitly illustrate sexual situations. Tijuana bibles, particularly popular during the Depression, lasted into the 1960's.

Comic strips also spawned mainstream comic books: At first, strips were collected, reprinted, and bound like magazines. Original material, aimed primarily at teenagers, appeared in the early 1930's. By the late 1930's, comic books were firmly established, and giants DC Comics and Marvel Comics dominated a booming field. For a decade, comic books flourished in a variety of genres: Westerns, romance, science fiction, combat, humor, and, especially, costumed crime fighters and superheroes. During the Golden Age, when characters such as Superman, Batman, Wonder Woman, Daredevil, and the Flash were created, comic books were widely considered a harmless, if not especially productive, form of youthful diversion.

Opinion radically changed in the early 1950's when EC Comics, under the direction of cartoonist Harvey Kurtzman, launched graphically explicit lines in crime, war, and horror genres. Titles such as *Tales from the Crypt*, *Weird Fantasy*, and *Frontline Combat* realistically depicted mayhem, showed scantily clad women

In the 1950's, comic books flourished in a variety of genres: Westerns, romance, science fiction, combat, humor, and especially costumed crimefighters and superheroes. (Time & Life Pictures/Getty Images)

in jeopardy, and denigrated societal institutions. Competing publishers copied EC, glutting the market with gore and arousing animosity from parents and authorities. A prominent voice in the anticomics crusade was New York court psychiatrist Fredric Wertham. In 1954, he published *Seduction of the Innocent*, a searing indictment of comic books as inspiration for criminal behavior. Wertham testified before the Senate Subcommittee on Juvenile Delinquency, which suggested comic book publishers voluntarily police content lest they face governmental suppression.

Comics' Seal of Approval

Fearing censorship, the industry reacted to the anticomics movement. A trade organization, the Comics Magazine Association of America, established a self-regulating Comics Code Authority in 1954. The Comics Code promised to show crime as undesirable: Good would triumph over evil, criminals would be punished, and authorities and established institutions would not be ridiculed. Excessive violence and torture would vanish. "Terror" and "horror" would not appear in comic book titles. Profanity and vulgarity were outlawed. Nudity, seduction, sexual situations, and perversions became taboo. Advertisements of items traditionally associated with criminality—weapons, tobacco, liquor, or sexually oriented materials—were proscribed.

Comics that adhered to the rules received a cover stamp: "Approved by the Comics Code Authority." Most periodical distributors would not carry unapproved material; thus, major comics producers quickly conformed to the code, while other publishers folded. EC dropped virtually all titles, except the irreverent Kurtzman project *MAD*, introduced as a comic book in 1952 but reformatted as a magazine in 1955 to exempt it from code restrictions. For a decade after the code was instituted, comic books became uncontroversial and formulaic, though superhero storytelling thrived.

Presses Go Underground

Conditions changed in the early 1960's with the emergence of underground presses, which were an outgrowth of student newspapers, college literary journals, and off-campus humor magazines that dabbled in subversive material and questioned authority. The first significant underground newspaper was the *Los Angeles Free Press*, begun in 1964. Other counterculture magazines—*The Berkeley Barb*, *The East Village Other*, *San Francisco Oracle*, and *Chicago Seed*—sprang up during the same period. By the end of the decade, dozens of such publications existed across North America. Similar underground newspapers cropped up in Australia, the United Kingdom, and Europe.

Aimed at a socially conscious, educated audience, underground tabloids were the leading edge of a revolutionary wave provoked by the Vietnam War, a catalyst for an examination of cultural issues. The presses espoused personal freedoms, delved into radical politics, and encouraged antiwar rhetoric. They published antiauthoritarian viewpoints about such subjects as recreational drug use, casual sex, current music, and alternative lifestyles. Underground presses offered nontraditional editorial content, exposés, rants, relevant news items, and advertising for merchandise aimed at young, aware adults. Most also featured political cartoons, offbeat art, and original comic strips that mocked or criticized aspects of established society.

Underground Comix

"Underground comix" (thus spelled to differentiate them from mainstream offerings and indicate X-rated subject matter) were by-products of underground papers. Major underground cartoonists were often first introduced in college- or alternative-press publications. In the early 1960's, when hippies supplanted the Beats, many creative types gravitated to San Francisco, headquarters of the counterculture.

Contributors to comix were many during an era that roughly paralleled U.S. military involvement in Vietnam (1961-1975). Certain cartoonists became instantly recognizable by their style and content. The works of countercultural favorites Robert Crumb, Gilbert Shelton, Vaughn Bodé, S. Clay Wilson, Spain Rodriguez, Robert Williams, Art Spiegelman, Denis Kitchen, Rick Griffin, Bill Griffith, Stanley Mouse, and Victor Moscoso made readers think and feel.

Though pioneers such as Frank Stack as Foolbert Sturgeon (*The Adventures of Jesus*, 1962) and Bodé

(*Das Kampf*, 1963) had self-published nontraditional material on a small scale, underground comics came of age in 1968. That year, Crumb published and hand-distributed the first issues of *Zap Comix* in San Francisco.

Comix: The Golden Age

The publication of *Zap* and Crumb-produced follow-ups—*Despair, Uneeda, Big Ass Comics, Home Grown Funnies, Hytone Comix*—was mind-expanding for underground readers. It was a revelation for cartoonists, too. Here was a genuine alternative to mainstream comics, a way to free expression and creative control.

Soon, comix exploded. Between the late 1960's and late 1970's, hundreds of adult-themed, X-rated cartoon anthologies were published, promoting everything

Art Spiegelman's *Maus* gave alternative comics a tremendous boost in legitimacy by winning the Pulitzer Prize. (Courtesy of Pantheon Books)

from gay lifestyles to women's rights. Many reveled in detailing deviant sex and glorified drug use. Others revealed innermost fantasies, condemned racial and ethnic injustice, or parodied and criticized facets of American society.

Some comix were hilarious, others deadly serious, and still others comprehensible only under the influence of mood-enhancing or perception-altering substances. Many were one-shots, and most lasted only a few issues. Financing was a perennial problem, so publication was uncertain. Distribution was sporadic until the early 1970's when head shops began stocking comix among other in-demand products such as rolling papers, posters, and beads.

Crumb's distinctive countercultural icons (Mr. Natural, Flakey Foont, Whiteman, Angelfood McSpade, and Fritz the Cat and the "Keep on Truckin'" logo) appeared everywhere. Other cartoonists made a similar splash. Bodé's Cheech Wizard fantasies became popular. Williams's surrealistic strips were seen in *Zap* and elsewhere. Griffin's elaborate psychedelic designs graced comix, posters, and album covers. Wilson's violent, sexually explicit "Checkered Demon" and randy pirates made readers squirm. Shelton's drug-oriented cartoons, featuring the Fabulous Furry Freak Brothers and Fat Freddy's Cat, drew grins. Griffith's politically incorrect *Zippy the Pinhead* (1971-   ), Rodriguez's biker art, and Moscoso's ethereal figures drew faithful followers until the countercultural movement fizzled in the early 1980's.

Impact

Individual underground comics and independent publishers came and went. Mainstay producers such as Apex Novelties, Print Mint, Kitchen Sink Press, Pacific Comics, and Eclipse Comics fell by the wayside; their catalogs are periodically recycled for nostalgia's sake or to introduce fresh generations of readers to work that once caused a sensation but seem tame when compared to the outrageous images easily accessible online. Several early underground publishers, such as Rip Off Press and Last Gasp, still produce new alternative material and reprint older works.

In 1977, an important addition to the mix, Fantagraphics Books, began *The Comics Journal*, which critically examines comics as an art form. In the late 1970's, comic book specialty stores improved distribution of independent releases. In the same period—borrowing a technique from Europeans, who routinely reprinted comics in high-quality permanent albums—the first American graphic novels were born, starting an ongoing trend.

Spiegelman's *Maus* (1986) boosted the legitimacy of alternative comics when it won a Pulitzer Prize Special Citation. Movies such as *Fritz the Cat* (1972) and *Crumb* (1994) attracted fresh attention to comix and their creators.

Many surviving underground cartoonists still work in the medium; talented new writers and artists have joined them to stretch the boundaries of acceptability. New independent presses, such as NBM Publishing, Dark Horse Comics, Image Comics, Oni Press, and Eros Comix, have arisen to print and distribute alternative works. Modern independent comics and graphic novels, often with content more controversial than the groundbreaking material of the 1960's, are now aboveground, commonly found on the shelves of public libraries and chain bookstores. In the twenty-first century, what was once confined to the underground is a vibrant part of modern alternative literature.

Jack Ewing

Bibliography

Dowers, Michael. *Tijuana Bibles: America's Forgotten Comic Strips*. Seattle: Eros Comix, 2009. Collects the first five volumes in a profusely, profanely illustrated eight-volume work that details the precursors to underground comics.

Kitchen, Denis, and James Danky. *Underground Classics: The Transformation of Comics into Comix*. New York: Abrams, 2009. A collection of essays that examines comix in terms of art and influence, focusing on both well-known and unknown contributors.

Skinn, Dez. *Comix: The Underground Revolution*. New York: Thunder's Mouth Press, 2004. A thorough, well-illustrated history of underground comics from a British perspective. Contains a list of underground publications released in the United States and the United Kingdom.

UNDERSTANDING COMICS: THE INVISIBLE ART

Author: McCloud, Scott
Artist: Scott McCloud (illustrator); Bob Lappan (letterer)
Publisher: Tundra Publishing; HarperCollins
First book publication: 1993

Publication History

Often considered to be comics theorist Scott McCloud's seminal work, *Understanding Comics: The Invisible Art* was first published by Tundra Publishing in 1993. HarperCollins later reprinted the work. The book has been translated into a number of languages, including Spanish, German, and Korean.

Prior to the publication of *Understanding Comics*, McCloud was best known as the creator of the superhero series *Zot!* (1984-1990), published by Eclipse Comics. After gaining recognition for his work as a comics theorist, he went on to write additional works about comics and the comics industry. *Reinventing Comics* (2000) focuses on the comic book industry and digital comics, while *Making Comics* (2006) explores the storytelling techniques used in comics, graphic novels, and manga.

Plot

Chapter 1 of *Understanding Comics*, "Setting the Record Straight," begins with a brief introduction by the narrator and then immediately delves into the problems of categorizing and defining comics. McCloud stresses that comics do not have to fit into the mold of immature reading material for children. Building on comics creator Will Eisner's definition of comics as "sequential art," McCloud considers how best to define the medium. The definition he ultimately settles on and repeats throughout the book is one that many scholars accept, or at least acknowledge, as one of the official definitions of comics. McCloud then begins to contextualize different forms of art and writing that, according to his definition, could fall under the heading of comics. Examples include a pre-Columbian picture manuscript and the Bayeux Tapestry. Hieroglyphics are quickly disregarded as comics, but Egyptian paintings certainly fit the bill. Modern comics originate with Rodolphe Töpffer, a French artist who essentially invented the panel, and other artists whose works can be considered as comics, even though they are rarely regarded as such. In fact, just about any work with a series of illustrations can technically be considered a comic, depending on one's standards, and McCloud encourages the reader to continue working out exactly what those standards should be.

Chapter 2, "The Vocabulary of Comics," begins with an example of how a representation of something does not equal the actual item or idea. Icons bring about meaning without the actual form; the icon itself can be an abstract depiction of its meaning or an almost realistic depiction of it. McCloud then goes on to address cartooning, describing it as "amplification through simplification," in that the lack of details makes the image more accessible and recognizable. The simplest icon to identify is that of the face, which the mind tends to project onto just about any visible surface or pattern. It is this simplicity and lack of detail that allow the average person to identify easily with the cartoon and the icon. The distinction between the most basic depiction of a concept and an almost photo-realistic representation of it is that they relay different forms of information, and this distinction becomes even more complex once language is defined as the abstract model of ideas. McCloud describes the concept using the image of a pyramid, which serves as both a chart and a map for comics. The three corners of the pyramid represent reality, the pictorial plane, and meaning. McCloud then arranges more than a hundred comics within the pyramid, ordering them based on how close they are to each corner and in relation to the others.

Chapter 3, "Blood in the Gutter," deals directly with how the mind completes that which goes beyond normal perception, which McCloud calls closure. Closure occurs almost automatically with just about everything the reader sees, and it is necessary for comics to function. It occurs between panels in a place called the gutter, where the different images come together to show changes in time and space. McCloud even argues that closure is an active choice, a leap taken voluntarily by the reader with his or her imagination to reach an intended meaning. He describes what he considers to be the six most basic (and self-defined) types of transition between panels—moment-to-moment, action-to-action, subject-to-subject, scene-to-scene, aspect-to-aspect, and non sequitur—and places them in a graph to see how American, European, and Japanese comics compare in terms of panel transitions. McCloud then discusses the number of panels necessary to tell a story and the importance of obtaining the right balance between too much and too little information with closure.

Chapter 4, "Time Frames," focuses on the element of time, especially within a single panel. Time is not uniform within a defined space, since even one panel depicts actions and not just a single moment. There is no way of knowing how much time actually elapses in comics; the direction of the panels gives a good sense of time, but how a reader observes those panels is not strictly defined. The linear progression of time and the impression of movement are represented differently in comics than in other forms of media, and cartoonists tend to play on readers' preconceptions to create meaning. Lines within a single panel of a still image can represent motion, while a stationary figure against a blurry background may have the same effect. The duration of time within a panel and the reader's perception of it are affected by a number of different factors.

Chapter 5, "Living in Line," deals with how the use of lines can evoke different meanings. This chapter includes a quick overview of different classical artists who used lines in their own ways to show something more. Cartoonists also follow a particular style to portray something unique. In comics, lines can be used to depict things that normally cannot be represented in a visual-only medium; for example, wavy lines often represent heat or a bad smell. Fonts and word balloons provide yet another way to depict meaning within comics.

Chapter 6, "Show and Tell," begins by asserting that over time, language becomes more abstract and pictures become more symbolic, with the two continuing to grow farther apart. Comics tend to join them together in varied ways, as McCloud shows with the previously mentioned pyramid chart. The standards of art and

writing have also changed, and these extend to comics as well. McCloud argues that comics should not be judged by the standards of previous forms, in part because comics are still growing in the way they can tell stories. He then provides different categories of ways in which words and pictures work together: word-specific, picture-specific, duo-specific, additive, parallel, montage, and interdependent. Separately, words and pictures can each tell a different story, but together they can achieve much more.

Chapter 7, "The Six Steps," starts by directly stating that comics are art, especially given a broad enough definition. McCloud defines art as anything that is not directly related to survival and reproduction. He ties art to a certain path that has six steps: idea/purpose, form, idiom, structure, craft, and surface. Many artists only vary the final parts of the path, and some do not even use any of the previous steps. With enough practice and study, artists can dedicate themselves to altering each of the steps until they change art itself. The goal of an artist need not be to transform art, but those artists who do allow for others to continue changing the path of art itself.

Chapter 8, "A Word About Color," consists of just eight pages and is the only chapter in the book to use color. McCloud gives a quick history lesson on how color first made its way into the print medium. Effectively, the early high costs of color and relatively low level of technology meant that only the standard primary colors were available. Comic book heroes were depicted in bright primary colors that came to represent them; Superman's blue, red, and yellow costume immediately comes to mind. While American comics were limited in their use of colors, McCloud notes that European comics had more colors available and strove to balance them all on the page. Other comics used completely different styles of palettes. Still, McCloud argues that black-and-white comics can evoke feelings just as well as full-color comics and should not be considered obsolete just because better technologies are available.

Chapter 9, "Putting It All Together," goes into the basics of communication, asserting that because the transmission of ideas is limited by medium, people must master their medium in order to communicate effectively. It is for this reason, McCloud claims, that it is important to understand comics, in order to use them better. Ignorance and preconceived notions about comics severely limit the message that can be conveyed via this medium. The medium of comics is still growing, and comics have the potential to communicate so much, if only given the chance to do so.

Characters

Scott McCloud is the author's avatar and the narrator throughout the entirety of the book. He wears large, round glasses and a *Zot!* T-shirt. McCloud is technically the only character within the book, although other familiar faces from the comic book world appear sporadically. He communicates directly with readers in order to help them achieve the titular goal of the book. However, for all of McCloud's knowledge, he rarely if ever appears to be arrogant or overly intellectual. Instead, he recognizes the limits of his own understanding and invites readers to join and engage in the debate about the nature of comics.

Artistic Style

The art in the book is fairly consistent, with McCloud's avatar being drawn in a simple manner against a blank background or different settings. However, examples of different panel layouts, the styles of other artists, and other aspects of drawing are presented in order to illustrate the differences between each, and sometimes the narrator's rendering shifts in order to match his surroundings. At first glance, the minimalist drawings might suggest to the average, casual reader that the book is a children's comic book featuring a man who talks too much; it is only upon careful reading that one comes to understand McCloud's exposition. The apparently simple artistic style helps both demystify the different aspects of comics and present them with an air of seriousness.

The book's typical layout, featuring McCloud's avatar addressing the audience via speech balloons for about twelve panels per page, makes *Understanding Comics* feel like a lively conversation rather than a boring lecture, manifesto, or treatise on the complexity of comics. From the iconic smiley face to a nearly photo-realistic portrait, McCloud draws and replicates

many distinct styles, depicting ancient cave paintings, famous works of art, and several familiar faces from the world of American, European, and Japanese comics to illustrate how varied comics, and even traditional art, can truly be. While the panel layouts and overall information can be dense throughout the majority of the book, there are no large sections of text that might thwart reader engagement or understanding.

Themes

McCloud expands on what Eisner first considered to be sequential art. Much of the book analyzes this art form and defends it as such, using various examples that range from ancient Egyptian art to the Bayeux Tapestry to contemporary diagrams. Distinctions are made as to what kinds of works do and do not qualify as comics, at least according to McCloud. The book serves as a pedagogical guide to the promised understanding of comics. If one were to classify the book, it would likely fall under the category of art criticism or even art history, though it is most likely to be found in the graphic novels section of the bookstore. While it can certainly serve as a textbook, the book's discourse is not preachy or overly authoritative; instead, McCloud presents his views on comics based on his personal experiences within the comic book industry and his own extensive research, expressing his ideas not as solutions but rather as considerations in the great debate on art and comics. If anything, *Understanding Comics* is highly democratic and inviting for all to participate. The last lines of the book sum up the purpose of the work: "This book is meant to stimulate debate, not settle it. I've had my say. Now it's your turn."

Impact

Understanding Comics became one of the most recognized and influential books about comics, winning several awards and prompting McCloud to write a number of other works on the subject. McCloud's definition of comics is rarely absent from any academic text on the subject, even those that disagree with his statements. The book has become one of the building blocks of the academic field of comics studies and has been used as a textbook in many academic programs. Ultimately, *Understanding Comics* goes beyond comic books and graphic novels, defining how images and text can be placed together to do something more than they can individually and redefining art along the way.

Gabriel Romaguera

Bibliography

Dardess, George. "Review: Bringing Comic Books to Class." *College English* 57, no. 2 (1995): 213-222.

Eisner, Will. *Comics and Sequential Art: Principles and Practices from the Legendary Cartoonist.* New York: W. W. Norton, 2008.

Wolfe, Gary K. "On Some Recent Scholarship." Review of *Understanding Comics: The Invisible Art,* by Scott McCloud. *Science Fiction Studies* 21, no. 3 (1994): 438-439.

Women as Readers

Definition

Comics originally had a wide-ranging readership in terms of both gender and age, but by the 1970's, the readership was largely composed of young males; however, the number of female comics readers began to increase by the 1990's. Scholars and publishers have frequently taken an interest in which graphic novels garner a female readership and how women read graphic novels in ways that seem associated with their gender.

Introduction

There have been periods in the history of comics in the United States in which women made up the majority of readers, but this has not been the case since the mid-twentieth century. During the 1940's, women were voracious readers of romance comics, which offered adult female readers more grown-up versions of the love-triangle dilemmas so common in the *Archie* comics. Women and girls of various ages were courted by publishing companies such as Timely Comics (the precursor to Marvel Comics), Harvey Comics, and MLJ Magazines (later Archie Comics), and by the late 1940's, female comic book readers outnumbered males in the United States.

Romance comics were among the casualties of the moral panic about comics that precipitated the implementation of the Comics Code in 1954. Like the horror comics that were also quickly neutered by the code, romance comics became so altered by the stipulations of the code that they lost their adult readers, who moved on to less censored reading material such as romance novels. In the wake of this decline in readership, publishers streamlined their output, and women were no longer courted with titles geared toward them as readers of comics. This difficult period for the industry saw a decline in the staple superhero genre as well, and the sharp drop in female readership of comics was followed by a slow but steady increase in focus on catering to males in their teens and early twenties.

By the 1970's, little comics content was geared toward female readers, and women had gotten the message that comics were not for them. There were some

Featuring teenage versions of female Marvel superheroes, *Marvel Her-Oes*, by writer Grace Randolph, debuted in 2010. (Courtesy of Marvel Comics)

prominent female cartoonists who were part of the underground comics movement; although this scene is more commonly linked to artists such as Robert Crumb and Gilbert Shelton, it also featured artists who created alternative comics for women, including Trina Robbins, Lisa Lyons, Meredith Kurtzman, and Hurricane Nancy Kalish. While these comics were clearly geared to an adult female readership, their circulation was not extensive beyond the underground circles of creators and readers. The comics anthology *Wimmen's Comix* continued to be published until the early 1990's, but it never circulated broadly. Some other independent comics have struck a chord with female readers, notably Jaime, Gilbert, and Mario Hernandez's *Love and Rockets* (1982-1996), but little else seemed to attract a female audience.

Comics for Female Readers

Throughout the 1980's, independently published black-and-white comics flourished, and some of that boom brought in female creators, publishers, and readers. For the most part, though, women were alienated by the move to direct sales in small comic shops staffed and frequented by the young men who were still being targeted by comics publishers long after female readers had been forgotten. *Archie* comics could still be purchased from newsstands and grocery stores, but most other comics had shifted to a direct-distribution model. Because readers often ordered or reserved titles in advance at local comic shops so that the shop owners would know how many copies to order from publishers, sales were for the most part geared toward elite readers who knew what titles were coming out and when. This direct-distribution method further concentrated readership among males, though the target age was increased, since the cost of comic books had also increased beyond the means of many young boys.

Some shops had large inventories of back issues that could help readers get caught up on a story once they discovered a title in progress, but most could not afford rent on spaces large enough to house many back issues for such readers. Generally, back issues were displayed in long drawer boxes and filed by title. This system continued to privilege elite readers with ties to comics fandom, which was also perceived as unwelcoming to females during this period.

Manga and Media Adaptations

When manga (Japanese comics) first hit the U.S. market in the 1980's, the titles being imported were primarily intended for male readers and sold in the same specialty comic stores as American comics. Since around 2002, sales in mainstream bookstores have fueled huge growth in manga's share of graphic novel sales, particularly of content geared specifically to female readers. The majority of titles found in bookstores are those written for a female audience, while comic shops have tended to give more space to manga aimed

at their regular customers, 85 to 90 percent of whom are men. A number of mainstream publishers broke into the translated manga business in the United States and targeted both bookstores and comic shops, also aiming primarily at female readers.

The Japanese publishing industry is divided into publications geared to specific age and gender demographics, and consequently there is a great deal of content that is deemed suitable for female readers and, more importantly, has gained a large readership and fan base among female readers. One genre that is specifically geared to female readers is *yaoi*, which features love stories between attractive young men. *Yaoi* is popular among older female readers, from teenagers through women in their forties and beyond, and has brought female readers into the direct-sales comic shops or to online bookstores and comics retailers; while many manga titles marketed to younger readers line the shelves of mainstream bookstores, there tend to be fewer *yaoi* titles in these more traditional book-buying venues.

The increase in female readers of manga due to sales in mainstream bookshops, sales through online booksellers, and growing online fan communities has had an impact on the North American comics industry as well. After decades of being largely ignored by the industry, women became the target audience of an increasing number of American comics, including mangalike titles and superhero miniseries such as *Marvel Her-Oes*, *Girl Comics*, and *Heralds*, all released by Marvel in the summer of 2010. In addition to these, comics publishers have produced an increasing number of comic book adaptations of works of literature that have long been associated primarily with female readers, such as the novels of Jane Austen or even parodies of her work such as *Pride and Prejudice and Zombies* (2009; graphic novel adaptation, 2010).

In addition to literature, comics have also been adapted from other female-targeted media, such as films and television shows. The publication of *Buffy the Vampire Slayer Season Eight*, the comic book continuation of Joss Whedon's television series, led many female fans of the show to venture into the world of comics. Other television-based series with sizeable female fan bases have also been adapted to comics, helping to expand the female readership. Titles such as *Buffy* are able to tap into existing fan bases to create a ready-made audience for new comics based on existing characters and stories.

Impact

Female readers may enjoy any genre of graphic novel, but as in other media, they tend to gravitate toward specific types of content. Stories that focus on relationships, have less action and more talking, and deal with emotion directly, while not exclusively the domain of female audiences and certainly not the only type of stories they enjoy, echo genres that are traditionally considered feminine, such as soap operas and romances, and are therefore more familiar to female readers. All these familiar aspects of female-targeted storytelling can be found in manga titles aimed at women and girls. Manga

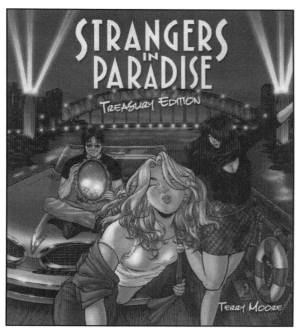

Written from a woman's point of view, *Strangers in Paradise* is popular with female readers. (Courtesy of Abstract Studio)

has been a significant factor in both the increase in female readers of graphic novels and the expansion of content geared toward a greater diversity of comics readership. In addition, the influx of manga into mainstream bookstores occurred simultaneously with the increase in publication of trade-paperback compilations of comic book series, which has made the back catalog of many comics more readily available. Many comics readers, both male and female, have begun to purchase these compilations, which can easily be bought online or in mainstream bookstores, instead of the individual issues of current comics. This broader availability of more diverse content has helped to expand female readership of American comics and works translated from other languages, and the subsequent increase in female readers has resulted in not only more comics content geared toward women but also a growing female audience for series not necessarily aimed at them.

June M. Madeley

Bibliography

Pohl-Weary, Emily, ed. *Girls Who Bite Back: Witches, Mutants, Slayers and Freaks.* Toronto, Ont.: Sumach Press, 2004. An edited volume of essays about female role models in popular culture, including several essays on graphic novel characters and readers.

Robbins, Trina. *From Girls to Grrrlz: A History of Women's Comics from Teens to Zines.* San Francisco: Chronicle Books, 1999. An analysis and history of comics read by women, including mainstream comics as well as works published by underground and alternative presses.

_____. *The Great Women Superheroes.* Northampton, Mass.: Kitchen Sink Press, 1996. An overview of female superheroes throughout the history of comics, from early characters such as Wonder Woman to the heroes of the 1990's.

THEME

ACTION AND ADVENTURE: DECLINE OF THE POSSIBLE IMPOSSIBLE

Definition

Comic books and graphic novels within the action-adventure genre focus on conflicts, often violent ones, that take place within the "real world" and eschew the fantastic plots, settings, or characters found within action-oriented superhero, fantasy, and science-fiction works. Action-adventure heroes and heroines perform unlikely or impossible derring-do under the tacit claim that such events could really happen.

Introduction

Action-adventure storytelling sets up a conflict that requires some form of violent resolution: a chase, a fight, or some other sort of destruction. The genre is narrow in that it traditionally does not include fantastic plot elements found in many other genres; yet, because it can encompass the whole of human history and all human societies, it can theoretically be used as a platform to tell stories about people and places at any point in the past or present. Thus, Westerns, samurai stories, Viking sagas, and modern-day police dramas may all fall under the action-adventure heading.

Pulp adventure characters such as the bronze giant Doc Savage and the cloaked vigilante the Shadow are not examples of action-adventure characters, as they are outlandish and exaggerated by their very nature and do not fit within the world that action-adventure stories seek to depict—a world like the real one. It is important, however, to note that the purported realism of the genre is itself a stylistic trope. The world of action-adventure stories is very similar to the real world, but such stories do not necessarily represent a one-for-one depiction of life as it is.

The somewhat fantastic realism of the action-adventure genre is particularly evident in the genre's treatment of violence. From comic book adaptations of Alexandre Dumas's novel *The Three Musketeers* (*Les Trois Mousquetaires*, 1844; English translation, 1846) to action comics pitting cops or spies against "the bad guys," action-adventure stories typically take a breezy approach to violent action. Little more than a token

mention is given to the real-world physical effects of violence on the characters, who shrug off gunshots and sprint down streets without becoming winded in the least. In terms of the frequency and nature of violent action, the adventure genre is actually a purer fantasy than fantasy itself—the stories present themselves as narratives that could really happen if one were merely to step outside the bounds of a dull, ordinary life.

Action-adventure stories are not as common in graphic novels and comic books as in other media, particularly film, but they do continue to constitute a small genre. The increasing popularity of more fantastic or speculative genres has lessened the influence of action-adventure, reducing the number of such stories published and raising questions about the fate of the genre. However, because nearly all popular genres include elements of the action-adventure story structure—often mirroring mythologist Joseph Campbell's "Hero's Journey," a narrative path found within myth, folklore, and popular media from a variety of disparate cultures, with its "call to adventure"—this change may be viewed more as a transformation than a true extinction.

The Lawless World

A basic assumption of the action-adventure genre is that merely one step beyond the visible or invisible bounds of everyday life waits a world of bold decision, savage action, and highly attenuated experience. The point-of-view character is generally a private investigator (as in Gil Kane's *His Name Is . . . Savage!*), a crime journalist (Michele Petrucci's *Due*), a police investigator (the *CSI: Crime Scene Investigation* adaptation from IDW Publishing), or a soldier (M. Zachary Sherman and Fritz Casas's *Bloodlines*). Action-adventure protagonists have one thing in common: They follow the formula of a hero who reacts to what a villain has done. The protagonist enters the world of violence and danger and may even relish it, but he or she is the instrument of its positive resolution. Like the hero of a Western, the action-adventure hero or heroine enters a place and time of chaos and restores order. There-fore, crime graphic novels such as Joshua Fialkov's *Tumor* and John Wagner and Vince Locke's *A History of Violence* are not properly within the purview of action-adventure storytelling, as they follow outlaw characters who play a role in instigating conflict.

Will Jacobs and Gerard Jones's *The Trouble with Girls* directly explores the central idea of the action-adventure genre: The protagonist need only make the slightest misstep for wild goings-on to ensue. Despite the general realism of the genre, such over-the-top events can present a problem for some readers. *The Trouble with Girls* is emblematic of the difficulty graphic novel audiences have in suspending disbelief when reading action-adventure stories. Warren Ellis's *Red* similarly deconstructs the idea of the adventure story in a modern world, taking situations and characters well over the top.

Literature and History

A number of action-adventure comic books and graphic novels have been based on classic works of literature. The venerable *Classics Illustrated* line of comics, originally published by the Gilberton Company, has been translated successfully to the larger-format graphic novel medium, enabling artists to produce adaptations of such novels as Robert Louis Stevenson's *Treasure Island* (1883) and Mark Twain's *The Adventures of Tom Sawyer* (1876). It would be impossible to argue that Steven Grant's adaptation of Dumas's *The Count of Monte Cristo* (*Le Comte de Monte-Cristo*, 1844-1846; English translation, 1846) is not an action-adventure story. Many comics storytellers writing in other genres, including *300* author Frank Miller, have cited the influence of literary adventure narratives on their works, and the structural crossovers are obvious. However, the *Classics Illustrated* line and similar works from publishers such as Penny-Farthing Press and Stone Arch Books are far from the mainstream of sequential art.

In keeping with the ability of the action-adventure genre to transcend boundaries of time and place, several significant works in the genre have been retellings or fictionalizations of historical events. Warren Ellis's *Crécy* presents a short, well-researched historical nar-rative concerning the fourteenth century Battle of Crécy, a major battle in the Hundred Years' War. *Age of Bronze*, by Eric Shanower, chronicles the legendary Trojan War and draws on both literary sources such as Homer's *Odyssey* and historical and archaeological evidence.

Evolution of the Genre

American and international consumer tastes have largely moved away from traditional action-adventure stories and toward fantastic genres in most areas. Non-real-world settings, situations, and characters are commercially popular and offer comics writers additional creative freedom, and publishing trends have reflected these factors. Stories with common action-adventure protagonists such as military personnel or police officers, for instance, are often set in fantastic or science-fictional worlds; non-real-world comics that display action-adventure charac-

G.I. Joe. (Courtesy of IDW Publishing)

teristics include the *Alien Legion* military series, created by Carl Potts, Alan Zelenetz, and Frank Cirocco, and Alan Moore's superhero police drama *Top 10*.

In addition to changing industry trends, the decrease in the number of action-adventure comics and graphic novels available is due in part to the narrow bounds of the genre. In a modern, industrialized setting, a wild series of adventures that are resolved through "action" would be illegal or, at best, the province of a national government's military, intelligence, or police agencies; therefore, many classic action-adventure protagonists would be considered dangerous or even criminal. Since one of the differences between the crime and action-adventure genres is that career criminals are antagonists rather than protagonists in action-adventure stories, comics featuring protagonists who work in opposition to the law do not fit the strict definition of action-adventure. Similarly, certain categories of stories, such as Westerns and pirate tales, have become subgenres unto themselves and are thus excluded from the action-adventure genre. This process of elimination leaves very few straightforward action-adventure comics and graphic novels.

The most successful action-adventure narratives of the Modern Age of comics appear to be those that mix traditional action-adventure concepts with fantasy, science-fiction, or superhero elements—titles such as *G. I. Joe*, a nonrealistic military series; *The Walking Dead* and *Y: The Last Man*, series featuring apocalyptic events that only vaguely resemble real disaster situations; and *Jonah Hex*, a rather hallucinatory approach to the American frontier of the nineteenth century. Even works such as Moore's *League of Extraordinary Gentlemen*, which brings together characters from a variety of literary sources, rely more upon the "sense of wonder" characters such as H. G. Wells's Invisible Man than "realistic" literary figures such as Kate Douglas Wiggin's Rebecca of Sunnybrook Farm.

Impact

The action-adventure genre has significantly influenced the comics industry, serving to inspire later publications that build on the classic tropes, situations, and character types of the genre. Although the popularity of traditional action-adventure comics has declined in favor of more fantastic or speculative stories, such popular fantasy, science-fiction, and superhero narratives are typically based on an action-adventure foundation, making them all subsets of the action-adventure story model. Audiences continue to seek the escape of freewheeling, fast-moving adventure and the catharsis of problems resolved through violent action, and the genre has shifted and transformed to meet its readers' needs.

Richard A. Becker

Bibliography

Benton, Mike. *The Comic Book in America: An Illustrated History*. Dallas: Taylor, 1993. An overview of the trends in graphic storytelling and the movement toward the fantastic and away from action-adventure realism.

Daniels, Les. *Comix: A History of the Comic Book in America*. New York: Outerbridge & Dienstfrey, 1971. An overview of the history of sequential storytelling in the United States, with reference to the rise and fall of various genres, including action-adventure.

Wright, Bradford W. *Comic Book Nation: The Transformation of Youth Culture in America*. Baltimore: Johns Hopkins University Press, 2003. Identifies the popular genres within comics, discusses the shifts in popularity among these genres, and explores how such changes have reflected trends among American youth.

ANIMAL INSTINCTS: DIVERSE DEPICTIONS OF ANTHROPOMORPHISM

Definition

Anthropomorphic comic books and graphic novels feature animal characters that adopt such human traits and abilities as speaking, gesturing, wearing clothing, walking upright, and using technology. Characters express emotions, pursue professions and hobbies, seek social relationships, and react to provocations and responsibilities similarly to how humans behave. Different literary techniques used to portray anthropomorphism, both contrary and compatible with animals' innate responses, convey themes to readers of varied ages.

Introduction

Writers have anthropomorphized animal characters in literature to express symbolism or propaganda or to voice opinions regarding contemporary issues since ancient times. Many anthropomorphic tales have been classified as children's literature, including enduring stories written by Beatrix Potter, Kenneth Grahame, A. A. Milne, and Rudyard Kipling that have influenced generations of readers. Since the nineteenth century, animal characters have entertained readers of comic strips, comic books, and graphic novels.

Narratives featuring anthropomorphic characters incorporate elements of various genres, particularly fantasy, science fiction, and mystery. They often contain references to folktales, myths, legends, and historical events that inspired their creators. Anthropomorphic characters are frequently used to explore cultural perceptions of gender, ethnicity, and socioeconomic class to achieve intended purposes such as satire or humor.

Animal characters frequently represent stereotypes based on readers' expectations for the behavior of such animals: dogs are loyal, wolves vicious, weasels deceitful, and reptiles venomous. While some graphic novels present gentle, kind animal characters such as Andy Runton's Owly, others focus on hedonists such as Dave Sim's Cerebus, emphasizing intense violence and bleak imagery. Graphic novels occasionally sub-

Teenage Mutant Ninja Turtles features four anthropomorphic turtles trained in the martial arts (Courtesy of IDW Publishing)

vert traditional interpretations of animal behavior, presenting anthropomorphism that defies both humans' and animals' instincts to maintain stability. Animals at times are depicted as opposites of their expected roles.

Roles and Relationships

Anthropomorphized animals in graphic novels play diverse roles representative of literary archetypes, serving as heroes, victims, tricksters, and villains. Forming unique identities, many animals are distinguished by human-derived names and demonstrate abilities implausible for their species' natural physiology. Some anthropomorphic characters retain behaviors attributed to animals: Juan Díaz Canales's John Blacksad, a cat, refers to his instincts when reacting to a rat he does not trust.

Anthropomorphic animals' interactions with humans vary. Animals comfort immigrants in Shaun Tan's *The Arrival*, and in Bryan Talbot's *The Tale of One Bad Rat*, abuse survivor Helen Potter relies on nurturing her pet rat while she heals emotionally. Animals also serve as guides and companions: Tintin's friendship with devoted terrier Snowy in Hergé's series exemplifies that canine's protective instincts. Some animals instigate transitions and plot movement, as when swarming locusts cause the protagonist of Jeff Smith's *Bone* to fall over a cliff into a hazardous valley.

Shape-shifting represents dual existences for anthropomorphic characters in Bill Willingham's *Fables* series and Jean-Phillipe Stassen's *Deogratias: A Tale of Rwanda*, in which a man traumatized by genocide is portrayed as a dog while coping with guilt and loss. Anthropomorphized animals portray historical figures such as a feline Adolf Hitler in Canales's *Red Soul*, reminiscent of sinister cat guards in Art Spiegelman's *Maus*. Humans sometimes manipulate animals' instinctual responses, as when criminals train a gorilla to attack strangers in Hergé's Tintin comic *The Black Island*. Nick Abadzis's *Laika* addresses complex ethical issues associated with animal experimentation.

Plots and Imagery

Anthropomorphic protagonists in graphic novels typically undertake journeys to seek better situations, avenge injustices, respond to betrayals, or protect weaker characters. Characters' movement is often provoked by stimuli challenging their instincts. These adventures sometimes appropriate plot elements from fairy tales: Blues singer Barnabus B. Wolf battles three racist swine he blames for killing his family and seizing his farm in J. D. Arnold's *BB Wolf and the Three LPs*, exposing the perils of revenge. Jennifer L. Holm and Matthew Holm's *Babymouse* series highlights daydreams in which the rodent protagonist interacts with notable animal characters from children's literature.

Many graphic novels pit "good" animals against "evil" animals, with the righteous not always prevailing. Characters' instinctual reactions frequently shape plot development, providing the basis for shifts in action and unexpected twists. Deceptions are plot catalysts when anthropomorphic characters are misled. Plots often feature heroes who protest social injustices and crimes against innocent victims, such as English badger Detective Inspector Archie LeBrock, who strives to defeat criminals and terrorists in Bryan Talbot's *Grandville* books. Historical precedents have inspired the creation of warriors such as the rabbit samurai protagonist of Stan Sakai's *Usagi Yojimbo*.

Anthropomorphic images are frequently drawn in black and white, sepia, or bold colors resembling illustrations from pulp magazines. Frames emphasize the juxtaposition of characters' fur, fangs, whiskers, and claws with human garments and mannerisms. Illustrations exaggerating animals' anatomy and contorting facial expressions and gestures call attention to absurd aspects of anthropomorphic characters.

Settings

Graphic novels populated with animals often take place in isolated wildernesses filled with forests and pollutant-free water resources that provide characters shelter and sustenance. Other rural sites, such as the wooded valley in Smith's *Bone* series, have sinister aspects. The Great Depression of the 1930's forms the backdrop for Matt Phelan's *The Storm in the Barn*, with images stressing the despair associated with drought. People nail dead snakes to fences, hoping that the sacrificial gesture will summon rain. Images of a jackrabbit drive include red panels showing those animals' terror as humans, enraged that the prairie setting has denied them prosperity, beat the hares to death.

While some animals remain in their indigenous settings, many function in places alien to their species' natural habitats. Cities are usually depicted as crowded, gritty places filled with buildings, industrial equipment, and paved roads. Escaped lions in Brian K. Vaughan's *Pride of Baghdad* wander through the war-damaged city, where their instinctual responses to acquire food and shelter fail. Some animal-driven graphic novels are implied to take place in postapocalyptic settings, such as the fantastical world through which the four lupine protagonists of Keiko Nobumoto's *Wolf's Rain* roam. In these settings, humans have vanished or been conquered, and animals control Earth and often must attempt to restore vitality to ecosystems damaged by humans. Alternate history landscapes frequently establish innovative premises such as a world in which Napoleon was victorious, as seen in *Grandville*.

Themes

Anthropomorphized animal characters in graphic novels represent themes compatible with traits and behaviors associated with animals as well as themes more relevant to human experiences and actions. The theme of desire is portrayed through characters' relationships, suggesting that they experience romantic love rather than the animal instinct to mate solely for reproduction. The theme of survival is constant for anthropomorphic characters who struggle in their surroundings, whether natural or artificial, much as animals in the wild seek shelter and gather food while eluding predators. Some anthropomorphic animals respond to hunger by using human agricultural tactics to grow and preserve food. They adapt to challenges, relying on their instincts to survive.

Many stories chronicle anthropomorphic animals' quests to attain power and status and confront threats posed by rivals. Themes of vengeance and justice coexist when anthropomorphized animals are motivated to attack characters who have wronged them by expressing derogatory comments or stealing property. Less antagonistic anthropomorphized characters, such as those in Susan Schade and Jon Buller's Fog Mound trilogy, endeavor to recover lost territories and possessions honorably, resorting to violence only when necessary to survive and restore belongings and lifestyles that sustain them. Redemption is a common theme associated with anthropomorphized characters: Expressing remorse about his past delinquency, Blacksad confronts and contains evil, helping people instead of harming them.

Impact

Graphic novels featuring anthropomorphic characters attract readership worldwide. Publishers issue translations of many such novels, offering international audi-

The anthropomorphic *Laika* is an Eisner Award winner. (Courtesy of First Second)

ences access to works with universal themes and archetypes they can apply to their cultures. Scholarly interest in anthropomorphic graphic novels has extended to related academic disciplines, incorporating expertise in literature, biology, history, anthropology, sociology, and animal sciences. Some educators assign anthropomorphic graphic novels for lessons or prepare literary guides analyzing specific books to teach students ranging from elementary grades to university levels.

Scholarly journals, including literary periodicals and publications focusing on animal issues, print analyses and reviews of anthropomorphic graphic novels and topics. Electronic magazines such as *Anthro* feature content and illustrations relevant to discussion of animal characters in graphic novels, reviewing new books and noting readers' reactions to stories. Since 1997, proponents of anthropomorphism in graphic novels and other media have gathered at Anthrocon meetings.

The Ursa Major Awards, presented by the Anthropomorphic Literature and Arts Association, honor graphic novels with animal characters. Eisner Award-winning graphic novels with anthropomorphic characters include *Laika* and *Fables*. *Deogratias: A Tale of Rwanda* won the Angoulême International Comics Festival's René Goscinny Prize. Anthropomorphic graphic novels have also received mainstream literary recognition, with *Maus* winning a Pulitzer Prize in 1992. Media outlets and such book-related organizations as the American Library Association often recognize graphic novels featuring anthropomorphic characters with literary awards, inclusion on best graphic novels of the year lists, and designation as outstanding books in various genre categories.

Elizabeth D. Schafer

Bibliography

Crist, Eileen. *Images of Animals: Anthropomorphism and Animal Mind*. Philadelphia: Temple University Press, 1999. Focuses on language used to depict animals' instincts and interactions, addressing naturalists' and scientists' commentary regarding animal behavior, particularly Charles Darwin's anthropomorphic descriptions.

Keen, Suzanne. "Fast Tracks to Narrative Empathy: Anthropomorphism and Dehumanization in Graphic Narratives." *SubStance* 40, no. 1 (2011): 135-155. Analyzes how literary and artistic styles shape depictions of animal and human characters and influence readers' responses to *Deogratias: A Tale of Rwanda* and *Pride of Baghdad*.

Mitchell, Robert W., Nicholas S. Thompson, and H. Lyn Miles, eds. *Anthropomorphism, Anecdotes, and Animals*. Albany: State University of New York Press, 1997. Presents scholarly studies of such topics as animal cognition and instincts to debate the definition, purpose, and effective presentation of anthropomorphism in literary works.

THE BIBLE: GRAPHIC REVELATIONS OF AN OLD MEDIUM

Definition

A number of comics creators have published graphic novels that adapt all or part of the Bible through a mixture of text and sequential illustrations. Such works have received recognition for making the Bible accessible to younger readers, encouraging children and teens to become engaged in the stories and their morals.

Introduction

It has been argued that popular culture is giving rise to new ways of conceptualizing religious, political, and social issues. The relationship between popular culture and society can be regarded as a process in which people's fears, ideas, and opinions are projected onto popular culture, thereby influencing media content; however, popular culture can also be regarded as informing people about religious and social issues. Religion is a prominent theme in comic books and graphic novels, with the works of many comics authors acknowledging the authors' personal interest in religious and esoteric imagery and ideas. Comics authors have shown that through the medium's unique combination of text and images, comics can be a platform from which to provoke serious discussion on such issues as social change, war, and religion.

Since 2000, there has been a surge in publications of graphic novel adaptations of the Bible, including Jeff Anderson and Mike Maddox's *Lion Graphic Bible: The Whole Story from Genesis to Revelation* (2004), Michael Pearl's *Good and Evil: The Bible as Graphic Novel* (2008), and Sergio Cariello's *Action Bible* (2010). Various graphic publications, not only adaptations of the Bible, demonstrate the importance of the Bible in contemporary comics. Strong references to biblical ideas can be seen in Neil Gaiman's *Signal to Noise* (1992), Frank Stack's *New Adventures of Jesus: The Second Coming* (2007), Jim Munroe's *Therefore Repent!* (2007), and Mark Millar's *American Jesus: Chosen* (2009).

Graphic Bibles can be divided into three categories: literal graphic adaptations such as Robert Crumb's *Book of Genesis* (2009), graphic interpretations such as

Ajibayo Akinsiku's *Manga Bible: From Genesis to Revelation* (2007), and spin-off variations, which draw heavily on biblical ideas but develop them in new contexts, such as Douglas Rushkoff's *Testament* (2006-2008). Two of the most successful graphic Bibles are Akinsiku's and Crumb's texts, which are extremely different in content and artistic style. However, both texts express the stories and messages of the Bible successfully through the graphic novel form.

The Manga Bible

First published in 2007, *The Manga Bible: From Genesis to Revelation* is a manga-style adaption of Today's New International Version Bible created by British Nigerian artist Ajibayo Akinsiku, also known by the pseudonym Siku. His brother, Akindele Akinsiku, also known as Akin, wrote the script. Siku has published several other graphic Bibles, including *The Manga Bible: NT Raw* (2007) and *The Manga Bible: NT Extreme* (2007); the "extreme" editions of his work include the manga as well as the full text of the Bible, while the "raw" editions include only the manga. Siku has also created *The Manga Jesus: The Complete Story* (2010), a graphic novel about the life and works of Jesus.

Siku's books target a teen audience with the hope of engaging young people in Christian belief. Unlike traditional Japanese manga, *The Manga Bible* is read from left to right. The volume includes a glossary of some key biblical terms, an interview with the creators, and preliminary sketches of the characters. Scattered throughout the novel are references to scriptural passages that can provide interested readers with more information about various topics.

A devout Anglican, Siku sees his work on graphic novels as part of an exploration of his faith. In the introduction to the book, he states that it was his intention not to cover the entirety of the Bible within the graphic novel but to select visually compelling biblical stories that demonstrate key Christian values. However, some critics have argued that the artwork is too sketchy and lacks sophistication, and the book has additionally been criticized for its content and interpretation of the Bible.

In particular, Siku's representation of Jesus as an action hero and rephrasing of scriptural passages have been met with negative responses from some critics. Notable biblical stories such as the temptation of Christ by the devil are given new interpretations in Siku's adaptation, and the Book of Revelation is told through the visions of a twelve-year-old girl in the twenty-first century, a radical interpretation that has been criticized as confusing the original content of the Bible. However, other readers have welcomed the adaptation's unique take on the Bible and deemed Siku's edgy and expressive art ideally suited for communicating the stories of the Bible to younger generations. In 2008, it was reported that the book had sold more than thirty thousand copies in Great Britain alone.

Genesis Illuminated

In 2004, American underground comics artist Robert Crumb began work on a graphic retelling of the Bible focusing specifically on the Book of Genesis. Crumb originally planned to create a spin-off graphic novel focusing on the story of Adam and Eve; however, he found this task to be too difficult. Instead, intrigued by the language of the Bible, he decided to create a literal interpretation of Genesis in a graphic format. Crumb particularly wanted to provide a visual retelling of Genesis that included the stories of rape, violence, and incest that other graphic Bibles do not include. In order to ensure his depictions of the stories of Genesis would be as detailed as possible, Crumb researched many different translations of the Bible and consulted many biblical commentaries. *The Book of Genesis*, first published in 2009, contains all fifty chapters of Genesis, accompanied by black-and-white illustrations. The work bears the disclaimer "adult supervision recommended for minors," calling attention to the mature nature of the subject matter.

Although Crumb rephrases a few lines in order to make the stories more accessible to a modern audience, the text largely reproduces biblical scripture, particularly referencing the King James Version of the Bible and Robert Alter's translation in *The Five Books of Moses* (2004). The book and its imagery have been generally accepted as theologically accurate. The illustrations represent a traditional Western understanding of the Bible, with God depicted as an elderly white man. The landscape, scenery, and characters' garments also reflect a traditional Christian understanding of the Bible. However, the imagery also relates closely to Crumb's signature artistic style; the women are buxom and the images are strongly caricatural, and despite the serious content of the book, there are elements of humor and playfulness, particularly in the story of Adam and Eve.

Crumb's innovative use of humor and unique style of drawing are often described as "zany," "grotesque," and "outrageous" and have subjected him to controversy throughout his career, with some readers criticizing his work's overt violence and sexuality. Crumb's visual interpretation of the Bible was therefore both enthusiastically anticipated and feared. However, in the book's introduction, Crumb stipulates that the book is "a straight illustration job" with no intention to offend or ridicule. While some have criticized the work as focusing too much on the sexual and violent nature of Genesis, the book has mostly received positive feedback due its adherence to biblical text and Crumb's depth of research.

In 2010, *The Book of Genesis* was nominated for the Will Eisner Comic Industry Award in the categories Best Graphic Album—New, Best Adaptation from Another Work, and Best Writer/Artist. The Hammer Museum at the University of California, Los Angeles organized the book's illustrations into the traveling art exhibition *The Bible Illuminated: R. Crumb's Book of Genesis*. As of early 2010, the book had sold more than 120,000 copies worldwide.

Impact

Graphic Bibles have become increasingly marketable in the twenty-first century as a result of their popularity among children, teens, and adults. Although such works are mostly targeted at readers between the ages of twelve and twenty-two, they range from children's graphic novels such as Anderson and Maddox's *Lion Graphic Bible* to adult works such as Crumb's *Book of Genesis*, allowing the biblical narrative to reach readers of all ages through the graphic novel format and through both Western and manga-style art.

Graphic Bibles have had a positive impact on perceptions of the comics medium, which for decades was considered cheap, inferior, and nonintellectual. The development of the graphic Bible has contributed to the debate over whether comics can be used effectively as educational tools, particularly demonstrating the ability of comics to communicate complex ideas to younger generations. Despite controversy, Crumb's and Siku's "humanized" biblical texts have made the Bible more accessible to young readers through their language and expressive illustrations.

Emily Laycock

Bibliography

Garrett, Greg. *Holy Superheroes! Exploring Faith and Spirituality in Comic Books*. Colorado Springs, Colo.: Piñon Press, 2005. Examines the presence of Christian ideas in American superhero comic books and graphic novels, particularly discussing the persistence of Christian themes and their relationship to American culture.

Holm, Douglas K., ed. *R. Crumb: Conversations*. Jackson: University Press of Mississippi, 2005. Collects interviews with Crumb in which he discusses his art style, influences on his work, and the controversies surrounding his work.

Lewis, A. David, and Christine Hoff Kraemer. *Graven Images: Religion in Comic Books and Graphic Novels*. New York: Continuum, 2010. Examines the significance of religion in comic books and graphic novels and the ways in which comics communicate religious ideas.

COMEDY, SATIRE, AND THE CODES OF GRAPHIC HUMOR

Definition

Humor is a vital component of comic books and graphic novels. From the beginnings of the medium to the Modern Age, creators of both mainstream and underground works have used humor to deconstruct the genres in which they work, call attention to political or social issues, and simply entertain.

Introduction

The graphic novel and its attendant formats—comic strips, comic books, cartoon magazines, and picture books—display a wide range of comedic themes and strategies. In some respects, the graphic novel seems designed to generate or sustain what French philosopher Henri Bergson called the "reciprocal interference" between message and meaning, or intention and result, that drives comedy. The pacing of specific events, experiences, or environments across panels and pages, and especially within the carefully sculpted composition of each frame, hinges on a carefully deployed fusion of interdependent cues between the images, text, and reader—exactly the same type of intimate, assumptive address that drives the gags and running jokes of many comedic forms. The graphic narrative's humorous potential hinges on its energetic, telegraphic sequencing.

It is also crucial to consider that almost all forms of graphic narrative apply some element of visual simplification to their subjects. The simplified caricatures embedded in the narrative systems of comics are highly stylized, insistently inviting minicomedies in and of themselves. The traces of style left by artists, inkers, and other designers in these predominantly drawn texts make the reading experience that much more personal. Readers are constantly aware that someone has drafted these pleasant pictures, and the more they learn to appreciate the artists' arbitrary aesthetic choices, the more amicable and intimate their interpretations become, regardless of the content or subject matter. At the most fundamental narrative levels, there may be some truth in the old assumption that sequential art moves across "funny pages."

Slapstick and Sequence

Physical humor and crisp, witty speech have been features of graphic novels from the medium's earliest ancestors. Beginning with the 1842 comic *The Adventures of Obadiah Oldbuck*, the comedic impact of interacting frames and captions often superseded concerns about continuity, plot, or visual polish. Other early comic strips such as Richard Outcault's *Yellow Kid*, Winsor McCay's *Little Nemo in Slumberland*, George McManus's *Bringing up Father*, or Bud Fisher's *Mutt and Jeff* also reveal how carefully early practitioners blocked their sight gags, deployed their scorching comebacks, and orchestrated their final "punch line" panels.

At the same time, these early works also absorb or remediate the full gamut of American comic traditions, especially silent film pantomime. Vaudevillian farce, blackface minstrelsy, and pioneer humor are evident in early graphic narratives such as George Herriman's *Krazy Kat*, E. C. Segar's *Thimble Theater*, Fontaine Fox's *Toonerville Trolley*, and Milt Gross's picture novel *He Done Her Wrong*. Even the notorious Tijuana bibles satisfied a common urge toward perverse desecration, depicting comic strip characters, movie stars, athletes, and other celebrities in rude, usually degrading scenes of pornography and violence. All of these comic strip ancestors have had a profound influence on the graphic novels of later decades.

Animal Antics and Kiddie Comedy

Funny animal or anthropomorphic graphic novels portray the generally humorous misadventures of personified animals in a variety of highly stylized situations. As original works or cross-marketed venues for such film, television, or advertising personalities as Donald Duck, Snoopy, Garfield, Opus, and the Animaniacs, the funny animal genre ranks among the most enduring traditions in international comic art. The seminal works of early auteurs have been republished in ornate treasuries and compendia, creating new, novelesque contexts for an otherwise forgotten heritage of humor. Archival collections of *Krazy Kat*, Carl Barks's Disney comics, and Walt Kelly's *Pogo* have created revealing new perspectives on later works such as Robert Crumb's *Fritz the Cat* or Art Spiegelman's *Maus*.

Experiments with funny animal forms can lead to surprisingly philosophical meditations on humanity's folly, as in Adam Sacks's *Salmon Doubts* and Dave Sim's *Cerebus*. In such cases, the allegorical implications of the funny animal conceit turn provocatively on the transmutation of human ethics and social constructions with the species-specific, instinctual behaviors of animals and their habitats. A number of funny animal novels ingeniously manipulate reader expectations to emphasize both comedy and suspense. Significant juvenile examples include Jeff Smith's *Bone* epic and Andy Runton's *Owly* graphic novels. David Petersen's *Mouse Guard* and Frank Cammuso's *Maxx Hamm, Fairy Tale Detective* offer equally hilarious preteen reading, while the moody, nearly mute multivolume works of European cartoonists such as Jason and Lewis Trondheim introduce darker comic fusions of violence, anxiety, and loneliness for adults.

Children's comics also thrive outside of anthropomorphic traditions, especially in the subtle worlds of Ernie Bushmiller's *Nancy* and Marjorie Henderson Buell's *Little Lulu*, both of which have been reprinted in collected volumes. Teen comedy remains a key theme in works such as IDW Publishing's collections of *Archie* comics and Tania del Rio's genre-bending *Sabrina the Teenage Witch: Magic Revisited*.

Parody in Tights

The superhero, a figure defined by pride, courage, and strength, is especially ripe with comic potential. In fact, superhumor functions across an extremely wide range. In its most faithful avatar, humor aids and abets the earnest superhero's cause, providing heroes with an extra defense against evil, or at least another method of irritating their opponents. Thus, Spider-Man's signature wisecracks, Hellboy's workaday asides, and Wolverine's one-liners are laced with a focalizing tension that allows the readers to feel the interior turbulence that makes the heroes' psychologies so attractive. Yet, the tradition of heroic and villainous monologuing, in which one gloats over a vanquished foe, cries out for hubris-punishing humiliation and parodic retribution.

The one-shot *The Punisher Kills the Marvel Universe* offers a satirical take on comic books in the 1990's. (Courtesy of Marvel Comics)

Perhaps Cerebus's and Gnatrat's send-ups of comics creator Frank Miller's ultramasculine interior monologues are the strongest examples of this leveling trend in superbanter. Another rich vein of comedy arises from catty supergroup melodrama. In superhero soap operas such as Joss Whedon's installments of *Astonishing X-Men* and J. M. DeMatteis, Keith Giffen, and Kevin Maguire's outrageous *Justice League International* comics, superhero rivalry, romance, and righteousness mix into turbulent, deliciously superhuman explosions of frustration, pettiness, and hilarity.

Numerous villains link comedy with menace or insanity. Embracing humor as a weapon, cause, or gimmick, mad geniuses such as the Joker, Arcade, and Mr. Mxyzptlk trade on the subversive qualities of madness, nonsense, and anarchy to frustrate supposedly well-adjusted do-gooders with their sadistic, unfathomable enigmas. In fact, humor, with its attendant themes of healing and growth, seems especially to antagonize driven vigilantes and avengers such as Batman, the Spectre, and the Crow. Offbeat stories such as Miller and Bill Sienkiewicz's *Elektra: Assassin* and Alan Moore and Brian Bolland's *Batman: The Killing Joke* include extended meditations on the ironic similarities between superheroic egos and schizophrenic lunacy. Such deconstructive superstories use humor poignantly to suggest the inherent contradictions and ethnical limitations of caped crusading.

Perhaps superhero comedy is most rewarding when it self-reflexively plays upon the inherent absurdities of the genre. For example, Jerry Siegel and Joe Schuster's superhero Funnyman rollicks through the traditions of Jewish American humor in a campy parody of Superman's more ennobling origins. The relentless parody of heroes, fans, comics continuity, and creators themselves that drives Keith Giffen's Ambush Bug and Don Simpson's Megaton Man allow for comical revisions of the inner conflicts and grandiose combat that readers have come to expect from superhero stories. Similarly, fan-centered farces such as Garth Ennis and Doug Braithwaite's *The Punisher Kills the Marvel Universe* and more allusive parodies such as Neil Gaiman and Andy Kubert's *Marvel 1602* toy knowingly with readers' allegiance to the complex motivations and continuities of superhero multiverses.

Politics, Parody, and Perversity

Some of the most inventive humor in graphic novels is found in works published by small or independent presses. For example, series such as Eric Powell's *Goon* have picked up gothic horror comedy where works such as Batton Lash's *Wolff and Byrd: Counselors of the Macabre* left off. Terry Moore's touching *Strangers in Paradise* and Alex Robinson's melodrama *Box Office Poison* are realistic "dramedies" with comic tension reminiscent of the Hernandez brothers' *Love and Rockets*. By contrast, Peter Bagge's *Everyone Is Stupid Except for Me*, Eddie Campbell's *Bacchus*, and Shannon Wheeler's *Too Much Coffee Man* present nearly surreal mixtures of oppositional humor and visual wit. Like many young humorists, these authors

The cover of issue #8 of *Mad* magazine shows a cartoon by Harvey Kurtzman of two men as they follow oversized footprints through a hole in a brick wall; one says to a terrified woman, "We're looking for a monster, ma'm! Has one been by here lately?" (Getty Images)

display the influence of *MAD* magazine pioneers such as Harvey Kurtzman, Sergio Aragonés, and Antonio Prohías, as well as underground satirists such as Crumb, Harvey Pekar, and Trina Robbins. Even more scathing political humor runs through Ted Rall's *Generalissimo El Busho*, Jen Sorensen's *Slowpoke*, and Michael Leunig's *Strange Creature*.

Many lesser-known works of comedy continue to surprise readers with their light-hearted ingenuity and amusing lyricism. These texts include Jennie Breeden's *The Devil's Panties*, Tom Beland's *True Story, Swear to God*, and Ken Knudsten's *My Monkey's Name is Jennifer*. Experimental forms of abstract or absurdist comedy inform Chris Ware's moody essays on hopelessness and failure, Jim Woodring's nasty psychedelic fables, and David Mazzuchelli's explorations of form in *Asterios Polyp*.

Impact

From comedic comic strips such as Charles Schulz's *Peanuts* to absurd graphic novels such as Mazzuchelli's *Asterios Polyp*, the forms of humor and amusement that march through cartoon and comic art are truly legion. Scholars of graphic narrative have begun to examine how multijointed connections across the comics page establish various reader experiences, but the speed of Ignatz's brick in Herriman's *Krazy Kat* or the depths of outrage in Aaron McGruder, Kyle Baker, and Reginald Hudlin's *Birth of a Nation* are truly difficult to pigeonhole. There are, of course, plenty of irresponsible and even hateful graphic amusements that indulge in grotesque fantasies of misogynist or racist objectification; the currents of comedy are by nature reckless, raw, and frequently mean-spirited. In general, however, humor infuses itself into graphic novels with great alacrity across time and genre, and it would be exceedingly difficult to comprehend the merits of any small sampling without a twinge of laughter.

Daniel Yezbick

Bibliography

Corrigan, Robert. *Comedy: Meaning and Form*. New York: Harper, 1981. Provides a critical and theoretical basis for studies of humor in comic books and graphic novels through essays on major theories of humor.

Gabilliet, Jean-Paul. *Of Comics and Men: A Cultural History of American Comic Books*. Translated by Bart Beaty and Nick Nguyen. Jackson: University Press of Mississippi, 2010. Chronicles the history of the American comic book as a cultural phenomenon and aesthetic signifier and explores the role of humor in the form's development.

Hatfield, Charles. *Alternative Comics: An Emerging Literature*. Jackson: University Press of Mississippi, 2005. Explores of the aesthetics of the graphic novel and deciphers the complex nature of comic book art styles and the implications of sequence.

CRIME PAYS: THE CRIME AND MYSTERY GENRE

Definition

The crime and mystery genre has played a significant role in the development of comic books and graphic novels. Widely popular in other media, crime stories have largely been marginalized in American sequential art, primarily because of changes and controversies within the comics industry.

Introduction

Tales of crime and criminals are very common. Most cultures have mythic tales that involve wily thieves and trickster con men, and it is no surprise that crime is one of the oldest and most enduring genres in the mass media. Crime and mystery works have played a particularly significant role in the comics industry, influencing the industry's development while also serving as fuel for those who considered comics to be harmful to society.

Defining the genre is somewhat difficult. During the anticomics controversy of the 1950's, some critics considered any comic in which a crime occurred to be a crime comic. The genre would thus range from violent gangster comics to the relatively innocuous Disney comics in which the Beagle Boys attempt to rob Scrooge McDuck. A more accurate but still somewhat facile definition would be that a crime story is a story focused on a crime or series of crimes. This still leaves in a number of well-defined genres (horror, kung-fu, Western, superhero) in which crimes are narratively important because they allow other aspects of these genres to exist. A better, though imperfect, definition would be that crime stories are thematically and narratively about the commission or investigation of a crime or series of crimes. By extension, works concerning the activities of criminals and those who investigate crimes, be they police officers, private detectives, amateur investigators, or crime scene analysts, would also be part of the genre.

In American comic books and graphic novels, the popularity of the crime and mystery genre has been cyclical. How and how often the crime genre has been represented in comic books has been largely shaped by three events: the adoption of the Comics Code in 1954,

Criminal accommodates a wide variety of crime and noir story patterns and archetypes. (Courtesy of Marvel Comics)

the development of the direct market in the 1980's, and the rise of the graphic novel and the bookstore market in the 2000's.

Pre-Comics Code Crime Comics

Drawing on both comic strips and the lurid pulp magazines of the 1920's and 1930's, crime comics became popular when the initial popularity of superhero comics began to decline after World War II. By many accounts, crime (though often conflated with horror) was the most popular genre in the late 1940's and early 1950's. There were a number of different types of crime comics during this period. The most common were lurid tales of colorful gangsters and their curvy girlfriends. While the message of these comics was theoretically anticrime, in practice, the stories often glorified the violent exploits and outlaw life-styles of their protagonists. Though there were some police-based series, crime comics were mostly anthologies that introduced new gangs and gangsters in each issue, showcased their crimes, and then ended with their deaths or imprisonment. Among the most well known of these comics were Lev Gleason Publications' *Crime Does Not Pay* and Fox Feature Syndicate's *Murder Incorporated*.

A second type of crime comic featured the incursion of crime into the everyday life of the middle class, typically as the result of a love affair gone wrong or an impulsive decision made by the protagonist. This style of comic, typified by EC Comics' *Crime SuspenStories*, was socially subversive because it undercut the perceived desirability and safety of middle-class life. While this type of narrative dominated the EC titles, stories of middle-class people led astray by sex or drugs into a life of crime also populated the other crime anthology titles.

After rising to prominence in the early 1950's, the crime and horror genres—and by extension the entire comic book industry—were drawn into a maelstrom of rising social concern about juvenile delinquency. In response to this concern, the industry adopted a code of self-regulation that was to be enforced by the Comics Code Authority, a branch of the newly formed Comics Magazine Association of America. The Comics Code prohibited certain depictions of violence as well as any sympathetic treatment of criminals or crimes. In the immediate postcode period, larger publishers reacted to the code in the same way that the film industry had initially responded to the somewhat similar Motion Picture Production Code (or Hays Code)—by transforming its gangster comics into police comics. However, these were not particularly popular. Ultimately, crime comics, with a few odd exceptions that were mostly television adaptations, had effectively disappeared from the American comic book industry by the mid-1950's.

The Era of Direct Sales and Independent Comics
Crime comics returned in the early 1980's following the advent of direct sales. Direct sales, a system in which retailers preordered comics on a nonreturnable basis, lowered the cost of entry into publishing and paved the way for the foundation of many new independent publishers. Marvel and DC Comics, historically the two largest pub-

lishers, were able to bring back genres that would not have been profitable under the previous system of distribution.

Eclipse Comics, one of the earliest influential independent publishers, initially brought crime back to comics with Max Allan Collins and Terry Beatty's character Ms. Tree. The private investigator debuted in Eclipse's multi-genre *Eclipse Magazine* in 1981 and later moved to her own series. A number of other crime-related books followed, emerging in spurts from the burgeoning independent press. The magazines *RAW* and *Heavy Metal* included some European crime comics, and independent publisher Fantagraphics Books published anthologies featuring crime stories. Even the major publishers resumed publishing crime comics, with Don McGregor and Gene Colan's *Nathaniel Dusk* published by DC Comics in two miniseries in 1984 and 1985.

As the direct market matured in the late 1980's and 1990's, many more crime comics were published, notably Frank Miller's *Sin City* series (1991-2000), Greg Rucka and Steve Lieber's *Whiteout* (1998), and David Lapham's *Stray Bullets* (1995-2005). Published in black and white by independent publishers, these titles, just as the European crime comics, were heavily influenced by film noir. This period also saw a trend toward the publication of standalone graphic novels; DC's graphic novel imprint Paradox Press produced a crime series that included John Wagner and Vince Locke's *A History of Violence* (1997) and Collins and Richard Piers Rayner's *Road to Perdition* (1998).

While the crime genre never became incredibly popular during the direct sales period, its reappearance was not surprising. Direct sales allowed the comic book industry to become much more profitable, and the print-to-order economics of direct sales made it possible for publishers to produce comics in a wide variety of genres, though superhero, crime, and science-fiction comics remained most popular. At the same time, this development led comics to give up its status as a mass medium. Comic book stores catering specifically to fans of the medium became the primary source of sales, while sales at newsstands and other venues that attracted casual readers declined.

Crime Graphic Novels in the Bookstore Market
In the early years of the twenty-first century, the trade book market became a significant sales channel for

graphic novels, supplementing the shrinking comic book store market. This change helped bring graphic novels more cultural prominence as well as the attention of wider audiences. An increasing number of trade paperback and hardcover graphic novels, both originals and collections of previously serialized comics, appeared on bookstore shelves. Graphic novels moved out of the humor or children's areas and into dedicated

Whiteout features a Deputy U.S. Marshal investigating a murder in Antarctica. (Courtesy of Oni Press)

sections of bookstores and libraries. This was driven, at least in part, by the popularity of manga, Japanese graphic novels that cover a wide variety of genres, including crime and mystery.

The move to bookstores has had mixed effects on the crime genre of graphic novels. The genre is popular in the book market, and exposure to wider audiences has been beneficial to the comics industry as a whole. The bookstore market reduces the advantage the superhero genre holds in comic book stores. However, it also opens up the field to many other genres, and as graphic novels in bookstores are generally mixed together without regard for genre, it can be difficult for crime and mystery graphic novels to stand out among all the others. Still, the shift to the bookstore market was significant in the major publishers' decisions to publish crime graphic novels such as Ed Brubaker and Sean Phillips's *Criminal* (2006-   ) and Jason Aaron and R. M. Guéra's *Scalped* (2007-   ). In 2009, DC established a line of original crime graphic novels through its Vertigo Crime imprint.

Impact

The crime and mystery genre has had a significant impact on the comics industry as a whole. Crime, along with horror, was at the forefront of the 1950's controversy about comics that led to of the creation of the Comics Code. The code restricted the possible genres for graphic narrative, making it harder for comics to compete with the rise of television. The code and the subsequent rise of the comic book store market led to the prevailing association of comic books with the superhero genre.

The visual influence of film noir came to graphic novels through the crime genre. European crime albums such as José Antonio Muñoz and Carlos Sampayo's *Alack Sinner* series and the independent crime comics of the 1980's featured noir elements such as the use of lighting and shadow that were particularly effective in black-and-white comics. This style crept into other comic genres, appearing in superhero titles such as *Daredevil* and *Batman* and becoming a common visual approach for comics of the grim and gritty style popular during the 1990's.

Like much of the comic book industry's output, crime and mystery comic books and graphic novels have proved a fertile ground for licensing, with crime stories frequently adapted to other media. *Sin City*, *Whiteout*, *A History of Violence*, and *Road to Perdition* were all made into feature films. Similarly, the popularity of the crime genre in other media has led to the publication of graphic novel adaptations of crime and mystery works such as Arthur Conan Doyle's Sherlock Holmes stories. Artist Darwyn Cooke has created graphic novels adapted from Richard Stark's Parker crime novels, and mystery authors Ian Rankin and Jason Starr have written graphic novels for Vertigo's graphic crime line.

Mark C. Rogers

Bibliography

Benton, Mike. *Crime Comics: The Illustrated History*. Dallas, Tex.: Taylor, 1993. Provides a history of the genre, focusing primarily on the pre-Comics Code era and including many examples of the covers of crime and mystery comics.

Gabilliet, Jean-Paul. *Of Comics and Men: A Cultural History of American Comic Books*. Translated by Bart Beaty and Nick Nguyen. Jackson: University Press of Mississippi, 2010. Discusses the Comics Code and the development of direct sales, both of which are important in understanding the position of the crime genre within comics.

Nyberg, Amy Kiste. *Seal of Approval: The History of the Comics Code*. Jackson: University Press of Mississippi, 1998. Explores the 1950's controversy about comics and the development of the Comics Code and reprints "The Whipping," a significant EC Comics crime story.

Espionage, Spies, and Skullduggery: Comic Book Counterintelligence

Definition

The clandestine world of international espionage has been a fixture in comic books and graphic novels for decades, offering readers culturally and politically charged adventures that throw a spotlight on the shadowy world beyond the headlines and reflect the United States' shifting relationship with spies.

Introduction

For as long as the comics medium has existed, writers and artists have offered readers a tantalizing glimpse into the lives of spies and saboteurs as they scheme and plot to defeat foreign powers, invaders from outer space, or supervillains planning global domination. Originating in the days of organized crime and bootlegging and continuing through World War II, the Cold War, and the most recent struggles against international terrorism, the spy genre has been well mined over the years by comic book creators. Occupying a middle ground between the unblemished good of heroes and the unashamed evil of villains, spies and secret agents are forced to walk the line between the two extremes. As the comic book medium matured, so too did the depiction of this morally muddy reality, with as much attention paid to questioning the authority of those who direct the spies as the motives of those whom the spies fight.

The birth of the modern comic book industry took place in the early 1930's, but it was arguably the 1940's and particularly World War II that cemented so much of the vernacular of comics in the American psyche. The superhero genre dominated during that time, thanks in no small part to those crusaders' status as ideal symbols of the United States' heroic role in the battle against the Axis forces. But spies also played a vital role in the comics of the period, often finding themselves rubbing shoulders with the spandex-clad heroes that occupied comic books' colorful covers and at times becoming akin to superheroes themselves.

Golgo 13 is a manga series about a master Japanese assassin. It was inspired by a four-issue James Bond manga. (Courtesy of VIZ Media)

Golden Espion-Age

When comic books first appeared on newsstands, crime fighting in burgeoning urban centers was of paramount importance, and the earliest secret agents in the paneled pages matched wits with bootleggers, criminal kingpins, and occasionally foreign agents trying to strike a blow against American sovereignty. Secret Agent X-9 appeared in a comic strip of the same name and eventually in comic books published around the world. Later known as Secret Agent Corrigan, he was created by detective novelist Dashiell Hammett in 1934 and illustrated by Alex Raymond. Over the years, and occasionally in cooperation with the FBI, Corrigan fought against smugglers, arms dealers, racketeers, and military saboteurs. By the time the United States entered World War II, a virtual renaissance in comic book storytelling was also occurring, and secret agents such as Corrigan were tasked with tracking down Nazi infiltrators and working to preserve peace and liberty.

Perhaps the most prominent figure associated with espionage in the Golden Age was not a spy himself but the scourge of all foreign spies determined to ferret out Allied secrets. Alan Armstrong, also known as Spy Smasher, debuted in issue 2 of *Whiz Comics* (1940) alongside Captain Marvel, Ibis the Invincible, and Dan Dare. He employed hand-to-hand combat and his Gyrosub to battle enemies of freedom throughout the 1940's, facing an agent known as the Mask and the Nazi America-Smasher, among other foes. Although not a secret agent in the same mold as the Cold War-era agent James Bond, Armstrong exemplifies the hybridization of the spy and superhero genres that proved popular during World War II.

Agents of Change

Trading the moral certitude of the Allied crusade against the Nazi threat for the uncertainty of the nebulous battle against communist forces in the protracted Cold War of the 1950's and 1960's, the United States found itself indulging in far more ambiguous entertainment as it struggled to reconcile prosperity with paranoia. Emblematic of the thinking pervading US sensibilities of the time is the comic book villain Yellow Claw, created by Atlas Comics, a precursor to Marvel Comics, and first appearing in *Yellow Claw* 1 (1956). In keeping with the Asian stereotypes that had permeated Western pop culture during World War II, the Claw is an unflatteringly depicted Chinese communist warlord who looms over American cityscapes and threatens the American way of life through his nefarious international network of spies and scientists. Later included among the characters in the Marvel Universe, the Yellow Claw was a symptom of the fear that would plague the United States for decades to come.

While the Cold War inspired some dark and disturbing storytelling and incorrect, insulting racial stereotypes, it also sparked satirical jabs at the conflict,

best captured in the sharp-witted *Spy vs. Spy* series that first appeared in *MAD* magazine in 1961. Created by Cuban expatriate Antonio Prohías, the strip blends humor with pointed political commentary as two identical beak-nosed secret agents—one dressed all in black, the other in white—and an occasional gray-clothed female spy match wits, set traps, and blow each other to bits hundreds of times. This satirical conflict has continued for decades, even long after Prohías's departure from the strip in 1987.

Patch on the Genre

Spies have always played a role in the crime-fighting escapades of the superhero world. Batman's faithful butler, Alfred Pennyworth, was revealed to be a former British intelligence operative, which shed some light on his ability to engage in reconnaissance and man the Batcave. The fate of Peter Parker's parents was initially a mystery, but *Amazing Spider-Man Annual* 5 (1968) reveals that they were secret agents who had fought Captain America's archenemy, the Red Skull.

Perhaps the most famous comic book spy is Colonel Nick Fury, the leader of S.H.I.E.L.D, an organization devised by Stan Lee as Marvel's answer to the clandestine agencies that employed Bond and his ilk. Having first appeared in *Sgt. Fury and His Howling Commandos* in 1963, Fury debuted in this Bondian role in *Strange Tales* in 1965 before moving to his own self-titled series filled with high-tech weaponry, robotic duplicates, and enemies such as Baron Strucker and HYDRA, A.I.M., and even the Yellow Claw. With Lee scripting and Jim Steranko providing expressive and visually inventive artwork, Fury's escapades were some of the most fondly remembered tales of the era and set the standard by which comic book spies would be measured.

Although he is likely the best-known spy in film and literature, Bond himself was notably absent from comics in the 1960's and 1970's, apart from a single-issue adaptation of *Dr. No* in DC Comics' *Showcase* 43 (1963). He later appeared in an adaptation of *For Your Eyes Only* (1981) published by Marvel, but further adaptations and attempts at original series from several publishers were met with limited success, making the quintessential secret agent a footnote in the history of comic book secret agents.

License to Thrill

Writer Greg Rucka, who had previously garnered acclaim for the miniseries *Whiteout* (1998) and *Whiteout: Melt* (1999-2000), made a significant contribution to espionage comics with *Queen & Country* (2001-2007). The series follows British secret agent Tara Chace and offers readers a more realistic look at the bureaucratic workings behind the exploits of espionage agents. Using her sexuality as a weapon in the war against her nation's enemies, Chace is not an invincible superheroine but a flesh-and-blood person capable of making mistakes. This grittier approach to the secret agent adventure, combined with artwork by Steve Rolston and other artists that juxtaposes cartoonish exaggeration

with realistic backgrounds, makes *Queen & Country* one of the more intriguing chronicles of genre.

Chace is not the only female character to redress the gender imbalance in espionage-themed comics. J. Scott Campbell's tongue-in-cheek *Danger Girl* first appeared in 1998, mixing *Charlie's Angels* kitsch with explosive action. Marvel's superhero/spy hybrid Black Widow, also known as Natasha Romanova, switched sides over the years, first appearing in the 1960's as a villain but becoming more visible as a hero in later decades through her work with groups such as S.H.I.E.L.D. and the Avengers. In 2007, DC introduced a new Spy Smasher, US government agent Katarina Armstrong. Described by her creators as somewhat inspired by antiterrorist agent Jack Bauer from the television show *24*, Armstrong blurs the lines between right and wrong in the pursuit of her goals.

Impact

By the end of the twentieth century and the beginning of the twenty-first, the increasingly complex relationship between citizens and governments, those with authority and those under it, had become a major concern within American popular culture. As such, the already murky world of secret agents became murkier, with loyalties difficult to determine and the traditional dynamic of good versus evil finding little parallel in contemporary storytelling. Writers found a way to take the more enticing, fanciful elements of the genre and balance them with a look at the political and bureaucratic forces that shape the secret agent's constantly shifting world. Spies in comics of this period often became victims of their own leaders, lost souls trapped between ethics and duty. Even those who donned masks or capes in the comic book world found their roles far less defined than they had been in the past.

Arnold T. Blumberg

Queen & Country. (Courtesy of Oni Press)

Bibliography

Cronin, Brian. *Was Superman a Spy? And Other Comic Book Legends Revealed.* New York: Plume, 2009. Collects anecdotes and trivia about the comic book industry's colorful characters, creators, and publishers, including those working in the espionage genre.

Hajdu, David. *The Ten-Cent Plague: The Great Comic-Book Scare and How It Changed America*. New York: Farrar, Straus and Giroux, 2008. Provides a detailed account of the comic book censorship movement, controversial comic stories published at the time, and the Cold War-era politics that motivated the individuals involved.

Jones, Gerard. *Men of Tomorrow: Geeks, Gangsters, and the Birth of the Comic Book*. New York: Perseus Books, 2004. Discusses the formation of the comics industry in America and presents anecdotal portraits of many of the prominent players and their sociopolitical leanings.

Wright, Bradford W. *Comic Book Nation: The Transformation of Youth Culture in America*. Baltimore: Johns Hopkins University Press, 2003. Chronicles the comic book industry's early years from a more socially oriented viewpoint, focusing on the young readers and the stories that shaped them.

FANTASY: AN OLD GENRE IN A NEW MEDIUM

Definition

Supernatural non-horror fiction—the broadly defined "fantasy" genre—is among the oldest literary divisions, encompassing fairy tale, legend, myth, fable, folklore, magical realism, and spirituality. Sequential fiction offers a new voice to this venerable storytelling tradition, uniting evocative graphic art with magical stories new and old.

Introduction

The fantasy genre in comics encompasses stories set in worlds in which magic works and the supernatural exists. These elements are not inherently inimical or malevolent, as in supernatural horror stories, and fantasy comics are generally distinguished from superhero comics in which magical elements appear. The fantasy genre does not necessarily exclude science-fiction concepts, but fanciful hybrids such as steampunk or space fantasy are not widely considered a part of the genre and are typically set aside into their own categories. The crucial element in the genre is magic in all its forms: wizardry, magical creatures and races, plants and substances with magical properties, and direct and indirect appearances of gods, spirits, and demons.

The fortunes of fantasy in comics and graphic novels have generally followed the genre's success or failure in other media. Graphic novels are a relatively recent expression of comics art, and their commercial success seems to have been limited mainly to superhero stories, manga, and the occasional breakout independent work. Among the earliest and most successful of these independent projects was Wendy and Richard Pini's creator-owned and self-published *ElfQuest*, which was published in multiple graphic novels over the course of twenty-five years.

Underground and International Works

While the mainstream comics industry was relatively slow to embrace the fantasy genre as more than a sidenote to superhero or horror comics, various creators working in the field of underground comics or publishing outside of the United States explored the genre

The Bone books by Jeff Smith paradoxically insert simple, humorous comic strip-style characters into realistically drawn settings and pit them against foes that range from normal human beings to the nightmarish "rat creatures" that infest Smith's detailed, complex fantasy world. (Courtesy of Cartoon Books)

to a considerable extent. Vaughn Bodé's stories featuring Cheech Wizard were among the underground creations that examined mainstream fantasy ideas—in the case of the Cheech Wizard stories, a magical forest and its denizens—in a hipper, more cutting-edge context. French comics creator Philippe Druillet's Lone Sloane stories as well as his *Yragaël* crossed the boundaries of the fantasy genre frequently in the 1970's, helping inspire American and British artists to new heights of invention. Less technologically oriented or science fiction-based than works by contemporaries such as Moebius (Jean Giraud), Druillet's often-mystical works strongly influenced the development of the fantasy genre in graphic novels.

For all his decades of work in mainstream superhero comics, artist and art instructor Jack Katz would receive his greatest recognition for his groundbreaking early graphic novel, *The First Kingdom*. Although the setting is science fictional in many of its trappings and overtones, particularly in later volumes, the presence of identifiable Greco-Roman deities and metaphysical implications shows that Katz, like fellow superhero comics creator Jack Kirby, felt that the fantasy genre's conventions were as adaptable in modern times as they had been in centuries past. This freedom to experiment with genre expectations was further explored in the supernatural elements of stories by creators such as Jim Starlin (*Dreadstar*). As a genre, fantasy has tended to offer the writers and authors of graphic novels a means of escaping conventional methods of reaching their audience.

Alien Worlds

Most fantasy graphic novels and comics are set in pre-industrial, pre-gunpowder societies of one sort or another. The exceptions to this rule, such as Matt Wagner's *Mage* and Mike Barr and Brian Boland's *Camelot 3000*, are usually very clearly set in places that are different enough from the real world that there is little risk of confusion. More clear-cut fantasy graphic novels may be set in a supernaturally augmented version of a documented historical period, as in the twelfth century Europe of Chris Claremont and John Bolton's *The Black Dragon*, or in an ancient or feudal setting reminiscent of J. R. R. Tolkien's *Lord of the Rings* or Robert E. Howard's Conan the Barbarian stories.

Even when fantasy graphic novels offer visions of preindustrial cultures, the worlds in which they are set are not always recognizably parallel to Earth. The *Bone* books by Jeff Smith paradoxically insert simple, humorous comic strip-style characters into realistically drawn settings and pit them against foes that range from normal human beings to the nightmarish "rat creatures" that infest Smith's detailed, complex fantasy world. Larry Marder's *Tales of the Beanworld* expresses real-world ideas of ecology and social interaction in a fanciful world that borders on the surreal. The World of Two Moons, the setting of *ElfQuest*, is a fully thought-out, workable fictional world, but its diminutive, savage, wolf-riding tribal elves are absolutely not of Earth. Like its cousin the fantasy novel, the fantasy graphic novel attempts to displace the reader's point of view to a strange and different world—not necessarily a utopian one, but always one that emphasizes qualities strangely changed from the world the reader knows.

Bloodstar

The first fantasy graphic novel known to have identified itself as such was Richard Corben's *Bloodstar*, a 1976 adaptation of Howard's fantasy short story "The Valley of the Worm," one of several to chronicle the adventurous past lives of protagonist James Allison. As a number of critics and comics historians have noted, *Bloodstar* was the first self-described "graphic novel" that was neither a collection of previously published comics nor a prose novel with interspersed illustrations; Will Eisner's *A Contract with God, and Other Tenement Stories*, commonly cited as the first graphic novel, was not published until 1978. Despite Corben's inclusion of some science-fiction elements in the story, *Bloodstar*'s provenance as fantasy is clear.

Although Corben uses a large portion of Howard's original text in dialogue and narration, vital portions of the story are conveyed almost completely through the illustrations. Along with Howard's straightforward story line, violence and sex are given graphic form in Corben's bravura manner. If *Bloodstar* lacks any claim to the title of first graphic novel, it may actually be in its reliance on imagery rather than words. The medium of the graphic novel relies on a balance between the word and the image, and there will always be those who advocate the primacy of the word in fiction.

Fantasy and Narrative

The argument is often made that all fictional characters are figures of fantasy, and it has been asserted that the superhero story is a subgenre of fantasy fiction rather than science fiction or adventure fiction. However, these notions make the genre definition too shapeless and far-reaching to mean very much for either marketing or intellectual purposes. Despite this, there is an increasingly popular category of person for writers and artists to include in fantasy graphic novels: ordinary people like the readers, and in some cases, the readers themselves.

Breaking the narrative fourth wall and addressing the readers—drawing them into the story, effectively making them participants as well as the audience—is a narrative technique with a long history. Because fantasy holds within its genre definition the implication that it concerns things that do not and cannot exist, generally only the most fanciful and lighthearted fantasy comics have allowed characters to wink to the reader and imply kinship. (Exceptions can also be made for supernatural horror stories, such as the metanarrative in Corben's story "The Slipped Mickey Click Flip" in *Creepy*, and for the supernatural assumptions made in religious comics as part of their message.) It was only in the late twentieth and early twenty-first centuries that this narrative leap came to be added to the repertoire of magically oriented titles such as those of Alan Moore and Grant Morrison, both of whom describe themselves as real-world magicians and certain of their works as actual magical "workings."

Whether taken literally or not, such experiments in enchantment call the reader's attention to the question of where the fictive act ends in the author's mind and where it begins in the audience's. Viewing art as an act with two accomplices—the creator and the consumer—lends weight to the idea that for the duration of a short suspension of disbelief, the reader actually does live in a magical world in his or her mind's eye. If Joseph Campbell's and Carl Jung's notions of a shared body of motifs, stories, and ideas across eras and cultures exists in any sense, it is surely allegorical to the rich body of cultural folklore that rises up through fantasy graphic novels only to pass into other creative minds and be changed and retold in other forms. This primal, intuitive, and polymorphic quality is part of the enduring power of fantasy in graphic novels. In many regards, the fantasy genre may be regarded as the mythmaking genre.

Impact

Graphic novels, like all other printed media, have faced increasing challenges in the marketplace in the early

Meddling gods and magic help to define Eric Shanower's *Age of Bronze*, a retelling of the mythological Trojan War, as fantasy. (Courtesy of Image Comics)

twenty-first century. However, the fantasy genre has been one of the few genres of printed media to experience a surge of interest during the period. In the wake of the success of motion pictures such as Peter Jackson's adaptation of *The Lord of the Rings* and fantasy novels such as J. K. Rowling's Harry Potter series, the fantasy genre has seen a healthy dose of matching success in the graphic novel medium. The groundswells of support for comic books featuring Howard's Conan and Red Sonja characters have also contributed to this success, as has the popularity of fantasy-tinged titles in DC's Vertigo line, notably Bill Willingham's *Fables*.

Thematically, the body of folklore and myth that underlies fantasy fiction informs other genres as well. Starlin's satirical *Gilgamesh II* pointedly takes off on the Babylonian tale, and the legends of ancient

Greece are frequently retold in youth-oriented educational graphic novels such as Charles R. Smith and P. Craig Russell's *The Mighty Twelve: Superheroes of Greek Myth*. Magic, the fabric of fantasy and much of its raison d'être, is so frequently utilized in graphic novels that a dollop of fantasy is often a useful ingredient for any sequential story, providing an insight into human nature and a frisson of the esoteric and the unknown.

Richard A. Becker

Bibliography

Benton, Mike. *The Comic Book in America: An Illustrated History*. Dallas, Tex.: Taylor, 1993. Offers an overview of the trends in graphic storytelling and the movement toward comics that fall within the fantasy genre or incorporate fantasy elements.

Gabilliet, Jean-Paul. *Of Comics and Men: A Cultural History of American Comic Books*. Translated by Bart Beaty and Nick Nguyen. Jackson: University Press of Mississippi, 2005. Provides a comprehensive history of the American comic book, including discussion of the development of the fantasy genre.

Petersen, Robert. *Comics, Manga, and Graphic Novels: A History of Graphic Narratives*. Santa Barbara, Calif.: Praeger, 2011. Discusses the history of the comic book and graphic novel both in the United States and elsewhere, exploring publication trends and major works.

FUNNY ANIMALS: WHIMSY AND WORRY IN THE WORLD OF ANIMAL NARRATIVES

Definition

A thriving, historically diverse genre of graphic novels, comic books, and newspaper comic strips, the funny animal genre features anthropomorphic animal characters who provide broadly comic, frequently satirical commentaries on human nature. Often misunderstood as simplistic or juvenile, such comics frequently tackle themes of sociopolitical conflict, ethnic difference, and ideological complexity.

Introduction

The funny animal genre represents a seminal tradition that pervades every form of graphic narrative. Featuring personified animals as endearingly cute innocents or morally ambiguous allegories, stories center on slapstick farce, witty screwball or situation comedy, sweet romantic escapades, or outlandish adventures involving exotic locales and extreme stereotyping. Gravely existential animal fables are also popular. Early auteurs brought incredible narrative and thematic sophistication to key characters who migrated back and forth between newspaper funnies, movie screens, comic books, and, later, television. In the late twentieth and early twenty-first centuries, treasuries have begun to collect and republish these milestone works, including George Herriman's Dadaist *Krazy Kat*, Carl Barks's Disney comics, and Walt Kelly's beautifully rendered woodland satires in *Pogo*. In the turbulent 1960's underground comics scene, the vulgarity of countercultural deconstructions such as Robert Crumb's *Fritz the Cat*, Dan O'Neill's notorious Disney parodies, and Chester Crill and Robert Armstrong's *Mickey Rat* broke ground for more ambitious anthropomorphic experiments such as Dave Sim's *Cerebus* and Art Spiegelman's Pulitzer Prize-winning *Maus*. Reaching back to the earliest forms of comic art, the funny animal mode encompasses a narrative tradition as resilient and resonant as superhero or fantasy genres.

Origin of the Species

The funny animal mode has roots in several interconnected milieu. Foremost are the intensely personal connections to cuddly stuffed playmates and holiday fantasies involving the Easter Bunny or to other anthropomorphized animals of childhood. Early-learning texts create didactic lessons about the difference and

Author Walt Kelly smoking a cigar; the artist had a strong influence on the funny animal genre. (Time & Life Pictures/Getty Images)

diversity of life through endearing animal characters. In such works, our intense childish love for this virtual fusion of human/beast perspectives embraces the bold exoticism of zoo animals such as elephants, the familiarity of barnyard animals such as horses, the companionship of domesticated creatures such as dogs, and even the danger or irritation of household pests such as rats.

More serious animal parables and satires often embrace the anthropomorphic contrast between human and beast to critique the failings, abuses, and vices of supposedly superior, enlightened beings. From Aesop's fables and Geoffrey Chaucer's "Parliament of Fowls" to George Orwell's *Animal Farm* and Richard Adams's *Watership Down*, works using such cautionary strategies inform numerous graphic novels, including Brian K. Vaughan and Niko Henrichon's *Pride of Baghdad*, Grant Morrison and Frank Quitely's *We3*, and Matt Dembicki's *Trickster*. In total, however, anthropomorphic graphic novels find their most immediate referents in newspaper strips, Hollywood animated cartoons, and the funny animal comic book boom of the late 1950's.

Several of the most influential funny animal texts originated in newspaper strips and pamphlet comic books. Later reprinted in book-length compilations, these texts represent the first serious collections of otherwise serial, ephemeral material, and the sense of rediscovery and reevaluation attached to them remains one of the most exciting elements of graphic novel studies. Perhaps the most important contribution to the preservation of endangered funny animal comics has been Fantagraphics Books' effort to collect the complete run of Herriman's *Krazy Kat* in volume form. These uniform editions build upon earlier efforts by past publishers to make the entire *Krazy Kat* oeuvre available for twenty-first century readers.

Boom and Barks

Much funny animal art derives from the smooth fusion of sequential formats and repurposed characters from animated cartoons. Young readers' periodicals brimmed with animal tales, and by the mid-twentieth century, comics marketed to very young or preliterate children began to feature characters from animated

films. Even lesser Hollywood characters found great success as comic book heroes, including Barney Bear, Felix the Cat, and Mighty Mouse.

The preeminent titles, in both sales and quality, were unquestionably Dell Comics' *Walt Disney's Comics and Stories* and *Four Color Comics*. *Walt Disney's Comics and Stories* began its run in 1940 as a successor to the innovative *Mickey Mouse Magazine* and soon became synonymous with middle-class children's culture. Featuring the full Disney pantheon of animal icons, the series remains one of the longest-running titles in American history, reaching well over six hundred issues by 2000. Dell's other landmark series, *Four Color Comics*, ran for more than thirteen hundred issues between 1939 and 1962. Both series enjoyed enormous popularity and greatly influenced later funny animal comics. A number of notable artists worked for these publications, including long-time Mickey Mouse artist Floyd Gottfredson and early Donald Duck designer Al Taliaferro. Artists Carl Barks and Walt Kelly, in particular, would have a strong influence on the genre.

A former Disney animator, Barks worked for both *Four Color Comics* and *Walt Disney's Comics and Stories*, producing numerous ten-page slapstick stories between 1943 and 1965 as well as many book-length *Four Color* one-shot adventures. He also created stories for the comic book *Uncle Scrooge*. In addition to creating Scrooge McDuck, Barks introduced such Disney characters as Gladstone Gander, Gyro Gearloose, Magica De Spell, and the Beagle Boys. Barks fashioned compelling tales of misanthropic adventure, imperialist exploration, and cunning satire, developing his Duckberg stories as microcosmic morality plays in which, in the oldest traditions of animal parables, he lambasted ignorance, arrogance, and affectation and celebrated the virtues of intellect, industry, and camaraderie.

The anthropomorphic works of Kelly, another former Disney animator, are even more richly conflicted in their mixture of funny animal themes, deft comedy, and bold political commentary. Unlike Barks, Kelly published his comics in newspapers as well as in volumes reminiscent of later graphic novels. More than thirty such volumes, collections of his *Pogo* strips,

Krazy Kat. (Courtesy of Kitchen Sink)

were published between 1951 and 1976. Kelly's work is especially known for its idiosyncratic dialogue; throughout his *Pogo* stories, his creatures speak, sing, and kvetch in a fascinating gumbo of Southern dialects, figurative metaphors, and half-baked malapropisms that continue to delight juvenile and adult readers. *Pogo* originally featured a nostalgic mixture of ethnic comedy, minstrel routines, and rube humor, but the series evolved into one of the most poignantly tolerant and creatively uncompromising works in graphic novel history. Uniquely political in its time, Kelly's work openly condemned McCarthyism, promoted environmental responsibility, and invoked liberal attitudes with a zesty diversity, grassroots spirit, and unabashed joy.

Bad Animals: Underground and Alternative Press
Funny animal comics also inspired some of the most vehemently revolutionary graphic narratives ever conceived. Underground comics creators Harvey Pekar, Crumb, O'Neill, and Spiegelman each credit the genre as a formative influence on their use of comic art as a countercultural weapon against conformity, boredom, and repression. In particular, Crumb's *Fritz the Cat* features lewd behaviors involving illicit sex, drug use, and even terrorist activities that helped to define the scandalously deconstructive sensibilities of adult and underground comics for decades. The underground press spawned genre-bending comics magazines such as *Funny Aminals*, which simultaneously lauded the masterworks of Herriman, Barks, and Kelly while paving the way for more ambiguously politicized comics such as *Maus*, *Cerebus*, and Kevin Eastman and Peter Laird's *Teenage Mutant Ninja Turtles*. The most belabored of the underground's funny animal protests involved the legal battle over O'Neill's unsanctioned use of trademarked characters in his *Air Pirates Funnies*. The decade-long controversy provided evocative proof of the genre's importance as a testing ground for trademarked icons as well as its seditious potential in the hands of renegade artists.

In 1970's and 1980's, small press anthologies such as Spiegelman and Françoise Mouly's *RAW* magazine, Antarctic Press's *Albedo*, and Fantagraphics Books' *Critters* and *Adventures of Captain Jack* revised funny animal comics in edgy New Wave scenarios. Originally published as pull-out pamphlets in *RAW*, Spiegelman's *Maus* was compiled as two graphic novels published in 1986 and 1991, respectively. The complete memoir received a Pulitzer Prize Special Citation in 1992. Spiegelman's Holocaust tale deploys the anthropomorphic conceit of German cats and Jewish mice to universalize his family history, and his awareness of the limitations of the animal metaphor raises the tensions of the funny animal genre with unparalleled gravitas.

Other animal comics of the 1980's were similarly ambitious in scope and content. Early Fantagraphics anthologies featured the first installments of Stan Sakai's *Usagi Yojimbo*, a long-running samurai series with an anthropomorphic rabbit protagonist. Sim's *Cerebus*, originally conceived as an homage to the sword and sorcery genre, was first published in 1977. Over time, the story evolved into a unique excoriation of every conceivable establishmentarian theme in comics, politics, and religion, self-consciously exploding the notion of sweet animal protagonists.

The 1980's saw anthropomorphism take on serious concerns of gender and sexuality. Funny animal comics began to gain sexual relevance when a minor anthropomorphic character from an underground sex anthology became the protagonist of a new series, Kate Worley and Reed Waller's *Omaha the Cat Dancer*. The series features the explicit sexual escapades of a feline exotic dancer and her associates and received critical attention for its treatment of social and political issues related to sexuality. Alternative comics such as Shary Flenniken's *Trots* similarly emphasize sexual politics, and well-developed themes of anthropomorphic eroticism and animal sensuality appear in later works such as Juan Díaz Canales and Juanjo Guarnido's *Blacksad*.

New Model Animals
Since 2000, funny animal narratives have migrated across astonishing artistic terrains. The autobiographical candor of *Maus* and *Cerebus* has been echoed in works by ambitious talents such as Jason, whose experiments with anthropomorphic malaise include *I Killed Adolf Hitler* and *Isle of 100,000 Graves*. French cartoonist Lewis Trondheim has developed uniquely

personal funny animal graphic novels such as *The Spiffy Adventures of McConey* and the series *Dungeon*, coauthored with Joann Sfar. The original innocence of traditional funny animal comics fuels preteen works such as Sara Varon's bittersweet *Robot Dreams* and *Sweaterweather* and Frank Cammuso's *Maxx Hamm, Fairy Tale Detective*. More raucous young-adult comedies include Steve Purcell's *Sam and Max* and Pepo's *Condorito*. Mature alternatives such as Tony Millionaire's *Maakies*, a comic strip that has been collected in numerous volumes, and Martin Kellerman's *Rocky*, about a reprobate but lovable canine reminiscent of Fritz the Cat, explore the decadence and profligacy that began with the Tijuana bibles and continued through the underground period. As an early twenty-first century mode of comic art, anthropomorphism continues to revise previous traditions of cuteness and comedy while pressing into deeper, and occasionally dangerous, habitats.

Impact

Funny animal comics have greatly influenced the field of comics studies, providing a wealth of thematic issues for analysis and interpretation. One primary concern is the depth or extremity of animalistic transformation in such narratives. In some cases, the principal metaphor or animal disguise is nearly transparent, little more than a mask. Such characters appear almost completely human except for a thin bestial veneer involving fur, wings, scales, or tails. In most cases, however, funny animals represent a fairly balanced mixture of human and bestial features. Animals speak, act, and feel in human terms rather than as people who have been retrofitted with slight or symbolic animal tropes. This mode can lead to contradictions, as in volume 2 of *Maus*, in which Spiegelman breaks from the narrative to discuss the thematic difficulty of introducing actual feline pets into his cat-and-mouse metaphor. Another major consideration involves whether funny animals interact with actual humans or if they populate their own closed anthropomorphic worlds. Various comics creators have explored these two possibilities, and both sorts of narratives have explored the meaning of humanity and humankind's place in the world. All told, the funny animal persists as one of the comics industry's most familiar and malleable traditions, continually urging creators and readers to use graphic novels and their brethren to examine their own tenuous grasp on humanity.

Daniel Yezbick

Bibliography

Gabilliet, Jean-Paul. *Of Comics and Men: A Cultural History of American Comic Books*. Translated by Bart Beaty and Nick Nguyen. Jackson: University Press of Mississippi, 2005. Provides a comprehensive history of the American comic book, including discussion of the development of the funny animal genre.

Gifford, Denis. *The International Book of Comics*. Rev. ed. London: Hamlyn, 1990. Discusses the history of comics art both in the United States and abroad and features chapters on early funny animal comic strips.

Keen, Suzanne. "Fast Tracks to Narrative Empathy: Anthropomorphism and Dehumanization in Graphic Narratives." *SubStance* 40, no. 1 (2011): 135-155. Presents a variety of concepts and critical praxis that are effectively applied to both classic and contemporary graphic novels featuring anthropomorphic characters.

HISTORY AND HISTORICAL FICTION: THE MANY FACES OF GRAPHIC HISTORY

Definition

History can take many forms in graphic novels. On the basis of the historicity of the depicted events, a work may fall into the category of nonfiction, historical fiction, or alternate history. Since history is omnipresent in many long-standing subgenres, overlap is inescapable; however, graphic novels that take place in distinct historical periods but do not offer any comment on humanity's past or present may be excluded from the historical genre.

Introduction

The often cruel but intriguing course of human history has provided writers and artists working in a variety of media with a plethora of stories that are frequently more fascinating than fiction. While the potentially usable historical material remains basically the same throughout these different media, the ways in which it is incorporated into the creative products vary widely. In graphic novels, history is likely to be represented rather subjectively because of the comics-specific combination of words and pictures. With all the laws of the medium involved, even the most documentary, historically faithful graphic novel will seem less objective than a written report on the same events. Moreover, since realistically filmed pictures will always appear more neutral than the most truthfully drawn images, history tends to be perceived as more fictional in graphic novels than in purely visual media.

Within this virtual impossibility of objectivity lies the particular appeal of the treatment of the historical in graphic novels. Obviously, not being the works of scholars, most historical graphic novels seek to show more than how things actually were. Nevertheless, creators of this type of graphic novel usually care a great deal about historical accuracy. Even those artists who introduce purely fictional characters or events tend to avoid anachronisms and other inaccuracies with respect to the depicted historical setting and props so that if such inaccuracies do appear, they have a purposeful effect.

It Was the War of the Trenches graphically depicts the horrors of the First World War. (Courtesy of Fantagraphics Books)

Several criteria can be used to break down the mass of historical graphic novels, the most obvious of which is the epoch in which the graphic novel's events take place. More fundamental, however, is the historicity of the shaped universe, which allows readers to separate the category of historical graphic novels into the subcategories of nonfiction, historical fiction, and alternate history.

Nonfiction

In nonfictional graphic novels, all significant characters are generally historical, and most of their story lines can theoretically be verified in history or reference books. In spite of its detractors, the comics medium has long been used to instruct children in national or world history, among other subjects. A highly realistically drawn story such as Jack Kirby's "April, 1861: Fort Sumter" in *Classics Illustrated* 162a (1961), about the outbreak of the American Civil War, is a fine example of the educational and ideological purposes of such histories.

The lives of famous people are also a favored subject of nonfictional graphic novels. Graphic biographies drawn in various styles (as in the *Edu-Manga* series narrated by Astro Boy) have chronicled the lives of historical figures as diverse as Ludwig van Beethoven, Isadora Duncan, Anne Frank, Malcolm X, Mother Theresa, and Leon Trotsky. Such works at times offer too many facts at the expense of a satisfying plot; in other words, they are too much history, too little novel.

History in graphic novels is often mediated by an autobiographical narrator who is to be identified with the named comics creator, as in Marjane Satrapi's *Persepolis* (2000-2003). The interweaving of individual experiences and personal linguistic and graphic styles with history inspiringly challenges the actual notion of nonfiction. The presence of an eyewitness emphasizes the near impossibility of reconstructing the historical truth. Of course, this booming subgenre (sometimes flirting with journalism, as in the work of Joe Sacco) is limited to contemporary events, the outcome of which the artists seldom know themselves.

Historical Fiction

Graphic novels in the historical fiction subgenre are less bound by historical fact than nonfiction comics. In such works, the main characters and even the very story lines may be entirely invented as long as the setting (and often some particular characters) is historical. As in historical prose novels, it is the interaction between a (fictional) hero and historical characters, events, laws, and customs that attracts readers interested in the past. For example, during his wanderings, Hugo Pratt's sailor Corto Maltese meets, joins with, or fights against historical figures such as those of the Russian Revolution (*Corto Maltese in Siberia*, 1975). Through their actions, such heroes seem to affect the historical events in which they become entangled; however, the artist will normally not let them change the course of history. The protagonist may also be historical, as in nonfiction, but in

historical fiction, the historical protagonist becomes involved in events that could have happened but generally did not actually occur. Such historical protagonists can interact with fictional characters, as in Frank Miller's *300* (1998).

In some works, historical characters are totally absent. In this case, the invented characters' behaviors and social conditioning allow the novel's creator to provide his or her unconstrained view on how life was in that period. The corresponding image of history may be romanticized, as in Hal Foster's medieval *Prince Valiant* (1937-), or it may be an indictment that transcends the time portrayed. Jacques Tardi effectively expresses the pointlessness of war in *It Was the War of the Trenches* (2010), a historically precise World War I graphic novel in which no character directly reminds the reader of concrete historical actors.

Alternate History

During the creative process, practically all creators of historical graphic novels must omit, add, or slightly distort elements of their historical stories. Such small changes are understood to be necessary in creating a historical work. If, on the other hand, the artist makes the characters substantially divert the course of history or depicts a past that must be the result of a crucial event or decision that never took place in the real world—the so-called point of divergence—the graphic novel is a work of alternate history.

In this subgenre, it is necessary that the point of divergence (and the depicted period thereafter) be situated in time before the first publication of the graphic novel in question. Otherwise, the work enters the realms of science fiction or fantasy, in which the alternative worlds usually differ far more from the real world than in the alternate history subgenre. Alan Moore and Dave Gibbons's *Watchmen* (1986-1987) is a case in point: Whether the reader chooses as its point of divergence the advent of masked vigilantes or the "rebirth" of scientist Jon Osterman as superbeing Dr. Manhattan, both events precede the creation and publication of *Watchmen*. In contrast, although twenty-first century readers may think of Moore and David Lloyd's *V for Vendetta* (1982-1989) as another example of alternate history, the work in fact takes place in the late 1990's and was conceived during the 1980's. Thus, *V for Vendetta* is actually an example of dystopian fiction.

Potentially much more playful than nonfiction and historical fiction, alternate history can offer keen and original visions of the mechanisms and futile coincidences of human history. This kind of graphic novel raises particular challenges for the creators because the alternate story world must be different from the real world but have a coherent history. Unlike *Watchmen*, most works in the alternate history genre reveal from the outset that they are "uchronical," as in Éric Corbeyran's *Uchronie(s)* series (2008-2011).

Other Parameters

In addition to the degree of historicity, criteria used to subdivide historical graphic novels can include the period in which the action takes place. There is no historical epoch that has not been evoked in the comics medium, from prehistory through the twentieth and early twenty-first centuries. Generally speaking, works about history from World Wars I and II onward are more likely to contain personal critical and political comments, especially autobiographical works. Historical fiction set against prehistoric backgrounds, such as Will Eisner's story "Humans" in *Will Eisner's Quarterly* 7 (1985), however, is just as able to provide the reader with insightful observations about the human race and its place in history.

Some graphic novels represent more than one time period. Probably the medium's most notorious device to realize this is the time machine (as in Larry Gonick's *Cartoon History of the Universe*, 1990-2009), but the very nature of the medium aptly allows for less incredible time traveling as well. Art Spiegelman's nonfiction work *Maus* (1986, 1991) presents scenes from his father's life in the 1930's and 1940's as well as

scenes depicting Spiegelman's work on the novel in the 1980's. Further parameters that can also be used to break up the historical genre include style, narrative perspective, and function.

Impact

The influence of human history on the graphic novel cannot be overestimated. From Rodolphe Töppfer, the Swiss pioneer of the modern comics medium, onward, artists have made their characters interact with history. The merely instructional use of the historical genre is still practiced with regard to young readers, but in the late twentieth and early twenty-first centuries, artists worldwide have conceived mature graphic novels about their individual, deliberately subjective thoughts regarding the past and present. Given the ever improving status of the graphic novel medium as an autonomous and thoughtful art form, the hybrid combination of words and pictures

Josh Neufeld's *A.D.: New Orleans After the Deluge* tells of seven real people from New Orleans as they experience the approach of Hurricane Katrina, the storm itself or the exodus to avoid it, and the aftermath. (Courtesy of Pantheon Books)

will likely continue to be used to give shape to artists' ideas about the often bizarre course of history.

History has influenced other genres as well, prompting superhero comics to comment on the state of the world following the terrorist attacks of September 11, 2001, for instance. In addition, the way in which graphic narrative has depicted and interpreted the past has had a significant impact outside the medium. Scholars of popular culture, literature, and historiography have begun to analyze graphic novels as historical documents, calling attention to the ways in which such narratives shed light on bygone ideologies.

Michel De Dobbeleer

Bibliography

Chute, Hillary. "Comics as Literature? Reading Graphic Narrative." *PMLA* 123, no. 2 (March, 2008): 452-465. Argues that the representation of history in graphic novels is at least as complex as in prose literature and includes examples from the work of Art Spiegelman and Joe Sacco.

McKinney, Mark, ed. *History and Politics in French-Language Comics and Graphic Novels.* Jackson: University Press of Mississippi, 2008. Discusses Franco-Belgian comics using academic tools that can be applied to graphic novels dealing with history regardless of the country of origin.

Witek, Joseph. *Comic Books as History: The Narrative Art of Jack Jackson, Art Spiegelman, and Harvey Pekar.* Jackson: University Press of Mississippi, 1989. Offers critical and aesthetic comments on the specific relations between graphic novels and history in the United States, focusing on the work of Jackson, Spiegelman, and Pekar.

HORROR COMICS: THE BIRTH, DEATH, AND REANIMATION OF A GENRE

Definition

Horror comics purposely attempt to produce fear and anxiety in the reader through the depiction of uncanny or distorted imagery, the expression of the psychological terror of the characters or narrative, or other means.

Introduction

Along with superhero and underground comics, horror comics have had a significant and problematic influence on comics and cultural perceptions of the form. Horror comics had a later start than many other comics genres, not fully emerging until the late 1940's and early 1950's. Under the guidance of editor William Gaines, EC Comics became the major horror comics publisher in the early 1950's. Following a series of congressional hearings in which a Senate subcommittee investigated the supposedly harmful effects of comics, the comic book industry established the Comics Code, a set of industry standards that greatly restricted the content of horror comics and led to a significant decrease in their publication.

Publishers had begun to circumvent the Comics Code by the late 1960's, and in 1971, the code itself underwent revisions that loosened its regulations. Horror surged during the 1970's with the major publishers but slowed into the 1980's. Independent publishers took up the gauntlet, publishing an array of horror comics, including Arrow Comics' *Deadworld* and Eclipse Comics' anthology series *Tales of Terror*. Horror comics remained on the periphery during the 1980's and 1990's. Series such as *Swamp Thing*, *Hellblazer*, *Ghost Rider*, and *Blade* were successful, but many horror series were short-lived and did not survive beyond the 1990's.

The rising popularity of the horror genre in prose fiction, film, television, and manga created a new demand for horror comics in the 2000's, prompting several new talents and regular series to emerge. Crossovers also served to increase the horror genre's popularity. For example, Ash Williams from the *Evil Dead* film series (1981-1992) appears in the Marvel

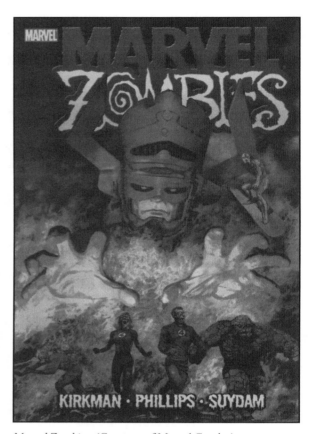

Marvel Zombies. (Courtesy of Marvel Comics)

Zombies universe in *Marvel Zombies vs. The Army of Darkness* (2007), and in *Freddy vs. Jason vs. Ash* (2007), he is pitted against Jason Voorhees and Freddy Krueger, characters with their own respective horror film and comics franchises. The success of horror comics during this period allowed creators to experiment with creating complex, macabre stories.

Early Horror Comics

The first horror comics were largely adaptations of literary works. Created by Dick Briefer, *The New Adventures of Frankenstein* became a regular feature in *Prize Comics* starting in 1940. The story pitted Mary Shelley's monster, erroneously identified as Frankenstein, against a variety of foes, including superheroes. By 1945, Briefer reinvented the series as a lighthearted, humorous narrative. An adaptation of Robert Louis Stevenson's *The Strange Case of Dr. Jekyll and Mr. Hyde* (1886) was published in 1943 as part of the *Classics Illustrated* line of graphic adaptations of literary works, and adaptations of *Frankenstein* (1818) and a collection of stories by Edgar Allan Poe followed.

For much of the 1940's, only a handful of horror titles made it into publication, since superhero, crime, and other genres still garnered the most attention. Beginning in 1944, the superhero anthology comic *Yellowjacket Comics* included the series *Tales of Terror*, which ran for two years. Publisher Avon Comics released the horror anthology *Eerie* in 1947, though it never saw a second issue. One of the few ongoing horror comics, *Adventures into the Unknown* was published by American Comics Group from 1948 into the 1960's. As crime comics caught on with comics readers, especially young men returning from World War II late in the decade, horror comics also became increasingly popular.

EC Comics and the Comics Code

Under editor William Gaines, the publisher EC Comics rose from obscurity to fame in the late 1940's and 1950's. Its major breakthrough series, *The Vault of Horror* and *Tales from the Crypt*, debuted in 1950 and triggered a cascade of similar horror comic publications over the ensuing years. Vying for readers, the publishers collectively pushed the limits of gore and violence with each issue. The violence of horror and crime comics drew attention to the comics industry, much of it negative. Psychiatrist Fredric Wertham linked comic books to juvenile delinquency, arguing in *Seduction of the Innocent* (1954) and other publications that the content of comics was having a negative effect on the children of the United States.

The resulting social controversy culminated in a series of hearings before a U.S. Senate subcommittee held in April and June of 1954. Gaines and Wertham both spoke at the meetings, but the committee ultimately sided with Wertham. Seeking to avoid government regulation, the Comics Magazine Association of America was formed and responded by establishing the Comics Code Authority (CCA), which self-regulated content for the comics industry in accordance with the newly drafted Comics Code. The code drastically diminished the range of horror stories that could be told, banning stories dealing with "walking dead, torture, vampires and vampirism, ghouls, cannibalism, and werewolfism," as well as "all scenes of horror, excessive bloodshed, gory or gruesome crimes, depravity, lust, sadism, masochism," and more. Comics could be published without the CCA's approval, but many vendors and distributors refused to stock comics without the CCA seal. A number of publishers went out of business following the implementation of the code.

Horror Comics Escape the Code

Throughout the 1950's and early 1960's, horror comics maintained a limited presence in the industry. EC Comics began to focus primarily on *MAD* magazine, and other surviving publishers either terminated their horror series or transitioned them into other genres such as mystery, science fiction, superhero, and suspense. What horror comics remained were predominantly monster stories that were derivative of 1950's monster films, developed in response to the rise of nuclear power and the escalating Cold War, or served as vehicles for superheroes to showcase their increasing powers.

Toward the middle of the 1960's, comic publishers circumvented the CCA and published horror comics as black-and-white magazines, which did not require the CCA's approval. Warren Publishing was the main publisher to explore this avenue for horror comics, publishing *Creepy*, an anthology of horror stories much like those from the early 1950's, beginning in 1964. By 1970, other publishers had followed this trend. The following year, the CCA lessened the severity of the code after Marvel Comics published several issues of *The Amazing Spider-Man* addressing drug abuse without CCA approval. The success of these comics proved to publishers that they could produce material that violated the code and be met with success. As the 1970's progressed, Marvel and DC Comics established a variety of horror series, both anthology comics such as *Chamber of Chills* and *Secrets of Sinister House* and ongoing series such as *Swamp Thing* and *The Tomb of Dracula*.

Modern Age Horror Comics

The rise of the direct-market system of distribution also lessened public concern about the nature of horror comics. Comics were increasingly sought out and purchased at comic book stores instead of the newsstands of the previous generation. By the 1980's, independent publishers dominated the genre.

During the 1990's and 2000's, the rise in popularity of the horror genre in prose fiction and film and the further loosening and virtual demise of the Comics Code contributed to a further increase in the publication of horror comics. The market was also increasingly influenced by the rise of manga, which included a significant influx of horror narratives by such creators as Hideshi Hino and Junji Ito. As publishers developed their own rating systems or simply sought out adult audiences, the public concern about the content and

Rex Mundi is one of the more notable horror comics. (Courtesy of Dark Horse)

graphic nature of horror comics was largely diminished.

Horror comics increased in popularity during the 2000's in part because of the success of Steve Niles and Ben Templesmith's *30 Days of Night* (2002) and Robert Kirkman's *The Walking Dead* (2003-). Though both were published by independent publishers, their popularity pushed DC and Marvel to publish a range of horror comics in the following years, often through their adult imprints. Horror comics returned to the mainstream with regular monthly publications of ongoing vampire, werewolf, zombie, and other horror-centered narratives.

Impact

The popularity of horror comics during the 1940's and 1950's and the subsequent controversy that led to the creation of the Comics Code played a significant role in creating the perception of comics as children's entertainment. With the Comics Code in place, comics were essentially banned from telling complex narratives for a generation, preventing the growth and development of comics as a sophisticated medium. However, the pre-Code horror comics had a significant influence on many horror storytellers of the twentieth and early twenty-first century; John Carpenter, Stephen King, George Romero, and R. L. Stine, among many others, credit horror comics with inspiring their forays into the genre. Horror comics remain a substantial niche within comics, with mainstream publishers DC and Marvel, as well as smaller companies, publishing horror series on a regular basis.

Horror comics served as the inspiration for the film series *Creepshow* (1982-2007) as well as the television series *Tales from the Crypt* (1989-1996). A number of comics have been adapted into films, including *30 Days of Night* (2007), the *Blade* series (1998-2004), and *Faust: Love of the Damned* (2001). In 2010, *The Walking Dead* was adapted into successful a television series, calling attention to the enduring popularity of the horror genre.

Lance V. Eaton

Bibliography

Benton, Mike. *Horror Comics: The Illustrated History*. Vol. 1 in the *Taylor History of Comics*. Dallas, Tex: Taylor, 1991. Gives a decade-by-decade breakdown of trends in horror comics from the 1940's to the 1990's, including images of covers and an extensive guide to horror titles.

Hajdu, David. *The Ten-Cent Plague: The Great Comic-Book Scare and How It Changed America*. New York: Farrar, Straus and Giroux, 2008. Provides an extensive look at the rise of horror comics and the factors leading to their decline, including the influence of Fredric Wertham and the congressional hearings.

Nyberg, Amy K. *Seal of Approval: The History of the Comics Code*. Jackson: University Press of Missis-sippi, 1998. Highlights the role that horror comics played in Wertham's attack on the industry and discusses the loosening of the Comics Code and the return of horror comics.

Wright, Bradford W. *Comic Book Nation: The Transformation of Youth Culture in America*. Baltimore: Johns Hopkins University Press, 2001. Chronicles the history of comics and their role in culture and provides context for the decline of horror comics in 1950's and their return during the 1970's and 1980's.

MANGA AND ITS IMPACT ON THE GRAPHIC NOVEL

Definition

Manga are comics and graphic novels produced in Japan. Since the 1990's, manga has become part of the larger global culture thanks to the international popularity of titles such as Naoko Takeuchi's *Sailor Moon*, Akira Toriyama's *Dragon Ball*, and Natsuki Takaya's *Fruits Basket*.

Introduction

Manga's roots have been traced back as far as the twelfth century, when Japanese artists created *emakimono*, or picture scrolls, depicting animals, humans, and objects. Such scrolls could reach up to eighty feet in length and did not contain the panels seen in later examples of graphic art. Some scrolls included text and images, while others were wordless. Japan's narrative art continued to evolve over time, and the first graphic narratives in booklet form were published in the eighteenth century. Japan was introduced to Western cartoons in the nineteenth century when the country's period of isolation ended, and improved printing technologies from the West allowed Japanese artists to mass-produce printed works quickly and inexpensively. The first serialized Japanese comic strip to feature recurring characters, *Tagosaku to Mokube no Tokyo kembutsu*, was created by Rakuten Kitazawa and published beginning in 1902.

Through the early twentieth century, Japanese artists drew inspiration from American comics and serialized many works of sequential art in Japanese publications. Following the outbreak of World War II, government censorship restricted the activities of Japanese artists. After Japan surrendered in 1945, artists gained more freedom to express themselves, and their cartoons shifted from political propaganda or commentary to depictions of family life. Beginning in this period, the manga industry was revolutionized by the work of Osamu Tezuka, who created the graphic narrative *Shin takarajima* (new treasure island) in 1947 and went on to create influential manga such as *Astro Boy* and *Princess Knight*. He expanded the boundaries of the medium, developing innovative story lines and cre-

Cartoonist Osamu Tezuka. (Getty Images)

ating a new style of art influenced by the work of American animators such as Walt Disney and Max Fleischer. Tezuka inspired numerous artists to develop complex narratives within the manga medium.

During the mid-twentieth century, serialized magazines such as *Manga Shōnen* became widely popular, creating a sizable audience for Japanese graphic narratives. Series originally serialized within manga magazines were collected into volumes, or *tankōbon*, which became a widely popular form of inexpensive entertainment. In the 1990's, anime (animated television shows often based on manga series) became increasingly popular outside of Japan. The international popularity of anime opened the door for manga, allowing translations of a wide variety of series to reach the global market. In the early twenty-first century, manga was translated into many languages and sold worldwide, attracting readers of all ages and genders.

Art and Layout

While there is no one style of manga art, a number of artistic and layout-related elements generally differentiate manga from comics published in other countries. Created by artists known as *mangaka*, manga are drawn and printed to be read from right to left, in keeping with the right-to-left orientation of Japanese writing. Thus, when reading a manga volume, one must begin at what Western readers might consider the back of the book and read the pages and the panels on the pages from right to left. The panels are often set up like frames of a film, showing the progression of movements to give the reader a sense of time and action, and at times, the panels run together or are not used at all. Manga also features many types of text, from spoken dialogue written inside text bubbles to the silent inner thoughts of the characters and onomatopoeic sound effects written in the background.

Backgrounds can be simple or detailed, and the level of detail often contrasts with the detail of the characters or objects in the foreground. Manga is particularly known for placing simple characters against complex, realistic backgrounds. *Shōjo* manga often feature floral backgrounds that indicate the characters' emotions, while *shōnen* manga often use sketchy backgrounds featuring motion lines to convey fast-paced action. Characters in all genres are frequently drawn with large eyes, a characteristic attributed to the influence of Disney's animated films on influential *mangaka* such as Tezuka. Exaggerated features such as large eyes serve to express emotion and further enhance the characterization within the narratives.

Subgenres and Story Lines

Manga is divided into a number of subgenres that refer to the age and gender demographics to which the manga magazines are targeted. It is important to note that these designations are not binding; while a series published in *Weekly Shōnen Jump* is marketed to teenage boys, its readership is not limited to that demographic. *Shōjo* re-

fers to manga written for preteen and teenage girls, while *shōnen* refers to manga written for boys of the same age. While each has its own conventions, there has been a great deal of blending between the two subgenres since the 1990's. *Josei* refers to manga that target women and older female teens. Often considered a grown-up form of *shōjo*, *josei* manga feature more realistic narratives that depict the complex reality of women's lives. Such series may include more mature subject matter and themes than their *shōjo* counterparts. Similarly, *seinen* manga are targeted at teenage and adult male readers and may feature more explicit portrayals of violence and sexuality than *shōnen* series. *Shōjo-ai* (sometimes referred to as *yuri* or "girls' love") refers to texts featuring romantic or sexual relationships between women, while *Shōnen-ai* (sometimes referred to as *yaoi* or "boys' love") refers to texts featuring romantic or sexual relationships between men. These latter types of manga should not be confused with manga marketed toward gay or lesbian readers; in fact, *shōnen-ai* manga is most popular among heterosexual women.

Manga encompasses a wide range of literary genres, from romance and action-adventure to crime and horror, and plots may be complex and multilayered. Nonetheless, a number of manga feature common story lines and narrative tropes. Series frequently draw influence from Asian folklore, Shinto, and Buddhism and combine the supernatural with the ordinary in fantasy and science-fiction texts. *Shōjo* manga often explore the dreams, hopes, and relationships of young, virginal female protagonists who yearn for romance. The relationships depicted are at times complex, as the female protagonist may be a cross-dresser or involved in a lesbian or incestuous relationship. The protagonist may also be involved in a relationship with a demon or other supernatural creature. In "magical girls" manga, a subset of *shōjo*, the female protagonist fights evil on a daily basis. *Shōnen* manga typically feature young male protagonists who seek adventure and camaraderie. They usually do not age or have children within the series. *Shōnen* manga are generally action-oriented and may feature lewd or scatological humor. Most manga, regardless of the intended demographic, provide deep insight into characters' thoughts and emotions, including those of characters other than the protagonist.

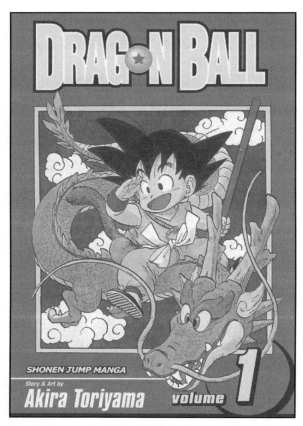

Japan's Agency for Cultural Affairs has named the *shōnen* series *Dragon Ball* as the third-best manga of all time based on its endurance and its impact on the genre. (Courtesy of VIZ Media)

Manga and the West

Manga has displayed Western influences since the nineteenth century, when printing technology from Europe was introduced to Japan, and in the period following the end of World War II, Western comics and animation shaped the style of manga artists such as Tezuka. *Mangaka* have combined elements from mythologies, folklore, and religions of the West with Japanese mythology, folklore, and religion. It is not uncommon to see both Shinto and Christian tones in the same manga. Manga began to have a particularly strong influence on the West in the 1990's, when anime and manga titles such as *Sailor Moon* and *Dragon Ball* became enormously popular with audiences in the United States and Europe. These titles paved the way for fur-

ther series to be exported. With multiple series becoming global successes, manga became a significant part of global culture.

During the 1990's and earlier decades, it was a common practice for publishers in the United States to edit manga severely when translating it into English. They often changed the characters' names to non-Japanese names and reversed the images so that the volumes could be read in the Western left-to-right reading order. However, in the early twenty-first century, companies recognized the readership's desire for uncut versions of their favorite manga that remained as true as possible to the original text. Companies such as TOKYOPOP began to market their publications as "authentic manga," retaining the original back-to-front structure of the novels and working to create faithful translations.

As publishers in the United States and Europe began to release an increasing number of manga, Western manga fandom grew immense in its scope and participation, encompassing fans of all ages, genders, and races. The creation of fan-made art and fiction featuring manga characters became popular, as did cosplay, an activity in which fans dress as manga or anime characters. Fans gathered at anime and manga conventions held globally and increasingly communicated with each other online. Adult fans working or seeking careers in academia began to write analyses and other scholarly works on manga series, the manga industry as a whole, and fan culture, publishing such works in academic journals such as *Mechademia*. Interest in the scholarly study of comics in general increased greatly throughout the late twentieth and early twenty-first centuries, and the study of manga has fallen within that overall trend.

Impact

Manga series sell globally and continue to be commercially successful, encouraging readers to read not only manga but also comics and graphic novels from the United States and other countries. *Shōjo* manga in particular has been credited with encouraging a significant number of women and girls to begin reading comics. In response to the popularity of manga, many publishers have imported comics from Asian countries such as

South Korea, expanding the selection of comics available to American readers. American artists inspired by manga have incorporated elements of manga's artistic and narrative styles into their work, with some going so far as to create graphic novels rendered completely in a manga-inspired style. Such works, sometimes known as original English-language manga, further call attention to the influence manga has had on comics artists, writers, and readers in the United States.

Rachel Cantrell

Bibliography

MacWilliams, Mark W. *Japanese Visual Culture: Explorations in the World of Manga and Anime*. Armonk, N.Y.: M. E. Sharpe, 2008. Examines the narratives and subgenres within manga and discusses how manga fits into Japanese culture and how the two affect one another.

Schodt, Frederik L. *Manga! Manga! The World of Japanese Comics*. Tokyo: Kodansha International, 1998. Provides a comprehensive background on the history of manga in Japan from its origins to the early 1980's, covering major influences and artistic styles. Includes a foreword by Osamu Tezuka.

Winge, Theresa. "Costuming the Imagination: Origins of Anime and Manga Cosplay." *Mechademia* 1 (2006): 65-76. Discusses the origins of anime and manga cosplay, providing insight into the community aspect of cosplay and examining why fans engage in the activity.

MANHWA: SOUTH KOREAN COMICS

Definition

The term *manhwa* is used to denote Korean comics, print cartoons, and sometimes animated cartoons. In the United States, the term refers to comics and graphic novels originally published in South Korea.

Introduction

The term *manhwa* came into popular use in Korea during the 1920's, when it was applied to cartoons. Korea was under Japanese occupation from 1910 to 1945, and during this time, elements of Japanese language and culture were incorporated into Korean society. The term *manhwa* is derived from the Japanese term for comics, *manga*.

During the early years of Japanese occupation, newspaper comics featured a great deal of social criticism. By the mid-1920's, most political newspapers were shut down, and political and social cartoons were abandoned in favor of children's and humorous illustrations. Political cartoons slowly reemerged following the establishment of the Republic of Korea (commonly known as South Korea) in 1948. Popular artist Kim Yong-hwan started Korea's first comic magazine, *Manhwa Haengjin*, in 1948, but it was quickly shut down because the authorities disapproved of the cover. During the Korean War (1950-1953), cartoons became a popular vehicle for propaganda.

For a period after the Korean War, children's comic books were quite popular. When sales began to decline, rental stores for comics began to open, allowing readers to rent comic books for lower prices than they would have paid to purchase them. While this system had its advantages, the quality of the comics suffered because of the lower prices, and the paper quality suffered as well. Artists created groups with the goal of improving the quality of the work: the Taehan Association of Cartoonists (later known as the Han'guk Association of Cartoonists) was an organization of children's cartoonists, and the Hyondae Association of Cartoonists was an organization for artists of adult comics.

The popularity of comics rose during the 1950's and 1960's, and the diversity of styles and subject matter led to the creation of new genres such as *sunjeong* (or *soonjung*), romantic stories aimed at young women. *Manhwabang*, comics cafés and stores that allowed readers to pay a set rate to sit and read comics, were also introduced to the public. In response to the increasing publication of comics and social and political changes within South Korea, the government began to enforce censorship laws and, by the mid-1960's, created a comics distribution monopoly that further censored *manhwa*.

During the 1970's, manga was increasingly imported from Japan, opening up the market to adults and allowing more risqué comics to find a market. However, the government stepped in once again and, in the 1980's, closed down many publishers and arrested publishers and artists for violation of the Juvenile Protection Law. A government measure introduced in 1987 stipulated that local publishers that registered with the government could publish without prior censorship, which prompted Korean publishers to import more adult-themed manga and either copy them outright or edit them for Korean audiences. By the 1990's, there was a rebirth of comic books in Korea as Korean artists fought against the influx of manga and demanded government intervention. *Manhwa* found an outlet online by the middle of the decade.

Impact of Manga on Manhwa

Manga influenced *manhwa* from the medium's beginnings during the Japanese occupation of Korea and continued to exert a powerful influence as the manga industry became a major force within Japanese culture and began to export comics abroad. *Manhwaga* (or *manhwa* artists) were not culturally isolated, and the influx of manga into the Korean comics market had a strong effect on the art and content of many artists' *manhwa*.

The extent of manga's influence on the artistic style of *manhwa* has been a topic of debate. Some artists claim there are no differences between the two styles, since both use a traditional Asian style of drawing that emphasizes black-and-white lines, white space, and other basic artistic styles and principles. However, some South Korean publishers have adapted manga for the Korean market by editing the art to suit cultural and social tastes, at times adding clothing to nude or scantily clad characters or otherwise altering the illustrations. Furthermore, the depiction of characters, though similar, is somewhat stylistically different: Eyes and faces are drawn more softly and realistically in *manhwa* than in manga.

Other artists claim there is a significant difference between manga and *manhwa* in terms of the content of the stories, arguing that while manga is more interested in plot, *manhwa* focuses on characters. *Manhwa* is generally more conservative than manga and typically deals with more realistic situations, though there are a significant number of science-fiction and other nonrealistic *manhwa* in circulation. One of the most obvious differences between the two forms concerns the directions in which works are read; manga is read from right to left, while *manhwa* is read from left to right in keeping with the orientation of Korean text.

Modern Manhwa

The 1990's ushered in a new age of comics for Korea, with sales and publications soaring. Japanese comics flooded the market despite the attempts of the Korea Ethics Committee on Books, Magazines, and Weekly Newspapers to hinder outright plagiarism of Japanese comics and to prevent violent and sexually graphic materials from entering the mainstream. In an attempt to gain government support for Korean comics and prevent manga from taking over the Korean comics industry, members of organizations such as the Korean Cartoonists Association led public demonstrations against manga and ridiculed Korean artists they claimed were heavily influenced by it. These efforts were at least somewhat successful, as the government began to recognize *manhwa* as a legitimate and popular art form, even using it to spread its own political messages. The government also established a number of initiatives to promote local production of comics, including government subsidies, grants, museums, and libraries.

Although the importation of manga did not stop, by the early 2000's, the Korean comics industry was flourishing. *Manhwa* finally began to be sold in traditional bookstores, which improved circulation and public perceptions of *manhwa*, making comics more respectable and accessible to readers who were uncomfortable visiting *manhwabang* and comics stores. More than one hundred universities and colleges established departments or majors dedicated to cartooning and illustration, further calling attention to the increasing acceptance of *manhwa* as an art form.

Impact

With manga proving to be both popular and commercially successful in Europe and the United States, a number of publishers imported and translated *manhwa* titles in the hope of reaching the same audience. The readability and left-to-right orientation of *manhwa* contributed to its growing popularity, as did the realism of the characters and the combination of Eastern and Western styles and mythologies. Popular *manhwa* in the U.S. and European markets include *Ragnarok*, *Priest*, *Island*, and *Tarot Café*. While some *manhwa* titles have been successful in these markets, the primary impact of *manhwa* has been local to South Korea, where artists have moved away from manga-style comics to develop their own art styles, characters, and story lines.

Michelle Martinez

Bibliography

Johnson-Woods, Toni. *Manga: An Anthology of Global and Cultural Perspectives*. New York: Continuum, 2010. Discusses *manhwa*'s cultural context as well as the influence of manga on the Korean cartooning industry, focusing in particular on the 1980's and 1990's.

Russell, Mark James. *Pop Goes Korea: Behind the Revolution in Movies, Music, and Internet Culture*. Berkeley, Calif.: Stone Bridge Press, 2008. Includes a chapter devoted to *manhwa* that details its rise during the 1990's and early twenty-first century and provides sidebars about important artists and works.

Sugiyama, Rika. *Comic Artists—Asia: Manga, Manhwa, Manhua*. New York: Harper, 2004. Introduces the work of comics artists in Japan, Korea, and Hong Kong through artist profiles and interviews that provide insight into their processes.

Nonfiction Graphic Novels: The Limits of Perspective

Definition

While the term "graphic novel" seems, by virtue of the word "novel," to refer to fictional works, it is also used to describe long-form nonfiction graphic narratives. The term "nonfiction," however, is also problematic, as the subjectivity of both words and images necessarily influences the factuality of such texts.

Introduction

Many of the most widely read graphic novels are works of nonfiction: biographies, autobiographies, memoirs, historical surveys, and even works of journalism. That these texts also overwhelmingly address significant historical events or social questions is not coincidental, suggesting that the multimodal medium of the graphic novel provides both the writer and the reader with a more complete, perhaps more cathartic, experience and allows the author to communicate personal, social, or cultural content more thoroughly.

The question of the validity and gravity of the graphic novel inevitably arises when discussing such important issues. Can comics credibly and accurately portray a major battle of the American Civil War? Can a mouse communicate the pain of the Holocaust? Both public and academic reaction to such texts suggests that they not only succeed in their portrayals but also do so with a complexity that requires in-depth study and analysis.

Such visual documentation of the past, used primarily to make sense of that past, distinguishes the nonfiction graphic novel from other works of nonfiction, providing the reader with a richer, more complex depiction of the relevant social or historical context. In memoir and biography, this

depiction not only reflects the author's journey of discovery but also allows readers to make that journey themselves. The value, then, of the nonfiction graphic novel is without question, whether the depicted past is social, cultural, or personal; however, the objectivity of such texts, in the context of their nonfiction designation, is problematic.

Autobiography and Memoir

In *Fun Home: A Family Tragicomic* (2006), Alison Bechdel describes her father's life and death with a map locating not only the titular home but also the major events of her father's life: his place of birth, the location of his death, and the site of his burial. Such information may seem supplemental, but Bechdel's map is integral to her experience. The proximity of

Alison Bechdel's *Fun Home: A Family Tragicomic.* (Courtesy of Mariner Books)

these places is the key to her (and the reader's) understanding of her childhood and her father's hidden homosexuality. Her father's sheltered existence appears to solve for Bechdel the riddle of his secret and helps to answer her own questions about the relationship between her sexuality and her father's. Bechdel's map is the text: The reader reads the map just as the reader of prose might read a description of the town. The map provides not only geographical but also personal context and is accompanied by text calling attention to the fact that while her father was worldly and well educated, he seemed inextricably tied to his hometown. Bechdel explains this paradox with a second map, one that locates the houses of her extended family and notes that many of their relatives had similarly remained in the town.

The close connection between images and written text is the crux of the graphic novel; the words and images function together to communicate a more complete message to the reader. One can imagine Bechdel's descriptions without the maps or the maps without the descriptions, and alone each would function adequately. Together, however, they provide the reader with an arguably more complete and complex message. The complexity comes not from the interaction between the visual and written but from the tension between the two. The reader is inclined to understand the text as captions, simple explanations of the maps, but the text serves a greater purpose. Bechdel suggests in her comparison of her father to other members of the Bechdel family the notion of genetic inheritance, an idea that she will later in the novel apply to her questions about sexuality.

Bechdel's work demonstrates the unique interrelationship between words and images in graphic texts: Together they create conceptual "threads" or themes that foreshadow events or frame the novel's focus. As a memoir (a genre differing from autobiography in its more specific focus), Bechdel's work has two related foci, her father and sexuality, addressed by both the words and images of her text.

As a story of memory, a memoir or autobiography allows an author to recall events that he or she has experienced. Communicating those memories visually is logical, yet written text is a necessary component to make sense of another's memories. Readers need labels and context that are not always apparent in images alone. As a gesture of sharing, the memoir or autobiography reaches its utmost power when the reader not only is interested in the author's life but also identifies with it. When reading Marjane Satrapi's *Persepolis* (2000-2003), for example, Western readers may have difficulty identifying with the Iranian child protagonist. Add to that story images of the Iranian child sitting at a school desk, playing on a playground, and dreaming in her bed, however, and readers can see a child not unlike themselves.

Personal, Societal, and Social Issues

While the motivation to write a memoir differs among authors, the general outcome is that an author shares his or her story with the public. Because of their focus, memoirs are usually couched in a particular historical, social, or experiential context such as war, discrimination, or personal tragedy. These texts therefore serve a dual purpose, as they are about both the author and the social context in which the author has placed his or her story. Not all nonfiction graphic novels are memoirs, however, and graphic novels about the terrorist attacks of September 11, 2001 (9/11), or Hurricane Katrina, for example, serve a similar purpose by contributing to social and political discourse.

While such graphic novels are told from an objective, journalistic point of view, the visual component of these texts results in a degree of subjectivity, even when the author's intention is to present an objective narrative. The subjectivity of images lies in their power to mislead. Readers, even practiced critical readers, are more willing to accept the truth of images. Clearly fictionalized images, such as Art Spiegelman's animals in *Maus* (1986, 1991), become factual to the reader, who quickly understands and accepts Spiegelman's allegory: Jews are mice, Germans are cats, Poles are pigs, and Americans are dogs. Therefore, while the nonfiction graphic novel succeeds in creating a closer bond between the reader and its subjects, it fails in presenting objective images. Spiegelman depicts real events, but his choice of animals is subjective: Jews are cowering victims, Germans are vicious predators, Poles are dirty and greedy, and Americans are submissive and loyal.

Though obvious symbols, such devices are often left uninterpreted by the casual reader or are taken for granted by the critical reader.

The way Spiegelman's father's racism is treated provides a significant example of the subjective power of Spiegelman's images. In a scene in which Spiegelman and his father, Vladek, are riding together in a car, Vladek erupts over Spiegelman and his wife's willingness to pick up an African American hitchhiker, portrayed as a black dog. While Vladek's racism and Spiegelman's disgusted reaction to it are clear from the dialogue between them, the portrayal of the African American man as a black dog masks the harsh truth of this incident. This sequence does provide the foundation for a powerful message: Most readers would find it ridiculous to discriminate against dogs based on color, and Spiegelman subtly suggests that such distinctions among people of different races are equally absurd.

The limit of memory further affects the objectivity of a narrative. Memory is clouded and biased. Satrapi's *Persepolis* is certainly about the Iranian Revolution, but more accurately, it is about *her* Iranian Revolution, her reactions to wearing a veil and buying Michael Jackson records on the black market. As the novel is based on the childhood memories of an adult and told from the perspective of a child, the politics are vague and generally gleaned only from Satrapi's parents and similarly thinking relatives and friends. While Satrapi makes no claims to tell *the* story of the revolution, some readers will read the novel as such, perhaps having little prior knowledge of the history and politics of the place and period. Satrapi's depiction of Muslim revolutionaries is biased, for to her, they are the enemy. They are drawn with sharp, angular faces, as compared to her friends and parents, who are drawn with soft, rounded faces, communicating to the reader that those with the liberal politics of her family are "right" and the others are "wrong."

Graphic novels written and drawn by those observing or reporting on events, such as Sid Jacobson and Ernie Colón's works about 9/11, tend to be more objective. However, despite Jacobson and Colón's journalistic distance and objectivity, the images still belie a certain bias. One can ignore the text altogether and tell from the images who the "good guys" and "bad guys" are in various events throughout the novels. Like Satrapi, Colón depicts the political players and nameless participants with some degree of visual bias.

Persepolis. (Courtesy of Pantheon Books)

History and Objectivity

Graphic novels about less recent historical events are perhaps the most objective nonfiction graphic novels, depicting events of such historical import as the creation and signing of the Declaration of Independence, the development of the U.S. Constitution, and the American Civil War. As compared to Satrapi's more personal depictions of the participants in the Iranian Revolution or Jacobson and Colón's characterizations of American politicians and Muslim leaders, the depictions of soldiers and politicians in these texts are markedly more objective.

Similar objective depictions are found in *Still I Rise* (1997). A survey of African American history created by Roland Laird, Taneshia Nash Laird, and Elihu Bey, the graphic novel presents white characters drawn in the same style as African American characters. The white aggressors are not visually stereotyped and are characterized not by their appearance but by their actions. As a historical survey, not a memoir, *Still I Rise* is a more objective text; such works, relaying facts and documented events, are generally more objective (though never completely objective) than one person's memory or story.

The complexity of any graphic novel lies in its multimodal text; that modality further complicates distinctions between fiction and nonfiction, objectivity and subjectivity. It is possible for a graphic novel's written text to be objective but its images subjective, or vice versa. With two modes of communication and often two levels of narrative, the degree of objectivity of any graphic novel is difficult to gauge, and readers must approach the graphic text with the understanding that even if a text is presented and intended as nonfiction, the bias of memory and the subjectivity of imagery will surely affect the degree of objectivity any text or author can claim. Such texts therefore require that readers of graphic novels be visually literate and intellectually equipped to read both written and visual text critically.

Impact

No graphic novel can be truly nonfiction, as the subjectivity of images requires some degree of interpretation by the artist or author. While memoirs are perhaps the most subjective, told from one person's memory and intended to tell the story or experiences of that individual, even historical surveys or graphic versions of historical documents involve some degree of interpretation and are, to some degree, made subjective by the images with which the written text is intertwined. As the study of graphic novels continues to develop, theorists will likely continue to address this interplay of words and images, urging readers to understand that like any texts purporting to be nonfiction, graphic novels have their limitations. Regardless, improvements in the naming and recognition of genres within the medium, from graphic biographies to graphic histories, help to remove the mark of fiction from these texts and allow inexperienced readers some degree of understanding of the works they may encounter.

Theresa Fine-Pawsey

Bibliography

Beaty, Bart. "Autobiography as Authenticity." In *A Comics Studies Reader*, edited by Jeet Heer and Kent Worcester. Jackson: University Press of Mississippi, 2009. Traces the rise of the autobiographical graphic novel, primarily in European works of the 1990's, and relates the genre of autobiography to the search for validity by authors of comic texts.

Constantino, Manuela. "Marji: Popular Commix Heroine Breathing Life into the Writing of History." *Canadian Review of American Studies* 38, no. 3 (2008): 429-447. Addresses the publication and reception of Satrapi's *Persepolis* and discusses the role of the individual in telling history, providing specific examples.

Pearl, Monica B. "Graphic Language: Redrawing the Family (Romance) in Alison Bechdel's *Fun Home*." *Prose Studies* 30, no. 3 (2008): 286-304. Explores the irony in the language of Bechdel's *Fun Home* as well as the contrast between the words and images.

Schwarz, Gretchen. "Media Literacy, Graphic Novels and Social Issues." *Simile* 7, no. 4 (November, 2007): 1-11. Discusses the significance of graphic novels in media literacy and in the instruction of social issues and provides examples of classroom use.

SATIRE AND PARODY IN GRAPHIC NOVELS

Definition
Satire is a literary form that calls attention to and ridicules human or societal failings through the use of parody, exaggeration, burlesque, and irony. Types of satire include formal or direct satire, in which the writer directly addresses the reader, and indirect satire, which allows the audience to draw their own conclusions.

Introduction
A satirical work is defined by its intent to make a specific point, criticize a specific person or institution, or persuade the reader of a specific point of view. Satire may be humorous or painfully serious. It often contains caricatures, which are exaggerated impressions of people or institutions that poke fun at their faults. The didactic purpose of the author—what the author intends to teach or convey to the reader—is the most important aspect of satire in graphic novels.

Satires are often specific to the time in which they were written, but because the purpose of the satire is to expose human failings, these characteristics are not bound to any one time period. Ted Rall's graphic novel *2024* (2001) satirizes George Orwell's *Nineteen Eighty-Four* (1949) and, in the process, the extent to which people will go to be happy. The message of Rall's book is that modern capitalist societies have created people who would rather be told what to do and remain under a totalitarian regime than be forced to make hard decisions and fight for their rights. A satire should always have an obvious point to its critique, and it must seek to persuade its audience.

The rhetoric of satire is also an important characteristic. Rhetoric is the voice of a text, the vocabulary it uses, and the way it presents its arguments. In rhetoric, there are three major categories: ethos, pathos, and logos. *Ethos* is how trustworthy the rhetor is seen to be; if he or she is trusted, persuasive, and believed, then he or she has good ethos and is more likely to persuade the reader. *Pathos* is the passionate and emotional side of the argument, which appeals to people's feelings, desires, and beliefs regarding what is good and right. *Logos* is the logical side of the argument, seeking to

An example of a satirical graphic retelling is *The New Adventures of Jesus* (1969), by Frank Stack. (Courtesy of Fantagraphics Books)

persuade based on the facts at hand. The success or failure of a work of satire depends on the persuasiveness of its rhetoric.

Rhetoric and the Graphic Novel
In graphic novels, the rhetoric is found not only in words but also in drawings. How the world is drawn, how people are drawn, the color scheme used, the size of the panels, and the color of the borders are all parts of the graphic rhetoric. Rall's *2024* is dominated by text with black-and-white illustrations. The people are drawn with simple faces, with two dots for eyes and one line for a mouth; this simplistic rendering empha-

sizes the fact that they have given up critical thinking. The background also creates atmosphere. On the first page, a building is painted with phrases such as "knowledge is impossible" and "exploitation is inevitable." The reader immediately knows that the country being depicted uses its citizens like objects and cares nothing about democracy, knowledge, or physical or intellectual freedom. This graphic novel operates from the standpoint that democracy, knowledge, and freedom are good things and criticizes the politicians and institutions that would have people sacrifice them for controlled happiness.

Hazed (2008), by Mark Sable and Robbi Rodriguez, satirizes sorority culture. In *Hazed*, the characters are drawn with significantly more attention to their faces and bodies, allowing for delineation between pretty and ugly on the page. This is necessary because the protagonist of the story, Ileana, transforms into an accepted sister of her sorority, changing her appearance, her behavior, and her goals to fit in. The exaggerated proportions of the "beautiful" sisters play on patriarchal stereotypes of feminine beauty and the damage done to women attempting to fulfill them. Without the more detailed artwork, the satire would not be as successful.

Graphic Retellings of Old Stories

Graphic novels can also be used to create graphic retellings of classic literary works. One example of this is Donald Lemke and Cynthia Martin's 2008 adaptation of Jonathan Swift's satire *Gulliver's Travels* (1726). A minimal narrative and glossy color illustrations retell the tale of Gulliver landing on Lilliput and his shock and dismay upon waking up tied down by the Lilliputians. The picture of the giant Gulliver at the mercy of the tiny people of Lilliput makes clear the ridiculousness of Gulliver bowing to the wishes of the Lilliputians, calling attention to Swift's satire of politics. While this graphic retelling does not replace the original text, it does make an excellent companion, providing the reader with visual satirical representation.

Another example of a satirical graphic retelling is *The New Adventures of Jesus* (1969), by Frank Stack. Certainly a more controversial work than Lemke's, Stack's satire is also pointed, humorous, and an influ-

ential example of what can be accomplished in the graphic medium. Satire often tries to make people angry; if it causes controversy, it has succeeded. By satirizing such an intensely emotional topic as Jesus, Stack provides a necessary criticism of religion and religious fervor, castigating those who would attack, fight, and kill in his name.

Alan Moore and Satire

Two of the most famous graphic novels that define satire in the medium were both written by Alan Moore: *Watchmen* (1986-1987, with artist Dave Gibbons) and *V for Vendetta* (1982-1989, with artist David Lloyd). In both cases, the characters are situated in a dystopian world brought about by society's own laziness and fear. In *Watchmen*, the idea of saviors is criticized through the failings of the retired superheroes, and humanity's penchant for destroying itself also comes under attack.

Hazed. (Courtesy of Image Comics)

In particular, Western ideas of imperialism are incorporated in the character of Ozymandias, while the Comedian represents the morally questionable identity of the American cowboy. *Watchmen* successfully critiques and rewrites the superhero genre, raising questions about the wisdom of allowing a few particularly powerful people to protect the world. The success of Moore and Gibbons's work demonstrated that graphic novels could question morality, ethics, government, and heroism more effectively than any other medium to date.

V for Vendetta, meanwhile, satirizes the conservative political environment in England under Margaret Thatcher, who served as prime minister from 1979 to 1990. An Orwellian world controlled by dictator Adam Susan and his secret police, the Fingermen, the graphic novel's version of London is a dark and vicious place. Through the story, Moore critiques society's fears of death, insecurity, and war. The world of V, and V himself, demonstrates that running from fear can lead to a fate as awful as the nightmare.

Despite a handful of predecessors such as Stack, in many ways Moore was the first author to demonstrate the satirical power of the graphic novel. Both *V for Vendetta* and *Watchmen* met with critical success and helped to reshape the graphic novel medium. Film adaptations of both titles, released in 2006 and 2009, respectively, have also demonstrated their enduring relevance to issues of society and government. Moore's works clearly critique the ideology of fear and totalitarian government while promoting individual responsibility and consciousness, serving as examples of the satirical potential of the graphic novel.

Impact

The use of satire in graphic novels has created a genre within the medium that is separate from superheroes, crime stories, and fantasy or science fiction. Within the safety of the much-abused and often ignored medium of comics, satirists have critiqued religion, country, and even their own readership. The importance of satire's move to the graphic novel lies in the necessity of this critique. As readers are bombarded by billboards, movies, books, and music, they are in danger, as always, of forgetting the ideology and values embedded in everything around them. Satire in graphic novels keeps people honest as readers, writers, and thinkers.

Graphic satire has also reshaped public opinion, as in the case of political cartoons, and finds itself perfectly situated to change ideas of morality and ethicality in popular culture. Because graphic novels are the home of dystopias, utopias, superheroes, and jokes, the satirizing of superheroes in titles such as *Watchmen* also calls into question what people find heroic and, by association, what they find moral. This is a lofty ideal for a satire; to question an ideology and also change it, as Moore and Gibbons's work did, is proof that satire is a defining force in cultural ideologies.

Jessica McCall

Bibliography

Griffin, Dustin. *Satire: A Critical Reintroduction*. Lexington: University Press of Kentucky, 1995. Provides a history of satire and critical theory dealing with it and considers satire's place in literature.

Ogborn, Jane, and Peter Buckroyd. *Satire*. Cambridge: Cambridge University Press, 2001. Offers a historical survey of satire in literature through the twenty-first century, plus techniques for reading and comprehension.

Sabin, Roger. *Comics, Comix, and Graphic Novels*. London: Phaidon Press, 1996. Chronicles the history of comics and graphic novels, including discussion of satirical works from both mainstream and alternative publishers.

SCIENCE FICTION: EXPANDING THE GENRE

Definition

Science fiction is a genre that presents a fictional narrative primarily supported by elements including science and technology. Settings tend to blend aspects of time and place to create futuristic imaginings that comment directly and indirectly on the author's present. While there is a great deal of variation among science-fiction graphic novels, many works use dystopian settings and conventions as part of their examinations of science and technology and the human condition.

Introduction

Science fiction has a long and complex history in many media, from text-only literature and graphic novels to film, television, and video games. Part of this complexity comes from the difficulty in defining the genre, while part comes from the fact that many of the key figures working in the genre, including authors Kurt Vonnegut and Margaret Atwood, have openly rejected the label. Broadly, science fiction is a genre of fiction that incorporates science and technology, usually with some twist on time, such as being set in the future. Science fiction tends to be allegorical and often builds social commentary and criticism into the narrative.

Science Fiction in Graphic Novels

Major science-fiction novels such as Arthur C. Clarke's *Childhood's End* (1953) and *Rendezvous with Rama* (1972) demonstrate the power of words to create and re-create entire worlds that would be nearly impossible to represent in reality. Such text-only works require a great deal of imagination on the part of the reader. While science fiction has been a powerful genre within film and television for many decades, much of that history has been marred by the inability of technology to reproduce faithfully what writers have produced in words. Comic books and graphic novels, then, have embraced

science fiction, since the medium lends itself to the futuristic and surrealistic nature of the genre.

A number of science-fiction books and films have been adapted as graphic novels, suggesting that the science-fiction genre lends itself well to sequential art as a medium. For example, the film *Blade Runner* (1982), an adaptation of Philip K. Dick's novel *Do Androids Dream of Electric Sheep?* (1968), was in turn adapted by Marvel Comics as *A Marvel Comics Super*

The Silver Surfer, whose homeworld is 3,000 light years from Earth, is one of Marvel's most popular science fiction characters. (Courtesy of Marvel Comics)

Special: Blade Runner in 1982. In 2009, *Do Androids Dream of Electric Sheep?* was adapted as a twenty-four-issue comic book series, eventually collected as several graphic novels that include every word of Dick's original text. Many science-fiction titles originally published in the comic book, graphic novel, or manga form are central works within the medium as a whole, among them *Astro Boy* (1952-1968), *V for Vendetta* (1982-1989), *Akira* (1982-1990), *American Flagg!* (1983-1988), *Watchmen* (1986-1987), *Hard Boiled* (1990-1992), *The Invisibles* (1994-2000), and *Y: The Last Man* (2002-2008).

Science fiction in graphic novels may include any of the following elements: speculative science; advanced technology; aliens; alternative history; time travel; space travel; multiple realities; totalitarian governments; medicine and drugs; artificial intelligence, such as robots, cyborgs, or androids; an automated or highly technical military or police force; distortions of procreation, such as artificial insemination or infertility; powerful and intrusive corporations; alienation and isolation; apocalyptic events; advanced computer intelligence or intrusion; and the existential hero, that is, the Western gunslinger archetype. One of the most highly praised graphic novels and works of science fiction is *Watchmen*, which represents well the influence of science-fiction elements on sequential art. In *Watchmen*, superbeing Dr. Manhattan embodies aspects of science, transformation, alien beings, space travel, and superhuman qualities. Further, the superheroes in both generations of the narrative, notably Nite Owl, often use technology as part of their efforts to fight crime. Artist Dave Gibbons and writer Alan Moore have commented that *Watchmen* was created in part to highlight the unique nature of sequential art as a medium that is reinforced by its ability to feature and make believable a character such as Dr. Manhattan.

Superheroes and Sci-Fi: How Do We Draw the Line?

The history of modern comic books dates back to the late 1930's, with the rise of graphic novels coming between the late 1970's and the mid-1980's, but the powerful connection between science fiction and sequential art can best be seen in the revitalization of the comic book industry in the 1960's and the attendant rise of Marvel Comics. At the core of their narratives, characters such as Spider-Man, the Fantastic Four, the X-Men, Iron Man, and the Incredible Hulk blend the superhero genre with science in ways that make genre distinctions difficult.

The rise of Marvel Comics has been in part attributed to this blending of genres—superhero, science fiction, romance—but science, technology, and alternate versions of reality have been central to most superhero comics and graphic novels since the very genesis of the genre, the introduction of Superman, and continuing through the rise of films based on comic books and graphic novels in the twenty-first century. Also at the center of superhero narratives is the "super" element, which tends to be connected in most cases to science or technology gone awry. The superhero narratives in sequential art also tend to take on allegorical aspects, as does most science fiction throughout all media.

Dystopia and Allegory

Elements of the dystopian narrative are common in text-only science fiction, and a number of influential graphic novels are set in dystopian worlds as well. Dystopian societies in science-fiction works provide a platform for removing the readers from the current time in order to make them more able to look critically at their own time. A classic example of this strategy is the novel *Nineteen Eighty-Four* (1949); author George Orwell simply inverted the year 1948 in order to give the dystopia the appearance of the future while he warned readers of their present. Similarly, Alan Moore and David Lloyd's graphic novel *V for Vendetta* serves to raise readers' awareness about 1980's British politics and society, mixing an antihero's obsession with the past with his assault on the dystopian present of the graphic novel in order to satirize the politics of Moore's contemporary society. Science-fiction graphic novels use the power of sequential art to create situations not bound by reality—distinct in this respect from text-only literature due to the presence of images, which are themselves distinct from other visual media in not being bound by the limits of film or computer-aided graphics—in order to satirize and warn. The use of utopian and dystopian structures to raise science fiction to

"Blade runner" Rick Deckard (actor Harrison Ford) in a scene from director Ridley Scott's futuristic thriller *Blade Runner* (1982). Marvel Comics published an adaptation of the science fiction film that same year. (Getty Images)

graphic novels in the early twenty-first century, science fiction and elements of the genre have been central to comic books, and the popular interest in science fiction has contributed to their success. In *Watchmen*, Moore and Gibbons make science-fiction elements central to their meta-analysis of the superhero genre, and the popular success of comic books and graphic novels being adapted to film represents the key role they have played in the mass media. The trilogy of *Spider-Man* films (2002-2007) directed by Sam Raimi demonstrates both the influence of sequential art as a powerful and mature medium and the value of science-fiction elements in narratives across media.

P. L. Thomas

the level of allegory is a key element in Orwellian science fiction like *V for Vendetta*. The graphic novel presents a dystopian world that is both like and unlike the real world many of its readers know. By removing the reader from the real world with a dystopia that has one foot in the reader's reality and the other in fiction, Moore presents an allegory that satirizes and criticizes the social and political reality of his society—England in the latter half of the twentieth century, notably the 1980's—and warns readers about topics and themes that transcend time and place, such as corporate and government oppression, hypocrisy, bigotry, and terrorism.

Impact

From the introduction of Superman, the foundational superhero in the medium of comic books, to the rise of films based on superheroes, comic books, and

Bibliography

Gravett, Paul. *Graphic Novels: Everything You Need to Know*. New York: Collins Design, 2005. Introduces readers to the graphic novel through chapters on various genres, recommends thirty essential graphic novels, and includes spreads to illustrate key thematic elements.

Roberts, Adam. *The History of Science Fiction*. New York: Palgrave Macmillan, 2006. Presents a scholarly consideration of science fiction as a literary and film/television genre, including discussion of science-fiction comics and graphic novels.

Seed, David, ed. *A Companion to Science Fiction*. Malden, Mass.: Blackwell, 2005. Includes a wealth of perspectives on science fiction as a genre, focusing on text and film and including discussion of comic books.

SEEING HOW COMICS WORK: DEFINING AND LEGITIMIZING COMICS AS VISUAL STORYTELLING

Definition

Visual storytelling theory recognizes that comic books utilize the complex relationships of word and image in juxtaposed panels to tell a story. This theory investigates and defines the visual storytelling method to legitimize the genre for scholarly study, critical attention, and understanding of the process of composing comics.

Introduction

Comic books have been associated with pulp-fiction plotlines and muscular superheroes for most of the twentieth century, and few scholars have seriously considered the visual grammar and meaning-making qualities of the comic book art form. While comic book innovators such as Will Eisner, Osamu Tezuka, and Art Spiegelman have expanded the art and narrative form of comics, the rich structure of the visual stories in comics went relatively unnoticed for most of the century. Hence, the subheading of comics theorist Scott McCloud's pivotal work on the subject, *Understanding Comics* (1993), notes that comics are an "invisible art." Comics are invisible because they are rarely seen as a complex mode of storytelling; however, many comic book theorists and educators have worked since the latter half of the twentieth century to change the perception of comics as a lesser art form, focusing on the complex mechanics and meaning inherent in the visual narrative of the comic book.

Works such as Eisner's *Comics and Sequential Art* (1985), McCloud's *Understanding Comics*, and Jessica Abel and Matt Madden's *Drawing Words and Writing Pictures* (2008) have established the comic book as a visual storytelling tool that highlights the relationships between word and image, frame panels and time, and the comic-creating process. These works maintain that comics need to be redefined in a way that recognizes them as a unique visual storytelling medium in literature. In *Comics and Sequential Art*, Eisner redefines comics as "sequential art"; Abel and Madden explain that this definition is an attempt to break away from stereotypes present in the genre. McCloud expands on this definition by explaining the intentionality of comics: Images are placed together deliberately to convey a story to the reader or viewer.

Eisner and McCloud demonstrate in their works that comics rely on the juxtaposition of image and text as well as space and time to tell a story, challenging the reader to understand a story in a different way: a way that integrates image and text with the reader's visual imagination so that the reader fills in gaps, and thus ultimately participates, in the narrative. Of course, these authors intend for comic book readers and creators to understand these underlying concepts in visual storytelling, and their works are typically labeled as educational texts. These texts seek to persuade audiences that comic books are a legitimate medium of storytelling that deserves critical attention.

Word and Image

A comic book helps readers make a close association between words and images in the reading process. After all, words are simply abstract symbols that people see and then interpret, so words and images are natural companions. When a person is reading a comic, he or she processes both images and alphabetic text at the same time to exercise the broad capabilities of his or her literacy. In combining image and word, the comics creator is not limited to describing what is happening in words but can present the viewer with an image that adds its own meaning to the story.

The interplay of word and image is the basis for the chapter "Show and Tell" in McCloud's *Understanding Comics*. This chapter discusses how word and image have become separate mediums that do not often comingle with each other in high literature or high art. Yet McCloud states that this separation only inhibits one's ability to tell a story. A comic book's power to tap into both the visual and the verbal literacy of the reader can create a more complete storytelling experience. Essentially, by combining word and image, the comic book creator can simultaneously show the story in pictures and tell it with words.

Frame Panels in Juxtaposition

Another essential component to the structure of a comic is the frame. The frame contains a momentary action, and its side-by-side connection, or juxtaposition, to other frames causes movement of action and story. A word following another word causes a verbal story to progress, and a comic book use this same progression with both word and image.

Additionally, juxtaposition of frames causes a movement of time and space in which the reader or viewer is transported from one time and space to another, compelling him or her to fill in the gaps between the two frames in order to make sense of what happened between the two images. In *Understanding Comics*, McCloud calls this act of filling in the gaps between frames "closure." The author gives the reader both image and text to enrich his or her reading experience, but the author also gives the reader the opportunity to create the parts of the story that are not visually depicted. As opposed to film, in which an image is rapidly replaced in the same space, or art, which typically features just one image in a space, a comic book is composed of a sequence of image frames. This makes comics a unique storytelling tool.

Education in Creating Comics

Once a student of comics understands how a comic book conveys a visual story through sequential images, he or she can embark on creating one. Just as writing should be an inclusive means of expression, so too should comics be inclusive for those who seek to tell visual narratives. A lack of artistic ability should not inhibit anyone from trying to create a comic; a sequential artist need not be an excellent artist. The message one is trying to convey is the most important part of the comic, and the images are meant to guide the reader to the message, however basic and abstract those images may be. Many storytellers distance themselves from creating comics because it is not considered a "serious" medium, but many others do so simply because they consider creating comics to be a specialized skill. However, with the advent of digital art and image-editing software, one need only have a minor grasp of drawing to create a comic.

Although it is a myth that one must be a superb artist to create a comic book, the creator must understand the fundamentals that go into making a comic. Juxtaposed panels are organized in a specific manner to tell a story on a page, just as characters, narrative arc, and world construction come alive in the story. The process of creating a comic involves layered steps of penciling a draft, lettering the text, and inking and coloring the final draft; these steps are often done by separate people, making comic book creation a collaborative endeavor.

Impact

Visual storytelling theory arose because comic books were not receiving critical attention as a form of literature and there was a need to define comic books as multifaceted visual texts. Theorists defined comics as sequential visual narratives in order to connect the act of creating comic books with early forms of storytelling, such as primitive cave drawings. These theorists not only helped to legitimize the art form of comics but also broadened the audience for this theory to include rhetoric and composition scholars, art scholars, and communication scholars, to name but a few.

Eisner is known as one of the first comic book creators to theorize the visual narrative process, which he did in conjunction with the sequential-art courses he taught at the School of Visual Arts in New York City. McCloud further popularized and built upon Eisner's concepts in *Understanding Comics*, an innovative work in which McCloud explains theories about comic book narrative form in the format of the medium itself. Both Eisner and McCloud shaped this theory in order for those studying comic books to have a better grasp of the functions and devices of this storytelling form.

Jim Haendiges

Bibliography

Caputo, Tony C., Jim Steranko and Harlan Ellison. *Visual Storytelling: The Art and Technique*. New York: Watson-Guptill, 2002. Discusses visual storytelling techniques and ways to use visual storytelling in educational contexts, providing information about the evolving field of comic books and comic book technique.

Eisner, Will. *Graphic Storytelling and Visual Narrative: Principles and Practices from the Legendary Cartoonist*. New York: W. W. Norton, 2008. Expands on Eisner's earlier work *Comics and Sequential Art* and focuses on visual narrative in comics and other visual media.

McCloud, Scott. *Making Comics: Storytelling Secrets of Comics, Manga, and Graphic Novels*. New York:

Harper, 2006. Focuses on the basic techniques of creating comics for those curious about creating their own graphic narratives.

_____. *Reinventing Comics: How Imagination and Technology Are Revolutionized an Art Form*. New York: Perennial, 2000. Discusses the ways in which comics are created and the digital revolutions that are occurring in the comic book industry.

SUPERHEROES: ARCHETYPES FOR THE MODERN MYTH

Definition

Works in the superhero genre feature characters, known as superheroes, with supernatural or otherwise extraordinary powers. Superhero protagonists often have a mission to right wrongs, protect the defenseless, or defeat supervillains, similarly gifted individuals with conflicting ideologies. Certain tropes distinguish the superhero from other fictional protagonists; usually a superhero will have a costume, and many maintain secret identities.

Introduction

Superhero comics are far and away the most popular genre within comic books. A confluence of historical and social events led to the emergence of the superhero genre in American comics during the 1940's, whereupon the vivid, action-packed color comic pages captivated the boundless imaginations of the children, mostly young boys, who consumed them. The superhero genre soon outstripped genres such as horror, mystery, and romance in popularity. Since then, the superhero has proved remarkably resilient, changing and evolving along with its audience.

The term and concept of the "superhero" originates with Friedrich Nietzsche's philosophy of the *Übermensch*, or superman, a person who is the pinnacle of human ability and thus something more than human. The concept of an individual person with unique abilities fits well into the hero archetype, and on the comics page, there are virtually no limits to the extent of the imagination. The archetype of the superhero can be continually reinvented to suit its audience, and thus superhero stories have been likened to modern-day myths. Superheroes have godlike powers, and though they are generally humans who can win the reader's empathy, they operate on a far grander scale than the average person. They are immortal within the pages of the comic, always changing but never growing, and they tell people stories about themselves, showing them the pageants they want to see, humanity's ideals in the form of muscle-bound heroes. Superheroes both reflect and affect popular culture, mirroring humanity's

Superman's debut in 1938 is universally recognized as the beginning of the Golden Age, as superheroes rapidly took over comics. (Getty Images)

greatest dreams and deepest fears. Perhaps it is for this reason the genre has grown so popular.

Superheroes, along with comics in general, now enjoy widespread acceptance in popular culture, having been adapted into books, toys, games, and major film franchises. In 2008, Christopher Nolan's Batman film *The Dark Knight* became the fourth film in history to earn more than one billion dollars in worldwide box-office revenue. Whether the superhero will continue to captivate imaginations remains to be seen, but for now, it appears firmly enshrined as a part of modern culture.

What Makes a Superhero

Certain motifs of the superhero genre, most of which have been present from the first Superman comic, are now so widespread they are considered clichés. Superheroes often have mysterious origins that give rise to their particular superpowers. Unlike traditional folk heroes, superheroes generally do not earn their abilities; rather, their powers are circumstantial or thrust upon them in a freak accident or otherwise traumatic event. This creates a mental or physical uniqueness in the hero, dispelling his or her former complacency. The hero then embarks on a mission of positive social justice that entails fighting crime, otherwise righting wrongs, or protecting his or her home, city, or planet.

Often superheroes will keep their identities secret in order to protect themselves and those close to them from unwanted attention and the vengeance of their enemies. This dual identity is the source of many difficulties for superheroes, who must go to great lengths to prevent both friends and foes from discovering who they are. Often it prevents them from maintaining consistent social relationships. Their actual identities tend to be vastly different from the superheroes' perceived traits, which can lead to further conflict; for example, Clark Kent longs for the affections of Lois Lane, who spurns him for Superman, unaware that the two are one and the same. Superheroes invariably wear costumes, which help to disguise their identities and distinguish them from one another.

Superheroes usually come into conflict with supervillains, antagonists who have origins similar to those of superheroes but are driven not by a desire to help others but by egotism, greed, or otherwise negative ideologies. These supervillains threaten the safety of whatever the superhero serves and protects, and a great deal of superhero plots revolve around their conflicts. The commercial demands of the comic book medium require that superheroes' adventures be serial, and thus new villains and obstacles are regularly introduced. Often superheroes will have an archenemy against whom they have a personal or otherwise more serious grudge, and that character will be repeatedly encountered and defeated, though never killed. Thus, another common motif of the superhero is that of the endless struggle, a conflict that can never be concluded because

superheroes' moral standards generally prevent them from killing their enemies.

The Superhero's Origin Story

Although themes of the superhero genre have been present in Western fiction since before comic books themselves—tales of the masked vigilante Zorro were first published in 1919, to name just one example—the first superhero to become widely popular was none other than Superman. Despite reluctance from major comics syndicates, Superman's creators, Jerry Siegel and Joe Shuster, managed to get their original character featured in *Action Comics* 1, published with the Man of Tomorrow on the cover in the spring of 1938. He struck a chord with readers, and when sales of *Action Comics* rose dramatically by the fourth issue, publishers discovered that the readers were not interested in the action so much as they were in Superman himself. The success of Superman marked the beginning of the Golden Age of comic books. Superman spawned hundreds of imitators, each new superhero hoping to match the popularity of the original. From 1939 to 1941, the number of comic book titles tripled, and more than 80 percent of them contained superheroes.

The comic book industry grew enormously during the years of World War II as a result of comics' popularity among U.S. troops. As more superhero titles were published, their heroes become patriotic and involved in conflicts closely related to the real world. Captain America debuted in 1941 and reflected the dominant social values in the United States at the time. He was both a soldier and a superhero, a man who epitomized American values and stood up to real-world villains such as Nazis. Comics featuring him and other "Allied" superheroes were as much propaganda as they were pulp.

The Superhero Reborn

Following the end of the war, comic books lost both their real-world villains and their military readers, and by 1949 the popularity of superhero comics had fallen dramatically. Most titles were ended, and the only superheroes not to see a break in publication were Batman, Superman, and Wonder Woman. Readers' interests shifted to crime, Western, and horror genres. In fact, the superhero genre might have fallen out of vogue entirely were it not for the infamous congressional hearings in 1954 regarding juvenile delinquency and comics, specifically those of the crime and horror genre. The instatement of the Comics Code Authority (CCA) led to a revival of superheroes, who were deemed acceptable role models and whose story lines did not have to contain explicit content or graphic violence.

The year 1956 marked the beginning of the Silver Age. In October of that year, the Flash returned with a new origin and a new costume, prompting the revival of other superheroes, such as Green Lantern and Aquaman, for new audiences. The first issue of the *Justice League of America* was published by DC Comics in 1960, inspiring Marvel Comics to release its own series featuring a superhero group, *Fantastic Four*. In 1964, Captain America was brought out of cold storage to become the leader of the Avengers. Overall, the Silver Age was a period of artistic achievement and commercial success for superhero comics. In 1966, the *Batman* television series debuted to very high ratings, boosting the sale of all comic books, especially *Batman* itself.

The Bronze Age of comics, a period from roughly 1970 to 1986, was marked by a growing maturity within comics and the superhero genre, as subjects of social relevance began to be addressed. Most notably, in 1971, *Spider-Man* defied the Comics Code Authority by featuring an antidrug story, thus flouting the ban on any mention of narcotics, and printing *Spider-Man* issues 96-98 without the CCA seal of approval. The issues sold very well, which led to a modification of the CCA standards. Other hallmarks of the Bronze Age were the introduction of black and other minority superheroes and a gradual shift in tone to more mature content. By the 1980's, the CCA's approval meant little, and numerous titles were being printed for comic books' growing mature audiences.

Superheroes Get Old

The superhero genre underwent a further transformation in the mid-1980's. Although ventures into the psychological dimensions of the superhero identity were not new, the superheroes during the 1980's were influ-

The Punisher, a militaristic vigilante driven by revenge, was one of many antiheroes that rose to prominence in the 1980's. (Courtesy of Marvel Comics)

enced by the mood of the times, and a sense of cynicism and discontent permeated their stories. It was in 1986 that two talented writers in the industry produced works that have affected most subsequent superhero comics: Frank Miller's *The Dark Knight Returns* and Alan Moore's *Watchmen*. These stories challenged the existing archetypes of comic book heroes, deconstructing and exploring the nature of the superhero to an unprecedented extent. It was this self-awareness regarding the limits of the genre that marked the beginning of the Modern Age of comics. It also instigated a wave of violence and brutality from writers and artists who sought to replicate the intensity of *The Dark Knight* and *Watchmen*. Amoral "superheroes" such as the Punisher arose, and revenge became an acceptable motivation for a heroic character.

Some scholars argue that in light of the global events in both Marvel and DC universes, comics have entered a postmodern age. DC's Infinite Crisis story line dealt with the inability of various superheroes to live up to the ideals expected of them, and Marvel's Civil War divided the superhero community in a conflict related to the privacy of the heroes' identities. With the incorporation of the deconstructive elements of the Modern Age into the mainstream comics universes, superheroes have transformed from the moral icons of their origin into fully human characters with the flaws and ambiguities of the average person.

Sexism and Notions of Masculinity

Since its inception, the comic book industry has been dominated by males, both as consumers and as creators. As a result, female characters have been consistently marginalized, and the superhero comic genre has often been criticized for its sexism. In the early days of superhero comics, most female characters were girlfriends of their heroic counterparts, and their roles in the plots consisted of nearly discovering the hero's secret identity or having to be rescued. Women who are otherwise portrayed as intelligent and capable frequently have no agency or existence outside the context of the superhero with whom they are associated. Even female superheroes who are powerful in their own right are portrayed as scantily clad or with sexual iconography, Wonder Woman's lasso being the most obvious example.

In addition, critics have pointed to homosocial tendencies in superhero iconography, to the point of exclusion of women. Superheroes generally reject or fail to win the affections of their female love interests, thus maintaining their secret identities and restoring the status quo. Love and intimacy are often associated with vulnerability and weakness, and to share secrets with a significant other is to confer power to them. In this way, superheroes reinforce traditional, mainstream notions of masculinity.

Impact

Superheroes were arguably the most significant factor in the development of American comics culture. Their influence permeates the genre; superhero lore and archetypes are appropriated and commented on even in unrelated genres and independent comics. Some scholars argue that the genre is a hindrance to the medium and that for years, puerile subject matter has prevented comics from being accepted into the canon of literature. Alan Moore has stated that he believes there is nothing more to say about the superhero, that the archetype has been completely explored. However, the superhero continues to elicit fascination in the popular sphere, and the genre has expanded into film, books, video games, toys, and music.

The superhero is firmly embedded in popular culture, the values of heroes such as Superman and Spider-Man are known the world over. They truly are modern mythological figures; like gods, they can be molded to whatever story needs to be told, and their histories can be continually reinvented to suit their audiences. Looking back on the history of American comics, one can see the history of American culture as well. At times, superheroes have influenced dominant social norms, as in World War II. They have revealed a fascination with spectacle and violence in modern culture. They reflect humanity's greatest dreams and deepest fears. It is fitting that so flexible a symbol of individualism should be emblematic of the comic book, a medium that is both boundless in its possibilities and widely accessible. Doubtless the superhero will continue to affect the graphic novel and popular culture for generations to come. The genre, like the superheroes themselves, can never truly die, only be reborn anew.

Sam Julian

Bibliography

Bongco, Mila. *Reading Comics: Language, Culture, and the Concept of the Superhero in Comic Books.* New York: Garland, 2000. Covers the development of comics from their pre-World War II American origins to the late 1980's, with specific attention paid to the superhero genre and its implications about popular culture.

Coogan, Peter. *Superhero: The Secret Origin of a Genre.* Austin, Tex.: MonkeyBrain Books, 2006. Provides an exploration of the superhero genre, from its mythological origins to its renaissance in film.

Garrett, Greg. *Holy Superheroes! Exploring the Sacred in Comics, Graphic Novels, and Film*. Louisville, Ky.: Westminster John Knox Press, 2008. Explores the portrayal of religious and spiritual concepts in comics, from dogmatic notions such as the apocalypse to moral issues such as the problem of evil and the notion of vigilante justice.

Wandtke, Terrence R., ed. *The Amazing Transforming Superhero! Essays on the Revision of Characters in Comic Books, Film and Television*. Jefferson, N.C.: McFarland, 2007. Collects essays offering social and cultural analysis of the superhero genre, focusing on trends in history, specific characters, and common themes.

VIOLENCE IN GRAPHIC NOVELS: HISTORICAL AND CULTURAL NECESSITY

Definition

Violence can be described as the use of physical force to cause injury, damage, or destruction to individuals, the environment, or surrounding objects. In graphic novels, this force may not necessarily be physical in the traditional sense, because characters such as superheroes, monsters, aliens, and other creatures or beings can have special powers and abilities (for example, mental capabilities) that can lead to violent results as well.

Introduction

Adults in American culture feel responsible for protecting young children, boys and girls alike, from the outside world's harsher realities. Since the Victorian period, childhood has been idealized and sentimentalized, transforming the general viewpoint of children as "little adults" into the sweeping belief that the young are innocent and naturally good and must be guarded from society's evil nature through education. Whereas the Victorians had no qualms about exposing children to violent and fantastical tales for instructional purposes or amusement, Americans in the twenty-first century see such entertainment as celebrating the dark, horrific, and brutal underbelly of humanity, a quality many would rather banish from reality—whether that means removing video-game gore, editing out violent lyrics and images from rap music videos, or confiscating graphic novels in which vigilante superheroes take justice into their own hands.

Largely more empathetic and literalistic than children, adults tend to become paranoid, automatically assuming that young people will emulate the violence shown in media such as comic books. What many fail to understand is that just as popular opinion changes throughout history, new generations of children have different needs and developmental rates. As research with children, parents, educators, and psychologists has demonstrated, young people's cravings for the elements of fantasy violence do not make them mere passive recipients of aggressive media trends. Rather, they are consumers and users of popular culture, developmentally quite capable of distinguishing between fantasy violence and reality at a young age with proper adult guidance. Instead of regarding the violence in graphic novels as a cause of real-world violence, American society must take note of the historically negative impact of censoring violent content and acknowledge the underlying benefits children and adolescents receive when reading about such violence. Easing cultural anxiety and disapproval will allow young people to find the freedom to enjoy graphic novel violence for the purposes it does serve, understanding themselves in a healthier manner along the way.

Golden and Silver Age Violence

The history of comic books and graphic novels is, essentially, a history of violence. From the Golden Age, beginning in the 1930's, up until the institution of the infamous Comics Code in 1954, popular superheroes such as Superman used righteous violence to aid oppressed citizens and those in need. Although these heroes often damaged or destroyed the environment and property, they exhibited an esteem for human life, no matter how corrupt or evil that life may be, that prevented them from killing. The perpetrators were therefore taught a lesson through either thrashings and beatings or witty, nonviolent means. As the superhero genre became supersaturated and comics became extremely popular with younger readers, however, creators moved to other subject matter, including tales of adventure, crime, horror, and lust. Since comic books at the time were viewed as innocent, harmless reading material for children, these low expectations and the lack of any monitoring system allowed the industry to turn out increasingly violent stories. True crime titles such as *Crime Does Not Pay* (1942-1955) featured graphic depictions of beheadings, stabbings, torture, shootings, and dismemberment. This trend toward luridly violent content outraged parents, as comics had surpassed what was considered socially acceptable even for adult amusement.

Based upon commentary from experts such as psychiatrist Fredric Wertham, who claimed that comic books were harmful to impressionable young people, schools, churches, and other community organizations held campaigns against comics and demanded legislative action. Accordingly, states banned or regulated titles, and eventually Congress put the comic book industry on trial. These hearings resulted in the creation of the Comics Code Authority, which enforced rigid restrictions on comic book content and artistic depictions, especially with regard to violence; for example, details and methods of a crime could not be addressed, and no gore, horror, depravity, excessive bloodshed, sadism, or masochism could be depicted. The code ushered in the Silver Age of comics, forbidding a wide variety of conflicts and essentially limiting production to innocent titles meant only for young children. The only really plausible option for comics creators was to revise their superheroes, creating unambiguous figures who were socially moral, never questioned authority, remained in control, and used brainpower and science (rather than physical violence) to defeat villains.

Bronze and Modern Age Violence

During the Bronze Age, which lasted from the 1970's to the mid-1980's, the Comics Code underwent important revisions in terms of violence. In the wake of a decade consumed by the controversial Vietnam War, a push for civil rights, and general youth rebellion against authority, the industry worked for more relevance by exploring timely social issues. Rather than simply pushing traditional values of the American adult populace onto young readers, publishers began to allow for the depiction of moral ambiguity, monsters, and corrupt government figures and police officers. Almost any situation that was not too provocative, obscene, or grisly was now permitted under the newly revised code—including instances of violence, as long as they were not extreme. Popular superheroes of the period still largely rejected violent responses to problems, but these changes to the code were a step toward acknowledging that children and adolescents already encountered real-life violent situations on the daily news and that by idealizing comic book story lines, society was insulting the general awareness of youths.

The Modern Age (1980's to the present) truly began to bring the comic book industry up to speed, matching the levels of violence already depicted in television and films. Seeking to appease the tastes of their young readers, who demanded more cynicism, violence, and moral ambiguity, and now able to sidestep the Comics Code though direct-market distribution, graphic novels finally lived up to the "graphic" portion of their name, introducing brutal story lines and characters. Vigilante superheroes, or more accurately antiheroes, who preferred taking the law into their own hands and exacting merciless punishment became the norm. Even mild superheroes who survived the Comics Code's harsh censorship now pursued revenge occasionally as well. Most notably, aggressive crusades for justice were depicted as reasonable alternatives, since social institutions frequently failed to punish criminals adequately or at all, helping the industry return to the trend of violent subject matter popular before the code was created.

Examples of Modern Age Violence

Even with violence reemerging in all types of Modern Age graphic novels, a few texts particularly pushed the bar in terms of brutality and shock value. Acclaimed writer Alan Moore has been noted for his ruthless, disturbing characters, whether they be villains or vigilantes. For example, because Rorschach in *Watchmen* (1986-1987) believes that life is meaningless and society apathetic, he freely administers his own form of violent justice, which he considers to befit his sick, rudderless society. As a ten-year-old child, he partially blinds a bully by forcing a lighted cigarette into the other boy's eye; as an adult, to punish a murderer who dismembered a six-year-old girl, he handcuffs the perpetrator to an appliance, dumps kerosene around the house, gives the man a handsaw, and drops a lighted match, leaving the criminal with the option of dying in the fire or severing his own hand to escape. Despite the heightened violence in the text's story line, Dave Gibbons's accompanying illustrations typically use a perspective or angle that leaves much of the graphic brutality to the audience's imagination—thus increasing the work's overall violent effect, because people's

Kick-Ass. (Courtesy of Marvel Comics)

imaginations tend to be more gruesome than any illustration could ever be.

Conversely, *Kick-Ass* (2008-2010), by Mark Millar and John Romita, Jr., utilizes realistic, ultraviolent images throughout, never skimping on over-the-top blood spatter or uncensored, cringe-worthy physical brutality. Especially disturbing to many conservative readers is the fact that such violence is carried out by an ordinary teenager named Dave, an avid comic book fan who possesses no superpowers. Even more shocking is ten-year-old Hit-Girl, also a "normal" child with no superhuman capabilities, who never hesitates to kill criminals: Using dual swords, she stabs completely through a drug dealer's chest while removing the heads, arms, and legs of his gang members before striking her final deathblows. Romita's illustrations in

Kick-Ass leave nothing to the imagination, prolonging every gory, bloody detail to the extreme in order to comment upon the nature of comics and society itself.

The Cultural Importance of Violence

Based upon the historical connection between graphic novels and violence and the trend's reemergence into the medium, violent depictions and story lines do serve an important role in modern culture and in the lives of youth. It may help ease social tension over brutal content in comic books to realize that even young children can easily recognize cartoonish depictions of violence as unreal, distinguishing between fantasy violence and real-life situations because they adhere to different laws. Once middle childhood has been reached, children have generally mastered the difference between their own personal fantasies and reality, gaining the ability to reason and reflect upon their new knowledge and compare themselves to society's standards.

Thus, as long as adult culture does not blur the boundaries between the worlds of fantasy and reality by reacting to fantasy violence in ways that befit a real-life situation, reading about and seeing violence in graphic novels can actually have positive benefits, such as allowing young readers to harness feelings of personal anxiety, access a range of emotions in order to reach a new developmental level, discover personal power and feel stronger as individuals, make sense of society and their places within it, have a cathartic experience and learn socially appropriate ways to handle true conflicts, and release strong feelings in order to exorcise emotional demons and prevent real experiences from being overwhelming. Once adults disregard the controversy over violent content in graphic novels, these benefits can become readily apparent, and youth audiences can continue to turn to brutal fantasy violence in order to cope with a reality that is also unreasonable and unkind.

Impact

Since the history of graphic novels was always interlaced with violent depictions, albeit to varying degrees, the Comics Code's attempts to remove violent imagery and story lines from the medium almost spelled the doom of the entire comics industry. At a time in which youth culture demanded conflict and challenges to authority, the industry was limited in the types of products it could release, and such comics did not meet the needs of the growing number of young consumers. While comics ranked as the most popular entertainment medium during the 1940's and early 1950's, after the code took effect, the industry dwindled down to fewer than a dozen publishers by 1962, with a total output of around 350 million comic books—a 50 percent decrease from the previous decade. With strict censorship of violence and sexuality leading to blacked-out portions of panels and whited-out spaces in dialogue, comics lost many of their unique artistic qualities as well as the escapism they provided for readers. Many talented writers and artists left the industry forever, and "comics" became a dirty, socially unacceptable word.

Despite losing readers, however, the comic book industry managed to survive the code. Unsurprisingly, the expansion of the industry during the 1980's and 1990's largely stemmed from the medium's increased violent content, with labels such as "For Mature Readers Only" generating more appeal for readers of all ages. When this graphic violence sparked media attention again, the public did not react with much concern the second time around; graphic novels were only starting to approach the level of violence already prev-

alent in music, films, and television, so the medium was left, once again, to its own devices.

Celeste Lempke

Bibliography

Hajdu, David. *The Ten-Cent Plague: The Great Comic-Book Scare and How It Changed America.* New York: Picador, 2009. Details the history of comics and comic books from the end of the nineteenth century to the 1950's, discussing the backlash that almost destroyed the industry.

Jones, Gerard. *Killing Monsters: Why Children Need Fantasy, Super Heroes, and Make-Believe Violence.* New York: Basic Books, 2002. Explains the benefits children receive from the fantasy genre, fantasy violence, superhuman characters, and sexuality in the realms of entertainment media.

Wright, Bradford W. *Comic Book Nation: The Transformation of Youth Culture in America.* Baltimore: Johns Hopkins University Press, 2001. Describes the cultural history of comic books, beginning largely in 1933 and proceeding through the Modern Age, emphasizing narrative trends, the comics business, and cultural insights revealed by comic book content.

THE WAR GENRE IN GRAPHIC NOVELS

Definition

The war genre of graphic novels comprises those whose primary concern is to represent, investigate, or report on wars, real or fictitious, or the effects of wars on the characters, cultures, or countries that experienced them.

Introduction

Though any genre is by nature constantly revising the boundaries by which it is defined, the war genre of graphic novels is particularly difficult to encapsulate within a single definition. Action and conflict are ubiquitous in graphic literature, and themes of conflict so routinely cross genre barriers that they alone cannot constitute a unique category of text. Similarly, many of the most celebrated graphic narratives that address war and warfare do so without presenting the conflict per se. As a result, a definition of the genre seems impossibly broad, but it might feasibly read as "graphic novels whose primary concern is to represent, investigate, or report on wars, real or fictitious, or the effects of wars on the characters, cultures, or countries that experienced them."

Graphic novels in the war genre have a mixed parentage that is evident in the myriad approaches to their chosen topics. Within the war genre are works of comics journalism, autographics, fictionalized historical warfare, and fictional warfare. The variety of approaches makes difficult a general theory of the genre, but it also testifies to the robust nature of the comic book medium.

Early comics purporting to portray narratives of real adventure stories and comics aimed directly at parents and educational systems often focused on American war heroes, from the Revolutionary War to expansionist battles in the American West. *True Comics*, published between 1941 and 1950 by Parents' Magazine Press, is one such antecedent to the war genre, though contrary to the titular emphasis on the veracity of the accounts, the narratives within were often sensationalized. *Classics Illustrated* (originally *Classic Comics*), published by the Gilberton Company from 1941 to

A fictional war is the setting for *Notes for a War Story*, which won several awards. The graphic novel recounts the tale of three young men as they travel in an unknown country ravaged by war. (Courtesy of First Second Books)

1971, is another antecedent to the modern war graphic novel. Unlike *True Comics*, however, the Gilberton comics emphasized historical accuracy in order to be more marketable to parents and educators. Together, these comics represent the parentage of the war genre of graphic novels, though the mixed genetics of sensationalism and veracity appear differently in the phenotypes of their many contemporary offspring.

Another important antecedent to representations of war in the graphic novel is the work of illustrator and editor Harvey Kurtzman. Kurtzman was himself enlisted in the army during World War II, though he never saw battle during his service. Instead, he contributed to the war effort by developing his artistic talent, authoring comics and single panels in Army publications such as *Yank* and the newsletter published out of his station, Camp Sutton, called *The Carry All*. Additionally, Kurtzman was among the many soldier-artists who designed instructional posters for training camps and American propaganda posters encouraging, among other things, donations to the Army Emergency Relief effort. It was Kurtzman's work after the war, however, as editor of two war titles published by Entertaining (EC) Comics, *Two-Fisted Tales* (1950-1955) and *Frontline Combat* (1951-1954), that is most relevant to the development of the war genre. The titles adhered to Kurtzman's pedagogical mission to educate children about the horrific realities of war. Marked by Kurtzman's narrative and illustrative concern for veracity as well as EC's penchant for explicit violence, prevalent as well in their horror and science-fiction titles, these two series are often cited as setting the standard for treatment of war in graphic literature.

The development of underground comics in the late 1960's and early 1970's also played an important role in the development of the war genre in graphic novels. While Kurtzman's work for EC Comics presented a realist argument against his country's involvement in the Korean War, that argument was articulated largely in humanistic rather than political terms. The counterculture generation that came after Kurtzman left as their legacy an urge to disparage, defile, and parody all that the dominant American ideology held sacrosanct. In their more explicit challenge to what they viewed as a repressive culture, the underground comics movement also introduced the autographic: an auteurist author's presence in the panels of the comics, narrating political events or depictions of events in his or her own life. In their passionate resistance to the accepted standards of comics, the pioneers of the underground comics expanded the use of the form, paving the way for many of the autographic and journalistic works in the war genre of graphic novels.

Graphic novels of the war genre have built upon these antecedents in their address of marginalized peoples and modern conflicts. The terrorist attacks of September 11, 2001, the Iraq War, and the American battle against terrorism have all become the focus of graphic narrative, as have conflicts in Macedonia, Bosnia, and Palestine. While these graphic novels, both fiction and nonfiction, have attracted much critical and academic acclaim, many prospective areas of research remain to be explored.

Comics Journalism and Autographics

Much of the most compelling work in the war genre of graphic novels derives its power from Kurtzman's model of intensive research and its focus from the independent voices of the underground comics movement. In establishing an ethos based on an academic concern for veracity and a humanist concern for providing a media outlet for the experiences of otherwise marginalized peoples, these graphic novels have instigated a return of the graphic narrative to the history classroom.

Jack Jackson's graphic novels *Comanche Moon* (1979) and *Los Tejanos* (1982) are early examples of work in this vein. In his work, Jackson seeks to address the complicated history of the relationship between the United States and Mexico from the point of view of Texan native peoples. His narratives of mixed-race Comanche chief Quanah Parker and the controversial revolutionary Tejano Juan N. Seguin are meticulously researched and include detailed bibliographies of prose sources. *Los Tejanos* is notably less explicit in its imagery than the earlier *Comanche Moon*, however, which suggests that Jackson's work, like that of others working in the nonfiction war-genre tradition, seeks to temper sensationalism in an effort to attract a wider audience to its minority perspectives.

Another way to verify the accuracy of the graphic text is through the first-person eyewitness perspective of its author. Comics journalists such as Joe Sacco, David Axe, and Ted Rall are reporters whose graphic novel work in the war genre is authenticated by their own personal testimony. Sacco's graphic novels *Palestine* (1993; published as a collected work in 2001) and *Safe Area Goražde* (2000) are two of the best-known examples of the genre, but also important is his *War's End* (2005), which furthers his reportage on the Bosnian War. Cementing the connection between war-genre graphic novels and underground comics is *Mace-*

donia: What Does It Take to Stop a War? (2007), a collaboration between Harvey Pekar and author Heather Robinson, the latter of whom visited Macedonia in search of evidence that war is not inevitable. Rall's *To Afghanistan and Back* (2002) and Axe's *War Fix* (2006) are other important contributions to the war genre of graphic novels made by traveling or embedded journalists.

War Fiction

Graphic fiction in the war genre has also taken up concerns related to real-world conflicts. In fictionalizing real events, however, these graphic narratives tread the dangerous line between sensationalism and respect for those who have suffered in the particular conflict. On the other hand, fictionalizing a true event may enable authors and illustrators to address very real concerns, such as military recruiting scandals,

Safe Area Goražde. (Courtesy of Fantagraphics Books)

the role of the media in modern warfare, and unforeseen casualties resulting from undischarged ammunition, through exaggeration, parable, or allegory. A prime example of the ambiguous ethics of fictionalized accounts is Kyle Baker's *Special Forces* (2007-2008), about a group of teenage American soldiers in Iraq whose characters are drawn with the broad strokes of cliché: a gay man, an autistic teenager, and the perpetually half-dressed hero, Felony, whose name references her criminal record. The narrative was inspired by reports of dishonorable U.S. Army recruitment policies, and the illustrations take pains to represent the horrors of children scarred by warfare. However, Baker addresses these issues through the adventures of his lead protagonist, who rushes from skirmish to skirmish in what is left of her ragged T-shirt and shorts, often foregrounding anatomy in a way that mitigates the implications of the satire.

Not all fictionalized accounts are as sexualized as *Special Forces*, however. Anthony Lappé and Dan Goldman's *Shooting War* (2006), a fictional account of an Iraq War correspondent, demonstrates another way in which fictionalizing allows for satire. The narrative is premised on an unending American quagmire in Iraq, and the protagonist, Jimmy Burns, is an embedded blogger whose reports seek to correct oversimplified understandings of the relationships between Middle Eastern national and religious groups as well as between the American military and corporate media.

A third intriguing approach to fictionalizing real events is represented by author Brian K. Vaughan and illustrator Niko Henrichon's *Pride of Baghdad* (2006). Vaughan and Henrichon use animal protagonists to tell their version of the true story of the animals who escaped from the Baghdad Zoo after a series of American bombing campaigns. The use of animal protagonists in a traumatic narrative recalls Art Spiegelman's *Maus* (1986, 1991), but Vaughan and Henrichon use the animals to a different effect. Unlike Spiegelman's illustrations, Henrichon's are naturalistic, creating a strange juxtaposition with the articulate thoughts Vaughan has scripted for the animals. The narrative challenges its audience to read for an allegory, while the violent images of weapons turned on animals is effective in ways that violence against people in the war genre might otherwise not have been.

Impact

Perhaps due to the difficulty of defining the genre, some aspects of the war genre in graphic novels have yet to receive a thorough theoretical treatment. One of the key issues not yet fully explored is the dark shadow of exploitation that lurks beneath comics reportage in the genre. For example, a graphic novel written by an American and covering the most recent American war in Iraq must confront the question of whether the author's profiting from the coverage of the trauma of native peoples is exploitative. The question is all the more pertinent for those working on fictionalized accounts. Similarly, while the underground comics movement exploded the limits of acceptable representation, theory should address the ethical implications of representations of lived trauma. While some studies have been published on the ethical interactions between author and subject, text and reader, in comics more generally, a similar study could focus on the war genre of graphic novels in particular.

A formal analysis of war-genre graphic novels is also missing. The genre houses work by many of the most ambitious authors and illustrators in the field of graphic novels, and in a genre dominated by both armed action and grim reportage, the stylistic decisions made by these creators deserve closer theoretical inspection. These graphic novels must not only express action in a still medium but also make editorial decisions regarding what images to include within the frames. One key area of inquiry, for example, is the role of the graphic novel format in representational decisions, as the format is much longer and therefore provides more room for development than traditional comic books, comic strips, and political cartoons.

Anthony Coman

Bibliography

Conroy, Mike. *War Stories: A Graphic History*. New York: HarperCollins, 2009. Provides an in-depth illustrated history of the war genre in comics and includes a ten-page cover gallery of comics from the late 1940's and early 1950's.

McAllister, Matthew P., Edward H. Sewell, Jr., and Ian Gordon, eds. *Comics and Ideology*. New York: Peter Lang, 2001. Focuses primarily on the various ideological implications of graphic literature, including essays that touch on issues of masculinity, feminism, queer theory, nostalgia, and mythology.

Versaci, Rocco. *This Book Contains Graphic Language: Comics as Literature*. London: Continuum, 2007. Addresses work by Kurzman, Sacco, and Spiegelman in depth, as well as touching on other war-genre graphic novels, such as Rall's *To Afghanistan and Back* (2002).

Witek, Joseph. *Comic Books as History: The Narrative Art of Jack Jackson, Art Spiegelman, and Harvey Pekar*. Jackson: University Press of Mississippi, 1989. Features a clear and provocative close reading of war-genre comics and argues that graphic novels play an important role in historical discourse.

WESTERN GENRE IN GRAPHIC NOVELS: THE TRANSFORMATION OF THE COWBOY, AND HIS FRONTIER

Definition

As the foremost metanarrative of American popular culture, the Western and its various tropes of the frontier, cowboys and Indians, and the changing American West became a crucial storytelling genre in the emerging comic book industry of the 1930's. Although the Western has waxed and waned in popularity over the decades, writers of comic books and graphic novels continue to explore its core thematic devices in innovative ways.

Introduction

As films such as *3:10 to Yuma* (2007) and *True Grit* (2010) have shown, the American West is making a slow but successful return to the silver screen. In comic books, however, the Western not only was one of the foundational genres of the medium but also has remained a popular and viable avenue with writers and fans alike since the 1930's, experiencing a resurgence during the 1960's that in turn gave way to tremendous growth during the 1970's against the backdrop of new Western films inspired by actor Clint Eastwood. By the 1980's, however, the Western genre in mainstream comic books and graphic novels had stagnated, resulting in the cancellation of numerous titles. While the shift toward darker heroes and villains and psychologically complex plots in the superhero comics of the period signified a maturation of the comics medium, attempts to reignite the Western by infusing it with horror, time travel, or dystopian themes largely failed to connect with readers.

Nevertheless, a new breed of Western comics that broke with traditional depictions of heroes and villains, race, and historical figures emerged in the late 1990's and early 2000's, demonstrating that comics have evolved into a serious medium that can, at times, deal with themes and topics that more mainstream film or television portrayals avoid. In the process, comics revitalized older Western characters while simultaneously introducing new, original characters who reflected a more inclusive, multicultural West, reinforcing their

Blueberry is a Franco-Belgian comic series that depicts the American Wild West. (Courtesy of Dargaud)

connections to the larger Western genre beyond comics while reaffirming their ability to mirror contemporary social interests.

Western Comics in the Formative Period, 1934-1961

When Malcolm Wheeler-Nicholson's National Allied Publications began operation in 1934, the American comic book was officially born. Although comics and syndicated newspaper strips predated National's debut, the establishment of National represented the birth of original material specifically created for the comic book medium. It is little surprise that the early freelance writers who published in National's earliest books, such as *New Fun* and *New Comics*, fell back upon tried-and-true genres, including the Western, for their early stories. Titles such as *New Adventure Comics* (originally *New Comics*, rebranded in 1937) featured short Western stories, sometimes even a single page in length, that told mostly formulaic tales of cowboys versus Indians and other frontier narratives.

The superhero genre dominated industry giants such as National Allied Publications and Timely Publications, the predecessors of DC Comics and Marvel Comics, respectively, throughout the Golden Age of comic books (c. 1938-1954). Western characters such as Vigilante (debuted in 1941) and Tomahawk (1947) did sporadically appear alongside mainstream leaders such as Superman, Batman, and Wonder Woman, and comics featuring licensed Western figures, as opposed to original comic book creations, shared the same shelves as the Golden Age superheroes. *Gene Autry Comics* was a regular staple from its inception in 1941 through its cancellation in 1959, and *Roy Rogers Comics* ran from 1944 through 1961. Comics such as *Red Ryder Comics* (1940-1957), *Hopalong Cassidy* (1943, 1946-1959), and *Tom Mix Western* (1948-1953) rounded out the early Western comics craze. Interestingly, the appearance of original American Indian characters as foils for superheroes predated the introduction of stock cowboy heroes and book titles of the late 1940's and early 1950's. One story line in *All Star Comics* (1940-1951) featured its Justice Society of America stopping an attempt by Nazis to infiltrate a Native American reservation in the West.

Because superheroes became so intrinsically tied to World War II, the war's conclusion in 1945 led to a decline in superhero comic book sales. Comic book publishers immediately shifted focus to accommodate the emerging Western craze that was reflected in film and television, transforming titles such as *All-American Comics* (1939-1948) and *All Star Comics* into *All-American Western* (1948-1952) and *All Star Western* (1951-1961), respectively. DC Comics' own *Western Comics* (1948-1961) would also be a premier venue for such stories. With characters such as Pow-Wow Smith, Wyoming Kid, Nighthawk, Rodeo Rick, and Matt Savage, Trail Boss in the DC Comics stable and the Two-Gun Kid, Kid Colt, the Apache Kid, the Ringo Kid, and the Rawhide Kid starring in Marvel Comics titles such as *Red Warrior* (1951) and *Two-Gun Western*

(1950-1952), original Western comic book stories found an eager audience in American children, who saw the West reinforced in television and film adaptations. Historical Western story lines based in fact also became popular, as Daniel Boone, Davy Crockett, Kit Carson, and Buffalo Bill Cody saw a resurgence in popularity in series such as *The Legends of Daniel Boone* (1955-1957) and *Frontier Fighters* (1955-1956).

Even the superhero comics were not immune to the Western craze of the postwar decades, as Superman, Wonder Woman, Green Arrow, and even Batman all had their own Western-themed adventures throughout the 1950's. Although superhero comics had taken a backseat to the Western books in the early 1950's, the introduction of newer heroes ushered in the Silver Age of American comics, which lasted from 1956 to 1970. While at first this shift had little effect on how the West and Western characters were portrayed in comics, it did signify a decrease in Western-themed books as superheroes reasserted their dominance. By the early to mid-1960's, most of the top Western anthology comics had been canceled, though individual titles such as *Rawhide Kid* (1955-1979) and *Kid Colt Outlaw* (1948-1979) successfully continued into the 1970's.

Western Comics Reborn, 1968-1985

Taking a cue from the shift in content in Western films such as *Cheyenne Autumn* (1964) and *Little Big Man* (1970) as well as the social upheavals of the era, comics began to reflect a new approach to the Western genre. The American Indian character Firehair first appeared in 1969 in DC Comics' *Showcase* (1956-1970, 1977-1978), which had also premiered the Western character Bat Lash a year earlier; Firehair later became a backup feature in *Tomahawk* (1950-1972). Even the classic title *Tomahawk* was not immune to the shifts in perception regarding the Western hero and issues of race, as themes of prejudice, sexuality, and bigotry began to appear in its pages.

In 1970, DC Comics resumed publication of *All Star Western* (1970-1972; rebranded *Weird Western Tales*, 1972-1980), which introduced characters such as Outlaw, El Diablo, and, most important, Jonah Hex. Far more violent and brutal than before, these early 1970's stories featured characters reminiscent of East

Clint Eastwood as The Man With No Name in the 1965 Italian-made Western *For a Few Dollars More*. (John Springer Collection/Corbis)

wood's "Man with No Name." Marvel followed suit in 1971 with the introduction of the bizarre character Red Wolf, who eventually received his own short-lived series, lasting from 1972 to 1973. Aside from Jonah Hex, the only popular Western figure of the 1970's was Brian Savage, also known as Scalphunter, who emerged in 1977 and eventually became a backup feature in Hex's series. Mounting fan complaints and the lack of innovative story lines ultimately doomed the *Jonah Hex* series, and the 1970's resurgence in Western comics died off by the early 1980's.

Western Comics' Golden Age Redux, 1997-2011

In the late 1990's, Vertigo began to publish Western miniseries, including a second *Weird Western Tales* (2001) that primarily featured bizarre story lines, gimmicks, and no-name characters and various series featuring recognizable Western comic book figures such as Tomahawk. The West also featured in DC's annual one-shot issues, which in 1997 were published under the banner "Pulp Heroes: Weird Western Tales" and showcased superheroes engaged in various Western scenarios with American Indian characters such as Pow-Wow Smith and Super-Chief.

The first successful attempt to fuse genres and reinterpret the West featured the preeminent superhero, Superman. DC Comics' *The Kents* (1997-1998) signified not only a reimagining of the Superman mythos but also a comeback for the Western in mainstream comic books, as historical characters and events were infused into the Man of Steel's legacy. Writer John Ostrander used the popularity of the series to launch a Western miniseries at Marvel, *Blaze of Glory* (2000), which he later followed with a sequel, *Apache Skies* (2002). Both miniseries saw a rebirth of classic Marvel Western characters, but with far more serious and contemporary social and cultural concerns and plotlines.

In 2005, DC Comics followed the success of *The Kents* with a relaunch of *Jonah Hex*, which ran until October, 2011, and inspired the 2010 film of the same name. Licensed products also returned in the first decade of the twenty-first century with the publication of Dynamite Publishing's *Lone Ranger* (2006-2011) and subsequent *Man with No Name* saga (2008-2009). Original series published include Jason Aaron's *Scalped*, created in 2007 for Vertigo, which showcases an all-American Indian cast and is set in a fictional Lakota reservation in South Dakota.

Impact

The Western genre has been the quintessential American national narrative of expansion since the foundation of the colonies and the generational movement into the interior of what would eventually become the continental United States. Although the West has shifted location as the frontier boundaries have been redrawn over the generations, its flexibility has allowed the genre to mirror contemporary social, cultural, economic, and political concerns of each era. From art, plays, and high literature to dime novels, international Wild West shows, early cinema and radio dramas, comic books, television, and Hollywood blockbusters, the Western has long been at the core of the American experience in popular culture.

More than simple cowboy-and-Indian adventures, the Western genre in comics encompasses frontier war, bandits and pirates, vigilantes and victims, and even the occasional superhero. Perhaps the most multicultural of all genres, the fictional graphic Western often showcases the diversity inherent in the historical West as different cultures and ethnicities came together or clashed in the contested spaces between "savagery" and "civilization."

Nathan Wilson

Bibliography

Green, Paul. *Encyclopedia of Weird Westerns: Supernatural and Science Fiction Elements in Novels, Pulps, Comics, Films, Television and Games*. Jefferson, N.C.: McFarland, 2009. Features an introduction that discusses the history of the "weird" Western in comics and other media, plus coverage of numerous Western comic book titles and characters.

Savage, William W., Jr. *Commies, Cowboys, and Jungle Queens: Comic Books and America, 1945-1954*. Hanover, N.H.: Wesleyan University Press, 1998. Focuses on the critical period of the 1950's, when the comic book medium underwent a dramatic shift following criticism from concerned parents and investigation by the United States government.

Wright, Bradford W. *Comic Book Nation: The Transformation of Youth Culture in America*. Baltimore: Johns Hopkins University Press, 2003. Provides a publishing history that situates the changing comic book medium within the larger cultural history of the United States and discusses the popularity of various genres, including the Western.

WOMEN IN GRAPHIC NOVELS: EVOLUTION AND REPRESENTATION

Definition

The depiction of women in graphic novels has changed significantly since the Golden Age of comics. Although women's roles in these stories continue to evolve, they also attract criticism regularly. Common roles women have embodied throughout the history of graphic novels include women seeking romance, women with superpowers, and "bad"/independent women.

Introduction

The roles women play in graphic novels have long attracted critical attention. Many female characters who are considered inspiring symbols of strength have also been criticized for their lack of complexity and highly sexualized roles. The representation of women in graphic novels has changed immensely throughout the twentieth and twenty-first centuries, with common female roles including the woman looking for love, the superheroine, and the "bad girl."

Women in graphic novels once functioned as little more than plot devices, usually to stimulate a man or provide him with opportunities to demonstrate his manliness via a sexual encounter or marriage proposal. Female characters in most popular 1940's graphic novels were also typically one dimensional, concerned with securing the attention and affections of men. The representation of women in graphic novels has evolved considerably since the Golden Age of comics, and female characters now form the crux of the plot in series such as *Elektra* and *Batgirl*. Similarly, female characters have become more complex, since series creators have also devoted more energy to developing layered and intriguing histories for female characters, such as Tulip O'Hare (*Preacher*) and Jenny Sparks (*Storm-watch, The Authority*).

Although women in graphic novels have become more multifaceted, they continue to be portrayed as sex objects. The majority of characters don revealing and form-fitting outfits, and illustrators often exaggerate female characters' body proportions to emphasize luscious curves and small waists. This representation has generated critical controversy, and some critics argue that the power associated with many female characters is subverted by their sexualized appearance. Representations of women in graphic novels, whatever form they take, call notions of power and sexuality into question.

Looking for Love . . . and Marriage

Women in graphic novels have long been portrayed as preoccupied with romance. Some of the most popular series of the 1940's and 1950's, including *Young Romance* (1947-1975), *Hi-School Romance* (1949-1958), *First Love Illustrated* (1949-1963), and *True Bride-to-Be Romances* (1956-1958), focused on romance, usually scandalous story lines, and traditional views of women. For example, the story "Afraid to Be Married" appeared in the June 1954 issue of *True Love Pictorial* (1952-1984) and focuses on Marge, a woman who devotes all of her energy to marrying the right man. Stories such as this reinforce the stereotype that women are primarily concerned with marrying, and marrying well. "My Beautiful Boss," from issue 39 of *Lovelorn* (1949-1954), tells a similar story: Jim loves his beautiful female boss, Rita, who embarrasses him by rejecting him. In the climax of the story, Jim refers to Rita as a "career woman" without feeling. This accusation infuriates Rita, and she expels her anger by pouncing on Jim and having sex with him. In the next frame, Jim reveals that he and Rita are married and living "happily ever after." This comic suggests that women focused on their careers are insensitive and that they will only find happiness after marrying. These representations of women, rooted in the romance genre of graphic novels, have continued to influence the way in which women are portrayed in graphic novels.

While creators of many romance series geared their stories toward adults, the pattern of women being preoccupied with romance also appears in comics for young readers. Perhaps the most notable example of women battling other women to secure a man's affection occurs in the *Archie* series of comics, first published in 1942. Betty Cooper and Veronica Lodge both love Archie and regularly compete with one another for his affections, even though he will not make a commitment to either of them, preferring instead to date them simultaneously. *Archie* remains a popular series, so the trope of women looking (and even fighting) for love, companionship, and security still exists as a popular trope for female characters. The women serve primarily as plot devices, providing Archie with opportunities for adventure.

Super (and Stereotypically Female) Powers

The most famous female graphic novel characters remain superheroines and villains. In contrast to the traditional depiction of women in 1940's comics, superheroines and villains do not seek to marry men but instead engage them in battle. Though their otherworldly abilities place them as equals with their male counterparts, their superpowers are often associated closely with sexuality and female stereotypes.

Wonder Woman and Catwoman are strong female characters, but they also radiate sexual messages. Though she was not the first comic book superheroine, William Moulton Marston's Wonder Woman, who debuted in 1941, remains the most notable and beloved in the graphic novel tradition. At her inception, she functioned as a rallying figure for Americans amid the strife of World War II, and as her character developed, she continued to be viewed as a symbol of female strength in general. Even so, she has always attracted criticism. Her special weapons, a lasso of truth and magic bracelets, are, as numerous critics have suggested, also objects associated with bondage; Wonder Woman's character confuses symbols of female strength with symbols of sadomasochism, further emphasized by her highly sexualized outfit of a leotard and thigh-high boots. Similarly, supervillain Catwoman possesses impressive physical prowess, but her form-fitting costume and her weapon of choice, a whip, regularly invite comparisons to a dominatrix.

Women such as Jean Grey, Rogue, and Julie Martin remain powerful figures in the graphic novel canon, but they also possess inherently female superpowers. Jean Grey, also known as Marvel Girl, was one of the first X-Men and initially the only woman in the group; her

Marjane Satrapi vibrantly depicts the concerns and lives of Iranian women in *Embroideries*. (Courtesy of Pantheon Books)

abilities include telepathy, which involves being able to identify and empathize with the situations of others, a stereotypically female trait. Rogue, another member of the X-Men, has the ability to absorb qualities and memories of those she touches, which suggests the stereotype that women are intuitive and feeling. Julie Martin of *Echo* (2008-2011) finds herself at the site of an explosion of an armored suit, the pieces of which fall on her and become part of her. The metal shards provide her with numerous abilities and also serve as a metaphor, suggesting that to survive difficulties—Julie is undergoing a divorce, for instance—women must adopt a steely exterior. The suit also affords Julie the ability to empathize with and protect others. Yet again, a superheroine's abilities focus on the stereotypical female trait of being empathetic. This pattern suggests that women rely on feelings and emotions to thrive, a stereotype long associate with women.

Bad Girls and Independent Women

A number of "bad girls" and independent women have appeared in graphic novels, primarily in the 1990's and 2000's. These women still often look to others for companionship or assistance, but they are celebrated by readers and critics for their take-charge attitudes, gumption, and reliance on their own physical and mental prowess, rather than some otherworldly ability, for survival. Female graphic novel characters such as Tank Girl, Gail, Hit-Girl, Alice, and Micchone all serve as prime examples of "bad girls" and independent women, adding to a thriving artistic tradition that portrays strong and autonomous women.

One of the most famous graphic novel "bad girls" is Jamie Hewlett and Alan Martin's character Tank Girl, star of the series of the same name. Tank Girl, who first appeared in 1988, wears ragged clothes, lives in a tank, and is known for her crude behavior and defiant spirit. Frank Miller presented his readers with a similar character in an early issue of his graphic novel series *Sin City* (1991-2000): Gail, one of the "Girls of Old Town," as they are affectionately called, is an Uzi-carrying prostitute. She and her fellow girls protect themselves and create sovereign spaces where they rule unopposed.

Both Tank Girl and Gail epitomize the "bad girl" tradition of the 1990's and laid the foundation for some of the most beloved and independent graphic novel female characters of the 2000's, including Hit-Girl, Alice, and Micchone. Hit-Girl, who appears in Mark Millar's series *Kick-Ass* (2008-2010), is highly trained in martial arts and devotes her energy to avenging her mother. Alice, of Warren Ellis's *Freak-Angels* (2008-2011), is known for her weapon and tactical knowledge and her ability to defend herself while fearlessly attacking enemies. Similarly, Robert Kirkman's character Micchone, of the series *The Walking Dead* (2003-   ), survives a zombie plague and walks two of the undead on leashes as if they were dogs. These female characters provide a stark contrast to the marriage-minded women of comics popular in the 1940's and 1950's.

Impact

The depiction of women in graphic novels remains especially relevant to the history of graphic novels because, like their male counterparts, female characters (often implicitly) reflect the cultural forces and pressures present during the period in which they were created. Since their inception, graphic novels have provided a cultural commentary on the roles of both men and women. The majority of readers of the 1940's expected women to be traditional, and thus the female figures in graphic novels of this era sought the love of men. This emphasis perhaps also existed because America was beleaguered by war, and finding security was a common goal and a luxury. In contrast, Wonder Woman sought to instill in women the strength and confidence to fight their own battles, much like the many women left to provide for their families while their husbands went to war. During the 1960's and 1970's, superheroines gained popularity, an undeniable reaction to the feminist movement. The bad girls and independent women of the 1990's and 2000's undoubtedly sprang from the flourishing superheroine tradition, providing readers with a vivid contrast to the women of 1940's graphic novels. As representations of women continue to develop and evolve, they deserve constant critical analysis. For many years, graphic novels were associated with their male protagonists; that reality has shifted with the careful creation and study of women in the graphic novel canon.

Karley Adney

Bibliography

Brown, Jeffrey A. *Dangerous Curves: Action Heroines, Gender, Fetishism, and Popular Culture.* Jackson: University Press of Mississippi, 2011. Addresses depictions of women in graphic novels as well as other media, providing detailed critical analyses in terms of sexuality, strength, and ethnicity.

Knowles, Christopher. *Our Gods Wear Spandex: The Secret History of Comic Book Heroes.* San Francisco: Weiser Books, 2007. Provides analyses of well-known comic book characters and discusses inconsistencies in the inspiration for Wonder Woman's character, comparing the Amazons to the portrayal of Wonder Woman as highly feminized sexual icon.

Madrid, Mike. *The Supergirls: Fashion, Feminism, Fantasy, and the History of Comic Book Heroines.* Ashland, Oreg.: Exterminating Angel Press, 2009. Examines female graphic novel characters and the evolution of their depiction, addressing the stereotypes associated with female characters and what the characters represent in terms of American culture.

Robbins, Trina. *The Great Women Superheroes.* Northampton, Mass.: Kitchen Sink Press, 1996.

Provides an overview of women in comics from the 1940's to the 1990's, including analyses of both major and minor characters and discussion of trends regarding the representation of women in graphic novels.

Robinson, Lillian. *Wonder Women: Feminisms and Superheroes.* New York: Routledge, 2004. Argues that graphic novels reflect American cultural values and emphasizes the importance of studying the depictions of heroines in various forms of media, including graphic novels.

TECHNIQUE

THE ART OF DESIGNING THE GRAPHIC NOVEL

Definition

Design determines the rhythm of a graphic novel, creating a synthesized narrative that combines visual and written modes of storytelling. The design similarly determines the pacing and mood of the work and provides the reader with a powerful reading experience not available through other media.

Introduction

Design is a key factor in the creation of a graphic novel. A comprehensive design permits the seamless blend of written and visual narrative characteristic of sequential art. Creating an experience for the reader that is unlike those of purely written or visual media, graphic novel design also has the ability to dictate the mood of the work through its unity of text and visual components. In many ways, the design of each graphic novel is customized to the needs of its narrative and builds upon the strengths of its illustrator and writer. Without a design customized to suit the artistic of vision of the creators, it is unlikely that a graphic novel would be fully appreciated by its audience.

Designing a graphic novel is a complex process that ultimately adds to the language each graphic novel embodies, creating a unique literary experience. There are several components that make up the overall design

Drawing Words & Writing Pictures offers a concise and illustrated look at the conceptualization and construction of graphic novels, examples from which have been provided to help guide readers. (Courtesy of First Second Books)

language, including paneling, spacing, and timing. Such factors determine the mood and pace of the piece. The comprehensive sense of time dictated by the spacing in a graphic novel allows for a new layer of emotional development, while spacing between and in panels adds to the drama of the narrative. These elements must function together to create an effective graphic novel.

The Function of Sequential Art

Graphic novels offer the reader the combined experience of a visual and a literary medium. The sequential nature of the art is key to the creation of a successful graphic novel. The images within the novel must not be static illustrations; rather, they must flow with the narrative. This provides continuity in the narrative and ultimately the entire novel. Even though the illustrations on their own are simply static images, the fact that they are followed by images that advance the narrative makes it possible for them to appear fluid. The spacing that exists in between the frames, which is called the gutter, helps to create this flow. These in-between spaces activate the reader, increasing his or her emotional investment in the work. To maintain the flow of the work and provide a full sensory experience, the novel's creators must weave the sequence of images and narrative together.

The creation of any graphic novel involves interweaving the talents of the creators as well. In the case of graphic novels for which the text and art are created by different people, design must merge not only two modes of storytelling but also two creative styles. Design utilizes the strengths of both written and visual media to create a cohesive work that effectively conveys a coherent narrative. The creation of time in motion is a difficult feat to achieve, and the sequence of the images is essential to this process.

Framing and Panels

Framing allows the creators of a graphic novel to capture particular moments for the reader, permitting them to dictate the importance of any given scene in a narrative. Single moments can be given more weight when they are depicted within a stand-alone frame, which forces the reader to contemplate only the words and

Drawing Words and Writing Pictures. (Courtesy of First Second Books)

image within that single frame. At times, the dialogue of the novel is suspended in such frames to reinforce the action that occurs within the specific moment. Conversely, panels function to set the pace of the narrative. A series of panels in a graphic novel develop a smooth transition from one idea to the next. This fosters a sense of movement throughout the still images that aids in creating a narrative pace and mood in the work as a whole.

The creators' framing choices inform the reader of what is important in the narrative. For instance, if the illustrator captures small moment-to-moment actions, such as a panel-by-panel zoom in, the framing builds anticipation for the reader. If the illustrator chooses to display the narrative through active frames that depict action scenes, the work takes on a different pace, and those moments become more important.

Some graphic novels feature a unique design that changes the mood of the work. Joe Kubert's *Dong Xoai, Vietnam 1965* (2010) abandons the typical design structure of contained, framed panels. Instead, Kubert uses powerful line work and a strong narrative to direct the reader from illustration to illustration. In this case, the lack of framing allows the reader to feel a lack of security akin to that felt by the soldiers in the narrative. By not including a clearly defined direction through paneling and framing, Kubert's design has a powerful and lasting emotional impact on the reader.

Timing and Spacing

Designing a work of sequential art requires the careful use of spacing, which allows the work to develop a mood and timing that synchronize with the narrative. The timing dictates the buildup and release of tension within the graphic novel. It permits the images to become energetic, losing the stagnant feel that still images inherently possess. In many ways, the development of a sense of time within a work infuses the narrative with reality. Time is real for the audience, and seeing its passage in a graphic novel fuses the reading experience with all the human emotions that are attached to the concept of time. Once the concept of time has been established in a novel, the reader is able to travel with the protagonist through memories and dreams with little confusion.

Unlike other narrative art forms such as literature and cinematography, graphic novels have the ability to mold the time that elapses. The form permits the creator to interact with the reader by creating emotional stress between and within panels and frames. That emotional buildup creates a richer narrative experience because the reader develops a personal emotional response unique to his or her own experience with the work, becoming invested in the story line of the graphic novel.

Impact

A seamless design is necessary in unifying the written narrative of the author and the aesthetic vision of the artist to create a graphic novel. Both components serve each other, making it possible for the graphic novel medium to exist. Creators must combine several design elements with the narrative to create the illusion of movement, time, and space. Will Eisner's series *The Spirit*, originally published throughout the 1940's and early 1950's, serves as an early example of creative design in sequential art, rejecting the typical style of page composition that had existed previously. This series forever changed the way artists and writers understood their medium; the page was no longer stagnant, and the rigid confines of page structure were beginning to bend. Such innovations from the Golden and Silver Ages of comics made it possible for Modern Age works such as John Layman's *Chew* (2009-   ) and Neil Gaiman's *Sandman* (1989-1996) to include creative use of design. Changing the design structure by breaking, merging, and bending the panels creates a new sense of movement that the rigidity of square panels could not offer. Design has evolved within the pages of graphic novels to serve the narratives as they transform with their content.

Jessica Gamache

Bibliography

Duncan, Randy, and Matthew J. Smith. *The Power of Comics: History, Form and Culture*. New York: Continuum International, 2009. Evaluates the evolution of graphic novels as a medium throughout the twentieth century and strives to chart the changes in audience, narratives, and function.

Eisner, Will. *Comics and Sequential Art: Principals and Practices from the Legendary Cartoonist*. New York: W. W. Norton, 2008. Provides a step-by-step guide on how to combine the visual art of cartooning with a written narrative to create a graphic novel, including discussion of design.

McCloud, Scott. *Understanding Comics: The Invisible Art*. New York: HarperPerennial, 1993. Demonstrates how elements such as framing and paneling affect the viewer's experience through a series of creative models, examples from classic graphic novels, and illustrations.

Basic Visual Trends in Comics, Manga, and Graphic Novels

Definition

A wide variety of illustration styles is discernible in graphic novels. Although many are adaptations or modifications of the visual styles associated with comic books and strips, techniques proximal to the fine arts, such as painting and mixed-media collages, are also used. Graphic novels from countries such as Japan and Belgium have also influenced the styles of US artists.

Introduction

There is no single graphic novel illustration style. On the contrary, graphic novels display a variety of styles, ranging from the linearity of Chris Ware's *Jimmy Corrigan* (2000) to the painterly realism of Kurt Busiek and Alex Ross's *Marvels* (2003). While many artists underscore the individuality of their style, others prefer to adhere to the conventions of visual narratives.

In *Jimmy Corrigan*, the stringent geometricality, recognized as Ware's trademark style, also alludes to the ordinariness of the protagonist's life.. (Courtesy of Pantheon Books)

However, individual traces within each conventional style are usually perceptible. The difference in the visual styles of graphic novels lies in their frequent emphasis on artistic individuality and enhancement of the story told: The stringent geometricality of *Jimmy Corrigan* is recognized as Ware's trademark style and also alludes to the ordinariness of the protagonist's life. While appearance is usually indicative of genre in many comic books, the multifarious means of visualization in graphic novels are accompanied by a greater degree of narrative relevance, as with the symbol-laden animal metaphors in Art Spiegelman's *Maus* (1986, 1991).

Given the proximity of graphic novels and comics, the most prominent visual trends in comics through the twentieth century provide an appropriate background for the styles used in graphic novels. Prominent comics styles were fostered by magazines, affecting both the creation and influence of the stories and artwork. Similarly dependent on publication contexts, the greater visual innovation in graphic novels has been propelled in part by an increasing demand for graphic novels and the consequently higher publication budgets, which enable the printing of high-quality images and sometimes even unusual formats.

The range of illustration styles for word-image narration has been singularly mapped by comics theorist Scott McCloud through his "Big Triangle" in *Understanding Comics*. This triangle is based on a horizontal axis of realism extending from the photorealistic to the iconic, with the vertex representing the greatest degree of conceptual abstraction. The somewhat problematic distinction between iconic and abstract styles in the diagram is symptomatic of any generalized chart for visual styles, since individualistic variations persist even among artists of the same movement.

Realistic and Cute Styles in American Comics

Illustration styles for all kinds of word-image narratives generally hover between the poles of realism and iconicity. Since narratives with visual material often target children, the legacy of a cartoonlike "cute" style deemed appealing to younger readers remains discernible in many works and overlaps with the caricatural and reductive tendencies in comics inherited from sa-

tirical newspaper cartoons or broadsheets. This stylistic trend also corresponds to the predominance of young or animal protagonists, as in early American comics such as *The Yellow Kid* (1895-1898) and *Krazy Kat* (1913-1944), which nonetheless targeted older readers.

From the 1930's onwards, caricatural exaggeration was superseded by the dramatic realism employed in the increasing numbers of superhero, horror, and crime comics. Fantasy and science-fiction works also rely on a considerably realistic visual mode. Just as the more caricatural or cute style is often proximal to animation, realism shares commonalities with certain genres of live-action films—film noir, for example, had a major influence on Will Eisner's *The Spirit* and Frank Miller's *Sin City*. Yet while realism persists as the preferred visual style for graphic novels targeting adults and has greater claims of seriousness, simplified styles are also common for tackling adult themes.

The Franco-Belgian Clear Line and the Marcinelle School

The styles dominating French and Belgian comics after World War II were represented by the two major comic magazines, Jijé's *Spirou* (1938-   ) and Hergé's *Les Aventures de Tintin* (1929-1976; *The Adventures of Tintin*, 1930-1976). Comparably relaxed regarding both style and content, *Spirou* favored far more dynamic drawings than those in *Tintin*. In 1977, the designer and cartoonist Joost Swarte introduced the term "clear line" to denote the style established by Hergé through his studios and followed by artists such as E. P. Jacobs. It is characterized by flat color and clear contours complemented by an equally clear story line. Despite the stylization of the characters, their stances and expressions are based on poses drawn from life. In contrast to the characters, the settings are drawn with meticulous detail. While the "new clear line" style that Swarte and some of his contemporaries adopted is formally similar to clear line, the stories drawn in the style can be less straightforward.

Although clear line is regarded as the dominant Franco-Belgian style with a far-reaching global impact, this is in part due to the avoidance of strict stylistic principles by the Marcinelle school. Associated with the highly diverse artwork of Jijé, which includes the realistic Western *Jerry Spring* (1954-1977) as well as the playful *Spirou and Fantasio*, the precise legacies of the Marcinelle school are difficult to define. Nevertheless, the visual freedom it endorsed has clearly continued.

The Underground's Ratty Line

Another style tied to the magazines in which it originated is the ratty line (also known as "ugly art" or "comix brut"), which appeared during the second wave of the American underground comics movement and is regarded as its characteristic style. Gary Panter is regarded as one of its chief initiators, and Robert Crumb's style is closely affiliated to it. Its main feature is the emphasis on the ugly and revolting, which corresponds with the adult and usually taboo themes taken up by these comics and combined with humorous and sometimes even ironic notes, as is notable in the works of Gilbert Shelton. Rebelling against the censorship imposed by the Comics Code Authority, the underground comics artists created a visual style that complemented the controversial themes, subject matter, and language of their works.

Over the course of more than a decade, the style changed from the more realistic and arguably more mocking mode of the magazines edited by Harvey Kurtzman, namely *MAD* and *Help!*, to the more distorted, wilder depictions in *RAW*, edited by Spiegelman and Françoise Mouly. Justin Green's 1972 autobiographical comic *Binky Brown Meets the Holy Virgin Mary*, an influential work drawn in this style, is particularly notable for its status as one of the first graphic novels to be published.

Manga

Manga, Japanese graphic novels, employ a distinctive visual vocabulary that maintains a considerable degree of similarity across genres. Since manga collections are larger and more numerous but cheaper than the average comic book, the printing

conditions and techniques have influenced the formulaic, monochrome visual style prevailing among most manga. In simple terms, this manner of illustration can be seen as varying between linear and rounded depictions. Since the founding father of modern manga, Osamu Tezuka, had been inspired by Disney and other Western comics and animation, the "cute" style is more pronounced in manga than in comics.

However, alterations of style within each manga are recurrent, including the use of sketchy figures for alternative views such as behind-the-scenes commentary. This in turn must be distinguished from the superdeformed style, which is also caricatural and exaggerated but refers to the style of the entire book or story instead of stylistic changes within it. *Gekiga*, more mature or alternative Japanese graphic novels, extend the formal conventions to darker and realistic or grotesque tendencies. The expressiveness of many *gekiga* artists recalls that of the underground comics artists, and stylistic nuances in this case are indicative of genre.

From *Town of Evening Calm, Country of Cherry Blossoms*; similar to other manga, the illustrative style has been described as "expressive" and "cute." (Courtesy of Last Gasp)

From Flat to Direct Color

Colored comics were originally created in flat color that was cheap to publish. The colorization process was based on a palette of cyan, magenta, and yellow, which were layered to create various other colors but did not allow for shading or other complex effects. This manner of coloring was common on both sides of the Atlantic and used by the American superhero comics as well as the clear line *bandes dessinées*. One of the earliest American full-color productions, Kurtzman's *Little Annie Fanny* series, began publication in October, 1962, in *Playboy*, the only magazine at that time willing to pay the high printing costs for all-color comics.

A more significant development is direct color, a technique in which color is applied directly to the artwork with paint. High-quality full-color reproduction of such artwork captures the nuances of both color and media, consequently rendering individual panels similar to works of fine art. In France, Enki Bilal is regarded as one of the earliest masters of this kind of illustration. The effect of this change of technique on the status of comics has been noted by comics theorist Thierry Groensteen. Contemporary *manhua* (Chinese-language manga predominantly from Hong Kong and Taiwan) such as *Orange* by Benjamin demonstrate the continuing popularity of graphic narratives featuring lavish, colorful artwork.

Impact

As advancements in printing techniques coincided with an increase in the popularity of graphic novels, elaborate or striking visuals are a characteristic feature of most such works. Many graphic novels retain a strong affiliation to traditional modes of depiction but usually transform them to suit aesthetic or narrative purposes. Thus, while the principle of using anthropomorphic animals in *Maus* recalls the tendency of illustration toward cuteness, the expressive and often unflattering portrayal of the figures and their surroundings takes up the antiaesthetic stance of the ratty line. Likewise, the superhero comics style was used by Dave Gibbons for Alan Moore's *Watchmen* (1986-1987), which transforms and subverts the concept of superheroes. A comparably stark, sparsely colored realism prevails over the dystopian *V for Vendetta* (1995), by Moore and David Lloyd.

Though realism is generally the dominant mode of illustration, extreme stylization is also used frequently and effectively to complement and sometimes even enhance a story, as in Paul Karasik and Dave Mazzucchelli's 1994 adaptation of the Paul Auster novel *City of Glass*. For similar reasons, the new clear line style has been taken up by several graphic novelists, including Chris Ware, Seth, and Marjane Satrapi. Expressionism—which has had different manifestations in superhero, horror, and crime comics as opposed to alternative comics—is a recurrent visual trend used by artists such as Craig Thompson and Eddie Campbell, though it is highly modified in accordance with the requirements of their stories. Ultimately, each graphic novel will have a distinctive visual style that is closely connected to the story; further generalizations based on genre or narrative style are largely insufficient.

Maaheen Ahmed

Bibliography

Groensteen, Thierry. *The System of Comics*. Translated by Bart Beaty and Nick Nguyen. Jackson: University Press of Mississippi, 2007. Explores the workings of the comics medium through numerous examples, many of which are drawn from Franco-Belgian comics.

Hatfield, Charles. *Alternative Comics: An Emerging Literature*. Jackson: University Press of Mississippi, 2005. Traces the history and visual style of the underground, alternative comics movement and analyzes the work of Gilbert Hernandez, Harvey Pekar, and other notable artists.

McCloud, Scott. *Making Comics: Storytelling Secrets of Comics, Manga, and Graphic Novels*. New York: HarperCollins, 2006. Explains the workings of sequential narration and discusses the various visual styles prevalent in comic books and graphic novels.

Schodt, Frederik L. *Manga! Manga! The World of Japanese Comics*. Tokyo: Kodansha International, 2001. Provides a history of Japanese comics and the visual styles used within them, focusing in particular on the enduring influence of Tezuka.

Screech, Matthew. *Masters of the Ninth Art: Bandes Dessinées and Franco-Belgian Identity*. Liverpool: Liverpool University Press, 2005. Analyzes Franco-Belgian comics in depth, discussing the works and visual styles of Jijé, Hergé, and a number of other artists.

SCRIPT, PENCILS, COLOR, COMIC! THE COLLABORATIVE PROCESS OF GRAPHIC NOVEL PRODUCTION

Definition

Though the production of graphic novels has evolved tremendously over the years, it remains a process involving numerous steps and, in most cases, the work of many individuals. Writers, artists, and editors all play an important role in graphic novel production.

Introduction

The production of graphic novels is most often a collaborative endeavor entailing the division of tasks such as writing, design, layout, penciling, inking, coloring, lettering, and editing amongst numerous individuals or entities. Unlike novels or paintings, which are generally the work of individual creators, graphic novels are typically produced via a process involving several individuals, and it is often the case that over the course of a series' run, multiple individuals will fill each role. The process of graphic novels' formal production is typically a group endeavor carried out by four categories of individuals: the creative teams and editorial staff, the writers, the interior and cover artists, and the colorists and letterers. However, there is often a great deal of overlap between these categories.

The Creative Team and the Editorial Staff

Writers of graphic novels generate scripts, the basis of graphic novels' verbal narratives. Within these scripts, writers usually include ideas and recommendations regarding how artists might illustrate the graphic novels' visual narratives. Artists vary greatly in function, and the order of their work on a comic is predefined; pencils precede inks, which precede color, and letters are almost invariably the final element to be added. Together, artists and writers make up what is known as the creative team. This team works closely with the editorial staff, which coordinates the various aspects of production. Editors review the work of artists and writers at every stage, frequently requesting revisions and determining limits so as to ensure that neither a text's verbal nor its visual narrative infringes upon the other.

Prior to a script's illustration, it is necessary to identify the right artists for the project, a decision ultimately made by the editors. Their selections take into consideration writers' recommendations and preferences but are made primarily on the basis of style and versatility—and, at times, availability. The continuity and consistency of visual and verbal narrative tracks over the course of a graphic novel is of the utmost importance; variations in style, color, or language can disrupt the reading experience and may cause readers to lose interest. For this reason, an artist or writer who joins a creative team subsequent to a project's commencement may be instructed to mimic, to the best of his or her ability, a previous artist's or writer's style. Indeed, there are even artists who specialize in stylistic mimicry.

Writers

The first step in the production of a graphic novel is writing, but the extent of a writer's role varies greatly depending on the project. Though a writer's primary responsibility is the creation or continuation of a graphic novel's verbal narrative, he or she often also plays a role in the text's design and layout as well as in the identification of artists whose styles compliment his or her own narrative objectives. Sometimes writers submit scripts detailing every aspect of design, layout, and even color; Alan Moore, author of *Watchmen* (1986-1987), generally includes such detailed instructions in scripts that the task of the artists becomes something akin to transcription. At other times, artists might work from rough outlines that develop alongside the art itself. This mode of production, commonly referred to as the "Marvel method," affords writers the opportunity to reflect artists' work and negotiate the relationship between the verbal and visual narrative tracks.

At times, editors ask writers to assume writing responsibility for a title already in print or assign writers projects that tie into or cross over with the narrative of another title. Writing a crossover requires writers to fulfill the stipulations of the assignment in a manner that furthers the plot of the story line to which their primary title is subordinate yet maintains the primary title's narrative integrity—which may prove difficult, given that a crossover may include characters with whom writers are unfamiliar or even characters owned by other publishers. On the other hand, it is often the case that writers, even those who have assumed authorship of a title from another, are at the helm of a story line's progress and exercise a wealth of narrative license. Perhaps the most prominent example of such is Chris Claremont, who scripted Marvel Comics' *Uncanny X-Men* (1963-   ) for almost seventeen years, along the way creating numerous characters who have secured prominence in the Marvel Universe.

Sometimes a single person will both write and illustrate mainstream comics, as in the case of writer-artist Frank Miller. In the case of alternative comics, writer-artists such as Marjane Satrapi and Joe Sacco frequently exercise total artistic control. Such writer-artists are often referred to as auteurs.

Interior and Cover Artists

Pencillers are the artists who work most closely with writers and editors, helping to determine page layouts and designs, and they are usually credited more prominently than other artists. Pencillers' ideas are vital to a project's success, but depending on the publisher, editorial office, or script itself, they may be asked to follow specific instructions. When pencillers are asked to work from a rough outline of the script, they play a far more influential role in the project's development. Pencillers usually record their ideas in sketchbooks and then refer to these sketches when they commence illustration. Illustrations for most comics are done on sheets of bristol board, which is often proprietary and provided by editors. Preliminary drawings are frequently done in blue pencil, followed by heavy lines of black.

Inkers are the second variety of specialist artist to work on a graphic novel. The inker's job is to trace and embellish the penciller's drawings in order to define lines and enhance visual impact. Inkers typically work directly on the same sheet of paper illustrated by pencillers. After an inker has finished inking a page, it is reviewed by editors, scanned, and forwarded to a colorist.

Cover artists are often distinct from interior artists, though cover art is similar to interior splash pages and splash panels in that it dominates the page, frequently articulating dramatic, climactic moments in a text. Cover art is intended to be eye-catching and will often deviate from the interior artwork's prescribed formula of consistency. At times, cover art is derived from interior art, but more often than not it is unique. It is not uncommon for cover art to be submitted by artists and retained by publishers or editorial offices for use in a future issue of a series. Given cover art's great attention to detail and composition, artists sometimes control multiple aspects of its design, but more often than not it proceeds through the same line of production as interior art.

Color and Letters

In the comics industry, it is rare for colorists to be provided with original art; rather, they work with high-resolution scans, either digitally or by hand, although the latter is becoming less and less frequent. Colorists work in consultation with editors and writers in order to determine the appropriate color palette for a graphic novel. The decision to use a particular palette is informed by factors such as the script's tone, its illustrators' style, and even the demographic to which it is intended to appeal.

Though writer-artists of alternative comics often refrain from including color, this decision is generally a matter of stylistic intent. Art Spiegelman is an example of a writer-artist who has at times followed unconventional production rules; when writing *Maus* (1986, 1991), he drew the pages at the same size they would be printed—rather than drawing them larger and shrinking them down, as is typical—and used a fountain pen to ink and letter each page. Both the absence of color from the interior art of *Maus* and the lettering of the text exert a strong influence on the story's tone and narration.

The final stage of production involves the addition of word balloons, thought bubbles, and captions. Editors typically determine where these should appear on the pages, coordinating them with numbered items in the script for the letterer's reference. In-house technicians most often add balloons, bubbles, and caption boxes before scans of the pages are sent to the letterers, who in turn add text either by hand or digitally. In the case of the latter, which is a general practice in mainstream comics, letterers may use proprietary fonts or even fonts created for a specific title.

Impact

Owing to the debate surrounding the origin and definition of the term "graphic novel," it is difficult to isolate the ways in which production has come to play a role in graphic novels' history. There is, however, a case to be made that the emergence of graphic novels had a greater impact on production than vice versa. With a few exceptions, the earliest examples of what might be referred to as graphic novels were bound collections of reissued serial comic books that appeared in the late 1970's. Despite the fact that most did not contain a single, unified narrative thread, these reissues met with great success, at least in the eyes of publishers; since the industry then operated under the work-for-hire system, publishers were not required to pay creators any additional compensation for the sale of collected series, thus earning a greater profit.

By the early 1980's, a backlash by creators mandated concessions on the part of publishers. The "limited series" format, which lends itself readily to compilation and resale, soon emerged, as did modest contractual guarantees regarding creators' rights. The latter encouraged creators to take a greater interest in the quality of their work, and this, coupled with the advent of the limited series, soon led to the term "graphic novel" becoming an industry standard. Around this time, the publication of alternative comics in graphic novel form also became more common, with some, such as Harvey Pekar's *American Splendor* (1976-2008) and Spiegelman's *Maus*, gaining popular attention. The publication of alternative comics in graphic novel form has become an industry unto itself, and few mainstream comics fail to lend themselves to compilation.

Stephen Marchand

Bibliography

Chute, Hillary L., and Marianne DeKoven, eds. *MFS Modern Fiction Studies* 52, no. 4 (Winter, 2006). Contains articles on graphic narrative by some of the leading scholars in the field as well as an article by Spiegelman and an interview with comics creator Alison Bechdel.

Hatfield, Charles. *Alternative Comics: An Emerging Literature*. Jackson: University Press of Mississippi, 2005. Provides both historical and theoretical information regarding alternative comics, including discussion of their creation, and argues that they are a form of literature worthy of serious academic consideration.

McCloud, Scott. *Understanding Comics: The Invisible Art*. New York: Harper Perennial, 1993. Addresses the production of comics, their creators, and their history as well as what visual literacy is and how it functions.

DRAWING THE GRAPHIC NOVEL

Definition

Drawing is one of the key steps in the creation of a graphic novel, as graphic narratives rely on both text and images to tell stories. Using a variety of techniques and styles, graphic novel artists draw images that transmit the mood of the written narrative and are essential to the emotional impact of a work.

Introduction

Graphic novels merge written narratives with visual language. The coupling of innovative visual and written narratives provides readers with a tangible reading and viewing experience unlike that of a purely written or purely visual work. The artwork that accompanies the written narrative deeply affects readers' perception of the entire graphic narrative. While graphic novels cannot exist without their narrative text, at times, the power of the image supersedes the text, creating a visceral emotional experience.

The process of drawing the images to accompany the text is a crucial step in the creation of an effective graphic novel. The artwork that accompanies any written narrative must be chosen to serve the strengths of the writer and artist involved. Each artist has a particular individual style, whether it is photorealistic or highly stylized. The artist chooses the style and other elements of drawing in order to create a rich experience that transcends the written narrative. The line work is the cornerstone of the drawing and the building block for the mood of the artwork in a graphic novel.

The Line

Drawing gives life to the graphic novel, making it an excitingly tactile medium that is unlike solely visual or written art forms. The most fundamental aspect of the drawing process is the line work. The weight of the line can set the mood for the work. For instance, graphic novel art that uses thick, dark lines without incorporating any color has an intensity that adds gravity to the narrative in a way that art featuring sharp, crisp lines does not. Some graphic novels consist almost entirely of simple, crisp line work, allowing readers to focus on the text. At times, pieces with sparse details allow readers to imagine themselves in the protagonist's situation, adding to the empathy that develops between reader and narrative.

The figures are the primary focus in most graphic novels, but other drawn elements aid in the creation of a cohesive work. The scenes and space that surround the main interactions of the characters also play a piv-

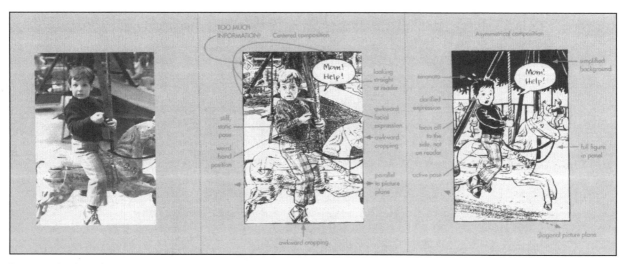

Drawing Words and Writing Pictures. (Courtesy of First Second Books)

otal role in establishing the mood of the work. While the weight of the line is different and may play a lesser role in the background, it nevertheless aids the flow of the narrative. Some graphic novels that have copious amounts of detail use the background space to reinforce the mood that the figures and the narrative have set, establishing the environment in which the characters exist. In graphic novels that focus primarily on the text, the few details that are included in the background typically serve to add gravity to the situation. The sparse background gives viewers a sense of the scene while keeping them actively engaged in the work.

Stylized Drawing

The style that the artist uses also contributes to the mood and effectiveness of the graphic novel. A tight, photorealistic style allows readers to rely on the text to understand the emotions of the characters. Conversely, a heavily stylized piece transmits the emotional weight of the narrative visually but can cause the weight of the written narrative to suffer.

Regardless of the graphic novel's style, the artwork is largely based on a shared understanding of visual language and cultural stereotypes. This understanding between creator and reader has allowed Clark Kent to conceal his true identity as Superman under glasses since the character's first introduction, for instance. Readers understand that according to cultural stereotypes, glasses distinguish the intellectual weaklings from the strong, dashing leading men. Such stereotypes and visual indicators have made it possible for graphic novels to transmit messages and symbols to their audience without expressing them directly.

Stylized drawing particularly serves to translate the emotions that manifest in a graphic novel, especially in conflict, presenting them visually to readers. Several graphic novels that focus on the events and brutality of warfare are drawn in particular styles to exemplify different emotional responses to warfare. For instance, in works related to twentieth and twenty-first century conflicts such as the Vietnam War and the terrorist attacks of September 11, 2001, some artists use expressive line work to capture the constant confusion that occurs during an attack. Loose line work can especially translate the turmoil that surrounds combat, allowing readers to experience the tumultuous nature of conflict. The stylization of the line continuously generates the mood embedded in the narrative.

Photorealism

Photorealism has existed within the fine arts for centuries and been used in graphic novels numerous times throughout their history. Art in this style is often based on photographs and itself appears nearly photographic. The use of photorealism in graphic novels continues to raise the question of what levels of abstraction and reality best support the narratives in these works. With the increasing ease of creating photorealistic images through computer software, a significant number of graphic novels have embraced this style.

While photorealism also relies on cultural stereotypes to establish an emotional grounding with readers, it does not need to adhere as closely to those traditions. Unlike stylized works, photorealistic works have an advantage in appealing to the casual reader. The style allows readers easy access into characters that are complex like themselves but appear to be entirely average. This is the case in Brian K. Vaughan and Tony Harris's series *Ex Machina* (2004-2010), the art of which was in part created using models and reference photographs. Although protagonist Mitchell Hundred is both the mayor of New York City and a superhero, readers are able to identify with him readily because he appears to be nothing more than a regular man.

Impact

Drawn images have an impact that can be far greater than that of the written word, and they serve to communicate the mood of the narrative in a way that words cannot. Inking, lettering, and other tasks are important parts of the graphic novel creation process, but drawing is the foundation on which the artwork is based. While the style of art in graphic novels has evolved and expanded since the Golden Age of comics, it continues to serve its purpose of unifying the mood of the graphic narrative. Creators of graphic novels must balance the art with the written text in order to create an effective narrative.

Jessica Gamache

Bibliography

Eisner, Will. *Comics and Sequential Art: Principles and Practices from the Legendary Cartoonist.* New York: W. W. Norton, 2008. Provides a step-by-step guide to combining the visual culture of cartooning with a written narrative to create a graphic novel, detailing various issues related to reader perception of the visuals.

_____. *Graphic Storytelling and Visual Narrative: Principles and Practices from the Legendary Cartoonist.* New York: W. W. Norton, 2008. Discusses how graphic novels unify their visual and literary components and includes numerous visual examples, drawing upon Eisner's decades of experience in the comics industry.

McCloud, Scott. *Understanding Comics: The Invisible Art.* New York: Harper, 1993. Analyzes how aspects of graphic novels such as realism and stylized line work affect the viewer's experience through a series of creative models, examples from classic graphic novels, and illustrations.

PENCILING AS PROCESS AND NARRATIVE TOOL

Definition

Penciling is an early and vital step in the translation of a script into a comic book or graphic novel. While pencil drawings are sometimes used as finished art, they are primarily an intermediate step in the creation of a graphic novel and are likely to be redrawn, either in ink or digitally.

Introduction

As one of the earliest stages in the creation of a comic book or graphic novel, penciling is crucial to the success of the final story. The penciller develops the figures and the layouts and makes sure both suit the story in every panel, often refining ideas in the process. As much as the writer, a good penciller must also be a good storyteller. The penciller provides a foundation on which the other creators build; if the penciller does not interpret the script or the rough layouts well, the inker, colorist, and production artist have less to work with. In this sense, the penciller is also responsible for consistency and continuity and can make the work of all who come after him or her both easier and of higher quality.

Penciling can be done with any tool that makes an irreproducible or erasable mark. The most common tools are artist-grade pencils, ranging in hardness from 9H (hardest) to 9B (softest); mechanical pencils and lead holders; nonphoto blue pencils, which are blue colored pencils whose color is not picked up in the printing process; and solid sticks of graphite, available in the same hardness range as pencils. A range of erasers is also necessary. Most pencillers prefer either white plastic or kneaded erasers. The penciller also chooses the material on which to draw—usually a bristol board, a smooth white board that is resistant to abrasion from erasing. This choice affects the work done by the inker, since different surfaces respond differently to different inking tools.

Steps in the Penciling Process

If the penciller is working from the layouts of another artist, a consultation with that artist may be necessary. Otherwise, the penciller begins by breaking the script into pages and each page into single images, or panels. The

penciller often must decide on the angle from which the panel is seen, the light source, and the composition, allowing for strategic placement of text and word balloons. He or she may try several variations before deciding on one. In order to maintain continuity, light sources and frame content must be consistent from one panel to the next. Setting and character appearances must remain consistent as well.

Depending on the project, a penciller's work may be reviewed by the writer, an editor, or both many times during creation of the art. After the pencils are approved, the pages are passed along for the next step in the creative process, usually inking. Following inking, pencil art is often erased.

An auteur, or single creator, has the flexibility to create a book without input from an outside writer or inker,

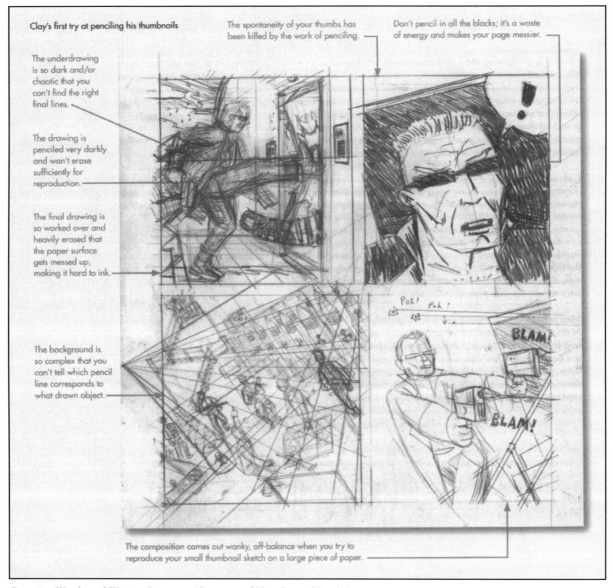

Drawing Words and Writing Pictures. (Courtesy of First Second Books)

though some auteurs do choose to work with editors. When a creator works this way, his or her pencils are not subject to outside review. Jon J. Muth, Matt Wagner, Will Eisner, and Colleen Doran are among those who have found success as sole creators of graphic novels.

Pencils as Final Art

As printing techniques began to improve in the early 1980's, stories were occasionally printed directly from pencils. Gene Colan's book *Ragamuffins* (1985) is notable in this area. Eisner's pencil preliminaries for many stories were printed in the magazine *Will Eisner's Quarterly* (1983-1986). The printing of pencils in fan publications was also fairly common, but the deliberate use of pencils as final art did not become more acceptable until the digital age. In two specific chapters of *Strangers in Paradise* (1993-2007), Terry Moore uses pencil art as final art.

This approach has advantages and disadvantages. In Colan's work, the pencil art in stories printed in black and white is sometimes too subtle for the dark blacks of inked panel borders and lettering and is subdued by those elements. However, when some of the stories were later collected in color, the strength of the pencil art became apparent. It imbues a subtle range of values, a quality of pencil art that can sometimes be muted by a heavy-handed inker.

Another notable example of the use of pencils as final art is Joe Kubert's *Yossel: April 19, 1943* (2003). Kubert, a creator with six decades of experience in the comics industry, made a conscious choice to have this work printed directly from pencils to preserve their immediacy as part of the story. As the story is told in first-person past tense by a young artist, the use of pencils as finished art lends an intimacy to the story.

Impact

Penciling has been an integral part of comic book and graphic novel creation since the early days of the comics medium. Historically, pencil art almost never

appeared in print because of limitations of the printing process and steps in the creation of comics. Despite this, some artists inking their own work were able to preserve the qualities of their pencil art; early creators Alex Raymond, Bernard Krigstein, and Alex Toth are notable in this respect.

For the most part, however, the work of a penciller was largely invisible for most of the early history the comic art form. Penciling's capacity for communicating the subtleties of narrative and emotion was lost to the printing process until around the 1980's, when the use of improved printing techniques and better paper made the printing of pencils as final art possible. As digital printing techniques were applied to comics and graphic novels, the problems associated with reproducing pencil art in graphic novels—fading, difficulty controlling value range, the art being outweighed by other page elements—became more manageable. By the early twenty-first century, printing technology had improved to the point that pencils could be very effective as final printed art.

Diana Green

Bibliography

Abel, Jessica, and Matt Madden. *Drawing Words and Writing Pictures*. New York: First Second Books, 2008. Offers individual lessons that take the reader through the process of creating a comic book and includes a section on penciling comics.

Janson, Klaus. *The DC Comics Guide to Pencilling Comics*. New York: Watson-Guptill, 2002.Discusses the fundamentals of penciling in detail and also addresses aspects of composition and storytelling.

McCloud, Scott. *Making Comics: Storytelling Secrets of Comics, Manga and Graphic Novels*. New York: HarperCollins, 2006. Analyzes the different aspects of creating graphic novels and how they come together as a whole.

INKING: ADDING DEPTH AND DEFINITION

Definition

Inking is the stage that follows penciling in the creation of hand-drawn comics. Inking involves going over finished penciled artwork with black india ink to make the art permanent and sharp. Inking pencils adds depth, focus, and texture to the drawings and historically allowed the artwork to be reproduced accurately in the printing process.

Introduction

Although inking began as simply the step of outlining penciled art darkly and cleanly enough to prevent the loss of information in the printing process, inkers have since become able to make a significant mark on the underlying structure of the artwork. As printing technology has evolved and improved, rendering dark ink outlines less necessary, inkers have nevertheless retained their importance to the process of creating comics, as their additional contributions to a finished work have allowed inking to transcend the simple tracing of the pencils. Over time, the inker's job has come to include creating a sense of depth, emphasizing certain objects within the page or panel, and otherwise adding to the penciled art through the use of a number of techniques and tools.

While the penciller is seen by many as the foundational artist of the comic, some artists prefer inking over penciling because of the satisfaction they derive from taking the pencils to their finished form. Although many artists ink their own pencils, controlling both pencil and brush with equal skill, most specialize as either a penciller or an inker. Regardless which artist ultimately inks a penciled work, a finished graphic work generally cannot exist without the efforts of several individuals; thus, the process of creating comic books and graphic novels is a highly collaborative one.

Many inkers have their own recognizable styles and are artists in their own right. Sometimes a specific inker is hired for a project because the inker's personal style is considered appropriate by the penciller or the editor of the comic or series. At other times, a project can require that an inker adopt the style that the project demands and work under the watchful direction of the penciller or editor. Some well-known inkers include Klaus Janson, inker of Frank Miller's *Batman: The Dark Knight Returns*; Karl Kesel, inker of such series as *The Fantastic Four*; Mike Perkins, inker of such series as *Captain America*; and Mike Esposito, who inked many issues of *The Amazing Spider-Man* and a number of other major Marvel Comics titles.

Tools

Like the penciller, the inker usually uses a drafting table and the equipment that goes with it when inking. This equipment may include an adjustable-height swing-arm lamp with incandescent and fluorescent bulbs, an adjustable-height drafting chair, a scanner, and a brush basin. The inker may use cutting tools such as a T square, a drafting triangle, a precision knife, and a ruler as well as basic tools such as erasers and white correction fluid.

In addition to copies of the penciled art, sable brushes and black india ink are the traditional tools of the inker. However, inkers also use other tools to create the many complex effects for which they are known. An inker's arsenal may include brush soap for keeping expensive sable

bushes clean between uses; gray wash, a mixture of black ink and water; white and pigmented ink; black pencils for providing rough textures; erasable colored pencils for achieving a softer line and more consistent tone; dip pens and flexible nibs for fine detail work and creating a more consistent line; pen brushes with their own built-in ink supplies; technical pens for creating uniform lines; and markers for creating somewhat fuzzy lines.

As technology has advanced, the computer has become one of the major tools used by some inkers. Though initial pencils are usually hand drawn, they can then be scanned and reworked on a tablet or monitor using virtual tools in a variety of illustration programs. While some pencillers choose to skip the inking stage altogether and just add color to their pencils, many believe that digitalization can never replicate traditional inking methods. Still, some of the repetitive and time-consuming work of the inker can be done electronically, allowing inkers to concentrate on more detailed work. Other benefits of digital inking include using the computer to blow up an artist's work to add details that have an interesting effect when the images are later reduced in size.

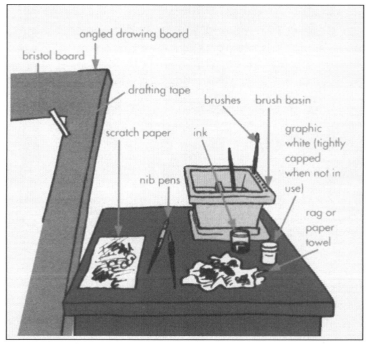

Drawing Words and Writing Pictures. (Courtesy of First Second Books)

Techniques

Inking techniques vary widely, from those that create a simple style to those that provide a more complex and layered look, depending on the effect the art is meant to have in relation to the story being told. In addition to making sure that all the information on the page is portrayed clearly, largely through outlines, inkers add shadow to certain planes and figures to emphasize the prominence of particular elements. Varying tones through a variety of techniques has a similar attention-capturing effect. Inkers also vary the weight, or thickness, of the lines of ink in order to give the art a sense of depth.

A number of common inking techniques rely on the use of many small lines or dots and on areas of black or gray tones. Feathering, or hatching, uses many close-set parallel lines of black ink to soften edges of lines and create gray tones. Cross-hatching and curved hatching fulfill similar functions but use crisscrossed lines and curved lines, respectively. Stippling also creates a variety of gray tones through the application of many small black dots. The tones created by these techniques give illustrations the illusion of texture. Large areas of black or gray are also essential to many comics. Known as spotting blacks, areas of solid black call the reader's attention to certain areas, provide dramatic shadows, and elicit emotional responses to the artwork. Areas of gray can be created using techniques such as watercolor wash, in which artists dilute black inks with water to apply gray tones in a manner similar to watercolor painting.

Impact

As comic book production becomes increasingly technologically sophisticated, some comics will be able to skip the inking stage because the pencil art can be reproduced in a way not possible before. Nevertheless, inking remains a crucial step in the creation of many comic books and graphic novels, even many of those created digitally. Inkers continue to be recognized for their significant contributions to comic book art, with awards such as the Inkwell Awards and the Eagle Awards honoring those working in the field.

Laurie Lykken

Bibliography

Eisner, Will. *Comics and Sequential Art: Principles and Practices from the Legendary Cartoonist.* New York: W. W. Norton, 2008. Labels and describes the various components of comic book art, including inking. Also discusses the collaborative nature of comic book creation.

McCloud, Scott. *Making Comics: Storytelling Secrets of Comics, Manga, and Graphic Novels.* New York: Harper, 2006. Discusses the steps involved in creating comics books and graphic novels and provides visual examples of various styles and techniques.

Schmidt, Andy. *The Insider's Guide to Creating Comics and Graphic Novels.* Cincinnati: Impact Books, 2009. Provides tips from comics professionals regarding various aspects of the comics creation process, including scripting, inking, and coloring.

EMBELLISHING: CREATING EFFECTS WITH INK

Definition

Embellishing is part of the inking process and involves using a variety of brush and pen strokes to add depth, focus, and texture to the penciled art. Though embellishing is traditionally done with black ink, advances in technology have allowed some of the work of embellishing to be done digitally.

Introduction

Originating as part of the inking process, embellishing expands the role of inking from its initial purpose of outlining penciled art, allowing inkers to add depth and texture to graphic novels' illustrations. The complexity of the embellishment can vary widely depending on the effect the art is meant to have in relation to the story line of the work. Sable brushes, nib pens, and fixed-width pens are the tools used most often in the embellishing process. Different artists prefer different tools and use these tools to create distinctive effects that define their work in ways fans admire and seek out.

Some embellishers add shadow to certain planes and figures to emphasize the prominence of a particular element or to indicate time of day or the mood of the scene. Embellishing also adds texture to surfaces, distinguishing, for example, cloth from concrete and concrete from dirt. A good knowledge of anatomy and an understanding of the structure of real-world surroundings help inkers to better depict these shadows and textures. Excellent embellishing can rescue mediocre pencils, but conversely, too little or too much layering and texturing can negatively affect the art. Good embellishing makes the essential figures stand out, while poor embellishing buries them. The inker must be

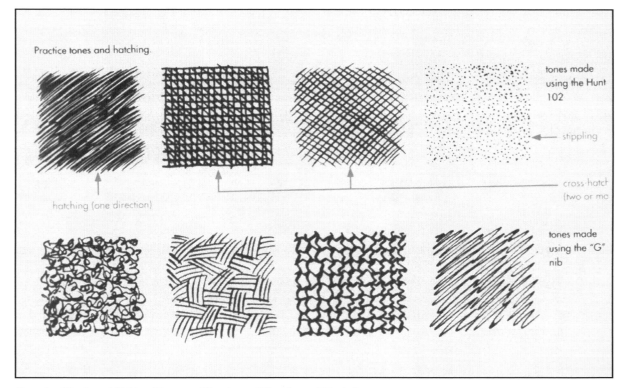

Drawing Words and Writing Pictures. (Courtesy of First Second Books)

mindful of balance and ensure that the reader can understand the part any given drawing plays in telling the graphic narrative.

Black Space, Black Lines, and Shadows

Solid black spaces placed in the art for specific purposes that connect to the story are referred to as spotting blacks. These totally black areas are used to give a drawing solidity and to help focus important elements in a picture by drawing the reader's eye toward a desired area. Solid black spaces create dramatic moods within the drawings. For example, black masses in vertical or horizontal shapes can create calm in a motionless scene. On the other hand, large, slanting black spaces can add a feeling of shock, unease, or impending danger and menace to a panel or page. Black spaces scattered all over a panel can create a sense of chaos and action.

Black ink lines define objects in comic book art. Going from a thick line in the foreground to a thin line in the background is one of the most widely used embellishing techniques. Varying the line weights gives the art a sense of depth and helps readers understand how the elements in a panel relate to one another spatially. Brushes are especially good for creating lines of varying width that give the artwork a fluid look. In contrast, nib pens produce uniform lines that are especially suited for adding detail. The use of a consistent line width can give the art an edgy, dry look.

Shadowing refers to varying tones created by a combination of gray washes, lighter pencils, and solid blacks. Shadowing emphasizes certain parts of the panel, controlling where the reader's eyes first hit the page and subsequently move. Watercolor wash, the process of creating gray areas by diluting inks with water, is one popular shadowing technique; darkening the figure or fixture in the foreground and placing it against a shadowless background is another. The type of paper used for the art, such as newsprint or glossy, and that paper's absorbency largely determine what an artist can do with shadows.

Texturing

Texturing, in the language of sequential art, means giving an object the distinct and identifiable illusion of texture through line direction and shape. Though time consuming, the texturing of substances such as fabric, brick, and water enhances the realism of the illustrations and thus of the narrative as a whole. One particularly common inking technique used for texturing purposes is feathering. Also known as hatching, the technique involves the use of close-set parallel lines of black ink to create shades of gray artificially, especially when the drawing situation does not allow for the use of watercolor wash or similar techniques. Fixed-width pens such as technical pens are often used when feathering to keep the lines uniform.

A number of similar techniques allow inkers to create particular shades and effects. Cross-hatching, a technique involving the use of crisscrossed lines of black ink, can create varying tones and show the uneven quality and folds of objects such as fabric. Curved hatching differs from standard hatching in that it fills space using curved, rather than straight, lines. This technique creates a fluid or smoky look that can represent clouds or water, for example. Stippling refers to black dots applied with a brush or pen that are used to create gray tones.

Impact

Embellishing has evolved into an essential inking step that makes an enormous contribution to the appearance of the finished comics artwork. As technology has advanced, a number of comics creators have begun to create comics digitally, and inkers have begun to experiment with new embellishing styles and techniques. While these digital processes have in some cases allowed for the elimination of the inking step, the resulting art often has a markedly different look than art created using traditional methods or colored digitally after the inking has been done. For this reason, although some artists forgo the inking stage, inking itself has remained a key part of the process of comics creation. Embellishing comics art with ink gives it a unique look, and the solid history behind that look makes the inking stage difficult, if not impossible, to eliminate entirely, regardless of technological advances.

Laurie Lykken

Bibliography

Eisner, Will. *Comics and Sequential Art: Principles and Practices from the Legendary Cartoonist.* New York: W. W. Norton, 2008. Labels and describes the various components of comic book art, including embellishment, and discusses the collaboration that is required in creating comics.

McCloud, Scott. *Reinventing Comics.* New York: Harper, 2000. Discusses the changes that occurred in the comics industry by the end of the twentieth century, including the advent of digital art creation.

McKenzie, Alan. *How to Draw and Sell Comic Strips.* Cincinnati: Impact Books, 2005. Examines the artistic choices artists make when creating comics and the effects of those choices on their art.

THE APPLICATION OF COLOR TO SEQUENTIAL ART

Definition

Coloring is the stage in the production of comic book art that traditionally follows inking. In this stage, the colorist adds color to the inked drawings. The colorist's goal is to maintain consistency in the colors from panel to panel and from page to page. Clarity is of equal importance to the colorist. To this end, a good colorist needs to understand the story so that the color choices place emphasis on the illustrations in ways that enhance the narrative.

Introduction

The coloring of comics began when technology made it possible to apply color to newsprint. The rivalry between newspaper owners William Randolph Hearst and Joseph Pulitzer for circulation numbers encouraged Pulitzer to experiment with printing full-color images on highly absorbent newsprint paper. When Pulitzer's attempt to reproduce fine art in his newspaper's pages failed, he turned to printing colorful comic strips. The colored comics were popular with readers and increased newspaper sales dramatically. Because of this proven popularity, colored comics soon came to be used as promotional material for businesses, such as gas stations. Eventually, comic strips became so popular that publishers began to sell collections of strips—the first comic books.

The Four-Color Process

The color in these early endeavors relied on what is known as the four-color process, a primitive method of colorization. In the four-color process, the intensity of the three primary colors—cyan, magenta, and yellow—is restricted to 100, 50, or 25 percent. Black ink is used for the line work and at times to create darker shades. A limited palette of colors could be created by combining the available colors and intensities of ink. The resulting bold, flat color became the standard look of comics in the United States. Artists rarely concerned themselves with the colorization process itself beyond establishing the colors of the costumes or hair colors of the main characters. Colors used for backgrounds and secondary characters were left up to the printer who handled the inks during the printing process.

In Europe, where color printing outpaced color printing in the United States, artists who used flat color did so out of preference rather than necessity. In the 1970's, influenced in part by a drop in sales, the high cost of color, and the need for smaller print runs, artists in the United States began to look past the four-color tradition and use a broader palate that would help express mood, depth, sensuality, and environment.

Media Choices

A number of different media can be used for coloring comics, and each creates a different look. The choice to work in a particular medium depends on the individual artist's preferences and what style of coloring best complements the story. Watercolor paints work well over inked drawings but are highly challenging to work with, requiring a lightness of touch. Watercolors can bleed, and coverage can be inconsistent. Colored inks also work well over India ink line work. Pelikan inks, for example, are transparent but permanent. Several coats must be applied to ensure that the colors stay intense and do not fade. Markers and colored pencils can also be used to achieve specific effects.

Advances in technology have revolutionized the coloring process, providing a variety of new tools and techniques. Digital coloring, for example, offers a vast palette of colors, shadings, and special effects. Even with the aid of such technology, the work of coloring a comic book page can be too much for one colorist. For this reason, many colorists employ specialists known as flatters, who lay down a flat layer of color on the art. Once this work is done, the colorist adds additional layers of color, incorporating shading, highlights, and special effects.

Impact

The use of color expanded the audience for sequential art. However, because color printing remains costly and therefore makes the finished books more expensive, many artists have chosen to skip coloring altogether.

Choosing black and white over color can also be an artistic choice made to create a certain look or support the tone of the narrative. Some artists believe that the ideas behind the art are communicated more directly in black and white, allowing art to approach printed lan-

guage. Nevertheless, as technology continues to offer artists more and more options for coloring comics, comic book fans can continue to look for and expect exciting developments in the use of color.

Laurie Lykken

Bibliography

Abel, Jessica, and Matt Madden. *Drawing Words and Writing Pictures*. New York: First Second Books, 2008. Explains the process of creating comics, including steps such as inking and coloring, through a series of fifteen lessons.

Eisner, Will. *Comics and Sequential Art: Principals and Practices from the Legendary Cartoonist*. New York: W. W. Norton, 2008. Labels and describes the various components of comic book art, which Eisner refers to as "sequential art."

McCloud, Scott. *Making Comics: Storytelling Secrets of Comics, Manga, and Graphic Novels*. New York: HarperCollins, 2006. Explores the process of making comic books and graphic novels and explains the importance of visual elements such as color to the narrative as a whole.

Sabin, Roger. *Comics, Comix & Graphic Novels: A History of Comic Art*. New York: Phaidon Press, 2001. Traces the history of sequential art from early woodcuts to modern times, focusing on such elements as storytelling, illustration, and coloring.

Schmidt, Andy. *The Insider's Guide to Creating Comics and Graphic Novels*. Cincinnati: Impact Books, 2009. Provides tips and advice regarding the creation of comics from professionals working in the industry, including prominent colorists.

LETTERING IN COMICS: GIVING SOUND TO A SILENT MEDIUM

Definition

In comics, lettering is the production step of adding words to the page layouts. It is the linguistic device by which characters speak and think and by which sounds occurring in the narrative are communicated to the reader. Lettering encourages readers to imagine the voices and sounds suggested by text in word balloons and by graphical onomatopoeias.

Introduction

Lettering is the step in the production process of comics and graphic narratives in which text, representing speech and thoughts as well as sound effects, is added to the pages. Comic strips are very often personally lettered by their creators; less frequently, creators of

comic books and graphic novels may provide the lettering for their own works. In such cases, the fonts used are intertwined with the artist's drawing style. In some cases, a single artist creates text and onomatopoeias that are harmonious with the drawing style and the page layout; the works of Will Eisner are particularly known for this quality. In most comic books and graphic novels, however, lettering is carried out by a distinct individual known as the letterer.

History of Comics Lettering

With the widespread popularization of the political cartoon in the early nineteenth century, the use of word balloons and lettering in humorous and satirical cartoons became familiar to the public. Building upon this

"Show of hands for a Liberal candidate" by the political cartoonist George Cruikshank (1792-1878). (Getty Images)

form, later artists began to mix illustrations and text in nonpolitical works. Images and text initially appeared in contiguous areas of the page or panel. Later, artists began to combine the two forms more directly, inserting captions and dialogues into the illustrated field and introducing the word balloon.

Early comics creators generally lettered their own works. However, during the comic book boom of the 1940's, a well-defined division of labor began to develop in comics studios. Under this system, different individuals carried out the many separate tasks required to create a comic book, which included penciling, coloring, and lettering. Individuals began to specialize, and the letterer became known as a distinct professional figure. This division of labor continues to be a common system of production into the twenty-first century, although a number of creators of Modern Age comics perform multiple or all of the necessary tasks. Lettering created by the artist of a comic typically displays similarities to the artistic style used throughout the rest of the work. In some cases, as in well-known francophone comics such as Hergé's *Les Aventures de Tintin* (1929-1976; *The Adventures of Tintin*, 1930-1976), lettering and visual onomatopoeias are embedded in the authors' overall graphic style.

Main Features of Comics Lettering

Lettering for comics consists of three complementary tasks: positioning bubbles and other enclosing areas used as captions or alternative places for speech or thoughts and choosing for them a shape and dimension correspondent to their linguistic function; writing the verbal texts inside these enclosing areas; and drawing and positioning the visual onomatopoeias that may be required by the scriptwriter.

In balloons, captions, and other areas of text, letterers convey specific meanings through a variety of graphical techniques. For instance, variations in the font's format and size can convey how a sentence is spoken by a character: Bold-formatted words indicate an emphasis, while tiny text within a large bubble indicates a sentence uttered in a low voice. Text is generally rendered entirely in capital letters, in part because capital letters have no tails, as do some lowercase letters, and thus will not overlap letters on the surrounding lines and make the lettering unclear. Clarity was especially important in early comics, as the limits of printing technology made elaborate hand-lettered texts difficult to render. In general, lower-case lettering is used in comics to convey specific meaning nuances, such as an elegant way of speaking. When used systematically, lower-case text can give the comics story a more literary air. Lettering can also involve creating new shapes and semiotic codes for text balloons. Although many classic styles of bubbles already exist, it is always possible to innovate their functions. Major contributors to innovation in this field include Eisner, Dave Sim, Todd Klein, and Osamu Tezuka.

Visual onomatopoeias convey the sounds heard within the narrative, such as "bang" or "crash." Before the development of digital technologies, letterers generally drew onomatopoeias by hand. Most letterers prefer to create their own visual sounds, adapting style, shape, effects, and colors to specific contexts. Onomatopoeias can describe sounds as distinct elements in a panel, take up two or more panels, or, in some instances, appear as word-shaped panels. In addition to a rich variety of consolidated noises and sounds normally used by most scriptwriters and letterers, onomatopoeias may also communicate particular effects.

Drawing Words and Writing Pictures. (Courtesy of First Second Books)

Until the 1980's, lettering was exclusively done by hand. With the advancement of computer technology, however, new methodologies have been developed. Computers have made it possible to scan handmade alphabets previously used for comics and reuse them digitally as well as to design new fonts aesthetically suitable for comics, the form and style of which expressly suggest a handmade creation.

Impact

The comics medium is both visual and auditory: Lettering aims not only to convey "mute" text but also to conjure certain sounds or even tones and timbres in the reader's mind. The impact of lettering on the linguistic, narrative, graphical, and artistic levels of comics stories has in turn had a significant effect on the self-organization of the comics industry, with the birth and development of lettering as a specific professional stage of the production process. A number of influential letterers have received critical praise, and a specific prize category for letterers exists in several comics awards, most notably the Eisner Awards.

Marco Pellitteri

Bibliography

Chiarello, Mark, and Todd Klein. *The DC Comics Guide to Coloring and Lettering Comics.* New York: Watson-Guptill, 2004. Includes explanations, examples, and illustrations regarding the processes of coloring and lettering, discussing both traditional and digital methods.

McCloud, Scott. *Making Comics: Storytelling Secrets of Comics, Manga, and Graphic Novels.* New York: Harper, 2006. Focuses generally on comics creation and includes discussion of traditional and digital lettering and how to evoke feelings with text.

Starkings, Richard, and John Roshell. *Comic Book Lettering: The Comicraft Way.* Los Angeles: Active Images, 2003. Provides a fully illustrated guide to lettering, particularly focusing on digital methods and software for comics lettering.

SCRIPTING A UNIQUE MEDIUM

Definition

Graphic novel writing melds many techniques used in writing comic books, novels, and screenplays into a new format with unique strengths and limitations. A graphic novel script must coordinate every visual and literary element to realize the format's full potential, using the interaction between words and images to fulfill the opportunities the graphic novel presents for larger scope, enhanced complexity, and greater maturity of subject matter, structure, and technique.

Introduction

The challenge of writing the graphic novel is to make the best use of both visual and literary media to tell a single thematically textured and richly layered story, which must be internally consistent, convey more meaning to the reader than it would in an episodic format, and be enriched by its larger scope. At its best, the graphic novel is much more than simply a long comic book. Writing a graphic novel is not like writing a novel or screenplay, and a graphic novel is not simply a collection of shorter graphic stories. A successful graphic novel must use words and images to reinforce and comment on one another in a way that offers more than either words or pictures can provide alone, and it must use its longer format to tell stories of greater scale and depth. The subject matter is not restricted to any particular genre or style, nor is there any single way in which a graphic novel should be published. However, if the story does not demand this greater physical length, then the graphic novel format becomes superfluous at best and gratuitous at worst. The story should be one that can only be told in a graphic novel.

Whether created by a writer-artist team or by an individual, a true graphic novel must present a single, harmonious narrative that explores unified characters, situations, themes, ideas, and more. This central artistic unity is of paramount importance. When the script is written, it must specify the ways in which words and pictures can work together to convey larger meaning and more complex detail. The format places greater demands on every creator involved; others involved in the creative process, such as colorists, letterers, and other specialists, must also look to the script for guidance in making their efforts meaningful to the overall story and aligned with its themes and objectives.

Format Shapes Message

A graphic novel tells a self-contained story, ideally one with layers of depth and meaning. The script for the graphic novel must address its visual component. While the writer must devote a significant portion of his or her time and energy (and space on the final printed page) to explaining what elements of the story the artist must convey visually, the format generates many new possibilities in storytelling. The graphic novel format has the potential to adopt many of the strengths of both novels and motion pictures without ever fully resembling either medium. The writer must recognize that the format is best used to attain a potential entirely its own.

The physical nature and visual component of graphic novels limit some of the strengths they borrow from literary novels. Because text must share physical space on the page with images, writing for graphic novels demands an economy of words that is far more stringent, minimizing verbal digressions and asides; however, it does enable their graphic equivalents. The writer may suggest fonts, point sizes, and other visual aspects of dialogue and narration to add further significance to what is said.

Graphic novels superficially resemble motion pictures, but as writer Alan Moore has explained, the temporal component of film enables filmmakers to dictate how the viewer will experience it, while graphic novel readers may revisit earlier sequences or look for details that would otherwise be merely subliminal. Unlike screenwriters, graphic novel writers may specify dense layers of visual detail for the artwork and carefully experiment with wordplay while ignoring film's time strictures.

Graphic Novel versus Trade Paperback

Critics of early graphic novels often complained that many were nothing more than extended comic books, and

many graphic novels are actually repackaged runs of monthly comics rereleased in trade paperback. Since the 1980's, the line has blurred between monthly comic books and graphic novels in terms of subject matter and treatment. The story arcs in many monthly titles have become more similar to chapters in a graphic novel, as publishers increasingly set aside considerations of self-contained stories and concern for the interest of the casual reader. It would appear on the surface that creators are encouraged to use their monthly assignments to tell longer-form stories than previous artists and writers were allowed.

However, many critics continue to argue that a re-packaged story arc from a monthly publication is not necessarily a graphic novel. Certainly a monthly magazine can convey a novel in short chapters, much as writers such as Charles Dickens serialized literary novels. However, a serialized graphic novel must be a novel first and a series of episodes second. Just as a properly written novel is not merely a linear series of unconnected events happening to a character, a properly written graphic novel must demonstrate true character progression, thematic depth, dense and detailed storytelling, and the possibility for reader immersion—and it must do so both verbally and visually.

Time and Meaning

As creators such as Will Eisner have asserted, the mechanics of combining visual art with words are not particularly different between serialized stories and graphic novels. Long form or short form, sequential storytelling requires that writers convey meaning in both words and pictures. However, the physical lengths and overarching structures of the two formats are entirely different, and both the creators and the audience have different expectations for each form.

In a serial publication, the reader may reasonably expect to find a complete story or a chapter of a complete story in every installment. In the serial format, the story is generally expected to unfold over time in a way that does not jump over or elide large portions of the characters' lives. In an equivalent number of pages or panels, the graphic novel may show only a sequence within a chapter, or possibly only a single scene within a sequence. It may also compress much more time into a given number of pages than any regularly serialized comic would do, because the reader's expectations are quite different for graphic novels. Such structural variations require careful thought from every member of the creative team in order both to convey that they are happening and to ensure that they are meaningful.

Continuity: A Separate Reality

Another differentiating factor is story continuity. Graphic novels require internal continuity but do not generally depend on or affect external continuity (though such continuity may be subjected to retroactive continuity, or "retconned," to match a popular graphic novel, as with DC Comics' 1996 miniseries *Kingdom Come*). As a platform for writers to tell stories of a richness, intellectual depth, and emotional power that shorter formats often lack, graphic novels offer creators the chance to experiment with structure, subject matter, and presentation without regard for any continuity other than what the novel needs to tell its story. If the graphic novel's potential must be made secondary to the demands of an ongoing open-ended story, such as a monthly publication, its literary quality must suffer to some degree.

Regardless of how many characters, plotlines, or parallel narratives the script includes, the creative team's efforts must be united by the script into a total continuity of both what is told and how it is told in order to present a coordinated story greater than the sum of its parts. This is achieved in a number of ways, including the use of visual and verbal storytelling structure and rhythm, themes that comment upon one another with how they look and what they say, symbolism and metaphors, and parallel narratives.

Impact

The writer of a graphic novel composes a long-form story in both words and instructions to the other members of the creative team, helping them to shape the visual message of the story. Although the writer-artist partnership may be well coordinated (if the writer and the artist are not the same person), the initial stage of planning and writing the graphic novel script is still quite demanding in this regard. Graphic novels demand structure and style to convey detail and meaning; self-reference and the gradual expression of story details are not matters of chance but narrative strategies that require profound consideration and planning. If the value of a long-form literary work lies in its ability to provide greater depth and complexity in storytelling, then writing a graphic novel requires creators to use every panel of the story to impart more information and emotion than they would in a shorter work. The subject matter need not be heavy, but the treatment of any subject must demand a larger stage. A graphic novel must do more with its words and pictures than merely enlarge them. It must make them a vehicle for a story with greater substance and dimensionality.

Richard A. Becker

Bibliography

Abel, Jessica, and Matt Madden. *Drawing Words and Writing Pictures*. New York: First Second Books, 2008. Addresses the process of crafting a graphic novel, focusing on both written and visual aspects of the narrative.

Chinn, Mike. *Writing and Illustrating the Graphic Novel: Everything You Need to Know to Create Great Graphic Works*. Hauppage, N.Y.: Barron's Educational Series, 2004. Explores the relationship between prose and art in the graphic novel medium, emphasizing the role of art more so than writing.

McCloud, Scott. *Making Comics: Storytelling Secrets of Comics, Manga and Graphic Novels*. New York: HarperCollins, 2006. Offers insights into the differences between writing a comic book and writing a graphic novel.

Moore, Alan. *Alan Moore's Writing for Comics*. Rantoul, Ill.: Avatar Press, 2007. Discusses writing fiction and scripting for comics, offering not only Moore's insights from his early career but also introductory comments about them in retrospect.

Appendixes

GLOSSARY OF TERMS AND TECHNIQUES

Airbrush: In this illustration technique an air-operated "gun" is utilized to spray paint onto a page from a short distance. While airbrush techniques date back to the nineteenth century, their use in comics emerged in the 1980's when changing printing technologies enabled greater levels of fidelity and clarity. Airbrushing is commonly used to create highly realistic representations in comics, and is closely tied to the development of science fiction and fantasy magazine illustration styles. With the rise of digital image processing programs, traditional airbrushing has been replaced to a large degree by computer-created effects.

Archetype: Often assumed to be universally understood, this figure or symbol is an exemplar upon which variations are patterned. In superhero comic books and graphic novels, many of the earliest heroes (like Superman) are archetypal, with more recently developed heroes being notable as variations or permutations of this original prototype. As graphic novels frequently rely on visual stereotypes as a form of shorthand, archetypes are widely used. The term is also used broadly in literary criticism to refer to recurrent character types, motifs, images, symbols, and plot patterns.

Bronze Age: The period in the production of American superhero comic books that ranges from approximately 1970 to approximately 1985. The period is frequently characterized by an increased focus on social relevance within the generic framework of superhero comics, and increasing levels of cross-title continuity. Bronze Age superhero comic books were typically produced by writers and artists who had grown up reading earlier superhero titles. This generation of creators was intensely concerned with pushing the limits of superhero comics.

Brushwork: The quality or style of the finished line created by an artist. Technically denoting the effects created by a brush but often used to describe marks made by a pen, in graphic novels there is a considerable variation in brushwork. Brushwork can be tight or loose, and lines can be long or short, among many other variations. Brushwork is unique to specific artists, and is one of the elements by which cartoonists are differentiated from each other in visual terms.

Captions: The text portions usually situated at the top of comic book panels and which are not attributed to a character by way of a scalloped tail. Captions are most frequently used to give voice to a narrator, whether in first- or third-person address.

Cartoon: In the context of graphic novels, a cartoon is a single-panel drawing with text included either in the image, or below it. Cartoons are the non-sequential form of comics. Editorial cartoons and gag cartoons have their own history dating back hundreds of years, and the style and format have strongly influenced the development of aesthetics in the comic strip, comic book, and graphic novel.

Chiaroscuro: An Italian term meaning "light-dark," chiaroscuro has its origins in the Renaissance and refers to the tonal contrasts that are used to suggest the volume of an object. In the practice of drawing, chiaroscuro refers to the way objects are rendered three-dimensional by varying the gradations of color or through the use of shading. The term can also be used to designate high-contrast lighting effects.

Close-ups: A visual technique in which a figure or item is shown in great detail. A character can be said to be drawn in close-up when only a small portion of their body (such as the face) is depicted. Close-ups are frequently used to draw attention to important details, whether related to the action or to the psychology of the characters.

Collage: An arrangement of different forms is brought to together in a single work. In comics, this technique was not widely used before the 1960's, when artists began responding to innovations in the world of fine arts by creating multimedia works. In comics, the most commonly used elements in collage are photos and drawings, but some artists have used elements that include tape, cloth, and string to add dimensionality to their work.

Conflict: The struggle that develops as a result of the opposition between the protagonist and another person, the natural world, society, or some force within the self. In short fiction, the conflict is most often between the protagonist and some strong force either within the protagonist or within the given state of the human condition.

Cross-hatching: Tone and shading effects are created in a drawing by the implementation of closely spaced parallel lines placed at an angle to each other. With its origins in engraving and etching, cross-hatching has a centuries-long tradition, and is most commonly used in black-and-white comics. Skilled practitioners can create variations in light and darkness by varying the line weight and proximity of the lines.

Crossover: The appearance of characters from one title in a title that is not their own. The tendency is particularly predominant in superhero comics, and has its origins very early in the genre when characters like Superman and Batman would appear in stories featuring the other character. In the 1960's, Marvel Comics particularly emphasized the crossover as a way to drive sales across its line of titles. In contemporary superhero comics the crossover is so normative that its absence is more notable than its presence.

Cyberpunk: A genre that offers a postmodern approach to science fiction and which rose to prominence in the 1980's. The genre emphasizes digital technologies in crime narratives, and is notable for the way that it privileges nostalgic attributes of pulp or noir crime writing in the context of cutting-edge technologies. In comics, the genre is most notable in manga.

Double-page spread: A visual effect in which two facing pages of a comic book compose a single image. The effect is frequently used for scenes featuring frenetic action or a multitude of characters, or to present a panoramic vista or establishing shot. In general, artists that use this effect seek to impress their readers with technical virtuosity by creating an expansive and immersive image that is presented as more important than the typical comic book drawing.

Drybrush: This is an illustration technique in which a paintbrush that is relatively dry—while still holding paint—is applied to paper, resulting in a "scratchy" stroke that highlights the bristles of the brush.

Though drybrush techniques are centuries old, they only emerged in comics relatively late as new printing techniques enabled a greater degree of clarity and fidelity to the artist's line.

Easter eggs: Jokes or messages that are intentionally hidden in the pages of comic books. The term itself is derived from the video game industry, and refers to items that need to be intentionally sought out by knowledgeable readers. In comics, Easter eggs are frequently used to place in-jokes into otherwise non-humorous stories.

Fable: One of the oldest narrative forms, it usually takes the form of an analogy in which animals or inanimate objects speak to illustrate a moral lesson. The most famous examples are the fables of Aesop, who used the form orally in 600 b.c.e.

Fairy tale: A form of folktale in which supernatural events or characters are prominent. Fairy tales usually depict a realm of reality beyond that of the natural world and in which the laws of the natural world are suspended.

Flashbacks: A narrative technique when a scene is interrupted to present another scene that takes place in the past. Flashbacks are frequently used to fill in backstory. In superhero comic books they are commonly used to refer back to earlier appearances by characters involved in the storyline. In comics, flashbacks are commonly signaled by changing the shape of panel borders, or by captions indicating that events took place at an earlier time.

Fold-out pages: Where certain pages are printed larger than the standard size and then folded into the book. When unfolded by the reader, the expanded page provides a much larger space for the art, generating a spectacular visual emphasis. As they are costly to produce, the technique is rarely used, and is reserved for situations where the aesthetic impact is maximized.

Folktale: A short prose narrative, usually handed down orally, found in all cultures of the world. The term is often used interchangeably with myth, fable, and fairy tale.

Foreground: The portion of the image or panel that represents diegetic space that is closest to the reader.

Unlike cinema or photography, in which mechanical camera processes frequently distort items in some planes if one plane is in sharp focus, the drawn nature of comics allows artists to render all planes with comparable levels of clarity. In traditional three-point perspective, items in the foreground are depicted as larger than those in the background.

Framework: The narrative setting within which other stories are told; usually used in connection with a frame story. The framework may also have a plot of its own. More generally, the framework is similar to structure, referring to the general outline of a work.

Golden Age: The time period developed by comic book sellers and collectors to refer to the period from the mid- or late-1930's to the late-1940's or mid-1950's. It represents the period that encompassed the origins of the American comic book industry, culminating at the approximate zenith of American comic book sales in 1952. The Golden Age was a period of great creativity and experimentation, at which time the American comic book moved from reprinting newspaper strips to developing new characters and titles. This was the period during which the basic narrative elements of the comic book were formalized.

Gutter: The space that exists between the panels of a comic book or comic strip. Usually white, this blank space formalizes the relationship between panels. Traversing the gutter generally involves a change in time or space, or both, particularly insofar as each panel can be read as a specific enunciation. Gutters do not have to be physically present on the comic book page, as certain artists (Jules Feiffer, for example) use implied gutters by leaving empty spaces between images.

Inking: Preparing lines for reproduction by use of a pen or brush. In the vast majority of comics, images are initially created in pencil so that they can be easily modified. When the image has been finalized, it is redrawn in ink, generally right over the penciled image on the same sheet of paper. Inking can either be done by the original artist or by a separate artist. The latter is the norm in superhero comics, and several artists have risen to prominence specifically on the basis of their inking.

Kirby dots: Sometimes known as "Kirby krackle," this is an illustration technique most closely associated with the artist Jack Kirby, in which the negative space around figures is filled with fields of black dots or fractal patterns that are used to represent energy forms, such as in explosions, lightning strikes, or solar effects. The effect is central to the cosmic look of much of Kirby's work beginning in the mid-1960's.

Layout: The entirety of a page in a comic book or graphic novel, particularly the relation of panels to each other and of images and word balloons within and across panels. Cartoonists are particularly aware of the limits and advantages of page layouts, and the best cartoonists structure their pages so that they can exist both as a totalizing unit and as a series of discrete elements.

Lettering: The process of adding text to comics pages. Lettering can be added to a comics page before or after the figures have been drawn, but it almost always come after the panels have put in place. While early comics strove for simple legibility in their lettering, and used all capital letters in order to help achieve it, contemporary comics and graphic novels frequently use other approaches to lettering, including varying colors and fonts to give text additional emphasis. Lettering is often done by the artist; in superhero comics, it is frequently outsourced to a lettering specialist known as a letterer.

Lighting: Unlike film or television, graphics novels are not technically "lit" by an external light source, but the illusion of light is created on the page by the careful and skillful deployment of light and dark areas. Using strong contrasts or areas of light color (or white), cartoonists are able to replicate lighting effects found in other media.

Line style: Refers to the way artists make specific marks on the comics page to delineate characters and their environments. While each cartoonist has their own unique line-making style, broad categories exist that allow artists who are stylistically similar to be grouped together. Perhaps the most famous line style is the clear line most closely associated with Belgian comics artist Hergé and his assistants and followers. Lines can vary a great deal in graphic novels—from thick to thin, from polished to ragged—and each line style creates a different aesthetic effect and communicates a different meaning.

Maxiseries: A long form of a miniseries: a comic book published for a predetermined number of issues intended to tell a complete story. Maxiseries rose to prominence in superhero publishing in the 1980's and have since become a central aspect of the superhero publishing logic. Maxiseries tend to be "event" publications involving a wide array of characters and creative teams, and are frequently used to fundamentally restructure the fictional world in which superhero comic book series unfold. Maxiseries are commonly collected as graphic novels, or as series of graphic novels.

Memoir: Usually written by a person prominent in public life, memoirs are the authors' recollections of famous people they have known and great events they have witnessed. Memoir differs from autobiography in that the emphasis in the latter is on the lives of the authors.

Metacomics: Similar to metafiction, this refers to fiction that manifests a reflexive tendency. Essentially, metacomics are comics in which the characters are aware that they exist in the pages of a comic, or they are comics that take other comics, or comics generally, as their subject. These are comics that are self-conscious and self-reflexive in addressing the devices of storytelling in order to undercut the illusion of fiction. Metacomics have a long history in the domain of comic strips, and became particularly common in comic books during the American underground period of the 1960's.

Miniseries: A series of comics whose run has a predetermined limit, often quite short. In the 1980's, it was common to test the market for new comic book series and comic book characters by creating miniseries which, if successful, could lead to the development of regular, ongoing series with no fixed ending. Many miniseries formed the basis for the earliest graphic novels in the superhero tradition, as their finite format made them easy to collect into trade paperback books.

Modern Age: The name given by comic book dealers and fans to the superhero comics produced after ap-proximately 1985. The Modern Age superhero comic book is defined by a high degree of intracompany continuity, crossovers, and event publishing. Modern Age comic books tend to be printed on better quality paper than were their predecessors, and have commonly included publishing gimmicks such as die-cuts and foil covers.

Myth: An anonymous traditional story, often involving supernatural beings or the interaction between gods and human beings and dealing with the basic questions of how the world and human society came to be as they are. Myth is an important term in contemporary literary criticism. Northrop Frye, for example, has said that "the typical forms of myth become the conventions and genres of literature." By this, he means that the genres of comedy, romance, tragedy, and irony (satire) correspond to seasonal myths of spring, summer, autumn, and winter.

Narration: Text in graphic novels provided through context rather than dialogue. In graphic novels this is most commonly provided by captions. Stories that are told by a narrator frequently incorporate the voice of that narrator in the text portion of the work, with the images operating as a complement to the text.

Noir: Taken from the cinema term "film noir," noir refers to certain generic expectations that are derived from hardboiled crime fiction in the immediate post-World War II era. French for "black," noir has come to be associated with storytelling styles that focus on crime and the underworld, and reflect a bleak pessimism about the state of the individual in society. Many comics versions of noir rely heavily on shadows and silhouettes to create a dark visual atmosphere.

One-shot: Most commonly used in superhero comic book publishing, this refers to a stand-alone comic book that is not part of a larger series. One-shots are commonly used to tell stories that fall outside of established continuity, or which involve crossovers between multiple comic book publishing companies. One-shots rarely compare to graphic novels in terms of length, and tend to feature short stories or novella length works.

Onomatopoeia: A word that mimics or suggests the sound that it describes. Many of the sound effects commonly used in graphic novels are onomatopoeias, ranging from the sound of explosions ("boom" or "bang") to the gentle sound of a clock ("tick tock"). Cartoonist Roy Crane was especially influential in the adoption of onomatopoeia in the comics form.

Palette: Originally signifying the board on which painters mix paints, in comics and graphic novels palette more generally refers to the range of colors available to or used by cartoonists. Limitations in printing technology in the mid-twentieth century meant that the palette of comic books during this period tended to be restricted to primary and secondary colors. Improved printing and, in particular, digitization has led to a greatly expanded color range in graphic novels. Many cartoonists deliberately restrict their palette to create aesthetic effects, including relying on only one or two colors throughout an entire work.

Panel: The base unit of the grammar of comics, the panel is the discrete unit—most often rectangular—that contains a single image representing a particular moment in time and space. Panels are commonly arranged in patterns, including a number of panels creating a strip along the same horizontal line (a tier) or in a regularized grid pattern. Panels can be any shape or size, and some artists use inset panels (panels within panels).

Parody: A work that imitates or burlesques another work or author for the purpose of ridicule.

Pen and ink: This medium has been the dominant illustration aesthetic in comic books and graphic novels since their origins. While other techniques are possible and have been widely practiced, pen-and-ink drawings account for the overwhelming majority of works produced in the form. In the early parts of the twentieth century, pen-and-ink drawings were the easiest—and cheapest—images to be produced and reproduced, and this history has structured comics to such a degree that the dominance of the approach has never been seriously challenged.

Perspective: In drawing, it is used to approximate images as they are seen by the human eye. Popularized during the Renaissance, though preceding it in some areas of painting, perspective is used to create the realistic illusion of depth, particularly through the use of fore-shortening and the practice of drawing objects in the distance as smaller than those in the foreground. Perspective can be produced in multiple manners, but two- and three-point perspective systems tend to be the most common.

Photorealism: This approach to illustration seeks to mimic the physical world as closely as possible in order to present an image that is in accordance with the world as it is. This approach frequently uses photographic reference as its basis and sometimes incorporates photography through collage effects. In the 1990's, photorealism was popularized in superhero comics by the painter Alex Ross, whose use of realist tendencies in the context of fantastic stories highlighted some of the central contradictions of the superhero genre.

Photoshop: This graphics editing program allows images to be manipulated digitally: to add color, change lines, and produce other visual effects. Photoshop is an Adobe software product and has been extensively adopted by artists working in comics. The term itself is well enough known as to stand in for a wide range of non-Adobe produced software that is used to manipulate images.

Pinup: A full-page image of a comic book character or characters and usually posed as if for a photograph. Often used as space fillers in early comic books, the pinup is of particular interest to collectors of original comic art for the way that it mimics the representational style of men's magazines.

Plot: The sequence of events in a play or story and how they are arranged. Authors also use this technique to suggest how those events are connected in a cause-and-effect relationship. There are a great variety of plot patterns, each of which is designed to create a particular effect.

Point of view: A term derived from the study of cinema, it refers to the practice of creating images in a comic book or graphic novel that reflect what a character is able to see. Point-of-view panels place the reader in the position of the character, and encourage readers to more closely identify with the character by placing them in his or her position for a brief moment of time.

Protagonist: Originally, in Greek drama, the "first actor" who played the leading role. The term has come to signify the most important character in a drama or story. It is not unusual for a work to contain more than one protagonist.

Pulp magazine: This inexpensive form of popular fiction was published in the United States from the 1890's to the 1950's. Pulps, which derived their name from the pulpy quality of the low-grade paper on which they were printed, were published in an array of genres, including science fiction and crime. The American superhero comic book is often regarded as an heir to the heroic pulps published in the 1920's. Many of the earliest publishers of comic books were also involved with the publication of pulps. The format was largely supplanted in the 1950's by television and the pocket book.

Satire: A form of literature that employs the comedic devices of wit, irony, and exaggeration to expose, ridicule, and condemn human folly, vice, and stupidity. Justifying satire, Alexander Pope wrote that "nothing moves strongly but satire, and those who are ashamed of nothing else are so of being ridiculous."

Scratchboard: In this illustration technique knives are used to cut a layer away from a layer of clay. This technique allows white lines to be carved into a black background. Illustrators often take advantage of the stark contrasts that the form offers.

Secret identity: In superhero comic books, this refers to the hidden personal identity of a public superhero or supervillain. A character uses an alternative name in his or her civilian life. Many stories have been built around the threat posed by the revelation of the civilian identities of superheroes.

Sequential art: A term coined by cartoonist Will Eisner in his 1985 book *Comics and Sequential Art*, it is often used to designate an array of creative practices that includes, but which is not limited to, comics. In general, the term signifies the production of cultural artifacts from a series of images, and can include cave paintings, hieroglyphics, and sculptures.

Shadow: An area shielded from a direct light source because it is obstructed by an object or a figure. They are frequently used in comics and graphic novels to balance white space on a page, and to create a more atmospherically pleasing layout. Following on the tradition of film noir, the use of shadows is commonly meant to create an atmosphere of fear or disorientation.

Silhouette: The outline of a person or an object whose interior has been filled in with a solid color, usually black. Silhouettes are commonly used in comics and graphic novels as a means of varying the representation of characters and creating a visually appealing page layout. As many graphic novels will frequently depict the same character in every panel on a single page, the use of silhouettes becomes a visually striking alteration to the flow of the story.

Silver Age: The time period used by comic book dealers and superhero fans to designate the period from approximately the mid-1950's to the early-1970's. While some critics tie the origin of the Silver Age to the creation of the Comics Code Authority (CCA) in 1954, others connect it to the introduction of a new version of the Flash in 1956. Superhero comics of this period were marked by the general renewal of the genre at Marvel Comics in the 1960's.

Sound effects: Artists denote sound, such as "slam" or "drip," through the deployment of lettering outside of captions and word balloons. The volume of the sound is generally signified by the size and prominence of the lettering, with explosions often written in block letters filling enormous spaces, and the sound of a dripping faucet often subtly placed in the background of a panel.

Splash pages: A single-image page that is used as the first page of a comic book or graphic novel. In superhero comic books, the splash page became a particularly popular way to open stories because it was dynamic, because it served to establish the locale for the action, and because it included the space to place story credits. As they are often carefully composed, splash pages are often sought out by art collectors.

Steampunk: A genre that blends elements of science fiction with action set in the past, notably the Victorian era and the age of steam power. The genre typically focuses on the technological possibilities of earlier periods and owes a debt to the vision of writers such as H. G. Wells and Jules Verne. Many of its best-known works are created to reflect attitudes toward science as they existed in the nineteenth century.

Storyboard: This visual guide allows for the previsualization of shots or sequences in motion pictures. Storyboards are created as a visual reference for a film crew and frequently contain very detailed information about framing, camera movements, lighting, and the movement of actors. Storyboards are similar to comics insofar as they are a type of sequential art. Some cartoonists use storyboards or breakdowns as a preliminary step in the establishment of page layouts while scripting a comic story.

Storytelling: The process of conveying a narrative through the combination of words and images. As comics and graphic novels are predominantly visual, most theories of storytelling follow the dictum that it is more important to show than to tell, and that the major plot elements of a work should be conveyed visually rather than through dialogue. Many critics argue that words and images should operate in a complementary fashion so as to enhance storytelling, and they frown upon works where images and text seem to be performing the same role or conveying the same information.

Tone: Strictly defined, it is the authors' attitude toward their subject, their persona, themselves, their audience, or their society. The tone of a work may be serious, playful, formal, informal, morose, loving, ironic, and so on; it can be thought of as the dominant mood of a work, and it plays a large part in the total effect.

Watercolor: A method of painting where the paint is dissolved in water, making it at least partially transparent and unable to hide errors. The medium became popular during the Renaissance, although its origins are much older. Watercolor techniques only became widely used in comics in the 1980's, when new printing technologies allowed original pages to be reproduced with clarity and fidelity.

White space: The portion of an image or drawing that is unmarked. This is the negative space, or the space between figures and objects in an image. The management of white space is an important compositional consideration for cartoonists who risk producing cluttered pages by omitting white space, but who must insert important visual information in a limited number of panels.

Widescreen storytelling: A method of storytelling that was highly cinematic and which used only a few page-width panels per page. They often contained very little dialogue, and were notable as quick reads. Widescreen storytelling was an aesthetic sensibility that was prominent in some superhero comics of the late-1990's and early-2000's. They were championed by a number of fan-favorite creators, including writers Warren Ellis and Mark Millar, and artists John Cassaday and Bryan Hitch.

Word balloons: The places where dialogue is presented on the comics page. Word balloons can appear anywhere in a comics panel, and generally have scalloped tails that indicate the character to whom the speech should be attributed. Thought balloons are a related phenomenon in which internal dialogue is indicated through differently shaped balloons and tails composed of a series of related bubbles. Many cartoonists have experimented with different visual effects in crafting word balloons, using subtle variations in line to signify the tone of speech.

Zine: Also referred to as a fanzine, it is a fan-produced magazine. These publications, often produced on photocopiers, circulate outside the channels of traditional book and magazine distribution. Zines have been published on virtually every topic imaginable, and they have been quite popular and influential in comics circles, with many notable cartoonists and critics having made their semi-professional debuts as zine creators. Zines are closely connected with mini-comics, which are essentially zines in comics form.

Bibliography

Abel, Jessica, and Matt Madden. *Drawing Words and Writing Pictures*. New York: First Second Books, 2008. Offers individual lessons that take the reader through the process of creating a comic book.

Aldama, Frederick Luis. *Your Brain on Latino Comics: From Gus Arriola to Los Bros Hernandez*. Austin: University of Texas Press, 2009. Reviews a number of Latino comics authors, generally emphasizing alternative, independent efforts. Includes images and lengthy interviews.

Altmann, Anna E., and Gail A. de Vos. *Tales, Then and Now: More Folktales as Literary Fictions for Young Adults*. Englewood, Colo.: Libraries Unlimited, 2001. A companion volume to *New Tales for Old*. Discusses comic book reworkings of four folktales and five literary fairy tales by Hans Christian Andersen.

Anders, Charlie. "Supergirls Gone Wild: Gender Bias in Comics Shortchanges Superwomen." *Mother Jones* July 30, 2007, 71-73. With a somewhat humorous tone, discusses the history of subjugating women in comic books. Provides a list of popular heroines and the fates that they meet. Examines how women have been viewed in the world of the superhero.

Avermaete, Roger. *Frans Masereel*. New York: Rizzoli, 1976. Discusses Masereel's life and career and contains illustrations, color plates, and samples of his many wordless novels.

Barnard, Rita. "Bitterkomix: Notes from the Post-Apartheid Underground." *South Atlantic Quarterly* 103, no. 4 (Fall, 2004): 719-754. Distinguishes between the interests of black and white African artists and writers, focusing on South Africa's *Bitterkomix* and the graphic novels that have come out of that magazine. Attempts slight comparisons between this "adult" satire magazine and other forms of African comics.

Beaty, Bart. "Autobiography as Authenticity." In *A Comics Studies Reader*, edited by Jeet Heer and Kent Worcester. Jackson: University Press of Mississippi, 2009. Traces the rise of the autobiographical graphic novel, primarily in European works of the 1990's, and relates the genre of autobiography to the search for validity by authors of comic texts.

Beaty, Bart. *Fredric Wertham and the Critique of Mass Culture*. Jackson: University Press of Mississippi, 2005. An in-depth examination of the life and works of Wertham, discussing his impact not only on comics but also on psychoanalysis.

Beaty, Bart. *Unpopular Culture: Transforming the European Comic Book in the 1990's*. Toronto: University of Toronto Press, 2007. An introduction to the scene of "alternative" European comics beginning in the 1990's.

Benton, Mike. *The Comic Book in America: An Illustrated History*. Dallas, Tex.: Taylor, 1993. Offers an overview of the trends in graphic storytelling and the movement toward comics that fall within the fantasy genre or incorporate fantasy elements.

Benton, Mike. *Crime Comics: The Illustrated History*. Dallas, Tex.: Taylor, 1993. Provides a history of the genre, focusing primarily on the pre-Comics Code era and including many examples of the covers of crime and mystery comics.

Benton, Mike. *Horror Comics: The Illustrated History*. Vol. 1 in the *Taylor History of Comics*. Dallas, Tex: Taylor, 1991. Gives a decade-by-decade breakdown of trends in horror comics from the 1940's to the 1990's, including images of covers and an extensive guide to horror titles.

Beronä, David A. *Wordless Books: The Original Graphic Novels*. New York: Abrams, 2008. Studies early wordless graphic novels and includes lengthy discussions of Ward and Gross as well as Europeans such as Masereel.

Bongco, Mila. *Reading Comics: Language, Culture, and the Concept of the Superhero in Comic Books*. New York: Garland, 2000. Covers the development of comics from their pre-World War II American origins to the late 1980's, with specific attention paid to the superhero genre and its implications about popular culture.

Booker, M. Keith. *May Contain Graphic Material: Comic Books, Graphic Novels, and Film*. Westport, Conn.: Praeger, 2007. Discusses the evolution of the comics behind the feature films, focusing on popular superhero comics and films as well as nonsuperhero films based on sequential art.

Brown, Jeffrey A. *Dangerous Curves: Action Heroines, Gender, Fetishism, and Popular Culture*. Jackson: University Press of Mississippi, 2011. Addresses depictions of women in graphic novels as well as other media, providing detailed critical analyses in terms of sexuality, strength, and ethnicity.

Caputo, Tony C., Jim Steranko and Harlan Ellison. *Visual Storytelling: The Art and Technique*. New York: Watson-Guptill, 2002. Discusses visual storytelling techniques and ways to use visual storytelling in educational contexts, providing information about the evolving field of comic books and comic book technique.

Carinci, Sherrie, and Pia Lindquist Wong. "Does Gender Matter? An Exploratory Study of Perspectives Across Genders, Age, and Education." *International Review of Education* 55, nos. 5-6 (2009): 523-540. Attempts to understand how a variety of factors, including age and education levels, impact perceptions of gender and other arenas of life.

Carter, James Bucky. *Building Literacy Connections with Graphic Novels*. Urbana, Ill.: National Council of Teachers of English, 2007. Presents articles about how to teach specific graphic novels, many of which include classroom exercises and black-and-white illustrations.

Cary, Stephen. *Going Graphic: Comics at Work in the Multilingual Classroom*. Portsmouth, N.H.: Heinemann, 2004. Looks at practical ways to integrate comics into a classroom with second-language learners, providing examples of classroom activities and samples of various graphic novels.

Caselli, Daniela. "*Androgyny in Modern Literature* (review)." Review of *Androgyny in Modern Literature*, by Tracy Hargreaves. *MFS Modern Fiction Studies* 54, no. 4 (Winter, 2008): 926-929. Looks at ways androgyny influences literature, including whether having androgynous characters affects how deeply characters are understood.

Chaney, Michael A. *Fugitive Vision: Slave Image and Black Identity in Antebellum Narrative*. Bloomington: Indiana University Press, 2008. An illustrated work dealing with the post-Civil War writings of former slaves, which have influenced the way African Americans see themselves in the modern world.

Chiarello, Mark, and Todd Klein. *The DC Comics Guide to Coloring and Lettering Comics*. New York: Watson-Guptill, 2004. Includes explanations, examples, and illustrations regarding the processes of coloring and lettering, discussing both traditional and digital methods.

Chinn, Mike. *Writing and Illustrating the Graphic Novel: Everything You Need to Know to Create Great Graphic Works*. Hauppage, N.Y.: Barron's Educational Series, 2004. Explores the relationship between prose and art in the graphic novel medium, emphasizing the role of art more so than writing.

Christiansen, Hans-Christian. "Comics and Films: A Narrative Perspective." In *Comics and Culture: Analytical and Theoretical Approaches to Comics*, edited by Anne Magnussen and Hans-Christian Christiansen. Copenhagen: Museum Tusculanum Press, 2000. Analyzes how cinematic devices are used differently in comics and in films, constructing different notions of time, space, and identification.

Chute, Hillary. "Comics as Literature? Reading Graphic Narrative." *PMLA* 123, no. 2 (March, 2008): 452-465. Argues that the representation of history in graphic novels is at least as complex as in prose literature and includes examples from the work of Art Spiegelman and Joe Sacco.

Chute, Hillary L., and Marianne DeKoven, eds. *MFS Modern Fiction Studies* 52, no. 4 (Winter, 2006). Contains articles on graphic narrative by some of the leading scholars in the field as well as an article by Spiegelman and an interview with comics creator Alison Bechdel.

Comic-Con: Forty Years of Artists, Writers, Fans, and Friends. San Francisco: Chronicle Books, 2009. A detailed and highly illustrated history of Comic-Con International: San Diego from its origins to its fortieth anniversary.

Conroy, Mike. *War Stories: A Graphic History*. New York: HarperCollins, 2009. Provides an in-depth illustrated history of the war genre in comics and includes a ten-page cover gallery of comics from the late 1940's and early 1950's.

Constantino, Manuela. "Marji: Popular Commix Heroine Breathing Life into the Writing of History." *Canadian Review of American Studies* 38, no. 3 (2008): 429-447. Addresses the publication and reception of Satrapi's *Persepolis* and discusses the role of the individual in telling history, providing specific examples.

Coogan, Peter. *Superhero: The Secret Origin of a Genre*. Austin, Tex.: MonkeyBrain Books, 2006. Seeks to define the superhero as a distinct genre of American entertainment. Addresses how the ages of superhero comic books reflect an introduction, solidification, deconstruction, and reinscription of the genre's components.

Cornog, Martha, and Erin Byrne. "Censorship of Graphic Novels in Libraries." In *Graphic Novels Beyond the Basics: Insights and Issues for Libraries*, edited by Martha Cornog and Timothy Perper. Santa Barbara, Calif.: Libraries Unlimited/ABC-CLIO, 2009. Contains statistical data garnered from surveys administered to libraries regarding challenges to graphic novel collections. Also discusses why materials are challenged and how to handle these challenges.

Corrigan, Robert. *Comedy: Meaning and Form*. New York: Harper, 1981. Provides a critical and theoretical basis for studies of humor in comic books and graphic novels through essays on major theories of humor.

Couch, Chris. "The Publication and Formats of Comics, Graphic Novels, and Tankobon." *Image [&] Narrative* 1 (December, 2000). http://www.imageandnarrative.be/inarchive/narratology/chriscouch.htm. Examines the parallel histories of book-form comics in the United States, Europe, and Japan by comparing such factors as readership demographics, economic models, and cultural specificities.

Crist, Eileen. *Images of Animals: Anthropomorphism and Animal Mind*. Philadelphia: Temple University Press, 1999. Focuses on language used to depict animals' instincts and interactions, addressing naturalists' and scientists' commentary regarding animal behavior, particularly Charles Darwin's anthropomorphic descriptions.

Cronin, Brian. *Was Superman a Spy? And Other Comic Book Legends Revealed*. New York: Plume, 2009. Collects anecdotes and trivia about the comic book industry's colorful characters, creators, and publishers, including those working in the espionage genre.

Daniels, Les. *Comix: A History of Comic Books in America*. New York: Bonanza Books, 1971. An early contribution to comics studies scholarship. Examines comic books as an artistic medium from a historiographic perspective and considers other roots of modern comics such as horror stories and funny animal books.

Dardess, George. "Review: Bringing Comic Books to Class." *College English* 57, no. 2 (1995): 213-222.

Dean, Michael. "A Comics Journal History of the Direct Market." *The Comics Journal*, February 15, 2010. http://www.tcj.com/history/a-comics-journal-history-of-the-direct-market-part-one. Provides a history and evaluation of the direct market's effect on both mainstream and independent comics from the 1970's to the 1990's.

De Vos, Gail A. *Stories from Songs: Ballads as Literary Fictions for Young Adults*. Westport, Conn.: Libraries Unlimited, 2009. Explores various renditions of traditional ballads in both North America and Western Europe and their literary reworkings, including graphic novels. Covers tragic love stories, murder ballads, otherworld beings, and tricks and disguises.

De Vos, Gail A., and Anna E. Altmann. *New Tales for Old: Folktales as Literary Fictions for Young Adults*. Englewood, Colo.: Libraries Unlimited, 1999. Gathers a number of popular folktale reworkings in a variety of genres and formats that appeal to young adults. Discusses Cinderella, the Frog King or Iron Henry, Hansel and Gretel, Little Red Riding Hood, Rapunzel, Rumpelstiltskin, Sleeping Beauty, and Snow White.

Dowers, Michael. *Tijuana Bibles: America's Forgotten Comic Strips*. Seattle: Eros Comix, 2009. Collects the first five volumes in a profusely, profanely illustrated eight-volume work that details the precursors to underground comics.

Duffy, Damian, and John Jennings. *Black Comix: African American Independent Comics, Arts, and Culture*. Brooklyn: Mark Batty, 2010. An illustrated discussion of the twenty-first century proliferation of independent black comics and graphic novels, featuring interviews with many of the major artists and writers in the genre.

Duncan, Randy, and Matthew J. Smith. *The Power of Comics: History, Form and Culture*. New York: Continuum International, 2009. Evaluates the evolution of graphic novels as a medium throughout the twentieth century and strives to chart the changes in audience, narratives, and function.

Eisner, Will. *Comics and Sequential Art: Principals and Practices from the Legendary Cartoonist*. New York: W. W. Norton, 2008. Provides a step-by-step guide on how to combine the visual art of cartooning with a written narrative to create a graphic novel, including discussion of design.

Eisner, Will. *Graphic Storytelling and Visual Narrative: Principles and Practices from the Legendary Cartoonist*. New York: W. W. Norton, 2008. Expands on Eisner's earlier work *Comics and Sequential Art* and focuses on visual narrative in comics and other visual media.

Eisner, Will. "Teaching and Learning Sequential Art for Comics in the Print and Digital Age." In *Comics and Sequential Art: Principles and Practices from the Legendary Cartoonist*. Rev. ed. New York: W. W. Norton, 2008. Explores some of the differences between traditional print distribution and online distribution in terms of artistic challenges, technology, process, delivery, and reading experience.

Ellis, Warren. *Do Anything: Thoughts on Comics and Things*. Rantoul, Ill.: Avatar Press, 2010. Explores an alternative history of comics from a postmodern perspective and discusses the comics medium as one open for experimentation.

Estrada, Jackie. "The Eisner Awards: A Brief History." *Comic-Con International*, n.d. http://www.comic-con.org/cci/cci_eisners_faq.shtml. Written by the second Eisner Awards administrator. Discusses the emergence and evolution of the awards.

Faludi, Susan. *Backlash: The Undeclared War Against American Women*. New York: Crown, 1991. Definitive work to date on the growth of antifeminism in American political and popular culture that accompanied the rise of the New Right of the 1980's. Gives perspective on how antifeminism became a major theme of popular discourse at the close of the twentieth century.

Feiffer, Jules. *The Great Comic Book Heroes*. New York: Dial Press, 1965. Provides a firsthand account of coming of age during the initial explosion of comic book heroes and explains the cultural impact of these texts.

Fenty, Sean, Trena Houp, and Laurie Taylor. "Web Comics: The Influence and Continuation of the Comix Revolution." *ImageText* 1, no. 2 (Winter, 2005). http://www.english.ufl.edu/imagetext/archives/v1_2/group/index.shtml. In-depth comparison between the Web comics uprising and the underground comics revolution of the 1960's. Focuses mostly on the content created during both comics movements.

"Full Cover Gallery." *Heavy Metal Magazine*, 2012. http://www.heavymetal.com. Includes little history on *Heavy Metal* magazine itself, but this information can be gleaned from the front covers, which highlight the authors and artists featured in each issue.

Gabilliet, Jean-Paul. *Of Comics and Men: A Cultural History of American Comic Books*. Translated by Bart Beaty and Nick Nguyen. Jackson: University Press of Mississippi, 2010. Chronicles the development of the American comic book industry, beginning with the comics of the 1930's and continuing into the Modern Age.

Gardner, Jared. "Autobiography's Biography, 1972-2007." *Biography* 31, no. 1 (2008): 1-26. Provides an overview of some of the autobiographical comics artists of the 1970's, including Justin Green, Pekar, and Spiegelman, along with visual examples of their work.

Garrett, Greg. *Holy Superheroes! Exploring Faith and Spirituality in Comic Books*. Colorado Springs, Colo.: Piñon Press, 2005. Examines the presence of Christian ideas in American superhero comic books and graphic novels, particularly discussing the persistence of Christian themes and their relationship to American culture.

Garrett, Greg. *Holy Superheroes! Exploring the Sacred in Comics, Graphic Novels, and Film*. Louisville, Ky.: Westminster John Knox Press, 2008. Explores the portrayal of religious and spiritual concepts in comics, from dogmatic notions such as the apocalypse to moral issues such as the problem of evil and the notion of vigilante justice.

Genter, Robert. "With Great Power Comes Great Responsibility: Cold War Culture and the Birth of Marvel Comics." *The Journal of Popular Culture* 40, no. 6 (2007): 957-978. Provides an outline of the rise of Marvel Comics, with a particular focus on the transition from conservatism to counterculture and the development of Marvel's adult fan base.

Gifford, Denis. *The International Book of Comics*. Rev. ed. London: Hamlyn, 1990. Discusses the history of comics art both in the United States and abroad and features chapters on early funny animal comic strips.

Goldstein, Lisa, and Molly Phelan. "Are You There God? It's Me, Manga: Manga as an Extension of Young Adult Literature." *Young Adult Library Services* 7, no. 4 (July, 2009): 32-38. Explores graphic literature as an introduction to reading for children. Notes how manga provides girls with the ability to mentally experiment with different sexual orientations. Suggests that young adults are growing up exposed to more open portrayals of sex and gender than their parents did.

Gordon, Ian. "Let Us Not Call Them Graphic Novels: Comic Books as Biography and History." *Radical History Review*, no. 106 (Winter, 2010): 185-192. Uses three graphic novels about politics to determine the appropriate classification of the texts and argues that the term graphic novel is a "marketing tool" for publishers.

Gordon, Ian, Mark Jancovich, and Matthew P. McAllister, eds. *Film and Comic Books*. Jackson: University Press of Mississippi, 2007. Collects essays on a wide range of topics, including the challenges faced in adapting comics to the screen and comics-related movies such as *Unbreakable* (2000).

Gorman, Michele. *Getting Graphic! Using Graphic Novels to Promote Literacy with Preteens and Teens*. Worthington, Ohio: Linworth, 2003. Focuses on practical issues librarians face when collecting graphic novels and includes a bibliography of graphic novel recommendations.

Goulart, Ron. *Over Fifty Years of American Comic Books*. Lincolnwood, Ill.: Mallard Press, 1991. Chronicles the publishing history of the first half century of modern comic books, from *Famous Funnies* (1935) through the beginning of the direct market and independent press boom of the late 1980's.

Gravett, Paul. *Graphic Novels: Everything You Need to Know*. New York: Collins Design, 2005. Introduces readers to the graphic novel through chapters on various genres, recommends thirty essential graphic novels, and includes spreads to illustrate key thematic elements.

Gravett, Paul. *Graphic Novels: Stories to Change Your Life*. London: Aurum, 2005. An introduction to masterpieces of the medium from all around the world, including various European graphic novels by artists such as Bilal, David B., Mattotti, Moebius, Pratt, and Tardi.

Green, Paul. *Encyclopedia of Weird Westerns: Supernatural and Science Fiction Elements in Novels, Pulps, Comics, Films, Television and Games*. Jefferson, N.C.: McFarland, 2009. Features an introduction that discusses the history of the "weird" Western in comics and other media, plus coverage of numerous Western comic book titles and characters.

Griffin, Dustin. *Satire: A Critical Reintroduction*. Lexington: University Press of Kentucky, 1995. Provides a history of satire and critical theory dealing with it and considers satire's place in literature.

Griffith, Paula A. "Graphic Novels in the Secondary Classroom and School Libraries." *Journal of Adolescent and Adult Literacy* 54, no. 3 (November, 2010): 181-189. Addresses the concerns of educators and librarians and provides concrete guidelines and suggestions for using graphic novels in the classroom and building school library collections.

Groensteen, Thierry. "Du 7e au 9e Art: L'Inventaire des singularités." *CinémAction* (Summer 1990):16-28. Analyzes the differences between comics and films in terms of the field of expression, process of creation, and mode of articulation. Considered a reference work in the field for its thorough examination of the steps of production of each medium.

Groensteen, Thierry. *The System of Comics*. Translated by Bart Beaty and Nick Nguyen. Jackson: University Press of Mississippi, 2007. Explores the workings of the comics medium through numerous examples, many of which are drawn from Franco-Belgian comics.

Grove, Laurence. *Comics in French: The Bande Dessinée in Context*. New York: Berghahn Books, 2010. A comprehensive introduction to francophone comics and their sociological implication.

Hahn, Joel. "Comic Book Awards Almanac." *Hahn Library*, 2006. http://www.hahnlibrary.net/comics/awards. Provides an overview of numerous awards, including the Kirby, Eisner, Harvey, Ignatz, Eagle, and Kodansha awards, along with other awards for comics given in Sweden, Germany, Spain, and Italy.

Hajdu, David. *The Ten-Cent Plague: The Great Comic-Book Scare and How It Changed America*. New York: Farrar, Straus and Giroux, 2008. Provides a detailed account of the comic book censorship movement, controversial comic stories published at the time, and the Cold War-era politics that motivated the individuals involved.

Hatfield, Charles. *Alternative Comics: An Emerging Literature*. Jackson: University Press of Mississippi, 2005. Traces the history and visual style of the underground, alternative comics movement and analyzes the work of Gilbert Hernandez, Harvey Pekar, and other notable artists.

Ho, J. D. "Gender Alchemy: The Transformative Power of Manga." *Horn Book Magazine* 83, no. 5 (September/October 2007): 505-512. Focuses on the "boy-love" genre of manga. Explores how manga may be able to allow youth both to experience life from a variety of different perspectives and to understand different sexual orientations and attitudes.

Holm, Douglas K., ed. *R. Crumb: Conversations*. Jackson: University Press of Mississippi, 2005. Collects interviews with Crumb in which he discusses his art style, influences on his work, and the controversies surrounding his work.

Hughes, David. *Comic Book Movies*. London: Virgin Books, 2003. Provides a history and discussion of comic book-related movies up to 2003, including cast lists, plot synopses, and critical evaluations.

Inness, Sherrie A. *Tough Girls: Women Warriors and Wonder Women in Popular Culture*. Philadelphia: University of Pennsylvania Press, 1999. Examines how the entertainment industry capitalized on and co-opted second-wave feminism. Contains a small section devoted to graphic literature, focusing on characters such as Elektra and Martha Washington. Discusses the rise of adventure-heroine programming in the mid-1970's, which helped impel the comics industry to embrace feminism more positively.

"An Inventory of the Comic Strip in Africa." *Africultures*, January, 2011. http://www.africultures.com/php/index.php?nav=article&no=5470. A history of the publication of various forms of comics in Africa, giving useful references for artist/writer associations as well as publishers of African comics.

Janson, Klaus. *The DC Comics Guide to Pencilling Comics*. New York: Watson-Guptill, 2002. Discusses the fundamentals of penciling in detail and also addresses aspects of composition and storytelling.

Jenkins, Henry. "Just Men in Tights: Rewriting Silver Age Comics in an Era of Multiplicity." In *The Contemporary Comic Book Superhero*, edited by Angela Ndalianis. New York: Routledge, 2009. Examines the comics ages in the context of wider genre theory and explores the enduring popularity of the Silver Age incarnations of superheroes and their adaptation to modern publications.

Johnson-Woods, Toni. *Manga: An Anthology of Global and Cultural Perspectives*. New York: Continuum, 2010. Discusses *manhwa*'s cultural context as well as the influence of manga on the Korean cartooning industry, focusing in particular on the 1980's and 1990's.

Jones, Gerard. *Killing Monsters: Why Children Need Fantasy, Super Heroes, and Make-Believe Violence*.

New York: Basic Books, 2002. Explains the benefits children receive from the fantasy genre, fantasy violence, superhuman characters, and sexuality in the realms of entertainment media.

Jones, Gerard. *Men of Tomorrow: Geeks, Gangsters, and the Birth of the Comic Book*. New York: Basic Books, 2004. A history of the comic book industry that focuses on the larger-than-life personalities of those involved.

Jones, Gerard, and Will Jacobs. *The Comic Book Heroes*. Rocklin, Calif.: Prima Books, 1997. Examines the comic book field from the Silver Age to the Modern Age and looks at the forces that shape the comics industry.

Jones, William B. *Classics Illustrated: A Cultural History, with Illustrations*. Jefferson, N.C.: McFarland, 2002. Traces the evolution of the publishing company that founded the *Classics Illustrated* series and provides an in-depth examination of the artists who contributed to the artwork in the series.

Kannenberg, Gene. *Five Hundred Essential Graphic Novels: The Ultimate Guide*. New York: Collins Design, 2008. Provides overviews of key graphic novels, including many award winners.

Keen, Suzanne. "Fast Tracks to Narrative Empathy: Anthropomorphism and Dehumanization in Graphic Narratives." *SubStance* 40, no. 1 (2011): 135-155. Analyzes how literary and artistic styles shape depictions of animal and human characters and influence readers' responses to *Deogratias: A Tale of Rwanda* and *Pride of Baghdad*.

Kitchen, Denis, and James Danky. *Underground Classics: The Transformation of Comics into Comix*. New York: Abrams, 2009. A collection of essays that examines comix in terms of art and influence, focusing on both well-known and unknown contributors.

Knowles, Christopher. *Our Gods Wear Spandex: The Secret History of Comic Book Heroes*. San Francisco: Weiser Books, 2007. Attempts to establish a link between modern mainstream superhero characters and Western mythologies. While more speculative than scholarly, this text further breaks down superheroes into archetypes such as messiah and wizard.

Kratina, Al. "Internet Liberates Comic Book Artists." The (Montreal) Gazette, November 14, 2008, E1. Examines the potential of Web comics to generate revenue outside of the typical publishing environment in which comics have traditionally existed.

Krensky, Stephen. *Comic Book Century: The History of American Comic Books*. Minneapolis: Twenty-First Century Books, 2008. Provides a detailed look at how comic books influenced American culture (and vice versa) in the twentieth century. Highlights the changing face of comic books during wartime and the evolution of masculinity.

Lacassin, Francis. "The Comic Strip and Film Language." *Film Quarterly* 26, no. 1 (1972): 11-23. Translated by David Kunzle. Draws a parallel between the properties of comic strip and film language, proving that comic strips developed their "basic expressive resources" before the influence of cinema.

Lamb, Annette, and Larry Johnson. "Graphic Novels, Digital Comics, and Technology-Enhanced Learning." *Teacher Librarian* 36, no. 5 (June, 2009): 70-75. Looks at graphic novels and Web comics written for young audiences as a form of both entertainment and education.

Lefkowitz, Emily S., and Peter B. Zeldow. "Masculinity and Femininity Predict Optimal Mental Health: A Belated Test of the Androgyny Hypothesis." *Journal of Personality Assessment* 87, no. 1 (August, 2006): 95-101. Examines the belief held by psychologists that embracing the masculinity and femininity inherent in all people is a step toward mental health.

Levitz, Paul. *Seventy-five Years of DC Comics: The Art of Modern Mythmaking*. Köln: Taschen, 2010. Provides access to decades of history of DC Comics' superhero publications, including rare and full-sized art samples. Breaks down the superhero ages with time lines on foldout pages that highlight the important points in the periods.

Lewis, A. David, and Christine Hoff Kraemer. *Graven Images: Religion in Comic Books and Graphic Novels*. New York: Continuum, 2010. Examines the significance of religion in comic books and graphic novels and the ways in which comics communicate religious ideas.

Lopes, Paul Douglas. *Demanding Respect: The Evolution of the American Comic Book*. Philadelphia: Temple University Press, 2009. Discusses the moral panic over comics during the 1950's as well as the aftermath during the 1960's and the subsequent evolution of fan culture.

Lyotard, Jean-François. *The Postmodern Condition: A Report on Knowledge*. Translated by Geoff Bennington and Brian Massumi. Minneapolis: University of Minnesota Press, 1984. Articulates postmodernism in a way that contributes to the understanding of graphic novels as works of art that adhere to the postmodern theory of working without a set of boundaries.

MacWilliams, Mark W. *Japanese Visual Culture: Explorations in the World of Manga and Anime*. Armonk, N.Y.: M. E. Sharpe, 2008. Examines the narratives and subgenres within manga and discusses how manga fits into Japanese culture and how the two affect one another.

Madrid, Mike. *The Supergirls: Fashion, Feminism, Fantasy, and the History of Comic Book Heroines*. Ashland, Oreg.: Exterminating Angel Press, 2009. Examines female graphic novel characters and the evolution of their depiction, addressing the stereotypes associated with female characters and what the characters represent in terms of American culture.

McAllister, Matthew P., Edward H. Sewell, Jr., and Ian Gordon, eds. *Comics and Ideology*. New York: Peter Lang, 2001. Focuses primarily on the various ideological implications of graphic literature, including essays that touch on issues of masculinity, feminism, queer theory, nostalgia, and mythology.

McCloud, Scott. *Making Comics: Storytelling Secrets of Comics, Manga, and Graphic Novels*. New York: Harper, 2006. Discusses the steps involved in creating comics books and graphic novels and provides visual examples of various styles and techniques.

McCloud, Scott. *Reinventing Comics*. New York: HarperCollins, 2000. Reviews the history, process, and consequences of different distribution methods, particularly direct distribution, and includes early speculation on the effects of digital distribution.

McCloud, Scott. *Understanding Comics: The Invisible Art*. New York: Harper, 1993. Analyzes how aspects of graphic novels such as realism and stylized line work affect the viewer's experience through a series of creative models, examples from classic graphic novels, and illustrations.

McGrath, Karen. "Gender, Race, and Latina Identity: An Examination of Marvel Comics' *Amazing Fantasy* and *Araña*." *Atlantic Journal of Communication* 15, no. 4 (2007): 268-283. Focuses on objectification, misrepresentation, and racial stereotyping of Araña, a teenage Latina character from Marvel Comics. Contains an image of the character.

McKenzie, Alan. *How to Draw and Sell Comic Strips*. Cincinnati: Impact Books, 2005. Examines the artistic choices artists make when creating comics and the effects of those choices on their art.

McKinney, Mark, ed. *History and Politics in French-Language Comics and Graphic Novels*. Jackson: University Press of Mississippi, 2008. Discusses Franco-Belgian comics using academic tools that can be applied to graphic novels dealing with history regardless of the country of origin.

Meskin, Aaron. "Comics as Literature?" *British Journal of Aesthetics* 49, no. 3 (July, 2009): 219-239. Within a broader debate about whether comics are legitimate literary works, Meskin looks briefly at Web comics and their continued reliance on hybridity, which he argues print comics are built on.

Mitchell, Robert W., Nicholas S. Thompson, and H. Lyn Miles, eds. *Anthropomorphism, Anecdotes, and Animals*. Albany: State University of New York Press, 1997. Presents scholarly studies of such topics as animal cognition and instincts to debate the definition, purpose, and effective presentation of anthropomorphism in literary works.

Molotiu, Andrei, ed. *Abstract Comics*. Seattle: Fantagraphics Books, 2009. Offers examples of postmodern comics, including works by Robert Crumb and those influenced by the work of artists such as Marcel Duchamp and Jackson Pollock.

Moore, Alan. *Alan Moore's Writing for Comics*. Rantoul, Ill.: Avatar Press, 2007. Critiques the comparison of comics with cinema and cinematic techniques and proposes some ways of breaking away from this comparison to move comics into new and interesting unexplored domains.

National Coalition Against Censorship, American Library Association, and Comic Book Legal Defense Fund. "Graphic Novels: Suggestions for Librarians." *National Coalition Against Censorship*, December 10, 2006. http://www.ncac.org/graphic novels.cfm. Provides a brief history of graphic novels and offers concrete suggestions for librarians, including where to shelve materials, talking points for media relations, and sample "challenging" questions and answers.

Nyberg, Amy Kiste. *Seal of Approval: The History of the Comics Code*. Jackson: University Press of Mississippi, 1998. Looks at the larger history of the anticomics movement beyond the work of Wertham, who is often erroneously portrayed as the sole force behind the campaign to regulate comic book content. Includes the text of various editions of the Comics Code in the appendix.

Ogborn, Jane, and Peter Buckroyd. *Satire*. Cambridge: Cambridge University Press, 2001. Offers a historical survey of satire in literature through the twenty-first century, plus techniques for reading and comprehension.

Pawuk, Michael. *Graphic Novels: A Genre Guide to Comic Books, Manga, and More*. Westport, Conn.: Libraries Unlimited, 2007. Organizes and describes more than twenty-four graphic novels and includes a cartoon preface touching on collection-development issues and the history of comics and graphic novels.

Pearl, Monica B. "Graphic Language: Redrawing the Family (Romance) in Alison Bechdel's *Fun Home*." *Prose Studies* 30, no. 3 (2008): 286-304. Explores the irony in the language of Bechdel's *Fun Home* as well as the contrast between the words and images.

Petersen, Robert. *Comics, Manga, and Graphic Novels: A History of Graphic Narratives*. Santa Barbara, Calif.: Praeger, 2011. Discusses the history of the comic book and graphic novel both in the United States and elsewhere, exploring publication trends and major works.

Pilchner, Tim. *Erotic Comics: A Graphic History from Tijuana Bibles to Underground Comix*. New York: Abrams, 2008. Uses graphics and text to give a history of erotica in comics from the 1920's to the late 1960's. Foreword discusses what makes a work erotic. Surveys a variety of subsections, including women artists, bondage and fetishism in art, and the rise of the Comics Code.

Pilchner, Tim. *Erotic Comics 2: A Graphic History from the Liberated 70's to the Internet*. New York: Abrams ComicArts, 2008. A critical history of erotic content in comics, beginning in the 1970's. Highlights comics magazines for mature audiences. Also includes sections on *Barbarella*, NBM, and *Heavy Metal*.

Pohl-Weary, Emily, ed. *Girls Who Bite Back: Witches, Mutants, Slayers and Freaks*. Toronto, Ont.: Sumach Press, 2004. An edited volume of essays about female role models in popular culture, including several essays on graphic novel characters and readers.

Pustz, Matthew J. *Comic Book Culture: Fanboys and True Believers*. Jackson: University Press of Mississippi, 1999. An extensive ethnography of comic book culture largely focusing on the comic book store as a locus of activity but also addressing the role of conventions.

Repetti, Massimo. "African Wave: Specificity and Cosmopolitanism in African Comics." *African Arts* 40, no. 2 (Summer, 2007): 16-35. An incisive historical essay by a curator of international events of African comics and graphic novels. Leans toward a Euro-centric view regarding how Europeans have helped to develop the African market for graphic novels and comics in general.

Reynolds, Richard. *Super Heroes: A Modern Mythology*. Jackson: University Press of Mississippi, 1994. Examines superheroes as modern myth while paying particularly attention to projects such as *Batman: The Dark Knight Returns* and *Watchmen*. Evaluates the artistic value of the graphic novel format versus that of monthly serials.

Riches, Adam, Tim Parker, and Robert Frankland. *When the Comics Went to War: Comic Book War Heroes*. Edinburgh, Scotland: Mainstream, 2009. Does not specifically examine war in graphic novels but, rather, in British comics in general. Contains a large number of illustrations.

Robbins, Trina. *From Girls to Grrrlz: A History of Women's Comics from Teens to Zines*. San Francisco: Chronicle Books, 1999. An analysis and history of comics read by women, including mainstream comics as well as works published by underground and alternative presses.

Robbins, Trina. *The Great Women Superheroes*. Northampton, Mass.: Kitchen Sink Press, 1996. Provides an overview of women in comics from the 1940's to the 1990's, including analyses of both major and minor characters and discussion of trends regarding the representation of women in graphic novels.

Roberts, Adam. *The History of Science Fiction*. New York: Palgrave Macmillan, 2006. Presents a scholarly consideration of science fiction as a literary and film/television genre, including discussion of science-fiction comics and graphic novels.

Robinson, Lillian S. *Wonder Women: Feminisms and Superheroes*. New York: Routledge, 2004. Examines the manner in which feminist principles have been communicated within the superhero genre since the 1940's. Focuses mostly on developments during the 1940's and early 1990's; briefly touches on the antifeminism of the 1960's. Provides insight into the impact the editors of *Ms.* magazine had on the comics industry in the early 1970's.

Russell, Mark James. *Pop Goes Korea: Behind the Revolution in Movies, Music, and Internet Culture*. Berkeley, Calif.: Stone Bridge Press, 2008. Includes a chapter devoted to *manhwa* that details its rise during the 1990's and early twenty-first century and provides sidebars about important artists and works.

Sabin, Roger. *Comics, Comix, and Graphic Novels: A History of Comic Art*. New York: Phaidon, 2001. Covers the rise of comics, including literary adaptations, and reviews thematic comics topics. Also highlights some of the various artistic styles and artists who have contributed to the industry.

Sabin, Roger. "Worldcomics." In *Adult Comics: An Introduction*. London: Routledge, 1993. A brief historical look at adult comics in Europe, focusing mostly on the evolution in the francophone region.

Savage, William W., Jr. *Commies, Cowboys, and Jungle Queens: Comic Books and America, 1945-1954*. Hanover, N.H.: Wesleyan University Press, 1998. Focuses on the critical period of the 1950's, when the comic book medium underwent a dramatic shift following criticism from concerned parents and investigation by the United States government.

Saxey, Esther. "Desire Without Closure in Jaime Hernandez' *Love and Rockets*." *ImageText* 3, no. 1 (Summer, 2006). http://www.english.ufl.edu/image text/archives/v3_1/saxey/. A scholarly article focusing on the relationship between Hopey and Maggie, two of the Hernandez brothers' most important characters.

Schelly, Bill. *The Golden Age of Comic Fandom*. Seattle: Hamster Press, 1999. A history recounting in detail the early years of comics fandom, from its initial publications to its first meetings, based on personal experience and interviews.

Schmidt, Andy. *The Insider's Guide to Creating Comics and Graphic Novels*. Cincinnati: Impact Books, 2009. Provides tips from comics professionals regarding various aspects of the comics creation process, including scripting, inking, and coloring.

Schodt, Frederik L. *Manga! Manga! The World of Japanese Comics*. Tokyo: Kodansha International, 1998. Provides a comprehensive background on the history of manga in Japan from its origins to the early 1980's, covering major influences and artistic styles. Includes a foreword by Osamu Tezuka.

Schumer, Arlen. *The Silver Age of Comic Book Art*. Portland, Oreg.: Collectors Press, 2003. Surveys the Silver Age of comic books and discusses the maturing illustrators who ushered in a new brand of storytelling.

Schwarz, Gretchen. "Media Literacy, Graphic Novels and Social Issues." *Simile* 7, no. 4 (November, 2007): 1-11. Discusses the significance of graphic novels in media literacy and in the instruction of social issues and provides examples of classroom use.

Scott, Darieck. "Love, Rockets, Race, and Sex." *The Americas Review: A Review of Hispanic Literature and Art of the USA* 23, nos. 3-4 (Fall/Winter, 1995): 73-106. Describes how the Hernandez brothers' work compares with mainstream comics in terms of race, sexuality, and even fan mail.

Screech, Matthew. *Masters of the Ninth Art: Bandes Dessinées and Franco-Belgian Identity*. Liverpool: Liverpool University Press, 2005. Analyzes Franco-Belgian comics in depth, discussing the works and visual styles of Jijé, Hergé, and a number of other artists.

Seed, David, ed. *A Companion to Science Fiction*. Malden, Mass.: Blackwell, 2005. Includes a wealth of perspectives on science fiction as a genre, focusing on text and film and including discussion of comic books.

Skinn, Dez. *Comix: The Underground Revolution*. New York: Thunder's Mouth Press, 2004. A thorough, well-illustrated history of underground comics from a British perspective. Contains a list of underground publications released in the United States and the United Kingdom.

Spiegelman, Art, and R. Sikoryak. *The Narrative Corpse: A Chain-Story by Sixty-Nine Artists!* Richmond, Va.: RAW Books, 1995. Serves as an example of a postmodern work created by sixty-nine comics artists, including influential figures such as Daniel Clowes, Crumb, Will Eisner, McCloud, and Ware.

Starkings, Richard, and John Roshell. *Comic Book Lettering: The Comicraft Way*. Los Angeles: Active Images, 2003. Provides a fully illustrated guide to lettering, particularly focusing on digital methods and software for comics lettering.

Strömberg, Fredrik. *Black Images in the Comics: A Visual History*. Seattle: Fantagraphics Books, 2012. An image-heavy history of how black people have been portrayed in comics from all over the world. Introduction by Charles Johnson.

Strömberg, Fredrik. *Comic Art Propaganda: A Graphic History*. New York: St. Martin's Griffin, 2010. A general, popular-culture approach to the subject of propaganda in comics, with a plethora of illustrations.

Strömberg, Fredrik. "Sexual Slander." In *Comic Art Propaganda: A Graphic History*. New York: St. Martin's Griffin, 2010. Demonstrates that creators expressed feminism and antifeminism through

comic book imagery in a variety of ways across time, companies, and genres.

Sugiyama, Rika. *Comic Artists—Asia: Manga, Manhwa, Manhua*. New York: Harper, 2004. Introduces the work of comics artists in Japan, Korea, and Hong Kong through artist profiles and interviews that provide insight into their processes.

Thurber, James. *Writings and Drawings*. New York: Literary Classics of the United States, 1996. Collects all of Thurber's work, from his early cartoons for *The New Yorker* to his attempts at creating a narrative form.

Ueno, Junko. "'Shojo' and Adult Women: A Linguistic Analysis of Gender Identity in *Manga* (Japanese Comics)." *Women and Language* 29, no. 1 (2006): 16-25. Examines graphic novels aimed at young girls and women. Analyzes the speech presented by female characters in these novels.

Versaci, Rocco. *This Book Contains Graphic Language: Comics as Literature*. New York: Continuum, 2007. Discusses graphic novel censorship, political imagery, and other adult topics in comics and graphic novels. Includes sample illustrations from graphic novels to support the text.

Wandtke, Terrence R., ed. *The Amazing Transforming Superhero! Essays on the Revision of Characters in Comic Books, Film and Television*. Jefferson, N.C.: McFarland, 2007. Collects essays offering social and cultural analysis of the superhero genre, focusing on trends in history, specific characters, and common themes.

Ward, Lynd. *Six Novels in Woodcuts*. New York: Library of America, 2010. Includes all six of Ward's woodcut novels as well as his writings and a lengthy introduction by graphic novelist Art Spiegelman.

Ware, Chris. *The ACME Novelty Library*. New York: Pantheon, 2005. Examines and critiques traditional comics from a Marxist perspective and inserts a design structure that breaks the sequentiality that both Eisner and McCloud suggest is at the heart of the medium.

Weiner, Robert G., ed. *Graphic Novels and Comics in Libraries and Archives: Essays on Readers, Research, History, and Cataloguing*. Jefferson, N.C.: McFarland, 2010. Deals directly with how naming has affected the delivery and reception of comics in libraries and examines how grouping comics together or throughout the library according to subject matter affects reader access.

Weiner, Stephen. *Faster than a Speeding Bullet: The Rise of the Graphic Novel*. New York: NBM, 2003. Includes a concise history of the medium as well as a guide to the most influential graphic novels of the 1980's and 1990's.

Weiner, Stephen. *The 101 Best Graphic Novels*. New York: NBM, 2005. Provides an introduction and a history of the medium for unfamiliar readers and lists significant graphic novels for young-adult or adult readers.

Winge, Theresa. "Costuming the Imagination: Origins of Anime and Manga Cosplay." *Mechademia* 1 (2006): 65-76. Discusses the origins of anime and manga cosplay, providing insight into the community aspect of cosplay and examining why fans engage in the activity.

Witek, Joseph. *Comic Books as History: The Narrative Art of Jack Jackson, Art Spiegelman, and Harvey Pekar*. Jackson: University Press of Mississippi, 1989. Features a clear and provocative close reading of war-genre comics and argues that graphic novels play an important role in historical discourse.

Wolfe, Gary K. "On Some Recent Scholarship." Review of *Understanding Comics: The Invisible Art*, by Scott McCloud. *Science Fiction Studies* 21, no. 3 (1994): 438-439.

Wolk, Douglas. *Reading Comics: How Graphic Novels Work and What They Mean*. Cambridge, Mass.: Da Capo Press, 2007. An excellent overview of the graphic novel genre, containing a section on theory and history as well as an extensive list of book reviews and commentary. Provides information about writing, understanding, and enjoying the genre.

Workman, John, ed. *Heavy Metal: Twenty-Five Years of Classic Covers*. Rockville Centre, N.Y.: Heavy Metal, 2002. Provides wonderful graphics. Introductions by Workman, the original art editor for *Heavy Metal*, and by artists such as Richard and Wendy Pini, Royo, and Simon Bisley.

Wright, Bradford W. *Comic Book Nation: The Transformation of Youth Culture in America*. Baltimore: Johns Hopkins University Press, 2003. Provides a publishing history that situates the changing comic book medium within the larger cultural history of the United States and discusses the popularity of various genres.

Wright, Nicky. *The Classic Era of American Comics*. London: Prion Books, 2009. A history of the comic book medium, focusing on its early years.

Guide to Online Resources

Center for Cartoon Studies
http://www.cartoonstudies.org/

A two-year institution based in White River Junction, Vermont, offering a Masters in Fine Arts degree program dedicated to elevating the cartooning profession. Provides a thoughtful meditation on the artistic value and role of comics in our society.

The Comic Book Database
http://www.comicbookdb.com/index.php

An online, user-created database, ComicBookDB compiles all things comics-related. Helpful in answering specific questions regarding issue numbers, contributors, character backgrounds, and series history. A useful resource for reference or cataloging.

Comic Book Legal Defense Fund
http://cbldf.org/

A nonprofit organization, founded in 1986, dedicated to fighting censorship and preserving freedom of expression in the drawing, writing, selling, and reading of comics.

Comic Book Resources
http://www.comicbookresources.com/

An online magazine devoted to comics and their adaptations in television, film, and video games, CBR provides comics-related news coverage and articles from comics writers, artists, and critics. Backed by Comic-Con International.

The Comics Journal
http://www.tcj.com/

A print and online magazine about comics featuring interviews, editorials, in-depth reporting, regular columns, industry news, and hard-line reviews. A blog highlights new content on the website.

The Comics Reporter
http://www.comicsreporter.com/

A useful collection of comics industry news, complete with commentary. Created and maintained by Tom Spurgeon, former editor of *The Comics Journal*. Publishes regular interviews with comics creators and reviews of recent publications.

Comics Worth Reading
http://comicsworthreading.com/

A collection of independent reviews of comics, graphic novels, and manga written from a predominantly female perspective. Established in 1999 by longtime comics fan and critic Johanna Draper Carlson, CWR provides up-to-date news coverage on the comics industry.

Diamond Bookshelf
http://www.diamondbookshelf.com/public/

A database hosted by the world's largest comic book distributor, Diamond Bookshelf is an informative resource for librarians and teachers. The site includes bestsellers, information on new and upcoming titles, and core lists by age group, as well as sample lesson plans and articles on using graphic novels in education and literacy.

Good Comics for Kids (SLJ blog)
http://blog.schoollibraryjournal.com/goodcomicsforkids

A blog maintained by *School Library Journal*, Good Comics for Kids reviews and recommends children's and all-ages comics, graphic novels, and manga.

Graphic Novel Reporter
http://www.graphicnovelreporter.com/

An offshoot of BookReporter.com, Graphic Novel Reporter is an online resource aimed at librarians. In addition to providing resources to help librarians collect and promote graphic novels in their libraries, GNR publishes feature articles and reviews useful to those with a cursory knowledge of graphic novels, comics, and manga.

Graphic Novels in Libraries listserv (GNLIB-L)
http://www.angelfire.com/comics/gnlib/

An email discussion group for librarians to ask questions and advise other librarians on graphic novels in their libraries—topics include popular titles, recommending graphic novels, shelving, resources, reading level, etc.

Graphic Novels: Resources for Teachers & Librarians
http://library.buffalo.edu/libraries/asl/guides/graphic-novels/index.php

An excellent starting point for librarians and teachers who want to become more comfortable with understanding, selecting, and recommending graphic novels for young adult patrons or students. Provides useful information on graphic novels publishers, formats, and genres.

Houston Public Library Graphic Books Next Reads Newsletters
http://www.nextreads.com/Display2.aspx?SID=797a1db1-f3d7-44c8-bb75-5176f6987699&N=388932

An online publication created by the staff at Houston Public Library, the bi-monthly newsletters *Graphic Books* and *Teen Graphic Books* highlight a thematic array of graphic novel titles, old and new.

Lambiek Comiclopedia
http://www.lambiek.net/

A collection of entries on over 11,000 comic artists from around the world, Comiclopedia has been maintained by the Lambiek comics shop in Amsterdam since 1994. Complete with representative illustrations, Comiclopedia is an excellent resource on comics contributors and their works.

Newsarama
http://www.newsarama.com/comics/

An online source for comics industry news, comic reviews, previews, press releases, articles, and commentary, Newsarama has covered comics for fans daily since 1998.

No Flying, No Tights
http://www.noflyingnotights.com/index2.html
No Flying, No Tights: Sidekicks
http://www.noflyingnotights.com/sidekicks/
No Flying, No Tights: The Lair
http://www.noflyingnotights.com/lair/

An online collection created by YA librarian Robin Brenner in 2002, the site features reviews of graphic novels and manga for teens. In addition to a blog, two more age-specific sister sites have been launched that review graphic novels and manga for kids (Sidekicks) and adults (The Lair).

Sequential Tart
http://www.sequentialtart.com/

A monthly webzine on comics and the comics industry, *Sequential Tart* is written with special attention paid to women as creators, characters, and fans—but is of interest to any comics enthusiast.

YALSA Great Graphic Novels for Teens
www.ala.org/yalsa/ggnt

This ann otated list has been compiled annually since 2007 by a Young Adult Library Services Association special committee. Great Graphic Novels for Teens provides graphic novels (published in the previous 16 months) recommendations for teen readers.

TIMELINE

c. 15000-12000 B.C.E.	Polychromatic prehistoric art, represented in the form of cave paintings of bison and deer, is created in a cave complex in Altamira, Spain. Other cave paintings date as far back as 25000 B.C.E.
c. 700's	Woodblock printing is brought to Japan from China.
c. 1070	The Bayeux Tapestry, an embroidered cloth which recounts the 1066 Norman conquest of England through hundreds of images and words, is created.
c. 1000's	*The Tale of the Genji*, by Murasaki Shikibu (early eleventh century), is adapted into an illustrated scroll. This era also marks the development of kamishibai, or a "paper drama" often enacted on the street with the aid of illustrated scrolls.
1401	In what is considered a pivotal event of the Renaissance, artists such as Lorenzo Ghiberti, Filippo Brunelleschi, and Donatello participate in a competition to illustrate the biblical story of the sacrifice of Isaac on the bronze doors of the Baptistery of San Giovanni in Florence, Italy.
c. 1600's	This century marks the development of ukiyo-e, consisting of woodblock prints depicting scenes from history, literature, and the environment.
18th-19th century	English poet and artist William Blake reinvigorates the medieval illuminated book, leading to much imitation later in the twentieth century. Cited as an influence by many graphic novelists, Blake's work would later be referenced in the seminal *Watchmen* (1986), among other graphic novels.
1814	The term "manga" is employed in the title of a collection of sketches by Japanese artist and printmaker Katsushika Hokusai, creator of the famous *The Great Wave off Kanagawa* print.
1837	Swiss schoolmaster Rudolphe Töpffer creates what is considered by many historians to be the first known comic book, *The Adventures of Obadiah Oldbuck*.
1874	The first manga magazine published in Japanese, *Eshinbun Nipponchi*, appears.
1895	American comic strip writer Richard F. Outcault, considered by many to be the foremost inventor of the comic strip, creates *The Yellow Kid*.
1909	Future manga publishing powerhouse Kodansha is founded.
1918	Artist Rakuten Kitazawa founds the Manga Kourakuki, an association for Japanese illustrators.

1919	Flemish artist Frans Masereel creates the "image novel" *Mon Livre d'Heures* (*Passionate Journey*), one of more than twenty wordless and woodcut novels he would create throughout his career.
1922	The major publishing company Shogakukan is founded.
1925	Shūeisha, an early manga publisher, is founded. Along with Shogakukan, it is now part of the Hitotsubashi Group.
1928	Osamu Tezuka, creator of *Astro Boy* and a major influence in the manga medium, is born.
1929	Working in wood engravings, American artist Lynd Ward creates *God's Man*, one of six wood-engraved novels he would produce between 1929 and 1937 that depict the troubled American landscape. It is often considered the first American graphic novel.
1930's	A depressed economy leads to the revival of kamishibai, which continues until after World War II. Many manga creators will get their start drawing kamishibai toward the end of and after the war.
1930's	Ippei Okamoto introduces Japanese audiences to Western comics, including *Bringing Up Father*, *Katzenjammer Kids*, and *Mutt and Jeff*.
1930	American illustrator and artist Milt Gross publishes *He Done Her Wrong*
c.1938	Beginning of the Golden Age of Comic Books, which marks the mainstream arrival of the comic book and the emergence of the superhero genre.
1938	*Action Comics* #1 is published, introducing the character of Superman, one of the first superheroes.
1939	The character of Batman is introduced in *Detective Comics* #27. The company producing the comic will eventually adopt the name DC Comics.
1939	The comic book series *Marvel Comics* is released by Marvel predecessor Timely Comics.
1941	Captain America makes his first appearance in *Captain America Comics* #1, battling the Axis alliance in a contemporary World War II setting. The cover depicts the title character punching Adolf Hitler in the face. That same year, Wonder Woman, the first female superhero, is also introduced.
1947	The monthly magazine *Manga Shōnen* is founded, and is published through 1955.

1949	Many trailblazing female *mangaka* (manga creators) are born, including Moto Hagio, Yumiko Oshima, Keiko Takemiya, Riyoko Ikeda, and Ryoko Yamagishi; collectively, these female *mangaka* are known as the "Fabulous Forty Niners."
1950	St. John Publications releases the "picture novel" *It Rhymes with Lust*, written by Arnold Drake and Leslie Waller (as Drake Waller), as part of a short-lived experiment in creating a mature comic book series for adults using a small paperback format.
1951	*Astro Boy*, or *Tetsuwan Atom*, by Osamu Tezuka, is first published, setting the tone and structure for young boys' (*shōnen*) manga.
1952	Humor magazine *MAD*, originally a comic book, makes its debut. *MAD*'s publisher, William Gaines, was also the co-editor of EC Comics, which specialized in publishing mature-audience comics across a wide range of genres, from horror to military fiction, in the 1940s and 1950s.
1954	Dr. Fredric Wertham, an outspoken opponent of comics, publishes *Seduction of the Innocent*, which links depictions of crime and horror in comics to juvenile delinquency.
1954	The Comics Code, a self-imposed censorship system on comics in the United States, is created.
1954	*Princess Knight*, or *Ribon no Kishi*, by Tezuka, is first published, setting the tone for young girls' (*shōjo*) manga.
1954	The *shōjo* magazine *Nakyoshi* begins publishing. One year later, in 1955, the *shōjo* magazine *Ribon* begins publishing.
1956	Beginning of the Silver Age of Comic Books, a period during which many of the conventions of the modern comic medium are established and many Golden Age characters such as the Flash and Green Lantern are revamped.
1956	The magazine *Weekly Manga Times* debuts. It is widely considered the first weekly manga publication.
1957	Yoshihiro Tatsumi reportedly coins the term "*gekiga*" to distinguish mature manga from what manga has come to mean—comics for kids.
1959	Two influential monthly manga anthologies, Shogakukan's *Shōnen Sunday* and Kodansha's *Weekly Shōnen Magazine*, are launched in the same month (May).
1961	The first anime series, *Manga Calendar*, is broadcast on Japanese television.

1961	Marvel Comics introduces the superhero group The Fantastic Four with the publication of *Fantastic Four* #1, marking the beginning of the collaboration between writer Stan Lee and artist Jack Kirby.
1962	Fictional comic book character Peter Parker dons the Spider-Man outfit for the first time in Marvel's *Amazing Fantasy* #15. The comic book series *The Amazing Spider-Man* was released shortly thereafter.
1962	Frank Stack's The Adventures of Jesus, a satirical view of the religious beliefs and society of Middle America, is published. It is regarded as the first underground comic ever published.
1964	The term "graphic novel" is coined by writer Richard Kyle in a newsletter circulated to all members of the Amateur Press Association.
1964	*Garo* magazine is founded to support adventurous comics for mature readers. It is published through 2002.
1968	In what is considered another significant step for the graphic novel medium, artist Gil Kane and writer Archie Goodwin collaborate on *His Name Is . . . Savage*, which Kane self-published.
1968	Robert Crumb, the leading figure of the underground comics movement, self-publishes his first solo comic, Zap Comix. Its publication is often regarded as the beginning of the underground "comix" movement.
1968	The magazine *Weekly Shōnen Jump* first publishes. It eventually becomes the best-selling manga magazine in Japan —which is to say, the world—giving birth to *Slam Dunk*, *Dragon Ball*, *Naruto*, *One Piece*, and countless other popular titles.
1969	Doraemon, a robotic cat and one of the most popular characters in Japanese pop culture, makes its debut in six different magazines.
c.1970	Beginning of the Bronze Age of Comic Books, a period marked by an increasing drive for realism and social relevance in comics.
1970	Renowned artist Jack Kirby leaves Marvel Comics to work for rival DC Comics. His Fourth World stories for DC are among the first attempts to create a cohesive, finite superhero narrative with the graphic novel medium in mind.
1970	The original Comic-Con International (organized initially as the Golden State Comic-Minicon) is first held in San Diego, California.
1970	Underground comics publishing pioneer Kitchen Sink Press is founded.

1972	Underground comics strip *Fritz the Cat*, by Robert Crumb, is adapted into an animated comedy film, becoming the first animated film to receive an X rating. Though Crumb took issue with many aspects of the film, it would become the most successful independent animated film of all time.
1975	The first Comiket convention is held for creators of self-published manga (*dōjinshi*).
1976	Author and illustrator Richard Corben's *Bloodstar*, generally considered the first self-proclaimed "graphic novel," is published by Morning Star Press. It is adapted from a short story entitled "The Valley of the Worm" by pulp writer Robert E. Howard.
1976	Harvey Pekar's *American Splendor*, a landmark title in the Underground Comix movement, begins publication.
1977	Early alternative comics publisher WaRP Graphics (later Warp Graphics) is incorporated, and begins publication of the long-running *Elfquest* series.
1978	Will Eisner's *A Contract with God*, considered by many to be the first modern graphic novel, is published. The same year, Marvel publishes The Silver Surfer, another early example of the format.
1978	Director Richard Donner's *Superman* film is released, marking the inauguration of the blockbuster era for comics cinema.
1981	The Hernandez brothers, Gilbert and Jamie, self-publish the first issue of Love and Rockets. Fantagraphics begins publishing the comic book series one year later.
1982	Katsuhiro Otomo's *Akira* begins serialization in *Young Magazine*. It runs through 1990.
1983	Frederik L. Schodt's *Manga! Manga! The World of Japanese Comics*, which presents a history of manga, is published.
1983	Frank Miller creates the American comic *Ronin*, which is strongly influenced by manga. He goes on to draw covers for the translated editions of *Lone Wolf and Cub*.
c. 1985	Beginning of the Modern Age of Comics, a period which ushers in more mature themes and revisionist approaches and introduces longer-form works and better-known artists.
1986	Art Spiegelman's *Maus*, considered one of the most significant graphic novels ever produced, is published.
1986	Frank Miller's *Batman*

1986	Dark Horse Comics, the largest independent comic book publisher, is founded.
1986	*Dragon Ball* by Akira Toriyama begins serialization in *Weekly Shōnen Jump*.
1986	The company VIZ (now known as Viz Media) is founded in the United States with the purpose of bringing translated Japanese manga to English readers.
1987	DC Comics collects the twelve issues of Alan Moore and Dave Gibbons's *Watchmen* as a trade paperback. Along with *Maus* and *Batman*
1988	Named in honor of cartoonist Will Eisner, the Will Eisner Comic Industry Awards are created, which recognize creative and outstanding achievement in American comic books.
1988	*Watchmen* wins a Hugo Award, given annually for the best in published fantasy and science fiction.
1989	Marvel Comics begins its full translated edition of Otomo's *Akira*.
1991	The *shōjo* manga *Sailor Moon* is first published.
1992	*Maus* becomes the first graphic novel to win the Pulitzer Prize.
1992	Comic book publisher Image Comics is founded by several high-profile artists who broke from Marvel and DC in a dispute over creators' rights and work-for-hire practices.
1996	Marvel creates Marvel Studios, which would later launch numerous successful and interconnected superhero film franchises, thus creating the Marvel Cinematic Universe.
1997	Independent publisher Oni Press is founded.
1997	Mixx, later known as TokyoPop, is founded in Los Angeles to license manga and anime. Eventually, the company will produce non-Japanese comics inspired by manga. TokyoPop will close its publishing division in 2011.
1999	*Pokemon* debuts on American television.
2001	The graphic novel series *Persepolis*, Marjane Satrapi's autobiographical account of growing up in Iran, wins the Angoulême International Comics Festival Coup de Coeur Award. The graphic novel series would later win several other awards, including the first Fernando Buesa Blanco Peace Prize in 2003 for its stance against totalitarianism.

2001	The film *Ghost World* is released to critical acclaim, becoming one of the first mainstream adaptations of an indie comic and earning alternative comic author Daniel Clowes an Academy Award nomination for Best Adapted Screenplay.
2002	*Shōnen Jump* magazine debuts in America.
2003	*Spirited Away*, directed by manga creator Hayao Miyazaki, wins the Academy Award for Best Animated Feature.
2005	Scholastic Inc., the world's largest publisher of children's books, announces the creation of a new graphic novel imprint, Graphix.
2005	*Watchmen* is the only graphic novel listed on *Time* magazine's "The 100 Best English Language Novels from 1923 to the Present."
2006	Gene Yang's *American Born Chinese* becomes the first graphic novel nominated for a National Book Award. It would later win the Michael L. Printz award for excellence in Young Adult literature.
2006	Alison Bechdel's *Fun Home* is a finalist for the National Book Critics Circle Award.
2008	The Japanese publisher Kodansha forms an American company, based in Manhattan.
2009	Fordham University hosts the first Graphic Novels in Education Conference.
2009	The *New York Times* introduces three different best seller lists for graphic novels
2010	The Japanese Digital Comic Association announces a joint venture with American publishers to fight online piracy.
2011	Borders Books and Music, which served a substantial amount of manga's American readership, closes its last U.S. store.
2012	*Shōnen Jump* magazine in America closes its print edition and moves online.

MAJOR AWARDS

Bill Finger Award for Achievement in Comic Book Writing

Awarded annually at Comic-Con International since 2005, the Bill Finger Award committee selects a living and a deceased writer to recognize for their body of work.

2005	Jerry Siegel Arnold Drake	2009	John Broome Frank Jacobs
2006	Alvin Schwartz Harvey Kurtzman	2010	Gary Friedrich Otto Binder
2007	Gardner Fox George Gladier	2011	Del Connell Bob Haney
2008	Archie Goodwin Larry Lieber		

Eisner Awards

Named in honor of cartoonist Will Eisner, the Eisner Awards were first granted in 1988. Category nominees are selected by a committee, and then final winners are chosen by representatives from all fields of the comics industry.

1988

Best Writer/Artist or Writer/Artist Team	*Watchmen*	Alan Moore and Dave Gibbons
Best Writer	*Watchmen*	Alan Moore
Best Single Issue (or One-Shot)	*Gumby Summer Fun Special #1*	Bob Burden and Art Adams
Best New Series	*Concrete*	Paul Chadwick
Best Limited Series or Story Arc	*Watchmen*	Alan Moore and Dave Gibbons
Best Graphic Album	*Watchmen*	Alan Moore and Dave Gibbons
Best Continuing Series	*Concrete*	Paul Chadwick
Best Black & White Series	*Concrete*	Paul Chadwick
Best Artist	*Nexus*	Steve Rude
Best Art Team	*Space Ghost Special*	Steve Rude, Willie Blyberg, and Ken Steacy

1989

Best Writer/Artist or Writer/Artist Team	*Concrete*	Paul Chadwick
Best Writer	*Batman: The Killing Joke*	Alan Moore
Best Single Issue (or One-Shot)	*Kings in Disguise #1*	James Vance and Dan Burr
Best New Series	*Kings in Disguise*	James Vance and Dan Burr
Best Limited Series or Story Arc	*Silver Surfer*	Stan Lee and Jean "Moebius" Giraud
Best Graphic Album	*Batman: The Killing Joke*	Alan Moore and Brian Bolland
Best Continuing Series	*Concrete*	Paul Chadwick
Best Black & White Series	*Concrete*	Paul Chadwick
Best Artist	*Batman: The Killing Joke*	Brian Bolland
Best Art Team	*Excalibur*	Alan Davis and Paul Neary

1990 – No Awards Given

1991

Best Writer/Artist or Writer/Artist Team	*Hard Boiled*	Frank Miller and Geof Darrow
Best Writer	*Sandman*	Neil Gaiman
Best Single Issue (or One-Shot)	*Concrete Celebrates Earth Day*	Paul Chadwick, Charles Vess, and Jean "Moebius" Giraud
Best Limited Series or Story Arc	*Give Me Liberty*	Frank Miller and Dave Gibbons
Best Inker		Al Williamson
Best Graphic Album—Reprint	*Sandman: The Doll's House*	Neil Gaiman and various artists
Best Graphic Album—New	*Elektra Lives Again*	Frank Miller and Lynn Varley
Best Continuing Series	*Sandman*	Neil Gaiman and various artists
Best Black & White Series	*Xenozoic Tales*	Mark Schultz
Best Artist	*Nexus*	Steve Rude

1992

Best Writer/Artist or Writer/Artist Team	*The Incredible Hulk*	Peter David and Dale Keown
Best Writer	*Sandman Books of Magic, Miracleman*	Neil Gaiman
Best Single Issue (or One-Shot)	*Sandman #22-#28: "Season of Mists"*	Neil Gaiman and various artists
Best Limited Series or Story Arc	*Concrete: Fragile Creature*	Paul Chadwick
Best Inker	*Batman Versus Predator*	Adam Kubert
Best Humor Publication	*Groo the Wanderer*	Mark Evanier and Sergio Aragonés
Best Graphic Album—Reprint	*Maus II*	Art Spiegelman
Best Graphic Album—New	*To the Heart of the Storm*	Will Eisner
Best Cover Artist	*Animal Man*	Brian Bolland
Best Continuing Series	*Sandman*	Neil Gaiman and various artists
Best Comics-Related Periodical	*Comics Buyer's Guide*	edited by Don and Maggie Thompson
Best Comics-Related Book	*From "Aargh!" to "Zap!": Harvey Kurtzman's Visual History of the Comics*	Harvey Kurtzman, edited by Howard Zimmerman
Best Comic Strip Collection	*Calvin and Hobbes: The Revenge of the Baby-Sat*	Bill Watterson
Best Coloring	*Legends of the Dark Knight, 2112, and Akira*	Steve Oliff
Best Artist	*Batman: Judgment on Gotham*	Simon Bisley
Best Anthology	*Dark Horse Presents*	edited by Randy Stradley

1993

Best Writer/Artist Team	*Nexus: The Origin*	Mike Baron and Steve Rude

Best Writer/Artist	*"Sin City" Dark Horse Presents*	Frank Miller
Best Writer	*Miracleman; Sandman*	Neil Gaiman
Best Single Issue (or One-Shot)	*Nexus: The Origin*	Mike Baron and Steve Rude
Best Short Story	*"Two Cities," in Xenozoic Tales #12*	Mark Schultz
Best Serialized Story	*"From Hell" in Taboo*	Alan Moore and Eddie Campbell
Best Publication Design	*Sandman: Season of Mists*	designed by Dave McKean
Best Penciller/Inker, Color	*Fairy Tales of Oscar Wilde; Robin 3000; Legends of the Dark Knight: "Hothouse"*	P. Craig Russell
Best Penciller/Inker, Black & White	*"Sin City" Dark Horse Presents*	Frank Miller
Best Penciller	*Nexus: The Origin*	Steve Rude
Best Painter/Multimedia Artist	*Aliens: Tribes*	Dave Dorman
Best Limited Series or Story Arc	*Grendel: War Child*	Matt Wagner and Patrick McEown
Best Lettering	*The Sandman Demon*	Todd Klein
Best Inker	*Batman: Sword of Azrael*	Kevin Nowlan
Best Humor Publication	*Bone*	Jeff Smith
Best Graphic Album—Reprint	*Sin City*	Frank Miller
Best Graphic Album—New	*Signal to Noise*	Neil Gaiman and Dave McKean
Best Cover Artist	*Animal Man; Wonder Woman*	Brian Bolland
Best Continuing Series	*Sandman*	Neil Gaiman and various artists
Best Comics-Related Publication	*Comics Buyer's Guide*	edited by Don and Maggie Thompson

Best Comic Strip Collection	*Calvin and Hobbes: Attack of the Deranged Mutant Killer Monster Snow Goons*	Bill Watterson
Best Coloring	*Legends of the Dark Knight #28-#30; Martian Manhunter: American Secrets; James Bond 007: Serpent's Tooth; Spawn*	Steve Oliff/Olyoptics
Best Archival Collection/Project	*Carl Barks Library album series*	
Best Anthology	*Taboo*	edited by Steve Bissette

1994

Best Writer/Artist	*Bone*	Jeff Smith
Best Writer	*Sandman; Death: The High Cost of Living*	Neil Gaiman
Best Single Issue (or One-Shot)	*Batman Adventures: Mad Love*	Paul Dini and Bruce Timm
Best Short Story	*"The Amazing Colossal Homer," in Simpsons Comics #1*	Steve Vance, Cindy Vance, and Bill Morrison
Best Serialized Story	*Bone #8-10: "The Great Cow Race"*	Jeff Smith
Best Publication Design	*Marvels*	designed by Comicraft
Best Penciller/Inker or Penciller/Inker Team	*Sandman #50*	P. Craig Russell
Best Painter/Multimedia Artist	*Marvels*	Alex Ross
Best Limited Series or Story Arc	*Marvels*	Kurt Busiek and Alex Ross
Best Lettering	*The Shadow; Dark Joker: The Wild; The Sandman Demon, Jonah Hex: Two-Gun Mojo, Hellblazer*	Todd Klein
Best Humor Publication	*Bone*	Jeff Smith

Best Graphic Album—Reprint	*Cerebus: Flight (Mothers and Daughters, Book 1)*	Dave Sim and Gerhard
Best Graphic Album—New	*A Small Killing*	Alan Moore and Oscar Zarate
Best Cover Artist	*Animal Man; Wonder Woman; Legends of the Dark Knight #50*	Brian Bolland
Best Continuing Series	*Bone*	Jeff Smith
Best Comics-Related Publication	*Understanding Comics*	Scott McCloud
Best Coloring	*Spawn*	Steve Oliff and Reuben Rude (Olyoptics)
Best Archival Collection/Project	*Complete Little Nemo in Slumberland,* Volume 6	Winsor McCay
Best Anthology	*Dark Horse Presents*	edited by Randy Stradley

1995

Best Writer/Artist-Humor	*Bone*	Jeff Smith
Best Writer/Artist	*Hellboy: Seeds of Destruction*	Mike Mignola
Best Writer	*From Hell*	Alan Moore
Best Single Issue (or One-Shot)	*Batman Adventures Holiday Special*	Paul Dini, Bruce Timm, Ronnie Del Carmen, and others
Best Short Story	*"The Babe Wore Red"* in *Sin City: The Babe Wore Red and Other Stories*	Frank Miller
Best Serialized Story	*"The Life and Times of Scrooge McDuck"* in *Uncle Scrooge #285-296*	Don Rosa
Best Publication Design	*The Acme Novelty Library*	designed by Chris Ware
Best Penciller/Inker or Penciller/Inker Team	*Martha Washington Goes to War*	Dave Gibbons
Best Painter/Multimedia Artist	*Mystery Play*	Jon J. Muth

Best New Series	*Too Much Coffee Man*	Shannon Wheeler
Best Limited Series or Story Arc	*Sin City: A Dame to Kill For*	Frank Miller
Best Lettering	*Batman vs. Predator II; The Demon, Sandman; Uncle Scrooge*	Todd Klein
Best Humor Publication	*Bone*	Jeff Smith
Best Graphic Album—Reprint	*Hellboy: Seeds of Destruction*	Mike Mignola
Best Graphic Album—New	*Fairy Tales of Oscar Wilde, Volume 2*	P. Craig Russell
Best Cover Artist	*Hellblazer*	Glenn Fabry
Best Continuing Series	*Bone*	Jeff Smith
Best Comics-Related Publication	*Hero Illustrated*	
Best Coloring	*Martha Washington Goes to War*	Angus McKie
Best Archival Collection/Project	*The Christmas Spirit*	Will Eisner
Best Anthology	*Big Book of Urban Legends*	edited by Andy Helfer

1996

Best Writer/Artist—Humor	*Groo*	Sergio Aragonés
Best Writer/Artist—Drama	*Stray Bullets*	David Lapham
Best Writer	*From Hell*	Alan Moore
Best Single Issue (or One-Shot)	*Kurt Busiek's Astro City #4: "Safeguards"*	Kurt Busiek and Brent Anderson
Best Short Story	*"The Eltingville Comic-Book, Science-Fiction, Fantasy, Horror, and Role-Playing Club in Bring Me the Head of Boba Fett"* in *Instant Piano #3*	Evan Dorkin

Best Serialized Story	*Strangers in Paradise #1-8*	Terry Moore
Best Publication for a Younger Audience	*Batman & Robin Adventures*	Paul Dini, Ty Templeton, and Rick Burchett
Best Publication Design	*The Acme Novelty Library*	designed by Chris Ware
Best Penciller/Inker or Penciller/Inker Team	*The Big Guy and Rusty the Boy Robot*	Geof Darrow
Best Painter/Multimedia Artist	*Batman: Manbat*	John Bolton
Best New Series	*Kurt Busiek's Astro City*	Kurt Busiek and Brent Anderson
Best Limited Series or Story Arc	*Sin City: The Big Fat Kill*	Frank Miller
Best Lettering	*Groo; Usagi Yojimbo*	Stan Sakai
Best Humor Publication	*Milk & Cheese #666*	Evan Dorkin
Best Graphic Album—Reprint	*The Tale of One Bad Rat*	Bryan Talbot
Best Graphic Album—New	*Stuck Rubber Baby*	Howard Cruse
Best Cover Artist	*Kurt Busiek's Astro City*	Alex Ross
Best Continuing Series	*Acme Novelty Library*	Chris Ware
Best Comics-Related Periodical/ Journalism	*The Comics Journal*	
Best Comics-Related Book	*Alex Toth*	edited by Manuel Auad
Best Coloring	*The Acme Novelty Library*	Chris Ware
Best Archival Collection/Project	*The Complete Crumb Comics, Volume 11*	R. Crumb
Best Anthology	*The Big Book of Conspiracies*	edited by Bronwyn Taggart

1997

Best Writer/Artist—Humor	*Walt Disney's Comics & Stories; Uncle Scrooge*	Don Rosa
Best Writer/Artist—Drama	*Hellboy: Wake the Devil*	Mike Mignola
Best Writer	*From Hell; Supreme*	Alan Moore

Best Single Issue (or One-Shot)	*Kurt Busiek's Astro City, Volume 2, #1: "Welcome to Astro City"*	Kurt Busiek, Brent Anderson, and Will Blyberg
Best Short Story	*"Heroes," in Batman: Black & White #4*	Archie Goodwin and Gary Gianni
Best Serialized Story	*Starman #20-23: "Sand and Stars"*	James Robinson, Tony Harris, Guy Davis, and Wade von Grawbadger
Best Publication for a Younger Audience	*Leave It to Chance*	James Robinson and Paul Smith
Best Publication Design	*Acme Novelty Library #7*	designed by Chris Ware
Best Penciller/Inker or Penciller/Inker Team	*Book of Ballads and Sagas; Sandman #75*	Charles Vess
Best Penciller	*Nexus: Executioner's Song*	Steve Rude
Best Painter/Multimedia Artist	*Kingdom Come*	Alex Ross
Best New Series	*Leave It to Chance*	James Robinson and Paul Smith
Best Limited Series or Story Arc	*Kingdom Come*	Mark Waid and Alex Ross
Best Lettering	*The Sandman; Death: The Time of Your Life; House of Secrets; The Dreaming; Batman; The Spectre; Kingdom Come*	Todd Klein
Best Inker	*Spider-Man, Untold Tales of Spider-Man #17-18*	Al Williamson
Best Humor Publication	*Sergio Aragonés Destroys DC and Sergio Aragonés Massacres Marvel*	Mark Evanier and Sergio Aragonés
Best Graphic Album—Reprint	*Stray Bullets: Innocence of Nihilism*	David Lapham
Best Graphic Album—New	*Fax from Sarajevo*	Joe Kubert
Best Cover Artist	*Kingdom Come; Kurt Busiek's Astro City*	Alex Ross

Best Continuing Series	*Kurt Busiek's Astro City*	Kurt Busiek, Brent Anderson, and Will Blyberg
Best Comics-Related Periodical/ Journalism	*The Comics Journal*	
Best Comics-Related Book	*Graphic Storytelling*	Will Eisner
Best Coloring	*Preacher; Death: The Time of Your Life; Dr. Strangefate; Challengers of the Unknown*	Matt Hollingsworth
Best Archival Collection/Project	*Tarzan: The Land That Time Forgot and The Pool of Time*	Russ Manning
Best Anthology	*Batman: Black and White*	edited by Mark Chiarello and Scott Peterson

1998

Best Writer/Artist—Humor	*Bone*	Jeff Smith
Best Writer/Artist	*Hellboy: Almost Colossus; Hellboy Christmas Special; Hellboy Jr. Halloween Special*	Mike Mignola
Best Writer	*Hitman; Preacher; Unknown Soldier; Blood Mary: Lady Liberty*	Garth Ennis
Best U.S. Edition of International Material	*Gon Swimmin'*	Masahi Tanaka
Best Single Issue (or One-Shot)	*Kurt Busiek's Astro City Volume 2 #10: "Show 'Em All"*	Kurt Busiek, Brent Anderson, and Will Blyberg
Best Short Story	*"The Eltingville Comic Book, Science-Fiction, Fantasy, Horror and Role-Playing Club In: The Marathon Men" in Dork! #4*	Evan Dorkin
Best Serialized Story	*Kurt Busiek's Astro City, Volume 2, #4-9: "Confession"*	Kurt Busiek, Brent Anderson, and Will Blyberg
Best Publication for a Younger Audience	*Batman & Robin Adventures*	Ty Templeton, Brandon Kruse, Rick Burchett, and others

Best Publication Design	*Kingdom Come deluxe slip-cover edition*	art director Bob Chapman/DC design director Georg Brewer
Best Penciller/Inker or Penciller/Inker Team	*Elric: Stormbringer; Dr. Strange: What Is It That Disturbs You, Stephen?*	P. Craig Russell
Best Painter/Multimedia Artist	*Uncle Sam*	Alex Ross
Best New Series	*Castle Waiting*	Linda Medley
Best Limited Series or Story Arc	*Batman: The Long Halloween*	Jeph Loeb and Tim Sale
Best Lettering	*Batman, Batman: Poison Ivy; The Dreaming, House of Secrets, The Invisibles, Uncle Sam; Uncle Scrooge Adventures; Castle Waiting*	Todd Klein
Best Humor Publication	*Gon Swimmin'*	Masahi Tanaka
Best Graphic Album—Reprint	*Sin City: That Yellow Bastard*	Frank Miller
Best Graphic Album—New	*Batman & Superman Adventures: World's Finest*	Paul Dini, Joe Staton, and Terry Beatty
Best Cover Artist	*Kurt Busiek's Astro City; Uncle Sam*	Alex Ross
Best Continuing Series	*Kurt Busiek's Astro City*	Kurt Busiek, Brent Anderson, and Will Blyberg
Best Comics-Related Periodical/Journalism	*The Comics Journal*	
Best Comics-Related Book	*The R. Crumb Coffee Table Art Book*	edited by Pete Poplaski
Best Coloring	*The Acme Novelty Library*	Chris Ware
Best Archival Collection/Project	*Jack Kirby's New Gods*	Jack Kirby
Best Anthology	*Hellboy Christmas Special*	edited by Scott Allie

1999

Best Writer/Artist—Humor	*You Are Here*	Kyle Baker
Best Writer/Artist	*300*	Frank Miller

Best Writer	*Kurt Busiek's Astro City; Avengers*	Kurt Busiek
Best U.S. Edition of International Material	*Star Wars: A New Hope—Manga*	Hisao Tamaki
Best Single Issue (or One-Shot)	*Hitman #34: "Of Thee I Sing"*	Garth Ennis, John McCrea, and Garry Leach
Best Short Story	*"Devil's Advocate" in Grendel: Black, White, and Red #1*	Matt Wagner and Tim Sale
Best Serialized Story	*Usagi Yojimbo #13-22: "Grasscutter"*	Stan Sakai
Best Publication for a Younger Audience	*Batman: The Gotham Adventures*	Ty Templeton, Rick Burchett, and Terry Beatty
Best Publication Design	*Batman Animated*	designed by Chip Kidd
Best Penciller/Inker or Penciller/Inker Team	*Superman for All Seasons; Grendel Black, White, and Red #1*	Tim Sale
Best Painter/Multimedia Artist	*Superman: Peace on Earth*	Alex Ross
Best New Series	*Inhumans*	Paul Jenkins and Jae Lee
Best Limited Series or Story Arc	*300*	Frank Miller and Lynn Varley
Best Lettering	*Castle Waiting; House of Secrets; The Invisibles; The Dreaming, etc.*	Todd Klein
Best Humor Publication	*Groo*	Sergio Aragonés and Mark Evanier
Best Graphic Album—Reprint	*Batman: The Long Halloween*	Jeph Loeb and Tim Sale
Best Graphic Album—New	*Superman: Peace on Earth*	Paul Dini and Alex Ross
Best Cover Artist	*The Invisibles*	Brian Bolland
Best Continuing Series	*Preacher*	Garth Ennis and Steve Dillon
Best Comics-Related Periodical/Journalism	*The Comics Journal*	
Best Comics-Related Book	*Batman: Animated*	Paul Dini and Chip Kidd
Best Coloring	*300*	Lynn Varley

| Best Archival Collection/Project | *Plastic Man Archives,* Volume 1 | Jack Cole |
| Best Anthology | *Grendel: Black, White, and Red* | Matt Wagner, edited by Diana Schutz |

2000

Best Writer/Artist—Humor	*I Die at Midnight;* "Letitia Lerner, Superbaby's Baby-sitter" in *Elseworlds 80-Page Giant*	Kyle Baker
Best Writer/Artist	*Eightball*	Dan Clowes
Best Writer	*League of Extraordinary Gentlemen, Promethea, Tom Strong, Tomorrow Stories, Top Ten*	Alan Moore
Best U.S. Edition of International Material	*Blade of the Immortal*	Hiroaki Samura
Best Single Issue (or One-Shot)	*Tom Strong #1:* "How Tom Strong Got Started"	Alan Moore, Chris Sprouse, and Al Gordon
Best Short Story	"Letitia Lerner, Superman's Baby Sitter" in *Elseworlds 80-Page Giant*	Kyle Baker
Best Serialized Story	*Tom Strong #4-7*	(Saveen/Ingrid Weiss time travel arc) by Alan Moore, Chris Sprouse, Al Gordon, and guest artists
Best Publication for a Younger Audience	*Simpsons Comics*	various
Best Publication Design	*300*	designed by Mark Cox
Best Penciller/Inker or Penciller/Inker Team	"Jack B. Quick" in *Tomorrow Stories*	Kevin Nowlan
Best Painter/Multimedia Artist	*Batman: War on Crime*	Alex Ross
Best New Series	*Top Ten*	Alan Moore, Gene Ha, and Zander Cannon
Best Limited Series or Story Arc	*Whiteout: Melt*	Greg Rucka and Steve Lieber

Best Lettering	*Promethea, Tom Strong, Tomorrow Stories, Top Ten; The Dreaming, Gifts of the Night, The Invisibles, Sandman Presents: Lucifer*	Todd Klein
Best Humor Publication	*Bart Simpson's Treehouse of Horror*	Jill Thompson, Oscar González Loyo, Steve Steere Jr., Scott Shaw!, Sergio Aragonés, and Doug TenNapel
Best Graphic Album—Reprint	*From Hell*	Alan Moore and Eddie Campbell
Best Graphic Album—New	*Acme Novelty Library #13*	Chris Ware
Best Cover Artist	*Batman: No Man's Land; Batman: Harley Quinn; Batman: War on Crime; Kurt Busiek's Astro City; ABC Alternate #1 covers*	Alex Ross
Best Continuing Series	*Acme Novelty Library*	Chris Ware
Best Comics-Related Periodical/ Journalism	*Comic Book Artist*	
Best Comics-Related Book	*The Sandman: The Dream Hunters*	Neil Gaiman and Yoshitaka Amano
Best Coloring	*The Authority; Planetary*	Laura Dupuy
Best Archival Collection/Project	*Peanuts: A Golden Celebration*	
Best Anthology	*Tomorrow Stories*	Alan Moore, Rick Veitch, Kevin Nowlan, Melinda Gebbie, and Jim Baikie

2001

Best Writer/Artist—Humor	*Maakies, Sock Monkey*	Tony Millionaire
Best Writer/Artist	*Age of Bronze*	Eric Shanower
Best Writer	*The League of Extraordinary Gentlemen, Promethea, Tom Strong, Top Ten, Tomorrow Stories*	Alan Moore
Best U.S. Edition of International Material	*Lone Wolf and Cub*	Kazuo Koike and Goseki Kojima

Best Single Issue (or One-Shot)	*Promethea #10: "Sex, Stars, and Serpents"*	Alan Moore, J. H. Williams III, and Mick Gray
Best Short Story	*"The Gorilla Suit" in Street-wise*	Sergio Aragonés
Best Serialized Story	*100 Bullets #15-18: "Hang Up on the Hang Low"*	Brian Azzarello and Eduardo Risso
Best Publication for a Younger Audience	*Scary Godmother: The Boo Flu*	Jill Thompson
Best Publication Design	*Jimmy Corrigan*	designed by Chris Ware
Best Penciller/Inker or Penciller/Inker Team	*Ring of the Nibelung*	P. Craig Russell
Best Painter/Multimedia Artist	*Scary Godmother*	Jill Thompson
Best New Series	*Powers*	Brian Michael Bendis and Michael Avon Oeming
Best Limited Series or Story Arc	*The Ring of the Nibelung*	P. Craig Russell, with Patrick Mason
Best Lettering	*Promethea, Tom Strong, Tomorrow Stories, Top 10; The Invisibles Dreaming; Castle Waiting*	Todd Klein
Best Humor Publication	*Sock Monkey,* Volume 3	Tony Millionaire
Best Graphic Album—Reprint	*Jimmy Corrigan*	Chris Ware
Best Graphic Album—New	*Safe Area Goražde*	Joe Sacco
Best Cover Artist	*Batman: Gotham Knights; The Flash; The Invisible*	Brian Bolland
Best Continuing Series	*Top 10*	Alan Moore, Gene Ha, and Zander Cannon
Best Comics-Related Book	*Wonder Woman: The Complete History*	Les Daniels
Best Coloring	*Acme Novelty Library #14*	Chris Ware
Best Archival Collection/Project	*The Spirit Archives,* Volumes 1 and 2	Will Eisner
Best Anthology	*Drawn & Quarterly,* Volume 3	edited by Chris Oliveros

2002

Best Writer/Artist—Humor	*Dork*	Evan Dorkin
Best Writer/Artist	*Eightball*	Dan Clowes
Best Writer	*Powers; Alias; Daredevil; Ultimate Spider-Man*	Brian Michael Bendis
Best U.S. Edition of International Material	*Akira*	Katsuhiro Otomo
Best Single Issue (or One-Shot)	*Eightball #22*	Dan Clowes
Best Short Story	*"The Eltingville Club in 'The Intervention'"* in *Dork #9*	Evan Dorkin
Best Serialized Story	*Amazing Spider-Man #30-35: "Coming Home"*	J. Michael Straczynski, John Romita Jr., and Scott Hanna
Best Publication for a Younger Audience	*Herobear and the Kid*	Mike Kunkel
Best Publication Design	*Acme Novelty Library #15*	designed by Chris Ware
Best Penciller/Inker or Penciller/Inker Team	*100 Bullets*	Eduardo Risso
Best Painter/Multimedia Artist	*Rose*	Charles Vess
Best New Series	*Queen & Country*	Greg Rucka and Steve Rolston
Best Limited Series or Story Arc	*Hellboy: Conqueror Worm*	Mike Mignola
Best Lettering	*Promethea; Tom Strong's Terrific Tales; Tomorrow Stories; Top 10; Greyshirt; The Sandman Presents: Everything You Always Wanted to Know About Dreams But Were Afraid to Ask; Detective Comics; The Dark Knight Strikes Again; Castle W*	Todd Klein
Best Humor Publication	*Radioactive Man*	Batton Lash, Abel Laxamana, Dan De Carlo, Mike DeCarlo, and Bob Smith
Best Graphic Album—Reprint	*Batman: Dark Victory*	Jeph Loeb and Tim Sale
Best Graphic Album—New	*The Name of the Game*	Will Eisner
Best Cover Artist	*Detective Comics; 100 Bullets*	Dave Johnson

Best Continuing Series	*100 Bullets*	Brian Azzarello and Eduardo Risso
Best Comics-Related Periodical/ Journalism	*Comic Book Artist*	edited by Jon Cooke
Best Comics-Related Book	*Peanuts: The Art of Charles M. Schulz*	edited by Chip Kidd
Best Coloring	*Ruse; Ministry of Space*	Laura DePuy
Best Archival Collection/Project	*Akira*	Katsuhiro Otomo
Best Anthology	*Bizarro Comics*	edited by Joey Cavalieri

2003

Best Writer/Artist—Humor	*House at Maakies Corner*	Tony Millionaire
Best Writer/Artist	*Age of Bronze*	Eric Shanower
Best Writer	*Powers; Alias; Daredevil; Ultimate Spider-Man*	Brian Michael Bendis
Best U.S. Edition of International Material	*Dr. Jekyll & Mr. Hyde*	Robert Louis Stevenson, adapted by Jerry Kramsky and Lorenzo Mattotti
Best Single Issue (or One-Shot)	*The Stuff of Dreams*	Kim Deitch
Best Short Story	*"The Magician and the Snake"* in *Dark Horse Maverick: Happy Endings*	Katie Mignola and Mike Mignola
Best Serialized Story	*Fables #1-5: "Legends in Exile"*	Bill Willingham, Lan Medina, and Steve Leialoha
Best Publication for a Younger Audience	*Herobear and the Kid*	Mike Kunkel
Best Publication Design	*Batman: Nine Lives*	designed by Amie Brockway-Metcalf
Best Penciller/Inker or Penciller/ Inker Team	*League of Extraordinary Gentlemen*	Kevin O'Neill
Best Painter/Multimedia Artist	*Wolverine: Netsuke*	George Pratt
Best New Series	*Fables*	Bill Willingham, Lan Medina, Mark Buckingham, and Steve Leialoha

Best Limited Series or Story Arc	*League of Extraordinary Gentlemen,* Volume 2	Alan Moore and Kevin O'Neill
Best Lettering	*Dark Knight Strikes Again; Detective Comics; Wonder Woman: The Hiketeia; Fables; Human Target: Final Cut; Promethea; Tom Strong; Castle Waiting*	Todd Klein
Best Humor Publication	*The Amazing Screw-On Head*	Mike Mignola
Best Graphic Album—Reprint	*Batman: Black and White,* Volume 2	edited by Mark Chiarello and Nick J. Napolitano
Best Graphic Album—New	*One! Hundred! Demons!*	Lynda Barry
Best Cover Artist	*Wonder Woman*	Adam Hughes
Best Continuing Series	*Daredevil*	Brian Michael Bendis and Alex Maleev
Best Comics-Related Publication (Periodical or Book)	*B. Krigstein,* Volume 1	Greg Sadowski
Best Coloring	*Hellboy: Third Wish; The Amazing Screw-on Head; Star Wars: Empire; Human Target: Final Cut; Doom Patrol; Tom Strong; Captain America*	Dave Stewart
Best Archival Collection/Project	*Krazy & Ignatz*	George Herriman
Best Anthology	*SPX 2002*	

2004

Best Writer/Artist—Humor	*Plastic Man; The New Baker*	Kyle Baker
Best Writer/Artist	*Blankets*	Craig Thompson
Best Writer	*The League of Extraordinary Gentlemen; Promethea; Smax, Tom Strong; Tom Strong's Terrific Tales*	Alan Moore
Best U.S. Edition of International Material	*Buddha,* Volumes 1 and 2	Osamu Tezuka
Best Single Issue (or One-Shot)	*Conan: The Legend #0*	Kurt Busiek and Cary Nord

Best Single Issue (or One-Shot)	*The Goon #1*	Eric Powell
Best Short Story	*"Death"* in *The Sandman: Endless Nights*	Neil Gaiman and P. Craig Russell
Best Serialized Story	*Gotham Central #6-10: "Half a Life"*	Greg Rucka and Michael Lark
Best Publication for a Younger Audience	*Walt Disney's Uncle Scrooge*	various
Best Publication Design	*Mythology: The DC Comics Art of Alex Ross*	designed by Chip Kidd
Best Penciller/Inker or Penciller/Inker Team	*Planetary; Planetary/Batman: Night on Earth; Hellboy Weird Tales*	John Cassaday
Best Painter/Multimedia Artist	*"Stray"* in *The Dark Horse Book of Hauntings*	Jill Thompson
Best New Series	*Plastic Man*	Kyle Baker
Best Limited Series or Story Arc	*Unstable Molecules*	James Sturm and Guy Davis
Best Lettering	*Detective Comics; Fables; The Sandman: Endless Nights; Tom Strong; Promethea; 1602*	Todd Klein
Best Humor Publication	*Formerly Known as the Justice League*	Keith Giffen, J. M. DeMatteis, Kevin Maguire, and Joe Rubinstein
Best Graphic Album—Reprint	*Batman Adventures: Dangerous Dames and Demons*	Paul Dini, Bruce Timm, and others
Best Graphic Album—New	*Blankets*	Craig Thompson
Best Cover Artist	*Batgirl; Fables*	James Jean
Best Continuing Series	*100 Bullets*	Brian Azzarello and Eduardo Risso
Best Comics-Related Periodical/Journalism	*Comic Book Artist*	edited by Jon B. Cooke
Best Comics-Related Book	*The Art of Hellboy*	Mike Mignola
Best Coloring	*Batman; Wonder Woman; 100 Bullets*	Patricia Mulvihill

Best Archival Collection/Project	*Krazy and Ignatz, 1929-1930*	George Herriman, edited by Bill Blackbeard
Best Anthology	*The Sandman: Endless Nights*	Neil Gaiman and others, edited by Karen Berger and Shelly Bond

2005

Best Writer/Artist—Humor	*Plastic Man*	Kyle Baker
Best Writer/Artist	*Concrete: The Human Dilemma*	Paul Chadwick
Best Writer	*Y: The Last Man; Ex Machina; Runaways*	Brian K. Vaughan
Best U.S. Edition of Foreign Material	*Buddha,* Volumes 3-4	Osamu Tezuka
Best Single Issue (or One-Shot)	*Eightball #23: "The Death Ray,"*	Dan Clowes
Best Short Story	*"Unfamiliar"* in *The Dark Horse Book of Witchcraft*	Evan Dorkin and Jill Thompson
Best Serialized Story	*Fables #19-27: "March of the Wooden Soldiers"*	Bill Willingham, Mark Buckingham, and Steve Leialoha
Best Publication Design	*The Complete Peanuts*	designed by Seth
Best Penciller/Inker	*Astonishing X-Men; Planetary; I Am Legion: The Dancing Faun*	John Cassaday
Best Penciller/Inker	*WE3*	Frank Quitely
Best Painter/Multimedia Artist (interior art)	*It's a Bird...*	Teddy Kristiansen
Best New Series	*Ex Machina*	Brian K. Vaughan, Tony Harris, and Tom Fesiter
Best Limited Series	*DC: The New Frontier*	Darwyn Cooke
Best Lettering	*Promethea; Tom Strong; Tom Strong's Terrific Tales; Wonder Woman; Books of Magick: Life During Wartime; Fables; WE3; Creatures of the Night*	Todd Klein
Best Humor Publication	*The Goon*	Eric Powell

Best Graphic Album—Reprint	*Bone One Volume Edition*	Jeff Smith
Best Graphic Album—New	*The Originals*	Dave Gibbons
Best Digital Comic	*Mom's Cancer*	Brian Fies
Best Cover Artist	*Fables; Green Arrow; Batgirl*	James Jean
Best Continuing Series	*The Goon*	Eric Powell
Best Comics-Related Periodical	*Comic Book Artist*	edited by Jon B. Cooke
Best Comics-Related Book	*Men of Tomorrow: Geeks, Gangsters, and the Birth of the Comic Book*	Gerard Jones
Best Coloring	*Daredevil; Ultimate X-Men; Ultimate Six; Captain America; Conan; BPRD; DC: The New Frontier*	Dave Stewart
Best Archival Collection/Project	*The Complete Peanuts*	edited by Gary Groth
Best Anthology	*Michael Chabon Presents The Amazing Adventures of the Escapist*	edited by Diana Schutz and David Land

2006

Best Writer/Artist—Humor	*Plastic Man; The Bakers*	Kyle Baker
Best Writer/Artist	*Shaolin Cowboy*	Geof Darrow
Best Writer	*Promethea; Top Ten: The Forty-Niners*	Alan Moore
Best U.S. Edition of Foreign Material	*The Rabbi's Cat*	Joann Sfar
Best Single Issue (or One-Shot)	*Solo #5*	Darwyn Cooke
Best Short Story	*"Teenage Sidekick" in Solo #3*	Paul Pope
Best Serialized Story	*Fables #36-38, 40-41 "Return to the Homelands"*	Bill Willingham, Mark Buckingham, and Steve Leialoha
Best Reality-Based Work	*It Was the War of the Trenches*	Kyle Baker
Best Publication for a Younger Audience	*Owly: Flying Lessons*	Andy Runton

Best Publication Design (tie)	*Acme Novelty Library Annual Report to Shareholders*	Chris Ware
Best Publication Design (tie)	*Little Nemo in Slumberland: So Many Splendid Sundays*	Philippe Ghielmetti
Best Penciller/Inker	*Astonishing X-Men; Planetary*	John Cassaday
Best Painter/Multimedia Artist (interior art)	*Hip Flask: Mystery City*	Ladronn
Best New Series	*All Star Superman*	Grant Morrison and Frank Quitely
Best Limited Series	*Seven Soldiers*	Grant Morrison and various artists
Best Lettering	*Wonder Woman; Justice; Seven Soldiers #0; Desolation Jones; Promethea; Top Ten: The Forty- Niners; Tomorrow Stories Special; Fables; 1602: New World*	Todd Klein
Best Graphic Album—Reprint	*Black Hole*	Charles Burns
Best Graphic Album—New	*Top Ten: The Forty Niners*	Alan Moore and Gene Ha
Best Digital Comic	*PVP*	Scott Kurtz
Best Cover Artist	*Fables; Runaways*	James Jean
Best Continuing Series	*Astonishing X-Men*	Joss Whedon and John Cassaday
Best Comics-Related Periodical	*Comic Book Artist*	edited by Jon B. Cooke
Best Comics-Related Book	*Eisner/Miller*	edited by Charles Brownstein and Diana Schutz
Best Coloring	*Acme Novelty Library #16*	Chris Ware
Best Archival Collection/Project—Strips	*The Complete Calvin & Hobbes*	Bill Watterson
Best Archival Collection/Project—Comic Books	*Absolute Watchmen*	Alan Moore and Dave Gibbons
Best Anthology	*Solo*	edited by Mark Chiarello

2007

Best Writer/Artist—Humor	*Billy Hazelnuts; Sock Monkey: The Inches Incident*	Tony Millionaire
Best Writer/Artist	*Batman: Year 100*	Paul Pope
Best Writer	*Captain America; Daredevil; Criminal*	Ed Brubaker
Best U.S. Edition of International Material—Japan	*Old Boy*	Garon Tsuchiya and Nobuaki Minegishi
Best U.S. Edition of International Material	*The Left Bank Gang*	Jason
Best Single Issue (or One-Shot)	*Batman/The Spirit #1: "Crime Convention"*	Jeph Loeb and Darwyn Cooke
Best Short Story	*"A Frog's Eye View"* in *Fables: 1001 Nights of Snowfall*	Bill Willingham and James Jean
Best Reality-Based Work	*Fun Home*	Alison Bechdel
Best Publication for a Younger Audience	*Gumby*	Bob Burden and Rick Geary
Best Publication Design	*Absolute DC: The New Frontier*	Darwyn Cooke
Best Penciller/Inker or Penciller/Inker Team	*Fables*	Mark Buckingham/Steve Leialoha
Best Painter/Multimedia Artist (interior art)	*"A Dog and His Boy"* in The Dark Horse Book of Monsters; *"Love Triangle"* in Sexy Chix; *"Fair Division,"* in Fables: 1001 Nights of Snowfall	Jill Thompson
Best New Series	*Criminal*	Ed Brubaker and Sean Phillips
Best Limited Series or Story Arc	*Batman: Year 100*	Paul Pope
Best Lettering	*Fables; Jack of Fables; Fables: 1001 Nights of Snowfall; Pride of Baghdad; Testament; Fantastic Four: 1602; Eternals; Lost Girls*	Todd Klein
Best Humor Publication	*Flaming Carrot Comics*	Bob Burden

Best Graphic Album—Reprint	*Absolute DC: the New Frontier*	Darwyn Cooke
Best Graphic Album—New	*American Born Chinese*	Gene Luen Yang
Best Digital Comic	*Sam and Max*	Steve Purcell
Best Cover Artist	*Fables, Jack of Fables; Fables: 1001 Nights of Snowfall*	James Jean
Best Continuing Series	*All Star Superman*	Grant Morrison and Frank Quitel
Best Comics-Related Periodical/ Journalism	*Alter Ego*	edited by Roy Thomas
Best Comics-Related Book	*The Art of Brian Bolland*	Joe Pruett
Best Coloring	*BPRD; Conan; The Escapists; Hellboy; Action Comics; Batman/The Spirit; Superman*	Dave Stewart
Best Archival Collection/Project— Strips	The Complete Peanuts, 1959-1960, 1961-1962	Charles Schulz
Best Archival Collection/Project— Comic Books	*Absolute Sandman*, Volume 1	Neil Gaiman and various
Best Anthology	*Fables: 1001 Nights of Snowfall*	Bill Willingham and various

2008

Best Writer/Artist—Humor	*The Goon*	Eric Powell
Best Writer/Artist	*Acme Novelty Library #18*	Chris Ware
Best Writer	*Captain America; Criminal; Daredevil; Immortal Iron Fist*	Ed Brubaker
Best U.S. Edition of International Material—Japan	*Tekkonkinkreet: Black & White*	Taiyo Matsumoto
Best U.S. Edition of International Material	*I Killed Adolf Hitler*	Jason
Best Single Issue (or One-Shot)	*Justice League of America #11: "Walls"*	Brad Meltzer and Gene Ha
Best Short Story	*"Mr. Wonderful"* in *New York Times Sunday Magazine*	Daniel Clowes

Best Reality-Based Work	*Satchel Paige: Striking Out Jim Crow*	James Sturm and Rich Tommaso
Best Publication for Teens	*Laika*	Nick Abadzis
Best Publication for Kids	*Mouse Guard: Fall 1152* and *Mouse Guard: Winter 1152*	David Petersen
Best Publication Design	*Process Recess 2*	James Jean and Chris Pitzer
Best Penciller/Inker or Penciller/Inker Team	*Y: The Last Man*	Pia Guerra/Jose Marzan, Jr.
Best Painter/Multimedia Artist (interior art)	*The Goon: Chinatown*	Eric Powell
Best New Series	*Buffy the Vampire Slayer, Season 8*	Joss Whedon, Brian K. Vaughan, Georges Jeanty, and Andy Owens
Best Limited Series or Story Arc	*The Umbrella Academy*	Gerard Way and Gabriel Bá
Best Lettering	*Justice, Simon Dark; Fables, Jack of Fables; Crossing Midnight; League of Extraordinary Gentlemen: The Black Dossier; Nexus*	Todd Klein
Best Humor Publication	*Perry Bible Fellowship: The Trial of Colonel Sweeto and Other Stories*	Nicholas Gurewitch
Best Graphic Album—Reprint	*Mouse Guard: Fall 1152*	David Petersen
Best Graphic Album—New	*Exit Wounds*	Rutu Modan
Best Digital Comic	*Sugarshock!*	Joss Whedon and Fabio Moon
Best Cover Artist	*Fables; The Umbrella Academy; Process Recess 2; Superior Showcase 2*	James Jean
Best Continuing Series	*Y: The Last Man*	Brian K. Vaughan, Pia Guerra, and Jose Marzan, Jr.
Best Comics-Related Periodical/Journalism	*Newsarama*	produced by Matt Brady and Michael Doran
Best Comics-Related Book	*Reading Comics: How Graphic Novels Work and What They Mean*	Douglas Wolk

Best Coloring	*BPRD; Buffy the Vampire Slayer; Cut; Hellboy; Lobster Johnson; The Umbrella Academy; The Spirit*	Dave Stewart
Best Archival Collection/Project—Strips	*Complete Terry and the Pirates,* Volume 1	Milton Caniff
Best Archival Collection/Project—Comic Books	*I Shall Destroy All the Civilized Planets!*	Fletcher Hanks
Best Anthology	*5*	Gabriel Bá, Becky Cloonan, Fabio Moon, Vasilis Lolos, and Rafael Grampa

2009

Best Writer/Artist	*Acme Novelty Library #19*	Chris Ware
Best Writer	*Fables, House of Mystery*	Bill Willingham
Best U.S. Edition of International Material—Japan	*Dororo*	Osamu Tezuka
Best U.S. Edition of International Material	*The Last Musketeer*	Jason
Best Short Story	*"Murder He Wrote"* in *The Simpsons' Treehouse of Horror #14*	Ian Boothby, Nina Matsumoto, and Andrew Pepoy
Best Reality-Based Work	*What It Is*	Lynda Barry
Best Publication for Teens	*Coraline*	Neil Gaiman, adapted by P. Craig Russell
Best Publication for Kids	*Tiny Titans*	Art Baltazar and Franco
Best Publication Design	*Hellboy Library Editions*	Cary Grazzini and Mike Mignola
Best Penciller/Inker or Penciller/Inker Team	*BPRD*	Guy Davis
Best Painter/Multimedia Artist (interior art)	*Magic Trixie; Magic Trixie Sleeps Over*	Jill Thompson
Best New Series	*Invincible Iron Man*	Matt Fraction and Salvador Larocca
Best Limited Series or Story Arc	*Hellboy: The Crooked Man*	Mike Mignola and Richard Corben

Best Lettering	*Acme Novelty Library #19*	Chris Ware
Best Humor Publication	*Herbie Archives*	"Shane O'Shea" (Richard E. Hughes) and Ogden Whitney
Best Graphic Album—Reprint	*Hellboy Library Edition*, Volumes 1 and 2	Mike Mignola
Best Graphic Album—New	*Swallow Me Whole*	Nate Powell
Best Digital Comic	*Finder*	Carla Speed McNeil
Best Cover Artist	*Fables; The Umbrella Academy*	James Jean
Best Continuing Series	*All Star Superman*	Grant Morrison and Frank Quitely
Best Comics-Related Periodical/Journalism	*Comic Book Resources*	produced by Jonah Weiland
Best Comics-Related Book	*Kirby: King of Comics*	Mark Evanier
Best Coloring	*Abe Sapien: The Drowning; BPRD; The Goon; Hellboy; Solomon Kane; The Umbrella Academy; Body Bags; Captain America: White*	Dave Stewart
Best Archival Collection/Project—Strips	*Little Nemo in Slumberland: Many More Splendid Sundays*	Winsor McCay
Best Archival Collection/Project—Comic Books	*Creepy Archives*	
Best Anthology	*Comic Book Tattoo: Narrative Art Inspired by the Lyrics and Music of Tori Amos*	edited by Rantz Hoseley

2010

Best Writer/Artist–Nonfiction	*Footnotes in Gaza*	Joe Sacco
Best Writer/Artist	*Asterios Polyp*	David Mazzucchelli
Best Writer	*Captain America; Daredevil; Marvels Project; Criminal; Incognito*	Ed Brubaker
Best U.S. Edition of International Material—Asia	*A Drifting Life*	Yoshihiro Tatsumi

Best U.S. Edition of International Material	*The Photographer*	Emmanuel Guibert, Didier Lefevre, and Frédéric Lemerier
Best Single Issue (or One-Shot)	*Captain America #601: "Red, White, and Blue-Blood"*	Ed Brubaker and Gene Colan
Best Short Story	*"Urgent Request" in The Eternal Smile*	Gene Luen Yang and Derek Kirk Kim
Best Reality-Based Work	*A Drifting Life*	Yoshihiro Tatsumi
Best Publication for Teens	*Beasts of Burden*	Evan Dorkin and Jill Thompson
Best Publication for Kids	*The Wonderful Wizard of Oz hc*	L. Frank Baum, Eric Shanower, and Skottie Young
Best Publication Design	*Absolute Justice*	Curtis King and Josh Beatman
Best Penciller/Inker or Penciller/ Inker Team	*Detective Comics*	J. H. Williams III
Best Painter/Multimedia Artist (interior art)	*Beasts of Burden; Magic Trixie and the Dragon*	Jill Thompson
Best New Series	*Chew*	John Layman and Rob Guillor
Best Limited Series or Story Arc	*The Wonderful Wizard of Oz*	Eric Shanower and Skottie Young
Best Lettering	*Asterios Polyp*	David Mazzuccheilli
Best Humor Publication	*Scott Pilgrim* Volume 5: *Scott Pilgrim vs. the Universe*	Bryan Lee O'Malley
Best Graphic Album—Reprint	*Absolute Justice*	Alex Ross, Jim Krueger, and Doug Braithewaite
Best Graphic Album—New	*Asterios Polyp*	David Mazzucchelli
Best Digital Comic	*Sin Titulo*	Cameron Stewart
Best Cover Artist	*Detective Comics*	J. H. Williams III
Best Continuing Series	*The Walking Dead*	Robert Kirkman and Charles Adlard
Best Comics-Related Periodical/ Journalism	*The Comics Reporter*	produced by Tom Spurgeon
Best Comics-Related Book	*The Art of Harvey Kurtzman: The Mad Genius of Comics*	Denis Kitchen and Paul Buhle

Best Coloring	*Abe Sapien; BPRD; The Goon; Hellboy; Solomon Kane; Umbrella Academy; Zero Killer; Detective Comics; Luna Park*	Dave Stewart
Best Archival Collection/Project—Strips	*Bloom County: The Complete Library,* Volume 1	Berkeley Breathed, edited by Scott Dunbier
Best Archival Collection/Project—Comic Books	*The Rocketeer: The Complete Adventures deluxe ed.*	Dave Stevens, edited by Scott Dunbier
Best Anthology	*Popgun* Volume 3	edited by Mark Andrew Smith, D. J. Kirkbride, and Joe Keatinge
Best Adaptation from Another Work	*Richard Stark's Parker: The Hunter*	Darwyn Cooke

2011

Best Writer/Artist	*Richard Stark's Parker: The Outfit*	Darwyn Cooke
Best Writer	*Lock & Key*	Joe Hill
Best U.S. Edition of International Material—Asia	*Naoki Urasawa's 20th Century Boys*	Naoki Urasawa
Best U.S. Edition of International Material	*It Was the War of the Trenches*	Jacques Tardi
Best Single Issue (or One-Shot)	*Hellboy: Double Feature of Evil*	Mike Mignola and Richard Corben
Best Short Story	*"Post Mortem" in I Am an Avenger #2*	Greg Rucka and Michael Lark
Best Reality-Based Work	*It Was the War of the Trenches*	Jacques Tardi
Best Publication for Teens	*Smile*	Raina Telgemeier
Best Publication for Kids	*Tiny Titans*	Art Baltazar and Franco
Best Publication Design	*Dave Stevens' The Rocketeer Artist's Edition*	designed by Randall Dahlk
Best Penciller/Inker or Penciller/Inker Team	*The Marvelous Land of Oz*	Skottie Young
Best Painter/Multimedia Artist (interior art)	*Blacksad*	Juanjo Guarnido

Best New Series	*American Vampire*	Scott Snyder, Stephen King, and Rafael Albuquerque
Best Limited Series	*Daytripper*	Fábio Moon and Gabriel Bá
Best Lettering	*Fables; The Unwritten; Joe the Barbarian; iZombie; Tom Strong and the Robots of Doom; SHIELD; Driver for the Dead*	Todd Klein
Best Humor Publication	*I Thought You Would Be Funnier*	Shannon Wheeler
Best Graphic Album—Reprint	*Wednesday Comics*	edited by Mark Chiarello
Best Graphic Album—New	*Return of the Dapper Men*	Jim McCann and Janet Lee
Best Graphic Album—New	*Wilson*	Daniel Clowes
Best Digital Comic	*Abominable Charles Christopher*	Karl Kerschl
Best Cover Artist	*Hellboy; Baltimore: The Plague Ships*	Mike Mignola
Best Continuing Series	*Chew*	John Layman and Rob Guillory
Best Comics-Related Periodical/Journalism	*Comic Book Resources*	produced by Jonah Weiland
Best Comics-Related Book	*75 Years of DC Comics: The Art of Modern Mythmaking*	Paul Levitz
Best Coloring	*Hellboy; BPRD; Baltimore; Let Me In; Detective Comics; Neil Young's Greendale; Daytripper; Joe the Barbarian*	Dave Stewart
Best Archival Collection/Project—Strips	*Archie: The Complete Daily Newspaper Strips, 1946–1948*	Bob Montana, edited by Greg Goldstein
Best Archival Collection/Project—Comic Books	*Dave Stevens' The Rocketeer Artist's Edition*	edited by Scott Dunbier
Best Anthology	*Mouse Guard: Legends of the Guard*	edited by Paul Morrissey and David Petersen
Best Adaptation from Another Work	*The Marvelous Land of Oz*	L. Frank Baum, adapted by Eric Shanower and Skottie Young

Glyph Comics Awards

Presented annually at the East Coast Black Age of Comics Convention, the Glyph Comics Awards were established in 2006 to honor the best works published in the comic industry which are either created by or are about people of color.

2006

Story of the Year	*Nat Turner*	Kyle Baker, writer and artist
Best Writer	*Lucifer's Garden of Verses: Darlin' Niki*	Lance Tooks
Best Artist	*Nat Turner*	Kyle Baker
Best Male Character	*Huey Freeman; The Boondocks*	
Best Female Character	*Darlin' Niki, Lucifer's Garden of Verses: Darlin' Niki*	Lance Tooks
Rising Star Award	*The Roach*	Robert Roach
Best Reprint Publication	*Birth of a Nation*	
Best Cover	*Nat Turner #1*	Kyle Baker, illustrator
Best Comic Strip or Webcomic	*The K Chronicles*	Keith Knight, writer and artist
Fan Award for Best Comic	*Black Panther: Who Is the Black Panther?*	Reginald Hudlin, John Romita, Jr., Klaus Janson, Axel Alonso

2007

Story of the Year	*Stagger Lee*	Derek McCulloch, writer, Shepherd Hendrix, artist
Best Writer	*Stagger Lee*	Derek McCulloch
Best Artist	*The Bakers*	Kyle Baker
Best Male Character	*Stagger Lee, Stagger Lee*	Derek McCulloch, writer, Shepherd Hendrix, artist; inspired by the life of Lee Shelton
Best Female Character	*Thomasina Lindo, Welcome to Tranquility*	co-created by Gail Simone, writer, Neil Googe, artist
Rising Star Award	*Templar, Arizona*	*Spike*
Best Reprint Publication	*Deogratias: A Tale of Rwanda*	

Best Cover	*Stagger Lee*	Shepherd Hendrix, artist
Best Comic Strip or Webcomic	*The K Chronicles*	Keith Knight, writer and artist
Fan Award for Best Comic	*Storm*	Eric Jerome Dickey, David Yardin & Lan Medina and Jay Leisten & Sean Parsons

2008

Story of the Year	*Sentences: The Life of MF Grimm*	Percy Carey, writer, Ronald Wimberly, artist
Best Writer	*Satchel Paige: Striking Out Jim Crow*	James Sturm
Best Artist	*Nat Turner: Revolution*	Kyle Baker
Best Male Character	*Emmet Wilson, Satchel Paige: Striking Out Jim Crow*	co-created by James Sturm, writer, and Rich Tommaso, artist
Best Female Character	*Amanda Waller, Checkmate*	Greg Rucka, writer, Joe Bennett & Jack Jadson, artists
Rising Star Award	*Aya*	Marguerite Abouet
Best Reprint Publication	*Aya*	
Best Cover	*Sentences: The Life of MF Grimm*	Ronald Wimberly, illustrator
Best Comic Strip or Webcomic	*The K Chronicles*	Keith Knight, story and art
Fan Award for Best Comic	*Fantastic Four: The New Fantastic Four*	Dwayne McDuffie, writer, Paul Pelletier & Rick Magyar, artists

2009

Story of the Year	*Bayou*	Jeremy Love, writer and artist
Best Writer	*Bayou*	Jeremy Love
Best Artist	*Bayou*	Jeremy Love
Best Male Character	*Black Lightning, Final Crisis: Submit*	Grant Morrison, writer, Matthew Clark, Norm Rapmund, Rob Hunter, and Don Ho, artists
Best Female Character	*Lee Wagstaff, Bayou*	Jeremy Love, writer and artist

Rising Star Award	*The Hole: Consumer Culture*	Damian Duffy & John Jennings
Best Reprint Publication	*Me and the Devil Blues V1*	
Best Cover	*Unknown Soldier #1*	Igor Kordey, illustrator
Best Comic Strip or Webcomic	*Bayou,*	Jeremy Love, writer and artist
Fan Award for Best Comic	*Vixen: Return of the Lion*	G. Willow Wilson, writer, Cafu, artist

2010

Story of the Year	*Unknown Soldier #13-14*	Joshua Dysart, writer, Pat Masioni, artist
Best Writer	*Archie & Friends*	Alex Simmons
Best Artist	*World of Hurt*	Jay Potts
Best Male Character	*Isaiah Pastor, World of Hurt*	created by Jay Potts, writer and artist
Best Female Character	*Aya, Aya: The Secrets Come Out*	created by Marguerite Abouet, writer, Clement Oubrerie, artist
Rising Star Award	*World of Hurt*	Jay Potts
Best Reprint Publication	*Aya: The Secrets Come Out*	
Best Cover	*Luke Cage Noir #1*	Tim Bradstreet, illustrator
Best Comic Strip or Webcomic	*The K Chronicles*	Keith Knight, writer and artist
Fan Award for Best Comic	*Luke Cage Noir*	Mike Benson & Adam Glass, writers, Shawn Martinbrough, artist

2011

Story of the Year	*Fist Stick Knife Gun*	Geoffrey Canada, writer, Jamar Nicholas, artist
Best Writer	*Unknown Soldier*	Joshua Dysart
Best Artist	*BB Wolf and the 3 LPs*	Richard Koslowski
Best Male Character	*Geoff, Fist Stick Knife Gun*	Geoffrey Canada, writer, Jamar Nicholas, artist

Best Female Character	*Selena, 28 Days Later*	Michael Alan Nelson, writer; Declan Shalvey & Marek Oleksicki, artists
Rising Star Award	*Fist Stick Knife Gun*	Jamar Nicholas
Best Reprint Publication	*Superman vs. Muhammad Ali Deluxe HC*	
Best Cover	*Unknown Soldier #15*	Dave Johnson, illustrator
Best Comic Strip or Webcomic	*The K Chronicles*	Keith Knight, writer and artist
Fan Award for Best Comic	*Captain America/Black Panther: Flags of Our Fathers*	Reginald Hudlin, writer, Denys Cowan, artist

Harvey Awards

Named for artist and writer Harvey Kurtzman, the Harvey Awards were established in 1988 to honor the best works published in the comics industry. Comic book professionals vote for the final winners in each category.

1988

Best American Edition of Foreign Material	*Moebius*	Jean "Moebius" Giraud
Best Artist	*Watchmen*	Dave Gibbons
Best Cartoonist	*Concrete*	Paul Chadwick
Best Colorist	*Watchmen*	John Higgins
Best Continuing or Limited Series	*Watchmen*	Alan Moore and Dave Gibbons
Best Domestic Reprint Project	*The Spirit*	Will Eisner
Best Graphic Album	*Watchmen*	Alan Moore and Dave Gibbons
Best Inker	*Daredevil*	Al Williamson
Best Letterer	*American Flagg!*	Ken Bruzenak
Best New Series	*Concrete*	Paul Chadwick
Best Single Issue or Story	*Watchmen #9*	Alan Moore and Dave Gibbons
Best Writer	*Watchmen*	Alan Moore
Special Award for Excellence in Presentation	*Watchmen*	Alan Moore and Dave Gibbons

1989

Best American Edition of Foreign Material	*Incal*	Alejandro Jodorowsky and Jean "Moebius" Giraud
Best Artist	*Batman: The Killing Joke*	Brian Bolland
Best Cartoonist	*Concrete*	Paul Chadwick
Best Colorist	*Batman: The Killing Joke*	John Higgins
Best Continuing or Limited Series	*Love & Rockets*	Gilbert and Jaime Hernandez
Best Domestic Reprint Project	*The Complete Crumb Comics*	Robert Crumb
Best Graphic Album	*Batman: The Killing Joke*	Alan Moore and Brian Bolland
Best Inker	*Daredevil*	Al Williamson
Best Letterer	*Mr. Monster*	Ken Bruzenak
Best New Series	*Kings in Disguise*	Vance and Burr
Best Single Issue or Story	*Batman: The Killing Joke*	Alan Moore, Brian Bolland, and John Higgins
Best Writer	*Love & Rockets*	Gilbert Hernandez
Special Award for Excellence in Presentation	*Hardboiled Detective Stories*	Charles Burns
Special Award for Humor in Comics		Bill Watterson

1990

Best American Edition of Foreign Material	*Akira*	Katsuhiro Otomo
Best Anthology	*A1*	
Best Artist	*Xenozoic Tales*	Mark Schultz
Best Biographical, Historical or Journalistic Presentation	*The Comics Journal*	
Best Cartoonist		Chester Brown
Best Colorist	*Akira*	Steve Oliff
Best Continuing or Limited Series	*Love & Rockets*	Gilbert and Jaime Hernandez

Best Domestic Reprint Project	*The Complete Little Nemo in Slumberland*	Winsor McCay
Best Graphic Album	*Ed the Happy Clown*	Chester Brown
Best Inker	*Daredevil*	Al Williamson
Best Letterer	*Black Kiss*	Ken Bruzenak
Best New Series	*Eightball*	
Best New Talent		Jim Lee
Best Single Issue or Story	*Eightball #1*	Dan Clowes
Best Syndicated Strip or Panel	*Calvin and Hobbes*	Bill Watterson
Best Writer	*Love & Rockets*	Gilbert Hernandez
Special Award for Excellence in Presentation	*Arkham Asylum*	Grant Morrison and Dave McKean
Special Award for Humor in Comics		Sergio Aragones

1991

Best American Edition of Foreign Material	*Lt. Blueberry*	Jean "Moebius" Giraud
Best Anthology	*RAW*	edited by Francoise Mouly and Art Spiegelman
Best Artist	*World's Finest*	Steve Rude
Best Biographical, Historical or Journalistic Presentation	*The Comics Journal*	edited Gary Groth and Helena Harvilicz
Best Cartoonist	*Hate*	Peter Bagge
Best Colorist	*Akira*	Steve Oliff
Best Continuing or Limited Series	*Eightball*	Dan Clowes
Best Domestic Reprint Project	*The Complete Crumb Comics*	Robert Crumb
Best Graphic Album of Previously Published Work	*Warts and All*	Drew Friedman
Best Inker	*Fafhrd and the Grey Mouser*	Al Williamson
Best Letterer	*Eightball*	Daniel Clowes
Best New Series	*Hate*	Peter Bagge

Best New Talent		Julie Doucet
Best Original Graphic Album	*Why I Hate Saturn*	Kyle Baker
Best Single Issue or Story	*Eightball #3*	Dan Clowes
Best Syndicated Strip or Panel	*Calvin and Hobbes*	Bill Watterson
Best Writer	*Sandman*	Neil Gaiman
Special Award for Excellence in Presentation	*Complete Little Nemo in Slumberland*	Winsor McKay
Special Award for Humor in Comics		Sergio Aragones

1992

Best American Edition of Foreign Material	*Akira*	Katsuhiro Otomo
Best Anthology	*Dark Horse Presents*	edited by Randy Stradley
Best Artist	*Xenozoic Tales*	Mark Schultz
Best Biographical, Historical or Journalistic Presentation	*The Comics Journal*	edited by Gary Groth and Helena Harvilicz; art directed by Dale Yarger
Best Cartoonist	*Cerebus*	Dave Sim
Best Colorist	*Akira*	Steve Oliff
Best Continuing or Limited Series	*Eightball*	Dan Clowes
Best Domestic Reprint Project	*The Complete Crumb Comics*	Robert Crumb
Best Graphic Album of Previously Published Work	*Maus II*	Art Spiegelman
Best Inker	*Love & Rockets*	Jaime Hernandez
Best Letterer	*Sandman*	Todd Klein
Best New Series	*Cages*	Dave McKean
Best New Talent		Joe Quesada
Best Original Graphic Album	*To the Heart of the Storm*	Will Eisner
Best Single Issue or Story	*Xenozoic Tales #11*	Mark Schultz and Steve Stile
Best Syndicated Strip or Panel	*Calvin and Hobbes*	Bill Watterson

Best Writer	*Sandman*	Neil Gaiman
Special Award for Excellence in Presentation	*Complete Little Nemo in Slumberland*	Winsor McKay
Special Award for Humor in Comics		Sergio Aragones

1993

Best American Edition of Foreign Material	*Akira*	Katsuhiro Otomo
Best Anthology	*Dark Horse Presents*	edited by Randy Stradley
Best Artist	*Xenozoic Tales*	Mark Schultz
Best Biographical, Historical or Journalistic Presentation	*The Comics Journal*	edited by Gary Groth and Frank Young; art directed by Dale Yarger
Best Cartoonist	*Invisible People*	Will Eisner
Best Colorist	*Tantalizing Stories Presents Frank in the River*	Jim Woodring
Best Continuing or Limited Series	*Sandman*	Neil Gaiman and various artists
Best Domestic Reprint Project	*The Complete Crumb Comics*	Robert Crumb
Best Graphic Album of Previously Published Work	*Hey Look!*	Harvey Kurtzman
Best Inker	*Spider-Man 2099*	Al Williamson
Best Letterer	*Sandman*	Todd Klein
Best New Series	*Madman*	Michael Dalton Allred
Best Original Graphic Album	*Fairy Tales of Oscar Wilde* Volume 1	P. Craig Russell and Oscar Wilde
Best Single Issue or Story	*Tantalizing Stories Presents Frank in the River*	Jim Woodring and Mark Martin
Best Syndicated Strip or Panel	*Calvin and Hobbes*	Bill Watterson
Best Writer	*Invisible People*	Will Eisner
Special Award for Excellence in Presentation	*Batman: Night Cries*	Archie Goodwin and Scott Hampton
Special Award for Humor in Comics		Sergio Aragones

1994

Best American Edition of Foreign Material	*Billie Holiday*	Jose Munoz and Carlos Sampayo
Best Anthology	*Blab!*	edited by Monte Beauchamp
Best Artist	*Marvels*	Alex Ross
Best Biographical, Historical or Journalistic Presentation	*Understanding Comics*	Scott McCloud; edited by Mark Martin
Best Cartoonist	*Bone*	Jeff Smith
Best Colorist	*Spawn*	Steve Oliff
Best Continuing or Limited Series	*Marvels*	Kurt Busiek and Alex Ross
Best Domestic Reprint Project	*Complete Little Nemo in Slumberland* Volume 6	Winsor McCay
Best Graphic Album of Previously Published Work	*Complete Bone Adventures*	Jeff Smith
Best Inker	*Spider-Man 2099*	Al Williamson
Best Letterer	*Spawn*	Tom Orzechowski
Best New Series	*Captain Sternn*	Bernie Wrightson and Shephard Hendrix
Best Original Graphic Album	*Understanding Comics*	Scott McCloud
Best Single Issue or Story	*Batman: Mad Love*	Paul Dini and Bruce W. Timm
Best Syndicated Strip or Panel	*Calvin and Hobbes*	Bill Watterson
Best Writer	*Understanding Comics*	Scott McCloud
Special Award for Excellence in Presentation	*Marvels*	Kurt Busiek and Alex Ross
Special Award for Humor in Comics		Jeff Smith

1995

Best American Edition of Foreign Material	*Druuna: Carnivora*	Paolo Eleuteri Serpieri
Best Anthology	*Dark Horse Presents*	edited by Bob Schreck and Randy Stradley
Best Artist	*Hellboy*	Mike Mignola

Best Biographical, Historical or Journalistic Presentation	*The Comics Journal*	edited by Gary Groth and Frank Young
Best Cartoonist	*Bone*	Jeff Smith
Best Colorist	*Spawn*	Steve Oliff/Olyoptics
Best Continuing or Limited Series	*From Hell*	Alan Moore and Eddie Campbell
Best Domestic Reprint Project	*The Complete Crumb Comics*	Robert Crumb
Best Graphic Album of Previously Published Work	*Marvels*	Kurt Busiek and Alex Ross
Best Inker	*Spider-Man 2099*	Al Williamson
Best Letterer	*Sandman*	Todd Klein
Best New Series	*Acme Novelty Library*	Chris Ware
Best Original Graphic Album	*Our Cancer Year*	Harvey Pekar, Joyce Brabner, and Frank Stack
Best Single Issue or Story	*Marvels #4*	Kurt Busiek and Alex Ross
Best Syndicated Strip or Panel	*Calvin and Hobbes*	Bill Watterson
Best Writer	*From Hell*	Alan Moore
Special Award for Excellence in Presentation	*Acme Novelty Library*	Chris Ware
Special Award for Humor in Comics		Sergio Aragones

1996

Best American Edition of Foreign Material	*Akira*	Katsuhiro Otomo
Best Anthology	*Drawn & Quarterly*	edited by Marina Lesenko
Best Artist	*Hellboy*	Mike Mignola
Best Biographical, Historical or Journalistic Presentation	*Crumb*	directed by Terry Zwigoff
Best Cartoonist	*Bone*	Jeff Smith
Best Colorist	*Acme Novelty Library*	Chris Ware
Best Continuing or Limited Series	*Sin City*	Frank Miller

Best Cover Artist	*Kurt Busiek's Astro City #1*	Alex Ross
Best Domestic Reprint Project	*The Complete Crumb Comics*	Robert Crumb
Best Graphic Album of Previously Published Work	*Hellboy: The Wolves of St. August*	Mike Mignola
Best Inker	*Superman vs. Aliens*	Kevin Nowlan
Best Letterer	*Acme Novelty Library*	Chris Ware
Best New Series	*Astro City*	Kurt Busiek and Brent Anderson
Best New Talent		Adrian Tomine
Best Original Graphic Album	*Stuck Rubber Baby*	Howard Cruse
Best Single Issue or Story	*Astro City #1*	Kurt Busiek and Brent Anderson
Best Syndicated Strip or Panel	*Calvin and Hobbes*	Bill Watterson
Best Writer	*From Hell*	Alan Moore
Special Award for Excellence in Presentation	*Acme Novelty Library*	Chris Ware
Special Award for Humor in Comics		Evan Dorkin

1997

Best American Edition of Foreign Material	*Gon*	Masashi Tanaka
Best Anthology	*Dark Horse Presents*	edited by Bob Schreck
Best Artist	*Kingdom Come*	Alex Ross
Best Biographical, Historical or Journalistic Presentation	*The Comics Journal*	edited by Gary Groth and Tom Spurgeon
Best Cartoonist	*Bone*	Jeff Smith
Best Colorist	*Acme Novelty Library*	Chris Ware
Best Continuing or Limited Series	*Eightball*	Dan Clowes
Best Cover Artist	*Kingdom Come #1*	Alex Ross
Best Domestic Reprint Project	*Batman: The Dark Knight Returns — 10th Anniversary Hardcover Edition*	Frank Miller

Best Graphic Album of Previously Published Work	*Astro City: Life in the Big City*	Kurt Busiek and Brent Anderson
Best Inker	*Xenozoic Tales*	Mark Schultz
Best Letterer	*Eightball*	Dan Clowes
Best New Series	*Leave It to Chance*	James Robinson and Paul Smith
Best New Talent		Jessica Abel
Best Original Graphic Album	*Fax from Sarajevo*	Joe Kubert
Best Single Issue or Story	*Acme Novelty Library #7*	Chris Ware
Best Syndicated Strip or Panel	*Dilbert*	Scott Adams
Best Writer	*Eightball*	Dan Clowes
Special Award for Excellence in Presentation	*Acme Novelty Library*	Chris Ware
Special Award for Humor in Comics		Sergio Aragones

1998

Best American Edition of Foreign Material	*Drawn & Quarterly*	various creators
Best Anthology	*Dark Horse Presents*	edited by Bob Schreck and Jamie S. Rich
Best Artist	Body of work in 1997 including *Elric: Stormbringer* and *Dr. Strange: What Is It That Disturbs You Stephen?*	P. Craig Russell
Best Biographical, Historical or Journalistic Presentation	*The Comics Journal*	edited by Gary Groth
Best Cartoonist	Body of work in 1997 including *Sergio Aragones' Louder Than Words*	Sergio Aragones
Best Colorist	Body of work in 1997 including *Acme Novelty Library*	Chris Ware
Best Continuing or Limited Series	*Kurt Busiek's Astro City*	Kurt Busiek and Brent Anderson

Best Cover Artist	*Kurt Busiek's Astro City; Batman: Legends of the Dark Knight #100; Squadron Supreme*	Alex Ross
Best Domestic Reprint Project	*Jack Kirby's New Gods*	Jack Kirby
Best Graphic Album of Previously Published Work	*Batman Black & White Collected*	various
Best Inker	Body of work in 1997 including *Black Hole*	Charles Burns
Best Letterer	Body of work in 1997 including *Ka-Zar, Castle Waiting,* and *Uncle Sam*	Todd Klein
Best New Series	*Penny Century*	Jaime Hernandez
Best New Talent		Steven Weissman
Best Original Graphic Album	*Sin City: Family Values*	Frank Miller
Best Single Issue or Story	*Eightball #18*	Dan Clowes
Best Syndicated Strip or Panel	*Mutts*	Patrick McDonnell
Best Writer	Body of work in 1997 including *Kurt Busiek's Astro City, Avengers,* and *Thunderbolts*	Kurt Busiek
Special Award for Excellence in Presentation	*Acme Novelty Library*	Chris Ware
Special Award for Humor in Comics		Sergio Aragones

1999

Best American Edition of Foreign Material	*A Jew in Communist Prague*	Vittorio Giardino
Best Anthology	*Oni Double Feature*	edited by Bob Schreck
Best Artist	*Penny Century*	Jaime Hernandez
Best Biographical, Historical or Journalistic Presentation	*The Comics Journal*	edited by Gary Groth and Tom Spurgeon
Best Cartoonist	*Bone*	Jeff Smith

Best Colorist	*300*	Lynn Varley
Best Continuing or Limited Series	*300*	Frank Miller and Lynn Varley
Best Cover Artist	*Kurt Busiek's Astro City, Superman Forever, Superman: Peace on Earth*	Alex Ross
Best Domestic Reprint Project	*DC Archives: Plastic Man*	Jack Cole
Best Graphic Album of Previously Published Work	*Cages*	Dave McKean
Best Inker	*Black Hole*	Charles Burns
Best Letterer	Body of work in 1998 including *House of Secrets* and *Captain America*	Todd Klein
Best New Series	*The Spirit: The New Adventures*	edited by Catherine Garnier
Best New Talent		Kevin Smith
Best Original Graphic Album	*You Are Here*	Kyle Baker
Best Single Issue or Story	*Penny Century #3*	Jaime Hernandez
Best Syndicated Strip or Panel	*For Better or For Worse*	Lynn Johnston
Best Writer	Body of work in 1998 including *From Hell* and *Supreme*	Alan Moore
Special Award for Excellence in Presentation	*Acme Novelty Library*	Chris Ware
Special Award for Humor in Comics		Sergio Aragones

2000

Best American Edition of Foreign Material	*Star Wars: The Manga*	Toshiki Kudo and Shin-Ichi Hiromoto
Best Anthology	*Tomorrow Stories*	edited by Scott Dunbier
Best Artist	*Hellboy: Box Full of Evil*	Mike Mignola
Best Biographical, Historical or Journalistic Presentation	*The Comics Journal*	
Best Cartoonist	*Bone*	Jeff Smith

Best Colorist	*Acme Novelty Library*	Chris Ware
Best Continuing or Limited Series	*Acme Novelty Library*	Chris Ware
Best Cover Artist	*Acme Novelty Library*	Chris Ware
Best Domestic Reprint Project	*DC Archive Series*	edited by Dale Crain
Best Graphic Album of Previously Published Work	*From Hell*	Alan Moore and Eddie Campbell
Best Inker	*Penny Century*	Jaime Hernandez
Best Letterer	*Acme Novelty Library*	Chris Ware
Best New Series	*Weasel*	Dave Cooper
Best New Talent		Craig Thompson
Best Original Graphic Album	*Batman: War on Crime*	Paul Dini and Alex Ross
Best Single Issue or Story	*Acme Novelty Library # 13*	Chris Ware
Best Syndicated Strip or Panel	*Peanuts*	Charles Schulz
Best Writer	*League of Extraordinary Gentlemen*	Alan Moore
Special Award for Excellence in Presentation	*Acme Novelty Library #13*	Chris Ware
Special Award for Humor in Comics		Sergio Aragones

2001

Best American Edition of Foreign Material	*Lone Wolf & Cub*	Kazuo Koike and Goseki Kojima
Best Anthology	*Drawn & Quarterly* Volume 3 #1	edited by Chris Oliveros
Best Artist	*Penny Century*	Jaime Hernandez
Best Biographical, Historical or Journalistic Presentation	*The Comics Journal*	
Best Cartoonist	*MAD Magazine*	Al Jaffee
Best Colorist	*The Authority*	Laura DePuy
Best Continuing or Limited Series	*Acme Novelty Library*	Chris Ware

Best Cover Artist	*Wonder Woman*	Adam Hughes
Best Domestic Reprint Project	*The Spirit Archives*	Will Eisner
Best Graphic Album of Previously Published Work	*Jimmy Corrigan*	Chris Ware
Best Inker	*Black Hole*	Charles Burns
Best Letterer	*Castle Waiting*	Todd Klein
Best New Series	*Luba's Comics and Stories*	Gilbert Hernandez
Best New Talent		Michel Rabagliati
Best Original Graphic Album	*Last Day in Vietnam*	Will Eisner
Best Single Issue or Story	*Superman & Batman: World's Funniest*	Evan Dorkin and various artists
Best Syndicated Strip or Panel	*Mutts*	Patrick McDonnell
Best Writer	*Promethea*	Alan Moore
Special Award for Excellence in Presentation	*Jimmy Corrigan*	Chris Ware
Special Award for Humor in Comics		Sergio Aragones

2002

Best American Edition of Foreign Material	*Lone Wolf & Cub*	Kazuo Koike and Goseki Kojima
Best Anthology	*Bizarro*	
Best Artist	*100 Bullets*	Eduardo Risso
Best Biographical, Historical or Journalistic Presentation	*Jack Cole and Plastic Man*	
Best Cartoonist		Dan Clowes
Best Colorist	*Acme Novelty Library*	Chris Ware
Best Continuing or Limited Series	*100 Bullets*	
Best Cover Artist	*Wonder Woman*	Adam Hughes
Best Domestic Reprint Project	*The Spirit Archives*	Will Eisner

Best Graphic Album of Previously Published Work	*Lone Wolf & Cub*	Kazuo Koike and Goseki Kojima
Best Inker	*Black Hole*	Charles Burns
Best Letterer	*Acme Novelty Library*	Chris Ware
Best New Series	*La Perdida*	
Best New Talent		Jason
Best Original Graphic Album	*Golem's Mighty Swing*	James Sturm
Best Single Issue or Story	*Eightball #22*	Dan Clowes
Best Syndicated Strip or Panel	*Mutts*	Patrick McDonnell
Best Writer	*100 Bullets*	Brian Azzarello
Special Award for Excellence in Presentation	*Spirit Archives*	
Special Award for Humor in Comics		Evan Dorkin

2003

Best American Edition of Foreign Material	*Lone Wolf & Cub*	Kazuo Koike and Goseki Kojima
Best Anthology	*Comics Journal Summer Special 2002*	
Best Artist	*100 Bullets*	Eduardo Risso
Best Biographical, Historical or Journalistic Presentation	*B. Krigstein* Volume 1	
Best Cartoonist	*Bone*	Jeff Smith
Best Colorist	*Hellboy*	Dave Stewart
Best Continuing or Limited Series	*League of Extraordinary Gentlemen*	Alan Moore and Kevin O'Neill
Best Cover Artist	*Wonder Woman*	Adam Hughes
Best Domestic Reprint Project	*Krazy and Ignatz*	George Herrimann
Best Graphic Album of Previously Published Work	*20th Century Eightball*	Daniel Clowes
Best Inker	*Love & Rockets*	Jaime Hernandez

Best Letterer	*Promethea*	Todd Klein
Best New Series	*Rubber Necker*	Nick Bertozzi
Best New Talent		Nick Bertozzi
Best Original Graphic Album	*Cartoon History of the Universe* Volume 3	Larry Gonick
Best Single Issue or Story	*League of Extraordinary Gentlemen* Volume II #1	Alan Moore and Kevin O'Neill
Best Syndicated Strip or Panel	*Mutts*	Patrick McDonnell
Best Writer	*Promethea*	Alan Moore
Special Award for Excellence in Presentation	*Krazy and Ignatz*	
Special Award for Humor in Comics		Evan Dorkin

2004

Best American Edition of Foreign Material	*Persepolis*	Marjane Satrapi
Best Anthology	*Drawn & Quarterly #5*	edited by Chris Oliveros
Best Artist	*Blankets*	Craig Thompson
Best Biographical, Historical or Journalistic Presentation	*Comic Art Magazine*	
Best Cartoonist	*Blankets*	Craig Thompson
Best Colorist	*Acme Novelty Datebook*	Chris Ware
Best Continuing or Limited Series	*League of Extraordinary Gentlemen* Volume II	Alan Moore and Kevin O'Neill
Best Cover Artist	*Black Hole*	Charles Burns
Best Domestic Reprint Project	*Krazy and Ignatz*	George Herrimann
Best Graphic Album of Previously Published Work	*Louis Riel*	Chester Brown
Best Inker	*Black Hole*	Charles Burns
Best Letterer	*Cerebus*	Dave Sim
Best New Series	*Plastic Man*	Kyle Baker

Best New Talent		Derek Kirk Kim
Best Original Graphic Album	*Blankets*	Craig Thompson
Best Single Issue or Story	*Gotham Central #6-10*	Greg Rucka and Michael Lark
Best Single Issue or Story	*Love & Rockets #9*	Gilbert and Jaime Hernandez
Best Syndicated Strip or Panel	*Maakies*	Tony Millionaire
Best Writer	*Louis Riel*	Chester Brown
Special Award for Excellence in Presentation	*Acme Novelty Datebook*	Chris Ware
Special Award for Humor in Comics		Tony Millionaire

2005

Best American Edition of Foreign Material	*Buddha*	Osamu Tezuka
Best Anthology	*Michael Chabon Presents: The Amazing Adventures of the Escapist*	edited by Diana Schutz
Best Anthology	*McSweeney's Quarterly Concern #13*	edited by Chris Ware
Best Artist	*DC: The New Frontier*	Darwyn Cooke
Best Biographical, Historical or Journalistic Presentation	*Comic Book Artist*	edited by Jon B. Cooke
Best Cartoonist	*Bone*	Jeff Smith
Best Colorist	*DC: The New Frontier*	Dave Stewart
Best Continuing or Limited Series	*The New Frontier*	Darwyn Cooke
Best Cover Artist	*Fables*	James Jean
Best Domestic Reprint Project	*The Complete Peanuts 1950-52*	Charles Schulz
Best Graphic Album of Previously Published Work	*Bone: Volume One Collection*	Jeff Smith
Best Inker	*Black Hole*	Charles Burns
Best Letterer	*Wonder Woman*	Todd Klein

Best New Series	*Michael Chabon Presents: The Amazing Adventures of the Escapist*	
Best New Talent		Andy Runton
Best Original Graphic Album	*Blacksad 2*	Juajono Guardno and Juan Diaz Canales
Best Single Issue or Story	*Eightball # 23*	Dan Clowes
Best Syndicated Strip or Panel	*Mutts*	Patrick McDonald
Best Writer	*Eightball*	Daniel Clowes
Special Award for Excellence in Presentation	*The Complete Peanuts 1950-52*	Charles Schulz
Special Award for Humor in Comics		Kyle Baker

2006

Best American Edition of Foreign Material	*Buddha*	Osamu Tezuka
Best Anthology	*Solo*	
Best Artist	*Promethea*	J. H. Williams III
Best Biographical, Historical or Journalistic Presentation	*The Comics Journal*	
Best Cartoonist	*Acme Novelty Library #16*	Chris Ware
Best Colorist	*Astonishing X-Men*	Laura Martin
Best Continuing or Limited Series	*Runaways*	Brian K. Vaughan
Best Cover Artist	*Fables*	James Jean
Best Domestic Reprint Project	*Little Nemo in Slumberland: So Many Splendid Sundays*	
Best Graphic Album of Previously Published Work	*Black Hole*	Charles Burns
Best Inker	*Black Hole*	Charles Burns
Best Letterer	*Acme Novelty Library #16*	Chris Ware
Best New Series	*Young Avengers*	

Best New Talent		R. Kikuo Johnson Roberto Aguirre-Sacasa
Best Online Comics Work	*American Elf*	James Kochalka
Best Original Graphic Album	*Tricked*	Alex Robinson
Best Single Issue or Story	*Love & Rockets* Volume 2 #15	Gilbert and Jaime Hernandez
Best Syndicated Strip or Panel	*Maakies*	Tony Millionaire
Best Writer	*Captain America*	Ed Brubaker
Special Award for Excellence in Presentation	*Little Nemo in Slumberland: So Many Splendid Sundays*	Winsor McKay
Special Award for Humor in Comics		Kyle Baker

2007

Best American Edition of Foreign Material	*Abandon the Old in Tokyo*	Yoshihiro Tatsumi
Best American Edition of Foreign Material	*Moomin*	Tove Jansson
Best Anthology	*Flight,* Volume 3	
Best Artist	*All-Star Superman*	Frank Quitely
Best Biographical, Historical or Journalistic Presentation	*Art Out of Time*	
Best Cartoonist	*Love & Rockets*	Jaime Hernandez
Best Colorist	*American Born Chinese*	Lark Pien
Best Continuing or Limited Series	*Daredevil*	Ed Brubaker and Michael Lark
Best Cover Artist	*Fables*	James Jean
Best Domestic Reprint Project	*Complete Peanuts*	Charles Schulz
Best Graphic Album of Previously Published Work	*Absolute New Frontier*	Darwyn Cooke
Best Inker	*Eternals*	Danny Miki
Best Letterer	*Usagi Yojimbo*	Stan Sakai
Best New Series	*The Spirit*	

Best New Talent		Brian Fies
Best Online Comics Work	*Perry Bible Fellowship*	Nicholas Gurewitch
Best Original Graphic Album	*Pride of Baghdad*	Brian K. Vaughn and Nino Henrichon
Best Single Issue or Story	*Civil War #1*	
Best Syndicated Strip or Panel	*The K Chronicles*	Keith Knight
Best Writer	*Daredevil*	Ed Brubaker
Special Award for Excellence in Presentation	*Lost Girls*	
Special Award for Humor in Comics		Bryan Lee O'Malley

2008

Best American Edition of Foreign Material	*Eduardo Risso's Tales of Terror*	Eduardo Risso
Best Anthology	*Popgun* Volume 1	edited by Joe Keatinge and Mark Andrew Smith
Best Artist	*All-Star Superman*	Frank Quitely
Best Biographical, Historical or Journalistic Presentation	*Reading Comics: How Graphic Albums Work and What They Mean*	Douglas Wolk
Best Cartoonist	*The Spirit*	Darwyn Cooke
Best Colorist	*Thor*	Laura Martin
Best Continuing or Limited Series	*All Star Superman*	
Best Cover Artist	*Hellboy*	Mike Mignola
Best Domestic Reprint Project	*Complete Peanuts*	Charles Schulz
Best Graphic Album of Previously Published Work	*Captain America Omnibus* Volume 1	Ed Brubaker, Steve Epting, and Mike Perkins
Best Inker	*Witchblade*	Kevin Nowlan
Best Letterer	*Daredevil*	Chris Eliopoulos
Best New Series	*Umbrella Academy*	
Best New Talent		Vasilis Lolos

Best Online Comics Work	*Perry Bible Fellowship*	Nicholas Gurewitch
Best Original Graphic Album	*Scott Pilgrim Gets It Together*	Bryan Lee O'Malley
Best Single Issue or Story	*All Star Superman #8*	
Best Syndicated Strip or Panel	*Doonesbury*	Garry Trudeau
Best Writer	*Y: The Last Man*	Brian K. Vaughan
Special Award for Excellence in Presentation	*EC Archives*	Various
Special Award for Humor in Comics		Nicholas Gurewitch

2009

Best American Edition of Foreign Material	*Gus and His Gang*	Chris Blain
Best Anthology	*Comic Book Tattoo*	edited by Rantz Hoseley and Tori Amos
Best Artist	*Umbrella Academy*	Gabriel Ba
Best Biographical, Historical or Journalistic Presentation	*Kirby: King of Comics*	Mark Evanier,
Best Cartoonist	*Tall Tales*	Al Jaffee
Best Colorist	*Umbrella Academy*	Dave Stewart
Best Continuing or Limited Series	*All Star Superman*	
Best Cover Artist	*Fables*	James Jean
Best Domestic Reprint Project	*Complete Peanuts*	Charles Schulz
Best Graphic Album of Previously Published Work	*Nat Turner*	Kyle Baker
Best Inker	*Thor*	Mark Morales
Best Letterer	*Marvel 1985*	John Workman
Best New Series	*Echo*	
Best New Talent		Bryan J.L. Glass
Best Online Comics Work	*High Moon*	Scott O. Brown, Steve Ellis, and David Gallaher
Best Original Graphic Album	*Too Cool To Be Forgotten*	Alex Robinson

Best Single Issue or Story	*Y: The Last Man #60*	Brian Vaughan and Pia Guerra
Best Syndicated Strip or Panel	*Mutts*	Patrick McDonnell
Best Writer	*All-Star Superman*	Grant Morrison
Special Award for Excellence in Presentation	*Kirby: King of Comics*	Mark Evanier
Special Award for Humor in Comics		Al Jaffee

2010

Best American Edition of Foreign Material	*The Art of Osamu Tezuka: The God of Manga*	Helen McCarthy
Best Anthology	*Wednesday Comics*	
Best Artist	*The Book of Genesis*	Robert Crumb
Best Biographical, Historical or Journalistic Presentation	*Art of Harvey Kurtzman*	Denis Kitchen and Paul Buhle
Best Cartoonist	*Richard Stark's Parker: The Hunter*	Darwyn Cooke
Best Colorist	*The Rocketeer: The Complete Adventures*	Laura Martin
Best Continuing or Limited Series	*The Walking Dead*	
Best Cover Artist	*Hellboy: The Bride from Hell*	Mike Mignola
Best Domestic Reprint Project	*The Rocketeer: The Complete Adventures*	Dave Stevens
Best Graphic Album of Previously Published Work	*Mice Templar*, Volume 1	Bryan J.L. Glass and Michael Avon Oeming
Best Inker	*Amazing Spider-Man*	Klaus Janson
Best Letterer	*Asterios Polyp*	David Mazzucchelli
Best New Series	*Chew*	
Best New Talent		Rob Guillory
Best Online Comics Work	*PVP*	Scott Kurtz
Best Original Graphic Album	*Asterios Polyp*	David Mazucchelli
Best Original Graphic Publication for Younger Readers	*The Muppet Show Comic Book*	

Best Single Issue or Story	*Asterios Polyp*	David Mazucchelli
Best Syndicated Strip or Panel	*Mutts*	Patrick McDonnell
Best Writer	*The Walking Dead*	Robert Kirkman
Special Award for Excellence in Presentation	*The Rocketeer: The Complete Adventures*	Dave Stevens
Special Award for Humor in Comics		Bryan Lee O'Malley

2011

Best American Edition of Foreign Material	*Blacksad*	Juan Diaz Canales and Juanjo Guarnido
Best Anthology	*Popgun #4*	edited by D.J. Kirkbride, Anthony Wu, and Adam P. Knave
Best Artist	*Richard Stark's Parker: The Outfit*	Darwyn Cooke
Best Biographical, Historical or Journalistic Presentation	*The Art of Jaime Hernandez: The Secrets of Life and Death*	edited by Todd Hignite
Best Cartoonist	*Richard Stark's Parker: The Outfit*	Darwyn Cooke
Best Colorist	*Cuba: My Revolution*	Jose Villarrubia
Best Continuing or Limited Series	*Love and Rockets,* Volume 3	Jaime and Gilbert Hernandez
Best Cover Artist	*Hellboy*	Mike Mignola
Best Domestic Reprint Project	*Dave Stevens' The Rocketeer Artist's Edition*	designed by Randall Dahlk and edited by Scott Dunbier
Best Graphic Album of Previously Published Work	*Beasts of Burden: Animal Rites*	Evan Dorkin and Jill Thompson
Best Inker	*Thor*	Mark Morales
Best Letterer	*Thor*	John Workman
Best New Series	*American Vampire*	Scott Snyder, Stephen King, and Rafael Albuquerque
Best New Talent	*Thor: The Mighty Avenger*	Chris Samnee
Best Online Comics Work	*Hark! A Vagrant*	Kate Beaton

Best Original Graphic Album	*Scott Pilgrim,* Volume 6: *Scott Pilgrim's Finest Hour*	Bryan Lee O'Malley
Best Original Graphic Publication for Younger Readers	*Tiny Titans*	Art Baltazar and Franco Aureliani
Best Single Issue or Story	*Daytripper*	Fabio Moon and Gabiel Ba
Best Syndicated Strip or Panel	*Doonesbury*	Garry Trudeau
Best Writer	*Thor: The Mighty Avenger*	Roger Landridge
Special Award for Excellence in Presentation	*Dave Stevens' The Rocketeer Artist's Edition*	designed by Randall Dahlk and edited by Scott Dunbier
Special Award for Humor in Comics	*The Muppet Show*	Roger Langridge

Ignatz Awards

Named in honor of the mouse from George Herriman's comic strip *Krazy Kat*, the Ignatz Awards were established in 1997 to recognize excellence in comics publishing by small press creators. Winners are chosen by attendees of the annual Small Press Expo convention.

1997

Outstanding Artist	*Palookaville*	Seth	Drawn & Quarterly
Outstanding Graphic Novel or Collection	*It's A Good Life If You Don't Weaken*	Seth	Drawn & Quarterly
Outstanding Story	*From Hell*	Alan Moore and Eddie Campbell	Kitchen Sink Press
Promising New Talent	*Nowhere*	Debbie Dreschler	Drawn & Quarterly
Outstanding Series	*Acme Novelty Library*	Chris Ware	Fantagraphics
Outstanding Comic	*Eightball #17*	Dan Clowes	Fantagraphics
Outstanding Mini-Comic	*The Perfect Planet*	James Kochalka	

1998

Outstanding Artist	*Cerebus*	Dave Sim	Aardvark-Vanaheim
Outstanding Graphic Novel or Collection	*Ghost World*	Dan Clowes	Fantagraphics

Outstanding Story	"Ghost World" serialized in *Eightball*	Dan Clowes	Fantagraphics
Promising New Talent	*Finder*	Carla Speed McNeil	Lightspeed Press
Outstanding Series	*Acme Novelty Library*	Chris Ware	Fantagraphics
Outstanding Comic	*Acme Novelty Library #9*	Chris Ware	Fantagraphics
Outstanding Mini-Comic	*Amy Unbounded*	Rachel Hartman	

1999

Outstanding Artist	*Liberty Meadows #1*	Frank Cho	Insight Studios Group
Outstanding Graphic Novel or Collection	*Cages*	Dave McKean	Kitchen Sink Press
Outstanding Story	*"David Boring" Eightball #20*	Dan Clowes	Fantagraphics
Promising New Talent	*Fireball #7*	Brian Ralph	Fort Thunder
Outstanding Series	*The Extended Dream of Mr. D*	Max	Drawn & Quarterly
Outstanding Comic	*Liberty Meadows #1*	Frank Cho	Insight Studio Group
Outstanding Mini-Comic	*Fireball #7*	Brian Ralph	

2000

Outstanding Artist	*Weasel*	Dave Cooper	Fantagraphics
Outstanding Graphic Novel or Collection	*From Hell*	Alan Moore and Eddie Campbell	Eddie Campbell Comics
Outstanding Story	*"Jimmy Corrigan, Smartest Kid on Earth" Acme Novelty Library*	Chris Ware	Fantagraphics
Promising New Talent	*Boswash*	Nick Bertozzi	Luxurious Comics
Outstanding Series	*Weasel*	Dave Cooper	Fantagraphics
Outstanding Comic	*The Acme Novelty Library No. 13*	Chris Ware	Fantagraphics

| Outstanding Mini-Comic | *LowJinx #2: Understanding the Horrible Truth About Re-inventing Mini Comics (The Bastard Format)* | various, edited by Kurt Wolfgang | |
| Outstanding Debut Award | *Dork #8* | Evan Dorkin | Slave Labor Graphics |

2001

Awards Cancelled

2002

Outstanding Artist	*Artichoke Tales #1, Non #5*	Megan Kelso	Highwater Books and Red Ink Press
Outstanding Graphic Novel or Collection	*The Golem's Mighty Swing*	James Sturm	Drawn & Quarterly
Outstanding Story	*Trenches*	Scott Mills	Top Shelf
Promising New Talent	*Catch as Catch Can*	Greg Cook	Highwater Books
Outstanding Series	*Sketchbook Diaries*	James Kochalka	Top Shelf
Outstanding Comic	*Eightball #22*	Dan Clowes	Fantagraphics
Outstanding Mini-Comic	*Artichoke Tales #1*	Megan Kelso	
Outstanding Online Comic	*Bee*	Jason Little	www.beecomix.com
Outstanding Debut Award	*Pulpatoon Pilgrimage*	Joel Priddy	AdHouse Books

2003

Outstanding Artist	*Shutterbug Follies*	Jason Little	Doubleday
Outstanding Graphic Novel or Collection	*Three Fingers*	Rich Koslowski	Top Shelf
Outstanding Story	*Flee*	Jason Shiga	Sparkplug Comic Books
Promising New Talent	*Same Difference and Other Stories*	Derek Kirk Kim	self-published
Outstanding Series	*Black Hole*	Charles Burns	Fantagraphics
Outstanding Comic	*Rubber Necker #2*	Nick Bertozzi	Alternative Comics
Outstanding Mini-Comic	*I Am Going to Be Small*	Jeffrey Brown	

Outstanding Online Comic	*American Elf*	James Kochalka	www.americanelf.com
Outstanding Debut Award	*Studygroup12 #3*	edited by Zack Soto	

2004

Outstanding Artist	*Blankets*	Craig Thompson,	Top Shelf
Outstanding Graphic Novel or Collection	*Blankets*	Craig Thompson	Top Shelf
Outstanding Story	"Glenn Ganges" *Drawn and Quarterly Showcase* Book 1	Kevin Huizenga	Drawn & Quarterly
Promising New Talent	*Kramers Ergot #4*	Lauren Weinstein	Avodah Books
Outstanding Series	*Finder*	Carla Speed McNeil	Lightspeed Press
Outstanding Comic	*Eightball #23*	Dan Clowes	Fantagraphics
Outstanding Mini-Comic	*Lucky #3*	Gabrielle Bell	
Outstanding Online Comic	*American Elf*	James Kochalka	www.americanelf.com
Outstanding Debut Award	*Teen Boat #6: VOTE BOAT*	Dave Roman and John Green	Cryptic Press

2005

Outstanding Artist	*Epileptic, Babel*	David B.	Drawn & Quarterly
Outstanding Anthology or Collection	*Diary of a Mosquito Abatement Man*	John Porcellino	La Mano
Outstanding Graphic Novel	*Persepolis 2: The Story of a Return*	Marjane Satrapi	Pantheon
Outstanding Story	*Dogs and Water*	Anders Nilsen	Drawn & Quarterly
Promising New Talent	*Owly*	Andy Runton	Top Shelf
Outstanding Series	*Finder*	Carla Speed McNeil	Lightspeed Press

Outstanding Comic	*Or Else #1*	Kevin Huizenga	Drawn & Quarterly
Outstanding Mini-Comic	*Phase 7*	Alec Longstreth	
Outstanding Online Comic	*Perry Bible Fellowship*	Nicholas Gure-witch	http://www. pbfcomics.com/
Outstanding Debut Award	*Will You Still Love Me If I Wet The Bed?*	Liz Prince	Top Shelf
Outstanding Artist	*Billy Hazelnuts*	Tony Millionaire	Fantagraphics

2006

Outstanding Anthology or Collection	*Black Hole*	Charles Burns	Pantheon
Outstanding Graphic Novel	*Tricked*	Alex Robinson	Top Shelf
Outstanding Story	*Ganges #1*	Kevin Huizenga	Fantagraphics
Promising New Talent	*Salamander Dream, Gray Horses*	Hope Larson	
Outstanding Series	*Owly*	Andy Runton	Top Shelf
Outstanding Comic	*Schizo #4*	Ivan Brunetti	Fantagraphics
Outstanding Mini-Comic	*Monsters*	Ken Dahl	
Outstanding Online Comic	*Perry Bible Fellowship*	Nicholas Gurewitch	http://www. pbfcomics.com/
Outstanding Debut Award	*Class of '99*	Josh Eiserike	self-published

2007

Outstanding Artist	*Love & Rockets*	Jaime Hernandez	Fantagraphics
Outstanding Anthology or Collection	*Curses*	Kevin Huizenga	Drawn & Quarterly
Outstanding Graphic Novel	*Don't Go Where I Can't Follow*	Anders Nilsen	Drawn & Quarterly

Outstanding Story	*"Felix" Drawn & Quarterly Showcase Vol. 4*	Gabrielle Bell	Drawn & Quarterly
Promising New Talent	*The Blot*	Tom Neely	I Will Destroy You
Outstanding Series	*The Mourning Star*	Kazimir Strzepek	Bodega Distribution
Outstanding Comic	*Optic Nerve #11*	Adrian Tomine	Drawn & Quarterly
Outstanding Mini-Comic	*P.S. Comics #3*	Minty Lewis	
Outstanding Online Comic	*Achewood*	Chris Onstad	http://www.achewood.com/
Outstanding Debut Award	*Papercutter #6*	edited by Alec Longstreth	Tugboat Press

2008

Outstanding Artist	*Do Not Disturb My Waking Dream*	Laura Park	self-published
Outstanding Anthology or Collection	*Papercutter #7*	edited by Greg Means	Tugboat Press
Outstanding Graphic Novel	*Skim*	Mariko Tamaki and Jillian Tamaki	Groundwood Books
Outstanding Story	*The Thing About Madeleine*	Lilli Carre	self-published
Promising New Talent	*How to Understand Israel in 60 Days or Less*	Sarah Glidden	self-published
Outstanding Series	*Snake Oil*	Chuck Forsman	self-published
Outstanding Comic	*Snake Oil #1*	Chuck Forsman	self-published
Outstanding Mini-Comic	*Bluefuzz*	Jesse Reklaw	
Outstanding Online Comic	*Achewood*	Chris Onstad	http://www.achewood.com/
Outstanding Debut Award	*Swallow Me Whole*	Nate Powell	Top Shelf

2009

Outstanding Artist	*Swallow Me Whole*	Nate Powell	Top Shelf
Outstanding Anthology or Collection	*Kramer's Ergot #7*	ed. Sammy Harkham	Buenaventura Press
Outstanding Graphic Novel	*Acme Novelty Library #19*	Chris Ware	Drawn & Quarterly
Outstanding Story	*"Willy," Papercutter #10*	Damien Jay	Tugboat Press
Promising New Talent	*Woman King*	Colleen Frakes	self-published
Outstanding Series	*Uptight*	Jordan Crane	Fantagraphics
Outstanding Comic	*Uptight #3*	Jordan Crane	Fantagraphics
Outstanding Mini-Comic	*Stay Away from Other People*	Lisa Hanawalt	
Outstanding Online Comic	*Year of the Rat*	Cayetano Garza	http://magicinkwell.com/?p=68

2010

Outstanding Artist	*Alec: The Years Have Pants*	Eddie Campbell	Top Shelf
Outstanding Anthology or Collection	*Masterpiece Comics*	R. Sikoryak	Drawn & Quarterly
Outstanding Graphic Novel	*Market Day*	James Sturm	Drawn & Quarterly
Outstanding Story	*Monsters*	Ken Dahl	Secret Acres
Promising New Talent	*"The Orphan Baiter," Papercutter #13*	Matt Wiegle	Tugboat Press
Outstanding Series	*Ganges,*	Kevin Huizenga	Fantagraphics
Outstanding Comic	*I Want You*	Lisa Hanawalt	Buenaventura Press
Outstanding Mini-Comic	*Rambo 3.5*	Jim Rugg	
Outstanding Online Comic	*Troop 142*	Mike Dawson	http://troop142.mikedawsoncomics.com/index.html/

Russ Manning Promising Newcomer Award

Awarded annually at Comic-Con International since 1982, The Manning Award is given to a new comics artist who displays exceptional talent.

1982	Dave Stevens	1997	Walk Holcomb
1983	Jan Duursema	1998	Matt Vander Pool
1984	Steve Rude	1999	Jay Anceleto
1985	Scott McCloud	2000	Alan Bunce
1986	Art Adams	2001	Goran Sudzuka
1987	Eric Shanower	2002	Tan Eng Huat
1988	Kevin Maguire	2003	Jerome Opena
1989	Richard Piers Raynor	2004	Eric Wight
1990	Dan Brereton	2005	Chris Bailey
1991	Daerick Gross	2006	R. Kikuo Johnson
1992	Mike Okamoto	2007	David Peterson
1993	Jeff Smith	2008	Cathy Malkasian
1994	Gene Ha	2009	Eleanor Davis
1995	Edvin Biukovic	2010	Marian Churchland
1996	Alexander Maleev	2011	Nate Simpson

Recommended Readings: Heroes

Titles with the asterisk (*) appear in the *Critical Survey of Graphic Novels* series.

Title	Author	Artist	Publisher	Year
*100%	Pope, Paul	Pope, Paul	DC Comics	2005
*100 Bullets	Azzarello, Brian	Risso, Eduardo	DC Comics	2000-2009
A. K. A. Goldfish	Bendis, Brian Michael	Bendis, Brian Michael	Caliber Comics, Image Comics	
Absolute Batman: The Long Halloween	Loeb, Jeph	Sale, Tim	DC Comics	2007
Acts of Vengeance Omnibus	Claremont, Chris; Lee, Jim; Layton, Bob; Gurenwald, Mark; Byrne, John; Mackie, Howard; Austin, Terry; Michelinie, David	Trimpe, Herb, and Ryan, Paul	Marvel	2011
Adam Strange: Planet Heist	Diggle, Andy,	Ferry, Pasqual	San Val	2005
A Disease of Language	Moore, Alan, and Campbell, Eddie		Knockabout Comics	2010
A God Somewhere	Arcudi, John, et al.	Snejbjerg, Peter	WildStorm	2010
*Alias	Bendis, Brian Michael	Gaydos, Michael	Marvel Comics	2003-2004
*All-Star Batman and Robin, the Boy Wonder	Miller, Frank	Lee, Jim	DC Comics	2008
*All-Star Superman	Morrison, Grant	Quitely, Frank	DC Comics	2007, 2009
Almuric	Thomas, Roy	Conrad, Tim	Dark Horse	1991

Title	Author	Artist	Publisher	Year
Amazing Adventures of Kavalier and Clay, The	Chabon, Michael	Rayn, Jay	Random House	2000
*Amazing Adventures of the Escapist, The	Chabon, Michael; Chaykin, Howard; McCarthy, Kevin; Pekar, Harvey; Vaughan, Brian K.	Barreto, Eduardo; Campbell, Eddie; Eisner, Will; Haspiel, Dean; Wight, Eric	Dark Horse Comics	2004-2006
Amazing Spider-Man Omnibus Vol. 1	Lee, Stan	Ditko, Steve	Marvel	2007
American Century	Chaykin, Howard, et al.	Laming, Mark	Vertigo	2001-2003
*American Flagg!	Badger, Mark; Chaykin, Howard; DeMatteis, J. M.; Grant, Steve	Badger, Mark, and Chaykin, Howard	First Comics	2008
American Vampire	Snyder, Scott; King, Stephen	Albuquerque, Rafael	Vertigo	2011
American Virgin	Segal, Steven T.	Cloonan, Becky, Rugg, Jim	Vertigo	2006-2008
Angel: After the Fall	Whedon, Joss, Lynch, Brian	Urru, Franco	IDW Publishing	2008-2009
*Animal Man	Morrison, Grant	Truog, Chas	DC Comics	1991-2003
Anita Blake, Vampire Hunter: Guilty Pleasures	Hamilton, Laurell K	Booth, Brett	Ace Books	2009
Anna Mercury, Volume 1: The Cutter	Ellis, Warren	Percio, Facundo	Avatar Press	2009

Title	Author	Artist	Publisher	Year
Annihilation	Giffen, Keith, et al.	Breitweiser, Mitch; Dazo, Bong, Kolins; Scot; Vella, Sheldon	Marvel Comics	2006-2007
Another Nail	Davis, Mark, Farmer, Mark	Farmer, Mark	DC Comics	2004
Astonishing X-Men	Whedon, Joss	Cassaday, John	Marvel Comics	2004-2008
Astounding Wolf-Man, The	Kirkman, Robert	Howard, Jason	Image Comics	2007-2010
Astro City	Busiek, Kurt	Anderson, Brent	Image Comics; DC Comics	1995-2011
Atomics, The	Allred, Michael		AAA Pop; Dark Horse Comics; Image Comics	2000-2001
Authority, The	Ellis, Warren, Millar, Mark	Barrionuevo, Al, Coleby, Simon	DC Comics	2000-2010
Avengers Forever	Busiek, Kurt, and Pachecho, Carlos	Pacheco, Carlos	Marvel Comics	1998-1999
Avengers Omnibus Vol. 1	Lee, Stan	Kirby, Jack	Marvel	2012
Avengers: Disassembled	Bendis, Brian Michael	Finch, David	Marvel	2006
Avengers: Kree/ Skrull War	Thomas, Roy	Buscema, Sal; Adams, Neal; Buscema, John	Marvel	2012
Avengers: The Contest	Mantlo, Bill; Gruenwald, Mark; Grant, Steven; Englehart, Steve; Defalco, Tom	Romita, John; Migrom, Al; Hall, Bob	Marvel	2010

Title	Author	Artist	Publisher	Year
Avengers: The Crossing	Harras, Bob; Kavanagh, Terry; Abnett, Dan; Lanning, Andy	Deodato, Mike; Wyman, MC; Morgan, Tom; Chueng, Jim	Marvel	2012
Avengers: The Korvac Saga	Shooter, Jim; Michelinie, David; Mantlo, Bill	Perez, George; Busema, Sal; Wenzel, Tom Morgan	Marvel	2010
Avengers: The Serpent Crown	Englehart, Steve	Perez, George	Marvel	2012
Batman and Robin: Batman Reborn	Morrison, Grant; Quitely, Frank; and Tan Phillip	Quitely, Frank, Tan, Phillip	DC Comics	2010
Batman Incorporated	Morrison, Grant	Paquette, Yankick	DC Comics	2012
Batman/Superman/ Wonder Woman: Trinity	Wagner, Matt	Wagner, Matt	DC Comics	2003
*Batman: Arkham Asylum	Morrison, Grant	McKean, Dave	DC Comics	1989
*Batman: Black and White, Volume 1	Bolland, Brian; Gaiman, Neil; Goodwin, Archie	Adams, Neal	DC Comics	1998, 2007
Batman: The Dark Knight	Miller, Frank		DC Comics	1986
*Batman: The Dark Knight Returns	Miller, Frank	Miller, Frank	DC Comics	1987
*Batman: The Dark Knight Strikes Again	Miller, Frank	Miller, Frank	DC Comics	2002

Title	Author	Artist	Publisher	Year
Batman: Dark Victory	Loeb, Jeph	Sale, Tim	DC Comics	2001
Batman: Ego and Other Tails	Cooke, Darwyn	Cooke, Darwyn	DC Comics	2005
Batman: Gothic	Morrison, Grant, and Klaus Janson	Janson, Klaus	DC Comics	1990
Batman: Hush	Loeb, Jeph, et al.	Lee, Jim	DC Comics	2002-2003
Batman: The Killing Joke	Moore, Alan	Bolland, Brian	DC Comics	1988
Batman: Knightfall	Dixon, Chuck	Moench, Doug	DC Comics	2012
Batman: The Long Halloween	Loeb, Jeph	Sale, Tim	DC Comics	1998
Batman: The Man Who Laughs	Brubaker, Ed, and Mahnke, Doug	Mahnke, Doug	DC Comics	2005
Batman: Nine Lives	Motter, Dean, et al.	Lark, Michael	DC Comics	2002
Batman: Year One	Miller, Frank	Mazzucchelli, David	DC Comics	1988
Batman: Year 100	Pope, Paul	Pope, Paul	DC Comics	2007
Beasts of Burden: Animal Rites	Dorkin, Evan, and Thompson, Jill	Thompson, Jill	Dark Horse	2010
Beauty and the Beast: Portrait of Love	Pini, Wendy	Pini, Wendy	First Publishing	1989
Big Guy and Rusty the Boy Robot, The	Miller, Frank	Darrow, Geof	Dark Horse Comics	1996
Billy the Kid's Old Time Oddities	Powell, Eric	Hotz, Kyle	Dark Horse Comics	2005
Blackest Night	Johns, Geoff	Reis, Ivan	DC Comics	2011

Title	Author	Artist	Publisher	Year
Black Orchid	Gaiman, Neil	McKean, Dave	DC Comics	1991
Black Panther	Hudlin, Reginald	Romita, John Jr.	Marvel Comics	2006-2008
Blacksad	Díaz Canales, Juan	Guarnido, Juanjo	Editions Dargaud (French); Dark Horse Comics (English)	2010 English translation of first three books
Blood: A Tale	DeMatteis, J. M.	Williams, Kent	Epic Comics, Vertigo	1997
Bloodstar	Howard, Robert E.; Corben, Richard; Jakes, John	Corben, Richard	Morning Star Press	1976
Bokurano	Kitoh, Mohiro	Kitoh, Moiro	Shogakukan	2004-present
Bone	Smith, Jeff	Smith, Jeff	Cartoon Books; Image Comics	1993
Bone: Tall Tales	Smith, Jeff, with Sniegoski, Tom	Smith, Jeff	GRAPHIX	2010
Boogeyman	Aragonés, Sergio, Evanier, Mark	Aragonés, Sergio	Dark Horse	1999
Books of Magic, The	Gaiman, Neil	Bolton, John	DC Comics	1993
Books of Magic, The	Rieber, John Ney, and Gross, Peter		Vertigo	1994-2000
Booster Gold	Johns, Geoff, and Dan Jurgens	Jurgens, Dan	DC Comics	2007-2010
Boys, The	Ennis, Garth	Robertson, Darick	DC Comics (issues 1-6); Dynamite Entertainment (issues 7-)	2007-present

Title	Author	Artist	Publisher	Year
*B.P.R.D.: Bureau for Paranormal Research and Defense	Mignola, Mike	Alexander, Jason Shawn	Dark Horse Comics	2002-2010
*Brat Pack	Veitch, Rick	Veitch, Rick	Tundra (comics); King Hell Press (book)	1992
Breathtaker	Wheatley, Mark, and Hempel, Rick		DC Comics	1990
Brightest Day	Johns, Geoff	various	DC Comics	2011
*Buffy the Vampire Slayer Season 8	Allie, Scott; DeKnight, Steven S.; Meltzer, Brad; Vaughan, Brian K.; Whedon, Joss	Jeanty, Georges	Dark Horse Comics	2007-2011
Bullet Points	Straczynski, J. Michael, and Lee Edwards, Tommy	Lee Edwards, Tommy	Marvel Comics	2007
Buzzard	Powell, Eric		Dark Horse Comics	2010- present
*Camelot 3000	Barr, Mike W.	Bolland, Brian	DC Comics	1988
Captain America	Brubaker, Ed, et al.		Marvel Comics	2005-2011
Captain America and the Falcon: Secret Empire	Englehart, Steve; Mike Friedrich; and Buscema, Sal	Buscema, Sal	Marvel Comics	2005
Captain America by Jack Kibry Omnibus	Kirby, Jack	Kirby, Jack	Marvel	2011
Captain America: Winter Soldier	Brubaker, Ed; Epting, Steve	Perkins, Mike; Lark, Michael	Marvel	2010

Title	Author	Artist	Publisher	Year
Captain America: Winter Soldier, Volume 2	Brubaker, Ed, et al.	Epting, Steve, Perkins, Mike	Marvel Comics	2006
Cartoon Guide to the Environment, The	Gonick, Larry, and Outwater, Alice	Gonick, Larry	Paw Prints	1996
Casanova	Fraction, Matt, and Bá, Gabriel	Bá, Gabriel	Icon Comics	2006-2008
Casanova: Luxuria	Fraction, Matt	Bá, Gabriel	Icon Comics	2006-2008
Catwoman: Relentless	Brubaker, Ed; Stewart, Cameron; Pulido, Javier	Stewart, Cameron, Pulido, Javier	DC Comics	2004
Catwoman: When in Rome	Loeb, Jeph, and Sale, Tim	Sale, Tim	DC Comics	2007
*Cerebus	Sim, Dave	Sim, Dave	Aardvark-Vanaheim	1986-2004
Chaos War	Pak, Greg; Van Lente, Red	Pham, Khoi	Marvel	2011
Chimichanga	Powell, Eric	Powell, Eric	Dark Horse Comics	2009-2010
Chronicles of Kull, The	Thomas, Roy, et al.	Wrightston, Bernie; Buscema, John; Chaykin, Howard; Chan, Ernie	Dark Horse Comics	2009
Chronicles of Solomon Kane, The	Thomas, Roy, and Macchio, Ralph	Chaykin, Howard	Dark Horse Comics	2009
Chronicles of Wormwood	Burrows, Jacen, and Ennis, Garth	Burrows, Jacen	Avatar Press	2007
Civil War	Millar, Mark, and McNiven, Steve		Marvel Comics	2006

Title	Author	Artist	Publisher	Year
Coffin, The	Hester, Phil, and Huddleston, Mike	Hester, Phil, Huddleston, Mike	Oni Press	2000
Come in Alone	Ellis, Warren	Ellis, Warren	AiT/PlanetLar	2001
Compleat Moonshadow, The	DeMatteis, J.M., et al.	Muth, Jon J.	DC Comics	1998
*Conan	Busiek, Kurt; Mignola, Mike; Nicieza, Fabian; Truman, Benjamin; Truman, Timothy	Giorello, Tomás	Dark Horse Comics	2005-2011
Conan and the Demons of Khitai	Yoshida, Akira	Lee, Pat	Dark Horse Comics	2006
Conan and the Jewels of Gwalhur	Russell, P. Craig	Russel, P. Craig	Dark Horse Comics	2005
Conan and the Songs of the Dead	Landsdale, Joe, and Truman, Timothy	Truman, Tim	Dark Horse Comics	2007
Conan the Barbarian	Thomas, Roy, et al.	Windsow-Smith, Barry	Dark Horse Comics	1970-1994
Conan: Book of Thoth	Busiek, Kurt, and Wein, Len	Jones, Kelley	Dark Horse Comics	2006
*Concrete	Chadwick, Paul	Chadwick, Paul	Dark Horse Comics	1994
Connor Hawke: Dragon's Blood	Dixon, Chuck, and Donovan, Derec	Donovan, Derec	DC Comics	2008
Cormac Mac Art	Thomas, Roy, and Thomas, Dann		Dark Horse Comics	1989
*Cosmic Odyssey	Starlin, Jim	Mignola, Mike	DC Comics	1992
*Criminal	Brubaker, Ed	Phillips, Sean	Marvel Comics	2007-present

Title	Author	Artist	Publisher	Year
Crisis on Infinite Earths	Wolfman, Marv	Pérez, George	DC Comics	1998
Daredevil Omnibus Companion	Miller, Frank, et al.	Sienkiewicz, Bill, Romita, Jr., John	Marvel Comics	2007
Daredevil: Born Again	Miller, Frank	Mazzucchelli, David	Marvel Comics	1987
Daredevil: Lowlife	Bendis, Brian Michael, and Maleev, Alexander	Maleev, Alex	Marvel Comics	2003
Daredevil: The Man Without Fear	Miller, Frank	Romita, Jr., John	Marvel Comics	1994
Daredevil: Underboss	Bendis, Brian Michael	Maleev, Alex	Marvel Comics	2002
Daredevil: Volume 1	Miller, Frank, et al.		Marvel Comics	2008
Dark Avengers	Bendis, Brian Michael	Deodato, Mike; Horn, Greg; Bachalo, Chris	Marvel	2011
Dark Rain: A New Orleans Story	Johnson, Mat, and Gane, Simone	Gane, Simone	Vertigo	2010
Daytripper	Bá, Gabriel, and Moon, Fabio	Bá, Gabriel, Moon, Fabio	Vertigo	2010-present
DC: The New Frontier Volume 1	Cooke, Darwyn, and Stewart, Dave	Cooke, Darwyn	DC Comics	2004
Death of Captain America Omnibus, The	Brubaker, Ed	Epting, Steve, Perkins, Mike	Marvel Comics	2009
Death of Captain America, The	Brubaker, Ed	Epting, Steve	Marvel Comics	2008

Title	Author	Artist	Publisher	Year
Death of Captain Marvel, The	Starlin, Jim	Starlin, Jim	Marvel Comics	1982
Death of the New Gods	Starlin, Jim	Banning, Matt, Thibert, Art	DC Comics	2007-2008
Death: The High Cost of Living	Gaiman, Neil	McKean, Dave	DC Comics	1994
Demo	Wood, Brian	Cloonan, Becky	AiT/Planet Lar	2005
Destiny: A Chronicle of Deaths Foretold	Kwitney, Alisa	Hampton, Scott	DC Comics	2000
DMZ	Wood, Brian	Burchielli, Riccardo	DC Comics	2006
Doc Savage	Malmont, Paul, et al.	Kubert, Adam	DC Comics	2010-present
Doctor 13: Architecture and Mortality	Azzarello, Brian, and Chiang, Cliff	Chiang, Cliff	DC Comics	2007
Dominic Fortune	Chaykin, Howard	Chaykin, Howard	Marvel Comics	2010
Doom Patrol	Morrison, Grant	Hughes, Rian	DC Comics	2000-2008
Dylan Dog Case Files, The	Marcheselli, Mauro; Sclavi, Tiziano	Brindisi, Bruno	Sergio Bonelli Editore (Italian); Dark Horse Comics (English)	2009
Earth X	Krueger, Jim; Ross, Alex	Leon, John Paul	Marvel Comics	2001
Echo	Moore, Terry		Abstract Studios	2008-present
Elektra	Miller, Frank, and Sienkiewicz, Bill	Miller, Frank	Marvel Comics	2008

Title	Author	Artist	Publisher	Year
Elektra Lives Again	Miller, Frank	Miller, Frank	Marvel Comics	1990
Elektra: Assassin	Miller, Frank	Sienkiewicz, Bill	Marvel Comics	1990
ElfQuest	Pini, Wendy; Pini, Richard	Pini, Wendy	WaRP Graphics	1981
Elric: The Making of a Sorcerer	Moorcock, Michael, and Simonson, Walter	Simonson, Walter	DC Comics	2007
End, The: Marvel	Starlin, Jim	Starlin, Jim, Milgrom, Al	Marvel Comics	2003
Enigma	Milligan, Peter, and Fegredo, Duncan	Fegredo, Duncan	Vertigo	1995
Escapists, The	Vaughan, Brian K., et al.	Rolston, Steve, Alexander, Jason Shawn	Dark Horse	2005-2007
Ex Machina	Vaughan, Brian K.	Harris, Tony	DC Comics	2005-2011
Fables	Willingham, Bill	Buckingham, Mark	DC Comics	2002-2011
Fallen Son: The Death of Captain America	Loeb, Jeph	Cassaday, John	Marvel Comics	2007
Fantastic Four by John Byrne Omnibus	Byrne, John; Claremont, Chris; Wolfman, Marv; Mantlo, Bill; Lee, Stan; Stern, Roger;	Byrne, John; Zeck, Mike; Wilson, Ron	Marvel	2011
Fantastic Four Omnibus Vol. 1	Lee, Stan	Kirby, Jack	Marvel	2007
Fear Itself	Fraction, Matt	Immonen, Stuart	Marvel	2012

Title	Author	Artist	Publisher	Year
*Filth, The	Morrison, Grant	Weston, Chris	DC Comics	2004
Final Crisis	Morrison, Grant, and Jones, J. G.	Jones, J.G	DC Comics	2008-2009
Flash: Flashpoint	Johns, Geoff	Kubert, Andy	DC Comics	2011
Flex Mentallo	Morrison, Grant, and Quitely, Frank	Quitely, Frank	Titan Publishing Company	1996
Flex Mentallo: Man of Muscle Mystery	Morrison, Grant	Quitely, Frank	DC Comics	2012
Fountain, The	Aronofsky, Darren	Williams, Kent	Vertigo	2005
Fray	Whedon, Joss, and Moline, Karl		Dark Horse Comics	2001-2003
Ghost Omnibus, Volume 1	Luke, Eric, et al.	Hughes, Adam; Dodson, Terry; Benefiel, Scott; Haley, Matt	Dark Horse Comics	2008
*Give Me Liberty: An American Dream	Miller, Frank	Gibbons, Dave	Dark Horse Comics	1990
God Save the Queen	Carey, Mike	Bolton, John	Vertigo	2007
*Goon, The	Powell, Eric	Powell, Eric	Albatross Exploding Funny Books; Avatar Press; Dark Horse Comics	2003-2011
Gotham by Gaslight	Augustyn, Brian; Mignola, Mike; and Russell, P. Craig	Mignola, Mike	DC Comics	1991
Gravel	Ellis, Warren, and Mike Wolfer	Wolfer, Mike	Avatar Press	1999-2011

Title	Author	Artist	Publisher	Year
Green Arrow, The	Kirby, Jack	Kirby, Jack	DC Comics	2001
Green Arrow: Quiver	Smith, Kevin; Phil Hester; Parks, Andé	Hester Phil, Parks, Ande	DC Comics	2000-2001
Green Arrow: The Longbow Hunters	Grell, Mike	Grell, Mike	DC Comics	1989
Green Arrow: Year One	Diggle, Andy	Jock	DC Comics	2008
Green Lantern: Emerald Twilight/ New Dawn	Marz, Ron, and Daryl Banks	Willingham, Bill	DC Comics	2003
Green Lantern: Rebirth	Johns, Geoff, and Van Sciver, Ethan		DC Comics	2005
Green Lantern: Secret Origin	Johns, Geoff	Reis, Ivan	DC Comics	2008
Green Lantern: The Sinestro Corps War	Johns, Geoff; Dave Gibbons; Peter Tomasi	Reis, Ivan; Gleason, Patrick; Van Sciver, Ethan	DC Comics	2008
Green Lantern: War of the Green Lanterns	Johns, Geoff	Tomasi, Peter J.	DC Comics	2011
Green Lantern-Green Arrow, the Collection: Hard Traveling Heroes	O'Neil, Dennis J.	Adams, Neal	DC Comics	1992
Green Lantern-Green Arrow, The Collection: Volume Two	O'Neil, Dennis J.; Maggin, Elliot S.; Adams, Neal	Van Sciver, Ethan	DC Comics	1992

Title	Author	Artist	Publisher	Year
Grendel	Wagner, Matt	Mireault, Bernie	Dark Horse Comics	1986-2009
Groo the Wanderer	Aragonés, Sergio; Evanier, Mark	Aragonés, Sergio	Dark Horse Comics; Eclipse Comics; Image Comics; Marvel Comics; Pacific Comics	1984
Gunfire, Issue 0	Wein, Len		DC Comics	1994
Hard Boiled	Miller, Frank		Dark Horse Comics	1990
Heavy Liquid	Pope, Paul	Pope, Paul	Vertigo	1999-2000
Hellblazer	Azzarello, Brian; Ennis, Garth; Morrison, Grant	Alfredo Alcala	DC Comics	1997-2010
Hellboy	Mignola, Mike; Byrne, John	Cassady, John	Dark Horse Comics	1994-2010
His Name Is . . . Savage!	Franklin, Robert (pseudonym of Archie Goodwin)	Kane, Gil	Adventure House Press	1968
Hitman	Ennis, Garth	McCrea, John	DC Comics	1997-2001
House of M	Bendis, Brian Michael, and Coipel, Olivier	Coipel, Olivier	Marvel Comics	2005
House of Mystery	Sturges, Matthew; Willingham, Bill; Rossi, Luca	Rossi, Luca	Vertigo	2008- present
Howard the Duck	Gerber, Steve, and Mayerik, Val	Mayerik, Val	Marvel Comics	1976-1979
Human Target	Milligan, Peter	Biukovic, Edvin	Vertigo	2000

Title	Author	Artist	Publisher	Year
*Identity Crisis	Meltzer, Brad	Morales, Rags	DC Comics	2005
In the Days of the Mob	Kirby, Jack		DC Comics	1971
Incorruptible	Waid, Mark, and Diaz, Jean	Diaz, Jean	Boom! Studios	2010-present
Incredible Hulk Omnibus Vol. 1	Lee, Stan; Friedrich, Gary; Kirby, Jack; Ditko, Steve; Severin, Marie	Kirby, Jack; Kane, Gil; Buscema, John; Everett, Bill; Romita, John; Ayers, Dick; Esposito, Mike; Powell, Bob	Marvel	2008
Incredible Hulk: Planet Hulk	Pak, Greg	Pagulayan, Carlo; Lopresti, Aaron; Santacruz, Juan; Frank, Gark; Miyazawa, Takeshi	Marvel	2008
Incredible Hulk: The End	David, Peter	Keown, Dale; Perez, George	Marvel	2011
Incredible Hulk: World War Hulk	Pak, Greg; David, Peter	Romita, John Jr.; Frank, Gark	Marvel	2009
Indiana Jones and the Tomb of the Gods	Williams, Rob, et al.	Scott, Steve	Dark Horse Comics	2008-2009
*Infinite Crisis	Johns, Geoff	Jimenez, Phil	DC Comics	2006
Infinity Gauntlet, The	Starlin, Jim	Lim, Ron	Marvel Comics	1992
Infinity War	Starlin, Jim	Lim, Ron	Marvel Comics	1992
*Invincible	Kirkman, Robert	Ottley, Ryan	Image Comics	2003-2010

Title	Author	Artist	Publisher	Year
*Invisibles, The	Morrison, Grant	Buckingham, Mark	DC Comics	1996
Iron Man: Armor Wars	Michelinie, David; Layton, Bob	Bright, Mark; Windsor-Smith, Barry	Marvel	2007
Iron Man: Demon in a Bottle	Michelinie, David	Layton, Bob; Romita, John Jr.; Infantino, Carmine	Marvel	2006
Irredeemable	Waid, Mark and Krause, Peter	Krause, Peter; Cassaday, John; Morrison, Grant	Boom! Studios	2009-present
iZombie	Roberson, Chris, and Allred, Michael	Allred, Michael	Vertigo	2010-present
Jack Cole and Plastic Man	Spiegelman, Art, and Kidd, Chip	Spiegelman, Art	Chronicle Books	2001
*Jack Kirby's Fourth World Omnibus	Kirby, Jack	Kirby, Jack	DC Comics	2007
Jinx	Bendis, Brian Michael	Bendis, Brian Michael	Image Comics	1996
JLA/Avengers	Busiek, Kurt, and Perez, George	Perez, George	DC Comics/Marvel Comics	2003
JLA: A League of One	Moeller, Christopher	Oakley, Bill, Moeller, Christopher	DC Comics	2000
*Joker	Azzarello, Brian	Bermejo, Lee	DC Comics	2008
*Jon Sable, Freelance	Grell, Mike	Grell, Mike	First Comics; IDW Publishing	2005-2010
Judge Death: Death Lives	Wagner, John; Grant, Alan; Bolland, Brian	Bolland, Brian, O'Niell, Kevin	2000 AD	2010

Title	Author	Artist	Publisher	Year
Judge Dredd	Ennis, Garth; Grant, Alan; Mills, Pat; Wagner, John	Bolland, Brian	Fleetway; IPC; Rebellion	2005-present
Just a Pilgrim	Ennis, Garth	Ezquerra, Carlos	Black Bull Comics	2001
Justice League of America	Meltzer, Brad, and Ha, Gene	Jurgens, Dan	DC Comics	2006-2007
Justice League of America: The Nail	Davis, Alan	Davis, Alan	DC Comics	1998
Kamandi, The Last Boy on Earth Omnibus	Kirby, Jack	Kirby, Jack	DC Comics	2011
Kick-Ass	Millar, Mark	Romita, John, Jr.	Marvel Comics	2010
Kickback	Lloyd, David	Lloyd, David	Panel Nine Publishing	2006
Killraven	Davis, Alan	Davis, Alan	Marvel Comics	2007
Kingdom Come	Waid, Mark	Ross, Alex	DC Comics	1997
Kull: The Shadow Kingdom	Nelson, Arvid		Dark Horse Comics	2009
Last Day, The	Sim, Dave, and Sim, Gerhard	Gerhard, Sim, Dave	Aardvark-Vanaheim	2004
League of Extraordinary Gentlemen, The	Moore, Alan	O'Neill, Kevin	DC Comics; Top Shelf Comics	2000
Lenny Zero and the Perps of Mega-City One	Diggle, Andy, and Jock	Jock; Flint Henry; Dillon, Steve	2000 AD	2011

Title	Author	Artist	Publisher	Year
Lex Luthor: Man of Steel	Azzarello, Brian, and Bermejo, Lee	Bermejo, Lee; Stewart, Dave; Gray, Mick; Story, Carl; Martin, Jason	DC Comics	2005
Life and Times of Martha Washington, The	Miller, Frank	Gibbons, Dave	Dark Horse Comics	2009
Light Brigade	Tomasi, Peter	Snejbjerg, Peter	DC Comics	2005
Local	Wood, Brian, and Kelly, Ryan	Kelly, Ryan	Oni Press	2008
Locke & Key: Welcome to Lovecraft	Hill, Joe	Rodriquez, Gabriel	IDW	2009
Losers, The	Diggle, Andy	Jock	DC Comics	2004-2006
Lucifer	Carey, Mike	Gross, Peter	DC Comics	2001-2007
M	Muth, Jon J	Muth, Jon J.	Abrams	2008
Madame Xanadu	Wagner, Matt, and Hadley, Amy Reeder	Hadley, Amy Reeder	Vertigo	2008-2010
Madman	Allred, Mike	Allred, Mike	Tundra; Dark Horse Comics; Image Comics	1996
Mage	Wagner, Matt	Wagner, Matt	Image Comics	1984-1997
Mage: The Hero Discovered	Wagner, Matt	Wagner, Matt	Image Comics	2004
Magnus, Robot Fighter	Manning, Russ	Manning, Russ	Dark Horse	1963

Title	Author	Artist	Publisher	Year
Marquis, The: Inferno	Davis, Guy	Davis, Guy	Dark Horse	2010
Marshal Law	Mills, Pat, and Kevin O'Neill	O'Neill, Kevin	Epic Comics, Dark Horse Comics	1987-2002
*Marvel 1602	Gaiman, Neil	Ditko, Steve	Marvel Comics	2004
*Marvel 1985	Millar, Mark	Edwards, Tommy Lee	Marvel Comics	2009
Marvel Apes	Kesel, Karl, and Bachs, Ramon	Bachs, Ramon	Marvel Comics	2009
Marvel Masters: The British Invasion	Grant, Alan, et al.	Gibbons, Dave; Davis, Alan; Hitch, Bryan; Dillon, Steve; Windsor-Smith, Barry; Neary, Paul; Quitely, Frank; Buckingham, Mark	Marvel Comics	2007-2008
Marvel Superheroes Secret Wars	Shooter, Jim; Zeck, Mike; Layton, Bob	Zeck, Mike, Layton, Bob	Marvel Comics	1984-1985
*Marvel Zombies	Kirkman, Robert; Layman, John; Van Lente, Fred	Phillips, Sean	Marvel Comics	2006-2010
*Marvels	Busiek, Kurt	Ross, Alex	Marvel Comics	1994
*Mask, The: Omnibus,	Arcudi, John	Mahnke, Doug	Dark Horse Comics	2008
Maximortal, The	Veitch, Rick	Veitch, Rick	King Hell Press	2002
Mighty, The	Tomasi, Peter, et al.	Snejbjerg, Peter, Samnee, Chris	DC Comics	2009

Title	Author	Artist	Publisher	Year
The Mighty Thor Omnibus Vol. 1	Lee, Stan; Lieber, Larry; Bernstein, Robert; Heck, Don; Hartly, Al	Kirby, Jack; Sinnott, Joe	Marvel	2011
Miracleman	Moore, Alan	Davis, Alan	Eclipse Comics	1988
Moon Knight: Countdown to Dark	Moench, Doug, and Sienkiewicz, Bill	Sienkiewicz, Bill	Marvel Comics	2010
Moonshadow	DeMatteis, J. M.	Muth, Jon J.	Marvel Comics	1989
Nemesis	Millar, Mark	McNiven, Steve	Marvel	2011
New Adventures of Abraham Lincoln, The	McCloud, Scott	McCloud, Scott	Image Comics	1998
New Avengers: Illuminati	Bendis, Brian Michael; Reed, Brian	Cheung, Jim	Marvel	2008
New Frontier, The	Cooke, Darwyn	Cooke, Darwyn	DC Comics	2004
New Gods	Kirby, Jack	Kirby, Jack	DC Comics	1971-1972
New X-Men	Morrison, Grant, et al.	Quitely, Frank; Van Sciver, Ethan; Leinil Francis, Yu; Kordey, Igor; Leon, John Paul; Jiminez, Phil; Bachalo, Chris; Silvestri, Marc	Marvel Comics	2004-2008
Nexus	Baron, Mike	Rude, Steve	Dark Horse Comics	2005
Nick Fury: Who Is Scorpio?	Steranko, Jim	Steranko, Jim	Marvel Comics	2001
Northlanders	Wood, Brian	Gianfelice, David	Vertigo	2008

Title	Author	Artist	Publisher	Year
Omega the Unknown	Lethem, Jonathan; Rusnak, Karl	Dalrymple, Farel	Marvel Comics	2008
Order, The	Fraction, Matt, and Barry Kitson	Kitson, Barry	Marvel Comics	2007-2008
Origin	Jemas, Bill, et al.	Kubert, Andy	Marvel Comics	2001-2002
Originals, The	Gibbons, Dave	Gibbons, Dave	DC Comics	2004
Other Side, The	Aaron, Jason, and Stewart, Cameron	Stewart, Cameron	Titan Books	2007
Outsiders, The: The Hunt	Tomasi, Peter, et al.	Mandrake, Tom	DC Comics	2010
Paradise X	Krueger, Jim, and Braithwaite, Doug	Leon, John Paul	Marvel Comics	2002-2003
Phoenix: The Untold Story	Claremont, Chris, and Byrne, John	Byrne, John	Marvel Comics	1984
Pigeons from Hell	Lansdale, Joe	Fox, Nathan	Dark Horse Comics	2009
Planetary	Ellis, Warren	Cassaday, John	DC Comics	2000-2010
Plastic Man Archives, The	Cole, Jack	Schelly, Bill	DC Comics	1999
Plastic Man	Baker, Kyle	Baker, Kyle	DC Comics	2004
Plastic Man: Rubber Bandits	Baker, Kyle	Baker, Kyle	DC Comics	2005
Pop Gun War	Dalrymple, Farel	Dalrymple, Farel	Dark Horse Comics	2003
Powers	Bendis, Brian Michael	Oeming, Michael Avon	Image Comics; Marvel Comics	2000
Preacher	Ennis, Garth	Case, Richard	DC Comics	1996

Title	Author	Artist	Publisher	Year
The Programme	Milligan, Peter	Smith, C.P.	Wildstorm	2008
*Promethea	Moore, Alan	Vess, Charles	DC Comics	2000-2005
Pulse, The	Bendis, Brian Michael, and Bagley, Mark	Bagley, Mark	Marvel Comics	2004-2006
Puma Blues, The	Murphy, Steven, and Zulli, Michael	Zulli, Michael	Mirage Studios	1986-1989
Punisher Max: Kingpin	Aaron, Jason, and Dillon, Steve	Dillon, Steve	Marvel Comics	2010
Punisher, The	Ennis, Garth, et al.	Dillon, Steve	Marvel Comics	2004-2009
Punisher: Welcome Back, Frank	Ennis, Garth, and Dillon, Steve	Dillon, Steve	Marvel Comics	2005
Rann-Thanagar Holy War	Starlin, Jim, and Lim, Ron	Lim, Ron	DC Comics	2008
Rat Catcher	Diggle, Andy, and Ibañez, Victor	Ibañez, Victor	Titan Publishing Company	2010
Red	Ellis, Warren, and Hammer, Cully	Hammer, Cully	WildStorm	2003
Richard Stark's Parker	Cooke, Darwyn and Stark, Richard	Cooke, Darwyn	Idea & Design Works	2009-present
*Rocketeer, The	Stevens, Dave	Stevens, Dave	Comico Comics; Dark Horse Comics; Eclipse Comics; IDW Publishing; Pacific Comics	1985
Rocketeer, The: The Complete Adventures	Stevens, Dave	Spiegle, Carrie	IDW Publishing	2009

Title	Author	Artist	Publisher	Year
Ronin	Miller, Frank	Miller, Frank	DC Comics	1987
Rose: Prequel to Bone	Smith, Jeff	Vess, Charles	Cartoon Books	2002
Runaways	Vaughan, Brian K.; Immonen, Kathryn; Moore, Terry; Whedon, Joss	Alphona, Adrian	Marvel Comics	2004-2009
Sacred and the Profane, The	Motter, Dean, and Steacy, Ken		Eclipse Books	1987
Saga of Solomon Kane, The	Thomas, Roy, et al.	Wenzel, David, Chaykin, Howard	Dark Horse Comics	2009
Sandman Mystery Theatre	Seagle, Steven T.; Wagner, Matt	Case, Richard	DC Comics	2004-2010
Sandman, The	Gaiman, Neil	Hempel, Marc	DC Comics	1990-1997
Sandman, The: Endless Nights	Gaiman, Neil, et al	Russel, P. Craig; Sienkiewicz, Bill; Manara, Milo; Prado, Miguelanxo; Storey, Barron; Fabry, Glenn; Quitely, Frank; McKean, Dave	Vertigo	2003
Savage Dragon	Larsen, Erik; Eliopoulos, Chris	Larsen, Erik	Image Comics	1996-present
Savage Sword of Conan, The	Thomas, Roy, et al.	Windsor-Smith, Barry, Buscema, John	Dark Horse Comics	
Savage Sword of Kull, The	Thomas, Roy, et al.		Dark Horse Comics	2010
Scalped	Aaron, Jason	Guéra, R.M.	Vertigo	2007

Title	Author	Artist	Publisher	Year
Scarlett	Bendis, Brian Michael, and Maleev, Alexander	Maleev, Alex	Marvel Comics	2010-present
Secret Invasion	Bendis, Brian Michael, and Yu, Leinil Francis	Yu, Leinil Francis	Marvel Comics	2008
Secret War	Bendis, Brian Michael	Dell'Otto, Gabrielle	Marvel	2009
*Secret Wars	Shooter, Jim	Layton, Bob	Marvel Comics	1992
Shazam! The Monster Society of Evil	Smith, Jeff	Smith, Jeff	DC Comics	2007
Showcase Presents: Warlord, Volume 1	Grell, Mike		DC Comics	2009
Siege	Bendis, Brian Michael	Coipel, Olivier	Marvel	2010
Silver Metal Lover, The	Lee, Tanith, and Robbins, Trina	Robbins, Trina	Spectra	1985
*Silver Surfer, The	Lee, Stan	Kirby, Jack	Marvel Comics; Simon & Schuster	1978
Silver Surfer, The: Rebirth of Thanos	Starlin, Jim	Edelman, Scott; Lim, Ron; Zeck, Mike	Marvel	2006
Silver Surfer: Parable	Lee, Stan, and Moebius	Moebius	Marvel	1988
Simon Dark: What Simon Does	Niles, Steve, et al.	Hampton, Scott	DC Comics	2008
Sin City: The Hard Goodbye	Miller, Frank	Miller, Frank	Dark Horse Comics	1991

Title	Author	Artist	Publisher	Year
Solomon Kane: Death's Black Riders	Allie, Scott	Robertson, Darick	Dark Horse Comics	2010
Solomon Kane: The Castle of the Devil	Allie, Scott	Guevara, Mario	Dark Horse Comics	2009
Space Ghost	Evanier, Mark, and Rude, Steve	Rude, Steve	Comico the Comic Company	1987
*Spawn	McFarlane, Todd; Gaiman, Neil; Miller, Frank; Moore, Alan; Morrison	McFarlane, Todd	Image Comics	1995-2001
Spectre, The: Tales of the Unexpected		Lapham, David, et al.		2007
Spider-Man: Birth of Venom	Shooter, Jim; DeFalco, Tom; Byrne, John; Simonson, Louise; Michelinie, David	Zeck, Mike; Frenz, Ron; Leonardi, Rick; LaRocque, Grag; MacFarlane, Todd	Marvel	2007
Spider-Man: Brand New Day	Slott, Dan; Guggenheim, Marc	Jimenez, Phil; McNiven, Steve; Larocca, Salvador	Marvel	2008
*Spider-Man: Kraven's Last Hunt	DeMatteis, J. M.	Zeck, Mike	Marvel Comics	1989
Spider-Man: Maximum Carnage	Defalco, Tom ; Kavanagh, Terry	DeMatteis, J.M.; Michelinie, David	Marvel	2006
Spider-Man: Sinister Six	Lee, Stan; Michelinie, David	Ditko, Steve; Larsen, Erik	Marvel	2009

Title	Author	Artist	Publisher	Year
Spider-Man: The Gauntlet	Slott, Dan; Van Lente, Fred; Waid, Mark	Kubert, Adam; Kitson, Barty; Azaceta, Paul; Pulido, Javier	Marvel	2010
Spider-Man: The Grim Hunt	Kelly, Joe, et al.	Lark, Michael	Marvel Comics	2010
Spider-Man: Torment	McFarlane, Todd	McFarlane, Todd	Marvel Comics	1990
*Spirit Archives, The	Eisner, Will; Feiffer, Jules; Cole, Jack	Eisner, Will	DC Comics	2000-2009
Spirit, The	Eisner, Will, et al	Eisner, Will	DC Comics	1941-1952
Squadron Supreme	Gruenwald, Mark, et al	Buscema, John; Hall, Bob; Ryan, Paul; Neary, Paul	Marvel Comics	1985-1986
Starman	Robinson, James, and Harris, Tony	Harris, Tony	DC Comics	1994-2001
Steampunk: Manimatron	Bachalo, Chris, and Kelly, Joe	Friend, Richard	Wildstorm	2001
Stormwatch	Ellis, Warren, et al	Raney, Tom	Wildstorm	2000
Stormwatch: A Finer World	Ellis, Warren; Hitch, Bryan; Neary, Paul	Hitch, Bryan	WildStorm	2000
The Strange Talent of Luther Strode	Jordan, Justin	Moore, Tradd ; Sobreiro, Felipe	Image	2012
Stumptown	Rucka, Greg, and Southworth, Matthew	Southworth, Matthew	Oni Press	2009-present
Superior	Millar, Mark	Yu, Leinil Francis	Marvel	2012

Title	Author	Artist	Publisher	Year
Superman for All Seasons	Loeb, Jeph	Sale, Tim	DC Comics	1999
Superman: Birthright	Waid, Mark, and Francis Yu, Leinil	Yu, Leinil Francis, Alanguilan, Gerry	DC Comics	2004
Superman: Distant Fires	Chaykin, Howard	Kane, Gil; Nowlan, Kevin; Hollingsworth, Matt	DC Comics	1998
Superman: Earth One	Straczynski, J. Michael, et al.	Davis, Shane	DC Comics	2011
Superman: Our Worlds at War	Loeb, Jeph, et al.		DC Comics	2006
Superman: Peace on Earth	Dini, Paul, and Ross, Alex	Ross, Alex	DC Comics	1999
Superman: Red Son	Millar, Mark	Dave Johnson	DC Comics	2004
Superman: Secret Origin	Johns, Geoff, et al.	Frank, Gary	DC Comics	2010
Superman: Speeding Bullets	DeMatteis, J. M.	Barreto, Eduardo, Dorscheid, Les	DC Comics	1993
Superman: The Man of Steel	Byrne, John	Byrne, John	DC Comics	1991
Swamp Thing	Moore, Alan	Bissette, Stephen R.	DC Comics	1987-2003
The Sword	Luna, Joshua ; Luna, Jonathan	Luna, Jonathan	Image	2008
Sword of the Atom	Strnad, Jan, et al	Kane, Gil, Broderick, Pat	DC Comics	2007

Title	Author	Artist	Publisher	Year
Tales of Asgard	Lee, Stan, and Kirby, Jack	Kirby, Jack	Marvel Comics	2011
Teenage Mutant Ninja Turtles	Laird, Peter, and Eastman, Kevin B.	Eastman, Kevin B., Laird, Peter	IDW Publishing	1984-1993
Tell Me Dark	Wagner, Edward; Karl, Rieber; John Ney; Williams, Kent	Williams, Kent	DC Comics	1992
Thanos Quest, The	Starlin, Jim, and Lim, Ron		Marvel Comics	1990
*Thor	Simonson, Walt	Simonson, Walt	Marvel Comics	2007
Thor: Rebirth	Straczynski, J. Michael, and Coipel, Olivier	Copiel, Olivier	Marvel Comics	2007
Tomorrow Stories	Moore, Alan	Veitch, Rick	Wildstorm	1999-2002
Tom Strong	Aylett, Steve; Brubaker, Ed; Moore, Alan; Vaughan, Brian K.	Baker, Kyle	DC Comics	2000-2011
*Tom Strong's Terrific Tales	Moore, Alan, et al.	Moore, Alan	WildStorm	2002-2005
*Top 10	Moore, Alan	Cannon, Zander	DC Comics	2000, 2002
*Transmetropolitan	Ellis, Warren	Robertson, Darick	DC Comics	1998
Truth: Red, White, and Black	Morales, Robert, and Kyle Baker	Baker, Kyle	Marvel Comics	2004
Ultimate Avengers: The Next Genera-tion	Millar, Mark, and Carlos Pacheco	Pacheco, Carlos	Marvel Comics	2010
*Ultimates, The	Millar, Mark	Bryan Hitch	Marvel Comics	2010

Title	Author	Artist	Publisher	Year
Ultimates, The: Super-Human	Millar, Mark, Bryan Hitch, and Currie, Andrew	Hitch, Bryan	Marvel Comics	2005
Ultimate Spider-Man	Bendis, Brian Michael, and Mark Bagley	Bagley, Mark	Marvel Comics	2002-2010
Ultimate Wolverine Versus Hulk	Lindelof, Damon, and Yu, Leinil Francis	Yu, Leinil Francis	Marvel Comics	2009
Ultimate X-Men	Millar, Mike, and Bendis, Brian Michael	Kubert, Andy	Marvel Comics	2006-2010
Umbrella Academy, The	Way, Gerard	Ba, Gabriel	Dark Horse Comics	2007-present
Uncanny X-Men	Claremont, Chris, et al.	Kirby, Jack, et al.	Marvel Comics	1975-1984
Uncanny X-Men Omnibus Vol. 1	Claremont, Chris ; Wein, Len	Cockrum, Dave ; Byrne, John	Marvel	2006
*Uncle Sam	Darnall, Steve; Ross, Alex	Ross, Alex	DC Comics	1998
Universe X	Krueger, Jim, and Braithwaite, Doug	Braithwaite, Doug	Marvel Comics	2000-2001
Unwritten, The	Carey, Mike, and Gross, Peter	Gross, Peter	Vertigo	2009-present
*V for Vendetta	Moore, Alan	Lloyd, David	DC Comics	1989
Victorian Undead	Edginton, Ian, et al.	Fabbri, Davide	DC Comics	2009-2010
Vigilante: City Lights, Prairie Justice	Robinson, James; Salmons, Tony; Blevins, Bret	Salmons, Tony, Blevins, Brett	DC Comics	2009

Title	Author	Artist	Publisher	Year
Walking Dead, The	Kirkman, Robert, and Moore, Tony	Moore, Tony	Image Comics	2003-present
*Wanted	Millar, Mark	Jones, J. G.	Image Comics	2005
Warlord: The Saga	Grell, Mike, et al.	Hardin, Chad, Prado, Joe	DC Comics	2010
*Watchmen	Moore, Alan	Gibbons, Dave	DC Comics	1987
Wednesday Comics	Gaiman, Neil, et al.	Bullock, Dave, Nowlan, Kevin	DC Comics	2010
Whatever Happened to the Man of Tomorrow?	Moore, Alan, and Curt Swan	Swan, Curt	DC Comics	1986
Will Eisner's The Spirit: Book 1— Action, Mystery, Adventure	Cooke, Darwyn, et al.	Eisner, Will	DC Comics	2007
*Wolverine	Claremont, Chris	Miller, Frank	Marvel Comics	1982
Wolverine Omnibus, Volume 1	Claremont, Chris	Buscema, John, Trimpe, Herb, McFarlane, Todd	Marvel Comics	2009
Wolverine: Enemy of the State	Millar, Mark, and Romita, John, Jr	Romita, John	Marvel Comics	2006
Wolverine: Old Man Logan	Millar, Mark, and McNiven, Steve	McNiven, Steve	Marvel Comics	2009
*Wolverine: Origin	Jemas, Bill; Jenkins, Paul; Quesada, Joe	Isanove, Richard	Marvel Comics	2002

Title	Author	Artist	Publisher	Year
Wolverine: The End	Jenkins, Paul, and Castellini, Claudio	Castellini, Claudio	Marvel Comics	2004
Wonder Woman: Gods and Mortals	Pérez, George; Wein, Len; Potter, Greg	Pérez, George	DC Comics	2004
*Wonder Woman: Love and Murder	Picoult, Jodi	Diaz, Paco	DC Comics	2007
Wonder Woman: Mission's End	Rucka, Greg	Lopez, David, Richards, Cliff	DC Comics	2005
*Wonder Woman: The Circle	Simone, Gail	Dodson, Terry	DC Comics	2008
Wonder Woman: The Hiketeia	Rucka, Greg	Jones, J.G	DC Comics	2002
X Omnibus, Volume 1	Mahnke, Doug, et al.	Kirby, Jack, et al.	Dark Horse Comics	2008
X-Men Omnibus Vol. 1	Lee, Stan; Thomas, Roy	Kirby, Jack; Gavin, Jay	Marvel	2009
X-Men: Age of Apocalypse	Scott Lobdell; Waid, Mark; Nicieza, Fabian; Loeb, Jeph	Cruz, Roger; Garney, Ron; Kubert, Andy; Chruchill, Ian	Marvel	2012
*X-Men: Days of Future Past	Claremont, Chris	Byrne, John	Marvel Comics	2004
*X-Men: God Loves, Man Kills	Claremont, Chris	Anderson, Brent	Marvel Comics	1982

Title	Author	Artist	Publisher	Year
X-Men: Inferno	Claremont, Chris; Simonson, Lousie; Simonson, Walter	Silvestri, Marc; Blevins, Bret; Bogdanove, Jon	Marvel	2009
X-Men: Messiah Complex	Brubaker, Ed; Carey, Mike; Kyle, Craig; Yost, Chris; David, Peter	Silvestri, Marc; Tan, Billy; Bachalo, Chris; Ramos, Humberto; Eaton, Scot	Marvel	2008
X-Men: Mutant Massacre	Claremont, Chris	Romita, John Jr; Guice, Jackson; Buscema, Sal	Marvel	2010
X-Men: Schism	Aaron, Jason	Acuña, Daniel; Davis, Alan; Kubert, Adam; Pacheco, Carlos; Cho, Frank	Marvel	2012
X-Men: The Complete Age of Apocalypse Epic, Book 1	Lobdell, Scott, et al.		Marvel Comics	-2006
*X-Men: The Dark Phoenix Saga	Claremont, Chris	Byrne, John	Marvel Comics	1990
X-Men: The Fall of the Mutants	Simonson, Louise; Claremont, Chris; Gruenwald, Mark; Nocenti, Ann	Blevins, Bret; Brigman, June; Silvestri, Marc; Simonson, Walter; Buscema, Sal	Marvel	2011
X-Men: The Hidden Years	Byrne, John	Byrne, John	Marvel Comics	2001

Title	Author	Artist	Publisher	Year
X-Statix	Milligan, Peter, and Allred, Michael	Dragotta, Nick	Marvel Comics	2002-2004
*Y: The Last Man	Vaughan, Brian K.	Chadwick, Paul	DC Comics	2003-2008
Young Avengers	Heinberg, Allan, and Cheung, Jim	Cheung, Jim, Di Vito, Andrea	Marvel Comics	2006
Zero Hour: Crisis in Time	Jurgens, Dan, and Ordway, Jerry	Ordway, Jerry	DC Comics	1994

Recommended Readings: Independents

Title	Author	Artist	Publisher	Year
*300	Miller, Frank	Miller, Frank ; Lynn Varley	Dark Horse Comics	1999
*30 Days of Night	Niles, Steve	Templesmith, Ben ; Robbins, Robbie	IDW Publishing	2003
*9/11 Report, The: A Graphic Adaptation	Jacobson, Sid	Colón, Ernie	Hill and Wang	2006
*A.D.: New Orleans After the Deluge	Neufeld, Josh	Neufeld, Josh	Pantheon Books	2009
Adventures in Oz	Baum, L. Frank, and Shanower, Eric	Shanower, Eric	IDW Publishing	2006
Adventures of Fat Freddy's Cat, The	Shelton, Gilbert	Shelton, Gilbert	Rip Off Press	1977
*Adventures of Luther Arkwright, The	Talbot, Bryan	Talbot, Bryan	Dark Horse Comics	1997
Adventures of Rabbi Harvey, The	Sheinkin, Steve	Sheinkin, Steve	Jewish Lights Pub	2006-2010
*Adventures of Tintin, The	Hergé	Hergé	Casterman (French); Little, Brown (English)	1930-1976 (English translation, 1958-1991)
After 9/11: America's War on Terror (2001-)	Jacobson, Sid, and Colón, Ernie	Colón, Ernie	Hill and Wang	2008
*Age of Bronze: The Story of the Trojan War	Shanower, Eric	Shanower, Eric	Image Comics	2001-present

Title	Author	Artist	Publisher	Year
Age of Reptiles	Delgado, Ricardo	Delgado, Ricardo ; Campbell, Jim (colorist); Sinclair, James (colorist)	Dark Horse Comics	1996
Airtight Garage of Jerry Cornelius	Moebius	Moebius	Les Humanoïdes Associés (French); Marvel Comics (English)	1979 (English translation, 1987)
Alan Moore's Hypothetical Lizard	Moore, Alan, et al.	Fiumara, Sebastian ; Lorente, Lorenzo	Avatar Press	2007
Alan's War: The Memories of G.I. Alan Cope	Guibert, Emmanuel	Guibert, Emmanuel; Merrien, Céline	L'Association (French), First Second (English)	2000 (English translation, 2008)
Alay-oop	Gropper, William	Gropper, William	Coward-McCann	1930
Alec	Campbell, Eddie	Campbell, Eddie	Top Shelf Productions	1981-present
Alec: The Years Have Pants	Campbell, Eddie	Campbell, Eddie	Top Shelf Productions	2009
Alex	Kalesniko, Mark	Kalesniko, Mark	Fantagraphics Books	2006
Alice in Sunderland: An Entertainment	Talbot, Bryan	Talbot, Bryan; Smith, Jordan	Dark Horse Comics	2007
Aliens	Byrne, John; Guinan, Paul; Verheiden, Mark	Aragonés, Sergio ; Bagge, Peter	Dark Horse Comics	2007-2009
Aliens vs. Predators	Stradley, Randy; Warner, Chris; Norwood, Phill	Warner, Chris; Norwood, Phill	Dark Horse Comics	1991
Alison Dare	Torres, J, and J Bone	Bone, J.	Tundra Books	2010

Title	Author	Artist	Publisher	Year
Al Williamson's Flash Gordon: A Lifelong Vision of the Heroic	Williamson, Al; Schultz, Mark; Aragonés, Sergio	Williamson, Al	Flesk Publications	2009
Amazing Screw-On Head and Other Curious Objects, The	Mignola, Mike	Mignola, Mike	Dark Horse Comics	2010
*American Born Chinese	Yang, Gene Luen	Yang, Gene Luen; Pien, Lark	First Second Books	2006
*American Splendor: From off the Streets of Cleveland	Pekar, Harvey	Budgett, Greg ; Crumb, Robert	Harvey Pekar; Dark Horse Comics; DC Comics	1987
American Splendor: The Life and Times of Harvey Pekar	Pekar, Harvey		Ballantine Books	2003
American Vampire	Snyder, Scott, and King, Stephen	Alburquerque, Rafael	Titan Publishing Company	2010-present
American Widow	Torres, Alissa, and Choi, Sungyoon	Choi, Sungyoon	Villard	2008
Anita Blake, Vampire Hunter	Hamilton, Laurell K	Lim, Ron ; Booth, Brett	Jove	1993-2010
Apex Treasury of Underground Comics, The	Donahue, Don, and Goodrick, Susan, eds.		Links Books	1981
*Arrival, The	Tan, Shaun	Tan, Shaun	Lothian Books	2006
Art School Confidential	Clowes, Daniel	Clowes, Daniel	Fantagraphics Books	2006

Title	Author	Artist	Publisher	Year
Asterios Polyp	Mazzucchelli, David	Mazzucchelli, David	Pantheon Books	2009
Asterix	Goscinny, René; Uderzo, Albert	Uderzo, Albert	Editions Dargaud; Editions Albert-René; Hachette	1961 (English translation, 1969)
Attitude: The New Subversive Political Cartoonists	Rall, Ted, ed.		NBM Publishing	2002
Auschwitz	Croci, Pascal	Croci, Pascal	Harry N. Abrams	2004
Awkward and Definition: The High School Comic Chronicles of Ariel Schrag	Schrag, Ariel	Schrag, Ariel	Touchstone	2008
Aya of Yopougon	Abouet, Marguerite	Oubrerie, Clément	Gallimard (French); Drawn and Quarterly (English)	2007
Babel	B. , David	B., David	Fantagraphics Books	2004, 2008
Bacchus	Campbell, Eddie	Campbell, Eddie	Harrier Comics; Dark Horse Comics; Campbell, Eddie Comics	1995-2010
Bakers: Do These Toys Belong Somewhere?, The	Baker, Kyle	Baker, Kyle	Baker, Kyle Publishing	2006
Ballad of Doctor Richardson, The	Pope, Paul	Pope, Paul	Horse Press	1994
Bambi and Her Pink Gun	Kaneko, Atsushi	Kaneko, Atsushi	Digital Manga Publishing	1998-2001

Title	Author	Artist	Publisher	Year
Bannock, Beans, and Black Tea: The Life of a Young Boy Growing Up in the Great Depression	Gallant, John, and Seth	Gallant, Seth	Drawn and Quarterly	2004
Barn Owl's Wondrous Capers, The	Banerjee, Sarnath	Banerjee, Sarnath	Penguin Global	2007
Batman vs. Predator	Gibbons, Dave; Kubert, Adam; Kubert, Andy	Kubert, Dave and Andy	DC Comics	1991-1992
Bayou	Love, Jeremy	Love, Jeremy	Zuda	2009
B. B. Wolf and the Three LPs	Arnold, J. D., and Koslowski, Rich	Koslowski, Rich	Top Shelf Productions	2010
Bear, The	Briggs, Raymond	Briggs, Raymond	Random House	1994
Berlin: City of Smoke	Lutes, Jason	Lutes, Jason	Drawn and Quarterly	2009
*Berlin: City of Stones	Lutes, Jason	Lutes, Jason	Drawn and Quarterly	2000
Beyond Palomar: A Love and Rockets Book	Hernandez, Gilbert	Hernandez, Gilbert	Fantagraphics Books	2007
Big Baby	Burns, Charles	Burnes, Charles	Fantagraphics Books	1999
Big Bad Bitterkomix Handbook, The	Kannemeyer, Anton, and Botes, Conrad		Jacana Media	2008
Big Fat Little Lit	Spiegelman, Art, and Mouly, Françoise		Puffin	2006
Biker Girl	Rocks, Misako	Rocks, Misako	San Val	2006

Title	Author	Artist	Publisher	Year
Binky Brown Sampler	Green, Justin	Green, Justin	Last Gasp	1995
Binky the Space Cat	Spires, Ashley	Spires, Ashley	Kids Can Press	2009
Birth of a Nation: A Comic Novel	McGruder, Aaron; Hudlin, Reginald; Baker, Kyle	Baker, Kyle	Three Rivers Press	2004
Bite Club	Chaykin, Howard; Tischman, David; Hahn, David	Hahn, David	Vertigo	2005
Black Hole	Burns, Charles	Burns, Charles	Kitchen Sink Press; Pantheon Books	2005
Blackmark	Goodwin, Archie; Kane, Gil	Kane, Gil	Bantam Books; Fantagraphics Books	1971 (Volume 1); 2002 (Volumes 1 and 2)
Blake and Mortimer	Jacobs, Edgar P., and de Moor, Bob	Jacobs, Edgar P.	Cinebook	1946-present
Blankets: An Illustrated Novel	Thompson, Craig	Thompson, Craig	Top Shelf Comics	2003
Blood Song: A Silent Ballad	Drooker, Eric	Drooker, Eric	Dark Horse Books	2002
Blueberry	Charlier, Jean-Michel; Corteggiani, François	Moebius	Editions Dargaud	1965-present (English translation, 1977-1993)
Bob and Bobette	Vandersteen, Willy	Vandersteen, Willy	Ravette Publishing	1945-present
Bone	Smith, Jeff	Smith, Jeff	Cartoon Books; Image Comics	1993

Title	Author	Artist	Publisher	Year
Book of Boy Trouble: Gay Boy Comics with a New Attitude, The	Kirby, Robert, and David Kelly, eds	Kirby, Robert	Greem Candy Press	2006
*Book of Genesis, The	Crumb, Robert	Crumb, Robert	W. W. Norton	2009
Bop! More Box Office Poison	Robinson, Alex	Robinson, Alex	Top Shelf Productions	2003
*Boulevard of Broken Dreams, The	Deitch, Kim; Deitch, Simon	Deitch, Kim	Pantheon Books; Fantagraphics Books	2002
*Box Office Poison	Robinson, Alex	Robinson, Alex	Antarctic Press; Top Shelf Productions	2001
Bradleys, The	Bagge, Peter	Bagge, Peter	Fantagraphics	2004
Breaking Up	Friedman, Aimee, and Norrie, Christine	Norrie, Christine	GRAPHIX	2007
Britten and Brülightly	Berry, Hannah	Berry, Hannah	Metropolitan Books	2009
Brought to Light: Thirty Years of Drug Smuggling, Arms Deals, and Covert Operations That Robbed America and Betrayed the Constitution	Brabner, Joyce, et al.	Sienkiewicz, Bill	Eclipse	1989
*Burma Chronicles	Delisle, Guy	Delisle, Guy	Delcourt (French); Drawn and Quarterly (English)	2007 (English translation, 2008)

Title	Author	Artist	Publisher	Year
Burnout	Donner, Rebecca, and Miranda, Inaki	Miranda, Inaki	DC Comics	2008
Cages	McKean, Dave	McKean, Dave	Tundra; Kitchen Sink Press; NBM; Dark Horse Comics	1998
Cancer Made Me a Shallower Person: A Memoir in Comics	Engelberg, Miriam	Engleberg, Miriam	Harper Perennial	2006
Cancer Vixen: A True Story	Marchetto, Marisa Acocella	Marchetto, Marisa Acocella	Alfred A. Knopf	2006
Caricature	Clowes, Daniel	Rosen, Mal	Fantagraphics Books	2002
Carnet de Voyage	Thompson, Craig	Thompson, Craig	Top Shelf Productions	2004
Cartoon History of the Universe, The	Gonick, Larry	Gonick, Larry	Rip Off Press; Kitchen Sink Press; Doubleday; HarperCollins	1990-2009
Case of the Winking Buddha, The	Stokes, Manning Lee, and Raab, Charles	Stokes, Manning Lee	St. John Publishing	1950
Castle Waiting	Medley, Linda	Medley, Linda ; Klein, Todd	Olio; Cartoon Books; Fantagraphics Books	2006
Cavalcade of Boys: Complete Collection	Fish, Tim	Fish, Tim	Poison Press	2006
Cecil and Jordan in New York	Bell, Gabrielle	Bell, Gabrielle	Drawn and Quarterly	2009

Title	Author	Artist	Publisher	Year
Chaos: Lone Sloane	Druillet, Philippe		Heavy Metal Magazine	2000
Che: A Graphic Biography	Jacobson, Sid, and Colón, Ernie	Rodriguez, Spain	Verso	2009
Chicken with Plums	Satrapi, Marjane	Satrapi, Marjane	L'Association (French); Pantheon Books (English)	Poulet aux prunes, 2004 (English translation, 2006)
Child in Palestine, A: The Cartoons of Naji al-Ali	Al-Ali, Naji	Al-Ali, Naji	Verso	2009
Chronicles of Conan, The; Volume 17: The Creation Quest and Other Stories	DeMatteis, J. M., et al.	Powell, Eric	Dark Horse	2009
City of Glass	Auster, Paul; Karasik, Paul; Mazzucchelli, David	Mazzucchelli, David	Avon Books	1994
Classics Illustrated	Kanter, Albert		Elliot Publishing Co. ; Gilberton Company ; Frawley Corporation	1941-1971
Clouds Above, The	Crane, Jordan	Crane, Jordan	Fantagraphics Books	2008
Clumsy	Brown, Jeffrey	Brown, Jeffrey	Top Shelf Comics	2002
Clyde Fans: Book One	Seth	Seth	Drawn and Quarterly	2004

Title	Author	Artist	Publisher	Year
*Color Trilogy, The	Hwa, Kim Dong	Hwa, Kim Dong	Daewon Culture Industry (Korean); First Second Books (English)	1995-1996 (English translation, 2009)
Comanche Moon	Jackson, Jack	Jackson, Jack	Reed Press	2003
Comix 2000	L'Association		Fantagraphics	1999
Complete Alice in Wonderland, The	Carroll, Lewis; Moore, Leah; Reppion, John; Awano, Erica	Tenniel, John	Wonderland Imprints	2010
Complete Crumb Comics, The	Crumb, Robert	Crumb, Robert	Fantsgraphics Books	1987
Complete Dirty Laundry Comics, The	Kominsky, Aline; Crumb, Robert; Crumb, Sophie	Crumb, Robert	Last Gasp	1993
*Complete Essex County, The	Lemire, Jeff	Lemire, Jeff	Top Shelf Productions	2007-2008
*Complete Fritz the Cat, The	Crumb, Robert	Crumb, Robert	Bélier Press	1978
Complete Wendel, The	Cruse, Howard	Cruse, Howard	Universe	2011
*Contract with God, And Other Tenement Stories, A	Eisner, Will	Eisner, Will	Baronet Books; Kitchen Sink Press	1978
Cotton Woods: The Comic Strip Adventures of a Baseball Natural	Gotto, Ray	Gotto, Ray	Kitchen Sink Press	1991

Title	Author	Artist	Publisher	Year
Courtney Crumrin	Naifeh, Ted	Naifeh, Ted	Oni Press	2003-2009
Criminal Macabre	Niles, Steve, and Templesmith, Ben	Niles, Steve	Dark Horse	1990-present
Curious Case of Benjamin Button, The	Fitzgerald, F. Scott; DeFilippis, Nunzio; Weir, Christina	Cornell, Kevin; Ashburn, Bryn	Quirk Books	2008
Curses: Glenn Ganges Stories	Huizinga, Kevin	Huizinga, Kevin	Drawn and Quarterly	2006
Cute Manifesto, The	Kochalka, James	Kochalka, James	Alternative Comics	2005
Daddy's Girl	Drechsler, Debbie	Drechsler, Debbie	Fantagraphics Books	1996
Daily Delirium	Prado, Miguelanxo	Prado, Miguelanxo	NBM Publishing	2003
Dark Rain: A New Orleans Story	Johnson, Mat, and Gane, Simon	Gane, Simone	Vertigo	2010
*David Boring	Clowes, Daniel	Clowes, Daniel; Kuramoto, John	Pantheon Books	2000
*Dead Memory	Mathieu, Marc-Antoine	Mathieu, Marc-Antoine; Rehm, Dirk	Delcourt (French); Dark Horse Comics (English)	Mémoire morte, 2000 (English translation, 2003)
*Dear Julia	Biggs, Brian	Biggs, Brian	Black Eye Productions; Top Shelf Comics	2000
*Deogratias: A Tale of Rwanda	Stassen, Jean-Philippe	Stassen, Jean-Philippe	Dupuis (French); First Second Books (English)	2000 (English translation, 2006)
Destiny: A Chronicle of Deaths Foretold	Kwitney, Alisa	Williams, Kent	Vertigo	2000

Title	Author	Artist	Publisher	Year
Devil's Panties, The	Breeden, Jennie	Breeden, Jennie	Jennie Breeden	2001-present
*Diary of a Mosquito Abatement Man	Porcellino, John	Porcellino, John	La Mano	2005
Diary of a Teenage Girl: An Account in Words and Pictures	Gloeckner, Phoebe	Gloeckner, Phoebe	Frog Books	2001
Different Ugliness, Different Madness	Malès, Marc	Malès, Marc	Humanoids - Rebellion	2005
Disease of Language, A	Moore, Alan, and Campbell, Eddie	Campbell, Eddie	Knockabout	2006
Do Androids Dream of Electric Sheep?	Dick, Philip K., and Parker, Tony	Parker, Tony; Sienkiewicz, Bill	Doubleday	1968
Dogs and Water	Nilsen, Anders	Nilsen, Anders	Drawn and Quarterly	2004
Dong Xoai, Vietnam 1965	Kubert, Joe	Kubert, Joe	Vertigo	2010
*Dropsie Avenue: The Neighborhood	Eisner, Will	Eisner, Will	Kitchen Sink Press	1995, 2006 (The Contract with God Trilogy)
Drunken Dream and Other Stories, A	Hagio, Moto	Hagio, Moto	Fantagraphics	2010
*Dykes to Watch Out For	Bechdel, Alison	Bechdel, Alison	Firebrand Books; Houghton Mifflin	1986-2008
Eddy Current	McKeever, Ted	McKeever, Ted	Image Comics	2008
*Ed the Happy Clown: The Definitive Ed Book	Brown, Chester	Brown, Chester	Drawn and Quarterly; Vortex Comics	1989

Title	Author	Artist	Publisher	Year
El Borrah	Burns, Charles			1984-2005
Elk's Run	Fialkov, Hale, Joshua	Tuazon, Noel ; Keating, Scott A. (colorist); Hanley, Jason (letterer)	Villard	2007
Embroideries	Satrapi, Marjane	Satrapi, Marjane	L'Association (French); Pantheon Books (English)	2003 (English translation, 2005)
Emiko Superstar	Tamaki, Mariko, and Rolston, Steve	Rolston, Steve	Minx	2008
Epicurus the Sage	Messner-Loebs, William, and Kieth, Sam	Kieth, Sam	WildStorm	2003
Epileptic	B., David	David B.	L'Association (French); Pantheon Books (English)	2005 (English)
Escape from "Special"	Miss Lasko-Gross	Lasko-Gross, Miss	Fantagraphics Books	2006
Ethel and Ernest: A True Story	Briggs, Raymond	Briggs, Raymond ; Devine, Carol (cover artist)	Jonathan Cape	1998
Eve	Waldman, Myron	Waldman, Myron	S. Daye	1943
Everybody Is Stupid Except for Me, and Other Astute Observations	Bagge, Peter	Bagge, Peter	Fantagraphics	2009
Exit	Kanan, Nabiel	Kanan, Nabiel	Caliber Comics	1996

Title	Author	Artist	Publisher	Year
*Exit Wounds	Modan, Rutu	Modan, Rutu	Coconino Press (Italian); Drawn and Quarterly (English); Am Oved (Hebrew)	2006 (English translation, 2007)
Fair Weather	Matt, Joe	Matt, Joe	Drawn and Quarterly	2002
Famous Fimmales: Witt Odder Ewents from Heestory	Gross, Milt	Gross, Milt	Doubleday, Doran & Company	1928
*Far Arden	Cannon, Kevin	Cannon, Kevin	Top Shelf Productions	2008 (self-published edition); 2009
Fate of the Artist, The	Campbell, Eddie	Campbell, Eddie	San Val	2006
Father Christmas	Briggs, Raymond	Briggs, Raymond	Random House Books	1973
*Fax from Sarajevo: A Story of Survival	Kubert, Joe	Kubert, Joe	Dark Horse Comics	1996
Femme Noir: The Dark City Diaries	Mills, Christopher	Staton, Joe	Ape Entertainment	2009
First in Space	Vining, James; Sherwood, Douglas; Major, Guy	Vining, James	Oni Press	2007
*Fixer, The: A Story from Sarajevo	Sacco, Joe	Sacco, Joe	Drawn and Quarterly	2003, 2005
*Flaming Carrot Comics	Burden, Bob	Burden, Bob; Starr, Roxanne	Dark Horse Comics	1997-2006

Title	Author	Artist	Publisher	Year
Flies on the Ceiling	Hernandez, Jaime, and Hernandez, Gilbert	Hernandez, Jaime and Gilbert	Fantagraphics Books	2003
Flood! A Novel in Pictures	Drooker, Eric	Drooker, Eric	Four Walls Eight Windows; Dark Horse Comics	1992
Footnotes in Gaza: A Graphic Novel	Sacco, Joe	Sacco, Joe	Metropolitan Books	2009
Francophone Bande Dessinée, The	Fosdick, Charles; Groves, Laurence; and McQuilan; Libbie, eds		Rodopi	2005
Frank Book, The	Woodring, Jim	Woodring, Jim	Fantagraphics Books	2003
French Popular Culture: An Introduction	Dauncey, Hugh, ed.		Hodder Education Publishers	2003
From Headrack to Claude: Collected Gay Comix by Cruse, Howard	Cruse, Howard	Cruse, Howard	Nifty Kitsch Press	2009
From Hell: Being a Melodrama in Sixteen Parts	Moore, Alan	Campbell, Eddie	Top Shelf Comics	1999
Fun Home: A Family Tragicomic	Bechdel, Alison	Bechdel, Alison	Houghton Mifflin	2006
Funny Misshapen Body	Brown, Jeffrey	Brown, Jeffrey	Touchstone	2009
Garage Band	Gipi	Gipi	Paw Prints	2007
Gemma Bovery	Simmonds, Posy	Simmonds, Posy	Pantheon Books	1999

Title	Author	Artist	Publisher	Year
*Get a Life	Berberian, Charles; Dupuy, Philippe	Berberian, Charles ; Dupuy, Philippe	Les Humanoïdes Associés (French); Drawn and Quarterly (English)	2006 (English translation of first three volumes)
Ghostopolis	TenNapel, Doug	TenNapel, Doug	GRAPHIX	2010
*Ghost World	Clowes, Daniel	Clowes, Daniel	Fantagraphics Books	1997
Girl Genius	Foglio, Kaja, and Phil Foglio	Foglio, Kaja and Phil	Studio Foglio	2002-2010
*Give It Up! And Other Short Stories	Kafka, Franz; Kuper, Peter	Kuper, Peter	NBM	1995
*Glacial Period	Crécy, Nicolas de	Ortho (letterer)	Musée du Louvre (French); NBM (English)	Période glaciaire, 2005 (English translation, 2006)
Glass Castle, The	Walls, Jeanette		Scribner	2005
God Save the Queen	Carey, Mike, and Bolton, John	Bolton, John	Vertigo	2007
*Golem's Mighty Swing, The	Sturm, James	Sturm, James	Drawn and Quarterly	2001
Golly!	Hester, Phil, and Turner, Brook	Turner, Brook	Image Comics	2008-2009
*Good-Bye, Chunky Rice	Thompson, Craig	Thompson, Craig	Top Shelf Comics	1999
Gordon Yamamoto and the King of the Geeks	Yang, Gene Luen	Yang, Gene Luen	SLG Publishing	2004
Grandville	Talbot, Bryan	Talbot, Bryan	Dark Horse Comics	2009

Title	Author	Artist	Publisher	Year
Graphic Storytelling and Visual Narrative	Eisner, Will	Eisner, Will	Poorhouse Press	2008
Great Walls of Samaris, The	Schuiten, François, and Peeters, Benoît	Schuiten, François, and Peeters, Benoît	Nantier Beall Minoustchine Publishing	1987
Great War and Modern Memory, The	Fussell, Paul		Oxford University Press	2009
Hal Foster's Prince Valiant: Far from Camelot	Gianni, Gary; Schultz, Mark; Foster, Harold R.	Gianni, Gary	Andrews McMeel Publishing	2008
*Hard Boiled	Miller, Frank	Darrow, Geof	Dark Horse Comics	1993
*Harum Scarum	Trondheim, Lewis	Trondheim, Lewis	Editions Dargaud (French); Fantagraphics Books (English)	1996 (English translation, 1997)
*Harvey Kurtzman's Jungle Book:	Kurtzman, Harvey	Kurtzman, Harvey	Ballantine Books; Kitchen Sink Press	1959
*Hate	Bagge, Peter	Bagge, Peter	Fantagraphics Books	1993-2001
Hat Trick	Burns, Jason M	Zanker, Armando M; Schomburg, Scott	Outlaw Entertainment	2010
*Haunted	Dupuy, Philippe	Dupuy, Philippe	Cornélius (French); Drawn and Quarterly (English)	Hanté, 2005 (English translation, 2008)
*He Done Her Wrong:	Gross, Milt	Gross, Milt	Doubleday; Fantagraphics Books	1930

Title	Author	Artist	Publisher	Year
Hey, Wait…	Jason (pseudonym of John Arne Sæterøy)	Jason	Jippi Forlag (Norwegian); Fantagraphics Books (English)	2002 (English translation, 2001)
Hicksville	Horrocks, Dylan	Horrocks, Dylan	Drawn and Quarterly	1998
History of Violence, A	Wagner, John	Locke, Vince	DC Comics	1997
Hoodoodad, The	Trondheim, Lewis		Fantagraphics	1998
Hookah Girl and Other True Stories, The: Growing up Christian Palestinian in America	Dabaie, Marguerite	Dabai, Marguerite		2007
Hothead Paisan: Homicidal Lesbian Terrorist	DiMassa, Diane	DiMassa, Diane	Cleis Press	1993
Houdini: The Handcuff King	Lutes, Jason	Bertozzi, Nick	Hyperion Paperbacks for Children	2007
How I Made It to Eighteen: A Mostly True Story	White, Tracy	White, Tracy	Roaring Brook Press	2010
How to Understand Israel in Sixty Days or Less	Glidden, Sarah	Glidden, Sarah	Vertigo	2010
Howard the Duck	Gerber, Steve, et al.	Mayerik, Val	Marvel Comics	1973-1978
Human Diastrophism	Hernandez, Gilbert	Hernandez, Gilbert	Fantagraphics Books	2007
Ice Haven	Clowes, Daniel	Clowes, Daniel	Pantheon Books	2005

Title	Author	Artist	Publisher	Year
I Die at Midnight	Baker, Kyle	Baker, Kyle	Vertigo	2000
I Kill Giants	Kelly, Joe, and J. M. Ken Niimura	Niimura, J. M. Ken	Image Comics	2009
Illuminated Poems	Drooker, Eric, and Ginsberg, Allen	Drooker, Eric	Four Walls Eight Windows	1996
*I Never Liked You: A Comic-Strip Narrative	Brown, Chester	Brown, Chester	Drawn and Quarterly	1994
*In the Shadow of No Towers	Spiegelman, Art	Spiegelman, Art	Pantheon Books	2004
Incal, The: Classic Collection	Moebius, and Jodorowsky, Alejandro	Moebius	Humanoids	2011
*Incognegro: A Graphic Mystery	Johnson, Mat	Pleece, Warren	DC Comics	2008
Insiders	Bartoll, Jean-Claude, and Garreta, Renaud	Garreta, Renaud	Cinebook	2009-present
Introducing Kafka	Mairowitz, David Zane, and Crumb, Robert	Crumb, Robert	Totem Books	1993
Invisible People	Eisner, Will	Eisner, Will	W. W. Norton	2000
Isaac the Pirate: To Exotic Lands	Blain, Christophe	Blain, Christophe	NMB Publishing	2003
I Shoulda Ate the Eclair	Gross, Milt	Gross, Milt	Ziff-Davis	1946
*It Rhymes with Lust	Waller, Drake	Baker, Matt; Osrin, Ray	Dark Horse Comics	1950

Title	Author	Artist	Publisher	Year
It's a Bird . . .	Seagle, Steven T.	Kristiansen, Teddy H.; Klein, Todd	DC Comics	2004
It's a Good Life, If You Don't Weaken:	Seth	Seth	Drawn and Quarterly	1996
It Was the War of the Trenches	Tardi, Jacques	Tardi, Jacques	Casterman (French); Fantagraphics Books (English)	C'était la guerre des tranchées: 1914-1918, 1993 (English translation, 2010)
Ivoire	Regnaud, Jean, and Bravo, Émile		Editions de la Pasteque	2006
iZombie	Roberson, Chris	Allred, Michael	Vertigo	2010-present
James Bond Omnibus	Fleming, Ian, et al	Lawrence, Jim; Horak, Yaroslav	Titan Books	2009-present
James Sturm's America: God, Gold, and Golems	Sturm, James	Sturm, James	Drawn and Quarterly	2007
Janes in Love	Castellucci, Cecil, and Rugg, Jim	Rugg, Jim	Vertigo	2008
Janet & Me: An Illustrated Story of Love and Loss	Mack, Stan	Mack, Stan	Simon & Schuster	2004
Jar of Fools: A Picture Story	Lutes, Jason	Lutes, Jason	Drawn and Quarterly	1996
Jew Gangster	Kubert, Joe	Kubert, Joe	ibooks	2005
Jew in Communist Prague, A:	Giardino, Vittorio	Giardino, Vittorio	Rizzoli Lizard (Italian); NBM (English)	Jonas Fink: L'infanzia, 1994 (English translation, 1997)

Title	Author	Artist	Publisher	Year
Jew of New York, The:	Katchor, Ben	Katchor, Ben	Pantheon Books	1998
Jews in America: A Cartoon History	Gantz, David	Gantz, David	The Jewish Publication Society	2001
Jimmy Corrigan: The Smartest Kid on Earth	Ware, Chris	Ware, Chris	Pantheon Books	2000
Job Thing, The	Tyler, Carol	Tyler, Carol	Fantagraphics Books	1993
Joe Sacco	Marshall, Monica		Rosen Pub. Group	2005
Johnny the Homicidal Maniac	Morrison, Grant, and Bond, Philip	Vasquez, Jhonen	SLG Publishing	(1995-1997)
Journey: The Adventures of Wolverine MacAlistaire	Messner-Loebs, William	Messner-Loebs, William	IDW Publishing	2008 (Volume 1); 2009 (Volume 2)
Journey into Mohawk Country	Bogaert, Harmen Meyndertsz van den	O'Connor, George	First Second Books	2006
Julius Knipl, Real Estate Photographer: Stories	Katchor, Ben	Katchor, Ben	Little, Brown	1996
Kabuki	Mack, David	Mack, David ; Mays, Rick ; Martin, Joe	Caliber Press; Image Comics; Marvel ICON Comics	1995-2009
Kafka	Mairowitz, David Zane	Crumb, Robert	Icon Books; Fantagraphics Books	1993 (Introducing Kafka); 2007
Kampung Boy	Lat	Lat	Berita	1979

Title	Author	Artist	Publisher	Year
*Kane	Grist, Paul	Grist, Paul	Dancing Elephant Press; Image Comics	2004-2006
Kill Your Boyfriend	Morrison, Grant, and Bond, Philip	Bond, Philip ; D'Israeli	DC Comics	1995
Kimmie66	Alexovich, Aaron	Alexovich, Aaron	Minx Books	2007
King, The	Koslowski, Rich	Koslowski, Rich	Top Shelf Productions	2005
*King: A Comics Biography	Anderson, Ho Che	Anderson, Ho Che	Fantagraphics Books	2005
*Kings in Disguise	Vance, James	Burr, Dan	Kitchen Sink Press; W. W. Norton	1990
Klezmer: Tales from the Wild East	Sfar, Joann	Sfar, Joann	First Second	2006
Lady Snowblood	Koike, Kazuo, and Kamimura, Kazuo	Kamimura, Kazuo	Carlsen Comics	2005-present
*Laika	Abadzis, Nick	Abadzis, Nick ; Sycamore, Hilary	First Second Books	2007
*La Perdida	Abel, Jessica	Abel, Jessica	Pantheon Books	2006
*Last Day in Vietnam: A Memory	Eisner, Will	Eisner, Will	Dark Horse Comics	2000
Late Bloomer	Tyler, Carol	Tyler, Carol	Fantagraphics Books	2005
Latino U. S. A.: A Cartoon History	Stavans, Ilan, and Alcaraz, Lalo	Alcaraz, Lalo	Basic Books	2000
Law of Love, The	Esquivel, Laura	Prado, Miguelanxo	Three Rivers Press	1996

Title	Author	Artist	Publisher	Year
Leave It to Chance	Robinson, James	Smith, Paul	Image Comics	1997-2003
Level Up	Yang, Gene Luen, and Pham, Thien	Pham, Thien	First Second	2011
Lewis and Clark	Bertozzi, Nick	Bertozzi, Nick	First Second	2011
Liberty Meadows: Eden, Book 1	Cho, Frank	Cho, Frank	Image Comics	2008
Life and Opinions of Tristram Shandy, Gentleman, The	Rowson, Martin, and Sterne, Laurence	Rowson, Martin	Dover	2010
*Life and Times of Scrooge McDuck, The	Rosa, Don	Rosa, Don	Gemstone Publishing; Boom! Studios	2005
Life, in Pictures: Autobiographical Stories	Eisner, Will	Eisner, Will	W. W. Norton	2007
*Life Sucks	Abel, Jessica; Soria, Gabe	Pleece, Warren ; Sycamore, Hilary	First Second	2008
Like a Sniper Lining Up His Shot	Manchette, Jean-Patrick, and Tardi, Jacques	Tardi, Jacques	Fantagraphics	2011
*Like a Velvet Glove Cast in Iron	Clowes, Daniel	Clowes, Daniel	Fantagraphics Books	1993
Literary Life	Simmonds, Posy	Simmonds, Posy	Jonathan Cape	2003
Little Nothings	Trondheim, Lewis	Trondheim, Lewis	NBM Publishing	2007
Living and the Dead, The	Jason	Jason	Fantagraphics Books	2006
*Long Time Relationship	Doucet, Julie	Doucet, Julie	Drawn and Quarterly	2001

Title	Author	Artist	Publisher	Year
Lost at Sea	O'Malley, Bryan Lee	O'Malley, Bryan Lee	Oni Press	2003
Lost Cause:	Jackson, Jack	Jackson, Jack	Kitchen Sink Press	1998
Lost Girl	Kanan, Nabiel	Kanan, Nabiel	NBM	1999
Lost Girls	Moore, Alan	Gebbie, Melinda; Klein, Todd	Kitchen Sink Press; Top Shelf Comics	1995
Louis	Chalmers, John	Marrs, Sandra	Metaphrog	2000-2010
Louis Riel: A Comic-Strip Biography	Brown, Chester	Brown, Chester	Drawn and Quarterly	2003
Love and Rockets	Hernandez, Gilbert; Hernandez, Jaime; Hernandez, Mario	Hernandez, Gilbert; Hernandez, Jaime; Hernandez, Mario	Fantagraphics Books	1985-present
Lucky	Bell, Gabrielle	Bell, Gabrielle	Drawn and Quarterly	2006
Lucky Luke	Morris, and Goscinny, René	Morris	Cinebook	1949-1967
Lute String, The	Woodring, Jim	Woodring, Jim	Fantagraphics	2005
Maakies	Millionaire, Tony	Millionaire, Tony	Fantagraphics Books	1994-present
Macedonia	Pekar, Harvey; Roberson, Heather; Piskor, Ed	Piskor, Ed	Villard	2007
Mail Order Bride	Kalesniko, Mark	Kalesniko, Mark	Fantagraphics Books; Paquet Editions (French); Ponet Mon (Spanish); Poptoon (Korean)	2001

Title	Author	Artist	Publisher	Year
Make Me a Woman	Davis, Vanessa	Davis, Vanessa	Drawn and Quarterly	2010
Man, The	Briggs, Raymond	Briggs, Raymond	Random House	1992
Man from the Ciguri, The	Moebius; Jean-Marc Lofficier; Randy Lofficier	Moebius	Dark Horse Comics	1996
Manga Bible: Names, Games, and the Long Road Trip—Genesis-Exodus	Lee, Young Shin, and Hwang, Jung Sun	Hwang, Jung Sun	Zondervan	2007
Mansion of Evil	Millard, Joseph		Fawett Gold Medal	1950
Map of My Heart	Porcellino, John	Porcellino, John	Drawn and Quarterly	2009
*Market Day	Sturm, James	Sturm, James	Drawn and Quarterly	2010
Marquis, The	Davis, Guy	Davis, Guy	Dark Horse Comics	2009
Masters of the Comic Book Universe Revealed!	Kaplan, Arie		Chicago Review Press	2006
Matrix Comics, The	Lamm, Spencer, et al.	Lamm, Spencer	Burlyman Entertainment	2003
*Maus: A Survivor's Tale	Spiegelman, Art	Spiegelman, Art	Pantheon Books	1986; 1991
Maus I: A Survivor's Tale: My Father Bleeds History	Spiegelman, Art	Spiegelman, Art	Pantheon Books	1986, 1991

Title	Author	Artist	Publisher	Year
Maybe Later	Dupuy, Philippe, and Berberian, Charles	Berberian, Charles; Dupuy, Philippe	Drawn and Quarterly	2006
Mendel's Daughter	Lemelman, Martin,	Lemelman, Martin	Free Press	2007
Meta 4: The Complete Series	McKeever, Ted	McKeever, Ted	Image Comics	2011
Metamorphosis, The	Kuper, Peter, and Kafka, Franz	Kuper, Peter	Turtleback	2003
*Metropol: The Complete Series + Metropol A.D.	McKeever, Ted	McKeever, Ted	Image Comics	2009
Mice Templar	Glass, Bryan J. L., and Oeming, Avon, Michael	Oeming, Avon, Michael	Image Comics	2007-present
Michael Moorcock's Elric: The Making of a Sorcerer	Moorcock, Michael, and Simonson, Walter	Simonson, Walter	DC Comics	2007
*Minor Miracles:	Eisner, Will	Eisner, Will	DC Comics; W. W. Norton	2000
Mister Wonderful: A Love Story	Clowes, Daniel	Clowes, Daniel	Vintage Books	2011
Modesty Blaise	O'Donnell, Peter, et al.	Holdaway, Jim	Souvenir Press	2003-present
Moebius 4: The Long Tomorrow and Other Science Fiction Stories	Giraud, Jean	Moebius	Marvel Enterprises	1988
Mom's Cancer	Fies, Brian	Fies, Brian	Abrams ComicArts	2006

Title	Author	Artist	Publisher	Year
Monologues for Calculating the Density of Black Holes	Nilsen, Anders	Nilsen, Anders	Fantagraphics Books	2009
*Monologues for the Coming Plague	Nilsen, Anders	Anders Nilsen	Fantagraphics Books	2006
More Than Complete Action Philosophers!, The	Van Lente, Fred, and Dunlavey, Ryan	Dunlavey, Ryan	Evil Twin Comics	2009
Motel Art Improvement Service	Little, Jason	Little, Jason	Dark Horse Comics	2010
*Mouse Guard	Petersen, David	David Petersen	Archaia Studios Press	2007-2010
Museum Vaults, The: Excerpts from the Journal of an Expert	Mathieu, Marc-Antoine	Mathiue, Marc-Antoine	ComicsLit	2007
*My Mommy Is in America and She Met Buffalo Bill	Regnaud, Jean	Bravo, Émile	Gallimard (French); Fanfare/Ponent Mon (English)	Ma maman est en Amérique, elle a rencontré Buffalo-Bill, 2007 (English translation, 2010)
My Most Secret Desire	Doucet, Julie	Doucet, Julie	Drawn and Quarterly	2006
My New York Diary	Doucet, Julie	Doucet, Julie	Drawn and Quarterly	1999
*Nat Turner	Baker, Kyle	Baker, Kyle	Harry N. Abrams	2008
Nat Turner's Slave Rebellion	Burgan, Michael, et al.	Burgan, Michael; Barnet III, Charles; Wiachek, Bob	Capstone Press	2006

Title	Author	Artist	Publisher	Year
Naughty Bits	Gregory, Roberta	Gregory, Roberta	Fantagraphics Books	1991-2004
New Adventures of Jesus, The: The Second Coming	Stack, Frank	Stack, Frank	Fantagraphics Books	2006
New York: Life in the Big City	Eisner, Will	Eisner, Will	W. W. Norton	2006
*Night Fisher	Johnson, R. Kikuo	Johnson, R. Kikuo	Fantagraphics Books	2005
Nightmare Factory, The	Ligotti, Thomas; Moore, Stuart; Harris, Joe	Ligotti, Thomas	Carroll & Graf	2007
Ninety-Nine Ways to Tell a Story: Exercises in Style	Madden, Matt	Madden, Matt	Jonathan Cape	2005
*Notes for a War Story	Gipi (pseudonym of Gianni Pacinotti)	Gipi	Coconino Press; First Second	Appunti per una storia di guerra, 2004 (English translation, 2007)
Olympians	O'Connor, George	O'Connor, George	First Second	2010
*Omaha the Cat Dancer	Worley, Kate; Vance, James; Waller, Reed	Waller, Reed	NBM	1987-1998
Ompa-pa	Goscinny, René, and Uderzo, Albert	Uderzo, Albert	Methuen	1977-1978
One! Hundred! Demons!	Barry, Lynda	Barry, Lynda	Sasquatch Books	2002
On the Odd Hours	Liberge, Eric	Liberge, Eric	NBM	2010

Title	Author	Artist	Publisher	Year
Optic Nerve	Tomine, Adrian	Tomine, Adrian	Drawn and Quarterly	1995-1998
Other Side, The	Aaron, Jason, and Stewart, Cameron	Stewart, Cameron	Titan Books	2007
*Our Cancer Year	Pekar, Harvey; Brabner, Joyce	Stack, Frank	Four Walls Eight Windows	1994
*Owly	Runton, Andy	Runton, Andy	Top Shelf Productions	2003-present
*Palestine	Sacco, Joe	Sacco, Joe	Fantagraphics Books	1994, 1996
*Palomar: The Heartbreak Soup Stories	Hernandez, Gilbert	Hernandez, Gilbert	Fantagraphics Books	2003
*Passionate Journey	Masereel, Frans	Masereel, Frans	Dover	Mon livre d'heures, 1919 (English translation, 1922)
*Paul	Rabagliati, Michel	Rabagliati, Michel	Les Editions de la Pastèque (French); Conundrum Press (English); Drawn and Quarterly (English)	1999-present (English translation, 2000-present)
Paying for It	Brown, Chester	Brown, Chester	Drawn and Quarterly	2011
*Pedro and Me: Friendship, Loss, and What I Learned	Winick, Judd	Winick, Judd	Henry Holt	2000
Peepshow	Matt, Joe	Matt, Joe	Drawn and Quarterly	1992-present

Title	Author	Artist	Publisher	Year
People's History of American Empire, A: A Graphic Adaptation	Zinn, Howard; Konopacki, Mike; Buhle, Paul	Konopacki, Mike	Metropolitan Books	2008
Percy Gloom	Malkasian, Cathy	Malkasian, Cathy	Fantagraphics Books	2007
Perfect Example	Porcellino, John	Porcellino, John	Highwater Books; Drawn and Quarterly	2000
Persepolis	Satrapi, Marjane	Satrapi, Marjane; Deluze, Eve; Merrien, Céline	L'Association (French); Pantheon Books (English)	2000-2003 (English translation 2003, 2004)
Photographer, The	Lefèvre, Didier	Guibert, Emmanuel; Lemercier, Frédéric; Lefèvre, Didier; Novgorodoff, Danica	Dupuis (French); First Second (English)	Le Photographe, 2003, 2004, 2006 (English translation, 2009)
Picture This	Barry, Lynda	Barry, Linda	Drawn and Quarterly	2010
Pinocchio: Vampire Slayer and the Great Puppet Theater	Jensen, Van	Higgins, Dusty	SLG Publishing	2010
Plain Janes, The	Castellucci, Cecil	Rugg, Jim; Fletcher, Jared K.	DC Comics	2007
Plastic Man: Rubber Bandits	Baker, Kyle	Baker, Kyle	DC Comics	2005
Playboy, The	Brown, Chester	Brown, Chester	Drawn and Quarterly	1992
Playboy's Little Annie Fanny	Kurtzman, Harvey	Kurtzman, Harvey	Playboy	2000

Title	Author	Artist	Publisher	Year
Plot, The: The Secret Stories of the Protocols of the Elders of Zion	Eisner, Will	Eisner, Will	W. W. Norton	2005
Poison River	Hernandez, Gilbert	Hernandez, Gilbert	Fantagraphics Books	1997
*Poor Bastard, The	Matt, Joe	Matt, Joe	Drawn and Quarterly	1997
Potential	Schrag, Ariel	Schrag, Ariel	SLG Publishing	2000
*Predator	Anderson, Kevin J, et al.	Alcatena, Enrique, et al.	Dark Horse Comics	1996-1999
*Pride of Baghdad: Inspired by a True Story	Vaughan, Brian K.	Henrichon, Niko; Klein, Todd	DC Comics	2006
Professor's Daughter, The	Guibert, Emmanuel, and Sfar, Joann	Guibert, Emmanuel	First Second	2007
*Pyongyang: A Journey in North Korea	Delisle, Guy	Delisle, Guy; Rehm, Dirk	L'Association (French); Drawn and Quarterly (English)	Pyongyang, 2003 (English translation, 2005)
*Queen and Country	Rucka, Greg; Johnston, Antony	Rolston, Steve et al.	Oni Press	2002-2007
*Rabbi's Cat, The	Sfar, Joann	Sfar, Joan; Findakly, Brigitte	Editions Dargaud (French); Pantheon Books (English)	Le Chat du Rabbin, 2002-2006 (English translation, 2005, 2008)
Rapunzel's Revenge	Hale, Shannon Nathan and Dean	Hale, Nathan	San Val	2008
R. Crumb's America	Crumb, Robert	Crumb, Robert	Last Gasp	1995

Title	Author	Artist	Publisher	Year
Rex Mundi	Nelson, Arvid	Eric J.	Image Comics; Dark Horse Comics	2004-2010
Richard Stark's Parker	Stark, Richard (pseudonym of Donald E. Westlake)	Cooke, Darwyn	IDW Publishing	2009-present
Ride Together, The: A Brother and Sister's Memoir of Autism in the Family	Karasik, Paul, and Karasik, Judy	Karasik, Paul	Washington Square Press	2004
Road to Perdition	Collins, Max Allan	Rayner, Richard Piers ; Lappan, Bob	DC Comics	1998
Robot Dreams	Varon, Sara	Varon, Sara	First Second	2007
Romeo and Juliet, the Graphic Novel: Original Text	Shakespeare, William, et al.	Volley, Will	Classical Comics	2009
Rose	Smith, Jeff	Vess, Charles	Cartoon Books	2002
Rude Girls and Dangerous Women	Camper, Jennifer	Camper, Jennifer	Jennifer Camper	1994
Sacred and Profane	Green, Justin		Last Gasp	1976
Safe Area Goražde	Sacco, Joe	Sacco, Joe	Fantagraphics Books	2000
Salamander Dream	Larson, Hope	Larson, Hope	AdHouse Books	2005
Salvatore	Crécy, Nicolas de	Crécy, Nicolas de	NBM Publishing	2011
Satchel Paige: Striking Out Jim Crow	Sturm, James	Tommaso, Rich	Hyperion Book CH	2007

Title	Author	Artist	Publisher	Year
Scalped	Aaron, Jason, and Guera, R. M.	Guera, R. M.	Vertigo	2007-present
*Scary Godmother: The Boo Flu	Thompson, Jill	Thompson, Jill	Sirius Entertainment	2000
*Scott Pilgrim	O'Malley, Bryan Lee	O'Malley, Bryan Lee	Oni Press	
Selina's Big Score	Cooke, Darwyn, and Hollingsworth, Matt	Torres, Daniel	Titan Books	2002
Sense and Sensibility	Austen, Jane; Butler, Nancy; Liew, Sonny	Liew, Sonny	Marvel	2011
Set to Sea	Weing, Drew	Weing, Drew	Fantagraphics	2010
Shazam! The Monster Society of Evil	Smith, Jeff	Smith, Jeff	DC Comics	2007
*Shenzhen: A Travelogue from China	Delisle, Guy	Delisle, Guy; Rehm, Dirk	L'Association (French); Drawn and Quarterly (English)	2000 (English translation, 2006)
*Shortcomings	Tomine, Adrian	Tomine, Adrian	Drawn and Quarterly	2007
*Shutterbug Follies	Little, Jason	Little, Jason	Doubleday Graphic Novels	2002
*Signal to Noise	Gaiman, Neil	McKean, Dave	VG Graphics; Dark Horse Comics	1992
Silver Metal Lover, The	Lee, Tanith, and Robbins, Trina	Robbins, Trina	Spectra	1985
*Sin City	Miller, Frank	Miller, Frank	Dark Horse Comics	1993-2000

Title	Author	Artist	Publisher	Year
Sin Titulo	Pope, Paul	Pope, Paul	Horse Press	1993
Six Novels in Woodcuts	Ward, Lynd	Ward, Lynd	Library of America	2010
Sketchbook, 1966-'67	Crumb, Robert	Crumb, Robert	Blue Angel	1981
*Skim	Tamaki, Mariko	Tamaki, Jillian	Groundwood Books	2008
*Skitzy: The Story of Floyd W. Skitzaf-roid	Freeman, Don	Freeman, Don	Self-published (1955); Drawn and Quarterly (2008)	1955; 2008
Sky over the Louvre, The	Carrière, Jean-Louis, and Yslaire, Bernard	Yslaire, Bernard	NBM Publishing	2011
Sleepwalk and Other Stories	Tomine, Adrian	Tomine, Adrian	Drawn and Quarterly	1998
*Sloth	Hernandez, Gilbert	Hernandez, Gilbert	Vertigo	2006
Small Favors	Coover, Colleen	Coover, Colleen	Eros Comix	2002
*Small Killing, A	Moore, Alan	Zarate, Oscar	VG Graphics	1991
Smile	Telgemeier, Raina	Telgemeir, Raina	GRAPHIX	2010
*Snowman, The	Briggs, Raymond	Briggs, Raymond	Random House	1978
Sof'Boy	Prewitt, Archer	Prewitt, Archer	Drawn and Quarterly	1997-present
Stagger Lee	McCulloch, Derek, and Hendrix, Shepherd	Hendrix, Shepherd	Image Comics	2006
Sticks and Stones	Kuper, Peter	Kuper, Peter	Three Rivers Press	2004
Stig's Inferno	Templeton, Ty	Templeton, Ty	Vortex Comics	1984-1986

Title	Author	Artist	Publisher	Year
Still I Rise: A Cartoon History of African Americans	Laird, Roland O; Laird, Taneshia N; Bey, Elihu Adolfo	Bey, Elihu Adofo	W. W. Norton	1997
Stitches: A Memoir	Small, David	Small, David	W. W. Norton	2009
Strangers in Paradise	Moore, Terry	Moore, Terry; Wiesenfeld, Josh; Zindzierski, Jessica	Antarctic Press; Image Comics; Abstract Studio	1995-2007
Strange Weather Lately	Chalmers, John, and Marrs, Sandra	Marrs, Sandra	Metaphrog	1999
Stray Bullets	Lapham, David	Lapham, David; Lapham, Mario	El Capitán	1996-2004
Stray Toasters	Sienkiewicz, Bill	Sienkiewicz, Bill; Novak, James	Marvel Comics	1991
Streak of Chalk	Prado, Miguelanxo	Prado, Miguelanxo	Norma Editorial (Spanish); NBM (English)	1993 (English translation, 1994)
Stuck Rubber Baby	Cruse, Howard	Cruse, Howard	DC Comics	1995
Students for a Democratic Society: A Graphic History	Pekar, Harvey, and Dumm, Gary	Dumm, Gary	Hill and Wang	2008
Subway Series	Corman, Leela	Corman, Leela	Alternative Comics	2002
Suckle: The Status of Basil	Cooper, Dave	Cooper, Dave	Fantagraphics Books	1996
Summer Blonde	Tomine, Adrian	Tomine, Adrian	Drawn and Quarterly	2002
Summer of Love, The	Drechsler, Debbie	Drechsler, Debbie	Drawn and Quarterly	2002

Title	Author	Artist	Publisher	Year
Superest, The: Who Is the Superest Hero of Them All?	Cornell, Kevin, and Sutter, Matthew	Cornell, Kevin; Sutter, Matthew	Citadel	2010
Swallow Me Whole	Powell, Nate	Powell, Nate	Top Shelf Productions	2008
Sweet Tooth: Out of the Deep Woods	Lemire, Jeff	Lemire, Jeff	Vertigo	2010
Sword of the Atom	Kane, Gil, and Strnad, Jan	Kane, Gil; Broderick, Pat	DC Comics	2007
*System, The	Kuper, Peter	Kuper, Peter	DC Comics	1997
System of Comics, The	Groensteen, Thierry		University Press of Mississippi	2007
*Tale of One Bad Rat, The	Talbot, Bryan	Talbot, Bryan; DeVille, Ellie	Dark Horse Comics	1995
*Tales of the Beanworld	Marder, Larry	Marder, Larry	Beanworld Press; Dark Horse Comics; Eclipse Comics	1990 (issues 1-16); 2009
Talking Animals and Other People	Culhane, Shamus	Culhane, Shamus	Da Capo Press	1998
*Tamara Drewe	Simmonds, Posy	Simmonds, Posy	Jonathan Cape	2007
Tangents	Prado, Miguelanxo	Prado, Miguelanxo	NBM Publishing	1995
*Tank Girl	Martin, Alan	Hewlett, Jamie; Chelnor, Chris	Penguin; Dark Horse Comics	1993-1996
*Tantrum	Feiffer, Jules	Feiffer, Jules	Alfred A. Knopf	1979
Teenage Mutant Ninja Turtles	Laird, Peter, and Eastman, Kevin	Laird, Peter; Eastman, Kevin	Mirage Studios	1984-1993

Title	Author	Artist	Publisher	Year
Temperance	Malkasian, Cathy		Fantagraphics	2010
They Found the Car	Gipi	Gipi	Fantagraphics	2006
Thoreau at Walden	Thoreau, Henry David, and Porcellino, John	Porcellino, John	Hyperion Book CH	2008
*Three Fingers	Koslowski, Rich	Koslowski, Rich	Top Shelf Comics	2002
*Three Shadows	Pedrosa, Cyril	Pedrosa, Cyril	Delcourt (French); First Second Books (English)	Trois Ombres, 2007 (English translation, 2008)
Tin-Pot Foreign General and the Old Iron Woman, The	Briggs, Raymond	Briggs, Raymond	Little Brown & Co	1984
T-Minus: The Race to the Moon	Ottaviani, Jim; Cannon, Zander; Cannon, Kevin	Cannon, Zander; Cannon, Kevin	Aladdin	2009
Too Cool to Be Forgotten	Robinson, Alex	Robinson, Alex	Top Shelf Productions	2008
Too Many Time Machines: Or, the Incredible Story of How I Went Back in Time, Met Babe Ruth, and Discovered the Secret of Home Run Hitting	Stamaty, Mark Alan	Stamaty, Mark Alan	Viking Juvenile	1999
Torso	Bendis, Brian Michael, and Anderyko, Marc	Anderyko, Marc	Image Comics	2002
Tower, The	Schuiten, François, and Peeters, Benoît	Schuiten, François, and Peeters, Benoît	NBM	1993

Title	Author	Artist	Publisher	Year
*Tragical Comedy or Comical Tragedy of Mr. Punch, The	Gaiman, Neil	McKean, Dave	Gollancz; DC Comics	1994
*Transit	McKeever, Ted	McKeever, Ted	Image Comics; Vortex Comics	2008
Treasury of Twentieth Century Murder, A	Geary, Rick	Geary, Rick	NBM	2008-present
*Treasury of Victorian Murder, A	Geary, Rick	Geary, Rick	NBM	1987-2007
Trial of the Sober Dog, The	Abadzis, Nick	Abadzis, Nick	The Times	2008
*Tricked	Robinson, Alex	Robinson, Alex	Top Shelf Comics	2005
Tumor	Fialkov, Hale, Joshua, and Tuazon, Noel	Tuazon, Noel	Archaia Entertainment	2010
Turok, Son of Stone	DuBois, Gaylord, et al.	Murphy, Matthew H.	Dark Horse Comics	1956-1982
*Twentieth Century Eightball	Clowes, Daniel	Clowes, Daniel	Fantagraphics Books	2001
Understanding Comics: The Invisible Art	McCloud, Scott	McCloud, Scott	William Morrow	1993
Unsinkable Walker Bean, The	Renier, Aaron	Reiner, Aaron	First Second	2010
Usagi Yojimbo: The Ronin, Book 1	Sakai, Stan	Sakai, Stan	Paw Prints	2002
Vernacular Drawings: Sketchbooks	Seth	Seth	Drawn and Quarterly	2001

Title	Author	Artist	Publisher	Year
Vietnam Journal	Lomax, Don	Lomax, Don	IBooks	2002
*Violent Cases	Gaiman, Neil	McKean, Dave	Dark Horse Comics	1987
*Walking Dead, The	Kirkman, Robert	Adlard, Charlie	Image Comics	2006-present
Walking Shadows: A Novel Without Words	Bousfield, Neil	Bousfield, Neil	Manic D Press	2010
*Wall, The: Growing Up Behind the Iron Curtain	Sís, Peter	Sís, Peter	Frances Foster Books	2007
*Waltz with Bashir: A Lebanon War Story	Folman, Ari	Polonsky, David	Metropolitan Books	2009
War's End: Profiles from Bosnia, 1995-1996	Sacco, Joe	Sacco, Joe	Drawn and Quarterly	2005
*We Are on Our Own	Katin, Miriam	Miriam Katin; Devlin, Tom	Drawn and Quarterly	2006
Werewolves of Montpellier	Jason	Jason	Fantagraphics	2010
We3	Morrison, Grant	Quitely, Frank	Titan Books	2004
*What It Is	Barry, Lynda	Barry, Lynda	Drawn and Quarterly	2008
*When the Wind Blows	Briggs, Raymond	Briggs, Raymond	Hamish Hamilton	1982
*Whiteout	Rucka, Greg	Lieber, Steve	Oni Press	1999
*Why I Hate Saturn	Baker, Kyle	Baker, Kyle	DC Comics	1990

Title	Author	Artist	Publisher	Year
Wilderness: The True Story of Simon Girty, the Renegade	Truman, Timothy	Truman, Timothy	Eclipse Books	1989
Will Eisner's New York: Life in the Big City	Eisner, Will	Eisner, Will	W. W. Norton	2006
Wilson	Clowes, Daniel	Clowes, Daniel	Drawn and Quarterly	2010
Wimbledon Green	Seth	Seth	Drawn and Quarterly	2005
Wobblies! The Graphic History of the International Workers of the World	Buhle, Paul, and Schulman, Nicole, eds.	Jones, Sabrina	Verso	2005
Wolverton Bible, The: The Old Testament and Book of Revelation Through the Pen of Basil Wolverton	Wolverton, Basil	Wolverton, Basil	Fantagraphics	2009
World War Robot	Wood, Ashley	Wood, Ashley	IDW Publishing	2009
Writing Without Teachers	Elbow, Peter		Oxford University Press	1998
X'ed Out	Burns, Charles	Burns, Charles	Pantheon	2010
Xenozoic Tales	Schultz, Mark	Schultz, Mark	Kitchen Sink Press; Marvel Comics; Flesk Publications	1989
Yossel	Kubert, Joe	Kubert, Joe	Ibooks	2003

Title	Author	Artist	Publisher	Year
*You Are Here	Baker, Kyle	Baker, Kyle	DC Comics	1999
You Can Never Find a Rickshaw When It Monsoons: The World on One Cartoon a Day	Willems, Mo	Willems, Mo	Hyperion Book CH	2006
You'll Never Know	Tyler, C.	Tyler, C.	Fantagraphics Books	2009
Zap Comix	Crumb, Robert, et al.	Crumb, Robert, et al.	Apex Novelties	1968-2005
Zeus: King of the Gods	O'Connor, George	O'Connor, George	First Second	2010
Zombies Vs. Robots	Ryall, Chris	Wood, Ashley; Robbins, Robbie	IDW Publishing	2008
Zot!	McCloud, Scott; Ratafia, Ivy	McCloud, Scott	HarperCollins	2008

Recommended Readings: Manga

Title	Author	Artist	Publisher	Year
A, A'	Hagio, Moto	Hagio, Moto	Viz	1997
Abandon the Old in Tokyo	Tatsumi, Yoshihiro	Tatsumi, Yoshihiro	Drawn and Quarterly	2006
A Bride's Story	Mori, Kaoru	Mori, Kaoru	Yen Press	2011-present
Absolute boyfriend	Watase, Yuu	Watase, Yu	Viz	2006-2008
A Certain Scientific Railgun	Kamachi, Kazuma	Fuyukawa, Motoi	Seven Seas	2011-2012
*Adolf	Tezuka, Osamu	Tezuka, Osamu	Bungei Shunju (Japanese); Cadence Books (English)	1992 (English translation, 1995-1996)
Afterschool charisma	Suekane, Kumiko	Suekane, Kumiko	Viz	2010-present
After school nightmare	Mizushiro, Setona	Mizushiro, Setona	Go! Comi	2006-2009
Age of Reptiles Omnibus	Delgado, Ricardo	Delgado, Ricardo	Dark Horse Comics	2011
Ai ore!	Shinjo, Mayu	Shinjo, Mayu	Viz	2011-present
Ai yori aoshi	Fumizuki, Kou	Fumizuki, Kou	Tokyopop	2004-2007
*Akira	Otomo, Katsuhiro	Otomo, Katsuhiro	Kodansha (Japanese edition); Marvel Comics (first U.S. edition); Dark Horse Comics (second U.S. edition); Kodansha (third U.S. edition)	1984-1993 (English translation, 2000-2002; authoritative edition, 2009-2011)

Title	Author	Artist	Publisher	Year
Akumetsu	Tabata, Yoshiaki, and Yugo, Yuki	Yugo, Yuki	Taifu Comics	2002-2006
Alice 19th	Watase, Yuu	Watase, Yuu	Viz	2002-2004
Amulet	Kibuishi, Kazu	Kibuishi, Kazu	Scholastic Books	
Andromeda Stories	Takemiya, Keiko	Takemiya, Keiko	Vertical	2007-2008
Apollo's Song	Tezuka, Osamu	Tezuka, Osamu	Vertical	1970
Astral Project	Marginal (Garon Tsuchiya), and Takeya, Syuji	Takeya, Syuji	CMX Manga	2008
*Astro Boy	Tezuka, Osamu	Tezuka, Osamu	Akita Shoten (Japanese); Dark Horse Comics (English)	1981 (English translation, 2002-2004)
Ayako	Tezuka, Osamu	Tezuka, Osamu	Vertical	2010
A Year in Japan	Williamson, Kate T.	Williamson, Kate T.	Princeton Architectural Press	2006
Baby and Me	Ragawa, Marimo	Ragawa, Marimo	Viz	2006-present
Bakuman	Ohba, Tsugumi, and Obata, Takeshi	Obata, Takeshi	Viz	2008-present
*Banana Fish	Yoshida, Akimi	Yoshida, Akimi	Shogakukan (Japanese); VIZ Media (English)	1996-1997 (English translation, 1998-2002, Volumes 1-7; 2004-2007, Volumes 1-19)
Baoh	Araki, Hirohiko	Araki, Hirohiko	Viz	1985-1986
*Barefoot Gen	Nakazawa, Keiji	Nakazawa, Keiji	Shūeisha (Japanese); Last Gasp Books (English)	English translation, 2004-2010

Title	Author	Artist	Publisher	Year
Battle Angel Alita	Kishiro, Yukito	Kishiro, Yukito	Shūeisha (Japanese); VIZ Media (English)	1991-1995 (English translation, 1995-1998)
Battle angel Alita: Last order	Kishiro, Yukito	Kishiro, Yukito	Viz	2003-2011
Beauty pop	Arai, Kiyoko		Viz	2006-2009
Berserk	Miura, Kentaro	Kentaro Miura	Hakusensha (Japanese); Dark Horse Comics (English)	1990-present (English translation, 2003-present)
Black bird	Sakurakoji, Kanoko	Sakurakoji, Kanoko	Viz	2009-present
Black Blizzard	Tatsumi, Yoshihiro	Tatsumi, Yoshihiro	Drawn and Quarterly	2010
Black butler	Toboso, Yana	Toboso, Yana	Yen Press	2010-present
Black cat	Yabuki, Kentaro	Yabuki, Kentaro	Viz	2006-2009
Black Jack	Tezuka, Osamu	Tezuka, Osamu	Akita Shoten (Japanese); Vertical (English)	1987-2004 (English translation, 2008-2011)
Blade of the Immortal	Hiroaki, Samura	Hiroaki, Samura	Dark Horse Comics	English translation, 1997-present
Blame!	Nihei, Tsutomu	Nihei, Tsutomu	TokyoPop	1998-2003
Bleach	Kubo, Tite	Kubo, Tite	Shūeisha (Japanese); VIZ Media (English)	2002-present (English translation, 2004-present)
Blue exorcist	Kato, Kazue	Kato, Kazue	Viz	2011-present
Bokurano: Ours	Kitoh, Mohiro	Kitoh, Mohiro	Viz	2010-present

Title	Author	Artist	Publisher	Year
Boys over Flowers	Kamio, Yoko	Kamio, Yoko	Shūeisha (Japanese); VIZ Media (English)	English translation, 2003-2009
Buddha	Tezuka, Osamu	Tezuka, Osamu	Ushio Shuppansha (Japanese); Vertical (English)	1974-1984 (English translation, 2003-2005)
Bunny drop	Unita, Yumi		Yen Press	2010-present
Buso renkin	Watsuki, Nobuhiro	Watsuki, Nobuhiro	Viz	2006-2008
Butterflies, flowers	Yoshihara, Yuki	Yoshihara, Yuki	Viz	2006-2008
Cain saga	Yuki, Kaori	Yuki, Kaori	Viz	2006-2007
Captive hearts	Hino, Matsuri	Hino, Matsuri	Viz	2008-2009
Cardcaptor Sakura	Clamp	Apapa, Mokona, Igarashi, Satsuki, Nekoi, Tsubaki	Kodansha (Japanese); TOKYOPOP (English)	1996-2000 (English translation, 2000-2003)
Ceres: Celestial Legend	Watase, Yuu	Watase, Yuu	Viz	2003-2006
Chi's Sweet Home	Konami, Kanata	Konami, Kanata	Vertical	2004-present
Chibi vampire	Kagesaki, Yuna	Kagesaki, Yuna	Tokyopop	2006-2009
Children of the sea	Igarashi, Daisuke	Igarashi, Daisuke	Viz	2009-2010
Chi's sweet home	Konami, Kanata	Konami, Kanata	Vertical	2004-present
Chobits	CLAMP	CLAMP	Tokyopop	2001-2003
Citizen 13660	Okubo, Miné	Okubo, Miné	University of Washington Press	1983
Claymore	Yagi, Norihiro	Yagi, Norihiro	Viz	2006-present
Codename: Sailor V	Takeuchi, Naoko	Takeuchi, Naoko	Kodansha Comics	2011-present

Title	Author	Artist	Publisher	Year
Cosplay Ai	Steinberger, Aimee Major		Go! Comi	2009
Crayon Shinchan	Usui, Yoshito	Usui, Yoshito	ComicsOne	2002-2004
Crime and Punishment	Dostoyevsky, Fyodor, and Tezuka, Osamu	Tezuka, Osamu	Todoko	1990
Crimson Snow	Tomoki, Hori		Tokyopop	2011
*Crying Freeman	Koike, Kazuo	Ikegami, Ryoichi	Shogakukan (Japanese); VIZ Media (English); Dark Horse Comics (English)	Kuraingu Furiiman, 1986-1988 (English translation, 1989-1990)
Cul de Sac	Thompson, Richard	Thompson, Richard	Andrews McMeel Publishing	2004-present
Dance in the vampire bund	Tamaki, Nozomu	Tamaki, Nozomu	Seven Seas	2008-present
Dawn of the arcana	Toma, Rei	Toma, Rei	Viz	2011-present
*Death Note	Ohba, Tsugumi	Ohba, Tsugumi	Shūeisha (Japanese); VIZ Media (English)	2004-2006 (English translation, 2005-2007)
Dengeki Daisy	Motomi, Kyousuke	Motomi, Kyousuke	Viz	2010-present
D. Gray-man	Hoshino, Katsura	Hoshino, Katsura	Viz	2006-present
Distant Neighborhood, A	Taniguchi, Jirō	Taniguchi, Jirō	Shogakukan (Japanese); Fanfare/Ponent Mon (English)	Haruka na Machi e, 1998 (English translation, 2009)
*Dr. Slump	Toriyama, Akira	Toriyama, Akira	Shūeisha (Japanese); VIZ Media (English)	1980-1985 (English translation, 2005-2009)

Title	Author	Artist	Publisher	Year
Dogs	Miwa, Shiro	Miwa, Shiro	Viz	2009-present
Dororo	Tezuka, Osamu	Tezuka, Osamu	Shogakukan (Japanese); Vertical (English)	1981 (English translation, 2008)
Dragon Ball	Toriyama, Akira	Toriyama, Akira	Shūeisha (Japanese); VIZ Media (English)	1985-1995 (English translation, Volumes 1-16, 2003-2004)
Dragon Ball Z	Toriyama, Akira	Toriyama, Akira	Viz	2000-2006
Drifting Classroom, The	Umezu, Kazuo	Umezu, Kazuo	Shogakukan (Japanese); VIZ Media (English)	1998 (English translation, 2006-2008)
Drifting Life, A	Tatsumi, Yoshihiro	Tatsumi, Yoshihiro	Seirin Kōgeisha (Japanese); Drawn and Quarterly (English)	2008 (English translation, 2009)
Drops of God	Agi, Tadashi	Okimoto, Shu	Vertical	2011-present
Earl Cain	Yuki, Kaori	Yuki, Kaori	Hakusensha	(2006-2008)
Elsewhere Chronicles	Nykko and Bannister	Bannister	Graphic Universe	2009-present
Emma	Mori, Kaoru	Mori, Kaoru	CMX Manga	2006-2009
Eternal Sabbath	Sōryō, Fuyumi	Jones, H.	San Val	2006-2007
Evil Blade	Shiono, Etrouji	Shiono, Etrouji	Square Enix	2005-present
Fairy Tail	Mashima, Hiro	Mashima, Hiro	Kodansha Comics	2008-present
Firefighter! Daigo of Fire Company M	Soda, Masahito	Soda, Masahito	Viz	2003-2007

Title	Author	Artist	Publisher	Year
*Fist of the North Star	Buronson	Hara, Tetsuo	Shūeisha (Japanese); VIZ Media (English); Gutsoon! Entertainment (English)	1984-1989 (partial English translation, 1995-1997)
*Four Immigrants Manga, The	Kiyama, Henry Yoshitaka	Kiyama, Henry Yoshitaka	Kiyama Yoshitaka gashitsu (Japanese); Stone Bridge Press (English)	Manga yonin shosei, 1931 (English translation, 1931, 1999)
*From Eroica with Love	Aoike, Yasuko	Aoike, Yasuko	Akita Shoten (Japanese); DC Comics (English)	1978-present (partial English translation 2004-2010)
*Fruits Basket	Takaya, Natsuki	Takaya, Natsuki	Hakusensha (Japanese); TO-KYOPOP (English)	1999-2007 (English translation, 2004-2009)
*Fullmetal Alchemist	Arakawa, Hiromu	Arakawa, Hiromu	Enix (Japanese); Square Enix (Japanese); VIZ Media (English)	2002-2010 (English translation, 2005-2011)
Fushigi Yugi	Watase, Yuu	Watase, Yuu	Viz	2003-2006.
Fushigi yugi: Genbu kaiden	Watase, Yuu	Watase, Yuu	Viz	2005-present
Gantz	Oku, Hiroya	Oku, Hiroya	Dark Horse	2008-present
Genshiken	Kio, Shimoku	Kio, Shimoku	Del Rey	2005-2007
Gentlemen's alliance+	Tanemura, Arina	Tanemura, Arina	Viz	2007-2010
*Ghost in the Shell	Shirow, Masamune	Shirow, Masamune	Kodansha (Japanese); Dark Horse Comics (English)	1991 (English translation, 1995)

Title	Author	Artist	Publisher	Year
Godchild	Yuki, Kaori	Yuki, Kaori	Viz	2006-2008
*Golgo 13	Saito, Takao	Saito, Takao	Shogakukan (Japanese); LEED (English); VIZ Media (English)	1973-present (partial English translation, 1986-1987)
*Gon	Tanaka, Masashi	Tanaka, Masashi	Kodansha (Japanese); DC Comics (English)	1992-2002 (English translation 2007-2009)
Good-Bye	Tatsumi, Yoshihiro	Tatsumi, Yoshihiro	Drawn and Quarterly	2008
Hana-kimi	Nakajo, Hisaya	Nakajo, Hisaya	Viz	2004-2008
Hellsing	Hirano, Kohta	Hirano, Kohta	Dark Horse	2003-2010
Hetalia Axis Powers	Himaruya, Hidekaz	Himaruya, Hidekaz	Tokyopop	2010
High school debut	Kawahara, Kazune	Kawahara, Kazune	Viz	2008-2010
Highschool of the dead	Sato, Daisuke	Sato, Shoji	Yen Press	2011-present
Higurashi when they cry	Ryukishi07	Houjyou, Yutori	Yen Press	2008-present
*Hikaru no go	Hotta, Yumi	Obata, Takeshi	Shūeisha (Japanese); VIZ Media (English)	1999-2003 (English translation, 2004-2011)
Honey and Clover	Umino, Chica	Umino, Chica	Viz	2000-2006
Hot gimmick	Aihara, Miki	Aihara, Miki	Viz	2003-2006
House of Five Leaves	Ono, Natsume	Ono, Natsume	Viz	2010-present
Hunter x hunter	Togashi, Yoshihiro	Togashi, Yoshihiro	Viz	2005-present

Title	Author	Artist	Publisher	Year
I am here!	Toyama, Ema	Toyama, Ema	Kodansha Comics	2010-present
Ikigami: The Ultimate Limit	Mase, Motoro	Mase, Motoro	Viz	2009-present
Inubaka: crazy for dogs	Sakuragi, Yukiya	Sakuragi, Yukiya	Viz	2007-2010
*InuYasha: A Feudal Fairy Tale	Takahashi, Rumiko	Takahashi, Rumiko	Shogakukan (Japanese); VIZ Media (English)	1997-2009 (English translation, 1998-2011)
Iron wok Jan	Saijyo, Shinji	Saijyo, Shinji	DMP	2002-2007
It's Better with Your Shoes Off	Cleveland, Ann		Tuttle Publishing	1955
Japan	Buronson and Miura, Kentarou	Miura, Kentarou	Dark Horse	1992
*Japan Ai: A Tall Girl's Adventures in Japan	Steinberger, Aimee Major	Aimee Major Steinberger	Go! Comi	2007
Japan as Viewed by Seventeen Creators	Boilet, Frédéric, ed.	Various	Toptron Ltd	2005
Jellaby	Soo, Kean	Soo, Kean	Hyperion Book CH	2008-2009
*JoJo's Bizarre Adventure	Araki, Hirohiko	Araki, Hirohiko	Shūeisha (Japanese); VIZ Media (English)	1987-present (English translation, 2005-2010)
Kamikaze Kaito Jeanne	Tanemura, Arina	Tanemura, Arina	CMX Manga	2005-2007
Kamisama kiss	Suzuki, Julietta	Suzuki, Julietta	Viz	2010-present
Kaze Hikaru	Watanabe, Taeko	Watanabe, Taeko	Viz	2005-present
Kaze no Hana	Mizta, Ushio	Mizta, Ushio	Yen Press	2008

Title	Author	Artist	Publisher	Year
Kekkaishi	Tanabe, Yellow	Tanabe, Yellow	Viz	2005-present
Kenichi: The Mightiest Disciple	Matsuena, Syun	Matsuena, Syun	Shogakukan	2002-present
Kimagure Orange Road	Matsumoto, Izumi	Matsumoto, Izumi	Community Home	1984-1987
Kimi ni todoke	Shiina, Karuho	Shiina, Karuho	Viz	2009-present
King City	Graham, Brandon	Graham, Brandon	Image Comics	2007-2010
Kobatao	CLAMP	CLAMP	Yen Press	2010-2012
Lady Snowblood	Koike, Kazuo, and Kamimura, Kazuo	Kamimura, Kazuo	Dark Horse	2005-2006
Legend of Zelda	Himekawa, Akira	Himekawa, Akira	Viz	2008-2010
Library wars	Yumi, Kiiro	Yumi, Kiiro	Viz	2010-present
Life, in Pictures: Autobiographical Stories	Eisner, Will	Eisner, Will	W. W Norton	2007
*Lone Wolf and Cub	Koike, Kazuo	Kojima, Gōseki	Dark Horse Comics	English translation, 2000-2002
Love hina	Akamatsu, Ken	Akamatsu, Ken	Tokyopop	2002-2003
Loveless	Kouga, Yun	Kouga, Yun	Tokyopop/Viz	2006-2008, 2012-present
*Lupin III	Monkey Punch	Monkey Punch	Futabasha (Japanese); TOKYOPOP (English)	1974-1975 (English translation, 2002-2004)
Magic Knight Rayearth	Clamp	Clamp	TokyoPop	1993-1995

Title	Author	Artist	Publisher	Year
Mai, the Psychic Girl	Kudo, Kazuya	Ryoichi Ikegami	VIZ Media	1985-1986 (English translation, 1989)
Maison Ikkoku	Takahashi, Rumiko	Rumiko Takahashi	Shogakukan (Japanese); VIZ Media (English)	1982-1987 (partial English translation, 1994-2000)
Melancholy of Haruhi Suzumiya	Tanigawa, Nagaru	Tsugano, Gaku	Yen Press	2008-present
MeruPuri	Hino, Matsuri	Hino, Matsuri	Viz	2005-2006
Meta-barons, The	Jodorowsky, Alejandro, and Giminez, Juan	Giminez, Juan	Humanoids Publishing	1992-2003
Michel Vaillant	Graton, Jean	Graton, Jean	Le Lombard	1957-present
Millennium snow	Hatori, Bisco	Hatori, Bisco	Viz	2007
Mixed vegetables	Komura, Ayumi	Komura, Ayumi	Viz	2008-2010
Mobile Suit Gundam	Yoshiyuki, Tomino, and Yasuhiko, Yoshikazu	Yoshikazu, Yasuhiko	Stone Bridge Press	2002-2003
Monster	Urasawa, Naoki	Urasawa, Naoki	Shogakukan (Japanese); VIZ Media (English)	1995-2001 (English translation, 2006-2008)
Mushishi	Urushibara, Yuki	Urushibara, Yuki	Del Rey	2007-2009
MW	Tezuka, Osamu	Tezuka, Osamu	Shogakukan (Japanese); Vertical (English)	1981 (English translation, 2007)
Nana	Yazawa, Ai	Yazawa, Ai	Shūeisha (Japanese); VIZ Media (English)	2000-2009 (English translation, 2005-2010)

Title	Author	Artist	Publisher	Year
*Naruto	Kishimoto, Masashi	Kishimoto, Masashi	Shūeisha (Japanese); VIZ Media (English)	2000-present (English translation, 2003-present)
Natsume's Books of Friends	Midorikawa, Yuki	Midorikawa, Yuki	Viz	2005-present
*Nausicaä of the Valley of the Wind	Miyazaki, Hayao	Miyazaki, Hayao	Tokuma Shoten (Japanese); VIZ Media (English)	1982-1995 (English translation, 1990-1997)
Negima!	Akamatsu, Ken	Palmer, Steve	Del Rey/Kodansha Comics	2004-present
Nemesis	Millar, Mark, and McNiven, Steve	McNiven, Steve	Marvel	2011
Neon Genesis Evangelion	Sadamoto, Yoshiyuki	Sadamoto, Yoshiyuki	Viz	2004-present
Neon Genesis Evangelion: Angelic Days	Hayashi, Fumino	Hayashi, Fumino	ADV Manga	2006-2007
Nora: The Last Chronicle Of Devildom	Kakei, Kazunari	Kakei, Kazunari	Viz	2008-2010
No Touching at All	Yoneda, Kou	Yoneda, Kou	Digital Manga Publishing	2010
Nura: Rise of the Yokai Clan	Shiibashi, Hiroshi	Shiibashi, Hiroshi	Viz	2011-present
Octopus Girl	Yamazaki, Toru	Yamazaki, Toru	Dark Horse Comics	2006
*Ode to Kirihito	Tezuka, Osamu	Tezuka, Osamu	Shogakukan (Japanese); Vertical (English)	1972 (English translation, 2006)
Ohikkoshi	Samura, Hiroaki	Samura, Hiroaki	Dark Horse Comics	2006

Title	Author	Artist	Publisher	Year
Oh My Goddess!	Fujishima, Kosuke	Fujishima, Kosuke	Kodansha (Japanese); Dark Horse Comics (English)	1989-present (English translation, 2002-present)
Old Boy	Tsuchiya, Garon	Minegishi, Nobuaki	Futabasha (Japanese); Dark Horse Comics (English)	1997-1998 (English translation, 2006-2007)
Omamori Himari	Matra, Milan	Matra, Milan	Yen Press	2010-present
One Piece	Oda, Eiichiro	Oda, Eiichiro	Shūeisha (Japanese); VIZ Media (English)	1997-present (English translation, 2003-present)
Ōoku: the Inner Chambers	Yoshinaga, Fumi	Yoshinaga, Fumi	Viz	2009-present
O-Parts hunter	Kishimoto, Seishi	Kishimoto, Seishi	Viz	2006-2009
Orpheus no Mado	Ikeda, Riyoko	Ikeda, Riyoko	Shueisha	1975-1981
Otomen	Kanno, Aya	Kanno, Aya	Viz	2009-present
Ouran High School host club	Hatori, Bisco	Hatori, Bisco	Viz	2005-2012
Pandora hearts	Mochizuki, Jun	Mochizuki, Jun	Yen Press	2009-present
Parasyte	Iwaaki, Hitoshi	Iwaaki, Hitoshi	Del Rey	2007
Path of the Assassin	Koike, Kazu, and Kojima, Goseki	Kojima, Goseki	Dark Horse Comics	1978-1984
Peacemaker Kurogane	Chrono, Nanae	Chrono, Nanae	ADV Manga	2002-2005
Peach Girl	Ueda, Miwa	Ueda, Miwa	Tokyopop	2000-2003
Peach Girl: Change of heart	Ueda, Miwa	Ueda, Miwa	Tokyopop	2003-2004

Title	Author	Artist	Publisher	Year
*Phoenix	Tezuka, Osamu	Tezuka, Osamu	Kodansha (Japanese), VIZ Media (English)	
*Pluto	Nagasaki, Takashi; Tezuka, Osamu; Urasawa, Naoki	Urasawa, Naoki	Shogakukan (Japanese); VIZ Media (English)	2009-2010
Pokemon Black and White	Kusaka, Hidenori	Yamamoto, Satoshi	Viz	2011-present
Prince of Tennis, The	Konomi, Takeshi	Konomi, Takeshi	Viz	1999-2008
Princess Knight	Tezuka, Osamu	Tezuka, Osamu	Vertical	1953-1956
Psyren	Iwashiro, Toshiaki	Iwashiro, Toshiaki	Viz	2011-present
Push Man and Other Stories, The	Tatsumi, Yoshihiro	Tatsumi, Yoshihiro	Drawn and Quarterly	2005
*Ranma 1/2	Takahashi, Rumiko	Takahashi, Rumiko	Shogakukan (Japanese); VIZ Media (English)	1988-1996 (English translation, 1993-2006)
Rebound	Nishiyama, Yuriko	Nishiyama, Yuriko	Tokyopop	2003-2007
Rin-ne	Takahashi, Rumiko	Takahashi, Rumiko	Viz	2009-present
Rosario+Vampire	Ikeda, Akihisa	Ikeda, Akihisa	Viz	2008-2009
Rosario+Vampire: Season II	Ikeda, Akihisa	Ikeda, Akihisa	Viz	2010-present
*Rose of Versailles, The	Ikeda, Riyoko	Ikeda, Riyoko	Shūeisha (Japanese); Sanyusha (English)	1972-1974 (partial English translation, 1981)

Title	Author	Artist	Publisher	Year
Rurouni Kenshin	Watsuki, Nobuhiro	Watsuki, Nobuhiro	Shūeisha (Japanese); VIZ Media (English)	1994-1999 (English translation, 2003-2006)
Sailor Moon	Takeuchi, Naoko	Takeuchi, Naoko	Kodansha (Japanese); TOKYOPOP (English); Kodansha Comics USA (English)	1992-1997 (English translation 1998-2001)
Sailor Moon (Pretty Guardian Sailor Moon)	Takeuchi, Naoko	Takeuchi, Naoko	Kodansha Comics	2011-present
Saint Seiya	Kurumada, Masami	Kurumada, Masami	Shūeisha (Japanese); VIZ Media (English)	1986-1991 (English translation, 2004-2010)
Sakura Hime	Tanemura, Arina	Tanemura, Arina	Viz	2011-present
Samurai Executioner	Koike, Kazuo, and Kojima, Goseki	Kojima, Goseki	Dark Horse Comics	2005-2006
Sanctuary	Fumimura, Sho	Ryoichi Ikegami	Shogakukan (Japanese); VIZ Media (English)	1990-1995 (English translation, 1993-1997)
Sand chronicles	Ashihara, Hinako	Ashihara, Hinako	Viz	2008-2011
S.A. special A	Minami, Maki	Minami, Maki	Viz	2007-2010
Sayonara, Zetsubou-Sensei	Kumeta, Koji	Kumeta, Koji	Del Rey	2009-present
Shaman king	Takei, Hiroyuki	Takei, Hiroyuki	Viz	2003-2011
Shugo chara!	Peach-Pit	Peach-Pit	Del Rey/Kodansha Comics	2007-2011
Skip beat!	Nakamura, Yoshiki	Nakamura, Yoshiki	Viz	2006-present

Title	Author	Artist	Publisher	Year
*Slam Dunk	Inoue, Takehiko	Inoue, Takehiko	Shūeisha (Japanese); Gutsoon! Entertainment (English); VIZ Media (English)	1991-1996 (partial English translation, 2003-2004)
*Solanin	Asano, Inio	Asano, Inio	Shogakukan (Japanese); VIZ Media (English)	2005, 2006 (English translation, 2008)
Soul eater	Ohkubo, Atsushi	Ohkubo, Atsushi	Yen Press	2009-present
*Speed Racer	Yoshida, Tatsuo	Yoshida, Tatsuo	Shūeisha (Japanese); Sun Wide Comics (Japanese); Fusosha (Japanese); NOW Comics (English); DC Comics (English); Digital Manga (English)	1966-1968 (English translation, 2008)
Spice & Wolf	Hasekura, Isuna	Ayakura, Ju	Yen Press	2010-present
Stepping on roses	Ueda, Rinko	Ueda, Rinko	Viz	2010-present
The Story Of Saiunkoku	Yukino, Sai	Yura, Kairi	Viz	2010-present
Strain	Buronson	Ikegami, Ryoichi	Viz	1998
Suicide Circle	Furuya, Usamaru	Furuya, Usamaru		2002
Sunshine sketch	Aoki, Ume	Aoki, Ume	Yen Press	2008-2012
Swallowing the Earth	Tezuka, Osamu	Tezuka, Osamu	Digital Manga Publishing	1968-1969
Teenage Mutant Ninja Turtles	Laird, Peter ; Eastman, Kevin	Laird, Peter ; Eastman, Kevin	Mirage Studios	1984-1993

Title	Author	Artist	Publisher	Year
Tegami Bachi	Asada, Hiroyuki	Asada, Hiroyuki	Viz	2009-present
Tenchi Muyo	Okuda, Hitoshi	Okuda, Hitoshi	Viz	2003-2006
Tenjo Tenge (2-in-1 eds.)	Oh! Great	Oh! Great	Viz	2011-present
*To Terra. . .	Takemiya, Keiko	Takemiya, Keiko	Asahi Sonorama (Japanese); Vertical (English)	1980 (English translation, 2007)
Tokyo Mew Mew	Yoshida, Reiko, and Ikumi, Mia	Ikumi, Mia	TokyoPop	2003-2004
Tomie	Ito, Junji	Ito, Junji	ComicsOne	2001
Toradora!	Takemiya, Yuyuko	Yasu	Seven Seas	2011-present
*Town of Evening Calm, Country of Cherry Blossoms	Kouno, Fumiyo	Kouno, Fumiyo	Futabasha (Japanese); Last Gasp (English)	Yūnagi no machi, Sakura no kuni, 2004 (English translation, 2007)
Tramps Like Us	Ogawa, Yayoi	Ogawa, Yayoi	TokyoPop	2000-2005
*Tsubasa: Reservoir Chronicle	Clamp	Clamp	Kodansha (Japanese); Random House (English)	2003-2009 (English translation, 2004-2010)
Tsubasa: Those with Wings	Takaya, Natsuki	Takaya, Natsuki	TokyoPop	1995-1998
Turok, Son of Stone	Murphy, Matthew H. et al.	Murphy, Matthew H.	Dark Horse Comics	(1954-1982; reprint 2009-present)
*20th Century Boys	Urasawa, Naoki	Naoki Urasawa	Shogakukan (Japanese); VIZ Media (English)	2000-2006 (English translation, 2009-present)
Tyrant	Bissette, Steve	Bissette, Steve	SpiderBaby Grafix	1994-1996

Title	Author	Artist	Publisher	Year
Usagi Yojimbo	Sakai, Stan	Sakai, Stan	Fantagraphics Books; Mirage Comics; Dark Horse Comics	1987-present
Uzumaki	Ito, Junji	Ito, Junji	Shogakukan (Japanese); VIZ Media (English)	1998-2000 (English translation, 2001-2002)
Vampire knight	Hino, Matsuri	Hino, Matsuri	Viz	2007-present
Video Girl Ai	Katsura, Masakazu	Katsura, Masakazu	Viz	1989-1992
Vinland Saga	Yukimura, Makoto	Yukimura, Makoto	Kurokawa	2005-present
Walking Man, The	Taniguchi, Jirō	Taniguchi, Jirō	Toptron Ltd	2004
Wallflower	Hayakawa, Tomoko	Hayakawa, Tomoko	Kodansha Comics	2004-present
We Were There	Obata, Yuki	Obata, Yuki	Shogakukan (Japanese); VIZ Media (English)	2002-2008, 2009-2012 (English translation, 2008-2012)
Wedding Peach	Yazawa, Nao, and Tomita, Sukehiro	Yazawa, Nao	Viz	2003-2004
Whistle!	Higuchi, Daisuke	Higuchi, Daisuke	Viz	1998-2003
With the light	Tobe, Keiko	Tobe, Keiko	Yen Press	2007-2011
Wonderful World of Sazae-San, The	Hasegawa, Machiko	Hasegawa, Machiko	Kodansha International	1997
xxxHOLic	CLAMP	CLAMP	Del Rey	2004-2012
Yakitate!! Japan	Hashiguchi, Takashi	Hashiguchi, Takashi	Viz	2006-2011

Title	Author	Artist	Publisher	Year
Yotsuba&!	Azuma, Kiyohiko	Azuma, Kiyohiko	Media Works (Japanese); ADV (English); Yen Press (English)	2003-present (partial English translation, 2005-2007)
Yu-gi-oh! 5D's	Hikokubo, Masahiro	Sato, Masashi	Viz	2011-present
Yu-gi-oh! GX	Kageyama, Naoyuki	Naoyuki	Viz	2007-present
Yu-gi-oh! R	Ito, Akira	Ito, Akira	Viz	2009-2010

INDEX

Note: Page numbers in **bold** indicate main discussion.